HARM REDUCTION: A NEW DIRECTION FOR DRUG POLICIES AND PROGRAMS

Edited by Patricia G. Erickson, Diane M. Riley, Yuet W. Cheung, and Patrick A. O'Hare

Since the First International Conference on the Reduction of Drug-Related Harm, held in 1990, the term 'harm reduction' has gained wide currency in the areas of public health and drug policy. Previously the field was characterized by heated struggle between proponents of prohibition and those advocating legalization of addictive substances, and this debate tended to obscure practical, collective approaches. Harm reduction, an approach which encompasses various policy directives and program initiatives, was inspired by the positive outcomes of such public measures as needle-exchange programs for reduction of HIV risk, methadone maintenance programs, education on the risks of tobacco use, and liquor licensing laws.

This collection of essays illustrates the scope and vigour of the emerging harm reduction model. The essays, drawn from seven international conferences on harm reduction, cover a wide variety of topics, including public policy, human rights, women and reproductive issues, the experiences of special populations, defining and measuring harm, and intervention.

Researchers and practitioners will benefit from the various papers in the volume, which combine insights into policy-making and front-line outreach efforts with comprehensive conceptual and empirical approaches. *Harm Reduction* represents an important initiative in making academic work accessible and useful to a larger community, and provides guidance for the development of effective policies and programs.

PATRICIA G. ERICKSON is Professor of Sociology at the University of Toronto and Senior Scientist with the Addiction Research Foundation. DIANE M. RILEY is Assistant Professor of Behavioural Science at the University of Toronto and Policy Analyst at the Canadian Foundation for Drug Policy. YUET W. CHEUNG is Professor of Sociology at the Chinese University of Hong Kong. PATRICK A. O'HARE is Executive Director of the International Harm Reduction Association.

Harm Reduction: A New Direction for Drug Policies and Programs

Edited by
PATRICIA G. ERICKSON
DIANE M. RILEY
YUET W. CHEUNG
PATRICK A. O'HARE

UNIVERSITY OF TORONTO PRESS
Toronto Buffalo London

© University of Toronto Press Incorporated 1997
Toronto Buffalo London
Printed in Canada

ISBN 0-8020-0756-2 (cloth)
ISBN 0-8020-7805-2 (paper)

∞

Printed on acid-free paper

Canadian Cataloguing in Publication Data

Main entry under title:

Harm reduction : a new direction for drug policies
and programs

Collection of papers drawn from 7 international
conferences on harm reduction.
ISBN 0-8020-0756-2 (bound)   ISBN 0-8020-7805-2 (pbk.)

Drug abuse – Congresses.   2. Drug abuse – Government
policy – Congresses.   3. Drug abuse – Treatment –
Congresses.   4. Drug abuse – Prevention – Congresses.
I. Erickson, Patricia G.

HV4998.H37 1997   362.29   C96-932461-8

University of Toronto Press acknowledges the financial assistance to its
publishing program of the Canada Council and the Ontario Arts Council.

Contents

PART V: COMMUNITIES AND SPECIAL POPULATIONS

Foreword

In the few years since the First International Conference on the Reduction of Drug-Related Harm (held in Liverpool in 1990), the term 'harm reduction' has gained wide currency in both public-health and drug policy. Perhaps this is because of the vacuum that existed before that time, when an often acrimonious struggle between prohibition and 'legalization' occupied the field. This dichotomy tended to exclude more pragmatic approaches such as those the Dutch began to explore in the late 1970s, with diminished criminalization and greater involvement of drug users themselves in the formation of policy and design of new programs. But, without doubt, it was the AIDS epidemic (first widely noticed among drug users in 1983–4) that changed the terms of reference of this issue. AIDS gave new traction to the search for more effective alternatives to drug policies based on prohibition and encouraged the development of harm reduction.

This volume represents the third collection of papers drawn from the seven international conferences on harm reduction. It is the most detailed to date in exploring a number of specific policy options and outlining several practical innovations, as well as framing the larger questions in ways that address the conceptual bases of harm reduction. Ranging from history and social theory to human-rights considerations (as well as the traditional matters of public health and clinical practice), this series of papers shows the scope and vigour of the emerging harm reduction approach. Evidence of this can be seen in the application of harm reduction thinking to a number of areas broadly associated with our current drug policies, for instance, prisons and incarceration, international security and order, development policies, and human rights. Also, for the first time, this volume assembles a number of clinical and laboratory studies that shed new light on the issues of drug testing, athletics, and pharmacology. It also develops the important dimension of community perspectives and those of 'special populations,' such as women drug users and ethnic minorities.

One of the sure signs of the growing significance of harm reduction thinking is the hostility it has provoked from those who subscribe to the 'war on drugs.' In an attempt to discredit it and its proponents, harm reduction is often presented as the 'wedge' for drug legalization. While totally untrue, this allegation does damage to the climate of open debate so vital to making needed progress in dealing with the huge problems associated with global drug markets and addiction's powerful association with the spread of AIDS. International organizational efforts to counter harm reduction have led to the formation of the European Cities Against Drugs (ECAD) and, in the United States, an *Atlanta Declaration*, which regularly attack harm reduction proposals and the dedicated professionals who advocate for them. Led by U.S. drug-enforcement officials, this backlash has even included the publication of instruction handbooks on how to argue against harm reduction. More ominously, the very use of the term harm reduction is embargoed by U.S. drug-research agencies and the United Nations Drug Control Program (UNDCP). They *do* use 'reduction of risk' as a 'safe' substitute (where no alternative exists), but still fail to acknowledge the legitimacy and common sense of specific harm reduction approaches such as needle and syringe exchange. For example, as of this writing (July 1996), U.S. policy still forbids the use of federal funds for support of needle exchanges.

Nonetheless, the lively vigour of the debate, the growing body of research and conceptual literature and, most important, the ever-expanding implementation of harm reduction innovations in practice are a testament to the generally positive flow of developments in the field. The reluctance of some politically conservative governmental programs to embrace harm reduction (especially in the United States) has been offset to a degree by an upsurge in private philanthropy and citizen activism. This movement has helped to establish harm reduction services and support the growing network of researchers, practitioners, and community-based organizations who draw encouragement and inspiration from harm reduction models and programs. This volume represents another milestone in that positive development.

ERNEST DRUCKER, Ph.D.
Director, Department of Community Health
Montefiore Medical Center
Bronx, New York

Acknowledgments

The conference from which this book emerged was sponsored by five agencies: the Addiction Research Foundation, the Canadian Centre on Substance Abuse, the Provinces of Quebec and British Columbia, and the Mersey Drug Training and Information Centre. Support for the conference's expenses came from several Canadian federal departments: Health, Communications, and the Solicitor General. This book was made possible by the support and work that made the conference of March 1994 a reality.

The editors wish to express our appreciation to Mrs Joan Moreau and Ms Victoria Vaag for their excellent technical assistance during the preparation of this manuscript.

The Executive Editor of the University of Toronto Press, Mr Virgil Duff, has been helpful and supportive through all the stages of this book's preparation. All his staff have been diligent and reliable with their contributions. We are most grateful to them.

We would also like to thank all those who submitted papers for review and consideration. While we could not include them all, the number and vitality of the submissions encourage us to see harm reduction as an expanding and dynamic field. We are confident that this volume will not be the last to chart the course of this new approach to drug problems in society.

The views expressed in this book are those of the authors and editors, and do not necessarily reflect the positions of the institutions with which they are affiliated.

HARM REDUCTION

Introduction:
The Search for Harm Reduction

This volume is a collection of selected, revised papers originally presented at the fifth International Conference on the Reduction of Drug-Related Harm held in Toronto, Canada, 6–10 March 1994. The series of international conferences began in Liverpool in 1990, and was triggered by two major factors. The first was the gradual recognition, by a growing number of countries, of the need for more pragmatic strategies for minimizing the risk of HIV transmission among injection drug users. The second factor was the success of certain pragmatic and innovative risk reduction programs that had been introduced in the Netherlands, Australia, and the United Kingdom in the 1980s, such as syringe-exchange schemes and prescribing of 'hard' drugs. They attracted a wide spectrum of people in the drug field to learn from each other's experience in reducing drug-related harm.

The success of the Liverpool conference sparked off the organization of subsequent international conferences, held in Barcelona in 1991, Melbourne in 1992, Rotterdam in 1993, Toronto in 1994, Florence in 1995, and Hobart in 1996. Three of these conferences led to the publication of books, one on the Liverpool conference (O'Hare, Newcombe, Matthews, Buning, and Drucker 1992), another on the Melbourne conference (Heather, Wodak, Nadelmann, and O'Hare 1993), and this volume on the Toronto conference.

Although the reduction, or minimization, of drug-related harm was by no means a new idea (Berridge 1993), the Liverpool conference marked the beginning of what formally may be called a 'harm reduction approach.' At past conferences, hundreds of participants, including scientists, academics, educators, service providers, health professionals, and policy makers from different parts of the world, had gathered together to hatch the egg of a harm reduction perspective. They had painstakingly explored the conceptual characteristics of such a perspective that would distinguish it from existing approaches, examined the potential applicability of such a perspective to practical programs, and discussed possible ways of enhancing the adoption of such a perspective into drug policies. Efforts made in these international conferences had stimulated discussions of the new perspective in many other conferences in related fields, in scientific journals, books, or other publications, and in the social and political arenas. By now, the harm reduction approach has gained tremendous momentum in many Western countries. It has also generated new debates in the drug field in some Asian societies, including Hong Kong (Ch'ien 1993; Day 1993).

To say that the search for a harm reduction perspective was a reaction to deficiencies of existing approaches is hardly an exaggeration. The *prohibitionist* approach assumes the existence of a consensus in society that use of drugs is a morally corrupt behaviour, one that violates the 'collective conscience' of the community (Durkheim 1950). The control of such 'bad' behaviour can best be achieved by legal sanctions, and a strong law-enforcement apparatus is thus required for such a purpose. This approach, most vividly represented by the 'War on Drugs' of the United States, has been widely criticized. These criticisms include its moral arbitrariness, its insensitivity to differential consequences of drug use, its stigmatization and thereby systematic marginalization of drug users, its manufacturing a drug-related 'moral panic' in society, its straining the criminal-justice system by turning drug users into criminals, its infringement on the civil rights of citizens, its indirect sustenance of a black market, and, most important of all, its inability to achieve what it promises to achieve – curbing illicit drug consumption and availability (e.g., Alexander 1990; Erickson 1992, 1993; Erickson and Cheung 1992; Erickson and Ottaway 1994; Erickson et al. 1994; Cheung and Erickson 1997; Cheung, Erickson, and Landau 1991; Nadelmann 1989; Riley 1993, 1994). Growing awareness of these serious drawbacks of prohibition, especially when aggressively pursued, have led the editors of this volume, as well as many of the contributors, to seek a new direction and a new model to guide drug policies and programs.

The apparent failure of the prohibition model in solving the 'drug problem' has served as a springboard for proponents of *legalization* to advocate their counter approach. If the root of the problem lies in the criminalization of drug use and users, a logical solution would be to remove all criminal penalties. Advocates of legalization are not satisfied with minor gestures of decriminalization of one of a few selected drugs or of penalty reduction. They maintain that all of the so-called illicit drugs should eventually be legalized, because only through such a measure could the black market be wiped out, the supply of psychoactive substances be regulated, appropriate advice be given to users in order to minimize problematic use, and resources for treatment and prevention work be greatly increased, as the enormous amounts of money allocated to law enforcement and the processing and institutionalization of drug-related offenders are saved (e.g., Nadelmann 1989; Stevenson 1990).

Although legalizers are able to provide the most thorough and penetrating criticisms against the prohibition approach, their somewhat extreme-liberalist perspective is too drastic, and perhaps too untested, to readily gain the confidence and acceptance of both the public and policy makers in the drug field. There is the fear that legalization would promote excessive use; it is not clear how the control and regulation of the supply and distribution of various drugs by the government could be effectively achieved, nor is it clear how the government could reconcile the fact that legalization may aggravate, by lengthening the list of licit drugs, the already heavy damages to health due to the more widespread use of alcohol and tobacco (e.g., Jacobs 1990; Beaglehole 1991; Goldstein and Kalant 1990). What is unresolved is the extent to which *harmful* use of the currently illicit drugs might increase in a legally regulated regime.

Another popular approach to drug use and treatment is the 'medical' model. Since the turn of the century, modern scientific medicine, based on the germ theory of disease, has become the dominant and mainstream school of medicine in the West (Brown 1979). The tremendous progress of scientific medicine in the conquest of diseases, and the confidence of the public in modern medicine, have not only allowed the medical profession to secure nearly total autonomy in medical and health matters, but also encouraged the profession to spread its reach to a wide range of 'deviant behaviours' previously not lying within the purview of medicine, a process described as 'medicalization of deviance' (Conrad and Schneider 1992). More and more deviant behaviours have come to be defined and treated as medical problems. The list of medicalized deviance includes, for example, mental illness, alcoholism, opiate abuse, hyperactivity and learning disabilities in children, child abuse, over- or under-eating, homosexuality, compulsive gambling, juvenile delinquency, and even crime (Conrad 1992; Conrad and Schneider 1992).

Medicalizing deviance means redefining deviance from 'badness' to 'sickness.' In a way, such redefinition has the advantage of lifting the moral, or criminal, stigma from the deviant. The deviant, now a patient in the 'sick role' (Parsons 1951) is not held responsible for his/her sickness, but is obligated to seek medical help in order to recover as soon as possible. Thus, the control of deviance shifts from legal authorities to the medical profession. In drug addiction, the drug addict is perceived as a sick person rather than a criminal, and he/she should be brought into the orbit of medical attention and control. However, as many critics of the modern medical institution have shown, the success of medicalization has been much more limited than the medical profession would have anticipated. Medicine has barely gained a foothold in deviant behaviours that do not have, or only marginally have, a medical component, such as child abuse, compulsive gambling, and delinquency. It fares better in dealing with types of deviance that seem to have a stronger medical component, including mental illness, alcoholism, drug addiction, and eating disorders. Nevertheless, even for these medically-related deviant behaviours, medicine has not come up with magical remedies that *alone* could cure the 'diseases' (Conrad 1992; Fox 1977). In the case of drug addiction, the use of drugs, and the treatment and rehabilitation of drug addicts, involve a multiplicity of factors at not only the physiological level, but the psychological, social, and cultural levels as well. Adopting only the medical model in understanding substance use and dealing with the drug problem is to commit a reductionist fallacy.

The three models discussed above differ greatly in how they define drug use, the user, the consequences of drug use, and what the appropriate societal reactions should be. Their limitations are such that they are by no means the ideal basis for the formulation of drug policy. The Harm Reduction Model is *not* another attempt to provide a new set of definitions of drug use that would exacerbate existing confusions in approaches to drug policy. Rather, it seeks to avoid falling into the snares of moral, legal, and medical-reductionist biases exhibited by other approaches. In fact, it is an approach to reducing drug-related harm 'with no strings attached.' By not associating itself with specific moral, legal, or medical interpretations of the phenomenon of drug use, the Harm Reduction Model releases itself from many of the unnecessary constraints on drug strategies set by existing approaches.

Before we go on to describe the harm reduction approach, it is worth mentioning that, whether by accident or by design, this model has many parallels with the current approach in the 'new' public health and the 'healthy cities' movement. Early public-health efforts, concerned primarily with prevention work such as sanitation and control of contagious diseases, were based on the above-mentioned medical model. Since the 1960s, public health has evolved into a broader perspective that embraces factors at the psychological, social, and environmental levels (Ashton and Seymour 1988; Duffy 1993; Berridge 1993). For example, the host, the agent, and the environment represented the three points of intervention adopted in the report of the Cooperative Commission on the Study of Alcoholism in the United States in the 1960s (Plaut 1967; Lee 1994). A more recent version of the agent-host-environment triangle was reformulated for the drug field as drug-set-setting (Zinberg 1984).

Since this latest version of public health accords an active and conscious, rather than passive and mechanical, role to the actor, recognizes the importance of interaction among physical, psychological, social, and cultural factors in shaping prevention and intervention outcomes, and makes no assumptions about the moral and legal natures of drug use, it is no wonder that Harm Reductionists found this 'new public health' approach appealing right at the beginning of the harm reduction initiatives, and looked to this approach for insights in building the conceptual and practical bases for the Harm Reduction Model. Indeed, harm reduction was inspired by the positive outcomes due to public-health measures such as the control of alcohol availability (Bruun, Edwards, Lumio, Mäkelä, Pan, Popham, Schmidt, Skog, Sulkunen, and Österberg 1975), public education on the health risks of tobacco use (Beauchamp 1990), methadone maintenance programs for opioid dependence (Sells 1977), and, more recently, needle-exchange programs for injection drug users for the reduction of the risk of HIV infection (Stimson 1990).

What, then, are the major features of the public-health-centred Harm Reduction Model? Although a more definite profile of this nascent perspective has yet to emerge, the extensive discussion at conferences and in books, journals, and other publications (e.g., O'Hare, Newcombe, Matthews, Buning, and Drucker 1992; Heather et al. 1993; Riley 1993, 1994; Erickson 1995; Single 1995; Room 1991; Cheung 1994) has offered some common themes that can be summarized as follows:

A. At the Conceptualization Level

1/A value-neutral view of drug use:

Harm reduction attaches no moral, legal, or medical-reductionist strings to drug use. Just like the use of 'licit' drugs, and just like other lifestyle practices, the use of 'illicit' drugs is not intrinsically immoral, criminal, or medically deviant. Drug use is one of many behaviours exhibited by individuals and populations that ranges from experimentation to problematic expressions.

2/A value-neutral view of user:

Since use of drugs is 'normal' behaviour, the user is a normal person rather than a morally, criminally, or medically deviant person.

3/Focus on problem:

Since drug use and the user are not defined as intrinsically problematic, the focus of harm reduction is on problems, or harmful consequences, resulting from use rather than on use per se.

4/The irrelevance of abstinence:

Harm reduction does not attach the requirement of abstinence to the user in treatment programs. Although harm reduction is not inconsistent with the long-term goal of abstinence, harm reduction accepts the fact that the user will continue to use drugs while in a drug program or in the community.

5/User's role in harm reduction:

The user is regarded as an active rather than a passive entity, capable of making choices about his/her own life, taking responsibility for these choices, and playing an important role in prevention, treatment, and the recovery process.

B. At the Practical Level

1/Prioritization of goals:

Harm reduction gives priority to strategies that can achieve more immediate and realizable goals of reduction of drug-related harm, rather than to those that are preoccupied with long-term intervention outcomes such as abstinence.

2/Pragmatic programs:

As such, harm reduction programs do not confine themselves to any specific, well-defined forms. Any strategy that helps to achieve the immediate and realizable goal of reduction of harmful consequences of drug use can be, quite eclectically, incorporated into a harm reduction program. With this flexibility, a range of innovative methods can be designed for reducing harms associated with various levels of drug problems.

3/User-centred programs:

Harm reduction programs solicit the cooperation and participation of drug users in determining the most appropriate prevention or intervention modalities. User-centred programs avoid marginalizing or stigmatizing users, and thus do not alienate them from the programs that are supposed to benefit them.

4/Emphasis of choice:

Harm reduction programs are not dogmatic and coercive structures. Rather, they are designed on the basis of accurate, scientific knowledge about drugs and drug use. Users are encouraged to voluntarily make their own choices regarding prevention and intervention issues; some of these choices may involve facing the current realities of what society is willing or able to provide, as well as a consideration of drug users' own responsibilties as members of communities.

C. At the Policy Level

1/A mosaic of middle-range policies:

As harm reduction provides a framework for asking practical questions and designing relevant strategies pertaining to harms associated with particular types of levels of use, it can generate an indefinite number of concrete, more down-to-earth policy measures that match a wide spectrum of types of patterns of drug use. It is therefore not the aim of the Harm Reduction Model to advocate a 'macro,' sweeping policy, to be rigidly and uniformly applied to all types and levels of drug use and drug-related harms. The advantage of 'middle-range' policies is that they disaggregate drug-related problems into manageable components, so that specific strategies can be worked out to deal with them.

2/Accommodation by existing policy:

Although harm reduction is at odds with the dominant legal-sanction-based policy, the middle range and pragmatic nature of harm reduction measures makes it possible for certain harm reduction strategies to be tolerated, accepted, or even incorporated by legal authorities, without completely dismantling the counter-productive punitive policy. The support and cooperation of the police in needle-exchange programs for injection drug users is one of several examples of the diffusion of genuine harm reduction elements into the existing drug policy, enabling change to occur, and thereby bringing about gradual policy reforms (Tawil, Verster, and O'Reilly 1995).

3/Focus on human rights:

The Harm Reduction Model encourages consideration of human rights and civil liberties as areas in which harms are to be reduced. This pertains not only to users but also to the broader violations of the rights of all citizens in the name of the 'war on drugs.'

At the moment, the characteristics of the Harm Reduction Model described above are by no means exhaustive and conclusive. There are still many gaps – in the definition of 'harm,' the assessment of harm resulting from drug use, the evaluation of harm reduction programs, the obstacles in the political arena for the harm reduction movement – to be filled, before a well-defined and coherent paradigm can appear (Cheung 1994; Strang 1993; Mugford 1993).

The building of a new paradigm is a lengthy process. This endeavour requires many participants to engage in countless dialogues and debates, and in reporting experiences in developing, running, and evaluating practical harm reduction programs. In this regard, the international harm reduction conferences have provided one vehicle for the journey towards a new paradigm. The three different books that have resulted from these conferences have slightly different foci, which in a way reflect the stages of developments in the state of the art of the Harm Reduction Model over the years. As did the earlier phase of harm reduction, the first book placed a heavy emphasis on HIV/AIDS prevention among injection drug users, so that one-third of its papers were about various practical programs on HIV/AIDS prevention. Conceptual and measurement issues were rather scanty. Other topics dealt with in the first book included stereotyping of drug users by the media and law-enforcement agencies, patterns of drug use the possible role of the police in harm reduction, and the shortcomings of current drug laws.

As more and more people participated, it soon became clear that to become a full-fledged perspective, harm reduction needed to step beyond the confines of prevention of HIV infection among injection drug users. Developments in this direction were heeded in the second book. More chapters were devoted to the conceptual components of harm reduction. The application of this approach was extended to non-injecting modes of drug use and to a wide range of illicit and licit psychoactive substances. Moreover, while the first book documented only experiences of Western countries, the second book collected several chapters discussing harm reduction issues in developing countries.

The present volume highlights several aspects of harm reduction that were not adequately addressed in the previous two books. These include social and legal policy, human rights, alcohol and public health, field studies utilizing a variety of methodologies, and special populations. While this volume highlights new aspects of harm reduction, conceptual measurements and intervention aspects are not neglected.

As harm reduction is still a developing, rather than a fully developed, perspective, it is understandable that authors of chapters in this volume do not necessarily share exactly the same definitions or standards of a Harm Reduction Model. This volume, then, is part of the ongoing evolution of the harm reduction paradigm. Its editors would also like to remind readers that reducing drug-related harm is an active construction. An approach based on doing many different things in order to reduce the ever-changing nature of the adverse consequences of substance use is bound to be dynamic and difficult to pigeon-hole. This dynamism and pragmatism are also part of the very nature of harm reduction. Its flexibility also poses the risk that harm reduction may become all things to all people and lose its distinctive features. Therefore, it is vital that all those engaged in the theory and practice of harm reduction move towards a common understanding and application in the future.

REFERENCES

Alexander, B.K. 1990. *Peaceful Measures: Canada's Way Out of the 'War on Drugs.'* Toronto: University of Toronto Press.
Ashton, J., and H. Seymour. 1988. *The New Public Health*. Bristol, PA: Open University Press.
Beaglehole, R. 1991. 'Science, Advocacy and Health Policy: Lessons from the New Zealand Tobacco Wars.' *Journal of Public Health Policy* 12: 175–83.
Beauchamp, D.E. 1990. 'Alcohol and Tobacco as Public Health Challenges in a Democracy.' *British Journal of Addiction* 85: 251–4.
Berridge, V. 1993. 'Harm Minimization and Public Health: An Historical Perspective.' In N. Heather et al., eds, *Psychoactive Drugs and Harm Reduction: From Faith and Science*, 55–64. London: Whurr Publishers.
Brown, E.R. 1979. *Rockefeller Medicine Men: Medicine and Capitalism in America.* Berkeley, CA: University of California Press.
Bruun, K., G. Edwards, M. Lumio, K. Mäkelä, L. Pan, R.E. Popham, W. Schmidt,

O.-J. Skog, P. Sulkunen, and E. Österberg, eds. 1975. *Alcohol Control Policies in Public Health Perspective*. Vol. 25. Helsinki: Finnish Foundation for Alcohol Studies.

Cheung, Y.W. 1994. 'Review of *The Reduction of Drug-Related Harm*, ed. P.A. O'Hare et al., and of *Psychoactive Drugs and Harm Reduction: From Faith to Science*, ed. N. Heather et al. *Contemporary Drug Problems* 21(2): 341–9.

Cheung, Y.W., and P.G. Erickson. 1997. 'Crack Use in Canada: A Distant American Cousin.' In C. Reinarman, and H. Levine, eds, *Crack in Context: Demon Drugs and Social Justice*. Berkeley, CA: University of California Press.

Cheung, Y.W., P.G. Erickson, and T. Landau. 1991. 'Experience of Crack Use: Findings from a Community-Based Sample in Toronto.' *Journal of Drug Issues* 21(1): 121–41.

Ch'ien, J.M.N. 1993. 'The Concept of Harm and Risk Reduction in Drug Abuse and Co-morbidity.' *Spotlight* (Publication of Hong Kong Council of Social Service) 20 (February): 2.

Conrad, P. 1992. 'Medicalization and Social Control.' *Annual Review of Sociology* 18: 209–32.

Conrad, P., and J.W. Schneider. 1992. *Deviance and Medicalization: From Badness to Sickness*. Philadelphia: Temple University Press.

Day, J. 1993. 'Harm Minimization: Concept or Convenience?' *Spotlight* (Publication of Hong Kong Council of Social Service) 20 (February): 3–4.

Duffy, J. 1993. 'History of Public Health and Sanitation in the West since 1700.' In K.E. Kiple, ed., *The Cambridge World History of Human Disease*, 200–6. New York: Cambridge University Press.

Durkheim, E. 1950. *Rules of Sociological Methods*. 8th ed. Trans. S.A. Solvay and J.H. Mueller. Glencoe, IL: Free Press.

Erickson, P.G. 1992. 'Recent Trends in Canadian Drug Policy: The Decline and Resurgence of Prohibitionism.' *Daedalus* 121(3): 239–67.

– 1993. 'The Law, Social Control, and Drug Policy: Models, Factors, and Processes.' *International Journal of the Addictions* 28(12): 1155–76.

– 1995. 'Harm Reduction: What It Is and Is Not.' *Drug and Alcohol Review* 14: 283–5.

Erickson, P.G., E.M. Adlaf, R.G. Smart, and G.F. Murray. 1994. *The Steel Drug: Cocaine and Crack in Perspective*. 2nd ed. New York: Lexington Books.

Erickson, P.G., and Y.W. Cheung. 1992. 'Drug Crime and Legal Control: Lessons from the Canadian Experience.' *Contemporary Drug Problems* 19(2): 247–77.

Erickson, P.G., and C.A. Ottaway. 1994. 'Policy – Alcohol and Other Drugs.' In P.E. Nathan, J.W. Langenbucher, B.S. McCrady, and W. Frankenstein, eds, *Annual Review of Addictions Research and Treatment*, 3: 331–41. New York: Elsevier.

Fox, R.C. 1977. 'The Medicalization and Demedicalization of American Society.' *Daedalus* 106: 9–22.

Goldstein, A., and H. Kalant. 1990. 'Drug Policy: Striking the Right Balance.' *Science* 249: 1513–21.

Heather, N., A. Wodak, E.A. Nadelmann, and P. O'Hare, eds. 1993. *Psychoactive Drugs and Harm Reduction: From Faith to Science.* London: Whurr Publishers.

Jacobs, J. 1990. 'Imagining Drug Legalization.' *The Public Interest*, 101: 28–42.

Lee, J.M. 1994. 'Historical and Theoretical Considerations: Implications for Multiculturalism in Substance Abuser Services.' In J.J. Gordon, ed., *Managing Multiculturalism in Substance Abuse Services*, 3–21. Thousand Oaks, CA: Sage.

Mugford, S. 1993. 'Harm Reduction: Does It Lead Where Its Proponents Imagine?' In N. Heather et al., eds, *Psychoactive Drugs and Harm Reduction: From Faith to Science*, 21–33. London: Whurr Publishers.

Nadelmann, E.A. 1989. 'Drug Prohibition in the United States: Costs, Consequences, and Alternatives.' *Science* 245: 240–6.

O'Hare, P.A., R. Newcombe, A. Matthews, E.C. Buning, and E. Drucker, eds. 1992. *The Reduction of Drug-Related Harm.* London: Routledge.

Parsons, T. 1951. *The Social System.* New York: Free Press.

Plaut, T.F.A. 1967. *Alcohol Problems: A Report to the National Cooperative Commission on the Study of Alcoholism.* New York: Oxford University Press.

Riley, D. 1993 'The Policy and Practice of Harm Reduction: The Application of Harm Reduction Measures in a Prohibitionist Society.' Ottawa: Canadian Centre on Substance Abuse.

– 1994. 'The Harm Reduction Model: Pragmatic Approaches to Drug Use from the Area Between Intolerance and Neglect.' Ottawa: Canadian Centre on Substance Abuse.

Room, R. 1991. 'Social Science Research and Alcohol Policy Making.' In P. Roman, ed., *Alcohol: The Development of Sociological Perspectives on Use and Abuse*, 315–39. New Brunswick, NJ: Centre of Alcohol Studies, Rutgers University.

Sells, S.B. 1977. Methadone Maintenance in Perspective.' *Journal of Drug Issues* 7: 13–22.

Single, E.W. 1995. 'Defining Harm Reduction.' *Drug and Alcohol Review* 14: 283–5.

Stevenson, R. 1990. 'Can Markets Cope with Drugs?' *Journal of Drug Issues* 20: 659–66.

Stimson, G.V. 1990. 'AIDS and HIV: The Challenge for British Drug Services.' *British Journal of Addiction* 85: 329–39.

Strang, J. 1993. 'Drug Use and Harm Reduction: Responding to the Challenge.'

In N. Heather et al., eds, *Psychoactive Drugs and Harm Reduction: From Faith to Science*, 3–20. London: Whurr Publishers.

Tawil, O., A. Verster, and K.R. O'Reilly. 1995. 'Enabling Approaches for HIV/ AIDS Prevention: Can We Modify the Environment and Minimize the Risk?' *AIDS* 9: 1299–1306.

Zinberg, N.E. 1994. *Drug, Set and Setting: The Basis for Controlled Intoxicant Use.* New Haven, CT: Yale University Press.

PART I: HISTORY, POLICY, AND SOCIAL THEORY

1 The Case of the Two Dutch Drug-Policy Commissions: An Exercise in Harm Reduction, 1968–1976

PETER D.A. COHEN

In the unruly times of the sixties, when a series of different political movements had unsettled the classic paternalistic ruling style in the Netherlands, youth had suddenly started to dance to strange music on strange intoxications. Sons and daughters of doctors, bricklayers, judges, and bank employees smoked a strange-smelling weed called marijuana. According to the law this was forbidden, and according to mostly American sources, marijuana provoked all kinds of psychic disturbance. Even worse, marijuana hunger was unsatisfiable and led to addiction, not only to the weed itself but also to other illicit drugs like cocaine and morphine.

At the onset of marijuana smoking and drug policy in the Netherlands, the authorities of the law and of medicine spoke out against marijuana use and described it as a dangerous evil (Maalsté 1993). However, the numbers of (mostly cannabis) users increased as did the difficulties of law enforcement against them. This trend led to a growing debate in professional journals and in the daily papers about the merits of the conventional views on drug use. At the end of the sixties time was ripe for a typical Dutch solution of very difficult problems, the setting up of a commission (Leuw 1994).

This presentation will deal with two important commissions that were set up at the end of the sixties with a small overlap in time. First, the composition of both commissions will be described, then their way of analysing the problem and their recommendations, to conclude with a few observations of why these commissions have been so influential and successful from a harm reduction point of view (de Kort 1994).

The Drug Commissions, 1968–1972

The first commission was set up in 1968 by the National Federation of Mental Health Organizations, a kind of umbrella organization. In the Netherlands, mental-health services used to be organized in a myriad of private and public-private settings along the lines of the different religious and political denominations. The previous year the National Federation of Mental Health Organizations had commissioned extensive research among drug users in the Netherlands. The investigator, Herman Cohen, a psychologist by training, worked at the Medical Faculty, Institute of Medical Sociology, University of Amsterdam. (H. Cohen was one of the members of both the Hulsman and Baan commissions.) It also set up a drug-policy commission of which the broadly defined task was 'to clarify factors that are associated with the use of drugs, to give insight into the phenomenon as a whole, and to suggest proposals for a rational policy' (Hulsman 1971). The members of the commission included law-enforcement officials, alcohol-treatment experts, psychiatrists, a drug-use researcher, and a sociologist. The commission was chaired by Louk Hulsman, a professor of criminal law at the University of Rotterdam who was very critical towards the use of criminal law in general. This commission presented its final report in October 1971. However, drafts of the final report had circulated before that date.

Also in 1968, the under-secretary of health, a medical man himself and worried about the use of marijuana, set up a state commission. After an unsuccessful chairmanship of an inspector of mental health, it was chaired from 1970 by Pieter Baan, a chief inspector of mental health. Health care in the Netherlands is divided into a number of areas, each having its own inspection structure. Addiction treatment has its own inspection, like dental health, physical health, and so on. This commission was asked 'to investigate causes of increasing drug use, how to confront irresponsible use of drugs, and to propose a treatment system for those who developed dependence of these drugs' (The Hague 1972). The Hulsman and Baan commissions had some members in common. In both we find Herman Cohen (a researcher of drug use trained in medical sociology), Mr Hartsuiker (a public prosecutor), Mr Krauweel (the head of the Jellinek Alcohol Treatment Clinic in Amsterdam), and Mr Witte (chief of the forensic laboratory of the Ministry of Justice). In the Baan Commission we find a few top officials of the Ministry of Justice, the chief of police of Amsterdam, a few psychiatrists, and two sociologists who did not participate in the Hulsman commission. The final report of the Baan Commission was presented to the Minister of Health in February 1972. Four years later, in 1976, the new Opium Law was adopted, including the articles that made decriminalization of cannabis use possible, as advocated by the Baan Commission. Decriminalization here meant to render former criminal behaviour or acts exempt from penal-law consequences.

The Hulsman Commission

The report of the Hulsman Commission is the more theoretical of the two. It gave an analysis of drug use, the social mechanisms behind drug problems, and the limited power of criminal law in these issues, and the outlines of a future drug policy for the Netherlands. It analysed drugs fundamentally from a heuristic point of view, in which the pharmaco-logical properties of drugs were integrated in set and setting, mostly conceptualized as the 'drug scene.' Herman Cohen was responsible for this innovative approach. He was the only one who had been research-ing drug use empirically from within, as it existed in the Netherlands, as well as being acquainted with the international social-scientific litera-ture on drug use. This gave him a substantial authority. About opiates, the Hulsman report states that these substances may give physical addiction. But also: 'Physiological, psychological and sociological fac-tors may keep a user connected to opiates, and if one detoxifies a heavy user, one does not have a "normal" individual but an unhappy ex junky, who maneuvers with difficulty in a huge emptiness' (p. 16).

The Hulsman report examines different risks associated with different substances as they occur in different use patterns. As its conclusion, the commission states: 'The different drugs have the risk in common that one does not restrict oneself to limited use, but that one evolves to long-lasting and intensive use. In that case they are harmful' (p. 19). This insight, that illicit drugs can be used in a controlled and limited way, was just as unconventional in those days as it is now. Furthermore, the report shows the negative effects of marginalizing drug-using subcultures. It also describes imprisonment of drug users as conflicting with the intended effect of separating the user from the heavier types of drug-using subcultures. As a clarification of this point, the commission quotes Herman Cohen that there is no evidence for a 'stepping stone'-like sequence of different drug use. However, becoming a member of a (mar-ginal) drug scene or drug-use subculture may make a cannabis user familiar with the existence of other drugs and other patterns of use. Here we see the roots of an important concept in present-day drug policy in the Netherlands: separation of the demand and the supply sides of different drug markets. The basic assumption underlying this concept is that one kind of drug user (of, for instance, heroin) will 'contaminate' another kind of drug user (of, for example, cannabis) when the two kinds of drug use are forced into one marginalized user subculture because the markets of two drugs can only jointly exist in one criminal arena.

About the use of state power, the Hulsman report says that 'the State can not have a disapproving point of view only on the ground that a certain behavior is not fitting in the concepts of life of those who carry State power' (p. 40). 'If an individual makes a choice that may be dangerous to herself as a private person (e.g. someone refuses blood transfusions) no one should deny her this right. Even when such behavior might endanger others (e.g. parents who do not allow their children to be vaccinated even if a danger for infection exists) the right of a personal choice will not be denied' (p. 42). Here the Hulsman Commission refers to a dearly won right of certain religious groups in the Netherlands to refuse vaccination for religious reasons.

About law enforcement against drug trafficking, the commission states that once on this road, police forces will have to be 'constantly enlarged to keep pace with the never ending escalation' (p. 49). 'If we opt for criminal law as the central means for opposing drug use, this option is inadequate and therefor also extremely dangerous. Time after time it will show that the means will fall short, upon which those who favor punishment will plead for increase of law enforcement, until it will be amplified a hundred fold from the present situation ... This will boost polarization between the different parts of our society and can result in increased violence' (p. 51). The commission says that full decriminalization is the right policy in the long run, but this should be done gradually.

The discussion of the seventy-page Hulsman report will be finished by summarizing its policy recommendations for the short term:

1/The use of cannabis and the possession of small quantities should be taken out of criminal law straight away. Production and distribution should for the time being remain within criminal law but as a misdemeanour.
2/The use and possession of other drugs will remain in the sphere of criminal law, as a misdemeanour, but in the long run have to be liberated completely.

3/Those who run into difficulties with their drug use should have adequate treatment institutions at their disposal.

An interesting detail of the proposals for the short term is that the production of non-cannabis drugs has to remain within criminal law as an offence. The background of this conclusion is not provided. It likely reflects the perspective of the commission on gradual long-term decriminalization of all drug use.

The Hulsman report strongly pleads for stepped-up research efforts in this field and the creation of a system for dissemination of information about drugs and for drug-treatment evaluation. The report still reads as a useful, rationally argued and humane blueprint of general drug-policy principles. It fully deserves translation into English.

The Baan Commission

The report of the Baan Commission gives a short overview of the risks associated with the use of drugs, and divides these risks into physical damage, psychological damage, and social damage. Quite consistently, the commission includes alcohol and tobacco in its overview.

The report describes the social aspects of drug use and the small drug trade in the Netherlands, showing that the special characteristics of youth culture and subculture are important determinants of the functions drug use have. If society, according to the Baan report, stigmatizes deviant behaviour by punitive measures, the probability of this behaviour intensifying is a serious danger, initiating a spiral that will make return of the individual to a socially accepted lifestyle increasingly difficult (p. 26).

Further, the Baan report discusses research results that counter hypotheses of drug use stemming from social misery or pathology. It literally quotes the research finding of a Dutch sociologist that drug-using youths 'not only read more about drugs but also read more about other things than drugs: art, politics, science and philosophy than youths from the two control groups' (p. 27).

Another topic the report deals with is the epidemiology of drug use in the Netherlands, and the demographic characteristics of users. It concludes that much drug use is short-lasting experimentation by young persons. Differences between metropolitan and non-metropolitan areas are quickly diminishing and are expected to disappear completely. According to the Baan report, cannabis use does not lead directly to other drug use. However, the report quotes an American source in showing that laws that declare cannabis an illegal drug will promote contacts between cannabis users and those who use heavier substances. This may lead to multiple drug use. Like the Hulsman report, Baan proposes the separation of drug-using subcultures, which has a particular social-scientific perspective at its base.

Looking at this 'stepping stone' thesis from empirical evidence now, after more than twenty years of factual decriminalization, one can observe the following: in Amsterdam drugs like cocaine and heroin are only used by persons who have some experience with cannabis. Lifetime prevalence of cocaine among cannabis users is just under 23 per cent (versus 7 per cent in the population as a whole), and of heroin, 4 per cent (versus 2 per cent). The large majority of cannabis users has no experience at all with other drugs. Last-thirty-days use of other drugs is very low among cannabis users (2 per cent for cocaine and 0.2 per cent for heroin). The idea that decriminalizing cannabis and other drugs for individual use would be followed by explosions of other drug use was not forecast by the commissions, and, as appears, rightly so (Cohen 1995).

In relation to law enforcement, the Baan Commission quotes a 1970 report by the Public Prosecutor's Office in which criminal law is described as inadequate regarding drug users. Users will be served better by drug information and prevention efforts than by prosecution.

One of the longer chapters of the Baan report is dedicated to cannabis, because, as Herman Cohen remarked twenty-five years later, 'the commission was firmly dedicated to ending this mess of youngsters going to prison for a few grams of hash' (Cohen 1994). The report describes the use of cannabis-products as relatively benign and the health risks as relatively limited. If sometimes unusual behaviour of cannabis-consuming youth is seen, this is more considered a result of specific subcultural norms and ideologies than of pharmacology. But cannabis use when driving or when operating machines in factories is 'not responsible.' 'Consumption [of cannabis] without risks for the individual or society can only take place during recreation' (p. 59).

The report proposes to design a 'danger scale' of drugs, in which concepts like 'soft' use and 'hard' use of a drug are incorporated. The Baan Commission adds a comment that is still as unusual as it is to the point: a danger scale that only takes pharmacological properties of a substance into account 'can not be an operational guide line for the State' (p. 64). Such a scale should divide drugs into those with 'acceptable' and those with 'unacceptable' risks. The commission states explicitly that controlled use of drugs is possible. The basis for state intervention should be to try to prevent the use of those drugs that present the greatest risks. Since opinions on risks are so diverse between experts, this topic should be further investigated.[1]

For cannabis use and trade a number of options are discussed. A suggestion is given to treat cannabis trade below a quarter of a kilogram as a misdemeanour only. The report discusses legal supply of cannabis as a means of preventing the development of cannabis-user subcultures that will reinforce 'hard' patterns of use and multiple drug use. But the commission considers this approach as being against the spirit of the 1961 Single Convention on Drugs. Although it proposes trying to change the Single Convention on this issue (of cannabis use and trafficking), it considers waiting for uncertain treaty changes as too impractical for the short-term goals the commission wants to reach.

About drugs other than cannabis, the Baan report has very little to offer. In spite of its remarks about the many complexities and uncertainties of rating the pharmacological and other potential dangers of a substance, it treats all other drugs than cannabis as substances 'with unacceptable risks' (p. 67). Trafficking these drug will have to remain an offence. However, for users of such drugs 'confrontation with criminal law is not an adequate approach' (p. 68). For the time being, the commission proposes looking at the use of these drugs as an offence, with complete decriminalization as a policy goal from such time as a good treatment system has been created. Until then, criminal law should be used as a tool for manoeuvring heavy user–patients into treatment.

We should understand this rather blunt and opportunistic approach towards non-cannabis drugs as the expression of a situation in which little non-cannabis use occurred. Some LSD, like amphetamine, use was found, but consumers of these drugs were considered a small minority among drug users. Opium was used by a small minority of all illicit drug users, of whom in the course of 1972 a still smaller minority would switch to heroin after the Amsterdam police cut off opium supply. Among *frequent* drug users, Cohen found 20 per cent opiate use (Baan report, p. 29). It is not clear if this figure reflected current use of opiates or lifetime prevalence.

Why Did the Baan Report Succeed in Shaping Dutch Drug Policy?[2]

To look for an answer to the question, 'Why did the Baan Commission (backed up by the more radical Hulsman report) succeed in shaping

Dutch drug policy,' we have to perceive the Baan Commission in the setting of the time in which it was asked to perform its task. Three possible factors could be relevant for an answer to this question.

First, Hulsman gives an important clue when he draws attention to the period of his employment at the Ministry of Justice. In 1959 he wrote a memo for the minister of justice about the draft Single Convention that had been sent to the Dutch government for comment. He states that the harsh law-enforcement approach of the draft was perceived as 'counter to our criminal law policies at the time' (Maalsté 1993, 140–1). At the end of the fifties, but certainly in the sixties, official policy was to restrict the reach of law enforcement, to prevent law breaking by adequate social policies, and to keep law breakers out of prison as much as possible. We should not forget that in those days lack of enthusiasm for expanding the realm of criminal law was a mainstream ideological background to the drug-policy issue. This means that, when the Hulsman and Baan commissions were writing their reports at the end of the sixties, participating high officials of the Ministry of Justice plus the Public Prosecutor's office did not discover the importance of diminishing the role of criminal law, *they simply applied it.*

The second important aspect for understanding the relative success of the policy recommendations by Baan is the social and publicity climate around cannabis use in that period. In 1969 the national and regional papers had published conspicuous articles on the results of Herman Cohen's survey of about a thousand drug users in the country. His conclusion was that addiction was a rare phenomenon, that most drug use occurred with persons of a relatively high level of education, and that (the threat of) imprisonment was the most harmful of all consequences of drug use (Cohen 1968).

In July 1970, the conservative *Elsevier*, a nation-wide weekly, reported extensively on the drug-use behaviour of a large crowd at an open-air pop concert in Rotterdam. It interviewed treatment experts present at the site to deliver assistance when needed, and a lot of people associated with drug policy, including the leading MPs on the public-health and justice subcommissions in parliament. The conclusion of all these interviews was that drug use was not a problem in the Netherlands, and that cannabis users were not 'addicts' but nice, controlled folks. An interesting detail of this article is that both police spokespeople and public prosecutors seemed to anticipate more formal changes would ensue in liberalizing drug legislation.

During the parliamentary discussions on the budget in 1970, a member of the large Labour Party confronted the under-secretary of public health with the pressing question that he was '[using] all his influence to prevent imprisonment of any drug user.' Moreover, the MP said, 'Available research results show that marijuana and hashish do not belong in the Opium Law.' (The 'Opium Law' [Dutch, 'Opium wet'] is the name for the Dutch Dangerous Drugs Act.) 'We request the Under secretary to bring the topic of cannabis legalization into consultation with the Ministry of Justice' (Handelingen 1970). At the time Mrs Padt-Jansen asked these questions the Baan Commission had just been expanded to its final composition and was working on its final report. These quotes serve to illustrate that for many in the country cannabis had to be lifted out of the sphere of law enforcement. The two commissions did not have to invent this viewpoint. It was exactly the same non-law-enforcement approach to social problems in general.

During the preparation of the new Opium Law, after the report of the Baan Commission had been presented to the cabinet, the minister of justice (a young law professor and progressive Catholic, Professor van Agt) found the Baan report too conservative! Professor van Agt had even written decriminalization of drugs into the party program of the Catholic Party (Hulsman 1994). The reason that the cabinet in which he took part accepted increased criminalization of non-cannabis drugs was, according to Hulsman, the Arab oil boycott of the Netherlands.[3] This made the Netherlands so dependent on neighbouring countries for its oil supply that strong pressure from the Ministries of Foreign Affairs and Economic Affairs forced van Agt and the cabinet to keep drug use within the realm of criminal law and to increase non-cannabis drug penalties from a maximum of four years' imprisonment to twelve.

If the new Dutch law in this area would be too unacceptable to Germany and the United Kingdom, they might reconsider their assistance with oil deliveries to the Netherlands. This alleged fear, based on an unforeseen complication of international oil politics, had nothing to do with other legal constraints as found in the Single Convention of 1961. If this analysis is correct, it would mean that decriminalizing cannabis use and retail selling, considered by all as the most important function of a new drug law, was bought for the price of a more severe criminal-law involvement for other drug trafficking. We should not exclude the possibility, however, that paying this price was understood as an unimportant cosmetic move. Non-cannabis drug use was, in the early seventies, not a problem. Then why not use a little cosmetics to make the decriminalization of cannabis a bit more palatable for foreign (and possibly domestic) opponents?[4]

The main purpose of remodelling the Opium Law was not to introduce a fundamentally different drug policy (perceived as impossible for the time because of existing global agreements), but to satisfy then existing needs to keep cannabis users out of prison. Keeping law breakers out of prison as much as possible already was accepted social policy. Only a modest change, official discrimination between 'drugs with acceptable risks' and those with 'unacceptable risks,' was needed to enable the new law, adopted in 1976, to fulfil that purpose.

A possible third reason for the success of the two commissions has to do with the limited experience of the Netherlands with prohibitive drug policies. Not only was such experience limited, it was also part of a distant past. In the Dutch Indies a profitable and highly regulated policy was developed on opium for smoking. In this state-run monopoly opium licences were sold to the highest bidders (mostly Chinese), who were then allowed to sell opium to all who wanted it. Marcel de Kort (1996) states that among sixty million inhabitants of the then Dutch East Indies, about 260,000 persons were regular opium smokers, most of whom were well-to-do Chinese. Later, Chinese immigrants in the Netherlands were allowed to smoke opium till well into the sixties, but only in their own homes or opium dens. This custom went undisturbed and practically unseen by the alcohol culture around them. For the few explorers during the sixties into the unknown worlds of opium dreams (students, artists, and weird university professors) opium was cheap and easily had from this enclave. The global opium treaties that had slowly developed since 1911 did not stop the Netherlands from continuing its opium policy within the Dutch East Indies, until the Japanese invaded during the Second World War. The American government forced the Netherlands to promise to cease its opium regime in the Dutch East Indies under the threat that no support would otherwise be given to ousting the Japanese from the Indies (de Kort 1995). When global treaties were designed from 1911 on, The Netherlands cooperated by signing treaties on cocaine, cannabis, opium, heroin, and morphine, but not because drugs were a problem.

Drugs had never been experienced as a problem within the Netherlands, because their use was almost unknown: opium use in the colonies was considered well confined to the locals and at most a foreign vice. Therefore, the treaties were signed because of opportunism and the requirements of global diplomacy, but without any attendant national motivation. In contrast with other countries, like the United Kingdom or the United States, the Netherlands had never been forced to look for solutions to (true or perceived) local or national drug-use epidemics, with the exception of alcohol. In that area, prohibition was considered but never adopted. This implied an absence of prohibitive drug-policy models and a presence of a certain 'naiveté' in these matters. This naiveté remained into the sixties and allowed drug-policy inventors in the Netherlands to look at foreign drug-policy ideologies from a detached perspective, certainly as far as cannabis was concerned. The same absence of experience may be at the base of the relative lack of concern for the rather 'theoretical' law-enforcement measures in relation to non-cannabis drug use proposed by Baan. We have to remember that in the late sixties such use was even more uncommon than later, in the seventies and eighties.

In summary: at the time of the Baan report, it was mainstream thinking that criminal law should be kept as restricted as possible. This innovation, made before drug legislation had to be adjusted, considerably eased the way for decriminalizing cannabis use, a drug-policy goal that had already made itself felt before the commissions started their work. A 'proper' sacrifice was made to foreign and domestic opponents by increasing maximum punishment for the trafficking of 'drugs with unacceptable risks' to the atypically high figure of twelve years. This increased punishment probably was more a cosmetic move than a choice grounded in principle, the more so since *non-cannabis* drug use was not a problem at the time (or ever before).

Relevance of the Commissions for Present-Day Drug Policies in the Netherlands

The reports of the Hulsman and Baan commissions did what was expected of them. The underlying arguments (e.g., for not arresting individual drug users, as a policy applying to all drugs, not only to cannabis, and on the counter-productive potential of criminal law in this area) were so solid they stand till this day.

Somehow the Dutch practice of not arresting individual drug users – unless they cause social nuisance or show criminal behaviour – has become so normal that the reasons why it originated went forgotten. They were reconfirmed, albeit in a fashion, in the most recent government policy paper (The Hague 1995). One of the consequences of the policy that large-scale production and trafficking should be suppressed, but individual drug use should not, is the subsidy state institutions pay to organizations that check so-called Ecstasy pills at the entrance of raves (dance festivities). Consumers bring their MDMA (XTC) pills there for checking, free of charge, if they suspect irregularities. Also, the Department of Health issued a set of guidelines that municipalities have to follow when checking the quality of raves where XTC use is assumed to occur. This is considered wise prevention of risks. At the same time, law enforcement works hard to locate and dismantle XTC laboratories, thereby driving XTC production and wholesale activities underground, which enlarges the dangers of 'impure' XTC pills being marketed, something that is considered very risky for the individual user! So, harm reduction in the sphere of XTC consumption is reduced in scope and quality because of the dominant presence of law enforcement in this area. Legislation, tied up as it is to international agreements and international cooperation between law-enforcement institutions, cannot be adjusted to harm reduction views on drug policy.

In the period after the two commissions prepared their reports a lot has changed in the Dutch drug scene. Heroin was introduced in 1972 after the police stopped opium sales, and became the focus of some Surinamese immigrants. It also became the drug of a small number of Dutch white youth who found no link with the highly regulated labour market in this country. As in other industrial countries, heavy heroin use led to social downfall and marginalization. The prevalence of such use has always been very low, and the proportion of street-dwelling junkies among heroin users is low as well. However, their conspicuous presence has etched a highly undesirable image of heroin on the public mind (Grapendaal, Leuw, and Nelen 1995).

Non-conspicuous and occasional use of opiates (mainly heroin) simply does not exist in both public and expert opinion, although it does occur certainly in Amsterdam. In the age cohort of 18 to 42 years of Amsterdam's adult population, Cohen and Sas (1995) found in 1991 a 9 per cent *lifetime* opiate experience (all licit opiates included). Among a representative sample of community-based non-deviant cocaine users in the same age category and the same year this figure is 40 per cent. Although last-thirty-days' use is far lower than lifetime experience, these figures show that occasional opiate use occurs. Recent heroin use is so low in the household population as a whole (last-thirty-days' use is around one or two-tenths of a per cent in Amsterdam) that it is almost irrelevant for an overview of drug use.

Cocaine, introduced in the early seventies as well, and peaking in the period from 1982 to 1985, is now an established albeit not widely used substance in the Dutch capital. Seven per cent of the Amsterdam adult population over twelve years has used this substance (Sandwijk et al. 1995). MDMA or XTC appeared in the mid-eighties.

Cannabis use has almost 'normalized' in the Dutch cities in the sense that it is culturally more or less accepted, and certainly no longer taboo. High-quality figures for cannabis-use prevalence in the Dutch population are non-existent except for Amsterdam. NIPO, a large Gallup-type research institute in Amsterdam, found in 1982 a lifetime cannabis use prevalence of 9 per cent in a national sample of respondents eighteen years and older (N = 1089); in 1992 it found 12% (N = 1123). In 1993 it found again 9% (N = 1635, twelve years and older). In the capital, lifetime experience with cannabis is highest in the age cohort of 20 to 24 years at 50%, and 29% in the adult household population – twelve years and older – as a whole (Sandwijk et al. 1995). See, for an overview of almost all available cannabis-use data in the Netherlands, Korf 1995.

Since our first household survey in Amsterdam, lifetime experience with cannabis has risen from 23% in 1987 to 29% in 1994 (N = 4400). Because last-twelve-months and last-thirty-days consumption has remained stable (at 10 and 6% respectively) we assume that the rise in lifetime prevalence is due to the decease of the elderly. According to the mayor of Amsterdam, S. Patijn, the city has 380 outlets for cannabis-type drugs, so-called coffee shops, as of April 1996.

The heritage of the two commissions is most strongly felt in the cannabis scene. The public fears about cannabis are substantially lower in the Netherlands than elsewhere, although (as for instance in the case of legalized abortion) fractions of the population deplore our present policies. Of the Dutch public, 50 per cent thinks that marijuana is dangerous, versus 83% in neighbouring Germany. For heroin these figures are 90% versus 96% (Eurobarometer 1992). In a national survey in 1996 (N = 1139), NIPO found that 52 per cent of the total Dutch population agrees to the open selling of cannabis (of which about half wants to legalize fully). In the combined respondents of the cities of Amsterdam, Rotterdam, and the Hague this figure rises to 66% (NIPO 1996). The theoretical notions and the scientific analysis of drug use as made in the report of the Hulsman Commission has remained relevant. What we need is to reflect on these notions and reapply them to today's drug situation.

Thanks to the two commissions and the Dutch system of accessible health care and housing for all, modern drug-policy discussion in the Netherlands has been deeply influenced by 'harm reduction.' Enabling the notion of harm reduction to play a role in drug policy is an important step away from the drug-political fundamentalism of the bureaucracies that expand, amplify, and control the obsolete UN drug treaties. What is needed, however, is more emphasis on community-drug-use data that show that for most persons drug use, as is the case with alcohol, is a matter of choice and leisure, not of compulsion.

The task for progressive politicians is to help find a way to convince society to consider drug use as a choice people are free to make and to reform the function of the state in the field of drug policy as a provider of harm-reducing conditions. This task existed before in such diverse areas as traffic regulations, abortion, divorce, alcohol distribution, and – many years ago – religious freedom.

NOTES

I thank Marcel de Kort for his remarks on this paper.

1 This has not been done. In the last paper written by a Dutch government on drug policy, the drugs with acceptable and unacceptable risks are still exactly the same as they were in the Baan Commission report. See The Hague 1995. I criticized the government drug-policy paper on this point in Vrij Nederland, 21 October 1995, p. 18–19.

2 I have used the verb 'shaping' rather than 'changing' because the initial prohibitive responses to drug use were more an automatic reaction with the help of the spirit of the law than a policy. We may therefore see the drug policy system after Baan as an argued policy and no longer as a non-shaped automatism.

3 About the same reasons were given to Eric Fromberg (1994) by the then minister of health, Mrs Irene Vorrink.

4 The same use of cosmetic moves was made by the Dutch government in 1995 when it proposed to cut down sales to private persons in coffee shops from 30 grams of cannabis to 5 grams. Most consumers never buy more than a few grams, let alone 30. The main reason for this proposed change was to placate French critics.

REFERENCES

Cohen, H. 1968. Drugs, *Drugs, druggebruikers en drugscene*. Alphen a/d Rijn: Samson.
– 1994. Personal communication. 20 February.
Cohen, P. 1995. 'Cannabis Use in Amsterdam.' Lecture given in Utrecht, June (available on Internet: http://www.frw.uva.nl/cedro/).

Cohen, P., and A. Sas. 1995. *Cocaine Use in Amsterdam II*. Amsterdam: University of Amsterdam.

de Kort, M. 1994. The Dutch Cannabis Debate, 1968–1976. *Journal of Drug Issues* 24 (3): 417–27.

– 1995. 'Tussen patient en delinquent. Geschiedenis van het Nederlands drugbeleid.' Dissertation, Erasmus University, Rotterdam (Between Patient and Criminal: A History of Dutch Drug Policy).

– 1996. Lecture in the Pauluskerk. 1 April.

Elsevier (weekly magazine). 11 July 1970: 13–19.

Eurobarometer. 1992. 'Intra Europe Report.' Brussels, Belgium, 22 October.

Fromberg, E. 1994. 'Dutch Drug Policy: Past, Present and Future.' 7th International Conference of the Drug Policy Foundation, 17–20 November, Washington, DC.

Grapendaal, M., E. Leuw, and H. Nelen. 1995. *A World of Opportunities. Lifestyle and Economic Behaviour of Heroin Addicts in Amsterdam*. Albany: State University of New York Press.

The Hague. 1972. 'Achtergronden en risico's van druggebruik.' Den Haag: Staatsuitgeverij (Backgrounds and Risks of Drug Use).

– 1995. 'The Drug Policy of the Netherlands: Continuity and Change.' Den Haag: Staatsuitgeverij (Backgrounds and Risks of Drug Use).

Handelingen. Parliamentary session, 1969–70, 40th meeting, 3 February 1970, Intervention by Mrs Padt-Jansen, MP, p. 1959.

Hulsman, L. 1971. *Ruimte in het drugbeleid*. Meppel: Boom (Opening up Drug Policy).

– 1994. Personal communication. 22 February.

Korf, D. 1995. 'Dutch Treat: Formal Control and Illicit Drug Use in the Netherlands.' Dissertation, University of Amsterdam.

Leuw, E. 1994. 'Initial Construction and Development of the Official Dutch Drug Policy.' In E. Leuw and I. Haen Marshall, eds, *Between Prohibition and Legalization. The Dutch Experiment in Drug Policy*. Amsterdam/New York: Kugler Publications.

Maalsté, N. 1993.) *Het kruid, de krant, de kroongetuigen. De geschiedenis van hennep 1950–1970*. Utrecht: Stichting WGU.

NIPO Press Release Archive Service. 1996. Telepanel CO 29, Amsterdam (with thanks to Henk Foekema).

Sandwijk, P., P. Cohen, S. Musterd, and M. Langemeijer. 1995. 'Licit and Illicit Drug Use in Amsterdam. Report of a Household Survey in 1994 on the Prevalence of Drug Use among the Population of 12 Years and Older.' University of Amsterdam.

2 Legalization of Drugs: Responsible Action towards Health Promotion and Effective Harm Reduction Strategies

LINE BEAUCHESNE

To feed a man without loving him is to treat him as cattle.
To love him without respecting him is to keep him as a pet.

Mencius, AD 300 (cited in Low, 1994, 320; our translation)

Canada, with its orientation towards a health-promotion policy, has distanced itself somewhat from repressive American drug policies. Health and Welfare Canada, in its 1986 publication *A Framework for Health Promotion*, adopted the definition of health promotion endorsed by the World Health Organization: 'health promotion is the process of enabling people to increase control over, and to improve, their health' (Health and Welfare Canada, 1986: 6). In other words, health cannot merely be defined as the absence of illness; health policy cannot simply be defined as investment in finding cures. Health promotion implies increasing a person's autonomy over the management of his or her own health:

Today we are working with a concept which portrays health as a part of everyday living, an essential dimension of the quality of our lives. *'Quality of life' in this context, implies the opportunity to make choices and to gain satisfaction from living.* Health is thus envisaged as a resource which gives people the ability to manage and even to change their surroundings. *This view of health recognizes freedom of choice* and emphasizes the role of individuals and communities in defining what health means to them.

Viewed from this perspective, health ceases to be measurable strictly in terms of illness and death. It becomes a state which individuals and communities alike strive to achieve, maintain or regain, and not something that comes about merely as a result of treating and curing illnesses and injuries. *It is a basic and dynamic force in our daily lives, influenced by our circumstances, our beliefs, our culture and our social, economic and physical environments.* (ibid.: 3; emphasis added)

This Canadian approach with respect to health promotion implies several challenges; according to Health and Welfare Canada the most important of these, without doubt, is the reduction of socio-economic inequalities: 'Within the low-income bracket, certain groups have a higher chance of experiencing poor health than others. Older people, the unemployed, welfare recipients, single women supporting children and minorities such as natives and immigrants, all fall into this category. More than one million children in Canada are poor. Poverty affects over half of single-parent families, the overwhelming majority of them headed by women. These are the groups for whom "longer life but worsening health" is a stark reality' (ibid.: 4).

The consequences of drug use, for example, vary depending on a person's overall health; drug users' state of health varies considerably with social class and living conditions. Also, many remain ignorant concerning the effects of various illicit drugs as a result of current penal laws that, rather than encouraging public autonomy, handicap the implementation of a health-promotion policy to address drug use. Furthermore, as emphasized by Health and Welfare Canada, prohibition of specific drugs obscures the effects of the drugs most responsible for public health problems: alcohol, nicotine, caffeine, and prescription medications (Health and Welfare Canada 1990). To implement a Canadian health-promotion policy, therefore, drug laws must be changed.

The foregoing is significant. To establish effective harm reduction strategies, that is, policies other than managing public 'disorder' resulting from substance abuse, or imposing a moral-medical approach with a primary aim of 'contamination containment' (such as policies for AIDS, tuberculosis, and hepatitis)[1] requires, from a health-promotion viewpoint, devising ways to improve living conditions, increase autonomy, improve access to services as well as provide information on managing dependency and thereby reducing harm (AITQ 1995). The quote from Mencius that prefaces this chapter refers directly to these elements. It highlights respect for the client as central to the strategies to be developed, rather than the maintenance of order, fear of contamination, or even pity (Boilard 1994).

This article maintains that among the tools required to develop effective harm reduction strategies within a health promotion framework, legalization of all drugs must be envisaged.[2]

1 Drug Legislation and Health Promotion: Overview of the Current Situation

Several study committees, government commissions of inquiry, and research projects that measured the effectiveness of prohibiting certain drugs to prevent associated risks or danger are unanimous in their principal conclusion: prohibition is not only ineffective as a means of promoting health, it has aggravated the situations it should have prevented by resulting in the expansion of a 'black market' for drugs, and by depriving thousands of persons of specific medical treatments.

More precisely, these studies found no correlation between drug prohibition and a reduction in drug use. Prohibitive laws at best reduced the use of specific drugs, where their application limited drug availability (de Choiseul-Praslin 1991). There is no evidence, however, that reducing the availability of a given product will not simply increase the use of an alternative product, often more harmful to health than the one prohibited. The reasons for drug use cannot be reduced to defiance of the law, or the fact that drugs are available, or a lack of information regarding toxicity. A decision to use drugs may be based on criteria as varied as the pursuit of pleasure or euphoria, the desire to overcome shyness, curiosity, conformity to adolescent peer pressure, the desire for tranquillity or relaxation, adaptation to employment demands, the desire to forget conflicts or escape problems, and so on. Furthermore, fear of the law is not significant in influencing decisions to reduce or stop drug use. According to Erickson's study, concern for health is in fact a determining factor of such decisions:

The use of marijuana, for example, is the most studied crime available for comparison. Conclusions from a number of studies consistently indicate that the perceived certainty and severity of punishment are insignificant factors in deterring use. Similarly, cocaine users have been found to view the legal threat as remote. What apparently has been much more important in reversing the trend of increasing illicit drug use that marked the 1970s has been the growth in perceived harmfulness of the activity, which has in turn likely augmented social disapproval of drug use behaviour. In any weighing of legal and health risks of drug use, concerns about health predominate.

Those who would claim that recent declines in illicit drug use are directly related to legal threat are overlooking the fact that dramatic increases occurred in the 1970s, when either no relaxing of laws against possession occurred or legal changes were demonstrably unrelated to use levels. Also, significant declines in cigarette smoking have occurred without arresting and jailing tobacco users, as the long-range impact of heightened awareness of the health hazards permeated through the population, and was reinforced by restrictions on smoking environments. As a primary prevention tool, criminal law is particularly ineffective against juveniles at the ages when much drug initiation occurs. Thus, declining illicit drug use has likely been independent of existing criminal law, and is unlikely to be affected by the easing of criminalization. Furthermore, it seems likely that greater flexibility in preventive programs and a consistent message of concern are more effective in the public health approach when they are not contradicted by the continued existence of punitive sanctions. (Erickson 1990: 565–6)

In the absence of a legitimate market, a black market responds to demands for illicit drugs. Drug-trafficking networks have developed where neither product quality nor places of distribution are regulated. Drug dealers are immersed in every environment: schools, discotheques, the street, the work place, and so forth. In most cases, products are adulterated to increase profits. The harmfulness of current laws prohibiting drugs is far more dramatic in this situation than were the laws prohibiting alcohol earlier in this century. Because such laws are international, the black market extends to more than sixty countries. Being so widespread, the black market has attracted a far broader range of drug traffickers, with far greater resources (Boustany 1993; Brouet 1991; Centre d'Études des Conflits 1991; de Choiseul-Praslin 1991; Fottorino 1991; Grimal 1993; de Kotchko et Datskevitch 1994; Makhlouf 1994; Observatoire Géopolitique des Drogues 1995; Sauloy and Le Bonniec 1992).

As a second health consequence of prohibiting specific drugs, their application for therapeutic use has been ignored. This applies especially in the case of marijuana or heroin. Persons who might otherwise benefit are deprived of their use to reduce pain, relieve anxiety, and so on. (Michka 1993). Another consequence is an increased difficulty in establishing harm reduction policies that would allow substance abusers sufficient autonomy to reduce the problems linked to their dependence (Brisson 1994). Without a change in existing legal prohibitions, persons with problematic illicit drug use habits cannot seek help without risking penal repression or social discrimination. Furthermore, adequate services to help such persons are difficult to implement in the context of prohibitive laws. Needle-exchange programs, for example, are too restrictive; few of the substance-abuse programs designed for injectable drugs, in any of the countries studied, will demonstrate correct injection practices, antidotes in case of overdose, access to helpful crisis-line numbers independent of police intervention, and so on (Caballero 1992; Cesoni 1996; Lauzon 1994; Schiray 1992).

In summary, studies of the effectiveness of prohibition as a means to promote health and to establish harm reduction aims and strategies with that objective have clearly demonstrated the old cliché: not only is the remedy ineffective against the disease, its effects are worse than the disease itself. Not only do these drug-prohibition measures fail to reduce illicit drug use, or risks associated with their use, they maintain a black market where product toxicity resulting from poor quality control or high concentration multiplies incidents of overdose and the risk of health problems. Thousands of persons are denied access to treatment at the cost of their lives (Bibeau and Perreault 1995). Finally, on an international scale, prohibition underwrites the sale of illicit drugs to pay for drug use or to generate income, the role of carriers or small-scale dealers, and the consolidation of international trafficking networks with insatiable appetites for money. The result is increased demand, supported by widespread cheating, and political and police corruption (Boustany 1993; Brouet 1991; Centre d'Études des Conflits 1991; de Choiseul-Praslin 1991; Fottorino 1991; Grimal 1993; de Kochko and Datskevitch 1994; Makhlouf 1994; Observatoire Géopolitique des Drogues 1995; Sauloy and Le Bonniec 1992).

2 Harm Reduction Strategies: The Foundations of Socio-Medical Control?

Until the early 1970s, an array of bureaucracies exercised a virtual monopoly over the production of publicly available drug information, a monopoly threatened by the Brecher Commission (Brecher et al. 1974) in the United States and the LeDain Commission (LeDain 1973) in Canada twenty years ago. This monopoly is largely responsible for the continued current dominance of the prohibitionist discourse, a moral debate in which entire populations are embroiled (Michka 1993). This debate increases the hold of penal and medical prohibitionist control, and precludes establishing effective harm reduction strategies that respect the individuals targeted for service.

To promote solidarity among members of a society, a state, or a geopolitical collective such as 'the West,' nothing is in fact more effective than a common enemy towards which public fear can be chanelled (Szasz 1994). History abounds with scapegoats whose principal function was to maintain social unity and cohesiveness in the group supporting the interests of leaders: 'We have throughout history observed holy or religious wars against persons professing a different faith; more recently we have witnessed racial and ethnic wars against persons with nonconforming physical attributes; currently we observe a medical or therapeutic war against those who use illicit drugs. Let us not forget that the modern State is a political apparatus which enjoys a monopoly on the power to declare war. It chooses its enemies, declares war on them, and profits from this enterprise' (Szasz 1989: 70).

It is simpler to create public solidarity *against* something than towards change, or towards challenging existing power and social norms. Opposition to a defined evil immediately places the person in opposition on the 'good' side, requires no effort towards making change, and does not challenge the popularly perceived need to 'control the enemy' – by violence if necessary (Barel 1982). If the drug addict continues to be used as the political enemy in national and international strategies, how can a context of services to drug addicts be created that is integrated with other services, and that gives the same respect to drug addicts as to any other persons (Bibeau and Perreault 1995)?

Mainstream information supports such political strategies. Even research is bent to the norms of laws that reinforce the legitimacy of prohibition (Alexander 1990). Only a small proportion of the population will examine research material directly to verify the validity of its methodology or the coherence of its results as proof of its findings. It is simple, therefore, to publicize weak and sensationalistic bits of research, generally through the media or through bureaucracies implicated in the management or enforcement of current drug laws, and to sow panic concerning the dangers of illicit drugs (Arnao 1989). The 'great illusion' (Comte-Sponville 1989) maintained by such information is that drugs themselves provide the motivation for drug abuse; solving any and all drug problems thereby becomes a matter of making them disappear. This reasoning evades critical reflection on quality-of-life issues, or on societal norms to which certain groups of persons adapt by using drugs that may eventually become problematic (Bibeau and Perreault 1995).

This comedy of errors is not funny. It stains the earth with blood and corrupts the fragile institutions of democracy. Worst of all, it diverts our attention from the real causes of the misery and violence that surrounds us. Cocaine is not a significant cause of crime, violence, addiction, heart disease, brain damage, unhealthy babies, student apathy, low productivity, or terrorism in the Third World. It is the destructive illusion that we can relieve these deeply rooted problems by attacking cocaine that is the real danger related to cocaine in our times. (Alexander 1990: 215)

Instead of establishing educational and preventive programs that teach better management of restricted drugs, instead of encouraging the implementation of better research, and instead of improving training or access to resources for addictions workers with a clientele in need, the prohibitionist discourse results in repressive police operations and drug-use detection, prevention, or treatment programs that constitute social-control activities, rather than health promotion and harm reduction strategies developed within a health-promotion perspective.

In other words, not only is police activity underwritten by a logic of social control, but other types of intervention are equally required to conform to legal norms and may easily evolve into control strategies (AITQ 1996). For example, institutional clinicians are generally required to frame drug problems according to legal norms; their employing institutions are unwilling or even unable, in this instance, to define problems outside of the context of law. To conform to institutional norms, clinicians must automatically consider the use of illicit drugs as a form of deviance that requires correction (Bertrand 1986). The treated person has even less power to change this clinical perspective, where few resources exist for support or assistance.[3]

In fact, the legal situation and social discrimination against drug addicts imposes on a clinician a role of authority that not only risks becoming an abuse of power, but is also antitherapeutic. How can clinicians establish a relationship of trust with the treated person when it is suspected that clinicians must report on their progress to referring institutions (Brochu 1995)?

In summary, within a context of prohibition, intervenors who wish to avoid becoming agents of social control, who hope to deliver a coherent, effective, and health-promoting message, and who work to establish effective harm reduction policies often find themselves in an uncomfortable position with respect to their employing institutions. They must avoid their own exclusion by the social control structures.

3 From Drug Prohibition to Regulating the Drug Market Place

From Decriminalization to Legalization

Approbation for the decriminalization of cannabis and its derivatives alone as the ultimate goal of improved judicial drug policies aimed at supporting harm reduction strategies has decreased among antiprohibitionists even while this remains an integral step towards more global strategies. This form of decriminalization would reduce certain abusive police controls and permits the social integration of a particular type of drug user, but remains a very limited solution in terms of health promotion, especially for users of intravenous drugs. It does not guarantee the quality control or improved distribution networks essential to reduce the dangers of intoxication; and it does not legitimate recreational drug use. Even with drug users who are adequately informed concerning their products, even with products of low concentration and quality control in a regulated market, users are not considered capable of managing their own usage. Finally, this policy does not leave room to challenge existing social-control measures.

A legislative strategy that represents responsible action toward health promotion aimed at implementing harm reduction strategies thus implies the legalization of all drugs. *Legalization is not, in itself, a solution to the problems of drug abuse.* Improved regulation to reduce the risk of harm, through improved conditions under which drugs are marketed, must be accompanied by the three inseparable tools of drug policies based on health promotion: adequate prevention programs, reasonable access to services and treatment, and socio-economic interventions that, by improving the quality of life of a certain sector of the population, facilitate their acquisition of healthier living habits (AITQ 1995).

From Legalization to Market Place Regulation

The three tools that must accompany drug regulation become even more important in a licit drug market, which tends to ensure its own expansion through stimulation of product demand. The weight of advertising currently aimed at promoting all types of medications, as well as alcohol, coffee, or tobacco (despite certain restrictions), testifies to this fact, as do drug-usage models validated by television programming.

The advertising of licit drugs encourages a close look at studies concerning the effectiveness of regulations that restrict drug advertising. All drug advertising, despite its apparent diversity, contains the same message: the user of medications, alcohol, tobacco, coffee, chocolate, or colas feels better, avoids pain, is more serene, or improves the quality of his or her life. Can the drug-promotion message be reduced by legal means, when it is constantly repeated to the public? Preliminary conclusions of studies on this question indicate that, even with advertising restrictions, new drug policies should not be created with the illusion that the drug-promotion message will disappear. Drug advertisers will always have sufficient imagination and resources to find new loopholes.[4] Specific restrictive measures may be required to support efforts towards prevention.

In summary, an examination of current drug laws clearly demonstrates that to determine new drug-marketing policies, based on a health-promotion viewpoint, requires challenging the current prohibition of illicit drugs and also the current marketing regulations concerning licit drugs.

4 Legalization of Drugs and Harm Reduction Strategies

The need to implement drug laws that promote health by ensuring cohesive and equitable regulations that include all drug marketing underlies the scenarios suggested by antiprohibitionists. Such regulations must not only consider economico-political obstacles to the modification of current laws; they must also take into account that any change challenges society's prevailing attitudes and drug-use habits (Evans 1990).

With new marketing methods for regulated drugs aimed at ensuring product quality and reduced concentration, it is reasonable to predict that an array of currently used adulterated products will disappear. These would either not be competitive in a new market place, or inadequate in terms of quality. Other drugs would be refined and sold in reduced and more manageable dosages. When alcohol use was legalized, bootleg liquor was not. Quality alcohol products were legalized, and products of regulated alcoholic content made available so that persons learning to use these products would not be poisoned. Legalization considerably lowered the price of alcohol, and placed its distribution under the control of liquor boards or specific liquor outlets. Similarly, it may be assumed that the expertise of persons who already have illicit drug-use habits would be accessed in defining appropriate dosages and consumption methods, and in determining the therapeutic value of such drugs.[5]

In any case, these are minor details in the scenario of a new drug market place. What is lacking, in light of current market trends, is the anticipation that pharmaceutical corporations would produce new synthetic drugs (Olievenstein 1989). New drugs – because of pharmaceutical companies' greater power to market their products, to produce them at lower cost, to offer a wider range of mood alterants, and in theory to ensure safer consumption (this will in any case be the approach promoted by pharmaceutical companies) – are likely to overtake the market.

Anticipation of the creation of such drugs includes concern that access to new mood-altering products will create new habits, not so much for recreational use as for increased employment productivity or for developing other potential skills. The popularity of Prozac is an eloquent example (Breggin 1994). Does this potential signify the use of new drugs to enforce even greater adaptation to the demands of employment, or to regulate our moods and those of our children? The question is not entirely frivolous (Cohen 1995). Drugs are already commonly used to regulate our bodies to meet employment demands. Many persons depend on Valium, Prozac, caffeine, or alcohol to reduce stress, to facilitate sleep, and so on. New drugs in a changed market place would not of themselves create drug-consumption models that differ greatly from current usage habits. It is not a fear of the development of new recreational drugs that animates the debate concerning a changed drug market place; it is concern that the development of new drugs will (or already does) prolong the drug-use habits that exist, and thus prolong habits that generate harm. Who will be the users and abusers of new drugs? New users or the same old faces?

These questions remind us that when looking for the best way to regulate a new drug market place, we must not lose sight of the political question of health promotion and harm reduction strategies that regulations should support. To maintain health promotion and harm reduction as a priority, analysing the impact of a new drug market place cannot be limited to analysing how illicit drugs may be used for recreational purposes. Such limitations too often omit consideration of the common attitudes and habits with respect to licit drugs.

Antiprohibitionists concur that while the economico-political controls maintaining current prohibitions must be countered, this is only a preliminary consideration. To come to terms with the entire range of drugs requires deeper reflection if regulations are to pursue health promotion for effective harm reduction strategies. Such terms imply a secondary level of consideration, which takes the role of drug use in post-industrial society into account.

Conclusion

Primary, secondary, and tertiary prevention practices currently being developed with the aim of harm reduction are confronted with a difficult situation. If they focus on drug-related harm and fear of AIDS rather than adopting a broader health-promotion focus, they risk accepting as normal the hopelessness and reduced opportunities for a certain segment of the population. But broader health-promotion policies contradict current drug laws (and projected changes such as the Controlled Drugs and Substances Act), as indicated by British Columbia Chief Coroner Cain in his 1994 drug-policy report:

I suggest that society must now reject negative criminal sanctions as the source of social control in drug abuse and turn rather to some other methods of control.

Time and time again I heard the following expressions: personal values, family values, role models, education, treatment, jobs, and housing. And yes, spiritual values ... Both body and mind must be involved, neither one to the exclusion of the other.

Agencies involved in the drug abuse problem will not conquer or reduce the personal and social harms until they know, understand, and challenge the root causes of these problems. (Cain 1994: 86)

Prohibitive laws may thus be considered a primary cause of harm:

This leads us to the need to establish a basic distinction between reducing drug related harms (health, family and violence problems, impaired driving, etc.) and harms related to drug controls, that is the prohibitionist context (marginalization, criminality, toxicity problems, reduced living standards and conditions, etc.) And if the maxim describing the cure as worse than the illness, referring to drug laws, is based on fact, we may globally consider the harms resulting from drug prohibition as greater and more in need of change than those resulting from legalized use (in spite of the undeniable seriousness and extent of harms linked to impaired driving). (Brisson 1994: 4)

While a great deal of research is currently being undertaken, much remains to be done. Reflection on this matter is important, and contributes towards understanding the strategies that must be developed on an international, national, regional, and local scale to meet these considerations. At stake are not only health promotion and harm reduction strategies, but also the democratic foundations of society.

NOTES

1 In this vein, many services offered to drug addicts are clearly based on fear of the spread of AIDS, and their basis thus becomes extremely fragile outside of this medical goal. The approach considerably reduces the potential of interacting honestly with drug addicts, of increasing their autonomy and their ability to manage, and eventually overcome, their dependence. Bibeau and Perreault 1995.
2 A more detailed presentation of these considerations is presented in Beauchesne 1992.
3 It is nevertheless true that drug users and addicts are increasingly trying to form organizations to lobby institutions: for example, ASSUD (Association des usagers de drogues) in France, or Citoyens comme les autres in Belgium, as well as the traditional Dutch organizations whose role in recent years has become less central.
4 These are the conclusions that have encouraged the Canadian Centre on Substance Abuse (CCSA) to propose the following recommendations in its memo to the CRTC: 'While it is impossible to prove that advertising increases consumption, the Centre underlines that it is equally impossible to prove that it is without effect. It is to be feared, however, that if advertising is prohibited, the alcohol producing industry will channel its enormous resources toward other forms of promotion. The result may be a decrease in price, an action which, it has been proved, will increase consumption.

   The industry also threatens to spend more money underwriting sports events or rock concerts, both of which attract a youthful public. "The short term economic effect of restricting advertising may increase consumption," stated Mr. Single.' Centre Canadien de Lutte 1991, *Action-Nouvelles; Bulletin* (p. 12).
5 For example, *kava* from the Fiji Islands has effects similar to those of alcohol but is much easier to manage, and has fewer side-effects than alcohol. Similarly, several drugs may be much safer than currently licit drugs such as tobacco. See Siegel 1990.

REFERENCES

AITQ. 1995. *Stratégies de réduction des méfaits en matière de drogues qui s'inscrivent dans une politique globale de promotion de la santé*. Montréal: Association des Intervenants en Toxicomanies du Québec.

– 1996. *Avec les toxicomanes: Aide ou contrôle?* Actes du XXIIIe Colloque de l'Association des Intervenants en toxicomanie du Québec, Laval, 22–25 October.

Alexander, B.K. 1990. *Peaceful Measures: Canada's Way Out of the War on Drugs.* Toronto: University of Toronto Press.

Arnao, G. 1989. 'Le coût de la bureaucratie dans la guerre à la drogue.' *Psychotropes* 5 (1–2): 83–8.

Bachmann, C., and A. Coppel. 1989. *Le dragon domestique.* Paris: Albin Michel. (Also 1991, under new title, *La drogue dans le monde, hier et aujourd'hui.*)

Barel, Y. 1982. *La marginalité sociale.* Paris: PUF.

Beauchesne, L. 1992. *La légalisation des drogues pour mieux en prévenir les abus.* 2nd ed. Montréal-Suisse: Édition du Méridien et Georg.

Bernat de Celis, J., and G. de Celis. 1992. *Fallait-il créer un délit d'usage illicite de stupéfiants?* Paris: CESDIP, no. 54.

Bertrand, M.A. 1986. 'Les intérêts professionnels: Obstacles premiers aux changements sur les drogues et à l'utilisation efficace des ressources pour toxicomanes.' In *Qualité de vie et drogues, Place aux jeunes,* 65–81. Montréal: Gaëtan Morin.

Bibeau, G., and M. Perreault. 1995. *Dérives Montréalaises. A travers des itinéraires de toxicomanies dans le quartier Hochelaga-Maisonneuve.* Québec: Boréal.

Boilard, J. 1994. 'Le modèle de la réduction des méfaits dans le champ de la réadaptation.' *L'écho-toxico* 6(2): 4–5.

Boustany, A. 1993. *Histoire des paradis artificiels. Drogues de paix et drogues de guerre.* Paris: Hachette Pluriel.

Brecher, E.M., et al. 1972. *Licit and Illicit Drugs: The Consumers Union Report.* Boston: Little Brown.

Breggin, P.R. 1994. *Talking Back to Prozac.* New York: St Martin's Paperbacks.

Brisson, P. 1994. 'La réduction des méfaits: Considérations historiques et critiques.' *L'écho-toxico* 6(2): 2–5.

Brochu, Serge. 1995. *Drogues et Criminalité, une relation complexe.* Montréal: Les presses de l'Université de Montréal.

Brouet, B. 1991. *Drogues et relations internationales.* Bruxelles: Éditions Complexe.

Caballero, F., ed. 1992. *Drogues et droits de l'Homme.* Les laboratoires Delagrange-Synthélabo, Collection Les empêcheurs de penser en rond. Paris.

Cain, J.V. 1994. *Report of the Task Force into Illicit Narcotic Overdose Deaths in British Columbia.* Office of the Chief Coroner, Burnaby, British Columbia.

Centre Canadien de Lutte contre l'Alcoolisme et les Toxicomanies. 1991. *Action-Nouvelles.* Ottawa: CCLAT.

Centre d'Etude des Conflits. 1991. *Mafia, drogue et politique.* Paris: L'Harmattan, cultures et conflits no. 3.

Cesoni, M.-L., ed. 1996. *Usage de stupéfiants: Politiques européennes.* Geneva: Georg.

de Choiseul-Praslin, C.H. 1991. *La drogue, une économie dynamisée par la répression.* Paris: CNRS.

Choquet, M., and S. Ledoux. 1992. *Drogues illicites et attitudes face au sida.* Paris: INSERM-Documentation française.

Cohen, D. 1995. *Guide critique des médicaments de l'âme.* Montréal: Éd. de l'Homme.

Comte-Sponville, A. 1989. 'La grande illusion.' *Autrement* 106: 69–72.

Cormier, D., S. Brochu, and J.P. Bergevin. 1991. *Prévention primaire et secondaire de la toxicomanie.* Montréal: Éditions du Méridien.

Debock, C. 1995. *Face à la drogue: Quelle politique?* Problèmes politiques et sociaux, no. 745, Paris: La Documentation française.

Del Brel, G., ed. 1991. *La géopolitique de la drogue.* Paris: La découverte.

Domic, Z. 1992. *L'état cocaine: Science et politique, de la feuille à la poudre.* Paris: PUF.

Ehrenberg, A. 1995. *L'individu incertain.* Paris: Calmann-Lévy.

Ehrenberg, A., and P. Mignon, eds. 1992. *Drogues, politique et société.* Paris: Éditions Descartes.

Erickson, P.G. 1990. 'A Public Health Approach to Demand Reduction.' *Journal of Drug Issues* 20(4): 563–75.

Evans, R.M. 1990. 'The Many Forms of Legalization: Beyond Whether to How.' In *The Great Issues of Drug Policies.* Washington: Drug Policy Foundation.

Fottorino, E. 1991. *La piste blanche: L'Afrique sous l'emprise de la drogue.* Paris: Balland.

Giffen, P.J., S. Endicott, and S. Lambert. 1992. *Panic and Indifference: The Politics of Canada's Drug Laws.* Ottawa: Centre Canadien de Lutte Contre l'Alcoolisme et les Toxicomanies.

Grimal, J.C. 1993. *L'économie mondiale de la drogue.* Paris: Le Monde poche.

Hanson, A. 1992. 'Le dépistage des drogues: Contrôle des drogues ou des esprits?' *Psychotropes* 7(3): 71–87.

Health and Welfare Canada. 1986. *Achieving Health for All: A Framework for Health Promotion.* Ottawa: Ministry of Supply and Services.

– 1990. *Drugs: Facts and Fictions.* Ottawa: Ministry of Supply and Services.

Henrion, R. 1995. *Rapport de la Commission de réflexion sur la drogue et la toxicomanie.* Paris: La Documentation française.

Jansen, A.C.M. 1991. *Cannabis à Amsterdam: Une géographie du haschish et de la marijuana.* Paris: Éditions du Lézard.

Jean-Pierre, T., and P. de Mertens. 1993. *Crime et blanchiment.* Paris: Fixot.

Johns, C.J. 1992. *Power, Ideology, and the War on Drugs.* New York: Praeger.

Kochko, D. de, and A. Datskevitch. 1994. *L'empire de la drogue: La Russie et ses marchés*, Paris: Hachette.

Labrousse, A. 1991. *La drogue, l'argent et les armes*. Paris: Fayard.

Labrousse, A., and A. Wallon, ed. 1993. *La planète des drogues, organisations criminelles, guerres et blanchiment*. Paris: Seuil.

Lascoumes, P. 1977. *Prévention et contrôle social*. Genève: Masson.

Lauzon, P. 1994. 'Le programme de méthadone et la réduction des méfaits reliés à l'usage des drogues.' *L'écho-toxico* 6(2): 7.

LeDain, G., et al. 1972. *Cannabis: A Report of the Commission of Inquiry into the Non-Medical Use of Drugs*. Ottawa: Information Canada.

– 1973. *Final Report of the Commission of Inquiry into the Non-Medical Use of Drugs*. Ottawa: Information Canada.

Low, K. 1994. 'Les jeunes, les drogues et la dépendance: Éléments d'une prévention radicale.' In P. Brisson, ed., *L'usage des drogues et la toxicomanie*, 2: 295–321. Montréal: Gaëtan Morin.

Makhlouf, H. 1994. *Culture et trafic de drogue au Liban*. Paris: L'Harmattan.

Michka. 1993. *Le cannabis est-il une drogue?* Geneva: Éditions Georg.

Observatoire Geopolitique des Drogues. 1995. *Géopolitique des drogues*. Paris: La Découverte.

Olievenstein, C. 1989. 'En désespoir de cause.' *Autrement* 106: 29–39.

Sauloy, M., and Y. Le Bonniec. 1992. *À qui profite la cocaine?* Paris: Calmann-Levy.

Schiray, M., ed. 1992. *Penser la drogue, penser les drogues*. Paris: Éditions Descartes.

Siegel, R. 1990. *Intoxication: Life in Pursuit of Artificial Paradise*. Washington: Dutton.

Sorman, G. 1992. *En attendant les barbares*. Paris: Fayard.

Stengers, I., and O. Ralet. 1991. *Drogues, le défi hollandais*. Paris: Delagrange, Collection Les empêcheurs de penser en rond.

Szasz, T. 1989. 'Plaidoyer pour la fin de la plus longue guerre du XXe siècle: La guerre contre la drogue.' *Psychotropes* 1:(1–2), 69–75.

– 1994. *La persécution rituelle des drogués*. Paris: Les éditions du Lézard.

3 The Battle for a New Canadian Drug Law: A Legal Basis for Harm Reduction or a New Rhetoric for Prohibition? A Chronology

BENEDIKT FISCHER

The Law in Canadian Drug Policy

In the late 1980s, Canadian drug policy seemed to be heading towards a paradigmatic change. In similar fashion to the United States, or even more vigorously at times, the country over decades had chosen a system of legal repression as its primary answer to 'illicit' drugs (Giffen et al. 1991; Solomon and Green 1988; Erickson 1992a). 'Illicit' drugs in the Canadian context are those substances that made their way onto the schedules of Canada's successively emerging prohibition laws, starting shortly after the turn of the century. This lengthy ideological crusade started in 1908 with the mobilization of police and justice resources against opium in western Canada, primarily because of socio-economic unrest that centred around the marginalized minority of Chinese labour immigrants (Comack 1985; Cook 1969). Subsequently, Canadian lawmakers added cannabis, cocaine, and opiates to the list of officially condemned substances in the first third of the century. Most of these additions onto the drug schedules were preceded by some form of moral-ideological panic, mobilizing politicians, the media, and eventually the public against a perceived social threat evolving around a new 'evil' substance. However, in some cases (i.e., cannabis), it is not clear why the substance was eventually included in the prohibition crusade, since evidence for its use or involvement with 'deviant' or 'criminal' people was sporadic or only started occurring after the drug had been banned (Solomon and Madison 1977; Giffen et al. 1991; Fischer 1995a).

Historically, the Canadian criminal laws were at the centre of most activities of state control against psychoactive substances outside the licit realm. Since their inception in the early 1910s, the laws had gradually become broader and more punitive, and were systematically upgraded by the justice bureaucracy primarily in response to requests from the enforcement apparatus. This drug-enforcement complex expanded around the prohibition laws in the first half of the twentieth century, largely under the leadership of the Bureau of Narcotic Drugs and the Royal Canadian Mounted Police. Since the Opium and Narcotic Drug Control Act in 1923, the law broadly prohibited possession, possession for the purpose of trafficking, as well as the various supply offences of production, sale, and import. Besides extremely harsh punishment that for many offences meant life imprisonment, the enforcement apparatus had managed to cut down the rights of the accused to a bare minimum; for example, the 'onus of proof' in many drug offences was shifted onto the accused to defend himself against the charges, instead of the prosecution to prove its case (Giffen et al. 1991; Fischer 1995b).

The emphasis on legal prohibition as the central response to drug control with the drug-prohibition law at its core was reinforced and modernized with the establishment of the 'Narcotic Control Act' (NCA) in 1961. The political approval of the law was preceded by an intense ideological battle between legal prohibitionists and representatives of an emerging treatment movement of health professionals arguing that not criminal punishment but treatment should be the answer to 'drug addiction.' The latter group's pressure indeed forced a 'treatment clause' into the draft of the law, providing for mandatory, indefinite institutionalized treatment of first-time addict offenders. However, the clause was never passed into law (Giffen et al. 1991; Fischer, forthcoming). Instead, the NCA provided the fertile legal basis for broad drug enforcement and prosecution, and subsequently harsh sentences (Solomon and Green 1988). Simple drug possession could be punished with up to seven years in prison, and most supply offences allowed for maximum life-imprisonment sentence. Starting mid-century, most drug enforcement in Canada started to concentrate on drug *users*. This enforcement emphasis emerged with the crusade against opiate users in the 1950s and was expanded in the late 1960s and 1970s, when enforcement began to concentrate on cannabis (Solomon and Madison 1977). In the 'cannabis enforcement era' starting around 1965, the scope of enforcement increased dramatically from some few hundred to ten thousands of drug offences in Canada per year. In the late 1970s, Canada had some 40,000 drug offences annually, 75 per cent of which were for cannabis-possession offenders – i.e., cannabis users – alone (Bryan

1979; Fischer 1995a). Numerous political promises or efforts – including the Le Dain Commission's fundamental recommendations to de-escalate criminal prohibition against cannabis users – to legally redirect prohibition efforts away from their primary target of the drug users failed sooner or later over the past twenty-five years (Le Dain 1972; Fischer 1994c; Giffen and Lambert 1988).

The Past Decade: Impulse for Reform?

In 1987, the Canadian government announced a principal redirection of its drug-policy efforts. Through the comprehensive federal policy program of 'Canada's Drug Strategy' (CDS), it proposed to shift the country's prohibitionist drug-control paradigm to a state approach emphasizing principles of 'harm reduction' and a 'balance of demand and supply reduction' measures (Government of Canada 1991; Erickson 1991). The federal administration underlined this claim with the launch of a \$270 million drug-policy program that devoted over 70 per cent of its resources to 'demand reduction' efforts in the areas of treatment, education, and prevention (Beatty 1991; Single et al. 1991). Most crucially, however, the government also announced that its drug-policy overhaul would include the introduction of a new drug law to constitute the 'legal backbone' of the new policy framework (Government of Canada 1991; Fischer 1994b).

After the announcement of the intended revision of its drug-policy principles that initially sounded like a fundamental departure from the 'War on Drugs' just re-proclaimed in the United States, the government took its time thinking about new drug legislation. In the meantime, the first substantial doubts had arisen among policy observers in regard to the serious commitment of the government to policy-restructuring efforts. Subsequently, policy analysts pointed out that for the first few years into the CDS policy period the enforcement rigour against users had hardly changed (Erickson 1992a, Fischer 1994a). In 1991, Canada featured almost 60,000 drug offences, with two-thirds resulting from law enforcement against drug users. The majority of those, still, were for cannabis possession (Moreau 1995; RCMP 1993). In comparison, Canada in the early 1990s thus criminalized even more cannabis users per capita than did the United States (BJS 1995; Drug Strategies 1996).

Also, the picture slowly emerged that most components of the publicized CDS policy program were better characterized as 'political window-dressing' than solid policy-reform efforts (Fischer 1994b). The largest part of the education and prevention funds seemed variously assigned to abstinence-promotion programs or went to police education programs. A comprehensive cost-sharing program between the federal and provincial levels that was to substantially increase the number of drug-treatment beds in the country proved to be a drastic policy failure. The provincial health administrations did not even invest half of the available funds into new treatment facilities. More generally, govern-mental policy makers had left their audiences in the dark as to what they actually meant in practical policy terms when they referred to a 'harm reduction' policy framework (Fischer 1994b; Single 1993). Had drug policy makers in Ottawa shot the rhetorical gun before thoroughly thinking about where to aim, or was the CDS just another episode of a hollow Canadian promise for drug-policy reform?

Confusion seemed complete in the spring of 1992, when the Conser-vative administration under Prime Minister Mulroney tabled its draft of Bill C-85, the Psychoactive Substances Control Act (PSCA), in Parlia-ment (Minister of National Health and Welfare Canada 1992). The bill, which was designed to replace the aged prohibitionist drug law, the NCA, triggered solid disillusionment among reform advocates. Bill C-85 basically presented a modernized version of the NCA, without any 'harm-reduction'-oriented reform. It featured the same list, philosophy, and structure of drug-offence categories, including those of drug possession as well as the ambiguous 'possession for the purpose of trafficking.' It also carried a new offence of 'seeking or obtaining' a substance, which would allow for enforcement against individuals attempting to purchase drugs or any substance held to be an illicit drug – a stipulation that would provide better prosecution potential follow-ing undercover operations. The PSCA's criminal penalty structure was equal in harshness to the NCA, featuring a maximum of seven years' imprisonment for simple drug possession and up to life imprisonment for most supply offences.

The drafters of the bill had not modified the irrational drug schedul-ing system of the NCA, compiling drug schedules against most princi-ples of modern pharmacology. For example, opiates were lumped together with cocaine-based substances as well as cannabis substances. The bill also did not feature any diversion provisions for drug-posses-sion offenders, and did not suggest distinctions with respect to the drug quantities involved or status of the offender. On top of the many sub-stantive queries in regard to the bill, the law was, as some of Canada's drug-law critics put it, 'poorly drafted, unnecessarily complex and difficult to comprehend,' as if written by persons 'whose skills had been honed drafting Income Tax legislation' (Usprich and Solomon 1993; see also Beauchesne 1994).

Initially, it seemed as if the government had sensed the substantial disappointment from some policy and media observers following the presentation of the draft. The government did not move on the bill for about a year. However, a sudden revival of interest on the government's side in passing the bill occurred in the summer of 1993, likely triggered by the prospect of a federal election in the coming fall and the intent of moving the bill through Parliament before then. Consistent with the practices of parliamentary law-making in the Canadian system, the bill was moved into a parliamentary subcommittee on health after second reading. This committee was to examine the legal draft in detail, hear submissions from drug-policy stakeholders and interest groups, and prepare the draft for the final reading in the House. These hearings provided an insight into not only how strongly many drug-policy stakeholders opposed the proposed bill, but how complex and inconsistent the government's positions were in regard to the role of the law as the central element of Canadian drug policy.

In a move that fundamentally undermined reform advocates' confidence that the government actually saw Bill C-85 as a crucial element of their overall drug policy as expressed in the CDS principles, its drafters claimed that it had to be understood as an 'independent' exercise in law-making, separate from other 'non-legal' policy efforts. 'In ... 1991 there was quite an important consultation process that went on by the Secretariat of the Canada Drug Strategy and I'm told that the bill was included and the intent and their overall principles, again were discussed ... The new legislation was not based on a fundamental reassessment of Canada's drug laws ... The purpose of this exercise was primarily to consolidate existing legislation. It was not to review, reassess and undertake substantial reform' (Paul Saint-Denis, Department of Justice, in House of Commons 1993).

Quickly, severe doubts were fostered in regard to what the government's actual intentions had been with the introduction of Bill C-85. While most observers had anticipated that this bill would constitute the promised 'legal backbone' for the progressive drug-policy principles announced with the CDS, a long list of government officials testified with statements to the effect that the 'first intention of the bill [was] to consolidate current legislation' (Marc de Gagne, Health and Welfare Canada, in House of Commons 1993) and that it constituted a 'legislative housecleaning' exercise. If the government, however, had seen the proposal of Bill C-85 as a 'tune-up' exercise for existing drug legislation (without any intention to modify the general profile of drug policy), the question remained as to what goals were being pursued with this particular exercise. The existing NCA seemed to work reasonably well with drug-enforcement and prosecution authorities, and – except for a few minor differences – the PSCA draft did not look much like a significantly modernized or enhanced legal 'piece of armour' for the Canadian version of the 'War on Drugs.'

On another front, however, the government subsequently emphasized that it did not consider the C-85 project as a process fundamentally embedded in its policy proceedings as initiated by the CDS program. As a symbolic indicator the parliamentary hearing process completely ignored the presence and potential advisory role of the Canadian Centre on Substance Abuse (CCSA). This multimillion-dollar, federal arm's-length agency had been created as part of the CDS in 1988, with the specifically assigned mandate to provide drug research and policy development within the federal jurisdiction (Single 1991). The occasion of new drug-control legislation in the midst of an alleged policy reform seemed like a tailor-made stage for the CCSA's mandate. By the time of the hearings, a few senior CCSA representatives had been on the record for criticizing existing drug policy and speaking out for fundamental changes towards a rationalization of drug control in Canada. Although not part of the official hearing proceedings, the CCSA in a separate statement summarized in frank language the perceived fundamental inconsistencies between governmental policy rhetoric and the proposed drug-control bill: 'C-85 perpetuates the illogicality of previous legislation ... [The] new legislation is neither a modernization nor an enhancement of existing policy. [There is] a lack of consistency between the CDS and Bill C-85. CDS stresses the use of harm reduction. This approach seems to be contrary to the PSCA ... A harm reduction approach would instead emphasize the policies and programs aimed at reducing the harmful consequences of illegal drug use ... A complete review of Canada's drug policy was expected [through the PSCA]' (Fralick 1993).

The only substantial political opposition to the bill within the parliamentary committee came from Liberal members – a crucial aspect in the developing paradoxicality of the emerging political battle for a new drug law. The key Liberal health critic, MP Ray Pagtakhan, pointed out the essential note of the drug law for the overall scope and impact of health policy that the government had obviously failed to consider. 'As we study this bill, we will be looking not only at the bill itself, but as it related to public health policy ... This legislation was not based on a fundamental reassessment of Canada's drug laws based on rational principles related to public health and safety concerns' (House of Commons 1993).

More precisely, he pointed out that this bill did not contain any explicit consideration of preventative, educational, or rehabilitative measures as they might have an effect on the general public, or might even be applied to drug users who have offended against legal norms of drug control: 'What would this bill do to help people get off drugs? ... If there is no real estimate, why was it not looked at so that we can give Canadians a feel as to what this tougher deal would do to help reduce substance abuse' (ibid.)?

Some MPs projected that the tough criminal law and the 'soft' measures introduced by the CDS could harmonically function 'hand in hand,' constructively complementing each other in dealing with drug offenders. This notion was in particular fuelled by some legislators' perceptions that Bill C-85 was not to be used as an enforcement tool against drug users, but against 'organized drug supply criminals.' If the law would become active against drug users, it was imagined, the legal process would do the necessary punishment, and then the soft 'harm reduction' measures – as emphasized by the CDS – would take care of the educational or rehabilitative 'follow-up.' It did not become clear that the two paradigms epitomized in Bill C-85 – drug control through legal repression – on one side, and the CDS – social and health measures for drug users – represented principally adversarial approaches. Epitomizing these contradictory assumptions, the bill's defenders said that it was 'not about the problem with the drug user' but constituted the state's central instrument to 'go after the trafficker' (MP Reimer in House of Commons 1993). The Member had obviously not examined existing drug-enforcement patterns, with approximately two-thirds of all drug offences being for simple possession of cannabis, cocaine, and heroin (Moreau 1995; RCMP 1993; Metropolitan Toronto Police 1996).

Various committee members insisted on the claim that non-legal elements of drug policy – in the form of prevention or treatment – and criminal enforcement and punishment aiming at drug users could be handled as two completely separate entities in policy practice, and that the bill discussed did not at all constrain the use of social and rehabilitative measures: '[T]here are various ways of perhaps looking at alternate forms of sentencing and dealing with the user and the educational role etcetera and reduce the demand side. But that's not what this bill is about. That's another aspect of drug policy' (MP Reimer in House of Commons 1993).

With these rather naive assumptions holding sway among parliamentarians in regard to the interdependency between the drug-control law and drug policy, it was left to non-governmental witnesses to thoroughly take issue with the bill. It was the rank-and-file police, represented by the Canadian Police Association, who assessed the C-85 draft practically from the perspective of 'harm reduction' and the objective of a 'balanced approach between supply and demand reduction' of the CDS. These principles, so the police argued, with the proposed legislation for the drug user would 'end at the courtroom doors.' As a suggestion for pragmatic improvement, the police picked up on a less-repressive model of cannabis-possession regulation that had first been suggested by the Trudeau government almost twenty years earlier (Giffen et al. 1991; Fischer 1995a). The police recommended that first-time possession be made into a non-criminal offence, processed by civil ticketing proceedings similar to a speeding offence that should allow the reduction of the 'enormous costs' of processing cannabis possession. They also argued that the bill needed modifications in its punishment provisions in regard to 'which drugs are possessed and how much is involved' (House of Commons 1993).

The only witness group who did not simply represent professional or corporate interests with respect to the proposed law, but considered its actual impact on potential subjects to the legislation, was the Ontario Addiction Research Foundation. Its representatives rejected the bill in principle, stating that in its general scope and prohibitionary focus, it was 'not in keeping with Canada's Drug Strategy.' The ARF called the bill a 'missed opportunity' for necessary drug-law reform, and advocated a bill that would be based on public health rather than legal-moralistic principles (ARF 1993).

A New Government – A New Drug Law?

Bill C-85, however, did not make it across the parliamentary finish line. It died on the order table when the Liberals ousted the Conservatives from Government office in the fall of 1993 (Fischer 1994a). This leadership change raised confidence in the prospect of drug-law reform, since the Liberals had been staunch critics of C-85. Also, the party had a history of calling for cautious moves to liberalize punitive repression of drug users, as it had proposed with Bill S-19 in 1974 (Bryan 1979; Fischer 1995b). But the unfolding events provided a shocking *déjà vu* experience of what had happened just two years earlier. In March 1994, the Liberal health minister tabled Bill C-7 – the Controlled Drugs and Substances Act (CDSA) – as the new government's proposed version of a 'new' drug-control law (Minister of Health 1994). To many observers' astonishment, the proposed bill was basically a carbon copy of C-85, even featuring some minor increases in the severity of penalties. The draft had been tabled in almost complete silence and in the media shadow of the massive tobacco tax cut initiated by the Liberals, without indication that any consultations with provincial administrations or other public-health officials had occurred (Beauchesne 1994; Boyd 1994).

Now forced to defend the bill that they had – voluntarily – inherited from their Conservative predecessors, Liberal government officials quickly developed a line of defence for C-7 that was quite similar to the previous government's statements on C-85. The parliamentary assistant to the minister of health argued, '[T]his bill is not a policy bill. It is really tidying up some of the loose ends we've had hanging around. [T]his is not a policy bill, so it should not be confused with drug policy. [I] don't think that it has anything to do with it at the moment' (Fry in House of Commons 1994).

Trying to ignore the criminal law's most central and decisive role in this field of social policy, the government argued that this bill was about 'enforcement issues' and that 'policy' was made through 'other instruments' – instead of recognizing that it was exactly the use of the criminal law as the central policy instrument against drug users with which the critics of C-7 were discontent. A second line of defence emerged over Canada's obligations to the international drug-control treaties. Though it was not clear at the point of discussion how Canada would have not been in full compliance with the three main international conventions, government officials underlined that the bill was necessary to 'satisfy our obligations ... under the international drug laws' (Rowsell in House of Commons 1994). Later, it emerged that Canada had been 'spanked' by a 1994 International Narcotics Control Board report for not having satisfactorily included Benzodiazepines in its drug-control regime – an omission that certainly did not require a completely new prohibition law (INCB 1994).

The following parliamentary hearings called a substantially longer list of non-governmental witness groups to Ottawa, largely testifying in opposition to the bill. The majority of these testimonies pointed to the antiquated prohibitionary principles of C-7, its continued features of inefficiency in dealing with drug users in particular as well as its lack of consideration of public-health principles. A symbolic testimony in this regard came from the Canadian Bar Association – representing some 37,000 Canadian legal professionals – whose representatives underlined that they 'opposed Bill C-7 in principle' although this was 'in direct contradiction to the self-interests of lawyers.' They argued that Bill C-7 meant an 'escalation' of prohibition against drug users, who ought to be considered a 'social and health problem.' The association predicted that C-7, based as it was on 'outdated' and 'ineffective' measures, would lead to 'significant increases in the rates of incarceration and in lengths of sentences, and will place additional stresses on an already overburdened criminal justice system. It will not contribute to public health but will exactly accomplish the opposite.' Instead, they advocated a 'more appropriate approach [within a] harm reduction framework [which would] emphasize a concern for health, focusing on prevention and treatment, while simultaneously minimizing the use of incarceration for drug offences that cause no evident harm to persons other than the user' (Canadian Bar Association 1994).

In looking at the obvious contradictions of the bill, government officials came up with an almost ironic suggestion from a law-making perspective for how to remedy this situation. High-ranking officials with the Ministry of Health suggested that 'as soon as this [C-7] is passed – if it's tidied up and put into some sort of omnibus bill,' law- and policymakers would be 'able to look at all those things' that seemed to be not in keeping with their image of a modern drug law (MP Fry in House of Commons 1994). Then, after this 'consolidation act' had been created, the government promised to look into the possibility of a 'substantive policy bill' (MP Szabo in ibid.). Did the government seriously believe that after not modernizing Canada's drug law for more than thirty years, lawmakers were willing to pass C-7 and then immediately thereafter look into building a completely new drug law?

While the Conservative party had almost been eliminated in the election, and the Reform party did not quarrel too much with C-7, it was left to the Bloc Québécois to play the role of primary opposition on the issue.[1] Asking federal Justice officials about the perceived impact and efficacy of the bill, the Bloc critic found out that C-7 had been pushed without much direction for policy development in mind. Asking about the anticipated effects of the suggested new law, he learned that

'[A]gain, we are talking about the potential impact of the legislation. [T]his is really an issue that should be raised with criminal policy makers. [I cannot] make predictions or tell you what might happen in the future. I am here only to explain the legislation. So, unfortunately, I am not in a position to answer that question' (Normand in House of Commons 1994).

While the Canadian Association of Chiefs of Police claimed that their position reflected the fact that 'society views drug abuse as more of a health and social problem than a criminal act, the testifying RCMP stated that the 'public health aspect' of drug policy had been taken into account by creating a 'hybrid offence for trafficking ... of marijuana or hashish.' The government's administration, however, made it clear that marijuana use was seen and dealt with as a legal problem in Canada.

Question: 'Over the years, it has developed that it [marijuana] is now more of a social health problem than a justice concern as it was in the past. Does this attitude reflect a change more on demand than on supply?'
Answer from the Health Canada official: 'No, I don't believe so' (House of Commons 1994).

Finally, the chair of the parliamentary committee and Liberal MP, Paul Szabo, set things straight when emphasizing that 'the government is not in favour of decriminalizing marijuana.' Taking the issue even farther, he asserted that there had never been any intention on the Liberal government's side to reassess its overall approach to drug use: 'The government has never made any indications in its platform or in its throne speech that there was going to be a change of strategy with respect to [illegal] drugs ... [If] for some odd reason, there was a need to make changes, you would have to withdraw bill C-7, introduce a brand new bill, and go through the whole process again. [This step] is extremely rare, and it doesn't reflect positively on the government. You would have to wonder who is driving the agenda' (Now 1995).

In the hearings, however, the government again tried to convince its audience as well as the public that current drug-law enforcement was primarily going after the 'big and bad guys,' contradicting drug-enforcement statistics indicating that drug enforcement was primarily targeting simple marijuana-possession offenders (Fischer et al. 1996; CCSA 1995): '[O]ur enforcement agencies are faced with priorities and they are trying to deal with the real criminal element, not with those charged with simple possession ... [T]heir real thrust is toward the criminal element that is trafficking and hitting a wide sector of the population' (Rowsell in House of Commons 1994).

The substantial resistance that mounted against Bill C-7 in the parliamentary-hearing process but also in the media was followed by a lengthy period of sudden silence starting in the fall of 1994. After nothing had happened with the bill in the spring of 1995, observers again wondered if the government had quietly decided to drop the controversial bill. This suspicion was nurtured by the fact that in the meantime, within the Liberal caucus, a substantial block of resistance had formed against the ideology behind and scope of the law and became increasingly vocal on the issue (Fischer, forthcoming). What had been unclear throughout the Liberal history of the bill was the Minister of Health Diane Marleau's stand on the issue. The minister supposedly in her first few weeks in office was talked into sponsoring the bill by some senior officials without knowing much about its implications. Stated a Liberal MP close to her, 'It is true that [Marleau] supported the bill in the first place, but she did so not realizing the other side of the story. She had been told one side of the story by her officials. Well officials will tell you what they want to' (Allmand in *Now* 1995).

The internal group of Liberals opposed to their own bill even produced a position paper pointing out the central weaknesses of the proposed law and, in effect, calling for major revision to the proposed legislation. A member of the 'unofficial' Liberal opposition to C-7 outlined at a drug-policy conference in September 1995 the major criticism that C-7 did not provide for any 'rehabilitation or treatment,' that it did not feature any diversion options 'as an alternative' to criminal sanctions for drug offenders, that it was based on pharmacologically 'outdated drug schedules,' that it confirmed the 'maximum prison terms' and legal status of cannabis-possession offences 'in contrast to current court practices and evolved societal attitudes,' and that it generally did not attend to principles of 'harm reduction'-based policy (Barnes 1995; Fischer, forthcoming). Coincidentally, a few months earlier, a highly publicized report by the chief coroner of British Columbia – investigating a recent dramatic increase in heroin deaths in the province – had blamed the inadequacies of the Canadian drug-control system for many of the over 350 annual fatalities in 1994. The report requested pragmatic modifications in drug-law and policy design with respect to user criminalization, health concerns, and treatment, many of which were now reflected in the Liberal criticism of C-7. Its recommendations called for 'harm reduction' in the form of needle exchanges, as well as methadone-and even heroin-substitution programs, and requested that lawmakers should 'seriously inquire into legalizing the possession' of illegal drugs in order to avert negative health consequences of a black drug market economy (Cain 1994).

A New Canadian Prohibition Law After All?

Finally, amidst the turmoil surrounding the upcoming Quebec referendum,[2] as well as some indication that drug – especially cannabis – use trends among North American students had rebounded after a decade of steady declines (Adlaf et al. 1994; 1995), the government tabled its revised version of C-7 for third reading in the House. Department of Health officials claimed that the revised draft contained substantial 'reforms' following the substantive criticism directed towards the bill in the hearings, and that it now 'enshrined an attitude of tolerance, compassion and concerns for the drug-addicted person' and reflected 'more liberal policy with regard to harm reduction, rehabilitation and societal aspects of drug use' (MP Fry in Hansard 1995).

A closer look revealed that the government in revising C-7 had again concentrated its efforts on political window-dressing in the form of symbolic reforms, but had not changed any of the substantive features of user repression contained in the bill (Fischer et al. 1996; ARF 1995). The main revisions included a technical revision to the provisions governing first-time cannabis possession offenders. They were to be regulated by a new schedule (for possession of small amounts), providing for 'summary conviction only' proceedings and a maximum penalty of six months' imprisonment and/or a thousand-dollar fine (penalties for subsequent offences in the same category were doubled respectively). By eliminating the indictment option for simple cannabis possession, the law would exclude offenders from being fingerprinted by police authorities and documented on the central police computer network.

Government officials, however, were quick to interpret this police procedural change as an elimination of the much-lamented 'criminal record' given to all convicted or discharged cannabis-possession offenders under the Criminal Records Act. Even with the revisions to C-7, however, this consequence had not been changed. In providing for the processing of cannabis possession under maximum amounts as 'summary conviction only,' the government had obviously tried to speed up court proceedings. It had basically only adjusted the letter of the law to actual prosecution and sentencing practices, since no first-time simple cannabis-possession offender would receive any disposition close to the old possible maximum penalty of seven years' imprisonment. Instead of initiating reform to drug-control policy through progressive legal initiative, the law reactively but slowly acknowledged sentencing practices towards cannabis users as they had been established over the last decade or so (Fischer et al. 1996; Canadian Bar Association 1994, 1996).

As another symbolic but practically meaningless reform provision, the revised C-7 introduced a vague and generalistic 'sentencing principle' section (s. 10/1), outlining that 'rehabilitation and treatment' for drug offenders was 'encouraged in appropriate circumstances' (Fischer et al. 1996; Allain 1996). It did not, however, provide concrete indicators of what defined such 'appropriate circumstances,' and, more important, did not offer any concrete guidelines or procedural provisions for social or medical rehabilitation within the actual sentencing paragraphs of the law. While the lawmakers had repeatedly referred to the necessity for the law to comply with international drug treaties, they had obviously ignored some explicit provisions from the international conventions offering non-criminal sanctioning alternatives for drug users. As the critical guideline, the 1988 Convention suggests that signatories put in place as an 'alternative to punishment ... measures for treatment, education, aftercare, rehabilitation or social reintegration of the offender' (INCB 1994; Fischer 1996).

In their final defence of the revised bill, government officials also promised that its passage would be linked with a thorough review of the principles and programs of Canadian policy after the new law had been put in place – a sequence of operation that was later criticized as being illogical and contradictory, since the scope and effects of the new drug-control law should have been considered as a crucial policy element in such a review exercise (ARF 1995). In another move of political strategizing, Bill C-7 was passed in the House on 30 October 1995 – exactly the day when the Canadian Confederation was put to the brink by the Quebec referendum, and the Bloc Québécois – the major opposition in the House to the bill – was absent from Parliament. Thus, the only explicit voice of criticism towards the bill in the final parliamentary debate came from one single MP of the New Democratic Party (MP Riis in Hansard 1995).

The defence and appraisal of C-7 during final reading again produced a number of paradoxical statements adding to suspicions that this law had to be considered as just another chapter in what P.J. Giffen had described as the 'Saga of Promise, Hesitation and Retreat,' being just one of the many failed efforts for drug-law reform in Canada (Giffen and Lambert 1988; Fischer 1995a). Even more so, some of the remarks triggered doubts that politicians had actually done their homework on background evidence around issues covered by the bill. For example, the chairman of the sub-committee on health, which had examined the bill earlier, MP Paul Szabo, claimed that the committee had seen no reason to 'decriminalize marijuana' since 'no evidence was presented ... on the attitudes of Canadians' with respect to cannabis control. Shortly before, coincidentally, the Department of Health – the 'home-department' of C-7 – had just released results from a large-scale public-opinion survey outlining that almost 70 per cent of the Canadian population favoured a non-imprisonment penalty (fine only) for, or the complete decriminalization (no legal punishment) of, simple cannabis possession as opposed to criminal punishment (Health Canada 1995).

These circumstances of C-7 as a case of 'legislation differing so dramatically from public opinion' were later interpreted as bringing 'the law into disrepute, rather than enhanc[ing] respect' for it (CBA 1996). These fundamental contradictions, however, were judged by a Member of Parliament to the effect that, through C-7's symbolic cannabis-possession revision, the law now incorporated a 'revised and more current understanding of how Canadians want to deal with marijuana' and now provided a 'more social responsible approach to dealing with cannabis' (Fry in Hansard 1995). Government officials again claimed that they had gone a great way to 'deal with the [criminal] consequences associated with marijuana [and the] negative impact ... on someone charged with this offence will be changed' since 'no traceable record' would appear anywhere about the conviction. It was further suggested that the bill's new 'sentencing principle clause' would make courts 'move toward treatment and rehabilitation instead of automatically treating all users as hardened criminals' (Hansard 1995).

The Department of Health's spokeswoman (it remains unclear why the health minister herself did not defend the controversial bill before the final reading) implicitly acknowledged the inappropriateness of its own politics, stating that 'drugs and drug abuse are basically a social and health problem' finding 'their way into the criminal justice system not because they naturally and necessarily belong there, but because we still have yet to devise a better method of control' (Hansard 1995). But while the parliamentary secretary of health had emphasized the lessening of the severity of penalties for cannabis possession, her Liberal MP colleague staunchly claimed that this was exactly what the law had not done, instead referring to the 'common sense' approach to the 'enforcement aspect of the bill': 'A recent article in the Telegraph Journal ... reported: "For possession of small amounts of cannabis, the amended sentence is six months and a $1000 fine instead of seven years and a $2000 fine." That is simply not true. It is misinformation and may lead the reader to believe the bill proposes the law to be more lenient on simple possession. Under Bill C-7, the penalty is identical to the [penalty for simple possession of marijuana as] under the existing Narcotic Control Act. That is the existing law. We did not deal with drug policy' (MP Szabo in Hansard 1995).

Approximately fifteen minutes later in the parliamentary discussion, Szabo's caucus colleagues called Bill C-7 the necessary and crucial vehicle 'intended to consolidate, modernize, enhance and streamline the government's drug policy ... which was to enhance the ability of the police and the courts to enforce our laws' (MP Ur) and that the bill 'moves Canada['s drug policy] 30 years in time from the sixties to the nineties' (MP Brown, both in Hansard 1995).

The previous substantial resistance to the bill from within the Liberal caucus had – at least in rhetoric and probably for the sake of party discipline – completely vanished from the political stage. The same MP who had attacked C-7 rather vigorously just a month earlier now, in the House, called it a 'harm reduction' law that 'takes a public health approach to the problem of drug abuse rather than a moralistic, punitive one which views such abuse as criminal in and of itself,' while claiming that 'concerns with the original Bill C-7 [regarding] harm reduction ... treatment and rehabilitation alternatives ... maximum prison terms ... [and] simple possession of cannabis [had now been] remedied' (MP Barnes in Hansard 1995).

The paradoxical, almost Kafkaesque nature of the bill's real face, its contradictory stance relative to the CDS principles, and finally the emerging ambiguity of where Canadian drug policy was going was probably best illustrated by the desperate attempt of one Liberal member to make sense of the lengthy legal drama in the following words: '[T]his new law will put Canada in the forefront ... of leading the War on Drugs from a perspective of harm reduction' (MP Alcock in Hansard 1995). This statement itself – probably better than any detailed legal analysis – expressed the obvious state of confusion of Canadian drug law and policy development that had dominated the political scene since lawmakers had reopened the issues almost ten years ago with the launch of the CDS.

Since the Canadian political system requires the Senate's approval of federal legislation before it is passed into law, Bill C-7 was moved into the Senate's Committee for Legal and Constitutional Affairs after its first and second reading in the upper chamber. The hearings there, which started in early winter 1995, basically saw a repetition of the opposition to C-7 from public-health and legal organizations as well as policy stakeholders and reform advocates. More than the parliamentary committee, it seemed, the Senate committee proved to be open, receptive, and concerned about the criticisms raised in regard to scheduling, cost-effectiveness, and the effects of drug-user criminalization. In their receptiveness the committee went so far as to request specific input from testifying witnesses in regard to making suggestions on how the bill could be pragmatically improved – underlining though that the bill had been 'fundamentally agreed to' by the Senate since it had passed second reading. The subsequent submission by the Canadian Foundation for Drug Policy (CFDP) then proposed major revisions to the law that would explicitly exempt drug users in possession of substances in small amounts for personal possession from criminal punishment (CFDP 1996). It practically suggested legally enshrining a system of partial prohibition in the new Canadian drug-control law (see McDonald et al. 1994).

In February 1996, Bill C-7 once again barely escaped complete elimination. It officially died on the order table when the prime minister prorogued Parliament ending that session. The pause was short lived, since the Government introduced the identical bill – under the same name but a new number, C-8 – to the new session of Parliament, where it was moved through the House and back to the Senate in a single day. By September 1996, after more hearings and clause-by-clause consideration of the bill, Bill C-8 survived nearly intact in the Senate Committee for Legal and Constitutional Affairs, and was passed by the Senate. The CDSA is expected to become the law of the land.

Conclusion

After a long journey, Bill C-8 shall become Canada's new drug-control law. Even if some of the many fundamental criticisms and suggestions for pragmatic improvement had been taken into consideration, the bill could never be a genuine 'public health' or 'harm reduction' law. It is legislation born of and grown on ideological and procedural grounds of prohibition against select psychoactive substances, a systemic process that in Canadian practice has traditionally meant criminal punishment of the drug users.

While the opportunity to enshrine 'harm reduction' principles into the law, and thus to provide a solid legal framework for a more rational 'public health'-based drug policy, has been wasted with C-85/C-7/C-8, the onus for possible progress along those lines will subsequently be shifted to the institutions and programs who work with or around the law in dealing with the issue of drug use. Many other jurisdictions – including some select American jurisdictions – have shown that more rational and public health-oriented drug policy for the benefit of drug users as well as their social environment can materialize even in the context of antiquated prohibitionist laws. The Dutch, and more recently so the Australian, Swiss, Spanish, and German systems, have proved that such change is possible by practising 'harm reduction' from a primarily 'un-legalistic' perspective, practising change despite the law, as opposed to through or against the law (Nadelmann et al. 1994; Erickson and Butters, forthcoming). These systems have started to reduce the 'harm' from inappropriate drug laws to drug users and communities by ignoring them or restricting their applicability according to 'public health' principles. It seems, however, that the players of Canadian public health – and this includes the different criminal-justice agencies, since they are responsible for a relevant element of community health and safety – have a hard piece of labour before themselves. The battle for a genuine 'harm reduction' drug law in Canada is lost for the time being. The future challenge is thus to prove that 'harm reduction' is primarily built on – more so than on the letter of the law – common sense and a rational, humanist approach to the 'drug problem.' Thus, there is still room for hope that 'harm reduction' will sooner or later be a reality in Canada – despite, with, or without the Controlled Drugs and Substances Act.

NOTES

1 In the Canadian Parliament elected in 1993, five political parties are represented: Liberals (Government party, centrist, 174 MPs), Bloc Quebecois (Quebec separatist party, official opposition, 53), Reform Party (right-wing, 51), New Democrats (social democrats, 3), Conservative Party (right-of-centre, 2).
2 For 30 October 1995, the provincial government of Quebec scheduled a referendum asking the people of Quebec if the province should seperate from the

Canadian confederation. Latest polls had shown a slim majority for separation before referendum day, and the country's social, political, and economic spheres had to anticipate the possibility of the end of Canada as one nation.

REFERENCES

Addiction Research Foundation. 1993. *A Response to Bill C-85, the Psychoactive Substance Control Act*. Standing House Committee on Health, Ottawa, 26 May. 1993.
– 1995. *A Response to Bill C-7, Controlled Drugs and Substances Act*. Submission to the Standing Senate Committee on Legal and Constitutional Affairs, Ottawa, 13 December.
Adlaf, E.M., F.J. Ivis, et al. 1994. *Alcohol and Other Drug Use among Ontario Adults in 1994 and Changes Since 1977*. Toronto: Addiction Research Foundation.
– 1995. *The Ontario Student Drug Use Survey, 1977–1995*. Toronto: Addiction Research Foundation.
Allain, J. 1996. *Bill C-8: The Controlled Drugs and Substances Act* (legislative summary). Ottawa: Library of Parliament (Research Branch).
Barnes, S. 1995. 'Bill C-7: The Controlled Drugs and Substances Act.' Paper presented at the 9th Annual Interdisciplinary Conference, 'Canadian Cannabis Policy,' Student Legal Society, University of Western Ontario, Faculty of Law, London, Ontario, 23 September.
Beatty, P. 1991. Foreword. *Journal of Drug Issues* 21(1).
Beauchesne, L. 1994. 'Le projet de loi C-7: Plus qu'un mauvais souvenir.' *L'Intervenant*, Octobre.
Boyd, N. 1994. 'The Liberals on Drugs: Ostriches in Search of More Sand.' *Options Politiques*, October.
Bryan, M. 1979. 'Cannabis in Canada: A Decade of Indecision.' *Contemporary Drug Problems* 8: 169–192.
Bureau of Justice Statistics. 1995. *Drugs and Crime Facts, 1994*. Rockville, MD: ONDCP Drugs and Crime Clearinghouse.
Cain, J. 1994. *Report of the Task Force into Illicit Narcotic Overdose Deaths in British Columbia*. Burnaby, BC: Province of British Columbia, Office of the Chief Coroner.
Canadian Bar Association. 1994. *Submission on Bill C-7*. Ottawa: National Criminal Justice Section of Canadian Bar Association.
– 1996. Letter to Senator Sharon Carstairs, Chair of the Senate's LCA Committee, on Bill C-7. Ottawa, 29 March.
Canadian Centre on Substance Abuse (CCSA). 1995. *Canadian Profile: Alcohol, Tobacco and Other Drugs, 1995*. Toronto: Addiction Research Foundation.

Canadian Foundation for Drug Policy. 1996. *Proposed Amendments to Bill C-7.* Ottawa: CFDP.

Comack, E. 1985. 'The Origins of Canadian Drug Legislation: Labelling versus Class Analysis.' In *The New Criminologies in Canada*. Toronto: Oxford University Press.

Commission of Inquiry into the Non-Medical Use of Drugs. 1973. *Final Report.* Ottawa: Information Canada.

Cook, S. 1969. 'Canadian Narcotics Legislation 1908–1923: A Conflict Model Interpretation.' *Canadian Review of Sociology and Anthropology* 6(1).

Drug Strategies. 1996. *Keeping Score.* Washington: Levine and Associates.

Erickson, P.G. 1991. 'Past, Current and Future Directions in Canadian Drug Policy.' *International Journal of the Addictions* 25(3A): 247–66.

– 1992a. 'Recent Trends in Canadian Drug Policy: The Decline and Resurgence of Prohibitionism.' *Daedalus* 121(3): 239–67.

– 1992b. *Commentary on 'Psychoactive Substance Control Act'* (prepared for the CCSA). Toronto: Addiction Research Foundation.

Erickson, P.G., and J. Butters. Forthcoming. 'The Emerging Harm Reduction Movement: The De-Escalation of the War on Drugs?' In E. Jensen and J. Gerber, eds, *The New War on Drugs: Its Construction and Impacts on Criminal Justice Policy in North America*. Chicago: ACJS series.

Erickson, P.G., and B. Fischer. 1995. 'Canadian Cannabis Policy: The Impact of Criminalization, the Current Reality and Future Policy Options.' Paper presented at the International Symposium on Cannabis Policy, Criminal Law and Human Rights, Bremen, Germany, 5–7 October.

Fischer, B. 1994a. 'Contemporary Canadian Drug Policy: Reducing the Harm or Improving the Image?' Paper presented at the 5th Annual Conference on the Reduction of Drug Related Harm, Toronto, March.

– 1994b. 'Maps and Moves: The Discrepancies between Rhetoric and Realities of Canadian Drug Policy.' *International Journal of Drug Policy* 5(2): 70–81.

– 1994c. 'The Persistent Tale of Prohibition: A Look at Canada's Failed Attempts for Drug Law Reform in the Past 25 Years.' Paper presented at the annual meeting of the American Society of Criminology, Miami, 9 November.

– 1995a. 'P.J. Giffen's "Saga of Promise, Hesitation and Retreat": Can the Cycle of Prohibition Be Broken This Time?' Paper presented at the American Society of Criminology meeting, Boston, November.

– 1995b. 'Drugs, Power and Politics: Historical Phases of Narcotics Control in Canada.' Unpublished manuscript. University of Toronto.

– 1996. 'Drug Treaties Don't Require a War on Users.' *The Journal* (Addiction Research Foundation), March/April.

– Forthcoming. 'Prohibition as the Art of Political Diplomacy: The Benign Guises of the War on Drugs in Canada.' In E. Jensen and J. Gerber, eds, *The New War on Drugs: Its Construction and Impacts on Criminal Justice Policy in North America*. Chicago: ACJS series.

Fischer, B., P.G. Erickson, and R. Smart. 1996. 'The New Canadian Drug Law: One Step Forward, Two Steps Backward.' *International Journal of Drug Policy* 7(3): 172–9.

Fralick, P. 1993. Comment on Bill C-85 (unpublished document). Ottawa: Canadian Center on Substance Abuse.

Giffen, P.G., S. Endicott, and S. Lambert. 1991. *Panic and Indifference: The Politics of Canada's Drug Laws*. Ottawa: Canadian Centre on Substance Abuse.

Giffen, P.G., and S. Lambert. 1988. 'What Happened on the Way to Law Reform?' In J.C. Blackwell and P.G. Erickson, eds, *Illicit Drugs in Canada: A Risky Business*, 345–69. Toronto: Nelson Canada.

Government of Canada. 1991. *Canada's Drug Strategy*. Ottawa: Minister of Supply and Services Canada.

– 1995. *Questions and Answers: The Controlled Drugs and Substances Act*. Ottawa: Canada's Drug Strategy Secretariat.

Hansard. 1995. *Debates of the House of Commons of Canada*. Ottawa, Monday, 30 October.

Health Canada. 1995. *Canada's Alcohol and Other Drugs Survey*. Ottawa: Minister of Supply and Services.

House of Commons. 1993. Minutes of Proceedings and Evidence of the Legislative Committee on Bill C-85 (11, 13, 26, and 27 May). Ottawa: Parliament of Canada.

– 1994. Standing Committee on Health. Minutes of Proceedings and Evidence of the Sub-Committee on Bill C-7, vol. 1–4. Ottawa, 28 April – 14 June.

– 1995. *Bill C-7* (as passed by the House of Commons, 30 October 1995). Ottawa: Canada Communication Group.

International Narcotics Control Board (INCB). 1994. *Report of the International Narcotics Control Board for 1994*. Vienna: United Nations.

Jensen, E., and J. Gerber. 1993. 'State Efforts to Construct a Social Problem: The 1986 War on Drugs in Canada.' *Canadian Journal of Sociology* 18(4): 453–62.

Le Dain Commission. 1972. *Cannabis Report*. Ottawa: Information Canada.

McDonald, D., R. Moore, J. Norberry, G. Wardlaw, and N. Ballenden. 1994. *Legislative Options for Cannabis in Australia*. Monograph series no. 26. Canberra: Australian Government Publishing Service.

Metropolitan Toronto Police Force. 1996. 'Drug Offence and Charge Data under the Narcotic Control Act, 1994 and 1995.' Toronto: Metro Police (unpublished data).

Minister of Health. 1994. *Bill C-7, 'The Controlled Drugs and Substances Act'; An Act respecting the control of certain drugs, their precursors and other substances and to amend certain Acts and repeal the Narcotic Control Act in consequence thereof.* Ottawa: Department of Health.

Minister of National Health and Welfare Canada. 1992. *Porposal for the 'Psychoative Substances Control Act' (presented to the third session of the thirty-fourth Canadian Parliament, June 8, 1992).* Ottawa: Health and Welfare Canada.

Moreau, J. 1995. 'Adult Charges for Various Drug Offences in Canada, 1971– 1993.' Unpublished internal document, Addiction Research Foundation, Toronto, Ontario. Tables based on data published in Canadian Crime Statistics, Statistics Canada Catalogue 85-215 Annual, Canadian Centre for Justice Statistics, Ottawa.

Nadelmann, E., P. Cohen, E. Drucker, U. Locher, G. Stimson, and A. Wodak. 1994. 'The Harm Reduction Approach to Drug Control: International Progress.' Paper presented at the 5th International Conference on the Reduction of Drug-Related Harm, Toronto, 6–10 March.

Now magazine. 1995. 'Stiff Pot Bill to Lose Political Popularity.' Toronto, 2 February.

Royal Canadian Mounted Police (RCMP). 1993. *Drug Intelligence Estimate 1990– 1992.* Ottawa: RCMP.

Single, E. 1991. *The Canadian Centre on Substance Abuse.* Ottawa: CCSA.

– 1993. *Assessing the Impact of Canada's Drug Strategy. Characteristics of Desired Indicators and Specification of Goals* (working paper). Ottawa: CCSA.

Single, E.W., J. Skirrow, P.G. Erickson, and R. Solomon. 1991. 'Policy Developments in Canada.' Paper presented at the congress 'The Window of Opportunity,' Adelaide, Australia, December.

Solomon, R., and M. Green. 1988. 'The First Century: The History of Non-Medical Opiate Use and Control Policies in Canada, 1870–1970.' In J.C. Blackwell and P.G. Erickson, eds, *Illicit Drugs in Canada: A Risky Business*, 88–116. Toronto: Nelson Canada.

Solomon, R., and T. Madison. 1977. 'The Evolution of Non-Medical Opiate Use in Canada – Part I: 1870–1929.' *Drug Forum* 5(3).

Standing Senate Committee on Legal and Constitutional Affairs. 1995. Evidence (transcript). Ottawa, 13 December.

United Nations Convention against Illicit Traffic in Narcotic Drugs and Psychotropic Substances, 1988 (adopted 19 December 1988). New York: United Nations.

Usprich, S.J., and R. Solomon. 1993. 'A Critique of the Proposed Psychoactive Substance Control Act.' *Criminal Law Quarterly*, 35: 211–40.

4 The De-Medicalization of Methadone Maintenance

MARSHA ROSENBAUM

The institution of methadone maintenance treatment in the United States represented a culmination of increased medicalization of American society during the first half of the twentieth century. Drug technologies had been developed that would alleviate all forms of pain that had been defined by Americans as uniformly intolerable (Illich 1976). During the 1950s deviant behaviour was redefined not as 'badness' but as disease, and addiction as an illness that could be treated with advancing medical technologies (Conrad and Schneider 1980). The *rehabilitative ideal* became the dominating solution to the crime problem, as thousands of offenders were reformed in a myriad of programs (American Friends Service Committee 1971).

In the mid-1960s, Doctors Vincent Dole and Marie Nyswander began to report on their initial findings in their research with methadone maintenance treatment (Dole and Nyswander 1965). Their findings constitute the basic ideology behind the proliferation of methadone maintenance: methadone could relieve the metabolic disorder created by addiction, and with doses high enough to block the physical craving for heroin, the individual would be immune to its euphoric effects. Thus, the methadone user would be in a favourable position to break his/her ties with heroin and go on to become a productive member of society. As such, methadone maintenance was the original form of drug harm reduction in the United States.

Although the outcome findings of the early proponents of methadone were tentative, '[t]he media immediately heralded it as the long-awaited "medical breakthrough," labeling methadone a "Cinderella drug" which could be economically applied to hundreds of thousands of addicts, and, in short order, solve the narcotics problem' (Newman

1977). With the methadone breakthrough, heroin addiction was further defined as a medical (as opposed to a social) problem, and the addict became a patient.

Having transformed heroin addiction into a treatable disease, and with proclamations about its salvific effects to society and the addict alike, methadone maintenance spread. Programs began to open officially in 1963 with Dole and Nyswander's original two patients. In March of 1965, the expanded program moved into an open ward of Beth Israel Hospital in New York, with six patients; by 1968 there were 1139 patients.[1]

During the 1970s and 1980s methadone providers and patients struggled with definition, implementation, and, ultimately, survival. In this paper we look at the first two decades of methadone treatment. We begin with the 1970s, when methadone expanded greatly. Next we look at the early 1980s, when the morality and fiscal austerity of the Reagan era created a treatment method that was largely containment of the addict population. Finally, we discuss the post-AIDS late 1980s when, just at a time when medical treatment was needed most, methadone became almost fully de-medicalized.

The 1970s: Methadone Expands and Comes under Attack

In the late 1960s and early 1970s, methadone treatment expanded rapidly. The spirit of rehabilitation laid the foundations for the growth of the treatment of deviant behaviour, including drug abuse, using the medical model. Three other variables entered into the picture that made more efficient *control* of drug abuse seem imperative. First, crime statistics indicated that the growing crime rate could be accounted for in large part by drugs. It was heroin addicts who were to blame for much of the increases in petty theft and burglaries. Second, the widespread addiction by Vietnam servicemen, who were becoming veterans, was alarming. Finally, the growing use of illicit substances (though, paradoxically, not opiates) by middle-class white youth (who saw themselves as part of the 'hippie' movement) redefined drug abuse as having reached epidemic proportions. According to Conrad and Schneider, 'The late '60s and early '70s marked a rise in public concern with "the drug problem," especially heroin addiction. Writers in the professional and popular media were declaring a virtual "heroin addiction epidemic" in America' (1980: 135).[2]

By 1972, drug abuse was proclaimed 'the major domestic crisis facing the nation' by the president of the United States (Nixon 1972). In the spirit of crisis with which Nixon characterized the drug problem, treatment in various forms proliferated: the drug-free therapeutic community, out-patient detoxification, and methadone maintenance.

By 1971 the estimated number of methadone patients nationwide had jumped to 25,000 (Brecher 1972). Accompanying this expansion was increased criticism, regulation, and bureaucratization. Perhaps topping the list of criticisms was the view that maintenance was the equivalent of substituting one drug for another, and patients 'never got off.' Ironically, methadone was initially attractive because it *was* an opiate substitute, and *maintenance* was recommended for this chronic relapsing condition of addiction. Methadone also came under attack because of *diversion* of the drug. This was another ironic criticism, since the diverted methadone was going largely to heroin addicts and other methadone patients. The idea that novices would become addicted to their first opiate through diverted methadone (on the schoolyard) proved completely unfounded. Even patients criticized methadone, claiming 'it takes your heart' (Hunt et al. 1985–6); had a host of side-effects (Rosenbaum and Murphy 1987); and tied them to the clinic (Rosenbaum 1981). Despite the criticism, extensive research continually found that methadone was expedient. It worked to reduce drug-related criminality in patients and stabilized their drug habits. In short, as one of my first study participants told me, 'Methadone removes the issue of drugs from my life.'

In response to the criticisms of methadone came the 'regulatory counter attack' in 1973 (V.P. Dole, as cited in Courtwright, Joseph, and Des Jarlais 1989). Indeed, clinics had to comply with a complex set of rules governing admission to treatment, attendance, dose level, take-homes, urinalysis, and record-keeping methods. If they did not comply with 'the regs,' they were out of business. From the perspective of clinic staff as well as patients, this hardly felt like the traditional delivery of medical services. It became clear that the proliferation of clinics in the 1970s had much more to do with stopping crime than the well-being of heroin addicts. Indeed, increased regulation moved methadone further away from purely medical treatment. As Zweben and Payte say,

Programs quickly learned that survival depended on the condition of the records and not the patients.

There has been considerable speculation as to the motivation or purpose for the regulations that represented an unprecedented intrusion into the practice of medicine. Some think there was a sincere intention to ensure quality care, others that the process was one of political compromise, and still others that the intention was to discourage the growth of this unpopular form of treatment. Evidently some provisions were made in the absence or disregard of scientific clinical investigations and experience. (1990: 594).

The Early 1980s: The New Morality, Fiscal Austerity, and Just Say No (to Methadone)

The New Morality and fiscal austerity of the Reagan administration had major implications for methadone treatment. Nancy Reagan's 'Just Say No' campaign and the emphasis on zero tolerance of illegal drugs ushered in an era (extending to the present) in which abstinence was seen as the only viable perspective and form of treatment.

The fiscal austerity of the early 1980s meant a general scaling back, often elimination, of social programs that hadbeen instituted in the 1960s and 1970s. Funding for methadone maintenance programs began to dry up, experiencing a 30 per cent decline between 1976 and 1987 (Gerstein and Harwood 1990). As a result private, fee-for-service clinics proliferated.

The original definitions of the nature of methadone maintenance treatment were further compromised in a effort to cut costs. If there were to be time limits in treatment, a new ideology had to be constructed. Hence, there was a shift in protocol from life-long to time-limited treatment. Methadone was seen as a means to an abstinent end rather than an end in itself.

The message was clear: methadone would be begrudgingly tolerated. The government would no longer pay for it, however, nor would they allow a methadone user to remain on a program indefinitely. This message lead to a further de-medicalization (what other medical regimen has a built-in time limit?) and increased demoralization of treatment staff as well as patients. Clinic staff were unable to act as medical personnel. With payment of fees and the movement away from a medical definition of addiction, the nomenclature changed. 'Patients' were increasingly called 'clients' in an effort to upgrade their status as consumers. A well-meaning gesture, it was hollow and ultimately counterproductive. None of the regulations changed that would empower clients, and they had gained no increases in decision-making vis-à-vis their own treatment. However, the shift in titles had the negative effect of moving methadone treatment even further away from medicine. As

Robert Kahn says, 'It is common for counselors to interchange the terms "client" and "patient" ... This may inadvertently contribute to negative perceptions. The term "patient" refers to someone manifesting an illness requiring expert care, and is more consistent with efforts to counteract the view of the heroin addict as a criminal with character defects' (Kahn 1992).

By the mid-1980s methadone usage had moved, essentially, from medical treatment to the *containment* of addicts – just as the criminal-justice system had moved from rehabilitation to containment of 'the rabble' (Irwin 1985). Methadone treatment was infused with the Reagan (abstinence) morality: dose levels were restricted despite evidence that treatment was more effective at higher levels (Ball and Ross 1991; Caplehorn and Bell 1991; Hargreaves 1983); time in treatment was limited despite research findings insisting that longer treatment stays produced better results (Cushman 1981; Dole and Joseph 1978; Hubbard et al. 1989; McGlothlin and Anglin 1981; Simpson 1979, 1981; Simpson and Sells 1982; Stimmel et al. 1978); private fees were instituted despite evidence that addicts needing methadone could not afford to pay for it (Rosenbaum, Murphy, and Beck 1987). Just as with other programs for the poor, the message was clear: it was no longer OK for lower-class people and their problems to be subsidized by the government.

The Mid-1980s: Enter AIDS

In the mid-1980s it was discovered that HIV could and was being transmitted through blood by the sharing of injection equipment. Intravenous drug users became the second largest group to be infected by HIV, which causes AIDS, and their numbers were growing quickly. It became obvious that a key method to stop the spread of the virus through drug users was to educate them to (1) clean their injection equipment, (2) use clean needles, or (3) stop using needles. Regarding the latter, methadone maintenance was seen as an already-in-place way to accomplish the cessation of needle-use. Indeed, methadone maintenance clients have demonstrated a lower seroprevalence rate (Abdul-Quadar et al. 1987; Hartel, Selwyn, and Schoenbaum 1988; Novick, Joseph, and Croxson 1990; Siddiqui et al. 1993; and Weber et al. 1990). When, all over the world, countries expanded programs in an effort to slow the spread of AIDS, stubborn morality and fiscal short-sightedness prevented the United States from utilizing methadone maintenance as a harm reduction strategy (Nadelmann, et al. 1994).

There was an effort by providers to reinstitute the original definition of addiction as a disease that would require lifelong treatment. This effort was consistent with the 'recovery' movement of the late 1980s, in which everything from alcohol problems to food abuse to gambling to relationship dependency was defined as a disease (Peele 1989). Whereas medicalization has proliferated in the form of defining so many problems and habits as diseases, the most popular solution has been the twelve-step programs. However, methadone maintenance, though a tried form of treatment for one of the oldest acknowledged diseases, has been systematically excluded as a viable option because its ultimate goal is not abstinence. Pragmatism, once again, was cast aside for the sake of morality.

Funding was cut, and although providers begged for increased client access to maintenance, the continuation of de-funding made methadone treatment inaccessible at $350 per month to the very people who needed it most (Rosenbaum, Murphy, and Beck 1987).

Morality Frustrates America's First Harm Reduction Effort

The War on Drugs initiated by the Reagan administration in the 1980s has Americans even more conflicted and inconsistent about drugs than ever. Even in the face of the AIDS epidemic, harm reduction efforts such as needle exchanges, marijuana use for the relief of nausea associated with AIDS and chemotherapy, and methadone for the cessation of injection drug use have been met with a stubborn moralistic resistance. Despite extensive research demonstrating its efficacy, as well as its legal status, methadone has been treated as an illicit drug and caught in a moral rather than medical debate: 'The reality is that those who reject methadone treatment have been unresponsive to intuition, empiricism, pragmatism, and scientific data. The reason seems clear (Dole and Singer 1979): the controversies over methadone treatment "stem almost entirely from philosophical differences – objections to the substitution of one drug for another – and not from doubts about the pharmacological safety and efficacy of methadone"' (Newman and Peyser 1991: 120).

Methadone maintenance has been a frustrating experience for nearly everyone concerned with it: clinic staff, clients themselves, and researchers. Methadone physicians and counsellors consistently express the exasperation of attempting to treat a medical problem with extensive regulatory mechanisms that more often than not interfere with sound medical treatment (Zweben and Payte 1990; Payte 1991). It is also difficult to practise medicine with the stigma attached to methadone, since that stigma ultimately extends not only to clients, but to clinic staff as well. As R.G. Newman said (in Kahn 1992), 'There is no other medication (methadone) ... that physicians rely on for which maximum dosages have been decreed ... Physicians in no other medical practice are constrained by law from treating more than a designated number of patients.' For this reason, some physicians have simply gotten out of this area (Payte 1991).

Methadone users have been victims of the political and social manoeuvring of the last twenty years. Initially, they expected a medical treatment that would allow them to function without having to procure an illegal drug (heroin) on a daily basis in order to feel normal. With the introduction of extensive regulations they found that being on methadone was no picnic (Rosenblum, Magura, and Joseph 1991; Rosenbaum 1994). Methadone users also felt stigmatized by the negative definitions of maintenance (Murphy and Irwin 1992; Rosenbaum 1982). They were in a perpetual state of identity 'limbo.' Ultimately, their real-life struggles are the most frustrating (Rosenbaum, Irwin, and Murphy 1988). The conditions experienced by clients have been exasperated by the de-medicalization of methadone treatment and its progressive marginalization.

Finally, those of us in the field of treatment research have learned that policy has little to do with science. Our research findings, largely in support of methadone maintenance as an effective harm reduction treatment, are widely acknowledged in the drug-abuse field. The National Institute on Drug Abuse, now a part of the National Institutes of Health, has funded methadone research for over two decades, and instituted policy consistent with the findings of their grantees. Nonetheless, to add to the frustration of researchers, state and federal bureaucracies often ignore such policy positions. Instead they opt for cost-cutting, politically expedient, but ultimately counter-productive means for dealing with drug abuse.

Perhaps, with increasing international adoption of harm reduction strategies, we can look forward to a shift in focus from a criminal-justice to a public-health view of drug use and the re-medicalization of methadone maintenance in the United States. Some providers believe methadone maintenance has been reintroduced and is already becoming less marginalized because of AIDS (Zweben and Sorenson 1988). Maybe Bill Clinton's drug-control strategy, which has emphasized, at least theoretically, the importance of prevention and treatment, will mean that methadone can once again be used as it was designed by

Doctors Dole and Nyswander: as a medical tool to reduce the harms of addiction and abuse.

NOTES

The author gratefully acknowledges the assistance of Jeanette Irwin, Sue Eldredge, and Ethan Nadelmann in the completion of this paper, as well as the support of the U.S. National Institute on Drug Abuse and Dr Bennett Fletcher, Project Officer.

1 Despite its growth and seeming acceptance, there was trouble early on for methadone *maintenance*. A 1919 amendment to the Harrison Act allowed physicians to prescribe narcotics only for legitimate medical purposes. Since addiction was not seen as a legitimate disease, the prescription of drugs for maintenance purposes was not allowed (Joseph and Appel 1993). In this instance, precedence was set for the reticence to endorse and then support maintenance treatment.

2 Although it was believed there was a heroin epidemic, some argued that it was actually manufactured by the reaction to increasing marijuana use by 'counterculture' types such as hippies, leftists, and other dissidents, including the Black Power movement (Lidz, Walker, and Gould 1980). The proliferation of programs to 'help' addicts and stepped-up law enforcement *created* statistics that proved after the fact there was an epidemic. The numbers of people in treatment andarrests had increased drastically.

REFERENCES

Abdul-Quadar, A.S., D.R. Friedman, D.C. Des Jarlais, M.M. Marmor, R. Maslansky, and S. Bartelme. 1987. 'Methadone Maintenance and Behaviour by Intravenous Drug Users That Can Transmit HIV.' *Contemporary Drug Problems* (Fall): 425–433.

American Friends Service Committee, A Working Party. 1971. *Struggle for Justice*. New York: Hill and Wang.

Ball, J.C., and A. Ross. 1991. *The Effectiveness of Methadone Maintenance Treatment*. New York: Springer-Verlag.

Brecher, E.M. 1972. *Licit and Illicit Drugs*. Boston: Little, Brown and Company.

Caplehorn, J.R.M., and J. Bell. 1991. 'Methadone Dosage and Retention of Patients in Methadone Treatment.' *Medical Journal of Australia* 154 (4 February): 195–9.

Conrad, P., and J.W. Schneider. 1980. *Deviance and Medicalization from Badness to Sickness*. St Louis, MO: C.V. Mosby Company.

Courtwright, D.T., H. Joseph, and D. Des Jarlais. 1989. *Addicts Who Survived: An Oral History of Narcotic Use In America, 1923–1965.* Knoxville: University of Tennessee Press.

Cushman, P. 1981. 'Detoxification after Methadone Treatment.' In J.H. Lowinson and P. Ruiz, eds, *Substance Abuse: Clinical Problems and Perspectives.* Baltimore: Williams and Wilkins.

Dole, V.P., and H.J. Joseph. 1978. 'Long-term Outcome of Patients Treated with Methadone Maintenance.' *Annals of the New York Academy of Sciences* 311: 181–9.

Dole, V.P., and M.E. Nyswander. 1965. 'A Medical Treatment for Diacetyl-morphine (Heroin) Addiction.' *Journal of American Medical Association* 193: 146–50.

Gerstein, D.R., and H.J. Harwood, eds. 1990. *Treating Drug Problems. A Study of the Evolution, Effectiveness, and Financing of Public and Private Drug Treatment Systems.* Vol. 1. Washington: National Academy Press.

Hargreaves, W.A. 1983. 'Methadone Dosage and Duration for Maintenance Treatment.' In J.R. Cooper, F. Altman, B.S. Brown, and D. Czechowicz, eds, *Research on the Treatment of Narcotic Addiction: State of the Art.* Maryland: National Institute on Drug Abuse, U.S. Department of Health and Human Sciences.

Hartel, D., P.A. Selwyn, and E.E. Schoenbaum. 1988. 'Methadone Maintenance Treatment and Reduced Risk of AIDS and AIDS-Specific Mortality in Intravenous Drug Users.' Abstract no. 8546. Fourth International Conference on AIDS, Stockholm.

Hubbard, R.L., M.E. Marsden, H.V. Rachal, H.J. Harwood, E.R. Cavanagh, and H.M. Ginzburg. 1989. *Drug Abuse Treatment: A National Study of Effectiveness.* Chapel Hill: University of North Carolina Press.

Hunt, D.E., D.S. Lipton, D.S. Goldsmith, D.L. Strug, and B. Spunt. 1985–6. 'It Takes Your Heart: The Image of Methadone Maintenance in the Addict World and Its Effect on Recruitment into Treatment.' *International Journal of the Addictions* 20: 1751–71.

Illich, I. 1976. *Medical Nemesis.* New York: Pantheon Books.

Irwin, J. 1985. *The Jail: Managing the Underclass in American Society.* Berkeley: University of California Press.

Joseph, H., and P. Appel. 1993. 'Historical Perspectives and Public Health Issues.' In Mark Perino, *State Methadone Maintenance Treatment Guidelines.* Rockville, MD: Center for Substance Abuse Treatment, U.S. Department of Health and Human Services.

Kahn, R. 1992. 'Methadone Maintenance Treatment: Impact of Its Politics on Staff and Patients.' *Journal of Psychoactive Drugs* 24(3): 281–3.

Lidz, C., A. Walker, and L. Gould. 1980. *Heroin, Deviance and Morality*. Beverly Hills, CA: Sage.

McGlothlin, W.H., and M.D. Anglin. 1981. 'Long-Term Follow-up of Clients of High- and Low-Dose Methadone Programs.' *Archives of General Psychiatry* 38: 1055–63.

Murphy, S., and J. Irwin. 1992. 'Living with the Dirty Secret: Problems of Disclosure for Methadone Maintenance Clients.' *Journal of Psychoactive Drugs* 24(3): 257–64.

Nadelmann, E., P. Cohen, U. Locher, G. Stimson, A. Wodak, and E. Drucker. 1994. 'The Harm Reduction Approach to Drug Control: International Progress.' Unpublished manuscript.

Newman, R.G. 1977. *Methadone Treatment in Narcotic Addiction*. New York: Academic Press.

Newman, R.G., and N. Peyser. 1991. 'Methadone Treatment: Experiment and Experience.' *Journal of Psychoactive Drugs* 23(2): 115–21.

Nixon, R. 1972. 'State of the Union Message.' *Congressional Quarterly* 118: 506.

Novick, D.M., H. Joseph, and T.S. Croxson. 1990. 'Absence of Antibody to Human Immunodeficiency Virus in Long-Term, Socially Rehabilitated Methadone Maintenance Patients.' *Archives of Internal Medicine* 150 (January): 97–9.

Payte, J.T. 1991. 'A Brief History of Methadone in the Treatment of Opiate Dependence: A Personal Perspective.' *Journal of Psychoactive Drugs* 23(2): 103–7.

Peele, S. 1989. *The Diseasing of America: Addiction Treatment out of Control*. Boston: Houghton Mifflin Company.

Rosenbaum, M. 1981. *Women on Heroin*. New Brunswick, NJ: Rutgers University Press.

– 1982. 'Surrender to Control: Women on Methadone.' Final Report. Rockville, MD: National Institute on Drug Abuse.

Rosenbaum, M., J. Irwin, and S. Murphy. 1988. 'De facto Destabilization as Policy: The Impact of Short-Term Methadone Maintenance.' *Contemporary Drug Problems* 15(4): 491–517.

Rosenbaum, M., S. Murphy, and J. Beck. 1987. 'Money for Methadone: Preliminary Findings from a Study of Alameda County's New Maintenance Policy.' *Journal of Psychoactive Drugs* 19(1): 13–19.

Rosenbaum, M., and S. Murphy. 1987. 'Not the Picture of Health: Women on Methadone.' *Journal of Psychoactive Drugs* 19(2): 217–26.

Rosenblum, A., S. Magura, and H. Joseph. 1991. 'Ambivalence toward Methadone Treatment among Intravenous Drug Users.' *Journal of Psychoactive Drugs* 23(1): 21–7.

Siddiqui, N.S., L. Brown, T. Meyer, and V. Gonzalez. 1993. 'Decline in HIV-1

Seroprevalence and Low Seroconversion Rate among Injecting Drug Users at a Methadone Maintenance Program in New York City.' *Journal of Psychoactive Drugs* 25(3): 245–50.

Simpson, D.D. 1979. 'The Relation of Time Spent in Drug Abuse Treatment to Posttreatment Outcome.' *American Journal of Psychiatry* 136: 1449–53.

– 1981. 'Treatment for Drug Abuse: Follow-up Outcomes and Length of Time Spent.' *Archives of General Psychiatry* 38: 875–80.

Simpson, D.D., and S.B. Sells. 1982. 'Effectiveness of Treatment for Drug Abuse: An Overview of the DARP Research Program.' *Advances in Alcohol and Substance Abuse* 2(1): 7–29.

Stimmel, B., J. Goldberg, M. Cohen, and E. Rotkopf. 1978. 'Detoxification from Methadone Maintenance: Risk Factors Associated with Relapse to Narcotic Use.' *Annals of the New York Academy of Sciences* 311: 173–80.

Weber, R., B. Ledergerber, M. Opravil, and R. Luthy. 1990. 'Cessation of Intravenous Drug Use Reduces Progression of HIV Infection in HIV+ Drug Users.' Abstract. The Sixth International Conference on AIDS. San Francisco.

Zweben, J.E., and J.T. Payte. 1990. 'Methadone Maintenance in the Treatment of Opioid Dependence: A Current Perspective.' *Western Journal of Medicine* (May): 588–99.

Zweben, J.E., and J.L. Sorensen. 1988. 'Misunderstanding about Methadone.' *Journal of Psychoactive Drugs* 20(3): 275–81.

5 Readiness for Harm Reduction: Coming to Grips with the 'Temperance Mentality'

BRUCE K. ALEXANDER and
GOVERT F. VAN DE WIJNGAART

The stringent anti-drug policy that has prevailed in North America for the last few decades has proved ineffective, costly, and cruel (Alexander 1990; Boaz 1990; Nadelmann 1989; Peele 1993; Trebach 1993; van de Wijngaart 1991; Wisotsky 1986). Fortunately, there are promising new directions, of which harm reduction appears the most realistic (Newcombe 1989; Watson 1991; Heather et al. 1993). However, it is not yet clear that society will tolerate any substantial deviation from the familiar policy.

We believe that Canadian society is very nearly ready for changes in the direction of harm reduction, but that the immediate prospects are less bright in the United States and some other countries, owing to widespread support for a way of thinking that we call the 'temperance mentality.' Therefore, we think that the harm reduction movement may be compelled to pay more attention to the temperance mentality in the future. These conclusions are based on hundreds of discussions with Canadians, Americans, and Europeans and on responses to two questionnaires that were administered to nearly 2000 university students in seven countries.[1]

Obviously, informal discussions and questionnaires administered to university students cannot reveal how all people of any particular country think about drugs or how they will react to policy proposals. However, we believe that our observations do provide a basis for cautious speculation about the readiness of various countries for harm reduction and that they suggest productive issues for future research.

Study 1: Readiness for Harm Reduction in Canada

The questionnaire data for Study 1 came from two samples of students:

Canadian anglophone university students from Simon Fraser University in Canada, and Dutch students from Utrecht University in the Netherlands. Comparison of Canadian and Dutch opinions seemed particularly pertinent to evaluating Canada's readiness for harm reduction, because Dutch society has accepted a number of harm reduction practices (Heath 1992; van de Wijngaart 1991). If Canadian students' opinions on drug issues were similar to those of Dutch students, it would suggest that harm reduction policy might be acceptable in Canadian society.

Method

A fifty-item 'Drug Attitudes Questionnaire' (DAQ) that addressed a wide variety of current issues concerning drugs and drug policy was prepared in 1989 and 1990. The DAQ was anonymously administered in 1990–91 to 226 students at Simon Fraser University in Vancouver, Canada, and 241 students at Utrecht University in the Netherlands. Most of the students were in their first or second year of university. The Simon Fraser students were registered in one of two sections of a course on 'Social Issues' taught by the first author, and the Utrecht students were registered in a variety of social-science courses, some of which were taught by the second author.

It was only possible to administer the questionnaire once to the Dutch students, during the first week of their courses. The Canadian students were asked to respond to the questionnaire on both the first and the last day of their course. The questionnaires were coded with pseudonyms so that the data collected from each student before and after the course could be matched without compromising anonymity.

Between the first administration of the DAQ and the last administration at the end of the semester, Canadian students were exposed to about thirty-five class hours of analysis and critique of the 'war on drugs' based upon current literature in psychopharmacology, medicine, psychiatry, and social science. There was no explicit mention of 'harm reduction' in the course, although there was considerable discussion of related ideas, especially the pros and cons of methadone maintenance, a controversial issue in the Vancouver media at that time.

Results

A full report on the results, including multivariate analysis of the data, is available elsewhere (Alexander et al. 1992). This article will focus on

TABLE 1
Students' responses to 'moral items' relevant to harm reduction (Average response ±
SD. Response categories: 1 = Strongly disagree, 2 = Disagree, 3 = Not sure, 4 = Agree,
5 = Strongly agree)

Using illegal drugs is immoral, even if there are no apparent bad effects.
    Canadian pre-course 2.7 ± 1.17   Dutch pre-course   2.3 ± 1.03**
                                         Canadian post-course   2.2 ± 1.17***

Total abstinence (no use at all) from all drugs, legal and illegal, is a goal of mine.
    Canadian pre-course 2.8 ± 1.35   Dutch pre-course   2.6 ± 1.03*
                                         Canadian post-course   2.4 ± 1.22**

Recreational drug use almost invariably leads to drug problems.
    Canadian pre-course 3.0 ± 1.22   Dutch pre-course   2.3 ± 1.04***
                                         Canadian post-course   1.6 ± 0.67***

Using illegal drugs should be punished more severely than it is now.
    Canadian pre-course 3.0 ± 1.15   Dutch pre-course   2.6 ± 1.09**
                                         Canadian post-course   2.0 ± 1.08***

$*p < 0.05$, $**p < 0.01$, $***p < 0.0001$. All comparisons are to the Canadian pre-course
data.

two subsets of items from the DAQ that seem directly relevant to the
readiness for change in the direction of harm reduction in Canada. DAQ
items of a moral nature are considered first, followed by items that tap
opinions on factual and policy matters.

Moral Items
Table 1 summarizes the students' responses to four DAQ items that concern the morality of drug use. We included items advocating abstinence
from drugs as 'moral items' because insistence on universal abstinence
seems to us intrinsically a moral, rather than pragmatic, position. A
pragmatic argument can be made that drugs should not be used excessively or that abstaining from a particular drug might be essential for
some or even most people, but, given the great variability of response to
all drugs, universal abstinence can only be advocated on a moral or religious basis.

    Acceptance of the four moral items identified in table 1 would logi-
cally and emotionally preclude support for harm reduction. To agree
with these items is to believe that drug use is immoral regardless of the
drugs' effects; to value abstention from all drugs, regardless of their
legal status; to hold the opinion, in spite of a large body of evidence to

the contrary, that recreational use almost invariably leads to drug problems; and/or to want to increase already Draconian punishments for people who use prohibited drugs.

People who think this way cannot be greatly concerned about reducing the harm that befalls drug users. For them, the important harm appears to lie in the immorality of drug use rather than in side-effects on health. To reduce the harm to the health of drug users is to be diverted from moral concerns, and to interfere with natural repercussions that could spur them to reform.

Table 1 indicates that the average Canadian student's response to each of these four moral items before taking the Social Issues course ('Canadian pre-course' scores) was close to the neutral midpoint (3.0) of the scale. However, these neutral averages did not indicate indifference. The responses to these moral items tended to be bimodally distributed and to have large standard deviations relative to the opinion items discussed below. In other words, the students were polarized by the moral items. Therefore, a substantial minority of the students had quite high scores on these moral items, even though the mean score was in the neutral range.

As table 1 shows, the Canadian pre-course average scores were significantly higher on all four moral items than the 'Dutch pre-course' scores. However, average scores on all four items had decreased among the Canadian students by the end of the course ('Canadian post-course' scores), and in every case the decrease was statistically significant. At the end of the course, the Canadian students expressed less support for these moral items than the Dutch students.

Opinion Items

Responses by Canadian and Dutch students to four representative opinion items that seem related to a person's likelihood of supporting harm reduction are listed in table 2. People who agreed with the first two opinion items would be likely to see harm reduction as entailing toleration of the intolerable: the continuing use of drugs that, even in low or moderate usage, are extraordinarily hazardous to the user and to unborn children. By contrast, people who agreed with the second two items would be likely to support harm reduction, because these items express approval for practices that form a part of the harm reduction program, namely maintenance of addicts with narcotic drugs.

The data on the opinion items tell a simple story. The distributions are unimodal, unlike the moral items described in table 1. Average Cana-

TABLE 2
Students' responses to 'opinion items' relevant to harm reduction
(Response categories: 1 = Strongly disagree, 2 = Disagree, 3 = Not sure,
4 = Agree, 5 = Strongly agree)

Occasional cocaine use causes a significant risk of heart attack.
Canadian pre-course 3.5 ± 0.83   Dutch pre-course   3.1 ± 0.62***
Canadian post-course 2.1 ± 0.90***

The use of small amounts of heroin or cocaine during pregnancy often causes
irreversible damage to unborn children.
Canadian pre-course 4.3 ± 0.80   Dutch pre-course   3.9 ± 0.83***
Canadian post-course 2.9 ± 1.10***

Medical doctors should be allowed to prescribe methadone on a regular basis to heroin
addicts.
Canadian pre-course 2.9 ± 0.78   Dutch pre-course   3.5 ± 0.98***
Canadian post-course 4.0 ± 0.80***

Medical doctors should be allowed to prescribe heroin on a regular basis to drug
addicts.
Canadian pre-course 2.0 ± 0.92   Dutch pre-course   2.5 ± 1.01***
Canadian post-course 3.6 ± 0.95***

***$p < 0.0001$. All comparisons are to the Canadian pre-course data.

dian students appeared to be unready for harm reduction policies
before they took the Social Issues course, because they tended to agree
with the first two items and to disagree with the second two, both on an
absolute scale and relative to students from the Netherlands. However,
at the end of the Social Issues course, the Canadian students' pattern of
agreement and disagreement was reversed and, in fact, the Canadians
students appeared more sympathetic towards harm reduction than the
Dutch students. All differences were statistically significant.

Discussion

These data suggest that a substantial number of the Canadian students
would have moral and opinion-based reasons to reject harm reduction
policy before they took the Social Issues course, but that this number
was reduced dramatically by the course. How seriously can these indications of readiness for harm reduction among Canadian university students be taken?

The Social Issues course that was the apparent agent of change towards readiness for harm reduction policy can be easily reproduced. It entailed little more than exposure to factual information that most of the students had not heard before. Because of university pressures against empirically unfounded rhetoric, the course was a self-consciously academic recitation and methodological analysis of the scholarly literature about drugs and drug policy, although critical conclusions that were empirically warranted were stated explicitly and the instructor did not conceal his own perspective. An indication of the factual and academic nature of the course is that the lectures were published in book form by a leading Canadian university press after reviews by established social scientists and pharmacologists (Alexander 1990). Although the course was critical of 'war on drugs' policy, its content was balanced by the inclusion of books and well-known guest speakers that took a conventional point of view (Malarek 1990; Appleton 1990).

It is possible that the students who took the Social Issues course were a self-selected sample of those who were atypically amenable to changing their opinions on drug issues, but this was not true of the majority of them. Each semester the Social Issues course at Simon Fraser University has a special topic that varies depending on which of several instructors teach it. Topics include the 'war on drugs,' sociobiology, AIDS, paranormal phenomena, and others. Although some of the students choose to take the course each semester because of the topic that is being taught, the majority do not. In fact, under current conditions of university over-enrolment, the majority are often enrolled by default, because they have failed to gain admission to smaller, more specialized courses in psychology and other social sciences.

It is possible that the students only changed their way of responding in class, without any deep transformation of their thinking. However, numerous face-to-face discussions with the students reinforced our opinion that the change from pre- to post-course data reflected a real and substantial transformation of thought. At the beginning of the course, many students were insistent and emotional in defence of 'drug war' doctrine, which was the routine content of media and educational experiences to which they had previously been exposed. Spirited arguments took place between students and teaching staff, and between students with different views. As the semester progressed, there was a visible shift in thinking. Students volunteered the following statements, and many similar ones: 'I had learned to think one way about drugs for my whole life and it changed in the fourth week of the course,' 'I have completely changed the way I look at drugs,' 'Why didn't they tell us about this before?' These statements were typical, but there were also students who were unmoved by the course, or who intensified their initial position in reaction against it.

Of course, the DAQ data were measured at the end of the university term and it might be expected that, as months and years passed, the students' opinions would gradually revert to the norm. However, even if this proves true, it will not weaken our view of these data as indications of the Canadian students' readiness for harm reduction. The crucial fact is that these students were ready to accept a point of view that was compatible with harm reduction when they were given access to a full range of information. Resistance to harm reduction, therefore, seems not to be a fundamental or unalterable part of these students' psychological make-up but rather the tenuous result of incessant exposure to 'drug war' propaganda and incomplete information.

On the basis of these data and our informal discussions with students in other parts of Canada, we would suggest that Canadian university students are very nearly ready for harm reduction. Although a substantial minority has an intensely held view of drug use as intrinsically immoral (table 1), and although the majority opinions justify the status quo in drug policy (table 2), the students are generally open to influence on a factual, pragmatic level. When students hear both sides of the issue, both moral values and factual opinions change, although the moral values appear to change less than the opinions.

Although there was a time when university students were best understood as intellectually distanced from the bulk of the population, there are reasons to view them differently today. Everywhere the proportion of people who receive post-secondary education has grown dramatically. Thus, university students are less and less atypical. More important, in the era of 'professional society,' the balance of power falls to professionals in medicine, education, the 'helping professions,' business management, law, civil service, and so forth (Perkin 1989). Virtually all of these influential professionals are university trained. In fact, universities have come to be the primary source of professional training in Western society (ibid.). Thus, university students may best be viewed, not as an isolated intellectual stratum, but as the future mainstays of the professional power structure in mainstream society.

The role of university-trained professionals is apt to be particularly important in determining drug policy. Room has pointed out that current pressure to restrict drug use 'has been more based in professional and bureaucratic groups, and in the normal political process, rather than taking the common earlier form of a social or religious movement outside parliamentary politics' (Room 1991: 38). The pressure against current drug policy has also come less from grass-roots organizations than from 'elite drug-control policy groups' (ibid.: 39).

It is our opinion that university students are not unusual among Canadians in their openness to reasoned argument on this topic. Both authors have had many discussions on drug policy with Canadians who are not students – for example, on radio talk shows, at public meetings, and in everyday discourse. We have found most Canadians willing to hear, and be influenced by, new facts and ideas if they are not presented too bombastically. On the other hand, there remain some whose embrace of conventional morality and opinion remains unshakable.

The Temperance Mentality

Principal component analysis[2] of the fifty DAQ items provided an indication, unforeseen when the DAQ was constructed, that the four moral items described above (table 1) may be part of an underlying dimension of thought and feeling with a historical foundation in North American culture.

In general, principal component analysis detects 'components' or clusters of items to which individuals respond consistently, whether they express agreement, disagreement, or neutrality. The first principal component that emerged from the multivariate analysis of the DAQ data was heavily weighted with moralistic, abstemious, punitive, and prohibitionistic items. Taken together, the items that loaded on this component were reminiscent of the literature of the North American temperance movement of the nineteenth century and early-twentieth century (see, for example, Rush, 1805/1947; Chenery 1890; Chiniquy 1847; Kellogg 1926; Smart and Ogborne 1986). We therefore named this component the 'Temperance Mentality.'[3] The four highest loading items on it are listed above in table 1, in descending order of their component loadings. By contrast, none of the opinion items in table 2 loaded heavily on this Temperance Mentality component, either positively or negatively.

The fact that the Temperance Mentality was the largest principal component that emerged from analysis of the DAQ data does not mean that most or all or the Canadian students agreed with the items that loaded on it; rather it means that they tended to respond for or against the lot of them, or with a consistent neutrality. The pre-course data showed that the Canadian students were about equally split for and against the Temperance Mentality principal component and, on average, supported it more than the Dutch students. Post-course scores on the Temperance Mentality component were significantly lower than pre-course scores for the Canadian students (See Alexander et al. 1992 for a more detailed presentation of these results).

Relatively high levels of pre-course support for the Temperance Mentality by many Canadian students fits with the observations of sociologist Harry Levine (1992), who has argued that Canada and the United States, along with several Protestant European countries (not including the Netherlands) can be classified as 'temperance cultures.' In temperance cultures, temperance claims were linked to political support for alcohol prohibition in the past and retain the support of many people – even now, a century after the temperance movement has lost its preeminence. Levine's analysis suggested to us that the temperance mentality might be measurable in other countries and that it might provide a comparative index of moralism about drugs and thus about the acceptability of harm reduction policy.

Study 2: The Temperance Mentality in University Students in Seven Countries

Study 2 was based on a 'Temperance Mentality Questionnaire' (TMQ) that we designed to assess acceptance of the claims that were promulgated by the temperance movement of nineteenth- and early-twentieth-century North America. All fifty items on the TMQ were drawn from North American temperance literature (for historical sources, see Burt et al. 1994). Although the substance of the temperance claims was not altered in preparing the TMQ, archaic words and phrases were replaced with contemporary alternatives. Construction of the TMQ was systematic, to ensure that it included all the mainstream claims of the historical temperance movement, but excluded both fringe claims from the temperance era (such as the belief in the 'spontaneous combustion' of drunkards) and claims from contemporary anti-drug rhetoric that could be retrospectively attributed to temperance doctrine. The resulting items were, for the most part, moralistic, punitive, abstemious, and prohibitionistic.

Because of the moralistic character of TMQ items, support for them would seem logically and emotionally incompatible with support for harm reduction. From the standpoint of a person with a high score on

Temperance Mentality, harm reduction policies would entail tolerance of immorality and protecting the welfare of those who deserve, and might benefit from, increased punishment. Responses to the TMQ, then, could provide some insight into readiness for harm reduction.

The twenty-eight items from the TMQ that, like the original temperance claims, were only directed against alcohol are here referred to as 'alcohol-only' items. Some alcohol-only items were 'Abstinence from alcohol in a community is the key to social progress' and 'Drinking leads to financial ruin.' Twenty-two other TMQ items were transformed by replacing references to alcohol with references to the objects of today's mainstream anti-drug sentiment, 'drugs,' 'illegal substances,' 'alcohol and other drugs,' 'marijuana,' 'crack cocaine,' and so on. These twenty-two transformed items are referred to here as 'drugs-and-alcohol' items. Some 'drugs-and-alcohol' items were 'Once they start, people spend every penny they have buying illegal drugs,' 'Citizens should take action if the government fails to enforce (maintain) drug laws,' and 'Alcohol and drug use lead to family breakdown and domestic violence.' About half of the alcohol-only items and the drugs-and-alcohol items were reversed and stated as negations of the original temperance claims, to control for the problem of 'acquiescence' in responses to the TMQ (Burt et al. 1994).

During 1993 and 1994 the TMQ was administered to populations of university students at Simon Fraser University in Vancouver, Canada; at l'Université d'Ottawa in Canada (in French); at Utrecht University in the Netherlands (in English); at Bologna University, Bologna, Italy (in Italian); at the University of Washington in Seattle, USA; at Cameron University in Lawton, Oklahoma, USA; at Trinity College, Dublin, Ireland; at Paisii Hilendarski University in Plovdiv, Bulgaria (in Bulgarian); and at the University of Teheran, Iran (in Farsi). Sample sizes at the various universities ranged between 107 and 471 students. The total number of students was 1938. Multivariate analyses showed that a remarkably similar Temperance Mentality component emerged as the first principal component in all nine samples. Detailed summaries of these multivariate analyses are being published elsewhere (Burt et al. 1994; Alexander et al., in preparation).

The data are summarized in tables 3 and 4 in a form that circumvents multivariate technicalities. Table 3 summarizes the responses of the various student samples to the twenty-eight 'alcohol-only' TMQ items. Table 4 summarizes the results for the twenty-two 'drugs-and-alcohol' items. Both tables give the percentages of students who supported the

TABLE 3
Percentage of students expressing support, neutrality, or opposition to 28 'alcohol-only' items in the Temperance Mentality Questionnaire (TMQ)

City, country	Overall support	Neutral or mixed	Overall opposition
Teheran, Iran	50.4	43.7	5.9
Paisii, Bulgaria	31.8	63.6	4.7
Lawton, USA	30.2	62.1	7.7
Seattle, USA	11.8	73.0	15.2
Bologna, Italy	8.2	82.2	9.7
Vancouver, Canada	5.5	67.1	27.4
Ottawa, Canada	4.2	69.2	26.4
Utrecht, Netherlands	3.4	65.4	31.2
Dublin, Ireland	2.0	62.1	35.9

$X^2 = 348.6$; df = 24; $p < .001$

TABLE 4
Percentage of students expressing support, neutrality, or opposition to 22 'drugs-and-alcohol' items in the Temperance Mentality Questionnaire (TMQ)

City, country	Overall support	Neutral or mixed	Overall opposition
Teheran, Iran	87.4	11.9	0.7
Paisii, Bulgaria	82.2	17.8	0.0
Lawton, USA	69.2	28.4	2.4
Seattle, USA	46.6	50.0	3.4
Bologna, Italy	36.3	58.6	5.1
Dublin, Ireland	35.4	61.6	3.0
Vancouver, Canada	31.8	57.7	11.0
Ottawa, Canada	21.5	68.1	10.4
Utrecht, Netherlands	19.5	67.3	13.2

$X^2 = 347.2$; df = 24; $p < .001$

temperance position (that is, agreed with more than half of the temperance claims), those who opposed it (disagreed with more than half of the temperance claims), and those who were unsure or neutral.[4]

Examination of tables 3 and 4 will show that the differences between the different university samples are large and that, with the exception of Ireland, the ordering of the samples was the same for the two types of items. The greatest support for TMQ items was found in the Iranian and Bulgarian students, followed by the two American student groups, the

Italian students, the two Canadian student groups, and the Dutch students. Compared to the other samples, the Irish students expressed the least degree of support for the alcohol-only items (table 3), but they were intermediate between the Canadian and Italian students on the drugs-and-alcohol items (table 4). Comparison of tables 3 and 4 will show that, in each sample, the drugs-and-alcohol items received greater support from the students than the alcohol-only items. This difference was statistically significant for each sample.

The greater support for the TMQ items by the Canadian students relative to the Dutch students reinforces Study 1's finding that, before the Canadian students were exposed to balanced information about drugs, they were less likely to support harm reduction than were Dutch students. In addition, tables 3 and 4 indicate that the anglophone Canadian students supported the Temperance Mentality more than the francophone Canadian students.

From a larger international perspective, however, the differences between the Canadian anglophone, Canadian francophone, Dutch, Irish, and Italian samples were relatively small. The Iranian, Bulgarian, and two American samples (particularly Oklahoma) expressed much greater support for both types of TMQ items (see tables 3 and 4).

The cities of Vancouver and Seattle constitute a well-matched pair to compare for indications of national differences between Canada and the United States, because although these two cities share geographic propinquity, similar economic status, west coast culture and climate, they sit on opposite sides of the international boundary between Canada and the United States. The greater acceptance of the TMQ items among Seattle students relative to Vancouver students was statistically significant. This indication of a Canadian-American difference can only be suggestive, however, because of strong regional differences within both countries, and the lack of a Canadian sample from a traditionally conservative area of Canada, such as Alberta. Better-controlled sampling will be required to provide an adequate demonstration of differences between any two countries.

The data in tables 3 and 4 do seem adequate to suggest that it is not yet propitious to plan an international harm reduction conference in either Iran or Bulgaria. Support for the alcohol-only TMQ items reached 50 per cent in Iran, the highest for any sample. In both Bulgaria and Iran, support for the drugs-and-alcohol TMQ items was over 80 per cent. The only other sample that approached this level was Lawton, Oklahoma, with almost 70 per cent support.

The Temperance Mentality and the Future of Harm Reduction

Obviously, samples of convenience drawn from students in particular universities cannot establish national trends. Our hope is that these data, in conjunction with our informal interview observations, can help to frame issues for future research on readiness for harm reduction policies. In this section we speculate further about the temperance mentality. At the end, we explain why, in spite of our optimism about the readiness of Canadian society for harm reduction, we think that the harm reduction movement may have to investigate the nature and origin of the temperance mentality in other parts of the world where it finds greater support.

Our data suggest that the temperance mentality, as defined by the North American literature of the nineteenth and early-twentieth century, is surprisingly widespread. But why? Various American and Canadian scholars have linked the temperance mentality to causes that are quintessentially North American: Puritanism, Protestantism, and the Protestant ethic, middle-class capitalist values, and U.S. communications media or political pressures – but these explanations may be too culture-bound. None of these explanatory factors are characteristic of Iran or Bulgaria, where student support for the Temperance Mentality appeared the strongest. Although Iran and other Moslem countries have a long tradition of alcohol prohibition, Bulgaria does not.[5] In Bulgaria, religious fundamentalism is uncommon even among the Muslim minority and there is no history of alcohol prohibition (I. Vlassev, personal communication). Excessive public consumption of alcohol might explain support for the Temperance Mentality in Bulgaria, but it cannot do so in Tehran, where most consumption of alcohol and illicit drugs is carried out in secret for fear of violent punishment (M. Sirdehi, personal communication).

Homogeneity of the Temperance Mentality in Diverse Cultures

It is possible that agreement with anti-drug and alcohol items grows from very different ways of thinking in different cultures. However, our data suggest that the temperance mentality may be surprisingly uniform where we have measured it. Table 5 compares the first principal component from the principal component analyses of the TMQ data for our nine student samples. The first column in table 5 ('Temperance sign test') shows that, in every sample but two, 49 or 50 of the 50 TMQ items

TABLE 5
First principal components from each sample compared

University, country loadings	Temperance sign test	Percentage of variance	Correlation of component
Vancouver, Canada	50/50	21.8	1.000*
Seattle, USA	50/50	19.0	0.970
Lawton (OK), USA	50/50	19.5	0.958
Utrecht, Netherlands	49/50	21.0	0.971
Ottawa, Canada	49/50	20.5	0.938
Plovdiv, Bulgaria	49/50	19.1	0.943
Dublin, Ireland	49/50	14.4	0.968
Bologna, Italy	48/50	18.3	0.938
Tehran, Iran	44/50	22.6	0.820

*Simon Fraser component loadings are the standard to which the other samples are correlated.

10 highest loading items, Simon Fraser sample:

Positive loadings: (Temperance Mentality items)
Item 45 + .665: Once they start, people spend every penny they have buying illegal drugs.
Item 14 + .659: Selling marijuana would be immoral even if it were legal.
Item 21 + .639: Abstinence from alcohol in a community is the key to social progress.
Item 47 + .595: Drugs are the underlying cause of much of the misery that children suffer.
Item 19 + .588: Drinking leads to financial ruin.

Negative loadings: (Reversed Temperance Mentality items)
Item 3 - 600: Moderate use of illegal substances does not result in serious health problems.
Item 57 – 563: Moderate use of illicit drugs in a community does not hinder social progress.
Item 7 – 554: Being 'under the influence' of alcohol or other drugs can be a rewarding, beneficial experience.
Item 48 – 506: Alcohol use does not commonly lead to family breakdown and domestic violence.
Item 46 – 488: Use of illicit drugs does not cause insanity.

load in the direction that would be predicted if this component was a measure of adherence to the claims of the North American temperance movement. In the remaining two samples, 48 and 44 of the TMQ items loaded in the predicted direction in Italy and Iran, respectively. Column 2 in table 5 shows that in every sample but one, the Temperance Mentality component accounted for about the same proportion of variance, between 18.3 per cent and 22.6 per cent. Column 3 in table 5 shows that

the magnitude of the loadings of the items on the first principal component was very similar from sample to sample. The index of similarity is
the correlation of the factor loadings of each sample with the factor loadings of the Vancouver sample. Those items that tend to load the most
and least on the Temperance Mentality component are quite similar in
all nine samples.

The similarity of the temperance components in all nine samples suggests a possibility that we did not foresee when this research began: that
the same constellation of views that constituted temperance doctrine in
North American a century ago might configure public opinion about
alcohol and other drugs in many areas of the world today. Much of the
world could be in the same frame of mind as North America a century
ago when most people could be identified as 'wets,' 'drys,' or somewhere in between. The conspicuous difference is that the target of
temperance sentiment has expanded from alcohol to a plethora of
psychoactive drugs, including alcohol.

The Temperance Mentality and Authoritarianism

Temperance thinking may be part of a broader constellation of attitudes
and ideologies, and, if so, may be quite refractory to long-lived change
simply on the basis of new information about drugs. A quantitative
indication that TMQ scores may be embedded in a larger constellation
of attitudes in Canada comes from the strong positive correlation (0.58)
of Temperance Mentality scores of Canadian students with their scores
on Altemeyer's Right Wing Authoritarianism (RWA) scale (Burt et al.
1994). The RWA scale is intended to measure adherence to a wide range
of right-wing attitudes. Relative to other scales of its sort, the RWA scale
performs impressively on statistical measures of validity, reliability, and
internal consistency (Altemeyer 1988). The items on the Altemeyer scale
are a bit startling in this era of political correctness, yet they were supported by Canadian students with high scores on Temperance Mentality. The RWA items include the following: 'The way things are going in
this country, it's going to take a lot of "strong medicine" to straighten
out the troublemakers, criminals, and perverts'; 'The facts on crime, sexual immorality, and the recent public disorders all show we have to
crack down harder on deviant groups and troublemakers if we are
going to save our moral standards and preserve law and order'; and
'One reason we have so many troublemakers in our society nowadays
is that parents and other authorities have forgotten that good old-

fashioned physical punishment is still one of the best ways to make people behave properly.'

A further indication that the temperance mentality is best understood as part of a larger constellation of thought comes from Schaler (1993), who has reported a high correlation in addiction counsellors between an Addiction Belief Scale that measured some aspects of the temperance mentality and several sociopolitical characteristics including hierarchical religious faith. If the temperance mentality is embedded in a larger complex of attitudes or ideology, be they to the left or right on the political spectrum, it may be difficult to modify simply by explaining the health benefits of harm reduction programs.

Can the Temperance Mentality Impede the Progress of Harm Reduction?

Our data and informal interviews suggest that the temperance mentality may not be popular in Canada and some European countries, that it may be significantly reduced by providing factual information, and that, in most of our samples, the majority of students are neutral on temperance items. Is the temperance mentality, then, a force to be reckoned with?

In spite of our optimism about prospects for harm reduction in Canada, we believe that substantial support for the temperance mentality in countries like Iran, Bulgaria, and the United States could constitute a serious impediment to the progress of harm reduction. Everyone who debates drug-policy reform knows the intensity of those who voice the temperance mentality. In public debates, these people identify drug use with every conceivable ill and radiate hostility at those who question their simple equation. They insist, in the face of strong evidence to the contrary, that abstention is the only healthy response to prohibited drugs. They seem unconcerned about harshly punitive measures imposed on those who disregard their injunctions. They rely on invective and ad hominem argument. All in all, they fit the grim stereotype of North American temperance zealots of a century ago, who matched their rhetoric with personal, political, and, when occasions arose, violent actions (Taylor 1966; Kobler 1973).

The events of recent history (for example, the abortion controversy in North America or the continuing violence in Northern Ireland) show that an outraged, moralistic minority can wreak havoc with the reasoned accommodations of a larger society. Those who uphold the temperance mentality in the United States seem determined to export it and enforce it globally. Moreover, our data highlight the possibility that the temperance mentality is not only a manifestation of American cultural hegemony. It could also be an indigenous, majority point of view in other parts of the world where new social policies are now taking form.

We do not believe that the temperance mentality is an irresistible force, but we do suspect that its fulminations will not subside of their own volition. The temperance mentality may prove to be a loud and irksome ghost that continues to haunt the movement towards harm reduction until scholars come to grips with its mysteries, and find ways to put it to rest.

NOTES

1 Many generous colleagues have helped us to collect the international data, including Thomas Atwater, Line Beauchesne, Shane Butler, Hans Ossebaard, Mahdi Sirdehi, Julien Somers, Inna Vlassev, and George Vlassev. Various forms of multifactorial analysis have been done with the help of Ray Koopman, Michael Maraun, Kim Bartholemew, Chris Roney, Gary Dawes, Colby Lewis, and other colleagues at Simon Fraser University.
2 An Orthogonal rotation BMDP 4M principal components analysis was used, which initially yielded 14 factors, which were reduced to five by a Scree test. The first principal component is here described as the 'Temperance Mentality.' A fuller description of this analysis is available in Alexander et al. 1992.
3 In the original publication, we called this dimension the 'temperance outlook,' but we have altered our jargon slightly for the sake of consistency in this presentation. We will use the capitalized expression 'Temperance Mentality' to refer to scores on the first principal component of the analysis described here, and the lower-case expression 'temperance mentality' to refer to a continuum of thinking that underlies these quantitative data.
4 These calculations incorporated a statistical correction to reverse the direction of the temperance claims that had been stated in a negative form.
5 Some areas of Bulgaria do have a strong Muslim influence, but Plovdiv is not one of these (I. Vlassev, personal communication).

REFERENCES

Alexander, B.K. 1990. *Peaceful Measures: Canada's Way Out of the 'War on Drugs.'* Toronto: Univeristy of Toronto Press.
Alexander, B.K., C. Lewis, J. van Wijngaarden, and G.F. van de Wijngaart. 1992. 'Dubious Consensus: Support for Anti-Drug Policy among Dutch and Canadian University Students.' *Journal of Drug Issues* 22: 903–22.

Alexander, B.K., G.A. Dawes, G.F. van de Wijngaart, H.C. Ossebaard, and M.D. Maraun. In preparation. 'The "Temperance Mentality": An Investigation of University Students in Six Countries.'

Altemeyer, B. 1988. *Enemies of Freedom: Understanding Right Wing Authoritarianism*. San Francisco: Jossey-Bass.

Appleton, P. 1990. *Billion $$$ High: The Drug Invasion of Canada*. Toronto: McGraw-Hill Ryerson.

Boaz, D., ed. 1990. *The Crisis in Drug Prohibition*. Washington: Cato Institute.

Burt, G., C. Roney, G.A. Dawes, D. Nijdam, B.L. Beyerstein, G.F. van de Wijngaart, H.C. Ossebaard, and B.K. Alexander. 1994. 'The "Temperance Mentality": A Survey of Students at a Canadian University.' *Contemporary Drug Problems* 21: 301–27.

Cheneryk, E. 1990. *Alcohol Inside Out from Bottom Principles: Facts for the Millions*. 2nd ed. Boston: The author.

Chiniquy, Rev. Father C. 1847. *Manual of the Temperance Society*. Montreal: Lovell and Gibson.

Heath, D. 1992. 'US Drug Control Policy: A Cultural Perspective.' *Daedalus* 121: 269–91.

Heather, N., A. Wodak, E.A. Nadelmann, and P. O'Hare, eds. (1993). *Psychoactive Drugs and Harm Reduction: From Faith to Science*. London: Whurr.

Kellogg, J.H. 1926. 'Alcohol – A Discredited Drug.' *Good Health* 61: 5–8, 28–9.

Kobler, J. 1973. *Ardent Spirits: The Rise and Fall of Prohibition*. New York: Putnam.

Levine, H.G. 1992. 'Temperance Cultures: Concern about Alcohol Problems in Nordic and English-Speaking Cultures.' In G. Edwards, M. Lader, and C. Drummond, eds, *The Nature of Alcohol and Drug Related Problems*. London: Oxford University Press.

Malerek, V. 1990. *Merchants of Misery*. Toronto: McClelland & Stewart

Nadelmann, E.A. 1989. 'Drug Prohibition in the United States: Costs, Consequences, and Alternatives.' *Science* 245: 939–47.

Newcombe, R. 1989. 'Preventing the Spread of HIV-Infection among and from Injecting Drug Users in the U.K.' *International Journal on Drug Policy* 1(2): 20–7.

Peele, S. 1993. 'The Conflict between Public Health Goals and the Temperance Mentality.' *American Journal of Public Health* 83: 805–11.

Perkin, H. 1989. *The Rise of Professional Society: England Since 1880*. London: Routledge.

Room, R. 1991. 'Drug Policy Reform in Historical Perspective: Movements and Mechanisms.' *Drug and Alcohol Review* 10: 37–43.

Rush, B. 1805/1947. 'The Effects of Ardent Spirits upon Man.' In D.D. Runes, ed., *The Selected Writings of Benjamin Rush*. New York: Philosophical Library.

Schaler, J.A. 1993. 'Addiction Beliefs of Treatment Providers: Factors Explaining Variance.' Unpublished PhD dissertation, University of Maryland.

Smart, R.G., and A.C. Ogborne. 1986. *Northern Spirits: Drinking in Canada Then and Now*. Toronto: Addiction Research Foundation.

Taylor, R.L. 1966. *Vessel of Wrath: The Life and Times of Carry Nation*. New York: New American Library.

Trebach, A.S. 1993. 'For Legalization of Drugs.' In A.S. Trebach and J.A. Inciardi, eds, *Legalize It: Debating American Drug Policy*. Washington: American University Press.

Watson, M. 1991. 'Harm Reduction – Why Do It?' *International Journal on Drug Policy* 2(5): 13–15.

van de Wijngaart, G.F. 1991. *Competing Perspectives on Drug Use: The Dutch Experience*. Amsterdam: Swets and Zeitlinger.

Wisotsky, S. 1986. *Breaking the Impasse in the War on Drugs*. New York: Greenwood.

6 Harm Reduction at the Supply Side of the Drug War: The Case of Bolivia

FERNANDO GARCÍA ARGAÑARÁS

Harm reduction is usually defined as a benign approach to drug use, one that rejects its criminalization and questions the punitive policies associated with it. In this paper, harm reduction is redefined so as to include the set of problems and characteristics that prevail at the supply side of the drug war. The perception that certain drugs – and not others – are an evil that must be eradicated at all costs, together with geopolitical considerations about the 'security' of the Andean region, have made 'fighting supply' the cornerstone of U.S. policy in the hemisphere since 1985. This work focuses on the harm derived from the pursuit of coca eradication and substitution policies in Bolivia, hoping to contribute to the reduction of such harm through greater awareness of the social 'price tag' of this war. In this sense, I reorient the notion of harm reduction to include the cultivation of coca leaves and the militarization of the so-called drug war – thus bringing into focus social actors other than consumers.

Defenders of supply-side counternarcotics policies claim that the drug war is being won in Bolivia, by reducing the acreage of coca cultivation, disrupting the major crime networks, and keeping under control the corruption of officials. Critics point out that reduction of acreage goes along with relocation of crops, rotation of trafficking networks, decentralization of cocaine production, and the increasing confusion between legal coca growers and illegal cocaine producers. They note that counternarcotics policies have a counterinsurgency dimension, which is leading to both the 'politicization' and the militarization of the drug war. In this context, the Bolivian government – under U.S. prodding – has put forth a set of 'Alternative Development' policies with the aim of reducing and eradicating with compensation the cultivation of coca leaves in Bolivia. At first sight such policies seem the least harmful available in the counternarcotics repertoire.[1]

Reducing Harm Through Alternative Development?

'Alternative Development,' in practice, refers to the main set of infra-structural, credit, and agro-industrial projects undertaken in the coca-growing region of the Chapare in Bolivia since 1984. The approach was the Bolivian government's response to the demands of peasant producers facing coca eradication in the mid-1980s at the prompting of the Reagan administration. Peasant producers had asked for a 'comprehensive' development effort that would go beyond the switch into 'alternative crops' favoured by the state.[2] Alternative Development, however, took on quite a different and specific meaning in U.S.-Bolivian agreements, where it was considered a form of assistance 'to facilitate the transition to an economy that will replace the one resting on coca' (CEDIB 1991: 42). Further into the document there is a specification as to the type of economy meant: one 'oriented towards exports.' By 1990, the application of this definition of development had led to a growing number of Alternative Development projects but also to widespread questioning and criticism of its 'alternative' nature (Aguiló 1992; Balderrama 1990).[3]

The prelude of the settlement process that laid the foundation of free-holding and coca cultivation in the Chapare was played in 1953, with the agrarian reform launched by the Nationalist Revolutionary Movement (MNR), and in the 1960s (García Argañarás 1992a, 1992b).[4] In the late 1970s, Chapare peasants had tried a variety of coca leaves (*erythroxylum novogranatense, erythroxylum truxillense, erythroxylum coca*), obtaining best results with the 'Coca Trujillo.' By the early 1980s the drastic decline of living standards of the urban working class, spiralling hyper-inflation, and the consolidation of the cocaine industry by Bolivian entrepreneurs and sectors of the state apparatus led to a 'mass movement of semi-permanent and seasonal migrants to the Chapare,' many of whom engaged in coca cultivation. Increased migration, accompanied by expanded demand for coca cutivation, led to a particular response on the part of the state: the provision of projects, programs, and financing for public and private works aimed at the substitution of coca leaves for other crops. These programs started with the 1985 MNR administration and were continued and refined by the ADN-MIR coalition government that came to an end in August 1993. The idea was to compensate producers within the framework of an export-oriented model.[5] This model goes in Bolivia by the name of neo-liberalism, since it seeks the maximum privatization of the economy and the maximum expansion of the rules of the market.

In 1989, it became clear that the 70 per cent eradication rule, imposed by the United States as a condition for the disbursement of compensation and other aid, was a failure. The National Directorate for Agricultural Reconversion (DIRECO) acknowledged that after one year of sustained efforts in the Chapare, only 4 per cent of 'excess' production (2190 Ha.) had actually been reduced. By mid-1991, the U.S. ambassador in La Paz was kindly engaged in negotiating and promoting the sale of substitute Chapare fruits and vegetables to Chile without consulting with the Bolivian government – a fact that led to some protestation in the local press (Los Tiempos, 30 August 1991).

The U.S. interest in Alternative Development goes beyond the 'economic,' however. Critics point out the common denominator of low-intensity warfare and Alternative Development: both are centred around the peasant producers. Current counter-insurgency policy seeks to defeat (or nip in the bud) guerrilla forces with actual or potential support on the part of the peasantry; counternarcotics policy aims at the arrest and prosecution of drug traffickers who offer lucrative markets for the coca leaves of the peasantry. These two sets of policies were conceived under the Cold War doctrine of containment, but have now been adapted to promote the post–Cold War strategy of 'enlargement.'[6] Two central components of this new mission entail expanding transnational market relations and dealing with dissent ('backlash states' and 'subversion') in the Third World. Insofar as low-intensity warfare (a counter-insurgency strategy) implies limited military operations together with 'civic action' programs to win the hearts and minds of peasants, it is in practice indistinguishable from low-intensity interdiction and eradication (a counternarcotics strategy). Both strategies have similar tactical objectives and methods vis-à-vis the peasantry (CEDIB 1990b; Andreas et al. 1991: 123).

Organized peasant resistance to eradication policies from above and without compensation played a significant role in the formulation of Alternative Development policies on paper, but the military linkages and infrastructure were gradually strengthened while peasant participation was in fact precluded.[7] Significantly, a confidential memorandum by a UN officer familiar with substitution policies concluded that 'there is nothing more profitable than coca [growing].'[8] While stating the obvious, the phrase hints at the anemic state and prospects of Alternative Development. The official view tends to promote it as a workable set of policies, but the view from the *cocaleros* is less sanguine. David Herrada, union leader of the coca growers, says, 'we have eradication without development,' echoing the message of producers in and around Villa 14 de Septiembre, Villa Tunari, and Chimoré.[9] The common criticism: peasants who eradicate coca leaves from their plots are now worse off than before. They lack sufficient credit to sustain their new crops, they owe money to banks because of initial investments in ill-conceived government-sponsored schemes, and their alternative crops are either a failure or take too long to become economically feasible (CIDRE-SEAMOS 1992: 22; CEDIB 1992a: 84–5, 91, 102). Indeed, the most complete study on the impact of Alternative Development in the Chapare estimates a net loss of some U.S. $17 million to coca producers between 1984 and 1991 as a result of eradication and substitution linked to Alternative Development-funded projects (CIDRE-SEAMOS 1992: 4).

At the end of 1995 Alternative Development seemed thus caught in a bind: the nearly U.S. $300 million spent since 1980 had not been enough to substantially raise the living standard of producers, and more money was not likely to create the jobs needed either. Part of the problem, no doubt, stems from the top-down approach used in the implementation of development projects.[10] But a large share of funds is also absorbed by the electrification and supply of other badly needed services to towns and villages of coca-growing regions, providing however little benefit to coca *producers* in the countryside (CIDRE-SEAMOS 1992; Palza Medina 1991: 53–5).

The Harmful Effects of Counternarcotics Policy

In the face of the questionable application and results of the Alternative Development approach to date, this section will analyse the three main harmful effects of counternarcotics policy in general: (1) The institutionalization of a 'Permanent army of the unwaged'; (2) the militarization of law enforcement; and (3) the Devaluation of 'political goods' in Bolivia's formal democracy.[11]

The Institutionalization of a 'Permanent Army of the Unwaged'

A conventional way to analyse market economies is to differentiate them in terms of economic 'sectors': primary, or raw materials and agri-

culture; secondary, or manufacturing; and tertiary, or services. Historically, the growth of the service sector in Europe and North America has
followed a significant expansion of the industrial sector of the economy
and the penetration of capitalist relations of production in agriculture.
In the Bolivian case, by contrast, the extraordinary expansion of the so-
called service sector since the mid-1980s has been attributed to a sort of
multiplier effect of the coca-cocaine economy and the stagnation of an
always incipient manufacturing sector.

In Latin America, the growth in the number of people making a precarious living in non-registered activities, in turn, has led to the division
of the tertiary sector into 'formal' and 'informal' components. Illicit coca
paste and cocaine hydrochloride production and marketing (some
55,000 small producers and traders and dozens of trafficking networks)
thus came to be included under the label of 'informal' economic activities, which in Bolivia are deemed to generate about 51 per cent of the
Gross Domestic Product (CEDIB 1989: 9). The economic weight of this
sector, on account of the highly profitable illicit component, hides the
poverty of the overwhelming majority of people – possibly 600,000 –
involved in informal activities not directly related to drug production or
distribution (Mansilla and Toranzo 1991: 41). Fully 32.6 per cent of the
labour force of Bolivia were involved in the 'informal' sector according to a 1991 study by the Instituto Nacional de Estadísticas (CEDIB
1993c: 47).

Counternarcotics policies of eradication, substitution, and interdiction
have, directly and indirectly, contributed to the mushrooming of this
unprotected, impoverished, and highly heterogeneous sector of Bolivians.[12] Instead of seeing the expansion of this sector as a 'temporary'
solution to Bolivia's economic crisis, it seems more pertinent to consider
it part and parcel of the restructuring of the labour market. While in
some respects this constitutes an addition to the 'reserve army of labour'
required by the market economy, in more fundamental respects we are
witnessing the formation of a 'permanent army of the unwaged.'

The growth of this sector can be understood as a structural outcome
of Bolivia's new form of accommodation to a world order in transition.[13]
Whereas the 1952–82 period was characterized by Bolivia's insertion
into the world order of the *pax americana* as a supplier of strategic miner-
als (mainly tin), the post-1982 period has seen a switch to its integration
as an exporter of non-traditional goods: oil and gas, soja, cotton and –
however illegal – coca paste and cocaine hydrochloride. If the political
economy of the former period can justifiably be labelled state capitalist,

with some protectionist overtones, the latter is unabashedly liberalizing and accommodating to the ideas, institutions, and practices proceeding from 'the community of major market democracies' and, especially, the remaining superpower. This new form of neoliberal accommodation has been achieved at the expense of massive expulsion of workers and employees from the state-capitalist, mining, and private industrial sectors (Mansilla and Toranzo 1991: 33–42). Fully two-thirds of the labour force of the state mining corporation (COMIBOL) had become permanently unwaged by 1989 and reductions continued until 1994. As a result, there has been a drastic shrinking in the state-capitalist sector as well as in the size and relative weight of private manufacturing. The process of economic restructuring therefore corresponds to a long-term trend of decline in the mining economy as well as to the complementary interests of a rising agro-exporting sector and U.S. policy that, through direct conditioning of economic and military assistance, promotes greater opening and privatization of the Bolivian economy (García Argañarás 1993). This restructuring has been the principal *generator* of the urban unwaged sector.

In this context, the institutionalization of the 'informal' sector helps local entrepreneurs and the market economy to lower the reproduction costs of the remaining urban wage-labour force, meeting some basic needs of this impoverished market – a market in dire need of cheaper transport, commodities, and services provided by street vendors and others. Here, the permanent army of the unwaged becomes three things at once: a subsidy to private entrepreneurs, a structural brake on wages for the labour force in the 'formal' sector of the economy, and a subsistence sector where moving from 'rags to riches' remains highly unlikely for all but a few.[14]

As indicated in the first section of this paper, Alternative Development policies – and, more generally, economic assistance – have been contingent on Bolivia's liberalization of the economy, its insertion in the world market as an exporter of primary products, and the expansion of military involvement in counternarcotics policy enforcement. The centrepiece of liberalization has been dubbed the New Economic Policy (NEP). Initiated by the MNR regime in 1985, the NEP has been dependent on 'progress' in the drug front in several interrelated ways.

First, U.S. assistance with the Bolivian balance-of-payments deficit has been linked to cooperation in the drug war – directly, through conditional disbursements of USAID funds and the process of 'certification' by the U.S. Congress, and indirectly, through approval of IMF loans for 'structural reforms' in line with the 'alternative economy' mentioned in the *Anexo 2* of 1987 (CEDIB 1992b: 5; García Argañarás 1996). As noted, these structural adjustments have led to mass lay-offs and cutbacks in public spending, enlarging considerably the permanent army of the unwaged.

Second, the NEP has provoked an explosion of smuggling from neighbouring countries, controlled by a small belt of prosperous merchants and resting on a mass of peddlers, 'who manage miniscule amounts of merchandise' (NACLA 1991: 20). The connection with counternarcotics policy here is two-fold: profits from the criminalized drug trade are laundered by large merchants with government ties through contraband, which has swelled the ranks of the small urban 'entrepreneurs' – otherwise known as vendors – who constitute two-thirds of the misnamed 'small business' sector. This sector covers a significant part of the permanent army of the unwaged. USAID mini-loans through NGOs have promoted the growth – and therefore the institutionalization – of this sector (ibid.: 23).

Third, the NEP has deepened Bolivia's agricultural crisis, lowering prices of agricultural products and increasing the country's dependence on food imports and donations. This crisis has harmed the subsistence and small farming sector of agriculture while favouring large agribusiness enterprises – which count on state and international support in the form of credit and subsidies. Peasants pushed out of the market have swelled the ranks of the permanent army of the unwaged. Meanwhile, U.S. food donations amount to some 30 per cent of national agricultural production and constitute another lever available to obtain compliance with U.S. directives.

The strings attached to USAID assistance, to IMF loans, and to counternarcotics efforts have not all, in and of themselves, aimed consciously at the growth of the permanent army of the unwaged. They have achieved this result, however, by virtue of their collective – and individual – weight in support of Bolivia's accommodation to the emerging world order on the basis of the 'alternative economy' of the NEP (García Argañarás 1995).

The Militarization of Law Enforcement

United States economic assistance between 1991 and 1995 included funding for rural projects in line with the 'export economy' advocated by the NEP and the *Anexo 2* (which sought to attract 'foreign investment through the formation of joint ventures, contracts or *maquilas'*). This assistance included advice on 'the labour force, installation costs and free export zones' (CEDIB 1992a: 113). The promotion of foreign investment in Bolivia by the U.S. government, like the promotion of fruit exports by the U.S. embassy, are symptomatic of a much wider process of convergence among security, economic, and political interests in Bolivia. A prime result of such confluence is the widening scope of military functions – and the consequent blurring between policing and defence roles.

Traditionally, the armed forces have seen themselves as a specialized institution to defend the nation against attacks by foreign governments. During the Cold War, the doctrine of national security extended this function to the preservation of 'internal order' against 'the enemy within.' Under this doctrine, Bolivia endured, like its Southern Cone neighbours, the heavy hand of anti-communist military dictatorships. The blurring between the official defence role of the military and its unofficial internal function has precedents in Bolivia's long history of military leadership. In fact, Bolivia holds the record in military coups, which outnumber its years as an independent nation. While the country is now enjoying its fourth consecutive civilian administration since 1982, counternarcotics policies have enhanced both the military role of the police and the policing role of Bolivia's military.

To begin, special forces have been created with the express purpose of fighting the drug war under the rubric of the Fuerza Especial de Lucha Contra el Narcotráfico (FELCN): the Unidad Móvil de Patrullaje Rural (UMOPAR); el Grupo de Inteligencia y Operaciones Especiales (GIOE); and other specialized support units. UMOPAR is a police unit with quasi-military functions, based in the Chapare region, the main source of coca leaves. Specialized units of the armed forces, under FELCN command and formed by members 'on special commission' who have received training in low-intensity conflict (by Fort Bragg, North Carolina, Bragg personnel), operate mostly in and around the Beni region of eastern Bolivia, where most traffickers have labs and clandestine air strips. Both types of forces are engaged in interdiction, search, patrolling, destroying of labs, and arresting of suspects (CEDIB 1993c: 125).[15]

The most immediate problem arising from these expanded functions is not the obvious blurring between the civil arena and military security, but the step-by-step encroachment upon civil liberties. Human-rights organizations, coca growers, the churches, journalists, and academics have noted the persistent reoccurrence of abuses and violations of civil and human rights not only on the part of Bolivian counternarcotics forces, but occasionally by the U.S. DEA and Especial Forces personnel who, at times, do not even comply with Bolivian law (Permanent Committee on Investigations, 26 September 1989: 22; Aguiló 1992: 111–17; CEDIB 1992b: 106–9; 1993c: 122).[16] These abuses cover the full spectrum, though the most extreme practices have become both less frequent and less intense: harassment and intimidation of peasants, unlawful incarceration, extortion, sexual molestation of women, unlawful seizure of belongings, beatings, torture, and killing of demonstrators. Most Bolivian citizens subject to this expansion of military and policing functions in the Chapare and eastern Bolivia can have no hope of redress in the courts, since violations take place in a framework of practical impunity – so victims bypass formal channels that may exist on paper and lodge complaints with union federations, the churches, and journalists, who, collectively, put pressure on the government to comply with the law.

The use of military intelligence in the drug war is another threat to Bolivian civil liberties. Bolivian and U.S. military intelligence agents necessarily collect information on Bolivian citizens at home and abroad, since the new security 'threats' – terrorism, drug trafficking, and so called backlash states – constitute not just national but international problems. Although there seems to be no lack of intelligence data, DEA and SOUTHCOM officials based in Panama have asked for 'an expanded support for intelligence efforts' (Permanent Committee on Investigations, 26 September 1989: 31). The expansion of intelligence activities with little, if any, public control lends itself all too easily to misuse against legitimate opponents of current policies and practices. This is especially the case with union leaders, politicians, and academics who question and criticize counternarcotics policies.[17]

Employing the Bolivian military as an agent of law enforcement against drugs and producers of coca leaves has brought the military directly into the civil arena in a new but no less worrisome guise. Given the country's history of military authoritarianism, it is not inconceivable that, in the event of a crisis, at least some military officers and some civilians would conclude that the military is, once again, better able to run the country.

The Devaluation of 'Political Goods' in Bolivia's New Democracy

The potential of military rule as an indirect result of the drug war brings us right into the process of democratization of the Bolivian state. Since 1982, four uninterrupted civilian governments have come to power through general elections. This is unprecedented in Bolivian history but coincides with the pattern of democratic liberalization in the rest of Latin America (Nun 1993). In advanced market economies, democratic liberalism has been extended to wider sectors of the population by enforcing a more or less strict separation between the purely 'political' sphere and the 'economy,' which allows for a unique form of juridical equality and social inequality. As we shall see, however, counternarcotics policies have reinforced the traditional lack of demarcation between 'political' and 'non-political' areas in Bolivia's state and society (García Argañarás 1992b). This fluidity comes at the price of the currency of democracy.

The 'political goods' of liberal democracy are well known: free and fair elections, political parties, separation of state powers, representativeness, and civil liberties. At the root of all this is the principle of popular sovereignty and participation, which legitimizes this form of political rule. Counternarcotics policies have, directly and indirectly, devalued these goods by fostering a formal allegiance to the official features of the political system while inducing practices that *minimize* or preclude popular participation and control of state policy. Peasant 'participation' in Alternative Development policies is a case in point. Unilateral U.S. efforts on behalf of Bolivia's exports from the Chapare is another instance.

More damaging, however, is the continued pressure on the executive, the Supreme Court, and the military to conform to U.S. directives even though these may contradict, violate, or bypass the Bolivian constitution, the will of voters, and international norms against foreign interference in the internal affairs of sovereign nations. Thus, in October 1993, U.S. troops arrived in Bolivia without congressional authorization, while further antinarcotics assistance was made conditional on judicial reforms (CEDIB 1993b: 132–3). These events came in the wake of a scandalous 'sting' operation organized by the U.S. embassy that implicated the Supreme Court chief in alleged acts of corruption and extortion (CEDIB 1993b: 15–30). At the centre of these U.S. efforts was the question of a new extradition treaty, proposed by the United States and resisted by previous Bolivian governments.[18] More recently, Washington has exerted more direct pressure by means of ultimatums and the process of 'certification' – eliciting full Bolivian compliance despite

widespread opposition in the country. Certification is a unilateral practice initiated by the U.S. government by virtue of which governments of
the Andean region are deemed to be performing or not performing well
in the Drug War. 'Decertified' countries, like Colombia under the pres-
idency of Ernesto Samper, are punished with a variety of political and
economic measures.

The vast majority of Bolivian citizens have little or no input in these
matters of national significance and have generally not been able to
change the course of events in one direction or another. When neither
the congress, nor the supreme court, nor the executive of a country can
operate independently from a superpower, and key decisions are taken
without consultation, it follows that some political goods obtained
through elections are circulating at less than their full value. Arguably,
these facts constitute a limitation on the assumed 'autonomy' of the
state.

Admittedly, the debate about state autonomy has referred mainly to
its relation to social classes and economic power. But the lack of citizen
consent regarding U.S. activities in Bolivia, together with the widespread perception that the political system serves 'only the rich' and not
'the people,' entails a devaluation in the legitimacy of the electoral system and raises serious questions about state autonomy in practice. This
is most significantly expressed in the increasing rates of electoral abstention in municipal elections, from 10 per cent in 1980 to 30 per cent in
1989; as well as in the high level of dissatisfaction with the political system. Indeed, according to public-opinion studies, only 16 per cent of
Bolivians see themselves being represented by this form of democratic
system (Lazarte 1993: 3, 6, 32, 285, 286). The municipal elections of
December 1993 confirmed this trend through the record level of abstention registered: nearly 50 per cent of the 2.5 million registered voters
failed to turn out – despite legislation in favour of compulsory voting
(LAWR 1993: 580).

We are seeing, in other words, a situation where the holders of (supposedly) authoritative means of domination and coercion wield them
less as an expression of the consent of the governed and more as instruments of enlargement of the market.[19] This, of course, is an illustration
of the fact that a set of procedural rules governing collective decisions –
such as multiparty elections and activities – do not suffice to define concrete practices (Nun 1993: 9). The rules may be 'democratic,' but their
implementation and enforcement may not.

Concluding Suggestions

If the supply-reduction policy has proved to be significantly less than successful, perhaps it may profitably be replaced by a harm-reduction one. The failure of the attempt 'to go at the source' has been acknowledged by some State Department and DEA documents, U.S. congressional reports, and agents in the field (though success has been claimed by the U.S. Information Service and others).[20] This duality is not merely a reflection of the double agenda of counternarcotics and counter-insurgency; it has something more fundamental to do with the application of neoliberal macroeconomic and social policies. The conditioning of all aid to the application of liberalization policies has come into contradiction with the stated objective of reducing supply. The operation and functioning of a market economy with a reducing state role do not neatly respond to conventional distinctions between 'formal' and 'informal' sectors, or between 'legal' and 'illicit.' As trivial as it may seem, the laws of supply and demand pay no heed to such categories. This contradiction has been expressed in the harmful effects discussed above. What follows are some harm reduction alternatives suggested by the analysis – some of which have already been put forth by people and organizations without access to policy making and implementation, such as the coca producers themselves.

1/Replace the regional policy of Alternative Development by a National Development Plan. An element of such a plan would be the industrial use and commercialization of coca leaves for medicinal products in coca-growing regions; another would promote food self-sufficiency and diversification in areas whose neglect is now pushing people toward urban centres and coca-growing regions as a strategy of survival.
2/Incorporate peasant participation and management in crop-substitution efforts.
3/Delink counternarcotics from counter-insurgency efforts, refocusing the drug war on the big trafficking networks.
4/Consider harm reduction policy alternatives, including legalization and decriminalization of the coca leaf.
5/Encourage the U.S. government to abide by international law and the laws of host countries.

Harm reduction on the supply side, therefore, entails maximizing the standards of living of actual and potential coca-leaf cultivators; finding a commercial outlet for their legal production and for medicinal and other products derived from the leaf; and making the local and foreign governments involved in substitution programs accountable to the citizenry.

NOTES

1 The following section is a significantly shortened, revised, and updated version of a paper presented at the conference 'Counternarcotics Policy in the Western Hemisphere,' hosted by CERLAC, York University, Toronto, on 30 January 1992.
2 See Javier Palza Medina. 1991: 195. All translations from the Spanish are the author's.
3 See CEDIB 1990b: 37.
4 Palza Medina's *La coca en la construcción nacional* has a good description of the establishment of coca cultivation in the Chapare.
5 It is rarely acknowledged, however, that some aspects of A.D. as a *substitution* approach are rooted in more than four decades of thinking by the U.N. Economic Commission for Latin America – known by the Spanish acronym CEPAL. CEPAL's thinking on development, however, was premised on Import Substitution Industrialization, and was therefore protective of the domestic market and production. The export-import model here refers to the attempt to fit new crops that would replace coca into the export economy that the U.S. favours. The focus on 'alternative crops' leaves aside related issues of peasant administration, human rights and the survival of small peasant production (threatened by international competition). The counterpart of non-traditional exports from Bolivia, and a declining small- and medium-sized agricultural sector, is increased dependence on food imports.
6 Anthony Lake, National Security Adviser, 21 September 1993: 'The successor to a doctrine of containment must be a strategy of enlargement – enlargement of the world's free community of market democracies. I see four components to a strategy of enlargement. First, we should strengthen the community of major market democracies – including our own – which constitutes the core from which enlarement is proceeding. Second, we should help foster and consolidate new democracies and market economies, where possible, especially in states of special significance and opportunity. Third, we must counter the aggression – and support the liberalization – of states hostile to democracy and markets. Fourth, we need to pursue our humanitarian agenda not only by providing aid, but also by working to help democ-

racy and market economies take root in regions of greatest humanitarian concern.' (Speech, 'Enlargement Should Succeed Containment,' published in *Aviation Week and Space Technology* 139: 64 0 4; see also Lake, 'From Containment to Enlargement,' *U.S. Department of State Dispatch* 4 [1993]: 658–64).

7 Taped transcripts of the meeting, Estación Experimental La Jota, Chimoré, Bolivia, 8 September 1992.

8 Given to the author by a UN functionary at La Paz, September 1992.

9 Among those interviewed between September and October 1992 and in the summer of 1993 were Evo Morales and David Herrada, from the Federación Especial de Trabajadores Campesinos del Trópico de Cochabamba; Alfonso Ferrufino, congressman from the Movimiento Bolivia Libre; Ramiro Avilés, from the Centro de Investigación y Educación Popular, CINEP; and scores of anonymous peasant producers in the Chapare.

10 Perhaps our UN source has stumbled upon something, judging by his memo, which asserts: 'there is a successive imposition of logics that are alien to the peasants, beginning with the logic of the financiers, who make disbursements to the degree that the repression of drug trafficking in their countries of origin is seen as less productive ... Later, the logic of national administrators prevails, seeking to obtain the maximum benefit for this and other purposes ... Finally, the technicians ...'

11 Field research for this section, between June and September 1993, was possible thanks to a grant by the York University Contract Faculty Grants Fund.

12 The prevailing view about the growth of the informal sector in Bolivia is, apparently, a positive one.

13 'Accommodation' is a concept that denotes the process and mechanisms that ensure the continuity of a given world order–national state relationship. This relationship rests on particular configurations of ideas, material conditions, and institutions. The period under discussion can be characterized as the *pax americana* (1973–96) in decline.

14 Street conversations between the author and *informales* in La Paz and Cochabamba have so far failed to yield evidence other than that the majority view their participation in this sector as a 'precarious survival strategy' dictated by poverty and lack of alternatives. Actually, it has been estimated that earnings among the *informales* has declined 37 per cent since joining this sector in 1985 (NACLA 1991: 18).

15 The expanded functions of both the police and the military are not confined to these special units. The 'Red Devils' and 'Blue Devils' battalions of the air force and the navy have long been providing logistical, communications, and search support to the FELCN (CEDIB 1996). Later, they have been joined by the 'Green Devils' battalion of the army (CEDIB 1993c: 126, 128). United

States nationals have reportedly been engaged in illegal riverine interdiction (stopping and searching boats in rivers) without the presence of Bolivian authorities or military personnel (CEDIB 1992c: 109).

16 U.S. concern about the 'implications of having military people, who are trained to shoot and kill, participate in and be in charge of law enforcement activities that heretofore have essentially involved matters of seizure and arrest' was expressed in 1989, in the context of a proposed expansion of Snowcap operations to include Special Forces personnel (Permanent Subcommittee on Investigations, 26 September 1989: 18).

17 In October 1993, for example, a UNDP functionary launched a most personal, public, and unsubstantiated campaign against Evo Morales, the executive secretary of the largest federation of coca-growers and Bolivian 'man of the year' in 1994. The campaign was launched on the basis of statements by the U.S. Embassy. He was accused of being 'the only one who has the capital' for 'an effective apparatus of communications, which includes a Fax to distribute his press releases' (CEDIB 1993b: 124).

18 The renewed interest in extradition came in the wake of Mexican, Colombian, and Bolivian expressions of concern and protest about the U.S. Supreme Court decision authorizing the kidnapping of alleged drug traffickers and terrorist suspects abroad for trial in the United States. This decision constituted a violation of international law and gave further impulse to the U.S. principle of extra-territoriality, culminating in the current process of 'certification' (CEDIB 1992b: 114–19, 125–7; García Argañarás 1996: 3). U.S. influence on judicial reforms in the Andean region has been noted to prop up 'a system of anti-terrorist legislation and the creation of judicial offices that are being used to repress legitimate social protest' (ILSA 1993).

19 The connection between the political economy of the NEP and human rights is the subject of the first report on Bolivia published by the Comisión Andina de Juristas (1988).

20 For a critical view, see for example the book by former DEA officer Michael Levine, *La guerra falsa* (1994); see also Andreas et al. 1991: 126).

REFERENCES

Andreas, Peter, et al. 1991. 'Dead-End Drug Wars.' *Foreign Policy* 85 (Winter).
Balderrama, Carlos. 1990. 'El potencial de violencia en el Chapare.' In ILDIS, *Las condiciones de la violencia en Perú y Bolivia*. La Paz: ILDIS.
CEDIB. 1989. *Realidad Nacional: Todo sobre la Coca y Cocaína*. Cochabamba, Bolivia: CEDIB.

- 1990a. 'Militarización ¡NO! Desarrollo ¡SI!' Dossier. Cochabamba: CEDIB.
- 1990b. 'Hacia Dónde va el Desarrollo Alternativo?' Dossier. Cochabamba, Bolivia: CEDIB.
- 1991. 'Bolivia: Coca y Lucha Contra las Drogas.' Documento. Cochabamba: CEDIB.
- 1992a. *30 Días*. Año I, no. 7. Cochabamba: CEDIB.
- 1992b. *30 Días*. Año I, no. 6. Cochabamba: CEDIB.
- 1992c. *De Cartagena a Texas*. Cochabamba: CEDIB.
- 1992d. *Coca – Cronología, Bolivia: 1986–1992*. Cochabamba: CEDIB-ILDIS.
- 1993a. *30 Días*. Año 2, no. 11. Cochabamba: CEDIB.
- 1993b. *30 Días*. Año 2, no. 10. Cochabamba: CEDIB.
- 1993c. *30 Días*. Año 2, no. 9. Cochabamba: CEDIB.
- 1996. 'La FELCN: Fuerza Especial de Lucha Contra el Narcotráfico.' *Dossier Informativo*. Cochabamba, June.
CIDRE-SEAMOS. 1992. *Estudio de impacto de los proyectos de desarrollo alternativo ejecutados en el trópico cochabambino*. Cochabamba, Bolivia: CIDRE.
Comisión Andina de Juristas. 1988. *Bolivia: Neoliberalismo y Derechos Humanos*. Lima: Comisión Andina de Juristas.
DIRECO. No date. Dirección Nacional de Reconversión Agrícola. *Plan Operativo 1992*. Cochabamba, Bolivia:
García Argañarás, Fernando. 1992a. 'Bolivia's Transformist Revolution.' *Latin American Perspectives* 19(2): 44–71.
- 1992b. 'The Mechanisms of Accommodation: Bolivia, 1952–1971.' *Review* 15(2): 257–308.
- 1993. *Reason of State and Bolivia's Deadlock: 1952–1982*. Toronto: MYE and LAL.
- 1995. 'Integration or Autonomy?: Bolivia in the New World Order.' Paper presented at the 26th Congress of the Canadian Association of Latin American and Caribbean Studies, Toronto, 9–11 November.
- 1996. 'La Diplomacia de la Certificación.' *Boletín Internacional – Coca, Drogas, Narcotráfico, Desarrollo* (La Paz) 5(1).
ILSA. 1993. 'Anti-Terrorist Legislation: The Hidden Agenda of the Judicial War Against Drugs.' Working paper. Bogotá: Instituto Latinoamericano de Servicios Legales Alternativos.
LAWR. 1993. Latin America Weekly Report, 16 December: 580. London: Latin American Newsletters.
Lazarte, Jorge. 1993. *Bolivia: certezas e Incertidumbres de la Democracia*. Cochabamba, Bolivia: Los Amigos de Libro.
Levine, Michael. 1994. *La guerra falsa*. Cochabamba, Bolivia: Acción Andina.
North American Congress on Latin America (NACLA): Report on the Americas. 1991. 'Bolivia' (several articles). 25(1): 10–38.

Nun, José. 1993. 'Democracy and Modernization.' *Latin American Perspectives* 20(4): 7–27.

Palza Medina, Javier. 1991. *La coca en la construcción nacional.* La Paz: Editorial Signo A & G.

Permanent Subcommittee on Investigations (U.S. Senate). 1989. 'Hearings on U.S. Government's Anti-Narcotics Activities in the Andean Region of South America.' Staff statement, 26 September.

Sanabria, Harry. 1989. 'Coca, Migration and Social Differentation in the Bolivian Lowlands.' In Edmundo Morales, ed., *Drugs in Latin America*, 81–123.

Sharpe, Kenneth. 1988. 'The Drug War: Going after Supply.' *Journal of Interamerican Studies and World Affairs*: 77–85.

PART II: HUMAN RIGHTS

7 Harm Reduction, Human Rights, and the WHO Expert Committee on Drug Dependence

ROBIN ROOM

The Tradition of WHO Expert Committees on Drug Dependence

Under the various international conventions on psychoactive drugs, the World Health Organization (WHO) has specific treaty responsibility to act as the source of scientific and medical advice to the international drug-control system. WHO's task, when it is asked for advice on a drug, is to evaluate a drug's dependence potential, its abuse liability, and its medical usefulness, and to recommend whether and in which schedule a drug should be placed under the control of the international drug-control machinery (Bruun et al. 1975).

The main WHO mechanism for accomplishing this task has been a series of expert committees, which used to meet every year, and now meet every second year. The 28th Expert Committee on Drug Dependence met in Geneva from 28 September to 2 October 1992.

The expert-committee mechanism is a well-established part of WHO's work. An expert committee is a relatively expensive mechanism, and thus is used judiciously, although in many different contexts. An expert-committee meeting on a topic may be a one-time affair or just one in a series. In 1992 and early 1993, for instance, WHO published non-recurring expert-committee reports on 'Recent advances in oral health,' 'Rehabilitation after cardiovascular diseases,' and 'Health promotion in the workplace: alcohol and drug abuse,' as well as reports from recurring series of expert committees on filariasis, rabies, the control of schistosomiasis, biological standardization, specifications for pharmaceutical preparations, the use of essential drugs, and food additives. WHO's style is to describe these recurring expert committees as if they are a continuing body. But the expert committee for each occasion is chosen for that occasion, and the turnover in composition between one meeting and the next in a series may be substantial.

The membership of an expert committee is carefully chosen with an eye to balance by geography, by social system, and by disciplines relevant to its topic. Members of the expert committee on drug dependence must already have been named to one of four WHO expert advisory panels – on drug dependence and alcohol problems, mental health, neurosciences, or drug evaluation – and may not come from 'industrial research units' (for instance in the pharmaceutical industry; WHO 1990b). In addition to the members of the committee, the meetings will include WHO staff and representatives of other intergovernmental organizations and recognized international non-governmental groups.

Normally, expert committees meet from Monday to Friday, and the report of the committee will be put together during the course of the week. It is a hard-and-fast rule that the committee's report must be adopted by its members before the committee disperses. These exigencies mean that there is thus usually much preparatory work for the meeting, in the form of commissioned papers and draft material from WHO staff, on which the committee can liberally draw in assembling its report. The committee is at liberty to ignore this material and start from scratch, but if it does it will have much work to do.

The form of organization of WHO meetings might be described as a guided democracy. Formally, the selection of the meeting's chair and vice-chair and of the rapporteur (or co-rapporteurs) who will be responsible for the report is democratic, but these choices are in fact organized by WHO staff beforehand. On the other hand, the role of WHO staff members in the committee's proceedings is limited; a staff member is named as secretary, but the committee's decisions are supposed to be autonomous and not constrained or guided by WHO staff. In principle, an expert committee's report is published just as the committee adopted it.

Expert committees in the drug dependence series have been meeting since 1949, the year WHO was founded (the first committee was on habit-forming drugs; the name has changed several times over the years). What drives the continuation of the meetings as a series, as noted above, is WHO's treaty obligations under the international drug conventions. The committee's evaluation of a particular drug is carried out under quite elaborate rules that allow for communications from interested parties, including Interpol and the pharmaceutical manufacturers (WHO 1990b).

In the 1950s and 1960s, expert committees on drug dependence had often taken a fairly broad view, concerning themselves, for instance, with matters of definition of addiction, habituation, and dependence. A landmark report was that of the twentieth committee, meeting in 1973, which had taken a broad view of policy and programs, adopting what would now be termed a harm reduction perspective, and had specifically brought alcohol into consideration (WHO 1974).

The expert committees that met between 1977 and 1990 adopted a narrower perspective, focusing mostly on the technical tasks of considering the scheduling of substances and preparations under the international control conventions. This narrower focus might be seen as reflecting the substantial burden of evaluating the many barbiturates, diazepides, and other compounds that the 1971 Convention on Psychotropic Substances potentially brought under international control. Psychopharmacology was the dominant expertise; in fact, an American pharmacologist, Harris, served as rapporteur or co-rapporteur to six of the seven meetings, and a Japanese pharmacologist, Yanagita, was a member of all seven committees and chair of the last three.

The new WHO Programme on Substance Abuse (PSA), separated from the Mental Health Division just before the 1990 expert committee met, had already decided at that time to expand the scope of the committee's work 'from reviewing psychoactive substances for recommendations on scheduling to a broader range of technical issues related to the reduction of demand' (WHO 1991: 1). The 1992 expert committee therefore met with a dual mandate. As with the immediately preceding committees, it had the duty of giving a preliminary consideration ('pre-review') to ten substances that had been put forward for possible scheduling, and deciding whether they should be given a critical review before the next committee made the decision on scheduling. But it was also given a broader charge, to pick up the thread that had been dropped after the 1973 meeting and 'look at the various strategies and approaches for reducing substance use and its harmful consequences in the light of the changes that had occurred since the twentieth meeting' (WHO 1993: 1).

The composition of committee reflected the double task it had been assigned. Yanagita and Schuster (U.S.) were retained from the roster of psychopharmacologists on previous committees. Ghodse (U.K.), an addiction psychiatrist, was the only other member who had previously been on an expert committee in the drug dependence series, although other members had been on other expert committees. Several members of the committee were known particularly for epidemiological or policy-oriented work in alcohol problems – Casswell (New Zealand, Poiko-lainen (Finland), and Room (Canada) – or for work in both alcohol and drugs – Edwards (U.K.) and Medina Mora (Mexico). Two members had strong connections with the United National Drug Control Pro-gramme in Vienna – Emafo (Nigeria) and Samarasinghe (Sri Lanka) – and Ghodse was chair of the International Narcotics Control Board. The French member, Jean-François, could draw on substantial experience in the national treatment system. No one in attendance at the twenty-eighth committee meeting had been at the twentieth meeting (Edwards had been invited to the latter but had been unable to attend).

The Production of the 1992 Expert Committee Report

Advance preparation for the committee's meeting did not turn out to have provided much in the way of raw materials for the report, except for the section on the pre-review of the ten substances, which was well prepared. The PSA staff were distracted with other concerns, and some-what split on what approaches to recommend to the committee in its broader task. Other than the pre-review materials, the main documents pre-circulated to the committee were the report of the 1973 committee (WHO 1974) and four short papers: a nine-page background document on the 'health sector's role in addressing drug- and alcohol-related prob-lems,' an eleven-page document on WHO's demand reduction strate-gies,' a commissioned working paper on 'human rights and licit and illicit drug use,' and a three-page note on dependence terminology.

One approach contemplated by some PSA staff members seemed to be simply to adapt the 1973 committee report. Committee members did not think this appropriate, however, and set out on the task of drafting and adopting the report during the five days of the meeting. The draft-ing had to proceed around the edge of a committee agenda filled from nine to five on each of the first four days with substantive discussions of an agenda prepared in advance by WHO staff.[1]

In the event, the report was finished and adopted within the pre-scribed time, although the committee was down to its minimum quo-rum by the time of the final report's adoption. There was a substantial amount of editing of the report by WHO staff in the weeks after the meeting, a process that introduced subtle changes into the final pub-lished version. As noted below, a further change after publication resulting in a new published version.

Themes in the Committee Meeting and the Report

Harm Reduction Redivivus

The committee was conscious that it was picking up a strand that had been dropped after the twentieth report. This was seen in terms of renewing a particular perspective as well as tackling a broader agenda than the intervening reports. As one influential member put it, 'I see the 20th Report as where we're coming back to after an intervening period of supply reduction. We're being forced back to it by the failure of supply reduction.'

The 1992 committee saw the twentieth committee report as having adopted a harm reduction perspective, although the term had not been used. The adoption of the perspective was explicit in the twenty-eighth committee report: 'The primary goal of national demand reduction programmes should be to minimize the harm associated with the use of alcohol, tobacco and other psychoactive drugs ... The Committee recommended that, for maximum efffectiveness, national policies should be oriented to explicitly defined "harm minimization" goals, with both short-term and long-term objectives' (WHO 1993: 35–6). The committee endeavoured to escape the dichotomy of supply versus harm reduction, and did not accept the proposition that its job and that of the World Health Organization was only to worry about 'demand reduction.'

The committee held relatively strongly to this position, but not without some grumbling. The chair, who had also served as chair of the International Narcotics Control Board, was initially suspicious of the term and its meaning, but the promised debate on adopting the perspective fizzled out when there was no substantial opposition.

Influenced by the alcohol expertise among its members, however, the committee adopted a relatively wide-ranging view of harm reduction, so that, for instance, regulation of the supply was seen as one of a number of potential harm reduction strategies.

The Spectrum of Psychoactive Drugs

The committee was invited to include alcohol in its consideration, and there was no dissent to doing so. Very early in its deliberations, it decided to include tobacco as well. This raised a slight awkwardness from WHO's point of view: the responsibility for tobacco at that point lay elsewhere in the WHO structure (but in 1994, tobacco was transferred to the PSA's responsibility).

The committee raised the issue of including steroids and other performance-enhancing drugs in the terms of reference of future committees,
although these drugs are not psychoactive and they are termed 'non-
dependence producing' in ICD-10 and other nosologies.

'Rational Use' of Drugs

The issue of the underuse of opiates for palliative care in cancer had
been identified by another WHO expert committee (WHO 1990a), and
was brought forward for discussion by staff of the relevant WHO unit.
Discussion of the issue was included in the report without any objection
(WHO 1993: 20–1). The formulation in terms of 'rational use' is curious,
but went largely unchallenged; it is a formulation that essentially
equates rationality with medical auspices. Implicitly, the formulation
includes a critique of overstrenuous drug control – that is, drug control
that impinges on the decision-making of doctors – as 'irrational.' Since
dependence tends to be regarded as something bad and to be avoided,
proponents of 'rational use' tended to want to shift the focus in definitions of dependence away from physical aspects like withdrawal and
towards drug-seeking behaviour; this was an argument put forward by
the representative of the International Federation of Pharmaceutical
Manufacturers Associations in one of her few interventions. A cancer
patient may go through withdrawal but not have drug-seeking behaviour; according to definition in terms of the latter, the patient would not
be dependent.

In connection with the discussion of 'rational use,' WHO staff laid out
to the committee the huge variations that exist between developed
countries in the medical use of opioids. For instance, in terms of defined
daily doses per capita, the use in France is 16 times that in Italy, and the
use in Denmark is 10.5 times that in the Netherlands. Denmark uses 37
times the amount of morphine per capita that Japan uses, although overall the Japanese spend more per capita on pharmaceuticals (over $300
per year) than anyone else. It was noted that the idea of 'rational use'
implies that comparable quantitative indicators of the appropriate level
of therapeutic use in a society can be arrived at, but this may not make
sense in view of the extent of variation in medical practice.

Traditional Use of Indigenous Psychoactive Plant Products

This issue came up in connection with a request from South America for a restudy of the dependence-producing potential of coca leaves, with the hope that a way would be found to remove traditional use from international control. Under the 1961 Single Convention on Narcotic Drugs, coca-leaf chewing was supposed to be abolished by 1989, and it is clear that this has not happened and is not likely to happen. The committee saw no point in recommending a restudy, since coca leaves were undoubtedly a precursor of cocaine, and thus would be covered by the convention whatever the dependence-producing potential of the leaves themselves.

The coca-leaf issue touched off a broader discussion of the wisdom of bringing traditional use of indigenous psychoactive plant products under international control. The social and health problems that had resulted from attempts to ban khat in Africa were described. But the international control machinery does not formally take into account the potential adverse effects of control. The committee, troubled by the possibility that a single complaining country could touch off inclusion of more of these indigenous psychoactive plant products in the international control regime, recommended studies looking towards possible changes in international control provisions concerning these traditional patterns of use (WHO 1993: 19–20). There was considerable correspondence after the meeting about keeping any language in the report that contemplated changes in the drug-control conventions; for some WHO staff, this was seen as an inappropriate recommendation for WHO or one of its expert committees to make.

Human Rights

The committee held a lively but somewhat confused discussion on the issue of human rights in the drug field. Although there were splits in the WHO staff on whether and how the issue should be brought up, a paper had been commissioned and was circulated. But committee members felt that the paper tried to apply analyses derived from the AIDS field too mechanically to the drug field. Given the shortness of time and the splits within the committee on what should be emphasized, the Committee decided to include the text of what is understood to be a WHO document as an annex,[2] and included in the text only a brief recommendation that listed issues that, it was felt, particularly needed to be addressed.[3]

Expert committee reports for the year are considered by the executive board of WHO at its annual meeting. The executive board is an elected executive body responsible to WHO's constituents, national ministries of health. So the twenty-eighth report was considered by the executive board in January 1994, shortly after it had been published. The Canadian and the Japanese representatives raised a question about the inclusion of an annex to the report, entitled 'WHO's contribution on drug use to the report *United Nations Action in the Field of Human Rights.*' As his objection is summarized in the summary record of the meeting, Larivière (Canada) felt that the annex 'was not a technical one, used fuzzy and confusing terms. The report would gain by its omission. In any event, as a WHO contribution to a United Nations report, it would be worded with a view not only to the concerns of the medical profession, but also to those of Member States where illegal drug users often transgressed the criminal code' (WHO 1994: 16). There was quick agreement by WHO staff to drop the annex, on the technical grounds that it had been discovered since the expert committee met that the document from which it quoted had missed a step in the WHO internal approvals process, and thus did not exist as a properly approved WHO document. However, the recommendation on human rights by the committee in the main text was retained. The report was then reprinted for publication without the annex.[4]

Human Rights as a Flashpoint for the Drug-Control System

Human rights is a flashpoint in international drug-policy debates for two reasons. One is that, almost by definition, it involves the clash between individual rights and state rights, and thus it is easily redefined into an argument about national autonomy. These days, with the significant exception of the United States, it is not by and large developed countries but rather the developing world that has the most extreme symbolic legislative punishments of drug trafficking, often including the death penalty, and arguments against a human-rights agenda are often couched in terms of the autonomy of developing societies. There is considerable irony in this, in view of the nature and history of the international drug-control regime and of the energetic intervention by the United States in other countries' legislative and policy decisions on drugs.

Human rights is also a flashpoint because, raised from the vantage of a health organization, it explicitly challenges the tidy separation between the 'soft' approaches of treatment and education and the 'hard' approaches of enforcement. The 'war on drugs' mentality has always been comfortable with the existence of the 'softer' approaches of treatment and education alongside the 'tough' approach of law enforcement, but this mentality insists that those responsible for the softer approaches stick to their knitting and not attempt to interfere in the actions of the tough side. In some definitions, harm reduction also breaks down this barrier between demand and supply approaches, but the meaning of the term has been elastic enough that it has been possible for those committed to the supply-and-demand dichotomy simply to classify harm reduction as a subcategory of demand reduction. The issue of human rights cannot, however, so easily be deflected. Though in part the committee's recommendation in this area was concerned with human rights in the context of the treatment and welfare systems, it does also refer to 'the protection of rights within the penal system.' The annex to the report more directly raised the issue that drug legislation 'may actually sanction the active contravention of human rights.' This turned out to be a challenge to the autonomy of penal approaches that could not be sustained.

The Canadian Role in International Drug Control

Writing in 1978, Lynn Pan and Kettil Bruun (1979), the historians of the international drug-control system, saw signs of change in the system in the nearly five years since their earlier book. In particular, there had been an 'attempt to reorientate the pursuit of goals towards the reduction of drug demand,' and some signs of a greater willingness to discuss alcohol in association with the other drugs. Both of these trends were already presaged in the landmark report of the 20th Expert Committee on Drug Dependence. Unfortunately, these changes in direction of the 1970s were largely swamped by the new wave of drug wars and drug hysteria in the 1980s. Now at last we have started again down the roads laid out in the twentieth report.

Canada played a strong role in the developments of the 1970s. David Archibald, the founding president of the Addiction Research Foundation, was a member of the 1973 expert committee, and both in its inclusion and in its substance the section on alcohol in the commnittee's report bears the hallmarks of the Foundation's approach. Pan and Bruun document that it was the Canadian delegation to the Commission on Narcotic Drugs that in 1975 'introduced a resolution on measures to reduce illicit demand for drugs which proved crucial for the shift of the focus of theoretical discussion in the Commission away from the supply and law enforcement aspects of drug abuse to the question of drug demand and prevention.' Pan and Bruun conclude concerning the 1970s: 'In terms of its contribution to policy-making, Canada has recently been important as an initiator. Because of its own keen espousal of the goal of demand reduction, its principal contribution to policy-making has been the enhanced legitimacy of that goal in the Commission. Canada's influence and membership of the inner circle of powerful countries stems also from the individual inclinations and attributes, including such assets as expert knowledge and negotiating ability, of its delegates. Furthermore, a key position, that of the director of the division [of narcotic drugs], is occupied by a Canadian national' (1979: 151). Unfortunately, the Canadian role in the international drug arena is now much more equivocal. In view of the generally positive role that Canada has played in the effort to get human rights onto the general international agenda, it is curious and extremely disappointing that the Canadian member of the WHO executive board played an instrumental role in securing the removal of the annex on human rights from the twenty-eighth expert-committee report.

NOTES

1 The writer of this paper served as co-rapporteur with primary responsibility for the broader agenda of the committee (other than the pharmacological reviews).
2 The text of the annex follows:

WHO's contribution on drug use to the report *United Nations Action in the Field of Human Rights*

Drug users represent a specific population in which there is a high risk that human rights and fundamental freedoms will not be respected. WHO recognizes that violations of the human rights of drug users may be considered under the following groupings:

Persecution: in some countries, there may be specific legislation that denies drug users their basic rights, and may actually sanction the active contravention of human rights through oppression, mistreatment and harassment;

Discrimination: in many countries, unwritten policies and cultural norms exist which sanction discriminatory practices against drug users; these may take the form of restrictions on freedom of movement (such as obtaining passports and visas), access to employment and access to quality services; and

Consequences of drug use and drug-using environment: the consequences of drug use may have an impact on the human rights of individuals, their families and the local community. Because of their reduced capacity to earn an income and the need to adopt certain lifestyles to support their drug use, drug users may be unable to fulfil both their own and their families' basic needs, and hence risk exploitation through cheap labour, criminal activity and prostitution. Women and youth are at the greatest risk. The promotion of health-damaging products such as alcohol and tobacco, using misleading information and targeted at high-risk populations, is common practice. Certain WHO projects specifically address these issues. These include projects geared to street children; the consequences of cocaine use by pregnant women; and appropriate drug interventions for indigenous populations that have retained their traditional cultures; and country and regional projects designed to develop national demand-reduction strategies, with due regard to human rights issues.

Although a footnote stated that this was 'reproduced from *United Nations action in the field of human rights*. New York, United Nations, 1993,' this publication had in fact been delayed beyond the middle of 1994, and it is reported that the text quoted in the annex was removed from it.

3 9.9.1: 'WHO should review ethical and human rights issues relating to the status of drug users, their families and others who may be affected by drug use, and encourage appropriate action by Member States on such issues. Particular attention should be paid to issues raised by compulsory treatment, the protection of rights within the penal system, data protection, rights of access to treatment and social assistance, child custody, the implications of drug-testing in the workplace, and the protection of research volunteers.'

4 The two English-language versions differ in the following ways: the omission of the annex (replaced by a page advertising Technical Report Series nos 771–89); the omission of Recommendation 9.9.3, which refers to it; the fixing of the sentence on page 18 that had implied that alcohol was covered by the international conventions; and an extra line in the printing record at the bottom of p. ii: '94/9990 – Benteli – 7000.' A replacement copy was mailed to those known to have received the earlier version with a slip page starting: 'For technical reasons, the first printing of this book has had to be withdrawn. The present volume replaces the earlier copy, which should be destroyed.' In the French edition of the report, the 'Annexe' was backed by a page of advertising rather than of text, so the French edition was distributed after the executive board decision (e.g., at the Vienna Narcotics commission meetings in May 1994) with the 'Annexe' page cut out.

REFERENCES

Bruun, Kettil, Lynn Pan, and Ingemar Rexed. 1975. *The Gentlemen's Club: International Control of Drugs and Alcohol.* Chicago and London: University of Chicago Press.

Pan, Lynn, and Kettil Bruun. 1979. 'Recent Developments in International Drug Control.' *British Journal of Addiction* 74: 141–60.

World Health Organization. 1974. *WHO Expert Committee on Drug Dependence: Twentieth Report.* WHO Technical Report Series no. 551. Geneva: WHO.

– 1990a. *Cancer Pain Relief and Palliative Care: Report of a WHO Expert Committee.* WHO Technical Report Series no. 804. Geneva: WHO.

– 1990b. *Revised Guidelines for the WHO Review of Dependence-Producing Psychoactive Substances for International Control.* Document PND/90.1, reprinted from EB85/1990/REC/1, ANNEX 7. Geneva: WHO.

– 1991. *WHO Expert Committee on Drug Dependence: Twenty-Seventh Report.* WHO Technical Report Series no. 808. Geneva: WHO.

– 1993. *WHO Expert Committee on Drug Dependence: Twenty-Eighth Report.* WHO Technical Report Series no. 836. Geneva: WHO. (As discussed in the text, there is a withdrawn version, with the printing mark at the bottom of p. ii '93/9682,' and a replacement version, with the added printing mark '94/9990.')

– 1994. Executive Board, *Provisional Summary Record of the Thirteenth Meeting of the Ninety-Third Session.* Document EB93/SR/13. Geneva: WHO.

8 Harm Reduction, Doping, and the Clashing Values of Athletic Sports

TRUDO LEMMENS

A harm reduction approach to the problems created by drug use should imply more than an assessment of the direct physical and psychological harms and benefits of drug use. This is recognized by a growing attention for human rights in the analysis and critique of current drug policies. Human rights indeed have their place in a harm reduction approach. They are not only a legal expression of values we share, but also shape our human identity. Oppressing human rights harms indi viduals directly in their roots. Nevertheless, human rights only reflect some of the core values of the specific social and cultural structure in which we find ourselves. They often function as a barrier to protect indi viduals against the interference of an always more powerful anonymous state or social surrounding and are a means to empower individuals. But other values also exist that, rather, represent aspects of our being a part of a larger social and cultural structure. In every human action a certain view of our relation to others and to the world is expressed. Such views can be found in, for example, aesthetic perceptions, social conventions, legal systems, and explicit moral rules. They can also be found in activities that at first seem 'neutral' or meaningless, such as sport activities. These values will not always be expressed in a rational or clearly understandable and logical way, but this does not mean that they are not present. Weight should be given to the symbols used to represent such values. As they are a constituent part of who we are, one should at least attempt to understand what those symbols mean to us. A clear awareness of the semantics behind certain social conventions, aesthetic perceptions, legal rules, and sport regulations enables a determination of their importance. It will allow a weighing of the consequences of the allegiance to those rules, in particular when this affects other values, such as the ones expressed by human rights.

Such an investigation of values is proposed in this paper in relation to doping in athletic sport. In order to understand common reactions towards doping, it is important to assess the values that are expressed in sports. Only by digging out these underlying values can we 'understand' the broader context of a prohibition on doping and the societal and cultural interests at stake. Such understanding should be an essential first step in a harm reduction approach. The unravelling of the abstract cultural/societal interests is nevertheless only one part of a harm reduction analysis. It is of course important to see how such values, and in particular the way they are enforced, are reconcilable with other values we share, including the physical well-being of individuals. The paper does not deal extensively with the practical issue of avoiding the physical harms linked with doping. It is an attempt to clarify attitudes and arguments used in the ethical debate on doping. The discussion is limited to so-called simple sports, which focus on speed, distance, or weight records and in which the Olympic ideals of *citius, altius, fortius* (faster, higher, stronger) are most clearly promoted. These sports reflect best the specific values that will be discussed further in this text.

The argument is as follows: (1) A doping prohibition is not an ethical obligation: there is nothing inherently unethical in doping. However, limiting individual freedom in the context of a sports game, by prohibiting doping, is also not problematic from an ethical perspective. A doping prohibition is a mere rule of the game that one accepts by entering into the game. (2) A doping prohibition has a very symbolic meaning. It expresses an idea of bodily purity. The body is perceived as a symbol of nature that we as humans try to control. Doping is a rejected stranger to the body. Controlling the 'pure' body seems to symbolize how humans always attempt to control nature. At the same time, athletic competition contains a symbol of how we are capable of exceeding previous limits, of how we are necessarily progressing by controlling our natural environment. This notion of progress, linked with the nearly unlimited economic interests at stake, pushes athletes to use performance-enhancing substances. (3) The way the enforcement of a doping prohibition is sought creates ethical and legal problems related to privacy, confidentiality, and consent. This forces us to assess whether there is a reasonable justification for the doping prohibition. (4) It seems then that, indeed, an efficient enforcement risks infringing fundamental values of our society without a balanced justification. Athletic competition seems to send out conflicting messages, by promoting an idea of physical 'purity' while pushing at the same time for limitless progress.

(A Ban on) Doping: Ethical or Unethical?

Some have attempted to point out the ethical need to prohibit doping in sports (for an interesting analysis and overview of the ethical debate, see Butcher and Schneider 1993). Others have argued on the contrary that a doping prohibition amounts to unacceptable paternalistic interference with personal autonomy.

1. 'Doping is cheating and creates an unfair advantage'

Two of the common justifications of a doping prohibition are that doping is cheating and that it creates an unfair advantage (see, for example, Coomber 1993). Both arguments have been criticized for the same reasons. Indeed, doping is not prohibited because it is cheating, but it is cheating because it is prohibited. And it is not merely because doping creates an advantage that it is unfair. Both notions of *cheating* and of *unfairness* require logically that there is a pre-existing rule that prohibits doping. They cannot be used to *justify* a ban on doping.

Doping is cheating because there is a rule stating that you cannot take some specific substances. The characterization of certain substances as dope depends solely on the context in which they are used. Certain medications, considered to be dope in the context of sports, are taken frequently by people suffering from the flu, sinusitis, and muscular pain or simply as a part of their daily nutrition. The use of these substances amounts to cheating only in the context of sports because the products are mentioned on the list of prohibited substances. The adoption by the International Olympic Committee (IOC) of doping regulations and the list of prohibited substances linked with it thus determines which actions will be considered as cheating in the context of sports. The status of caffeine, for example, has changed three times under the IOC regulations: for a long time it remained unregulated and thus permitted, subsequently it was classified as a banned substance, while its use is now permitted up to a certain level. Moreover, the threshold limit differs according to different sport organizations (Fuentes et al. 1994).

An interesting point has also been made by some authors who discuss whether some forms of prima facie cheating might not be considered a part of the game (Shapiro 1991; see also Lehman 1988). Some suggest that doping may have become such an intrinsic practice of professional sports that beating the technological means for detecting doping has become an element of winning a game (Fairchild 1989). A national survey for the Canadian Centre for Drug-free Sport also indicated that one of the rationalizations young Canadian adolescents use to justify their steroid use is the argument that doping does not amount to cheating if others are doing the same (Price-Waterhouse 1993).

Another argument that cannot be used to justify the need to ban doping in sports is the notion of unfair advantage. Doping does not per se create an unfair advantage. It only does so because there is a rule that prohibits its use, and because athletes are supposed to respect that rule. Shapiro correctly indicates that '[t]he ideas of equality and fairness in contests thus suggest only that if PE [performance-enhancement mechanisms] is banned, the ban should be enforced. It does not show that PE should be banned in the first place' (Shapiro 1991: 65; see also 63: 'the inequality argument makes some sense when PE ... is forbidden and people cheat'). If doping would be freely available, every athlete would be put on an equal footing and an athlete using forbidden substances would not have the advantage of being able to take a substance to which other obedient colleagues do not have access. As Fost stated: 'Legalizing all drugs, or even distributing them free at the training table or at game time, would moot charges of unfairness. Athletes would be free to eschew such aids, just as they are free to avoid training hard, or risking injury through weight-training. However, they could no longer claim their opponents' advantage was unfair' (1986: 6).

Some might object by saying that, even if doping were allowed, there would still be an unfair advantage, because not every athlete may have equal access to doping. Athletes from industrialized countries would be supported by a sophisticated doping industry, while athletes from the developing world would often be deprived of such ergogenic aids. However, this line of argument is not very solid. If we would follow it, we would have to prohibit all high-tech training facilities and all the medical support to which some athletes of industrialized countries have access. Few people speak about the ethical 'unfairness' of the advantage of having medical support and institutionalized training, let alone that it would not be possible to establish what kind of technological and medical support creates an unfair advantage and what does not. Do sophisticated high-energy meals create an unfair advantage?

A more sophisticated version of this argument is that 'athletes do not have equal access to the proper medical supervision that is necessary when taking these potent prescription drugs' (Fuentes et al. 1994: 225). However, this policy argument has more to do with the presumed harms of doping. It suggests that doping should not be freely available because some people, in particular those who cannot pay for appropriate medical supervision, will be suffering from the potential detrimental effects of doping. In this strain of thought, the unfairness lies in the divergent accessibility of medical supervision, which results in greater harm to some and more benefits to others. However, here again one may object that a difference in the standard of medical care does not only affect athletes who are taking doping but is already a source of inequality in sports. Furthermore, as will be discussed in the following section, the harms of doping are equivocal and cannot be generalized. Doping does not always require medical supervision.

2. 'Doping is harmful'

A more solid argument to defend the necessity of a ban on doping is that doping creates harm, both to the individual user and to the sports community. Allowing doping, it is argued, will stimulate athletes to inflict harm upon themselves. Moreover, because of the coercive power of doping, the whole sports world, and especially young people, is eager to imitate the behaviour of their sport heroes and will be sucked into a spiral of drug use. Two discussions are traditionally distinguished here. The first one has to do with the question whether it is legitimate to restrict the behaviour of individuals in order to protect them against self-harm. The second discussion deals with the extent to which we are or should be allowed to restrict individual freedom for the protection of others.

2.1. The Alleged Harms of Doping
Before entering into the theoretical discussion of the legitimacy of freedom-restricting measures, it is essential to point out what, if any, the potential harms of doping are. Why is it that sport institutions propagate the notion that doping is so dangerous? It seems difficult to talk about the harms of doping in any general way. Indeed, as mentioned earlier, what constitutes doping is determined by prohibitory lists generated by sport organizations. Doping thus includes an assortment of products such as anabolic steroids, beta blockers, erythropoietin and blood doping, amphetamines, growth hormone, and a variety of stimulants, anti-inflammatories, and analgesics (for an interesting overview see Wagner 1991). Using products that are freely available and consumed on a regular basis by the general population may be classified as doping if sport organizations so decide. Often, the consumption of these

products is not health-threatening in any significant way. It is therefore clear that the assumed harms of doping cannot always be invoked to justify a doping ban. However, several prohibited substances do seem potentially detrimental to athletes' health. Today, the debate on the harmfulness of doping is mainly concentrated on these substances, and in particular on anabolic-androgenic steroids, the popularity of which has caused a lot of concern in the last decades.

While an in-depth discussion of the harms of different products is outside the scope of this essay, the example of anabolic steroids tells us something about the enigmas of the harms debate. Several studies indicate that anabolic steroids have gained an immense popularity, not only among professional and semi-professional athletes, but also among non-competitive recreational athletes (see Perry et al. 1992). Their consumption among youth has reached unanticipated heights. A Canadian study indicates that 83,000 Canadian youths between eleven and eighteen had used anabolic steroids in the past year (Price-Waterhouse 1993). Surveys of college students and adolescents in Scotland and in the United States lead to the conclusion that from 5 to 11 per cent of males were using or had used anabolic steroids (Fuentes et al. 1994). They do so in order to improve athletic performance or their physical appearance. Sport officials, health authorities, and medical experts have sounded the alarm in light of this problematic popularity of anabolic steroids. However, the effect of anabolic-steroid consumption outside a controlled medical context is unclear. Medical use of anabolic steroids has been the subject of clinical trials, which led to their approval as effective drugs for medical purposes. The effect of their use in the sports and 'beauty' business is more difficult to assess. Nevertheless, case reports and studies indicate that the harms associated with anabolic-androgenic steroid use may be serious. Anabolic steroids may be the cause of several reported cases of myocardial infarction among athletes (Kennedy 1993; Welder and Melchert 1993; Ferenchick and Adelman 1992; Ferenchick 1991). Major mood disturbances, including severe depression, mania, and aggressive behaviour, have also been associated with steroid use (Pope and Katz 1994; Fuentes et al. 1994; Smith and Perry 1992; Pope and Katz 1990). Anabolic steroids may also have an effect on the reproductive system. Testicular atrophy and gynaecomastia (enlargement of male breast tissue) among men have been attributed to anabolic steroids (Pope and Katz 1994; Fuentes et al. 1994). In women, steroid use can have an effect on body and facial hair growth and can result in a lowering of the voice. The normal growth of adolescents may be affected seriously by steroids

(Fuentes et al. 1994; Plowright 1993). Changes in liver functioning, liver failure, and even liver tumours are associated with long-term steroid consumption (Fuentes, et al. 1994; Cabasso 1994; see, however, Coomber 1993a,b and Plowright 1993). Finally, medical experts warn that anabolic steroids may have a destructive effect on muscle strength and may lead to tissue disruption (Laseter and Russell 1991).

From a harm reduction perspective, it is worth mentioning that scientists also affirm that further research has to be undertaken on the health risks of doping and, in particular, of anabolic steroids (Lucas 1993; Plowright 1933; Wagner 1991; Laseter and Russell 1991). There are often contradictory reports. For example, contrary to the studies mentioned above, a study on the psychological consequences of anabolic steroids did not find any significant difference between users and non-users according to existing scientific scales, while the users reported, among other effects, increases in enthusiasm, aggression, and irritability. The authors concluded that perceived or actual psychological changes may occur, but that the effects are too subtle, or the inventories used insensitive, to detect the changes (Bahrke et al. 1992). Smith and Perry indicate that studies on the effects of anabolic steroids in sports were often poorly designed and that reference is generally made to anecdotal reports (1992). Coomber therefore argues that clinical studies do not offer clear proof that doping is much more harmful than other accepted practices of competition sports (1993). It has been questioned whether the current attitude towards doping contributes to the development of sound scientific research in this field. Legal prohibitions reduce the willingness of users to be identified and to participate in research (Plowright 1993). Moreover, certain harms associated with anabolic steroids are the result of covert consumption. The risk of HIV infection has been associated with anabolic-steroid injection (Scott 1989; Nemechek 1991). HIV transmission through needle sharing is more likely to occur when steroid consumers are driven underground. Reports indicate that anabolic-steroid users are frequent clients of needle-exchange programs and that needle sharing among steroid users occurs (Coomber 1993b; Fuentes et al. 1994), be it sometimes on a very low scale compared with some other drug-injecting groups (Plowright 1993). Illegal production and sale of steroids has increased. The risks associated with using counterfeit or non-steroid products are clear. They result from a lack of quality control and difficulty in controlling the dosage.

Interestingly, some authors suggest that evidence of the positive properties of anabolic steroids for athletic performance are equivocal

(Plowright 1993; Van Helder et al. 1991), or even that steroids have a negative impact on performance (Welder and Melchert 1993). Should further research confirm these possibilities, steroid users may more easily be convinced to alter their behaviour. In contrast, the often-exaggerated warnings about the detrimental effects of steroids do not have such an effect. Steroid users are mostly aware of the potentially detrimental health consequences but do not change their behaviour (Plowright 1993). In fact, the large sums spend on detecting anabolic-steroid use in sports increase, according to some, the credibility of anabolic steroids as efficient ergogenic aids (Coomber 1993).

Some medical experts further point out that doping may sometimes remedy the physical damage resulting from the excesses of competition sports. Noret (1985), for example, indicates that professional athletes very often do not allow their bodies to recuperate after prolonged physical efforts, as a result of which their level of testosterone decreases considerably. The administration of some milligrams of testosterone per day could re-establish a normal, more healthy level.

2.2. A Doping Ban to Protect against Harm

For the sake of argument, one may accept the idea that doping is harmful. It is then often argued that athletes should be prohibited from inflicting harm on themselves. This argument sees in the doping prohibition a protective measure comparable with, for example, anti-smoking legislation, regulations obliging motorcyclists to wear helmets, and the like. Some libertarians will in principle reject legislation that is aimed at interfering with what they would call 'purely self-regarding behaviour.' They will argue on the basis of autonomy that nobody should intervene if people act in a way that is harmful only to themselves. However, this liberal view does not provide us with a lot of answers. Indeed, what constitutes self-regarding behaviour? As Weinreb indicates, conventional understandings determine whether behaviour is self-regarding or other-regarding (1987: 135–48). Conventional understanding can change over time. Conduct that was originally considered as harming only the individual actor can later be assessed as being harmful to others. Weinreb gives as an example the shift in our societal attitude towards smoking, which only in part may be explained by our increased scientific awareness of its harmfulness. In a majority of cases, one could argue that individuals have an obligation towards the public health system, which is funded by the community of taxpayers, not to put their health at unnecessary risks. Harming oneself can thus easily be reframed by society such that society has an interest in prohibiting or regulating this behaviour. The freedom to engage in an activity is normally not dependent on the 'neutral,' 'objective nature' of that particular activity. Whether one is free to engage in an activity reveals whether society considers that certain values are threatened by it or not. The argument of libertarians that we should not prohibit doping because it harms only the individual user does not add anything to the debate. It tells us more about how libertarians perceive the use of doping as a trivial issue than it clarifies the societal rationale behind a doping prohibition. It is therefore legitimate to argue that individual doping consumption affects others. The question remains whether it affects in such ways that something should be done about it. And if something has to be done, what is the most appropriate way to go about it?

How others are affected by doping, or what kind of symbolic order is protected by a doping prohibition, should be specified. Indeed, traditional arguments to defend such prohibition are often flawed. For example, reference is frequently made to the notion of coercion. If we allow athletes to use doping, it is argued, others will be forced to do the same in order to be capable of competing with their doped colleagues (on the notion of coercion, see Murray 1983 and the correct critique of Butcher and Schneider 1993). Not intervening amounts therefore to taking away the liberty of athletes not to engage in a harmful activity. However, the use of the notion of coercion in this context is rather far-fetched. The idea of coercion could then also be invoked against intensive training programs. Allowing athletes to train seven days a week forces competing athletes to do the same. It could thus be argued that, as intensive quasi-professional training is harmful to an athlete's body, such training should be prohibited. Yet, it is generally accepted that athletes are free to invest as much energy in their training as they want. They are free to harm themselves by such actions and others are free to do the same.

Libertarians will also point out that the notion of harm does not justify in itself the attitude towards doping in sport as there are so many other aspects of sports that endanger the physical well-being of athletes. Indeed, it can be questioned whether some forms of high competition sports are not per se harmful because they demand too much from an athlete's body (Noret 1985). Certain sport disciplines, such as boxing, skiing, and mountain climbing, are moreover characterized by the existence of the danger of physical harm (see Fost 1986, who cites studies on the harmfulness of professional football, and statistics on deaths from boxing, football and auto racing). Libertarians will require at least some serious justification of the argument that allowing doping will cause significantly more harm to athletes or to others. If the harmfulness of doping is the reason to prohibit it, they will argue, one might as well prohibit many other harmful sport activities.

2.3. Prohibiting Doping Thus Unjustified?
This does not mean that prohibiting doping amounts to unjustifiable paternalism and constitutes a denial of personal autonomy. The debate on the ethics of doping essentially misses the point. Prohibiting doping in sport is perfectly justifiable without reference to an ethical principle. A prohibition on doping in sports is essentially a rule of the game and could be compared with those rules that set out the context of the game, the conditions for participation, and the technical instruments that can be used. Arguing that prohibiting doping in sports denies the autonomy of athletes therefore does not make sense. Playing a game always implies limiting one's own behaviour to the rules of the game. The latter are enforced by a system of sanctions that players implicitly accept by participation in the game. However, this does not imply that there are no limits as to what persons who participate in such games can be submitted to. There are limits to our possibility to give away our freedom. These limits often have to do with what it means to be a human being. For example, we do not accept that people submit themselves to slavery. We also require a certain reasonableness in the way the rules of a game are enforced. We would not find it acceptable that an athlete who violated a rule of a game would be asked to fast for a month in order to be allowed to participate again. We request a certain relation between the violation of a rule and the 'punishment,' even in the context of a game that we freely engaged in. This rationality requirement is reflected in the way courts are more and more allowed to intervene when private bodies, such as professional bodies, disciplinary committees, but also golf clubs and athletes' organizations, make decisions that affect individual members.

In light of the difficulties in finding a 'rational need' to prohibit doping, it is important to understand why doping is so strongly opposed in sports. Why are athletes so severely punished when they are caught after having doped themselves, more severely than when they trip up an opponent or hit her/him deliberately in the ribs? The seriousness of the sanction tells us something about the importance that is attributed to the value behind drug-free sports. In order to measure the reasonableness of the sanctions it is therefore essential to unravel what kind of values are promoted by sports. A harm reduction approach implies a balancing of 'interests,' 'benefits,' and 'harms' in order to find an appropriate solution. This solution should not only be the least 'physically' harmful, but also be the least intrusive on fundamental rights and have the least effect on certain core values in our society. In the context of doping, it is therefore essential to understand why it is prohibited, what the consequences of the prohibition are, and how one can balance the negative consequences of a prohibition against the importance of the reasons behind it.

The Values of Athletic Sports

Two values seem to be preponderant in athletic sports. First, athletic sports seem to be a symbol of how we as humans are capable of control over our own bodies, our own resemblance with nature, through the exercise of will and personal endurance. The body we have to control in athletic sports seems to be linked to a state of purity, a purity that refers to our existence through nature. There is an idea of bodily purity in athletic sports, and a notion that athletes, while resembling the rest of us, are capable of a superior control over their bodies. At the same time, this resemblance and superiority make athletic sports a valuable mirror, one that is supposed to show us our potential for human excellence. In order for there to be a certain resemblance between athletes and 'ordinary people,' athletes need to be seen as being 'fully human.' In this context, it has been argued that 'we wish to view the athletes as the counterparts not of gods but of demigods ... Elite athletes exceed what average human beings are capable of achieving, but they do not break the rules of humanness. Athletes do what normal human beings do but their performances are faster, higher, farther and stronger. Such performances are considered exemplary because they are viewed as demonstrations of the ultimate capabilities that are accessible to human beings, as such' (Gardner, cited in Butcher and Schneider 1993: 75).

This of course raises questions such as, What is so *unnatural* about doping, and what then are *human* limits? Why doping would lead us beyond the limits of humanness is indeed not so clear. The distinction between what remains within human boundaries and what not may be arbitrary and not rationally founded. It could be argued that, among other things, the attitude towards doping in sport not only reflects but to a certain extent also creates the limits between 'natural' and 'unnatural' and defines what is considered to be human. It does so by reference to how 'ordinary' human beings are supposed to behave in their everyday life, and by adding a requirement of absolute bodily purity, as being that which gives athletes their exemplary status. At the same time, this attitude may be influenced by the general disapproval of drug use in society and the images linked with drugs. Indeed, one can easily identify a growing discomfort towards all forms of drugs in our society, including more 'institutionalized' drugs such as alcohol and tobacco. This societal disapproval of drug use may, apart from being based on health concerns, in its turn be linked with the obligation to control oneself physically and psychologically. This pressure to control oneself both physically and psychologically, without 'external' aids, is put to an extreme test in the context of sports.

In the second place, this control over our 'pure nature' allows us to overcome limits, to progress in an untrammelled way. This is reflected in the value attributed to record breaking. As Ortega y Gasset stated: 'It is a constant and well-known fact that in physical effort connected with sport, performances are "put up" to-day which excel to an extraordinary degree those known in the past. It is not enough to wonder at each one in particular and to note that it beats the record, we must note the impression that their frequency leaves on the mind, convincing us that the human organism possesses in our days capacities superior to any it has previously had' (as cited in Hoberman 1984: 8). Sport as an activity of human beings, controlling their own nature, may in that sense be the counterpart of our technological control over nature. Both reflect the idea that humans, through rational control, continuously exceed the limits placed on them by nature.

There are ample examples in the history of the Olympic Games of how the performance of athletes has been used and abused as a symbol of progress made in the culture to which they belonged. Berry, then professor at Harvard University, wrote in 1927 that athletics and team games are a substitute for war and labour, since 'they combine both these essential qualities and also have for their ethical basis the survival and supremacy of the race' (1927: 38). The comparison with the use of the Berlin Olympic Games by Nazi Germany is easily made. In the more recent past, we can see how Olympic Games have been dominated by a competition between two ideologies, represented by the USSR and the United States. It seems as if the achievements in the Olympic stadium are used as a reflection of the development of a given society, a sign of the progress and advantage of the particular culture to which the winning athlete belongs. Sport as a symbol of control of the individual athlete over his own pure body is used in the same way as technological progress: as a means to indicate the greatness of the nation, the way in which a particular society is progressing in its control over nature. Bob Beamon's fabulous leap of 29'2½" in 1968 had the same significance as Neil Armstrong's first hesitating step on the moon in 1969: it was perceived as a symbol of American superiority and used as a sign of the development of American society.

The importance attributed to sport as a symbol of human striving for progress, enabled by control over our own pure, 'natural' body by the exercise of will, explains why the description of Canadian sprinter Ben Johnson in the popular press changed so fundamentally. From being a symbol of human possibilities, he was made into a beast, a racehorse, after the discovery of his use of doping. Johnson was not only morally condemned for his cheating (contra Butcher and Schneider 1993). The public reaction went further. It was suddenly pointed out how ugly his pumped-up musculature was, that he was rather unintelligent, in short, that he resembled a beast. It shows us how the attitude towards doping reinforces in a strange way our view of being human. Ben Johnson's 'body beautiful' before the doping detection did not differ from that after the detection, but the public perception of his body changed. He was not any longer a powerful, admirably muscled athlete, but was described as an ugly, unnaturally blown-up cheater. Pictures were suddenly appearing that compared how he 'normally' was to how he looked now, as if one was talking about another being. Ben Johnson was suddenly dehumanized (see also Fairchild 1989 and a critique by Butcher and Schneider 1993: 69–74).

Ethical Issues of the Enforcement of the Ban

So far, it has been argued that prohibiting doping is neither ethical nor unethical, but that a doping prohibition tells us something about the values promoted by athletic sports. However, the way those values are promoted, and in particular the way the doping prohibition is *enforced*, along with the outcomes, raises ethical and legal problems. These problems can be linked with, among other issues, the inviolability of the human body, the respect for a person's privacy, consent, and the confidentiality of personal medical information.

1. Problems Related to Adequate Control

In the context of the anti-doping campaign, more and more sophisticated means of doping have been developed, enabling athletes to escape mechanisms of control. This has led to the development of new techniques of detection, the scientific reliability of which has sometimes been put into question. In order to curb the problem of avoidance of tests, a system of random out-of-competition testing and blood testing has been proposed and implemented. This move extends the power of sport authorities from the sport arena into the private life of athletes. It can be questioned whether such an intrusion into private life would survive legal scrutiny. Submitting employees to drug tests that reveal information on private behaviour outside any work context, and that do not always have a rational relation to an individual's performance at work, has been criticized as unwarranted interference with the private lives of individuals. The Privacy Commissioner of Canada argued that there is no reason to treat athletes differently from other employees with respect to their privacy. In his report *Drug Testing and Privacy* he stated that 'athletes should not be forced to abandon their *Charter* rights at the locker room' (1990: 43). He therefore strongly opposed proposals of Sport Canada to introduce random, mandatory, and unannounced urine analysis, which in his view 'trample[s] upon the basic right to a reasonable expectation of privacy which athletes share with other Canadians' (ibid.).

The Canadian Human Rights Tribunal, while rejecting the view that a mandatory urinalysis program to detect drug use by employees constituted a discriminatory action on the basis of disability, denounced such a program as intrusive: 'As a blanket policy, it does represent a major step in the invasion of privacy of many individuals in the employment field. This method could only be seen as reasonable in the face of substantial evidence of a serious threat to the Bank's other employees and the public, its customers' (*Canadian Civil Liberties Association v. Toronto Dominion Bank*, 16 August 1994, no. T.D. 12/94: 35). For the Ontario Law Reform Commission, mandatory drug and alcohol testing in the workplace could constitute a violation of a person's reasonable expectation of privacy and even be 'a serious affront to human dignity' (Ontario Law Reform Commission 1992: 70).

The introduction of blood testing has been criticized even more severely. It has been argued that such testing is certainly to be avoided as it would per se infringe more upon the privacy of persons than urinalysis. As the Privacy Commissioner argued, '[u]rinalysis is intrusive, but at least it does not involve entering a person's body to remove body fluids, as blood testing would' (1993: 53). He considered it 'frightening to think that some people will contemplate violating the very physical integrity of human beings, an integrity protected for centuries by law, in the name of men and women playing games' (ibid.). In the course of blood testing and also urinalysis, information is gathered on a person's health and private life. This information has sometimes no relation to doping use. Should sporting institutions, or even sport doctors, be allowed to have access to such information? It might be argued that obligatory testing of athletes undermines their right of confidentiality of medical information. Examples in the past have also proved how difficult it is to keep test results secret. It is to be feared that even medical information obtained through doping tests that is unrelated to doping will not always be kept secret. In the future, we can also imagine an escalation of genetic testing to ensure that athletes have not been 'genetically enhanced.' Genetic tests performed to determine the sex of athletes are a very clear onset to such practices. Indeed, such tests, the first genetic tests for non-medical purposes, have already taken place in the context of sports. Can we accept the idea that sporting institutions have access to such intimate information, which may affect not only the 'consenting' athlete but also his or her family?

Some will immediately object and argue that athletes are free to participate in sporting competition and thus free to consent to being tested. However, the validity of this argument can be questioned if we consider the growing economic importance of sports for individuals and their families who already build their lives around the activity of sports. It is more and more accepted that individuals in 'weak positions' cannot be required to consent to measures that intrude too much on their privacy.

In this context, reference can again be made to the necessary limitation of the power of employers. Their demands for consent have to bear some rational relation to the obligations of the employee. In relations of power, the possibility of demanding consent is often limited in order to protect the weaker party from being forced to consent to procedures that intrude in an unreasonable way upon privacy. As the Ontario Law Reform Commission argues in its *Report on Drug and Alcohol Testing in the Workplace*: '[A] convincing argument can be made that an employee who submits to a urine, breath, blood, hair or other test involving the extraction of a bodily sample for the reason that a refusal to comply will result in loss of employment, demotion or the imposition of other disciplinary measures, cannot be considered to have waived his s.8 constitutional rights' (1992: 79).

2. The Severity of the Sanctions

Sanctions of a violation of an ordinary sports rule are normally limited to the context of the game in question. In some cases, athletes are deprived of their victory or are excluded from the playground, but they are generally not prohibited from participating in later sport events. The sanction on doping use, however, clearly exceeds the boundaries of a particular game, as it can result in an all-encompassing prohibition from participating in further competition. To the extent that sport has become the primary activity of the athlete, such an exclusion is comparable to prohibiting a physician or a lawyer from exercising his or her profession. These prohibitions are normally linked with actions that fundamentally violate the purpose, dignity, or essence of the profession. Because of the seriousness of such sanctions, decisions on their implementation are not taken lightly but will be subjected to severe legal scrutiny. The argument that a lawyer or a physician agreed to a rule by entering into the profession will not constitute a sufficient justification for such sanctions. The sanctions have to be in proportion to the importance of the rule. People cannot be pushed to consent to unreasonableness when other important values are at stake.

Inherent Contradictions as a Problem for Justifying Harsh Consequences of Doping Control

The consequences of the doping regulations clearly exceed the strict limits of a given game. They affect individual athletes in their physical integrity, their privacy, and their capacity to retain control over an important part of their life. In this way, other values of our society enter into the game. These values are protected by social institutions such as the legal system. It seems, therefore, that the harsh consequences of enforcing the ban on doping will be subjected to a rule of reasonableness.

In that respect, there might be some difficulties because of the inherent contradictions in the values that athletic sports try to promote. On the one hand, there is the idea of control over a pure, physical body. On the other hand, we value the idea of untrammelled progress as reflected in the importance of records. The second value, linked with the economic interests at stake, pushes athletes to take performance-enhancing substances, while the first requires complete abstinence. It seems that the values of control over a 'pure' body and of unlimited progress are to a large extent irreconcilable. Endless progress seems to be impossible without technological means, certainly if there is such pressure to obtain record-breaking performances. As Shapiro states, 'If a sport entails not just competition against current opponents but the possibility and desirability of record-setting, it is not obvious why PE (Performance Enhancement) ... is always conceptually excluded' (1991: 62).

Conclusion

It may be unreasonable to violate basic values of our society, as reflected in human-rights codes, by subjecting athletes to intrusive tests or punishing them in an extreme way, if the sole basis of the intervention is to protect inherent values of sport that, on the other hand, partly promote rule-breaking behaviour. Sport institutions push for limitless progress of athletes' performances while they introduce intrusive doping control measures and sanctions. No boundaries for human performance are accepted, yet being human is defined in a way that could imply the existence of boundaries. According to the Olympic Ideal, athletes have to go faster and higher and become stronger, but one of the ways to overcome physical limits, namely doping, is considered to render athletes inhuman.

It might be interesting to refer here to a new tendency in economics and environmental policy, which tries to correct the criticized concept of endless growth and introduces the notion of 'sustainable development.' This notion implies an acceptance of the limits of our natural resources. It might be necessary to apply the same kind of reasoning to sports if we reasonably want to avoid doping. Sport institutions can play a major role in this regard by stressing the value of control over the 'pure' body instead of stimulating an untrammelled breaking of limits. (For an attempt to develop a new approach, stimulating drug-free sports, see Butcher and Schneider 1993: 99–155.) They may also try to take away some of the economic incentives for rule-breaking behaviour. If they do not, they may face difficulties in defending the harsh consequences of the control of doping use. Moreover, a more coherent approach towards doping may include the promotion of sound medical research on the negative *and* positive effects of doping. This research may, for example, convincingly demonstrate that anabolic steroids are not effective as ergogenic aids. As an argument against doping, such a conclusion is likely to be more convincing than intrusive doping tests. Moreover, an exclusively prohibitory approach may well result in other serious harms associated with concealed doping consumption.

NOTES

Research for this paper was funded by Social Sciences and Humanities Research Council Canada (SSHRCC) grant 21936. An earlier version was presented at the 2nd International Congress on Sports Law in Olympia (Greece) on 30 October 1993. The Canadian Centre for Drug-free Sport generously provided funding for this presentation. I am particularly indebted to C. Elliott, R. Jürgens, D. Riley, and C. Weijer for their insightful comments on the final version of this text. Thanks also to R. Butcher, A. Schneider, and M.A. Somerville for their helpful comments on an earlier version and to N. Gilmore for allowing me to devote a portion of my research time to this subject. I retain full responsibility for any errors.

REFERENCES

Bahrke, M.S., J.E. Wright, R.H. Strauss, and D.H. Catlin. 1992. 'Psychological Moods and Subjectively Perceived Behavioral and Somatic Changes Accompanying Anabolic-Androgenic Steroid Use.' *American Journal of Sports Medicine* 20(6): 717–24.
Berry, E. 1927. *The Philosophy of Athletics, Coaching and Character*. New York: A.S. Barnes.
Butcher, R., and A. Schneider. 1993. *Doping in Sports: An Analysis of the Justification for Bans and the Ethical Rationale for Drug-Free Sport*. Ottawa: Canadian Centre for Drug-free Sport.
Cabasso, A. 1994. 'Peliosis Hepatitis in a Young Adult Bodybuilder.' *Medicine and Science in Sports and Exercise* 26(1): 2–4.
Coomber, R. 1993a. 'Drugs in Sport: Rhetoric or Pragmatism.' *International Journal of Drug Policy* 4(4): 169–78.
– 1993b. 'Drug Use in Sports as a Health Problem.' *Bulletin of Medical Ethics* 87 (April): 5–6.
Fairchild, D. 1989. 'Sport Abjection: Steroids and the Uglification of the Athlete.' *Journal of the Philosophy of Sport* 16: 74–88.
Ferenchick, G.S. 1991. 'Anabolic/Androgenic Steroid Abuse and Thrombosis: Is There a Connection?' *Medical Hypotheses* 35(1): 27–31.
Ferenchick, G.S., and S. Adelman. 1992. Myocardial Infarction Associated with Anabolic Steroid Use in a Previously Healthy 37-Year-Old Weight Lifter.' *American Heart Journal* 124(2): 507–8.

Fost, N. 1986. 'Banning Drugs in Sports: A Skeptical View.' *Hastings Center Report* 16(4): 5–10.

Fuentes, R.J., A. Davis, B. Sample, and K. Jasper. 1994. 'Sentinel Effect of Drug Testing for Anabolic Steroid Abuse.' *Journal of Law, Medicine and Ethics* 22(3): 224–30.

Hoberman, J.M. 1984. *Sport and Political Ideology.* Austin: University of Texas.

Kennedy, C. 1993. 'Myocardial Infarction in Association with Misuse of Anabolic Steroids.' *Ulster Medical Journal* 62(2): 174–6.

Laseter, J.T., and J.A. Russell. 1991. 'Anabolic Steroid-Induced Tendon Pathology: A Review of the Literature.' *Medicine and Science in Sports and Exercise* 23(1): 1–3.

Lehman, C. 1988. 'Can Cheaters Play the Game?' In W. Morgan and K. Meier, eds, *Philosophic Inquiry in Sport*, 283–8. Champaign, IL: Human Kinetics Publishers.

Lucas, S.E. 1993. 'Current Perspectives on Anabolic-Androgenic Steroid Abuse.' *Trends in Pharmacological Sciences* 14(2): 61–8.

Melchert, R.B., T.J. Herron, and A.A. Welder. 1992. 'The Effect of Anabolic-Androgenic Steroids on Primary Myocardial Cell Cultures.' *Medicine and Science in Sports and Exercise* 24(2): 206–12.

Murray, T.H. 1983. 'The Coercive Power of Drugs in Sports.' *Hastings Center Report* 13(4): 24–30.

Nemechek, P.M. 1991. 'Anabolic Steroid Users: Another Potential Risk Group for HIV Infection.' *New England Journal of Medicine* 325(5): 357.

Noret, A. 1985. 'Le dopage des sportifs.' *Psychotropes* 2(2): 43–58.

Ontario Law Reform Commission. 1992. *Report on Drug and Alcohol Testing in the Workplace.* Toronto: Ontario Government Publications Services.

Perry, H.M., D. Wright, and B.N. Litlepage. 1992. 'Dying to Be Big: A Review of Anabolic Steroid Use.' *British Journal of Sports Medicine* 26(4): 259–61.

Plowright, S. 1993. *Harm Minimisation and Anabolic Steroids.* Australian Capital Territory: Assisting Drug Dependants Inc.

Pope, H.G., and D.L. Katz. 1990. 'Homicide and Near-Homicide by Anabolic Steroid Users.' *Journal of Clinical Psychiatry* 51(1): 28–31.

– 1994. 'Psychiatric and Medical Effects of Anabolic-Androgenic Steroid Use. A Controlled Study of 160 Athletes.' *Archives of General Psychiatry* 51(5): 375–82.

Price-Waterhouse. 1993. *National School Survey on Drugs and Sport: Final Report.* Ottawa: Canadian Centre for Drug-free Sport.

Privacy Commissioner of Canada. 1990. *Drug Testing and Privacy.* Ottawa: Minister of Supply and Services.

– 1993. *Annual Report 1992–1993.* Ottawa: Canada Communication Group.

Scott, M.J. 1989. 'HIV Infection Associated with Injections of Anabolic Steroids.' *Journal of the American Medical Association* 262: 207–8.

Shapiro, M.H. 1991. 'The Technology of Perfection: Performance Enhancement and the Control of Attributes.' *Southern California Law Review* 65(1): 11–114.

Smith, D.A., and P.J. Perry. 1992. 'The Efficacy of Ergogenic Agents in Athletic Competition. Part I: Androgenic-Anabolic Steroids.' *Annals of Pharmacotherapy* 26(4): 520–8.

Van Helder, W.P., E. Kofman, and M.S. Tremblay. 1991. 'Anabolic Steroids in Sports.' *Canadian Journal of Sport Sciences* 16(4): 248–57.

Wagner, J.C. 1991. 'Enhancement of Athletic Performance with Drugs.' *Sports Medicine* 12(4): 250–65.

Weinreb, L.L. 1987. *Natural Law and Justice*. Cambridge: Harvard University Press.

Welder, A.A., and R.B. Melchert. 1993. 'Cardiotoxic Effects of Cocaine and Anabolic-Androgenic Steroids in the Athlete.' *Journal of Pharmacological and Toxicological Methods* 29(2): 61–8.

9 Will Prisons Fail the AIDS Test?

RALF JÜRGENS

What has gone wrong with HIV/AIDS policies in prisons? As stated by Harding and Schaller (1992a: 761–2), 'despite clear recommendations made by international bodies in 1987/88 ... and the substantive policy change in some countries, the overall picture is bleak. Discrimination, breaches of medical confidentiality, and segregation remain widespread. Treatment programs for HIV-infected prisoners are inadequate. Tuberculosis is increasing in prison populations ... No effective measures for preventing HIV transmission through injection drug use are applied in most countries.'

This situation persists although international and national recommendations on HIV/AIDS and drug use in prisons are all consistent in favouring 'equivalence of treatment of prisoners,' meaning that the same standards of health care and protection that apply outside prisons should also apply to prisoners. These recommendations stress the importance of prevention of transmission of HIV in prisons, and suggest that condoms and clean needles or bleach should be available to prisoners (see, for example, WHO 1987, 1993; Council of Europe 1988, paras. 14A(i)–14A(viii); United Nations 1990a: 167).

In Canada, the National Advisory Committee on AIDS (1987, 1989), the Royal Society (1988), the Parliamentary Ad Hoc Committee on AIDS (1990), the Federal/Provincial/Territorial Advisory Committee on AIDS (1991), and the Prisoners with AIDS/HIV Support Action Network (PASAN) (1992) have all issued recommendations aimed at reducing the spread of HIV infection and the harms from drug use in prisons. As early as 1988, making condoms and bleach available to inmates was recommended.

In March 1994, the (Canadian) Expert Committee on AIDS and Prisons (ECAP) released its final report (Correctional Service Canada 1994a,b,c). ECAP's mandate was to assist the Canadian government to promote and protect the health of prisoners and staff, and to reduce the harms from HIV/AIDS and drug use in federal penitentiaries. The committee found that what needed to be done to resolve the problems raised by HIV/AIDS and by drug use in prisons was obvious and had in many cases already been articulated by others. As a result, it focused on strategies for making necessary changes possible. In its final report, the committee expressed its hope that the Correctional Service of Canada (CSC) would act quickly upon its recommendations, pointing out that 'steps have to be taken immediately in order to avoid rates of infection reaching the high levels observed in some other prison systems' (CSC 1994a: 121).

However, the implementation of ECAP's recommendations has proved to be disappointingly slow. As a result, individuals and organizations consulted during phase 1 of a Project on Legal and Ethical Issues Raised by HIV/AIDS, undertaken jointly by the Canadian HIV/AIDS Legal Network (Network) and the Canadian AIDS Society (CAS), indicated that issues raised by HIV/AIDS in prisons remain a priority in Canada. In particular, they expressed concern about CSC's reluctance to implement some of ECAP's major recommendations, such as the recommendation to undertake a pilot study of needle distribution in at least one prison. They suggested that the joint Network/CAS Project examine whether governments and the prison systems have a legal obligation to provide prisoners with the means that would allow them to protect themselves against contracting HIV, and address the issue of the potential liability for not providing condoms, bleach, and sterile needles and for the resulting transmission of HIV in prisons.

In July 1996, after extensive consultations, the Project released a report (Jürgens 1996), concluding that

[c]learly prison systems have a moral, but also a legal, responsibility to act without further delay to prevent the spread of infectious diseases among inmates and to staff and the public, and to care for inmates living with HIV and other infections. Canadian prison systems are failing to meet this responsibility, because they are clearly not doing all they could: measures that have been successfully undertaken outside prison with government funding and support, such as making sterile injection equipment and methadone maintenance available to injection drug users, are not being undertaken in Canadian prisons, although other prison systems have shown that they can be introduced success-

fully, and receive support from prisoners, staff, prison administrations, politicians, and the public. (Jürgens 1996)

This article will briefly review what is known about HIV/AIDS, tuberculosis, and drug use in prisons. It will then discuss what is being done to prevent HIV infection and to reduce the harms from drug use in prisons and, importantly, what is not being done. Some of the reasons why responding to HIV/AIDS in prisons has been slow will be identified and ways to overcome barriers to implementation of harm reduction measures will be suggested.

The Extent of the Problem

1. HIV/AIDS

Worldwide, rates of HIV infection in inmate populations are much higher than in the general population (Harding and Schaller 1992a: 762; Heilpern and Egger 1989: 21). They are, in general, closely related to two factors: (1) the proportion of prisoners who injected drugs before imprisonment and (2) the rate of HIV infection among injection drug users in the community. The jurisdictions with the highest HIV prevalence in prisons are areas where HIV infection in the general community is 'pervasive among IV drug users, who are dramatically overrepresented in correctional institutions' (Hammett 1988: 26). Commenting on the situation in the United States, the U.S. National Commission on AIDS (1991: 10) stated that 'by choosing mass imprisonment as the federal and state governments' response to the use of drugs, we have created a de facto policy of incarcerating more and more individuals with HIV infection.'

Particularly high rates of prisoner HIV infection have been reported from countries in southern Europe; for example, 26 per cent in Spain and 17 per cent in Italy (Harding and Schaller 1992a: 762, with reference to Harding 1987). High figures have also been reported from France (13 per cent; testing of 500 consecutive entries), Switzerland (11 per cent; cross-sectional study in five prisons in the Canton of Berne), and the Netherlands (11 per cent; screening of a sample of prisoners in Amsterdam). In contrast, some European countries, including Belgium, Finland, Iceland, and some Länder in Germany, report low levels of HIV prevalence. Relatively low rates of HIV prevalence have also been reported from Australia. In the United States, the geographic distribution of cases of HIV infection and AIDS is remarkably uneven. Many correctional systems continue to have rates under 1 per cent, while in a few rates approach or exceed 20 per cent (seroprevalence data are from CSC 1994a: 18–19 and 1994c: 47–79).

In Canada, seroprevalence studies undertaken in federal and provincial correctional institutions have shown rates of HIV infection between 1 and 7.7 per cent (see CSC 1994a: 15–18, with references; Jürgens 1996: appendix 2, with references). In federal prisons, the number of inmates who are known to be infected increases at an alarming rate: in January 1991, 27 inmates were known to be infected, while in March 1996, 159 inmates (more than 1 per cent of the total inmate population) were so identified (CSC 1996a).

2. Tuberculosis

The spectre of TB looms particularly large in congregate settings like prisons (Greifinger 1992). Tuberculosis is not a new problem in prisons. During the mid-nineteenth century the annual TB mortality in some prisons in the United States exceeded 10 per cent of the inmate population, and at the beginning of the sanatorium era, 80 per cent of prison deaths were attributed to TB. Several studies undertaken in prisons in New York City, New Orleans, and Arkansas between the mid-1940s and the late 1970s revealed higher rates of TB infection and disease among inmates than in the outside population, and documented the transmission of TB infection among inmates and from recently released inmates to persons in the community outside prisons (Greifinger, Heywood, and Glaser 1993: 332). It should therefore not come as a surprise that the recent resurgence of TB in the United States and elsewhere has had a disproportionate effect on prisons. At least eleven TB outbreaks in prisons in eight states were reported between 1985 and 1989. In 1992, the annual incidence of TB disease among prisoners in New York State was 189 cases per 100,000, an increase of more than 1300 per cent since 1977–80. The vast majority of inmates with TB disease were also HIV-infected (Hammett and Harrold 1993: 11). So severe is the increase in the TB caseload that a federal judge ordered that a special unit for inmates with TB be constructed in a jail in New York City. High incidence and prevalence rates of TB among inmates are not limited to New York State, but have been reported from other prison systems in the United States. An increasing incidence of active TB among HIV-infected prisoners has also been confirmed in prisons in France, Spain, and Switzerland (Harding and Schaller 1992a: 769).

Outbreaks of multiple-drug-resistant tuberculosis (MDR-TB) in prison systems in the United States have been widely reported in the press. The most serious of these occurred in New York State in 1990–2. At least nineteen correctional facilities and two hospitals where inmates were treated were involved, and a total of forty-one inmates were diagnosed with MDR-TB. Thirty-six of these and one correctional officer died, and a number of health-care workers were also infected with an MDR-TB strain (Hammett and Harrold 1993: 12).

In Canada, neither TB nor MDR-TB appear as yet to be a major problem and it may be too early to suggest that Canadian prisons are facing a TB crisis. Only 63 of 1996 TB cases reported in Canada in 1990 involved resistant organisms. Of these, only one was found to be resistant to four or more drugs. In Canadian federal correctional institutions, four new cases of active TB were reported in 1992, while in 1993 eighteen new cases were reported, with five new cases in the first six months of 1994 and, in the first four months of 1996, five new cases (CSC 1994d, 1996b). While it is too early to establish whether new cases of TB in prison are actually increasing, or whether more cases are reported as a result of increased screening, it is agreed that there is reason for concern: in Canada as elsewhere, HIV and TB converge in prisons in ways that favour transmission of TB among HIV-infected persons. 'The world [and prisons in particular] must come to terms with the fact that the concurrence of AIDS and MDR tuberculosis has primed a time bomb' (Ryan 1993: 413, cited in Greifinger, Heywood, and Glaser 1993).

3. Drug Use

More and more data are becoming available on the prevalence of drug use in prisons. In Canada, 53.7 per cent of all federal inmates were classified as having a serious substance-abuse problem (Riley 1994, with reference to CSC 1990), and the Parliamentary Ad Hoc Committee on AIDS heard evidence that up to 50 per cent of inmates may use drugs (1990: 47). Others have estimated that up to two-thirds of all prisoners use drugs while in prison (Appleby 1991: A1). In a recent survey, almost 40 per cent of 4285 federal inmates self-reported having used drugs since arriving in their current institution (CSC 1996c: 144–8). As Riley has pointed out, many inmates use drugs as a part of their lifestyle. Drugs relieve tension, boredom, and hopelessness, and it should come as no surprise that they are popular among inmates (Riley 1994: 154). Inmates often turn to drug use 'as a means to cope with the harsh reality of prison life' (PASAN 1992: 15).

Injection drug use is also prevalent in prisons, and the scarcity of needles often leads to needle sharing. During its prison visits, ECAP was told on some occasions by inmates that injection drug use and needle sharing are frequent and that sometimes fifteen to twenty people will use one needle without cleaning it between each use. Many CSC staff, in their responses to a questionnaire ECAP sent them, also acknowledged that drug use is a reality in federal correctional institutions, saying that 'drugs are part of prison culture and reality,' that 'drug use is widespread in institutions,' that 'there does not seem to be a way to ensure that there will be no use of drugs,' and that there are 'many needles in the prisons' (see CSC 1994a: 73–4, and 1994c: 85–109).

The following are accounts of the personal experiences of two prisoners in a federal institution (personal communication, received 4 March 1994):

Mr P is a 43-year-old male serving life. He has served twenty years on his sentence. He started using injectable drugs after he was incarcerated; this was his method of dealing with his loneliness. Mr P states his early experiences were with anyone willing to share a hit. After watching one of his peers die of AIDS two years ago, Mr P has his own rig (which is seven years old) and he shares it with no one.

Mr S is a 37-year-old male serving nine years for drug-related crimes. Mr S does not use injectable drugs but has found a market for his thirteen rigs inside the institution. Mr S rents out his needles for one hour at a time for three to five packages of cigarettes. Three packages of cigarettes rents a needle older than two years. Five packages of cigarettes rents a needle less than two years old. Mr S has needles that are less than six months old but they go strictly for cash or stamps valued at $50–100 depending on the demand. All his needles are cleaned with bleach (when he can steal it) or toilet bowl cleaner (if he has no bleach).

Anecdotal evidence of the existence and extent of injection and other drug use in prisons is confirmed by an increasing number of scientific studies undertaken in Canada and elsewhere (for a comprehensive overview, see Jürgens 1996, with many references). A study on HIV transmission among injection drug users in Toronto found that '[o]ver eighty per cent [of the participating injection drug users] had been in jail overnight or longer since beginning to inject drugs, with twenty-five per cent of those sharing injecting equipment while in custody' (Millson 1991). Eleven per cent of Canadian federal inmates self-reported having injected an illegal/non-prescription drug since coming to the particular institution in which they were currently staying; of these, only 57 per cent thought that the equipment they used was clean, while 17 per cent thought that it was not clean and the rest did not know (CSC 1996c: 138, and 1996d: 348–9). In Australia, '[a]ll commentators agree that [injection drug use] occurs and that needle sharing is almost always associated with IV drug use in prisons because of the lack of availability of syringes' (Heilpern and Egger 1989: 38, with many references). In an early survey of 'HIV Risk-Taking Behaviour of Sydney Male Drug Injectors While in Prison,' approximately 75 per cent of respondents reported having injected drugs at least once while in prison. Of these, two-thirds provided data on the frequency of sharing of injection equipment in prison, with 75 per cent reporting sharing (Wodak 1991: 240–1). Other more recent studies have confirmed that HIV risk behaviours are frequent in Australian prisons (Dolan et al. 1994b; and forthcoming). In the United Kingdom, a number of surveys found that the use and availability of injectable drugs greatly exceeds official estimates and that needles and syringes are commonly shared out of necessity (Thomas 1990: 7–10; Pickering and Stimson 1993; see also Bird et al. 1995 and Gore 1995). One study found that injection drug use decreased in prisons among inmates who had been injection drug users on the outside. However, inmates were more likely to inject in an unsafe manner when they did inject. The study concluded that imprisonment increased the risk of contracting HIV infection (Turnbull, Dolan, and Stimson 1992). This is consistent with the results of two other studies of drug-using behaviour in Scottish prisons. In the first, 11 per cent of a purposive sample of 234 prisoners had injected during their current sentence, while 32 per cent were injecting before imprisonment. However, of those who were injecting in prison, 76 per cent were sharing equipment, while only 24 per cent of those who were injecting before imprisonment were sharing (Shewan, Gemmell, and Davies 1994). In the second study, 76 of 227 prisoners (33 per cent) had injected drugs at some time in their lives, and 33 (15 per cent) admitted to injecting in prison. While injectors tended to use drugs on a daily basis outside prison, they would normally inject only weekly or monthly while in prison. However, all those who had injected in prison had shared equipment at least sometimes. Twenty prisoners had always shared it, compared to only two prisoners who had always shared outside (Taylor et al. 1994). In Germany, nearly 20 per cent of injection drug users who participated in a large epidemiological study were HIV-infected, and about 60 per cent of them had served a prison sentence. While only 10 per cent of participants with no prison experience tested HIV-positive, 26 per cent of those with prison experience tested HIV-positive, and 67 per cent of participants indicated that they continued to inject while in prison (CSC 1994c: 60).

4. Sexual Activity

Homosexual activity occurs inside prisons, as it does outside, as a consequence of preferred sexual orientation. In addition, prison life produces conditions that encourage the establishment of homosexual relationships within the institution (Thomas 1990: 5). The prevalence of sexual activity in prison is difficult to estimate, but is based on such factors as whether the accommodation is single-cell or dormitory, the duration of the sentence, the security classification, and the extent to which conjugal visits are permitted (Heilpern and Egger 1989: 40, with reference). Studies of sexual contact in prison have shown 'inmate involvement to vary greatly' (Saum et al. 1995). In Saum's study of the nature and frequency of sexual contact between male inmates in a Delaware prison, respondents were questioned extensively about sexual activities they themselves engaged in, directly observed, and heard about 'through the grapevine.' Saum concluded that 'although sexual contact is not widespread, it nevertheless occurs,' and that most sexual activity is consensual. Mahon conducted a focus-group study among fifty inmates in state prisons and city jails in New York, in which prisoners and former prisoners reported frequent instances of unprotected sex behind bars. One woman summarized the prevalence and range of sexual activity described by participants in the study when she stated: 'Male CO's are having sex with females. Female CO's are having sex with female inmates, and the male inmates are having sex with male inmates. Male inmates are having sex with female inmates. There's all kinds, it's a smorgasbord up there' (Mahon 1996). In Canada, 6 per cent of federal inmates self-reported that they had had sex with another inmate since coming to the institution in which they were currently incarcerated; of these, only 33 per cent reported using condoms (CSC 1996c).

5. Evidence of HIV Transmission in Prisons

Until recently, few data were available on how many prisoners become infected while in prison (for a review of five studies, see Parts 1991). According to Hammett and Harrold, the available data from studies undertaken in the United States suggested that transmission does occur in correctional facilities, but at quite low rates (1993: 43).

The results of these studies have sometimes been used to argue that HIV transmission in prisons is rare, and that consequently there is no need for increased prevention efforts. However, as pointed out by Hammett and Harrold (1993: 47), regardless of the rates of HIV seroconversion documented in studies, it is clear that sex and drug use continue to occur in prisons and that they represent high-risk activities for transmission of HIV. Anecdotal evidence that HIV transmission is occurring in prison is abundant. For example, a Louisiana inmate who tested positive for HIV in 1989 reported he was infected through sexual intercourse and/or needle sharing with a cell mate during an eight-month period in which they did 'every unsafe thing you could do' (ibid., with reference to Wikberg and Rideau 1992). In a survey conducted by the Deutsche AIDS-Hilfe, about 17 per cent of HIV-positive participants stated that they believed they had acquired HIV infection while in prison. The author of the study commented: 'Probably many justice ministries will say that this is a subjective opinion not supported by hard evidence. I ask myself, however, why these prisoners should give false testimony' (CSC 1994c: 60, with reference).

Recent events suggest that the extent of HIV infection occurring in prisons has been underestimated. In 1994, a study undertaken in Glenochil prison for adult male offenders in Scotland provided definitive evidence that outbreaks of HIV infection can and will occur in prisons unless HIV prevention is taken seriously. Of forty-three inmates who admitted having injected at some point in their lives, but not in Glenochil, thirty-four were tested. Of these, none tested positive. In contrast, twelve of twenty-seven inmates who admitted having injected in Glenochil tested positive, seven tested negative, and the remaining eight tested negative, but had recently been exposed to the risk of transmission. Certain characteristics of the positive test results made it clear that in most, if not all, cases the infection had been acquired in prison (Taylor et al. 1994; see also Christie 1995, Taylor et al. 1995, and Jürgens 1995a). Following the outbreak, twelve HIV-positive inmates and ten other drug injectors were interviewed about their risk behaviours in prison. From the interviews emerged a vivid description of random sharing with a limited number of needles and syringes, which were mostly blunt, broken, or fashioned out of a variety of materials. The researchers who conducted the interviews concluded by saying that, if another outbreak of the type reported from Glenochil is to be avoided, the 'same efforts that have gone into preventing HIV transmission among drug injectors outside prisons must be given to the prevention of spread inside' (Taylor and Goldberg 1996).

Evidence of HIV transmission in prisons in the United States (Mutter et al. 1994), Australia (Jürgens 1994: 5, with reference to Dolan et al. 1994a; Dolan et al. 1996), and other countries (Wright et al. 1994) has also been published, providing compelling reasons for the need to take HIV transmission in prisons seriously. In Canada, there have thus far been no documented cases of HIV transmission in prisons. However, the only reason for this is the absence of research in this area; everyone knows that HIV transmission is in fact occurring.

HIV Prevention in Prisons

This article does not intend to discuss the variety of measures such as education that are being undertaken in prisons to prevent HIV infection. While these measures are important, information is not of much use if inmates do not have the means to act on it. Inmates themselves have said that educational sessions are simply frustrating when they get information about how to protect themselves but the means to do so are not made available to them. An example of this is educating prisoners about safer injection drug use, but not making bleach and/or sterile needles available to them. The article will therefore focus on the availability in prisons of the means that are necessary to prevent HIV transmission.

1. Condoms and Lubricant

According to the World Health Organization's network on HIV/AIDS in prison, twenty-three of the fifty-two prison systems sampled allow condom distribution (Harding and Schaller 1992a: 767). Significantly, no country that has adopted a policy of making condoms available in prisons has reversed the policy.

In Canada, condoms have been available in federal penitentiaries since January 1992. Each penitentiary has established its own system for making them available. Some of the provincial prison systems have also started making condoms available to prisoners. Other provinces, however, are still refusing to make them available, and generally, with the exception of some federal institutions and provincial institutions in British Columbia, condoms are not easily and discreetly available, but only upon request and through prison health-care services. Lubricant, although essential for the practice of safer sex with a condom, is often not available.

2. Bleach, Sterile Needles, and Methadone

Measures aimed at drug use in prisons have traditionally aimed at eliminating drug use rather than at reducing the harms from it. Stress has been placed on interdiction and apprehension, education, and the treatment of addicted offenders. Some of the measures undertaken or planned, such as implementation of effective drug education, are uncontroversial and widely supported, but others have been criticized. Drug-testing programs such as those undertaken in Canadian federal prisons are not only costly and hardly a good use of scarce resources, but are intrusive and likely to have a negative impact on efforts to reduce the harms from drug use. In theory, drug testing should reduce the amount of drug use in prisons because people should be dissuaded from using drugs through fear of disciplinary action. However, there is concern that it could lead to an increased frequency of injection drug use. Drug use in prison may shift from marijuana to other drugs such as cocaine, heroin, PCP, and LSD, which have much shorter windows of detection (CSC 1994a,c, with reference to Oscapella 1993). Respondents to a discussion paper written as part of the joint Network/CAS Project (Jürgens 1995b) confirmed that this is already happening (Jürgens 1996), as did 28 per cent of federal prisoners responding to CSC's inmate survey (CSC 1996c: 150).

Bleach is made available to inmates in a growing number of prison systems. As reported by Harding and Schaller (1992b: table 4.1), sixteen of fifty-two systems surveyed late in 1991 made bleach available to prisoners, often accompanied by instruction on how to clean needles. For example, in Spain a bottle of bleach is included in the sanitary kit that inmates receive at entry into the prison system and monthly thereafter, and 'more is provided whenever needed' (Spanish Ministry of Justice 1992: 1). In Switzerland, 'first-aid kits' containing small bottles of bleach have been given to inmates since June 1991. In Canada, bleach is already made available to inmates in some provincial prison systems and has been made available in federal institutions since the fall of 1996.

While CSC rejected ECAP's recommendation to undertake a pilot study of distribution or exchange of sterile injection equipment, distribution of such equipment has been a reality in some Swiss prisons since 1993. In June 1994, a one-year pilot AIDS prevention program including needle distribution started at Hindelbank institution for women. One year later, a decision was taken to continue the program because evaluation by external experts demonstrated clear positive results: the health status of prisoners improved, no new cases of infection with HIV or hepatitis had occurred, an important decrease in needle sharing was observed, there was no increase in drug consumption, and needles were not used as weapons (Nelles and Fuhrer 1995).

Hindelbank was not the first institution to distribute sterile injection equipment to inmates, but was the first to scientifically evaluate such a program. It was in another Swiss prison, the Oberschöngrün prison for men, that sterile injection equipment first became available to inmates in 1993:

Dr Franz Probst, a part-time medical officer, working at Oberschöngrün prison in the Swiss canton of Solothurn was faced with the ethical dilemma of as many as 15 of 70 inmates regularly injecting drugs, with no adequate preventive measures. Unlike most of his fellow prison doctors, all of whom feel obliged to compromise their ethical and public health principles daily, Probst began distributing sterile injection material without informing the prison director. When this courageous but apparently foolhardy gesture was discovered, the director, instead of firing Probst on the spot, listened to his arguments about prevention of HIV and hepatitis, as well as injection-site abscesses, and sought approval from the Cantonal authorities to sanction the distribution of needles and syringes. Thus, the world's first distribution of injection material inside prison began as an act of medical disobedience. (Nelles and Harding 1995)

Three years later, distribution is ongoing, has never resulted in any negative consequences, and is supported by prisoners, staff, and the prison administration. As a result of the positive experiences in Swiss prisons, more and more prison systems around the world are announcing that they will also make sterile injection equipment available. At a symposium on harm reduction strategies in prisons in Berne in February 1996, representatives of several German prison systems, as well as the Spanish system, presented their programs or talked about their intention to start one soon – probably the best evidence that the lessons learned in Switzerland can be applied elsewhere (for a detailed review of such programs, see Jürgens 1996).

Treatment with methadone as a substitute for opiate use has been adopted in several prison systems worldwide (for a review, see Dolan and Wodak 1996). It is seen as an AIDS prevention strategy that allows people dependent on drugs an additional option to get away from needle use and sharing. There are ample data supporting the effectiveness of methadone maintenance programs in reducing high-risk injecting behaviour and, thereby, the risk of contracting HIV (Riley 1994, with many references). There is also evidence that people who are on methadone maintenance and who are forced to withdraw from methadone because they are incarcerated often 'return to narcotic use, often within the prison system, and often via injection' (response to ECAP's working paper by B. Kearns, acting chief executive officer, Alberta Alcohol and Drug Abuse Commission). For participants in a study of drug-using behaviour in Scottish prisons, being prescribed methadone before imprisonment was associated with a move towards either stopping, or reducing, injecting and sharing. On entry to prison, however, where all methadone prescriptions were abruptly discontinued, there was a strong trend for prior methadone prescribing to become closely identified with subsequent sharing of injection equipment. The study concluded that 'a rethink is necessary on the response within prisons to prisoners who are on prescriptions in the community,' and that a 'detoxification programme with reduction based oral prescribing should be routinely offered, and administered on a contractual basis, to all prisoners on admission who present with a drug problem' (Shewan, Gemmell, and Davies, 1994). Others have suggested that methadone is the best available option to prevent needle sharing in prisons (McLeod 1991: 248) and that increasing the number of places available for methadone treatment in prisons should be considered a 'matter of urgency for HIV positive drug dependent prisoners' (Heilpern and Egger 1989: 94).

Time to Rethink Prison Policy

Initially, responding to the problem of HIV/AIDS in prisons in Canada and elsewhere was very slow. Only small steps were made to develop policies and provide educational programs for staff and prisoners. In many systems, prisoners with HIV infection or AIDS were segregated from the rest of the prison population and were subject to a variety of discriminatory measures. Neither condoms nor bleach were made available to prisoners, and educational programs often appeared inadequate.

In recent years a growing number of prison systems have started undertaking efforts to address the problems raised by HIV/AIDS and drug use in prisons. Often this was done only after they were confronted with sharp increases in the numbers of prisoners with HIV infection or AIDS in their custody. Some systems have made condoms, bleach, and even sterile injection equipment available, abandoned segregation policies, and introduced better educational programs delivered or supplemented by community-based outside organizations and/or peers.

In Canada, the federal prison system accepted many of the recommendations issued by ECAP (see CSC 1994b), acknowledging that AIDS represents 'a serious public health problem for all of society and that there are particular concerns about inmates in federal penitentiaries' (CSC 1994e). The Commissioner of Corrections added that, '[g]iven that over 80 per cent of inmates are serving fixed sentences and will eventually be returned to the community, the Correctional Service is particularly sensitive to its responsibility to protect the public, including staff and inmates, from the consequences of HIV/AIDS transmission.' He concluded by saying that CSC has 'a responsibility to do all we can to prevent the spread of this fatal disease' (ibid.). Despite this, however, the Service will not provide methadone maintenance programs or pilot test needle-exchange programs in prisons.

CSC has been praised for implementing many of ECAP's recommendations, but criticized for rejecting 'critical parts of [ECAP's] plan' relating to drug use in prisons. PASAN issued a press release stating that CSC 'has chosen to ignore the issue of injection drug use and the high risk of HIV transmission through needle use within the prison context. How can CSC admit that there is a drug problem in the prisons and still refuse to even try a pilot needle exchange program for prisoners? This contradiction will cost lives' (PASAN 1994). Similarly, an editorial in the *Vancouver Sun* (1994) found that the '[p]rison system [is] guilty of AIDS complacency,' and that 'prison reform maintains its snail-like pace.' The editorial concluded: '"There is no room for delay or complacency in responding to this threat," Dr. Gilmore [chairman of ECAP] said when his committee's recommendations for preventing the spread of AIDS in prisons were made. But that's exactly the response he got from corrections officials. If any lesson should be learned from the continuing outcry over the Red Cross's sluggish response to the threat of AIDS transmission through the blood supply, it's that such attitudes can be lethal.'

Instead of implementing methadone maintenance programs and undertaking a pilot project for needle distribution, CSC announced a war on drugs in federal prisons. Many of the measures proposed as part of the new 'strategy to combat drugs' are controversial at best and, as stated by ECAP, 'may create risks or harms that outweigh the benefit being sought, namely the reduction of drug use' (CSC 1994a: 66).

Barriers to HIV Prevention in Prisons

It is generally agreed that responding to the threat of HIV/AIDS in prisons is more difficult than it is outside. At the same time, prisons represent a 'window of opportunity' for the prevention of HIV transmission because a significant proportion of people engaging in high-risk activities, injection drug use in particular, pass through them (Brewer 1991). The following paragraphs outline some of the barriers to prevention of HIV infection in prisons, and suggest ways to overcome them.

1. The Underlying Conflict of Values between the Penal System and Medical Care

The common reply to early criticism of government inaction was that medical recommendations had to be balanced with correctional concerns. Correction is a public-safety (law enforcement) rather than a public-health activity (Brewer 1991), and prison life is not organized on the basis of care, but of coercion. Outside the prison setting, it has long been recognized that coercive interventions are counter-productive in controlling HIV transmission and its consequences; that HIV/AIDS interventions need to be based on respect for persons and their rights and dignity; and that personal responsibility has to be encouraged. Prevention of disease and the provision of medical care in prisons, however, require reconciling or balancing a medical model of prevention, diagnosis, care, and treatment with the correctional requirements of custody and control (Dubler et al. 1990: 365). The punitiveness inherent in the prison system and security concerns have often been seen as obstacles to effective prevention of HIV/AIDS in prisons.

However, the promotion of health in prisons does not necessarily entail lessening the safety and security of prisons. The interest of prisoners in being given access to the means necessary to protect them from contracting HIV infection are compatible with the interest of staff in their security in the workplace and of prison authorities in the maintenance of safety and order in the institutions. Indeed, promotion of health in the prison population and the education of both prisoners and staff may be the best ways to create safety and security (PASAN 1992: 3). Any measure undertaken now to prevent the spread of HIV infection will benefit prisoners, staff, and the public. First, it will protect the health of prisoners, who should not, by reason of their imprisonment, be exposed to the risk of a deadly condition. Offenders are imprisoned *as* punishment and not *for* punishment, and their rights must be respected 'except for those limitations that are demonstrably necessitated by the fact of incarceration' (United Nations 1990b: para. 5). Moreover, as prisoners' rights as human persons are necessarily curtailed to some extent, they are also entitled to more protection (Somerville 1979: 96). In particular, they are entitled to protection from contracting diseases.

Second, any measure to protect prisoners will also protect staff in correctional institutions. Lowering the prevalence of infections in prisons means that the risk of exposure to these infections will also be lowered.

Finally, measures to prevent the spread of HIV infection in prisons also protect the public. Indeed, they are mandated by a sound public-health policy. Most inmates are in prison only for relatively short periods of time and are then released into their communities. In order to protect the general population, HIV/AIDS prevention measures need to be available in prisons, as they are outside.

2. Misperceptions of the Public

In Canada and elsewhere the public probably holds as many misperceptions and is as misinformed about prisoners and prisons as it is about drugs. The public's perception is that the majority of prisoners are violent offenders, that prisoners deserve to be punished, and that prisons constitute a world that is entirely separate from the world we live in. In reality, most prisoners are non-violent offenders and are released from prison after relatively short periods of time, meaning that any delay in implementing effective AIDS prevention in prisons will severely affect not only prisoners but also the public. The public's misperceptions are fuelled by parts of the media that engage in a 'war against criminals' by advocating a more restrictive approach to the policy and practice of criminal justice. Because of existing prejudices and false perceptions, it is politically useful to engage in a war on drugs, but not on AIDS, while it would be politically hazardous to implement harm reduction measures in prisons. We need to educate the public about the reality of prisons, instead of letting its prejudices influence government politics.

3. Political Commitment

Political and institutional commitment are necessary if approaches to deal with HIV/AIDS and drug use in prisons are to be implemented effectively. The decisions involved are often political decisions, and so far there has not been enough political commitment to resolve the problems raised by HIV/AIDS and drug use in prisons. As pointed out by Dr Michael O'Shaugnessy, then chairman of the Canadian National Advisory Committee on AIDS, the most important reason why effective AIDS prevention measures, including needle exchanges, are not available in prisons is lack of political commitment (statement at the closing session of the Second National Workshop on HIV/AIDS, Drugs and Alcohol in Edmonton, Canada, February 1994).

4. Condoning Drug Use or Condoning HIV Transmission?

Many prisoners are in prison because of drug offences or drug-related offences. Preventing their drug use is seen as an important part of their rehabilitation. Even in countries that have officially embraced a harm reduction philosophy, abstinence is still seen as the primary goal in prisons. In the eyes of many, acknowledging that drug use is a reality in prisons would be to acknowledge that prison authorities have failed in their mandate: 'And doesn't this mean that the government is basically admitting defeat – saying it can't control illegal drug use in prisons ...?' (*Edmonton Sun* 1994).

Another argument that is often used is that making condoms, bleach, or sterile needles available to inmates would mean condoning behaviour that is illegal in prisons. Far from condoning sexual activity and drug use in prisons, however, making available to inmates the means that are necessary to protect them from HIV transmission acknowledges that protection of prisoners' health, rather than elimination of drug use, needs to be the primary objective of drug policy in prisons. On the other hand, refusing to make condoms and bleach or sterile needles available to inmates, while knowing that activities likely to transmit HIV are prevalent in prisons, could be seen as condoning the spread of HIV among prisoners and to the community at large. Governments and prison administrators have the duty to face up to the risks of the spread of HIV infection. Because HIV has such devastating consequences, contradictions resulting from making condoms and bleach or clean needles available in prisons when both sexual activity and drug use are prohibited should be tolerated (Kirby 1991: 263). As stated by Martin Lachat, interim director of Hindelbank institution, the Swiss prison for women in which the pilot project of syringe provision started in 1994, '[t]he transmission of HIV or any other serious disease cannot be tolerated. Given that all we can do is restrict, not suppress, the entry of drugs, we feel it is our responsibility to at least provide sterile syringes to inmates. The ambiguity of our mandate leads to a contradiction that we have to live with' (Lachat 1994).

This unavoidable contradiction has also been recognized by police forces in many countries, including Canada, which, although continuing their fight against drugs, allow and even promote needle exchanges and other harm reduction approaches. As the head of the Merseyside Police Drug Squad, Mr Derek O'Connell, has stated (cited in Riley 1994: 156): 'As police officers, part of our oath is to protect life. In the drugs field that policy must include saving life as well as enforcing the law. Clearly, we must reach injectors and get them the help they require, but in the meantime we must try and keep them healthy, for we are their police as well ... People can be cured of drug addiction, but at the moment they cannot be cured of AIDS.'

5. Drug Laws

At least in part, the high prevalence of HIV in prisons is a result of current drug laws that prohibit drug use or possession and force many drug users into a life of crime and imprisonment. Prisons are the single largest response to the drug problem in most countries and more resources are used in moving drug users through the criminal-justice system than any other form of management, medical or social (Harding 1990). As the World Health Organization (1987) has stated, '[g]overnments may ... wish to review their penal admission policies, particularly where drug abusers are concerned, in the light of the AIDS epidemic and its impact on prisons.' Indeed, reducing the number of drug users who are incarcerated needs to become an immediate priority. Many of the problems created by HIV infection and by drug use in prisons could be reduced if alternatives to imprisonment, particularly in the context of drug-related crimes, were developed and made available.

Conclusion

In Canada and elsewhere, prison systems are starting to react to the problems raised by HIV infection and AIDS in the correctional environment. However, much remains to be done. Prison systems are still reluctant to acknowledge the existence of drug use in prisons and to undertake the steps that are necessary to prevent HIV transmission through sharing of unclean needles. As Riley has stated, '[f]or those of us who have started to feel that we have begun to make headway in introducing harm reduction as an acceptable policy in our countries, the situation in prisons should make us realize how much is still to be done. Reducing drug-related harm in society means reducing harm in prisons too, and in that regard we have clearly failed' (1994: 160).

NOTES

Parts of this text are based on the reports that the author prepared for the Expert Committee on AIDS and Prisons (Correctional Service 1994a); and for the Joint Project on Legal and Ethical Issues Raised by HIV/AIDS of the Canadian HIV/AIDS Legal Network and the Canadian AIDS Society (Jürgens 1996; the latter report can be obtained through the Canadian HIV/AIDS Legal Network, 4007 de Mentana, Montréal H2L 3R9). The author would like to thank Diane Riley, Jean Dussault, Bruno Guillot-Hurtubise, and Anne Stone for their assistance, and the members and external observers of the Expert Committee for their input in and comments on earlier versions of the text. The text is dedicated to Anne Malo, Health Canada, and formerly National Coordinator of the AIDS Programs of the Correctional Service of Canada, for her dedication to the issues raised by HIV/AIDS in prisons.

REFERENCES

Appleby, T. 1991. 'AIDS Adds Lethal Element to Widespread Drug Use in Jails.' Toronto *Globe and Mail*, 5 November.
Bird, A.G., et al. 1995. 'Anonymous HIV Surveillance with Risk Factor Elicitation at Scotland's Largest Prison, Barlinnie.' *AIDS* 9: 801–8.
Brewer, T.F. 1991. 'HIV in Prisons: The Pragmatic Approach.' *AIDS* 5: 897.
Castro, K., R. Shansky, V. Scardino, et al. 1991. 'HIV Transmission in Correctional Facilities.' Poster presented at the 7th International Conference on AIDS, Florence, Italy.
Christie, B. 1995. 'Scotland: Learning from Experience.' *British Medical Journal* 310(6975): 279.
Correctional Service Canada. 1990. Research and Statistics Branch. 'Findings from the National Alcohol and Drug Survey.' *Forum on Corrections Research* 2(4): 3–6.

– 1994a. *HIV/AIDS in Prisons: Final Report of the Expert Committee on AIDS and Prisons*. Ottawa: Minister of Supply and Services Canada.

– 1994b. *HIV/AIDS in Prisons: Summary Report and Recommendations of the Expert Committee on AIDS and Prisons*. Ottawa: Minister of Supply and Services Canada.

– 1994c. *HIV/AIDS in Prisons: Background Materials*. Ottawa: Minister of Supply and Services Canada.

– 1994d. 'TB Statistics.' Ottawa: The Service's Health Care Services.

– 1994e. Backgrounder: 'CSC Response to the Expert Committee on AIDS and Prisons (ECAP)' and News Release: 'Correctional Service of Canada Announces Response to Final Recommendations Submitted by the Expert Committee on AIDS and Prisons.' Ottawa: The Service, 24 March.

– 1996a. 'Reported Cases of HIV/AIDS in Federal Penitentiaries.' Ottawa: The Service's Health Care Services.

– 1996b. 'TB Statistics.' Ottawa: The Service's Health Care Services.

– 1996c. *1995 National Inmate Survey: Final Report*. Ottawa: The Service, Correctional Research and Development.

– 1996d. *1995 National Inmate Survey: Main Appendix*. Ottawa: The Service, Correctional Research and Development.

Council of Europe. 1988. 'Recommendation 1080 on a Co-ordinated European Health Policy to Prevent the Spread of AIDS in Prisons of 30 June 1988.'

Dolan, K., W. Hall, A. Wodak, and M. Gaughwin. 1994a. 'Evidence of HIV Transmission in an Australian Prison.' *The Medical Journal of Australia* 160: 734.

– 1994b. 'Bleach Availability and Risk Behaviours in New South Wales.' Technical Report no. 22. Sydney: National Drug and Alcohol Research Centre.

– 1996. 'A Network of HIV Infection among Australian Inmates.' Abstract no. 6594, 11th International Conference on AIDS, Vancouver, 7–11 July.

– Forthcoming. 'HIV Risk Behaviour of IDUs before, during and after Imprisonment in New South Wales.' *Addiction Research*.

Dolan, K., and A. Wodak. 1996. 'An International Review of Methadone Provision in Prisons.' *Addiction Research* 4(1): 85–97.

Dubler, N.N., et al. 1990. 'Management of HIV Infection in New York State Prisons.' *Columbia Human Rights Law Review* 21: 363.

Edmonton Sun. 1994. 'Terribly Modern.' 29 March, p. 10.

Federal/Provincial/Territorial Advisory Committee on AIDS. 1991. 'Draft Statement on HIV/AIDS in Correctional Facilities.' Ottawa: National AIDS Secretariat.

Gore, S.M. 1995. 'Drug Injection and HIV Prevalence in Inmates of Glenochil Prison.' *British Medical Journal* 310: 293–6.

Greifinger, R.B. 1992. 'Tuberculosis behind Bars.' In *The Tuberculosis Revival: Individual Rights and Societal Obligations in a Time of AIDS*, 59–65. New York: United Hospital Fund.

Greifinger, R.B., N.J. Heywood, and J.B. Glaser. 1993. 'Tuberculosis in Prison: Balancing Justice and Public Health.' *Journal of Law, Medicine and Ethics* 21(3–4): 332–41.

Hammett, T.M. 1988. *AIDS in Correctional Facilities: Issues and Options*. 3rd ed. Washington: U.S. Department of Justice.

– 1993. *1992 Update: AIDS in Correctional Facilities: Issues and Options*. Cambridge, MA: Abt Associates Inc.

Hammett, T.M., and L. Harrold, 1993. *Tuberculosis in Correctional Facilities*. Final draft report. Cambridge, MA: Abt Associates Inc.

Harding, T.W. 1987. 'AIDS in Prison.' *The Lancet* 2: 1260–3.

– 1990. 'HIV Infection and AIDS in the Prison Environment: A Test Case for the Respect of Human Rights.' In J. Strang and G. Stimson, eds, *AIDS and Drug Misuse*, 197–207. New York: Routledge.

Harding, T.W., and G. Schaller. 1992a. 'HIV/AIDS Policy for Prisons or for Prisoners?' In J.M. Mann, D.J.M. Tarantola, and T.W. Netter, eds, *AIDS in the World*. Cambridge: Harvard University Press.

– 1992b. *HIV/AIDS and Prisons: Updating and Policy Review. A Survey Covering 55 Prison Systems in 31 Countries*. Geneva: WHO Global Programme on AIDS.

Heilpern, H., and S. Egger. 1989. *AIDS in Australian Prisons: Issues and Policy Options*. Canberra: Department of Community Services and Health.

Jürgens, R. 1994. 'Taking HIV Prevention Seriously: Provision of Syringes in a Swiss Prison.' *Canadian HIV/AIDS Policy and Law Newsletter* 1: 1–3.

– 1995a. 'Alarming Evidence of HIV Transmission in Prisons. *Canadian HIV/AIDS Policy and Law Newsletter* 1(2), 2–3.

– 1995b. *HIV/AIDS in Prisons: A Discussion Paper*. Montréal: Canadian HIV/AIDS Legal Network and Canadian AIDS Society.

– 1996. *HIV/AIDS in Prisons: Final Report*. Montréal: Canadian HIV/AIDS Legal Network and Canadian AIDS Society.

Kirby, M. 1991. 'AIDS in Prisons in Australia.' *Medico-Legal Journal* 59: 252–65.

Lachat, M. 1994. 'Account of a Pilot Project for HIV Prevention in the Hindelbank Penitentiaries for Women – Press Conference, 16 May 1994.' Berne: Information and Public Relations Bureau of the Canton.

McLeod, F. 1991. 'Methadone, Prisons and AIDS.' In J. Norberry et al., eds, *HIV/AIDS and Prisons*. Canberra: Australian Institute of Criminology.

Mahon, N. 1996. 'New York Inmates' HIV Risk Behaviors: The Implications for Prevention Policy and Programs.' *American Journal of Public Health* 86(9): 1211–15.

Millson, P. 1991. 'Evaluation of a Programme to Prevent HIV Transmission in Injection Drug Users in Toronto.' Toronto: Toronto Board of Health.

Mutter, R.C., R.M. Grimes, and D. Labarthe. 1994. 'Evidence of Intraprison Spread of HIV Infection.' *Archives of Internal Medicine* 154: 793–5.

National Advisory Committee on AIDS. 1987. Minutes of meeting. Ottawa, 22 April.

– 1989. 'Statement Concerning Correctional Settings.' In Parliamentary Ad Hoc Committee on AIDS 1990.

Nelles, J., and A. Fuhrer. 1995. 'Drug and HIV Prevention at the Hindelbank Penitentiary.' Abridged Report of the Evaluation Results. Berne: Swiss Federal Office of Public Health.

Nelles, J., and T. Harding. 1995. 'Preventing HIV Transmission in Prison: A Tale of Medical Disobedience and Swiss Pragmatism.' *The Lancet* 346: 1507.

Oscapella, E. 1993. 'The Impact of Drug Policy on the Risk of HIV Infection in Prisons: Prohibition vs. Harm Reduction.' Submission to ECAP of 24 January.

Parliamentary Ad Hoc Committee on AIDS. 1990. *Confronting a Crisis: The Report of the Parliamentary Ad Hoc Committee on AIDS*. Ottawa: The Committee.

Parts, M. 1991. 'The Eighth Amendment and the Requirement of Active Measures to Prevent the Spread of AIDS in Prisons.' *Columbia Human Rights Law Review* 22: 217–49.

Pickering, H., and G.V. Stimson. 1993. 'Syringe Sharing in Prison.' *The Lancet* 342: 621–2.

Prisoners with AIDS/HIV Support Action Network (PASAN). 1992. *HIV/AIDS in Prison Systems: A Comprehensive Strategy*. Toronto: The Network.

– 1994. 'Prisoner HIV/AIDS Activists Challenge Correctional Service Canada's Inadequate Response to HIV/AIDS and Prisons.' Press release, 25 March.

Riley, D. 1994. 'Drug Use in Prisons.' In Correctional Service Canada 1994c: 152–61.

– 1994.'The Policy and Practice of Harm Reduction.' In P. Brisson, ed., *L'usage des drogues et la toxicomanie*. Montreal: Gaetan Morin.

Royal Society of Canada. 1988. *AIDS: A Perspective for Canadians. Summary Report and Recommendations*. Ottawa: The Society.

Ryan, F. 1993. *The Forgotten Plague: How the Battle Against Tuberculosis Was Won – and Lost*. New York: Little, Brown and Company.

Saum, C.A., et al. 1995. 'Sex in Prison: Exploring the Myths and Realities.' *Prison Journal*. December.

Shewan, D., M. Gemmell, and J.B. Davies. 1994. 'Prison as a Modifier of Drug Using Behaviour.' *Addiction Research*.

Somerville, M.A. 1979. *Consent to Medical Care*. Study paper prepared for the

Law Reform Commission of Canada. Ottawa: Ministry of Supply and Services Canada.

Spanish Ministry of Justice. 1992. 'Program for the Prevention and Control of AIDS in Spanish Prisons.' Madrid: The Ministry.

Taylor, A., and D. Goldberg. 1996. 'Outbreak of HIV in a Scottish Prison: Why Did It Happen?' *Canadian HIV/AIDS Policy and Law Newsletter* 2(3): 13–14.

Taylor, A., D. Goldberg, S. Cameron, and J. Emslie. 1994. 'Outbreak of HIV Infection in a Scottish Prison.' Paper presented at the 10th International Conference on AIDS, Yokohama, August.

Taylor, A., et al. 1995. 'Outbreak of HIV Infection in a Scottish Prison.' *British Medical Journal* 310(6975): 289–92.

Thomas, P.A. 1990. 'HIV/AIDS in Prisons.' *Howard Journal of Criminal Justice* 29: 1–13.

Turnbull, P.J., K.A. Dolan, and G.V. Stimson. 1992. 'Prison Decreases the Prevalence of Behaviours but Increases the Risks.' Poster abstract no. PoC 4321. 8th International Conference on AIDS, Amsterdam, 19–24 July.

United Nations. 1990a. 'Infection with Human Immunodeficiency Virus (HIV) and Acquired Immunodeficiency Syndrome (AIDS) in Prisons.' Resolution 18 of the Eighth United Nations Congress on the Prevention of Crime and the Treatment of Offenders, Havana, Cuba, 27 August–7 September. In *Report of the Eighth United Nations Congress on the Prevention of Crime and the Treatment of Offenders*. U.N. Doc. A/CONF.144/28 of 5 October 1990.

United Nations. 1990b. 'Statement of Basic Principles for the Treatment of Prisoners.' Annex to General Assembly resolution 45/111 of 14 December 1990.

U.S. National Commission on AIDS. 1991. *Report: HIV Disease in Correctional Facilities*. Washington: The Commission.

Vancouver Sun. 1994. 'Prison System Guilty of AIDS Complacency.' 2 April: A18.

WHO. 1987. *Statement from the Consultation on Prevention and Control of AIDS in Prisons*. Geneva: WHO Global Programme on AIDS.

– 1993. *Guidelines on HIV Infection and AIDS in Prisons*. Geneva: WHO Global Programme on AIDS.

Wikberg, R., and W. Rideau. 1992. 'The Medusa Strain.' *The Angolite* 17 (March/April): 22.

Wodak, A. 1991. 'Behind Bars: HIV Risk-Taking Behaviour of Sydney Male Drug Injectors While in Prison.' In J. Norberry et al., eds, *HIV/AIDS and Prisons*, 181–91. Canberra: Australian Institute of Criminology.

Wright, N.H., et al. 1994. 'Was the 1988 HIV Epidemic among Bangkok's Injecting Drug Users a Common Source Outbreak?' *AIDS* 8: 529–32.

10 Is Prenatal Drug Use Child Abuse?: Reporting Practices and Coerced Treatment in California

AMANDA NOBLE

A number of women in the United States have been prosecuted for their drug use during pregnancy; there have been approximately 150 such cases reported nationwide. This chapter discusses a different form of punishment, one that is far more common. In California, poor women and women of colour are often tested for illicit drugs when they arrive at hospitals to deliver their babies. Sometimes the infant's urine is tested, sometimes the mother's urine is tested and sometimes both are tested. If they test positive for drugs, hospital workers frequently call child-welfare workers, who begin an investigation of child abuse that can lead to loss of custody.

These practices occur, in part, because of the politicization of the problem of drug use during pregnancy in the United States and its connection to the recent war on crack cocaine. Media reports and images of drug use during pregnancy have spawned a kind of moral panic.[1] Scientific and popular reports on the ill effects of drug and alcohol use have contributed to the panic and led to concerns on the part of both hospital personnel and child-welfare workers that the health and well-being of infants and children be protected. Drug use during pregnancy is not good or exemplary behaviour and the impetus for concern is understandable. But this method of identifying such women and children is racist and punishes the poor. Under the guise of 'helping' children and their mothers, the children of poor women and women of colour are singled out as victims, labelled as damaged, and their mothers are coerced into 'getting well' via treatment programs.

This chapter is drawn mostly from a study of the social and political construction of drug and alcohol use during pregnancy in the state of California. Qualitative methods were used, including attendance at state and local government meetings about the problem; conferences and training sessions; legislative hearings for relevant bills; and meetings of organizations that were politically active in their attempts to persuade legislators to take specific positions on bills. Key players were also interviewed. Other data sources for this analysis include direct observations of two state agencies that were involved in attempting to solve the problem of drug-exposed babies during the years 1988–91, recent epidemiologic research in California, and a survey of California counties related to their practices.

Identifying and Reporting Drug-Using Pregnant Women

The identification of drug-using mothers is accomplished through hospital protocols. The protocols are constructed so that women are categorized by the degree of risk they pose for delivering a drug-exposed baby. The main point in using a protocol is to justify a urine test and to collect further information about the woman and her family that are likely to be turned over to child-welfare workers when hospital workers file a suspected-child-abuse report.

A 1990 California law required that counties construct protocols for the handling of this population. Counties were to bring together health, child-welfare, and hospital personnel to agree upon such practices, and, in theory, adopt them on a county-wide basis. Typically, the protocols list risk factors that are used as keys in identifying drug users. Urine toxicology tests are taken when sufficient risk exists, and the test is to be followed by an assessment of the family's needs and the risks to the child. A recent study of the law's adoption by counties revealed that, for most counties with protocols, their use was more consistent in public hospitals than in private hospitals. By way of explaining the inconsistent use of protocols in private hospitals, many counties remarked that private hospitals, serving primarily white, middle-class delivering women, were reluctant to screen such patients. In addition, counties reported that one problem experienced in constructing such protocols was the reluctance of private physicians and hospitals to adopt protocol policies (Noble 1994). These findings echo other studies that report reluctance on the part of physicians and private institutions to test and otherwise question delivering women about their alcohol and drug use (Zellman et al. 1993; Robin-Vergeer 1990).

When many such medical protocols are reviewed, it becomes clear that the most important risk factor was always whether or not the

woman had received prenatal care. In the United States, coverage for
prenatal care is limited to those who have job-related (or marriage-
related) health benefits or who can afford to pay out of pocket.
Although publicly assisted medical coverage for the poor exists in theory, it is often quite difficult to find physicians who are willing to take
such patients (Noble 1992; Perkins and Stoll 1987). It is clear that this
risk factor penalizes those who are unable to pay for prenatal care or
find doctors willing to treat them. As Tsing has pointed out, contemporary standards of middle-class respectability require attention to
conventions of health and personal care. Middle-class people expect
themselves and others to follow the advice of medical experts. For the
case of pregnancy, obstetric care is an important class marker: 'Those
who do not use these services are, according to the voice of respectability, stupid, lazy, and irresponsible – precisely the qualities seen as causing poverty itself. While it may be reprehensible to let these qualities
control one's self-care, it is seen as *criminal* to operate with these traits
around children' (Tsing 1991: 294, emphasis hers). Other risk factors
that led to drug tests or assessments were those related to a woman's
social class or race/ethnicity: for instance, the woman was homeless or
without a telephone, the woman had no husband, she had an untreated
sexually transmitted disease or a history of such, or she or her husband
or partner had previous histories of drug-abuse treatment or had been
previously arrested or incarcerated. Poor women and women of colour
are more likely to live in impoverished conditions and to have had contact with criminal-justice agencies (Noble 1994, 1992).

Other commonly occurring risk factors are highly subjective in
nature: a mother's mental confusion or bizarre behaviour, uncoopera-
tive behaviour with medical staff, a 'gut feeling' or suspicion, a mother's
impaired bonding or lack of attachment, her weak support system, or
the appearance that friends and visitors are using drugs. Complicating
matters is the fact that a positive toxicology screen for either the mother
or the infant is often listed as a risk factor, which allows for discretion on
the part of medical personnel to make a decision to test regardless of the
presence of further risk factors (Noble 1994; Noble 1992).

Race/ethnic-group membership does not appear as a risk factor on
protocols – to do so would clearly discriminate. We do know, however,
that African American women are more likely than white women to be
poor and dependent on public funds for their medical care. And several
studies have documented that medical personnel are far more likely to
suspect and report cases of child abuse, including prenatal drug use, if

the mother is poor, publicly insured, and a woman of colour (Hampton and Newberger 1985; Chasnoff et al. 1990; Wiley et al. 1991, Wulczyn 1992). The discrimination against women of colour does not only occur when women deliver their children. Discrimination may also take the form of neglect when women are pregnant. There is recent evidence that African American women receive very different kinds of advice than white women from health-care providers when pregnant. A U.S. nation-wide survey revealed that African American women were less likely to receive advice about drinking and smoking during pregnancy than white women (Kogen et al. 1994).

Do these types of risk factors reflect drug and alcohol use in the population of delivering women? A recently completed population-based study of the prevalence of alcohol and drug use[2] by nearly 30,000 women delivering in more than two-thirds of the maternity hospitals in California provides some answers. In this anonymous study women's urine was tested and the results linked to basic demographic and medical information, including self-reported current tobacco smoking (Vega et al. 1993). Focusing on two variables, race/ethnic group and the method of payment for birth,[3] provides data related to the use of alcohol and drugs by race and class. Race/ethnic-group variations appear as figure 1 (p. 178). African American women had the highest rates for all substances, including tobacco by self-report. Hispanic women had the second-highest rate for alcohol, and white women had the second-highest rate for illicit drugs and self-reported tobacco use. Asian women's rates were lowest for all substances.

Race/ethnic-group findings were also analysed based on the projected numbers of substance-exposed births. As figure 2 (p. 179) shows, white and Hispanic women were the largest race/ethnic groups of pregnant alcohol and drug users in the state. In California, Hispanic women constitute one-half of the delivering population. Despite their low rates for illicit drugs, their relatively high rates for alcohol meant that almost one-half of the alcohol-exposed births were to Hispanic women. White women had the highest overall incidence of alcohol- and drug-exposed births. Also relevant are findings related to the woman's expected source of payment, collected as a general indicator of socio-economic status. In California, approximately one-half of births are publicly assisted. Women whose births were publicly assisted had higher prevalence rates than those with insurance; they were twice as likely to use illicit drugs and to smoke. This finding, however, should not be interpreted to mean that the use of substances by insured women was minimal. Among

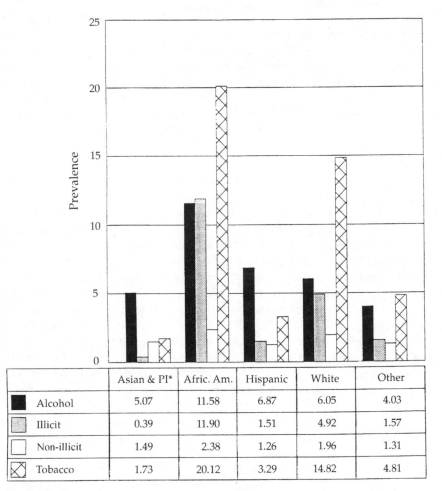

		Asian & PI*	Afric. Am.	Hispanic	White	Other
■	Alcohol	5.07	11.58	6.87	6.05	4.03
▨	Illicit	0.39	11.90	1.51	4.92	1.57
□	Non-illicit	1.49	2.38	1.26	1.96	1.31
⊠	Tobacco	1.73	20.12	3.29	14.82	4.81

*Pacific Islanders

FIGURE 1 Statewide prevalence rates (per cent positive) by race-ethnicity in California, 1992 (Source: Perinatal Substance Exposure Study – General Report, California Department of Alcohol and Drug Programs, September 1993)

pregnant women tested, insured women (figure 3, p. 180) constituted approximately 40 per cent of alcohol users, 25 per cent of illicit drug users, and 30 per cent of those who reported they were smokers.

In sum, prevalence study findings both do and do not support the decision to test and report based on risk factors.[4] If one pays attention to

Births

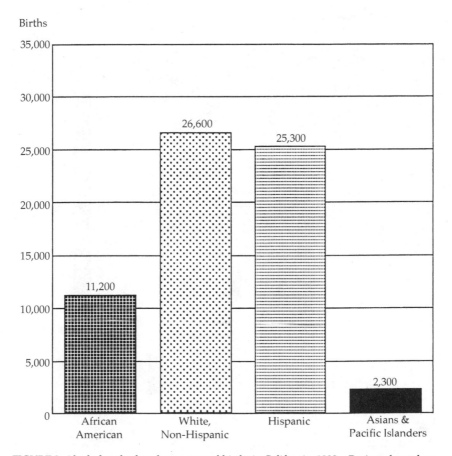

FIGURE 2 Alcohol and other drug-exposed births in California, 1992 – Projected number of drug-exposed births

rates alone, one can rationalize their use, but when incidence is considered, white women were the race/ethnic group with the highest numbers of alcohol- or drug-exposed births, and women with private health insurance were also using in substantial numbers. These are women who will probably escape detection when they deliver. They don't fit the profile of the poor, publicly insured, and likely African American woman who will not escape.

It is important to point out that many hospitals test 'high-risk' women without informed consent. There is wide variation among hospitals in

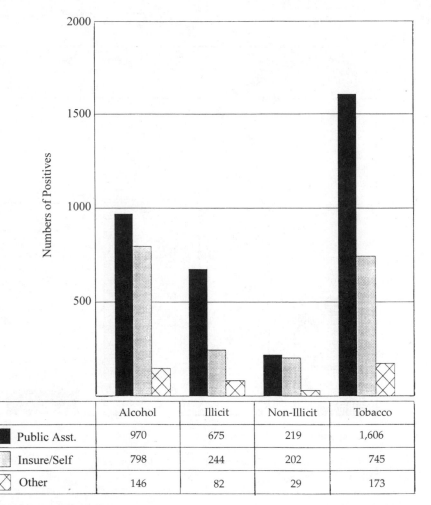

	Alcohol	Illicit	Non-Illicit	Tobacco
■ Public Asst.	970	675	219	1,606
▨ Insure/Self	798	244	202	745
⊠ Other	146	82	29	173

* Payment source definitions:

Insure/Self = Private or commercial insurance, CHAMPUS, or self-pay; Public Asst. = MediCal/Medi-Cal Managed Care or Pending MediCal, or other public assistance; Other = any other means of pay.

FIGURE 3 Distribution of perinatal substance exposures by primary payer* in California, 1992 (Source: Perinatal Substance Exposure Study – General Report, California Department of Alcohol and Drug Programs, September 1993)

their approach to obtaining consent for drug test. Many hospitals rely on the conditions-of-admission form that patients are asked to sign authorizing the hospital to perform a variety of medically necessary routine procedures (Noble 1992). Other facilities require pregnant women to sign a consent form authorizing numerous tests including toxicology screens. Others avoid the issue of informed consent by testing the urine of infants rather than mothers. There is also wide variation in hospitals' assessment whether testing and reporting are legitimate activities. Studies have documented that public hospitals, and others that routinely treat poor women, are more likely to test (Noble 1992; Humphries et al. 1992; Robin-Vergeer 1990). Hospitals that mainly treat middle-class women with health-insurance policies are more likely to be nervous about testing without consent. As a consequence, these hospitals are more likely to rely on subjective factors in their determinations to test. This allows for discretionary practices by hospital nurses and physicians that, of course, potentially result in discriminatory decisions about who gets tested. One study revealed that one such hospital had a policy that infant drug tests could be ordered if the mother simply 'acts strangely,' and that the children of poor women and women of colour were more likely to be singled out than wealthier white women, even when their mothers' behaviour was equally bizarre (Robin-Vergeer 1990).

An informed consent explains the risks and benefits associated with a procedure and ensures that the patient's consent is voluntary (English 1990). At least one legal advocate has suggested that where a positive toxicology screen triggers mandatory reporting and potential criminal prosecution or deprivation of custody, these consequences should be disclosed to the patient is she if to make an informed decision to undergo drug testing (Moss 1990).

Recent studies reveal that, for the hospital as an organization, the issue of drug screening and reporting of delivering women or their infants is sometimes quite contentious. A nationwide survey of the medical training program queried obstetricians and pediatricians about their views on reporting cocaine use and exposure. Nearly twice as many pediatricians favoured reporting than did obstetricians, a view that perhaps reflects the patient with whom they most identify. Also important, pediatricians were twice as willing as obstetricians to want a policy of involuntary drug treatment (Pelham and DeJong 1992).

Similarly, a study of screening and reporting policies in five large hospitals in two California counties found that physicians in these two

specialties often disagreed about policy and practices, and such dis-
agreements resulted in the hospitals operating without formal policies
and protocols and thus with discretionary screening and reporting.
Nurses and social workers tended to support pediatricians in their
desire to enact policies to identify perinatal substance use, while obstetricians acted as obstructionists, claiming that there was not enough
drug treatment available, and a lack of information about whether treatment 'works' for this population. Obstetricians further worried that
women might be prosecuted or otherwise punished, and that testing
and reporting would lead to a lack of business (Zellman et al. 1993).

Consequences of Reporting

When a child-abuse report is made, there are several possible consequences. Many counties put police holds on children so that their mothers cannot remove them from the hospital until an investigation is
complete. Workers can make 'family maintenance' contracts with parents, where parents agree to certain forms of 'help' that include random
drug screening, drug treatment, and parenting classes. The duration of a
family-maintenance contract is open-ended. The welfare worker has the
power to decide when to close the case, or whether more drastic action
should be taken.

But mothers are not always given the option of family-maintenance
contracts. Their cases can be taken to the juvenile court for a dependency hearing, and the court may decide to dismiss the petition and
enact a family-maintenance agreement. The court may allow the baby to
remain in the home and order the mother into services and treatment.
The family, welfare worker, and judge meet at various intervals to
assess progress.

There is another common outcome: drug-exposed babies are removed
from the home and placed in foster care or with relatives. Parents are
allowed to spend very little time with their children, and are given
eighteen months to fulfil a plan in order to regain custody. Such plans
revolve around the mother's willingness to enter drug treatment and be
a successful client. If she doesn't fulfil such a plan, she may lose custody
altogether.

Just as poor women and women of colour experience an increased
likelihood of being tested and reported for drugs when they deliver
their children, poverty and race/ethnic-group status may determine
child-welfare dispositions. A recent study of custody decisions made

about cocaine-exposed infants in a large New York City hospital revealed that the major predictors to children being placed in foster care were that their mothers were African American and that they had previous records with child-welfare agents (Neuspiel et al. 1993). The authors point out that previous child-welfare records may act as a convenient way to identify mothers 'at risk' for subsequent parenting deficiencies, especially when such agencies are overtaxed. They also elaborate that the African American population under study, like African American communities in most U.S. inner cities, have less available extended-family support because of the severity of drug addiction, unemployment, homelessness, and limited access to basic health care. Lack of social resources for housing, employment, and health care, they argue, may predispose to loss of child custody.

A study in one large county in northern California followed referrals to child protective services for infants with positive drug screens. The researchers found that Hispanics and African Americans were overrepresented by 11 per cent and 28.5 per cent respectively. Mothers were predominantly single, and the majority had not completed high school and were unemployed. Nearly 50 per cent of the infants in this study were temporarily removed from their mother's care, and 57 per cent of those cases ended with a permanent placement outside of the home (Sagatun-Edwards et al. 1995).

In the United States, the national foster-care population was in decline in the early 1980s, but since then has soared. By 1989, there were 360,000 children in foster care, and most of the increase had occurred since 1987. More than half of the increase occurred in just two states: New York and California. In New York, the numbers of infants placed in foster care soared during the 1980s, coinciding with the crack cocaine 'drug war.' In 1989, there were more than 5000 such infants, nearly four times as many as in 1985 (Wulczyn 1992). In California, the numbers are strikingly similar. By 1989, there were about 4400 infants in foster care, also four times as many as in 1985 (CWDAC 1990). Most child-welfare officials will testify that the increases in foster care were due to the perceived drug epidemic.

Confirming those studies (Neuspiel et al. 1993; Chasnoff et al. 1990) that point to the likelihood that African Americans will be reported and their children removed is California's data on the race/ethnicity of children in foster care. Approximately 49,000 minority children were in out-of-home care in 1989, representing 62 per cent of all children in placement. African American children were especially disproportionately involved with the child-welfare system. African American children represent 7 per cent of California's total population and 26 per cent of children entering foster care (CWDAC 1990). In addition, African American children represent 34 per cent of children residing in foster-family homes and 44 per cent of children residing with relatives as guardians.

These actions are meant to protect children, and in that sense they are understandable. There is literature that attests to the problems of parenting while heavily using alcohol or other drugs (Bays 1990; Famularo et al. 1992). The concerns about parenting while using or drinking are linked, for the most part, to risks of child neglect rather than child abuse. For example, one commonly cited concern is that parental time and resources are occupied with obtaining and using drugs, so that significant amounts of time and money are not available to children. Also common are concerns about parental engagement in criminal activity, bringing stress to households and possible arrests and separations. Parents who are addicts or alcoholics are also likely to be physically and mentally vulnerable, which may affect their parenting abilities (Bays 1990).

Still, many have pointed to reasons for reconsidering such protective actions, beyond issues of the discriminatory manner in which identification and disposition take place. Often these actions are based on the outcome of urine toxicology tests, a technology that gives us very limited information. Such tests can only detect very recent use, and tell us nothing about the extent of the person's use. That such tests are linked to serious interventions has been a matter of concern for policy-making groups (Task Force on Substance Exposed Infants 1990). Such groups have argued against the presumption that if one tests positive for drugs, one is likely to be an abusive or neglectful parent. Others point to the fact that there is no research that demonstrates that the use of drugs during pregnancy is *predictive* of child abuse or neglect (Larson 1991).

That infants are often removed from parental custody in drug cases can be devastating for both women and children. Researchers have noted that motherhood is often the woman addict's only claim to personal and social worthiness. Losing custody often begins a downward spiral in women's drug careers (Rosenbaum 1981). Moreover, these laws and practices have produced what is known in the United States as the 'boarder baby' crisis, wherein newborns sometimes languish in hospitals for months awaiting investigations and foster homes (Humphries et al. 1992). In New York City, medical experts testified that the lining-up of infants in bassinets resembled army barracks, and that once the infants learned to walk, the tops of their cribs were covered with bars in order to control them (Bussiere and Shauffer 1990). Lawsuits led to limitations on the amount of time infants stayed in hospitals, but also increased the recruitment of new foster-care providers and foster-care placements.

The psychological damage experienced by children placed in foster care is only part of what drug-exposed children might experience. Such children, especially cocaine-exposed children, have been labelled as irremediably damaged. At best, such labels result in lowered expectations. These children will be treated as 'different' by teachers and other adults who interact with them. If their mothers lose custody, such children will ultimately have more difficulty than most in the foster-care system. Foster parents are reluctant to care for children with 'impairments.' That same reluctance is bound to be experienced by potential adoptive parents. These labelling problems are so severe that a group of physicians wrote an opinion piece for the *Journal of the American Medical Association* asking that social, health, and educational institutions and policy makers suspend judgment about the developmental outcomes of cocaine-exposed children until solid scientific data were available (Mayes et al. 1992).

Doing Time in Treatment

What happens to women once identified as drug users? What is the nature of the prescribed treatment? Using a case study of a day-treatment program in southern California will help to illustrate the services women are expected to participate in, once identified as using while pregnant. In this particular county, every identified drug-exposed baby was taken from hospitals to a facility that held infants and children for foster care and adoptions. A dependency hearing was held for every reported case. In January 1990, twenty-five such cases were reported per month or about three hundred cases per year. Mothers temporarily lost custody and were ordered into treatment. One program they were referred to was a highly structured day-treatment program. Treatment was a combination of group and individual therapy, with the real emphasis on group therapy. In addition, clients were urine-tested twice a week. Because judges considered a 'no show' for a urine test to amount to dirty urine, clients had incentive to show up for tests. Dirty urines were strong evidence against regaining custody (Noble 1992).

It was a demanding nine-month program, done in phases. There were very strict rules with which the client had to comply. Rules included being on time for appointments, regular attendance, and regular urine testing. Non-compliance meant that clients must re-enter at the first phase. Clients were allowed three re-entries. After the third violation, they were restricted from receiving treatment at any county drug facility for ninety days. The director of the program said: 'These actions aren't meant to be punitive, but to keep them motivated. The restriction from other county clinics keeps them focused here. If they drop out, it doesn't necessarily mean they've failed. It's part of the disease [addiction]. If they come back, we count that as a success. She [client] knows she has a problem.' The problem with this explanation is that it didn't appear that child-welfare workers and the courts shared the disease ideology. When clients dropped out of the program, or even performed poorly in the beginning, it looked bad for them in court, and resulted in serious custody consequences.

The original intent of the program was that it serve pregnant and parenting women. Only 10 per cent of clients, however, were pregnant at any given time in the program. According to the director: 'We've learned that pregnant addicts won't seek treatment even if it is available to them. It makes no sense to target that population. They are afraid to seek treatment because they think they will either be sent to jail or have their babies taken away.' The fears expressed by pregnant drug users were justified. Most of the clients, at least 95 per cent, were women who had been referred to the program by Child Protective Services (CPS). They had lost temporary custody of their children because of what CPS and the courts had determined was child abuse or neglect related to their drug use while pregnant. It was mandatory that those clients attend and do well in the program in order to regain custody of their children.

Clients tended to drop out in the early phases of the program, which their therapists characterized as most difficult for everyone. One therapist said, 'The women are angry because they are mandated to be here. They tend to be openly hostile.' This was a very personally demanding program, and the women had no choice about 'working it' if they wanted to get their children back. Another source of anger for the clients was that fathers were not similarly ordered into such programs. Unless a father admitted to drug use or had a history of drug arrests, he might not be ordered to do anything. If he was, programs for men were less structured, time consuming, and personally demanding. Fathers were not, for example, required to attend parenting classes (Noble 1992).

This program was heralded as a model program at both state and national levels, and, as such, is disturbing. According to the director, the program had attempted but failed to convince pregnant women to enter the program voluntarily. The women were reluctant to do so because they feared arrest or the loss of their children. These fears were discredited and the absence of safe medical care for pregnant drug users ignored. Instead, the solution was to coerce women into treatment when they had given birth to drug-exposed babies.

The availability of publicly funded prenatal care is a serious problem in the United States. In many California counties, there is simply no prenatal care available. In others, women are on waiting lists for up to six months. This is a complex issue involving eligibility criteria, reimbursement rates, malpractice-insurance premiums, and the ability of physicians to refuse to treat patients they consider high-risk (Perkins and Stoll 1987). Even when system capacity is adequate and providers are willing to take publicly funded patients, participation may be limited for other reasons. Services are often poorly coordinated, service hours are inconvenient, waits are lengthy, personnel are rude, and surroundings are uncomfortable. Women may also face transportation problems, cultural and language barriers, and problems arranging for child care.

These factors combine to leave many women without prenatal care or with extremely limited care (Brown 1989). Meanwhile, medical solutions to the problem take the form of demands for more alcohol- and drug-treatment dollars, and these funds have been forthcoming. California now spends approximately $40 million annually on treatment programs for pregnant and parenting women. The problem of access to health care is shoved aside, and the 'solution' appears to lie in suspecting those who haven't been able to get health care, drug testing them, mandating treatment, and using the possibility of loss of custody as punishment if women don't 'get well.'

Conclusion

There are medical forms of coercion and punishment that confront women who are suspected of delivering drug-exposed babies. Simply put, medical and treatment officials and practitioners work hand in hand with child-welfare agents and the family and juvenile courts to define such women as child abusers. These control measures are largely focused on poor women and women of colour. Such practices make already limited access to prenatal care and drug treatment unsafe. A pregnant woman with a drug problem understands that the threat of arrest or loss of custody originates from those to whom she might turn for help.

Once identified, the woman is handed to a treatment community that psychologizes her problems. Her experiences with poverty, unemployment, racial and ethnic discrimination, and strained familial or social resources are flattened. She is forced to participate in a program like the case study presented above, where sessions are held during normal working hours, preventing her from working. She may have to travel long distances and make arrangements for the care of her children while she is 'working the program.' She endures these conditions in order to prove herself worthy of motherhood.

The absence of accessible and safe medical care and drug and alcohol treatment should not serve as justification for mandated approaches to 'getting well.' The use of legal sanctions, however, has assumed a position of prominence in California. This is due to the construction of social and public-health policies that individualize problems. Blaming individual women leads to detection efforts that are based on class and race, and to involuntary treatment. 'Getting well' becomes a matter of internalizing white middle-class notions of the etiology of addiction and putting aside the social factors that may have led to alcohol or drug use. This response to the problem ignores its social base, and blames, rather than helps, its victims.

Many Californians embrace the notion that their state's policies on pregnancy and drug use are progressive and public health–oriented. They focus on the fact that legislation that would prosecute pregnant drug users was defeated. They also point to the expansion of drug and alcohol treatment now available for pregnant and parenting women. That such programs are important is not disputed, nor is the fact that many states suffer from a lack of programs willing to admit pregnant women and women with small children. It is important nevertheless to point to the racism and the punishment of the poor that is inherent in the current system of 'risk factors' that lead to testing, reporting, and coerced treatment.

It is true that in California pregnant women with drug or alcohol problems are largely viewed as 'sick,' but this definition is not without punitive consequences. Such women are 'bad' as well as 'sick.' Medical professionals attribute 'badness' to such women when they identify and report them to child protective workers. Treatment providers accommodate the 'badness' definition as well, working with social workers and judges on cases. Officially, California defined this problem as a 'disease,' but the mothers who deliver drug-exposed babies have a special 'disease' for which they receive special attention: they are child abusers as well.

NOTES

1 The U.S. war on crack cocaine and the role of the media in creating a moral panic about drugs are explicated by Reinarman and Levine 1989. Also see Cohen 1980 on moral panics in general.
2 Illicit drugs refers to methamphetamines, cannabinoids (marijuana, hashish), cocaine, phencyclidine (PCP), and opiates not available by prescription. Non-illicit drugs refers to amphetamines, barbiturates, benzodiazepines, methadone, and opiates that are available by prescription but were not prescribed by the attending physician before urine was tested
3 The categories of method of payment for birth appearing in figure 3 are insured/self-pay, publicly assisted, and other. Included in the insured/self-pay category are those women with private, commercial, or military insurance policies, or those who were uninsured but could pay for the birth. Included in the publicly assisted category are those women who were eligible for MediCal (California's version of Medicaid, available to those who meet certain low-income eligibility criteria), those who were assessed as probably eligible for MediCal, and those whose births would probably be covered by county forms of assistance for low-income women who are not eligible for MediCal. The other category means any other means of pay.
4 Prevalence study findings include rates for alcohol, a substance that is not, to my knowledge, routinely tested for in hospitals. I have argued elsewhere (Noble 1992) that alcohol, when used in excess during pregnancy, can cause far greater fetal damage than any other substance, including cocaine. That hospitals don't test for alcohol can be explained, in part, because it is legal, but also because it is used by many white, middle-class women.

REFERENCES

Bays, J. 1990. 'Substance Abuse and Child Abuse: Impact of Addiction on the Child.' *Pediatric Clinics of North America* 37: 881–904.
Brown, S.S. 1989. 'Drawing Women into Prenatal Care.' *Family Planning Perspectives* 21: 73–80.
Bussiere, A., and C. Shauffer. 1990. 'The Little Prisoners.' *Youth Law News* 11: 22–6.

Chasnoff, I., H.J. Landress, and M.E. Barrett. 1990. 'The Prevalence of Illicit Drug or Alcohol Use during Pregnancy and Discrepancies in Mandatory Reporting in Pinellas County, Florida.' *New England Journal of Medicine* 322: 1202–6.

Cohen, S. 1980. *Folk Devils and Moral Panics: The Creation of the Mods and the Rockers*. 2nd ed. New York: St Martin's Press.

CWDAC (Country Welfare Directors Association of California.) 1990. 'Ten Reasons to Invest in the Families of California: Reasons to Invest in Services Which Prevent Out-of-Home Placement and Preserve Families.' Report published by the Association, Sacramento.

English, A. 1990. 'Prenatal Drug Exposure: Grounds for Mandatory Child Abuse Reports?' *Youth Law News* 11: 3–8.

Famularo, R., R. Kinscherff, and T. Fenton. 1992. 'Parental Substance Abuse and the Nature of Child Maltreatment.' *Journal of Child Abuse and Neglect* 16: 475–83.

Hampton, R.L., and E.H. Newberger. 1985. 'Child Abuse Incidence and Reporting by Hospitals: Significance of Severity, Class, and Race.' *American Journal of Public Health* 75: 56–60.

Humphries, D., J. Dawson, V. Cronin, P. Keating, C. Wisniewski, and J. Eichfield. 1992. 'Mothers and Children, Drugs and Crack: Reactions to Maternal Drug Dependency.' *Women and Criminal Justice* 3: 81–99.

Kogen, D., M. Kotelchuck, G.R. Alexander, and W.E. Johnson. 1994. 'Racial Disparities in Reported Prenatal Care Advice from Health Care Providers.' *American Journal of Public Health* 84: 82–8.

Larson, C.S. 1991. 'Overview of State Legislative and Judicial Responses.' *The Future of Children* 1: 72–84.

Mayes, L.C., R.H. Granger, M.H. Bornstein, and B. Zuckerman. 1992. 'The Problem of Prenatal Cocaine Exposure: A Rush to Judgment.' *Journal of the American Medical Association* 267: 406–8.

Moss, K. 1990. 'Legal Issues: Drug Testing of Postpartum Women and Newborns as the Basis for Civil and Criminal Proceedings.' *Clearinghouse Review* 23: 1406–14.

Neuspiel, D.R., T.M. Zingman, V.H. Templeton, P. DiStabile, and E. Drucker. 1993. 'Custody of Cocaine-Exposed Newborns: Determinants of Discharge Decisions.' *American Journal of Public Health* 83: 1726–29.

Noble, A. 1992. 'Law, Medicine and Women's Bodies: The Social Control of Pregnant Drug Users.' Doctoral dissertation, University of California – Davis.

– 1994. 'Efforts to Identify and Assess the Needs of Substance-Using Delivering Women: The Implementation of Senate Bill 2669 in California's Counties.' California Department of Alcohol and Drug Programs, Sacramento.

Pelham, T.R., and A.R. DeJong. 1992. 'Nationwide Practices for Screening and

Reporting Prenatal Cocaine Abuse: A Survey of Teaching Programs.' *Child Abuse and Neglect* 16: 763–70.

Perkins, J., and K. Stoll. 1987. 'Medical Malpractice: A "Crisis" for Poor Women.' *Clearinghouse Review* 16: 1277–86.

Reinarman, C., and H. Levine. 1989. 'The Crack Attack: Politics and Media in America's Latest Drug Scare.' In J. Best, ed., *Images of Issues: Typifying Contemporary Social Problems*, 115–37. Hawthorne, NY: Aldine de Gruyter.

Robin-Vergeer, B. 1990. 'The Problem of the Drug-Exposed Newborn: A Return to Principled Intervention.' *Stanford Law Review* 42: 745–809.

Rosenbaum, M. 1981. *Women on Heroin*. New Brunswick, NJ: Rutgers University Press.

Sagatun-Edwards, I.J., C. Saylor, and B. Shifflet. 1995. 'Drug-Exposed Infants in the Social Welfare System and the Juvenile Court.' *Child Abuse and Neglect* 19: 83–91.

Task Force on Substance Exposed Infants. 1990. *Final Report*. Sacramento, CA: Joint Publications.

Tsing, A. 1991. 'Monster Stories: Women Charged with Perinatal Endangerment.' In F. Ginsburg and A. Tsing, eds, *Uncertain Terms: Negotiating Gender in American Culture*, 282–99. Boston: Beacon Press.

Vega, W.A., A. Noble, B. Kolody, P. Porter, J. Hwang, and A. Bole. 1993. 'Profile of Alcohol and Drug Use during Pregnancy in California 1992: Perinatal Substance Exposure Study General Report.' California Department of Alcohol and Drug Programs, Sacramento.

Wiley, K., B. Gibbs, S. Kahn, R. Karlman, A. Tse, and R. Perez-Woods. 1991. 'Prevalence of Illicit Drug Use among Prenatal Patients and Predictive Validity of Nurses' Judgments.' *Journal of Perinatology* 11: 330–5.

Wulczyn, F. 1992. 'Status at Birth and Infant Foster Care Placement in New York City.' Report for the New York State Department of Social Services.

Zellman, G.L., P.D. Jacobson, H. DuPlessis, and M.R. DiMattio. 1993. 'Detecting Prenatal Substance Exposure: An Exploratory Analysis and Policy Discussion.' *Journal of Drug Issues* 23: 375–87.

PART III: ALCOHOL AND PUBLIC HEALTH

11 Towards a Harm Reduction Approach to Alcohol-Problem Prevention

ERIC SINGLE

Harm reduction was developed as an approach to deal with problems associated with illicit drug use, and we tend to think of it in this context. The basic thesis of this paper, however, is that the trend towards harm reduction in illicit drugs is closely paralleled by a similar trend in measures aimed at reducing the consequences of heavy-drinking occasions.

A variety of prevention measures have developed in the recent past that focus not so much on restricting drinking occasions, but rather on reducing the harm that may arise when drinking takes place. In the following discussion several examples will be presented, including measures to reduce non-beverage alcohol consumption by skid-row inebriates, measures to reduce intake of alcohol by drinkers (e.g., promotion of low-alcohol beverages and server training programs), and measures to reduce the consequences of intoxication. It will be argued that increased attention is likely to be given to prevention measures that focus on preventing problems associated with drinking rather than on restricting access to alcohol. The trend to harm reduction approaches for alcohol is supported by evidence that it is more effective to target heavy-drinking occasions rather than level of drinking in prevention programming. Data from a recent national survey in Canada indicate that the number of heavy-drinking occasions is a better predictor of alcohol problems than an individual's overall level of consumption.

Whereas the contrast between harm reduction approaches for illicit drugs and a 'zero tolerance' approach is almost self-evident, the parallel differences between harm reduction approaches for alcohol and prevailing conceptualizations of alcohol prevention are perhaps less obvious. Table 1 (p. 197) contrasts the conceptual differences between harm reduction and alternative approaches to alcohol prevention. The alternative approaches are temperance, the disease concept of alcoholism, and the public-health approach to alcohol problems.

– Temperance: According to the temperance perspective, the primary problem with alcohol is drinking per se. Alcohol use is viewed as an indicator of moral weakness and it inevitably leads to a decline in moral behaviour. The goal of prevention is abstinence for the entire population, to be achieved through moral education and legal prohibition.

– The disease concept: With the repeal of Prohibition in the early part of this century in many Western societies, the temperance perspective was largely displaced by the disease concept. According to this perspective, the primary problem of alcohol is the disease of alcoholism. Alcoholics are seen as fundamentally different from normal, social drinkers. The purpose of public policy is to provide access to alcohol for the majority of drinkers who do not suffer from this disease, and to provide treatment and encourage abstention for those who do. While clearly preferable in many ways to the moralistic attitudes of temperance, the disease concept shifted the locus of blame for alcohol problems from the bottle to the drinker, and helped to justify the liberalization of alcohol-control policy. As stated in an alcohol-industry brief to government, 'Just as sugar is not the cause of diabetes, alcohol is not the cause of alcoholism.'

– The public-health perspective: In the 1960s and 1970s, the disease concept was increasingly questioned by epidemiologists. The primacy of alcoholism as the major alcohol problem was challenged. It was noted that for many alcohol-related disorders, there are risks associated with moderate consumption as well as heavy drinking. Therefore, research and prevention programming began to focus on individual levels of consumption rather than alcoholism. The use of controls over alcohol availability was advocated, not to the point of Prohibition (and not to prevent immorality), but as a means to reduce (or at least prevent further increases in) levels of alcohol-related health and social problems. The public-health perspective uses the classic paradigm of agent (i.e., alcohol), individual, and environment to explain variations in problem levels and to address prevention efforts. Research focuses not only on the individual but on the impact of environmental factors and public policy towards alcohol. The focus of prevention has shifted from medical treatment to (a) the agent: reasonable controls over production and distribution of alcohol, (b) the individual: early

TABLE 1
The emphases of harm reduction versus alternative models

	Temperance	Disease concept	Public-health perspective	Harm reduction
Primary problem	Immorality of use per se, evidenced by related immorality	Dependence and health effects	Health and social consequences	Particularly severe consequences, such as AIDS, impaired driving
Underlying problem and process	Moral weakness – inevitable	Disease – progressive for those vulnerable	Interaction of agent, individual, and environment; increasing risk of adverse effects for all	Consequences largely stem from circumstances of use, not use per se
Intervention point	Total population	Alcohol-dependent	Continuum of risk	Highest priority to most severe problems
Intervention goal	Abstinence	Abstinence for those suffering from disease	Reduced risk (controlled drinking may be appropriate)	Reduced harm
Prevention measures	Prohibition	Medical treatment	(a) Agent: production and quality controls; (b) individual: education, brief intervention, treatment; (c) environment: availability controls	Safer supply (e.g., low-alcohol drinks), measures to avoid adverse effects (e.g., safe transport), education
Focus of education	Morality	Biomedical aspects, genetic predisposition	Level of consumption, early detection	Avoiding heavy drinking and/or related problems

detection and intervention, and (c) environment: social norms concerning the appropriate use of alcohol.
– Harm reduction: Harm reduction is not an alternative but rather a specific aspect of the public-health approach to alcohol prevention. It represents that aspect of the public-health model that applies to acute alcohol problems, particularly among heavy users. Unlike temperance, harm reduction focuses on the consequences of use, not use per se, as the primary problem to be addressed. Unlike the disease concept, it does not view abstinence as the only treatment goal. Prevention focuses on the provision of a safer supply (e.g., low-alcohol-content drinks) and measures to avoid adverse consequences (e.g., provision of safe transport).

Examples of Harm Reduction in the Prevention of Alcohol Problems

Harm reduction differs from (and thus complements) prior alcohol prevention in that it focuses on decreasing the risk and severity of adverse consequences arising from alcohol consumption without necessarily decreasing the level of consumption. It is essentially a practical rather than an idealized approach: the standard of success is not some ideal drinking level or situation (abstention or low-risk levels), but whether or not the chances of adverse consequences have been reduced by the introduction of the prevention measure.

An excellent example of a harm reduction approach to alcohol is provided by the introduction of special early opening hours for a store of the Alberta Liquor Control Board in downtown Edmonton. The objective of the early opening was to reduce the use of potentially lethal non-beverage alcohol by skid-row inebriates. The measure was not intended to reduce their consumption; indeed, it was expected to increase their consumption of *potable* alcohol. It was focused exclusively on reducing adverse consequences from drinking things like shoe polish. Other examples of harm reduction measures for the prevention of alcohol problems include the following:

– Measures that reduce the consequences of intoxication: This would include measures not specifically aimed at reducing drinking problems, such as the introduction of airbags into cars (which reduce the number of alcohol-related traffic injuries and fatalities) as well as measures aimed at reducing the consequences of intoxication, such as changes in the physical structuring of drinking establishments that minimize the harm that may result if a fight breaks out (e.g., compartmentalization of space and padding of furniture). Another example of a measure aimed specifically at reducing the consequences of drinking is the 'Nez Rouge' program in Quebec, which is a community-based service providing two drivers (one for the drinker and one for his or her car) to anyone who feels that he or she has had too much to drink at a party or a licensed establishment to drive home safely.

- The promotion of low-alcohol beverages: Light beers, low-alcohol-content wines, and even light spirits have been introduced in many countries in recent years. These beverages can reduce ethanol intake without reducing the overall volume (i.e., liquid intake) of drinking. Thus, they maintain industry profitability and serve a public-health purpose at the same time.

- Server training programs: Server training represents a harm reduction measure in several respects. Most programs involve the development of house policies to promote moderation (for instance, quality upgrading, pricing lower-alcohol-content beverages below higher-strength beverages, avoiding Happy Hours, and other volume discounts or specials). They may also involve policies (e.g., designated driver programs) or environmental modifications (e.g., via monitoring of entrances to prevent the entry of underage or intoxicated persons) to reduce the likelihood that problems will occur. Staff are trained to recognize and gradually cease service to intoxicated patrons, offering low-alcohol or non-alcoholic alternatives. To deal with situations in which these prevention efforts fail, servers are also trained to manage intoxicated patrons in the appropriate manner, including strategies to provide safe transport home. Thus, server training attempts to reduce the problems associated with drinking without generally restricting drinking by the majority of drinkers or adversely affecting the profitability of licensed establishments. (In fact, evaluation studies have generally shown that establishments that have undergone server intervention training tend to attract more customers and be more profitable as a result of the introduction of responsible serving practices.)

- Controlled drinking programs: The provision of controlled drinking as a treatment alternative for alcohol-dependent persons might also be thought of as a harm reduction measure, although it could reasonably be argued that the harm from drinking is not merely reduced but eliminated if drinking is successfully controlled. The often acrimonious debate concerning controlled drinking versus abstinence as a treatment goal for persons with alcohol problems parallels in many ways the conflict between harm reduction and zero tolerance approaches regarding illicit drug use.

The Trend towards Harm Reduction in Alcohol Problem Prevention

Most of these examples of harm reduction measures are relatively new. There is a distinct trend towards prevention measures aimed not so much at the reduction of drinking per se as at a reduction in the harmful consequences of drinking. There are several reasons for this shift in alcohol problem prevention towards a harm reduction approach.

There is declining political support for controls over the availability of alcohol, especially in light of declining consumption in many countries and the erosion of international trade barriers. This trend is likely to continue as new evidence regarding the potential benefits of moderate consumption becomes more widely publicized. Increased attention is likely to be given to prevention measures that focus on preventing problems associated with drinking rather than restricting access to alcohol. The harm reduction approach focuses on preventing problems associated with heavy-drinking occasions. Rather than attempting to persuade light and moderate drinkers to reduce their level of consumption (e.g., on the grounds that they contribute to overall levels of consumption and may therefore influence someone else to drink excessively), this perspective focuses on environmental controls such as server intervention and preventive education to convince drinkers at all levels of consumption to avoid drinking to intoxication and to minimize the harm that may result from drinking.

Furthermore, there is empirical support for the focus on heavy-drinking occasions. An analysis of data from a Canadian national survey conducted in 1989 (Single and Wortley 1993) indicates that it is more efficient to focus on heavy-drinking occasions among all drinkers rather than focus on the individual's level of consumption per se. In this analysis, both the level of consumption and number of times respondents reported consuming five or more drinks on an occasion were related to a series of alcohol problems. It was found that

– the number of heavy-drinking occasions is a stronger predictor of drinking problems than level of consumption, and
– there is an interaction effect regarding the joint impact of the number of heavy-drinking occasions and level of consumption, with particularly high rates of alcohol problems among low-level drinkers who occasionally drink immoderately.

TABLE 2
Probability of experiencing a drinking problem by heavy-drinking occasions and level of consumption

	Number of heavy-drinking occasions*			
Drinks per year	None	One	Two to six	Seven and more
1–51	2%	8%	7%	17%
52–364	2%	8%	10%	21%
365 and more	7%	5%	14%	35%

*Number of times in the past twelve months respondent consumed five or more drinks on one occasion.

Table 2 presents more recent data from the 1993 General Social Survey in Canada on the joint impact of level of consumption and number of heavy-drinking occasions on the likelihood of a person's experiencing a drinking problem. It can be seen that the likelihood of experiencing drinking problems is greater for a moderate-level drinker who occasionally drinks immoderately than for a high-level consumer who rarely or never drinks immoderately.[1] This finding may be associated with physical tolerance as well as the tendency for high-volume drinkers to develop social supports and other mechanisms to minimize the adverse consequences of their drinking. Of course, there are limits to which heavy drinkers can control adverse consequences: over time, heavy drinking will greatly elevate the risk of chronic health consequences such as cirrhosis. Nonetheless, for many of the more acute alcohol problems, such as impaired driving, alcohol-related family dysfunction, or employment problems, relatively low-level consumers who occasionally drink immoderately contribute substantially to problem levels.

These findings indicate that it may be most efficient to focus specifically on reducing heavy-drinking occasions among all drinkers. This approach contrasts with that of focusing on high-volume consumers or on the aggregate level of consumption per se. This is not to say that programs specifically targeted at high-risk drinkers, such as early identification and intervention programs, should not be supported. These would undoubtedly result in the reduction of alcohol problems. However, programs focusing on reducing overall levels of alcohol consumption should not be adopted to the exclusion of approaches that focus instead on heavy-drinking occasions. Indeed, the findings above indicate that the most efficient approach may be to target preventive education at the general population (as it is persons who consume alcohol at levels below that associated with alcohol dependence who contribute the most to problem levels), but focus on safe drinking limits and the avoidance of intoxication and other behaviours likely to cause problems rather than on the individual's overall level of consumption.

In conclusion, the trend towards harm reduction in illicit drugs is paralleled by a similar trend in alcohol prevention towards measures aimed at reducing the consequences of heavy-drinking occasions. With the erosion of political support for alcohol control measures and the emergence of new evidence about potential health benefits associated with low-level alcohol consumption, it may be expected that alcohol prevention will increasingly focus on the reduction of the harmful consequences of alcohol rather than on monitoring individual levels of consumption to avoid dependence.

NOTES

1 A multivariate regression analysis controlling for socio-demographic variables and drinking venues shows that the number of heavy-drinking occasions is a far stronger predictor of alcohol-related problems than is level of consumption.

REFERENCES

Single, E., and S. Wortley. 1993. 'Drinking in Various Settings as It Relates to Socio-Demographic Variables and Levels of Consumption: Findings from a National Survey in Canada.' Journal of Studies on Alcohol 54: 590–9.
Stockwell, T., E. Lang, P. Rydon, and A. Lockwood. 1992. 'High Risk Drinking Settings: The Association of Serving and Promotional Practices with Harmful Drinking.' Mimeo, National Centre for Research into the Prevention of Drug Abuse, Perth.

12 Reducing Alcohol-Related Harm: A Balanced and Disaggregated Perspective*

MARTIN PLANT

This paper reviews some evidence related to the minimization of alcohol-related problems. Two types of data are considered. The first of these is an impressive array of evidence suggesting that abstainers share with 'heavy drinkers' a high rate of premature mortality from coronary heart disease and other causes. This evidence, from a variety of different countries, suggests that there are tangible health benefits derived from moderate, and even not-so-moderate, levels of alcohol consumption. One possible explanation for this is that drinking stimulates the production of high-density lipoprotein cholesterol. It is recommended that evidence on this protective effect should be integrated with the 'problem-oriented' epidemiology of alcohol. Public policy should be based upon a 'holistic' perspective.

Second, several local and national initiatives are considered. These indicate that it is possible to reduce the levels of alcohol-related problems significantly. These measures include policies on drunken driving, the use of local by-laws and policing strategies, and, finally, new evidence on the possible merits of 'toughened' beer glasses. It is widely and repeatedly acknowledged that 'heavy' or 'inappropriate' alcohol consumption incurs a massive toll of adverse consequences. The latter include illness, dependence ('alcoholism'), accidents, mortality, and a host of social, legal, occupational, and family problems. It is also evident that overall levels of 'alcohol-related problems' commonly fluctuate, at least in general terms, in association with levels of per capita alcohol consumption (Bruun et al. 1975; Royal College of Psychiatrists 1986; Sales et al. 1989).

* This text was processed by Ms Sheila McLennan. The Alcohol & Health Research Group receives core funds from the Portman Group.

Is Drinking Beneficial?

Preventive Paradox health based in public action risk reduction Ledermann dist.- of con-... models.

Adapting the work of Rose (1981), Kreitman has argued (1986) that the 'Preventive Paradox' is important in relation to alcohol-control policies. In essence this infers that if all drinkers in a population, even light and moderate drinkers, reduced their alcohol consumption, this would lead to a marked fall in alcohol-related problems. This view is based upon the assumption that although the heaviest drinkers have the highest rates of such problems, these people are in a small minority. Accordingly, it is argued, lighter drinkers, being far more numerous, have a bigger role to play in contributing to the total number of alcohol-related problems: lighter drinkers are urged to reduce their levels of alcohol consumption, thereby reducing their levels of risk as well as the total level of alcohol problems for society as a whole. This view is appealing: 'If everyone drank a bit less, we would all be better off.' Another way of interpreting this view is that if 'light' and 'moderate' drinkers consumed less this might redefine social norms and, possibly, influence heavier or 'higher risk' consumers. Conversely, it has also been argued that this view is as illogical as attempting to cope with one person's fever by having others taking a cold shower!

The force of argument supporting the relevance of the 'Preventive Paradox' is greatly weakened if there are health benefits associated with less than heavy alcohol consumption. In addition, if it is the case that it is healthier to drink than to abstain, it may not be sensible to urge *all* drinkers to consume less.

Much of the 'mainstream' literature on alcohol use and alcohol problems has examined the possible connections between levels and patterns of alcohol use and adverse effects. Econometric analyses have also emphasized the 'debit' rather than the 'credit' side of the alcohol equation: the latter is generally attributed to the fact that most of the possible benefits of drinking are intangible, or at least difficult to measure in economic terms. The consequence of this emphasis has been a problem-oriented epidemiology. The development of the latter is understandable since alcohol-related problems are commonplace and very serious in many cultures. Even so a mounting body of evidence has been produced that warrants close attention. This evidence also deserves to be integrated into the overall framework of alcohol epidemiology, not only for scientific reasons (to be complete) but also to guide clinical practice and public policy. A vast array of evidence supports the conclusion that 'heavy drinking' (variably defined) incurs elevated risks of illness, premature death, and other adverse effects. A growing and already impressive additional body of evidence supports another conclusion: abstainers die younger than do people who drink low/intermediate amounts (variably defined). The strength of this conclusion is derived from the fact that it is now supported by a series of independent studies from a variety of widely differing cultures. A heated debate has focused on this topic. As brilliantly observed by Haskell (1993), the alcohol field is highly politicized and some of the interlocutors have been motivated by ideology and emotion, rather than by the force of the evidence itself.

Several of important points have been raised. For example, it has been suggested that abstainers may be 'sick quitters' – former heavy drinkers who stopped drinking because of ill health. It has further been suggested that abstainers are a highly stressed, deviant minority, or possibly they are religious fundamentalists. These and several other possibilities have been examined, controlled, and discounted. Study after study had supported the view that drinking does have tangible health benefits. Moreover, most drinkers appear to consume levels consistent with these benefits. This fact appears to make some people uncomfortable. As noted by Mäkelä (1993), 'It may be inevitable that the bulk of alcohol research pays attention to the negative consequences of drinking. The institutional existence of alcohol studies as a special field is due to the fact that drinking causes problems. If this would not be the case, what would be left of alcohol research would be immersed in general studies of culture, general studies of consumer behavior, and so on. We drink alcohol because it is good for us, we study alcohol because it is bad for us.' Mäkelä further noted (in relation to a paper by Gusfield [1993]: 'If we adopt a narrowly pathological frame, we indeed cannot understand the very phenomena we are supposed to study.'

A number of studies indicate that myocardial infarction and coronary heart disease are less common amongst light/moderate drinkers than amongst abstainers or heavier drinkers (for example, Klatsky, Friedman, and Sieglelaub [1974] [USA]; Hennekens, Rosner, and Cole [1978] [USA]; Blackwelder et al. [1980]; [Honolulu]; Marmot et al. [1981] [UK]; Dyer et al. [1980] [USA]; Colditz et al. [1985] [USA]; Kaufman et al. [1985] [USA]; Kono et al. [1986] [Japan]; Shaper, Wannamethee and Walker [1988] [UK]; Boffetta and Garfinkel [1990] [USA]; Jackson, Scragg and Beaglehole [1991] [New Zealand]; Kono et al. [1991] [Japan]; Farchi et al. [1992] [Italy]).

Moreover, some studies also indicate that mortality from all causes is lowest amongst those who drink light/moderate amounts (see, for instance, Cullen, Knuiman, and Ward [1993] [Australia]; and Groen-baeck et al. [1994] [Denmark]). Several studies support the conclusion that moderate alcohol intake exerts a protective effect on heart disease: a recent report suggested that this may be due to alcohol stimulating the production of high-density lipoprotein (Gaziano et al. 1993) (USA).

As yet, there have been few attempts to either acknowledge the importance of this evidence or integrate it into the more general information about alcohol and its effects. This failure is curious and clearly warrants rectification. Selective epidemiology is poor science. One implication is that there may be no general health benefits to be derived from moderate drinkers becoming abstainers. In fact, such a transition might elevate mortality rates. Moreover, existing assumptions and guidelines related to 'low risk' or 'recommended' levels of alcohol consumption now need to be reconsidered in the light of *all* available evidence (Royal College of Psychiatrists 1986). A recent Danish study (Groenbaek et al. 1994) indicated that, for male and females, the lowest mortality risk was evident amongst those who consumed one to six alcoholic beverages per week. Even so, amongst drinkers this risk only rose significantly amongst those drinking more than forty-two (UK) drinks a week.* Surveys of alcohol consumption in Britain indicate that only a small minority, (less than 2 per cent of women and 10–12 per cent of men) consume such high levels (Foster, Wilmot, and Dobbs 1990). Evidence on the *apparent* beneficial effects of moderate drinking deserves acknowledgment and serious attention. It now needs to be weighed in the context of the impact of specific levels and patterns of alcohol consumption on other possible adverse consequences. As noted by Duffy (1993), this assessment has yet to be attempted. In the meantime it appears to be possible that the health benefits attributable to moderate drinking may at least equal the toll of ill health (if not the many behavioural problems) associated with heavy or inappropriate drinking. For example over 100,000 people die annually from acute myocardial infarction in Britain. The corresponding number of (mainly alcohol-fostered) liver cirrhosis deaths is around 3500 (Registrar General Scotland 1993; Government Statistical Office 1991). The distinction could usefully be emphasized by health education and public policy.

It has been suggested that evidence about the protective effects of

---

* Roughly equivalent to 26 standard U.S. drinks. A UK standard drink or unit contains approximately 1 centilitre/7.9 grams of absolute alcohol.

alcohol might complicate or confuse 'clear messages' for the general public. This view is patronizing in the extreme. It should be emphasized that the integration of these two rather separate alcohol epidemiologies is not intended to conceal or to minimize the scale of the adverse consequences of heavy or inappropriate drinking. It should further be acknowledged that many alcohol-related problems involve intermediate-level consumers and that many are attributable to acute intoxication rather than to chronic heavy drinking or alcohol dependence ('alcoholism'). Even so, epidemiologists have a duty to examine – and to present – the big picture, not just part of it.

Towards a Disaggregated Approach to Minimizing Alcohol Problems

Alcohol-control policies may be attempted at the macro or micro level. Macro-level policies, such as fiscal manipulation, are controversial and appear to be unpopular in most countries. Political support for such policies tends to fall if, as at present, national per capita levels of alcohol consumption are stable or declining. At the micro level a number of strategies have led to marked declines in rates of specific types of alcohol-related problems, quite independent of overall national levels of per capita alcohol consumption. Three examples of these are briefly considered.

1. Policies on Alcohol-Impaired Driving

Random breath testing (RBT) was introduced in Finland in 1977. It has also been introduced in Australia. In both countries this policy was followed by considerable decreases in levels of alcohol-impaired driving as measured by traffic surveys (Dunbar, Pentilla, and Pakkarainen 1987). A review by Peacock (1992) concluded that the most important factor behind the success of policies to deter the intoxicated or alcohol impaired driver is the *perceived* risk of being detected. It should be noted that, in both Finland and Australia, the fall in impaired driving vastly exceeded concurrent changes in per capita alcohol consumption in these countries. An interesting contrast is provided by British experience. Legislation on drunken driving in the United Kingdom is far less rigorous than that in Finland or Australia. In spite of this, between 1979 and 1989 the proportion of drivers killed in road accidents who were above the legal blood-alcohol level fell by approximately 50 per cent (Department of Transport 1990). During the same period, UK per capita alcohol consumption remained virtually unchanged (Brewers' Society 1993). The reason for this improvement – particularly evident among younger drivers – is unclear. Public attitudes towards drinking and driving have certainly been transformed, as clearly have behaviour patterns: driving under the influence has become socially unacceptable.

2. Police Policy: Enforcing the Law

There is evidence that a considerable impact may be made upon local rates of alcohol-related crimes by the rigorous enforcement of existing laws. Four examples are available from the United Kingdom, though a description of only one of these initiatives has been published in a scientific journal. Jeffs and Saunders (1983) described an experiment conducted in Torquay, a small coastal town in southern England. There was a local problem of public disorder and other offences associated with harbour-side bars. For the period of one year the town's police adopted vigorous activity in and around these bars. Bar owners were advised that liquor licensing laws would be stringently enforced. In particular, attention would be paid to legal closing times, serving drinks to under-age patrons, and the serving of drink to intoxicated people. During the experimental year (1978) all arrests in this town fell by 20.9 per cent. There was no change in a comparison town. After the experimental period, arrest rates rose again by 20 per cent.

This classic study has been widely discussed inside Britain. There is evidence that a comparable impact on levels of alcohol-related crimes (and in some cases other offences too) has been achieved in Sussex (Abbot 1993). In addition, local by-laws, the rigorous enforcement of existing laws, or the restriction of the late-night opening of licensed premises has been reported to have produced significant falls in rates of alcohol-related offences in two areas of Scotland, Motherwell (Ilgunas 1993) and West Lothian (McKenzie 1993).

3. Toughened Glasses: Safer Bars?

The classic Canadian work of Graham (1985) has suggested that the design and organization of the bar-room environment might influence levels of intoxication and aggression. Work by Shepherd, a British surgeon, and his colleagues has created interest in the possibility that accidental and non-accidental bar-room injuries may be reduced by the use of 'toughened' or 'tempered' beer glasses.

Drinking glasses are often used as weapons in bar-room assaults. Such assaults often inflict seriously disfiguring facial wounds. Some of these injuries blind or kill. It has been reported that the police in England and Wales annually record between 3,400 and 5,400 violent crimes in which glasses are used as weapons. Shepherd, Kinder, and Huggett (1991) have suggested that 'tempered' or 'toughened' glasses might be safer for use in licensed premises (note also Shepherd et al. 1990 and Shepherd, Price, and Shenfine 1990).

Linked pilot studies have been conducted in Scotland. The first of these involved a survey of the experiences of a random sample of one hundred public-bar managers in Edinburgh (Plant et al. 1994). The second involved the mechanical testing of toughened and non-toughened (or 'annealed') one-pint glasses. These later studies indicated that there is no such thing as a completely 'safe glass.' In spite of this both studies support the general conclusion that toughened glasses are stronger, safer and more durable. Even so, used or damaged glasses lose much of their initial safety advantage. It is recommended that national and international safety standards be required to minimize the potential dangers, not only of drinking glasses, but also of beer bottles (Alder 1993).

Conclusion

Alcohol and alcohol-related problems are complicated phenomena. Simple or reductionist 'solutions' are frequently impractical or ineffective. Accordingly, it is suggested that an experimental, balanced, and pragmatic approach should be adopted to the reduction of alcohol-related problems.

First, it is important to examine the whole picture – both the benefits and the harm – associated with alcohol consumption. A 'holistic' or integrated epidemiology is now required. This should take account of the apparent benefits of 'moderate' drinking as well as the harm associated with heavy or inappropriate use. Second, there are many national and local examples of proven strategies to reduce specific types of alcohol-related problems. Experimentation with such strategies should be encouraged. The implementation of such initiatives will require the creation of local or national coalitions. Such strategies, whenever possible, should be evaluated. In addition, if tangible gains are to be prolonged, the implementation of successful initiatives must be sustained.

REFERENCES

Abbott, J. 1993. 'The Sussex Experiment.' Presentation at conference 'Safer Bars? Safer Streets?' London, 15 April.

Alder, G. 1993. Personal communication.

Blackwelder, W.C., K. Yano, G.G. Rhoads, A. Kagan, T. Gordon, and Y. Palesch 1980. 'Alcohol and Mortality: The Honolulu Heart Study.' *American Journal of Medicine* 68: 164–9.

Boffetta, P., and L. Garfinkel. 1990. 'Alcohol Drinking and Mortality among Men Enrolled in an American Cancer Society Prospective Study.' *Epidemiology* 1: 342–8.

Brewers' Society. 1993. *UK Statistical Handbook*. London: The Brewer's Society.

Bruun, K., G. Edwards, M. Lumio, K. Makela, E. Osterberg, L. Pan, R.E. Popham, R. Room, O-J Skog, and P. Sulkenenen. 1975. *Alcohol Control Policies in Public Health Perspective*. Helsinki. Finnish Foundation for Alcohol Studies.

Colditz, G.A., L.G. Brunch, R.J. Lipnick, W.C. Willett, B. Rosner, B. Posner, and C.H. Nennekens. 1985. 'Moderate Alcohol and Decreased Cardiovascular Mortality in an Elderly Cohort.' *American Heart Journal* 109: 886–9.

Cullen, K., H.W. Knuiman, and N.J. Ward. 1993. 'Alcohol and Mortality in Busselton, Western Australia.' *American Journal of Epidemiology* 137: 242–8.

Department of Transport (UK). 1990. *Blood Alcohol Levels in Fatalities in Great Britain 1988*. London: Transport and Road Research Laboratory.

Duffy, J.C. 1994. 'Current Weekly Limits Too Mean.' Letter, *British Medical Journal* 308.

Dunbar, J.A., A. Penttila, and J. Pakkarainen. 1987. 'Drinking and Driving: The Success of Random Breath Testing in Finland.' *British Medical Journal* 295: 101–3.

Dyer, A.R., J. Stamler, P. Oglsby, O. Paul, M. Lepper, R.B. Skekelle, H. McKean, and D. Garside. 1980. 'Alcohol Consumption and 17-Year Mortality in the Chicago Western Electric Company Study.' *Preventive Medicine* 9: 78–90.

Farchi, G., F. Fidanza, S. Mariotti, and A. Menotti. 1992. 'Alcohol and Mortality in the Italian Rural Cohorts of the Seven Countries Study.' *International Journal of Epidemiology* 21: 74–81.

Foster, K., A. Wilmot, and J. Dobbs. 1990. *General Household Survey 1988*. London: HMSO.

Gaziano, J.M., J.E. Buring, J.L. Breslow, S.Z. Goldlhaber, B. Rosner, M. Van Denburgh, W. Willett, and C.H. Hennekens. 1993. 'Moderate Alcohol Intake Increased Levels of High Density Lipoprotein and Its Subfractions and the Decreased Risk of Myocardial Infarction.' *New England Journal of Medicine* 329: 1829–34.

Government Statistical Office. 1991. *Mortality Statistics*. London: HMSO.

Graham, K. 1985. 'Determinants of Heavy Drinking and Drinking Problems: The Contribution of the Bar Environment.' In E. Single and T. Storm, eds, *Public Drinking and Public Policy*, 71–84, Toronto: Addiction Research Foundation.

Groenbaeck, M., A. Deis, T.I.A. Sorensen, U. Becker, K. Borsch-Johnsen, C. Muller, P. Schnohr, and G. Jensen. 1994. 'Influence of Sex, Age, Body Mass Index and Smoking on Alcohol Intake and Mortality.' *British Medical Journal* 308: 302–6.

Gusfield, J. 1993. 'No More Cakes and Ale: The Rhetorics, Frame and Politics of Alcohol Research.' Paper presented at Kettil Bruun Society, 19th Annual Alcohol Epidemiology Symposium, Krakow, Poland, June.

Haskell, R.E. 1993. 'Realpolitik in the Addictions Field: Treatment-Professional, Popular-Culture Ideology, and Scientific Research.' *Journal of Mind and Behavior* 14: 257–76.

Hennekens, C.H., B. Rosner, and D.S. Cole. 1978. 'Daily Alcohol Consumption and Fatal Coronary Heart Disease.' *American Journal of Epidemiology* 107: 196–200.

Ilgunas, M. 1993. 'Prohibition of Alcohol Consumption in Designated Areas: An Assessment.' Presentation at conference 'Alcohol: Problems and Solutions,' Glasgow, 13 October.

Jackson, R., R. Scragg, and R. Beaglehole, 1991. 'Alcohol Consumption and Risk of Coronary Heart Disease.' *British Medical Journal* 303: 211–16.

Jeffs, B.W., and W. Saunders. 1983. 'Minimising Alcohol-Related Offences by Enforcement of Existing Legislation.' *British Journal of Addiction* 78: 67–78.

Kaufman, D.W., L. Rosenberg, S.P. Helmrich, and S. Shapiro. 1985. 'Alcoholic Beverages and Myocardial Infarction in Young Men.' *American Journal of Epidemiology* 121: 548–54.

Klatsky, A.L., G.D. Freidman, and A.B. Sieglelaub. 1974. 'Alcohol Consumption Before Myocardial Infarction.' *Annals of International Medicine* 81: 294–301.

Kono, S., K. Handa, T. Kawano, T. Hiroki, Y. Ishihara, and K. Arakawa. 1991. 'Alcohol Intake and Nonfatal Acute Myocardial Infarction in Japan.' *American Journal of Cardiology* 68: 1011–14.

Kono, S., M. Ikela, S. Tokudo, M. Nkhizum, and M. Karatsume. 1986. 'Alcohol in Mortality: A Study of Male Japanese Physicians.' *International Journal of Epidemiology* 15: 527–32.

Kreitman, N. 1986. 'Alcohol Consumption and the Preventive Paradox.' *British Journal of Addiction* 81: 353–63.

McKenzie, K. 1993. Personal communication.

Mäkelä, K. 1993. Comments in discussion at Kettil Bruun Society, 19th Annual

Alcohol Epidemiology Symposium, Krakow, Poland, June (personal communication, 25 February 1994).

Marmot, M.G., G. Rose, M.J. Shipley, and B.J. Thomas. 1981. 'Alcohol and Mortality: A U-Shaped Curve.' *Lancet* 8219: 580–3.

Peacock, C. 1992. 'International Policies on Alcohol-Impaired Driving: A Review.' *International Journal of the Addictions* 27: 187–208.

Plant, M.A., P. Miller, M.L. Plant, and P. Nichol. 1994. 'No Such Thing as a Safe Glass.' Letter, *British Medical Journal* 308: 1237–8.

Registrar General (Scotland) 1993. *Annual Report 1992*. Edinburgh: HMSO.

Rose, G. 1981. 'Strategy of Prevention: Lessons from Cardiovascular Diseases.' *British Medical Journal* 282: 1847–51.

Royal College of Psychiatrists. 1986. *Alcohol: Our Favourite Drug*. London: Tavistock.

Sales, J., J. Duffy, M.A. Plant, and D.F. Peck. 1989. 'Alcohol Consumption, Cigarette Sales and Mortality in the United Kingdom: An Analysis of the Period 1970–1985.' *Drug and Alcohol Dependence* 24: 155–60.

Shaper, A.G., G. Wannamethee, and M. Walker. 1988. 'Alcohol and Mortality in British Men: Explaining the U-Shaped Curve.' *Lancet* 8597: 1267–73.

Shepherd, J.P., G. Kinder, and R. Huggett. 1991. 'Impact Resistance of Drinking Glasses.' *British Medical Journal* 303: 133.

Shepherd, J.P., M. Price, and P. Shenfine. 1990. 'Glass Abuse and Urban Licensed Premises.' *Journal of the Royal Society of Medicine* 83: 276–7.

Shepherd, J.P., M. Shapland, N.X. Pearce, and C. Scully. 1990. 'Pattern, Severity and Aetiologies of Injuries in Victims of Assaults.' *Journal of the Royal Society of Medicine* 83: 75–80.

13 Harm Reduction and Licensed Drinking Settings

TIM STOCKWELL

In relation to illicit drugs, law enforcement and harm reduction strategies are usually viewed as being mutually incompatible. In this chapter it will be argued, however, that once a drug becomes legally available, law-enforcement efforts can shift from the stereotype of 'zero tolerance' to being a powerful tool for reducing harm.

To understand this point it is helpful to imagine an alternative universe in which heroin is legally available and in which it is necessary to devise a set of laws regarding its sale and distribution. In order to promote low-risk use this legislation would need to include some of the following features:

1/ A stated objective to allow access to heroin in a manner consistent with minimizing the harm associated with its use.
2/ A licensing system to ensure that traders were responsible and informed about the safest ways to use.
3/ A range of different categories of licence with different restrictions and stipulations, for instance, for the sale of take-home heroin only, as opposed to use on the premises.
4/ Authorization for the government to collect some kind of sales tax, though this could involve lower taxes for heroin provided in a form suitable only for smoking as opposed to injecting.
5/ Licensees and their staff would be required to attend training courses to enable them to understand both their legal obligations and how to sell heroin in a responsible fashion.
6/ A system of fines for offences such as selling heroin to very intoxicated customers, promotions that encourage excessive use, and failure to provide clean injecting equipment.

7/Licensing boards would be established with teams of inspectors who would monitor compliance with regulations on an undercover basis.

8/Arrangements would have to be created with extreme care so as to minimize the enormous potential in such a system for corruption.

While such a scheme may seem fanciful in the extreme, there are just such arrangements in place with regard to the sale, supply, and promotion of a drug that causes far greater harm than does heroin – namely, alcohol. Unfortunately, the tremendous potential of existing liquor-licensing legislation to reduce harm is rarely realized.

There has been an increasing interest in many countries in incorporating public-health objectives into liquor legislation. However, public-health concerns are a latecomer into an arena already crowded with some powerful competing agendas, such as the desire of most adults to enjoy ready access to their favourite recreational drug; the concern of alcohol producers to have as few restrictions as possible placed on their market place; the concern of retailers to trade at the hours that suit them and with a minimum of competition; and the opportunity for governments to collect taxes on a non-essential commodity.

The challenge is to find ways to reduce alcohol-related harm through the instrument of liquor laws that do not overly compromise these other objectives. It will be argued here that, with some rare exceptions, the manner in which liquor-licensing systems are constructed at present ensures that public-health objectives are not met. This argument will be illustrated with examples, primarily from Australia, where the author has recently completed a review of liquor-licensing laws across all states and territories (Stockwell 1995).

The Preventive Potential of Liquor Licensing Laws

There are several reasons for supposing that liquor-licensing laws have tremendous potential for preventing alcohol-related harm. Licensed premises are the settings where most heavy-drinking occasions occur and that precede most of the harmful consequences of drinking.

In Australia, about one-third of all alcohol is consumed in licensed premises, but its consumption is associated with about two-thirds of subsequent problems of intoxication (Stockwell et al. 1993b). Studies from other countries demonstrate a similar pattern (Martin, Wyllie, and Casswell 1992; Single and Wortley 1993). Existing legislation in most countries has provisions that seek to reduce some of these harmful out-

comes, for instance, those concerned with serving intoxicated customers, limiting crowding, and managing aggressive behaviour (Solomon
and Prout 1995). Creating the perception among licensees and their staff
that these licensing laws are likely to be enforced has been shown to
result in marked improvements in standards of service and a significant
reduction in problems (Jeffs and Saunders 1983; McKnight and Streff
1992). However, in Australia at least, there are wide variations in standards of practice with regard to the sale and promotion of alcohol across
jurisdictions, with most having considerable room for improvement
(Rydon 1995). Such variations occur despite the existence of a significant
degree of public support for the enforcement of relevant laws, for
instance, those concerned with the service of alcohol to intoxicated customers (Lang, Stockwell, and White 1995).

Our understanding of the means by which harm reduction can be
achieved is, however, at an early stage, and there is an urgent need for
more research and resources to be directed into this area. A number of
strategies are available to licensing authorities to reduce alcohol-related
harm. The following list places these in order of increasing 'tolerance' of
the use of alcohol:

1/ Controls over physical access by determining the permitted hours of
   trading, number and type of outlets, and restrictions on who may
   purchase alcohol.
2/ Controls over the economic availability of alcohol by the levying of
   taxes and regulation of cheap-drink promotions.
3/ Controls over customers' levels of intoxication.
4/ Requirements to ensure customers have alternatives to regular-
   strength alcoholic drinks, such as low-alcohol beers, and food continuously available.
5/ Requirements that licensees, managers, serving staff, and door staff
   are adequately trained and understand their legal obligations.
6/ Requirements that seek to modify other risk factors for alcohol-
   related harm without influencing alcohol consumption, for instance,
   the use of plastic glasses, serving of beer in cans rather than bottles,
   adequate levels of security staff, and limits on crowding and on
   parking.

Most of these approaches have high levels of public acceptability and
all are consistent with a harm reduction approach (Lang, Stockwell,
and White 1995). In recent years economic rationalists have favoured

the deregulation of industries and hence controls over the numbers of outlets and hours of trading have been especially unpopular with conservative governments (Nieuwenhuysen 1988). These various strategies are available in some form or degree in most jurisdictions in most countries. There is, however, a widespread failure to utilize them effectively.

The Failure of Enforcement

Evidence from most of the English-speaking world suggests that levels of enforcement of liquor laws relevant to the prevention of alcohol-related problems are inadequate for achieving a significant deterrent effect. This is especially true of the law regarding service of alcohol to intoxicated customers, as illustrated by quotes from the authors of the two case studies referred to above that report successful enforcement strategies. Jeffs and Saunders note the irony of the following contrasts in a typical year in Scotland: 'there were some 32,000 arrests for breach of the peace and 12,600 arrests for drunkenness, yet prosecutions of licensed premise operators for selling alcohol to intoxicated people were extremely rare' (1983). In a similar vein, the authors of a U.S. study note, their study aside, that 'laws prohibiting the service of alcohol to already intoxicated patrons of bars and restaurants are seldom enforced' (McKnight and Streff 1992).

It is frequently asserted that there is great difficulty in establishing whether a person is intoxicated at the time they are served alcohol. The difficulty with determining degree of intoxication appears to be peculiar to cases involving a person being served alcohol on licensed premises. There appears to be no such difficulty in relation to public drunkenness. For example, in 1989 in Western Australia there were approximately 13,000 arrests for public drunkenness and none at all for serving a person in a bar who was already drunk.

Regardless of the type of liquor offence, there is evidence of a widespread bias towards prosecuting drinkers rather than the servers of alcohol or licensees. For example, in 1991 the ratio of liquor-law violations involving drinkers as opposed to servers or licensees was 34:1 in Tasmania, 20:1 in Western Australia, and 6:1 in Queensland (Craze and Norberry 1995). A major reason for this bias is likely to be the strong sympathy that appears to exist between licensees and some enforcement personnel in Australia, particularly in times of economic hardship (Rydon 1995).

TABLE 1
Number of infractions reported by Ontario (Canada) licensing inspectors
from 1 January to 11 December 1992

Complaint type	No.
Breach of advertising regulations	92
Discount pricing	63
Liquor/food menus unavailable or incomplete	435
No light meals	243
Under-age drinking	43
Serving intoxicated patrons	114
Intoxicated patrons on premises	79
Offer or give inducement to drink*	15

*Includes promotions intended to increase consumption; for example,
offering doubles at the same price as single shots.

Further evidence that there is simply a lack of will to enforce the legislation is provided by the number of infractions of liquor laws reported
by licensing inspectors in Ontario, Canada (Stockwell 1993), as depicted
in table 1. A wide variety of offences are prosecuted in that province, for
the sole purpose of reducing the harm associated with the consumption
of alcohol.

The Failure of Server Training Programs

Responsible Beverage Service, or 'RBS,' has become an international
movement in recent years. It had its origins, however, in the need for
proprietors in the United States to reduce their exposure to legal liability
for the actions of drunken patrons. One strategy for achieving this end
has been to send staff on courses concerning the responsible service of
alcohol. Despite early evaluations of model server training programs
(Russ and Geller 1987) being encouraging, the benefits of the training
appear to be greatly diluted when delivered on a community-wide basis
(McKnight 1987; Mosher et al. 1989; Stockwell et al. 1993a).
    McKnight (1987) describes how a high-profile and well-funded pro-
gram attempted to offer state-of-the-art server training to managers and
staff of eighty establishments in two U.S. communities of similar size.
Only about one-third of available staff took up this offer. While these
personnel demonstrated significant pre- to post-training improvements
in knowledge about alcohol and the laws regulating its sale, there was

no clear evidence of benefits on a critical measure of server behaviour – refusing service to an apparently intoxicated 'pseudo-patron.'

In another major evaluation of server training, Mosher et al. (1989) conducted observations of the drinking behaviour of several thousand customers in Monterey and Santa Cruz in California both before and after training. Despite the massive sample size, no significant change was found in the number of customers leaving the premises with estimated blood-alcohol levels in excess of 0.10 mg/ml.

An attempt to train managers and bar staff of 'high risk' licensed premises in the Western Australian community of Fremantle was evaluated by the National Centre for Research into the Prevention of Drug Abuse (Stockwell et al. 1993a). The training in question was conducted jointly by the WA Police Department and the local Hotels Association ('hotels' are the common name for pubs or bars in Australia). The key finding was that the training program had no significant overall impact on the outcome measure of service refusal to actors feigning the signs of extreme intoxication. The 'pseudo-patrons' were only refused a drink eight times during the whole project out of a total of over two hundred attempts to purchase alcohol. There was one hotel in the study where there were marked improvements on all outcome measures following training. It is probably not coincidental that the management at this establishment gave the most enthusiastic support to the training program and its objectives.

While much can be learned from the detailed reports of these studies, the inescapable conclusion appears to be that, outside of small-scale demonstration projects, server training in isolation from other interventions has no measurable benefit.

These negative findings should be compared with those of an evaluation of a far simpler and cheaper form of intervention. In James McKnight's more recent research in Michigan, it was found that a police enforcement strategy resulted in a threefold increase in rates of service refusal to 'intoxicated' pseudo-patrons. Unless the quality of pseudo-patrons in Michigan has taken a downturn recently, these findings merit serious attention. The successful strategy involved first warning licensees, via the media, of an imminent campaign to enforce the existing liquor-licensing laws. Following this a systematic program of surveillance of serving practices and the issuing of positive or negative feedback to licensees at regular intervals was instigated – the latter being accompanied with an infringement notice if appropriate (McKnight and Streff 1992).

Harm Reduction as a Primary Objective of Liquor Legislation

Over the past five years an increasing number of jurisdictions in Canada, New Zealand, and Australia have explicitly incorporated into their liquor legislation the goal of minimizing alcohol-related harm. The 1989 Sale of Liquor bill in New Zealand states that its principal objective is the reduction of 'liquor abuse.' For Canada, Single and Tocher (1992) have described the processes leading to pioneering legislation in Ontario that has succeeded in placing harm reduction at the centre of licensing decisions – as evidenced by the figures quoted above. In Australia, Queensland's and Victoria's acts provide explicit mention of the prevention of alcohol-related problems in the statement of their objectives (Craze and Norberry 1995).

These developments represent the beginnings of public-health input to liquor legislation. A variety of commentators have noted that the major trend this century in liquor legislation has been the gradual dismantling of the restrictions imposed on alcohol availability as a consequence of the worldwide temperance movement that reached its height in the 1920s. New Zealand and parts of Australia came very close to joining parts of the USA in having a total prohibition on alcohol. The lifting of these restrictions has, of course, been actively promoted by alcohol manufacturers and some sections of the retail alcohol trade too. However, it is important to note that liquor licensees and their associations have also actively campaigned against the relaxing of licensing laws where this would jeopardize their own commercial interests. Thus, retail associations worldwide have objected to the lifting of restrictions on the numbers of licences permitted – the fewer there are, the less the competition (Boots 1993).

It has been argued that the retail industry in Australia succeeded in 'capturing' liquor legislation (Foster and Nieuwenhuysen 1988) to the extent that the largest and most powerful association (representing the hoteliers) has ensured that the status quo remains undisturbed. Licensing legislation has created and preserved distinct market niches, the occupants of which have been able to influence licensing authorities so as to gain further advantage – for instance, by gaining more generous trading hours or by opposing the introduction of new licences. In some Australian jurisdictions these authorities have become completely tied up with the resolution of such industry 'turf wars' without reference to any broad social purpose. As a consequence, it has been recommended that the purpose of licensing legislation, rediscovered and reflected in all aspects of the administration of liquor laws, be that of 'reducing the harm associated with the use of alcohol' (Stockwell 1995).

Impediments to Harm Reduction in Liquor Licensing

The main impediment to achieving a reduction in alcohol-related harm through enforcement of liquor licensing laws can be summarized as a lack of political will to take on a powerful industry lobby, compounded by a system designed to keep community input to licensing decisions to a minimum. The following are some illustrations of this lack of serious intent drawn from the author's home state of Western Australia.

1. No Clear Statement of a Public-Health Objective

From the point of view of the judiciary, the 'scheme' of a piece of legislation is critical in helping to resolve the degree of weight to give competing claims. The scheme is determined by the stated objectives of the legislation. Western Australia is an example of a jurisdiction in which there is no mention of health- or alcohol-related problems in the stated objectives of liquor-licensing laws. In a recent decision, the judge of the WA Liquor Licensing Court gave an indication of his view of the scheme of current legislation when he stated that 'it can be viewed as primarily promoting the sale of liquor' as he quashed a complaint against the granting of a new licence (*Charlie Carter v. Ausgen and Quality Pacific Management*, 1991). Liquor licensing has come a long way in WA since temperance times!

2. Unclear and Obscure Terminology and Definitions

The WA Liquor Licensing Act 1988 (1989) provides what appears to be a definition of intoxication, as follows: 'For the purposes of this Act a person shall be taken to be drunken if, at the time, the person is visibly affected by liquor to the extent that any further consumption of liquor is liable to induce drunkenness' (section 115, 3). Suffice it to say that, despite the good intentions behind this clause, neither magistrates nor police find that it greatly assists them in their work. As discussed previously, there are major problems in defining what constitutes drunkenness. It may be better to simply state 'visibly affected by liquor' and/or provide examples of the well-known visual signs of extreme drunkenness. This is an important issue as, until recently, 'drunkenness' was interpreted as meaning literally 'incapable of looking after oneself' or, in effect, incapable of purchasing another drink! Our own research with licensees and bar staff in Perth suggests that they perceive little difficulty with identifying drunk customers. Rather, the problem lies in how to handle refusal of service without creating an awkward situation (Stockwell et al. 1993a).

3. Lack of Knowledge of Liquor Laws

Indicative of the lack of enforcement of key provisions of WA liquor laws is the finding in a 1990 survey that persons who had been recently employed in the hospitality industry had less knowledge of these provisions than the general public (Lang et al. 1992). Community police who were recently interviewed openly acknowledged that they did not know the contents of liquor licensing legislation and suggested that it would help them to receive summaries of its main contents in plain English (Stockwell 1995). Posters and leaflets with such summaries were well received by bar staff and managers who participated in a responsible-service training program (Stockwell et al. 1993a).

4. Priorities of the Liquor Licensing Authority

These are well illustrated by the chosen performance indicators as stated in their last annual report (Office of Racing and Gaming 1994). These refer only to the speed with which new licence applications are dealt with and the amount of serious under-reporting of liquor purchases, that is, attempts to evade paying liquor taxes.

A recent interview conducted by the author with the director of the authority revealed that approximately 95 per cent of his resources were dedicated to either tax collection or processing of new licence applications (Stockwell 1995). Matters examined by inspectors in applications included proposed numbers of toilets and length of bars. Hardly any resources were available for monitoring the conduct of those holding existing licences and virtually no information was passed on to his department by the police other than the criminal records of prospective licensees. Clearly, the authority has no capability to determine whether licenced premises are being conducted responsibly, or whether they are likely to be in the future.

5. Preoccupation with Industry 'Turf Wars'

It emerged in a recent interview with the judge of the WA Liquor

Licensing court (Stockwell 1995) that this court is rarely used for any-thing other than for resolving disputed applications for new liquor licences. The disputing parties almost invariably are existing operators fearful of losing trade.

In the last two years the licensing authority has begun to receive applications for extended trading hours from hotels and taverns. Most of these have been vehemently opposed by an association representing nightclub owners who, until now, have had a monopoly on trading after midnight. The applications are so many and the disputes so involved that the quasi-judicial hearings required appear to have greatly preoccu-pied the authority.

6. Keeping the Community in the Dark

The authority has a complaints procedure that is activated if ten or more persons living near licensed premises sign a petition and present it to the director. A recent household survey revealed that, while some 24 per cent of Perth residents experienced some form of serious nuisance emanating from nearby premises, only 3 per cent knew about the com-plaints procedure (Lang et al. 1992). Last year the authority dealt with five complaints.

When a variation to a licence is applied for, the applicant is required to advertise this fact in the public-notices column of the main daily newspaper. In response to the charge that this was not an adequate means of inviting community participation, applicants seeking after-midnight trading permits were required to place a large sign outside their premises that would be visible from the road. In large letters this sign stated 'Application under Liquor Licensing Act 1988,' under which was an A4 sheet of paper explaining what this referred to. In the unlikely event that anyone passing would want to find out, this has been made more difficult by the practice of making the notices visi-ble only from a side-street or, worse still, at four feet above head-height!

A large number of these applications are being granted, even though recent public-opinion research has shown that only 10 per cent of West Australians favour extended trading hours (Beel and Stockwell 1993).

7. Inappropriate Enforcement Strategies

The main responsibility for enforcement of existing licensing laws in

Western Australia falls to a special squad within the police department known as the Liquor and Gaming Squad. While this squad has begun to prosecute a tiny number (four in the last year) of licensees for serving drunk customers, there appear to be powerful structural impediments to the squad's being an effective deterrent to irresponsible service. Officers work the same area for up to four years and become well known to managers and servers. Many are middle-aged and are readily identified as being police even though they are in plain clothes. As the only plain-clothes branch currently operating, they frequently get called away to a variety of general police matters such as high-speed pursuits and investigating drug trafficking (Rydon 1990). The recent review exercise conducted by the author and colleagues was presented with many allegations of corrupt practice by this squad (Stockwell 1995).

The Way Forward

It can confidently be predicted that the next five years will see dramatic changes to liquor-licensing law and its enforcement in Australia. The recent national review identified a previously unacknowledged consensus within government, industry, and academia. The clearest expression of this was the endorsement by most stakeholders of the following proposal: 'A primary objective of liquor licensing laws should be the minimisation of alcohol-related death, injury and other harm' (Stockwell 1995). This recommendation was also recently upheld at a national symposium convened by the Commonwealth Department of Health that was well attended by industry, police, and health representatives. Other recommendations to be so endorsed included the introduction of compulsory training of licensees and managers in responsible serving practices and licensing laws, the simplification and explanation of liquor laws for serving staff, police, and the community at large, and the granting of greater priority and resources to the enforcement of liquor laws.

This consensual position is likely to find expression in new legislation as each jurisdiction reviews its laws, usually every five years. Wide-ranging bureaucratic reforms will, however, be required in the structure of liquor-licensing authorities if these grand objectives are to be fully realized. Nonetheless, directors of licensing authorities are also beginning to use their existing powers in order to reduce alcohol-related problems in specific ways. Two examples will be given.

1. The Control of Irresponsible Alcohol Promotions in Victoria

In the middle of 1993, the director of the Victoria licensing authority announced guidelines for licensees wishing to promote their premises with special offers on alcoholic drinks. Some practices such as drinking competitions were banned entirely, while rules were provided for others. For example, the ubiquitous 'happy hour' was retained, but was not permitted late at night, and drinkers were not allowed to stack or hoard these cheap drinks. The guidelines were distributed to all licensees and announced through all media outlets. A significant enforcement effort ensued and a few test cases were prosecuted; for example, one licensee was fined $10,000 for holding a drinking contest. In the directors' opinion, these practices have now virtually ceased (personal communication).

2. Control over the Supply of Alcohol in Halls Creek, Western Australia

Halls Creek is a remote community in Western Australia with a significant Aboriginal population and a reputation for heavy drinking and violence. Community representations to the licensing authority about the seriousness of this problem resulted in some unprecedented controls being imposed on local licensees. To someone unfamiliar with drinking culture in the remote areas of Australia these may seem unimpressive; they have, however, been widely applauded by local community members and agencies. Liquor stores were not allowed to sell any alcohol before noon and sales of four-litre wine casks were only permitted between 4 pm and 6 pm, with a limit of one per person per day (Holmes 1995). Perhaps the most significant aspect of this case was the willingness of the director of liquor licensing to exercise his powers at the behest of a local community concerned about drunkenness and alcohol-related violence.

There is a real danger in discussing these issues of giving the impression that law enforcement is the best or the only solution to preventing alcohol-related problems. It should be emphasized that liquor-licensing laws are a neglected aspect of what needs to be a coordinated and comprehensive response involving education, early intervention, and treatment approaches. To quote from the report on Australian liquor laws: 'The responsibility for minimising the harm associated with alcohol use cannot be placed entirely on any single group in society whether this be the liquor industry, the police, health departments, individual drinkers, liquor licensing authorities or local communities. Rather each of these sectors have unique responsibilities and capabilities to reduce the harm. These need to be clarified and taken seriously in every instance. 'Liquor legislation should support and enable positive, cooperative initiatives to reduce alcohol problems through such means as encouraging the input of local communities in licensing matters, supporting preventative policing methods and fostering industry responsible service initiatives' (Stockwell 1995: xvii).

Some readers would probably favour, or at least consider, some form of licensing system as a means of supplying drugs that are currently illegal in most countries. It has been argued here that there is a great and largely unrealized potential within current licensing systems for reducing harm associated with our favourite legally available recreational drug, namely, alcohol.

REFERENCES

Beel, A., and T. Stockwell. 1993. *The Introduction of 0.05 in Western Australia: A Preliminary Research Report*. Perth: National Centre for Research into the Prevention of Drug Abuse.
Boots, K. 1993. 'An Odious and Loathsome Sin.' *Substance* 4(2): 6–10.
Craze, L., and J. Norberry. 1995. 'The Objectives of Liquor Licensing Laws in Australia.' In T. Stockwell, ed., *Alcohol Misuse and Violence 5: The Appropriateness and Efficacy of Liquor Licensing Laws across Australia*. Canberra: Australian Government Publishing Services.
Foster, W., and J. Nieuwenhuysen. 1988. 'Victoria's New Liquor Laws: A Case Study in Deregulation and Industry Capture.' *National Economic Review* 8: 75–88.
Government of Western Australia. 1989. *Liquor Licensing Act 1988*.
Holmes, M. 1995. 'The Halls Creek Initiative.' *Pro-Ed* 10(1): 21–2.
Jeffs, W.B., and W.M. Saunders. 1983. 'Minimising Alcohol Related Offences by Enforcement of the Existing Licensing Legislation.' *British Journal of Addiction* 78: 66–77.
Lang, E., T. Stockwell, P. Rydon, and C. Gamble. 1992. *Drinking Settings, Alcohol Related Harm, and Support for Prevention Policies. Results of a Survey of Persons Residing in the Perth Metropolitan Area*. Bentley, WA: National Centre for Research into the Prevention of Drug Abuse.
Lang, E., T. Stockwell, and M. White. 1995. 'The Acceptability of Reforms of Liquor Licensing Laws to the General Public and to Key Stakeholders.' In

T. Stockwell, ed., *Alcohol Misuse and Violence 5: The Appropriateness and Efficacy of Liquor Licensing Laws across Australia.*' Canberra: Australian Government Publishing Services.

McKnight, A.J., and F.M. Streff. 1992. *The Effect of Enforcement upon Service of Alcohol to Intoxicated Patrons of Bars and Restaurants.* Landover, MD: National Public Services Research Institute.

McKnight, J. 1987. *The Effectiveness of a Field Test of a Responsible Alcohol Serving Program.* Volume 1: Research findings. Washington: National Highway Traffic Safety Administration.

Martin, C., A. Wyllie, and S. Casswell. 1992. 'Types of New Zealand Drinkers and Their Associated Alcohol-Related Problems.' *Journal of Drug Issues* 22(3): 773–98.

Mosher, J.F., C. Delewski, R. Saltz, and M. Hennessy. 1989. *Monterey – Santa Cruz Responsible Beverage Service Project.* Final report. San Rafael, CA: Marin Institute for the Prevention of Alcohol and Other Drug Problems.

Nieuwenhuysen, J. 1988. 'Liquor Control Policy and Alcohol Availability-Consumption Relationships: Reflections on the Victorian Debate.' *Australian Drug and Alcohol Review* 7(3): 263–72.

Office of Racing and Gaming. 1994. *Annual Report 1993–4.* Perth: Government of Western Australia.

Russ, N.W., and E.S. Geller. 1987. 'Training Bar Personnel to Prevent Drunken Driving: A Field Evaluation.' *American Journal of Public Health* 77: 952–4.

Rydon, P. 1990. 'Enforcing Liquor Licensing Laws.' Update: the Alcohol Advisory Council of Western Australia, Spring 1990: 2–3.

– 1995. 'Alcohol Industry Practices Relating to Liquor Licensing Regulations.' In T. Stockwell, ed., *Alcohol Misuse and Violence 5: The Appropriateness and Efficacy of Liquor Licensing Laws across Australia.* Canberra: Australian Government Publishing Services.

Single, E., and B. Tocher. 1992. 'Legislating Responsible Alcohol Service: An Inside View of the New Liquor Licence Act of Ontario.' *British Journal of Addiction* 87: 1433–43.

Single, E., and S. Wortley. 1993. 'Drinking in Various Settings as It Relates to Socio-Demographic Variables and Level of Consumption: Findings from a National Survey in Canada.' *Journal of Studies on Alcohol* 54: 590–9.

Solomon, R., and L. Prout. 1995. 'A Summary of Provisions Contained in Liquor Legislation of Possible Relevance to Violence.' In T. Stockwell, ed., *Alcohol Misuse and Violence 5: The Appropriateness and Efficacy of Liquor Licensing Laws across Australia.* Canberra: Australian Gvernment Publishing Services.

Stockwell, T. 1993. 'Can Liquor Laws Regarding Service to Intoxication Ever Be Enforced?' *CentreLines* 15 (September): 3–6.

Stockwell, T., ed. 1995. *Alcohol Misuse and Violence 5: The Appropriateness and Efficacy of Liquor Licensing Laws across Australia*. Canberra: Australian Government Publishing Services.

Stockwell, T., E. Lang, P. Rydon, and A. Beel, eds. 1993a. *An Evaluation of the 'Freo Respects You' Responsible Alcohol Service Project*. Perth: National Centre for Research into the Prevention of Drug Abuse.

Stockwell, T., E. Lang, P. Rydon, and A. Lockwood. 1993b. 'High Risk Drinking Settings: The Association of Serving and Promotional Practices with Harmful Drinking.' *Addiction* 88(11): 1519–26.

14 Reducing Alcohol-Related Harm in Communities: A Policy Paradigm

CLAIRE NARBONNE-FORTIN, RENÉ LAUZON, and RONALD R. DOUGLAS

Alcohol, an accessible and legal drug, is sometimes underestimated as a potentially harmful substance. As a result, a greater emphasis is often placed on the harmful consequences of illicit drug use. The Addiction Research Foundation, a provincial drug agency in Canada, reported that in 1994, 82 per cent of adults and 56 per cent of students between the ages of twelve and nineteen reported having used alcohol in the previous year. This compares to 0.7% and 1.5% respectively having used cocaine during the same period. The same report indicated that approximately 10% of Ontario deaths in 1991 were associated with alcohol use (Addiction Research Foundation 1995).

The development of policies to manage alcohol in municipally owned recreation facilities is a pragmatic response by politicians to citizens wanting access to alcohol while being concerned about its associated negative consequences. In the Canadian province of Ontario, where Municipal Alcohol Policies began appearing in the early 1980s, individuals and groups wishing to serve alcohol for community celebrations, fund-raisers, sport banquets, and other social events held in non-licensed facilities are required to obtain a Special Occasion Permit (SOP).* In Ontario, it is estimated that 84,000 SOPs were issued in 1994 (LLBO 1995). In a review of special permit drinking in Ontario (1988), Smart identified drinking at such events as a problem area that is receiving little attention from social policy researchers.

These special one-time drinking events are often operated by well-intentioned, inexperienced, and untrained community volunteers. As a

---

* The SOP application form, issued by the Liquor Licence Board (LLBO), informs the signatory of his/her responsibility for the 'safety and sobriety' of those attending the event.

result, alcohol-related problems, such as impaired driving, fights, and drunkenness have a potential for occurring owing to over-consumption. Since the prohibition of alcohol at weddings, club dances, and receptions would not be supported by the majority of a community's residents, strategies for reducing heavy consumption and inappropriate drinking, while maintaining the availability of alcohol, are required. A harm reduction approach, using a policy intervention to govern the provision of alcohol, has been developed in order to reduce harm to the partying participants and other members of a community while maintaining the benefits of increased socializing, generating funds for worthy causes, and attracting tourism dollars to communities.

As a harm reduction intervention, Municipal Alcohol Policies (MAPs) contain many of the conceptual elements identified in Newcombe's description of a harm reduction framework (1992), albeit from a community rather than individual perspective and at the policy rather than the therapeutic level. The policy-formulation process considers the positive and negative results of alcohol use. Health, social, and economic consequences are considered by planners in relation to the individual and his/her community. Risks are tackled through specific strategies impacting on 'quantitative dimensions (dosage, potency, and frequency) and qualitative dimensions (access, administration, and setting)' (Newcombe 1992). Application of this public-health approach to reduce potential problems is illustrated in table 1 (p. 230), with subsequent tables describing some health, social, and economic consequences of policy intervention.

Policy Formulation Process

Since 1980, Ontario municipalities and First Nations (Aboriginal) communities have increasingly collaborated with the Addiction Research Foundation in the development of alcohol management policies. Traditionally, First Nations have resorted to prohibition as a way to resolve alcohol problems. This practice too frequently served to displace the problem to neighbouring communities or ignored illegal drinking in the community. In the mid-1990s, some First Nations have begun to develop policy to manage the use of alcohol as an alternative to outright banning.

Throughout this paper, 'MAP' will refer to policies being developed by municipal councils for cities, towns, and townships, by band councils for First Nation communities, and by area planning boards for rural,

TABLE 1
Potential harm caused by alcohol mismanagement

	Health		Social		Economic	
	Short-term harm	Long-term harm	Short-term harm	Long-term harm	Short-term harm	Long-term harm
Individual/family	• Hangovers/ sickness • Impaired motor skills • Impaired decision-making skills • Risk taking/ decision making	• Serious injury • Permanent disability • Chronic liver damage • Fetal Alcohol Syndrome/Effect • Psychological/ emotional problems • Death	• Embarrassing behaviour • Risky behaviour • Family dysfunction • Family violence episodes • Peer influence • Marital problems	• Loss of friends • Limited social network • Loss of respect • Marital breakdown • Unhealthy work relationships • Criminal record	• Missed work days • Excessive spending to buy alcohol • Legal fines • Loss of driver's licence	• Jail term resulting in loss of income • Loss of insurance eligibility • Lawsuits
Community/societal	• Vehicle accidents • Violent episodes • Assaults	• Lack of concern for others • Diminished physical and mental health • Risk of harm to community members • High suicide rate	• Shoddy appearance of facilities • Poor maintenance • Reduced social events • Vandalism	• Poor community image • Destruction of facilities • Family breakdown • High unemployment • Increased delinquency • Tolerance of alcohol misuse • Poor societal norms • Attitude change regarding use of health-care facilities • Reluctance to host social events	• Increased maintenance costs • Expensive repairs • Increased cost of correctional system	• Loss of rental revenue • Lawsuits • High insurance premiums • Insurance disqualification • High health-care costs • Increased welfare costs • Increased unemployment • Increased levels of liability • Loss of liquor-licence privileges

unorganized community populations. The policies are designed to designate band and municipally owned facilities suitable for accommodating drinking events, to establish knowledge and training standards for event operators, and to provide operating guidelines for those managing alcohol-related events.

The process of MAP development is unique in that it is not dominated by the traditional agents of social control, but is instead shifted to the community itself. A policy committee, normally appointed by municipal or band council and representing a cross-section of community interests, meets approximately eight times over a period of six months. Committee members review information on the local and provincial use of alcohol as well as the literature on drinking practices. Facilities anticipated to be covered by the policy are inspected and discussions are held regarding prior problems and existing management practices. During their deliberations, the committee members also examine alcohol policies implemented in other communities. They familiarize themselves with the Liquor Licence Act of Ontario, paying special attention to sections that deal with SOPs, responsible service, serving to the point of intoxication, under-age drinking, and civil liability. Throughout the policy process, the committee solicits input from staff, volunteers, and other groups. No matter the population, the process of policy development is similar, with an emphasis on direct contact with the community at large and easy access to the committee by interested parties. Committee members draft a series of recommendations that are presented to the municipal or band council for approval (see Thomson et al. 1984; Thomson and Douglas 1983; Douglas 1986; and Else, Douglas, and Becks 1992 for further descriptions of the policy-development process).

Once adopted, the policy or specific regulations within the policy become a municipal by-law. Community members, facility user groups, and individuals who wish to rent a municipal facility for an alcohol-related event are informed of the policy through an intense promotional campaign involving a mix of signs being posted, news items appearing in the press and on the electronic media, pamphlet distribution, public meetings, and server training sessions (see Thomson et al. 1985; Murray and Douglas 1988; and Gliksman et al. 1990 for a further description of a promotional campaign).

Policy Examples

While the specific regulations contained in a MAP may vary according to the unique circumstances of each community, policies tend to be similar in that they contain the following: a list of facilities at which alcohol can be served, restrictions on serving patrons to the point of intoxication, provision of safe transportation for the intoxicated, prohibiting the serving of under-age participants, making available low-alcohol-content drinks, and required server training for those managing the event. A policy also lists numerous operating requirements such as limiting the number of drinks that can be served at one time, supervision at the entrance to keep out troublemakers, serving in paper cups, prohibiting 'last call' (that is, announcing that the bar is about to close), and specifying the number of supervisors needed for the size of the event (see Symons and Douglas 1991; Douglas, Pyette, and Anstice 1990; Pollard, Abraham, and Douglas 1989; Narbonne-Fortin 1993; and Lauzon et al. 1995 for sample policies).

In applying the harm reduction framework (as described by O'Hare, Newcombe, Matthews, Buning, and Drucker [1992] and others) to the components of a municipal or band alcohol-management policy, the strategies for reducing potential short- and long-term health, social, and economic harm to individuals and their communities become apparent.

Reducing Health Harm to the Individual, Family, and Community

MAP interventions can be directed at reducing potential short- and long-term negative health effects so as to benefit the individual, family, and community. For example, as illustrated in table 2, the likelihood of an individual experiencing the short-term consequence of sickness or hangover as a result of excessive consumption can be reduced by the policy regulation that prohibits serving patrons to the point of intoxication. The additional requirements of posting a visible statement on intoxication (see example), providing low-alcohol drinks and food substitutes, and requiring servers to be trained in responsible serving practices work together to reduce the probability of the drinker becoming drunk or ill.

STATEMENT ON INTOXICATION

Our community strives to provide recreation facilities for the enjoyment of all. Servers are required by law not to serve an intoxicated person or to serve anyone to the point of intoxication. Low-alcohol beverages, coffee, soft drinks, and food items are available upon request.

TABLE 2
Some health benefits of policy interventions

Short-term harm	Long-term harm	Policy intervention	Harm reduction benefits
		Individual/family	
• Hangovers/sickness • Stress • Assaults • Injury	• Alcoholism/problem drinking • Chronic liver damage • Fetal Alcohol Syndrome/effect • Permanent disability	• Server training • Provision of low-alcohol and no-alcohol beverages • Posting a statement on intoxication • Food availability • Proper and adequate supervision • Maintaining safe premises, e.g., adequate lighting	• Reduced incidence of intoxication • Reduced alcohol-related illness and disabilities • Slower rate of alcohol absorption • Decrease in violent occurrences • Reduced injuries
		Community/societal	
• Vehicle accidents • Injury and suffering for victims of drunk drivers	• Permanent disability • Psychological/emotional problems • Diminished physical and mental health • Risk of harm to community members • High suicide rate • Dysfunctional families	• No 'last call' announcing bar closing • Proper supervision • Designated Driver Program • Alternative transportation options • Roadside spot checks	• No last-minute rush to the bar • Reduction in impaired driving charges • Reduction in alcohol-related vehicle accidents • Decreased stress on the health system • Increased positive family interaction and relationships

On an extended basis, this policy practice interrupts the pattern of drinking for the purpose of getting intoxicated, which can contribute to alcoholism.

When applying the harm reduction framework to the above-noted interventions, the application of risk-reduction strategies is demonstrated. They restrict access to alcohol, reduce the frequency of service, manage the amount served and strength of drink provided (dosage and potency), and determine the rate and style of serving practices (administration, setting).

The policy decision not to serve people to intoxication, when combined with the additional policy requirements to no longer provide a 'last call' for drinks at closing time, to provide free or low-cost non-alcoholic drinks to designated drivers, and to warn participants of police roadside checks for impaired drivers helps to reduce the risk of drivers experiencing a vehicle crash. Thus, for the driver, consumption of alcohol is moderated or reduced so as to avoid immediate injury and suffering or long-term disabilities. Similarly, family and friends are less likely to be involved in an impaired driving crash while travelling with a 'drinking driver' whose consumption was moderate.

Integrated with the above-noted MAP interventions is the requirement to provide adequate supervision of the event. In addition to being trained, the volunteers must be adults (18 years and over), refrain from drinking alcohol during the time of the event, and perform their assigned duties (door coverage, floor supervision, ticket sales, bar serving, and so on). The combination of these specific interventions further reduces the possibility of patrons becoming intoxicated and engaging in violent behaviour such as fights at the event or later at home with a spouse or children. As a result, personal injuries, prolonged stress leading to mental-health problems for family members, and retaliation by victimized community members is reduced.

Reducing Social Harm to the Individual, Family, and Community

Liberal serving practices leading to excessive consumption of alcohol increase not only the possibility of the individual drinker becoming intoxicated but also the likelihood that his or her immediate drinking group will do the same. Unfortunately for family and community members, as this drinking group continues to increase its alcohol consumption and drinking occasions, it has been hypothesized (Bruun et al. 1975), its heavy drinking can also adversely affect the drinking patterns of others with whom it comes into contact, thus elevating the overall consumption and extending this risky drinking style into the home and community (Douglas et al. 1986; Douglas and Giesbrecht 1993).

Heavy drinkers tend to experience states of drunkenness that result in abusive behaviour to others. As a result, it is not uncommon to witness their removal from social gatherings. The short-term consequence of being 'bounced' from the event, when done frequently, can lead to long-term social isolation from the mainstream moderate drinking behaviour of the community. The policy interventions require trained servers to cut drinkers off before they reach a state of intoxication, prohibit volume discounts and drinking contests, limit the number of people sitting at a table, and restrict the buying of rounds. Isolated deviant groups would only tend to reinforce inappropriate drinking patterns that could lead to other social problems, such as charges, court appearances, incarceration, and family alienation. A MAP reduces the previously mentioned short-term problems while retarding the possibility of having individuals or groups barred from events.

Uncontrolled drinking events lead to damaged facilities, thereby projecting a shoddy appearance. Unattractive buildings deter participation and further prevent social interaction among community members. As a result, a negative image is projected. Residents are less likely to volunteer for social functions and may take less pride in their community. By implementing the above-listed MAP interventions (illustrated in table 3, p. 236) as an integrated risk-reduction strategy, community groups can sponsor drinking events to accommodate consumers, ranging from light to heavy drinkers, while avoiding social conflicts. Community members and visitors will tend to participate more readily in functions viewed as free from the hassles caused by a few intoxicated participants. This results in increased gatherings at which residents take pride and share in a positive community spirit.

Reducing Economic Harm to the Individual, Family, and Community

Heavy drinking can lead to economic harm, whether to the individual drinker, his or her family, or community. The heavy drinker spends a disproportionate amount of money on alcohol, often at the expense of needed staples. Prolonged drinking bouts can result in missed work days and eventually conclude in dismissal, thus placing the drinker and his or her dependents in the community's social-services system. For a

TABLE 3
Some social benefits of policy interventions

Short-term harm	Long-term harm	Policy intervention	Harm reduction benefits
		Individual/family	
• Heavy drinking • Peer influence to drink excessively • Influencing friends and families to drink frequently and drink more • Removal from social activities: 'bounced' • Fights/assaults • Disruptive behaviour • Dysfunctional behaviour • Criminal charges	• Limited social network • Barred from events • Heavy group drinking • Marital breakdown • Unhealthy work relationships • Family alienated from community • Criminal record	• Server training • Limited alcohol tickets per purchase • Limited number of drinks per serving from the bar (no 'rounds') • No volume discounts • No drinking contests • No serving to intoxication	• Continued positive interaction with community • Family harmony • Good working relationships • No criminal involvement/record
		Community/societal	
• Shoddy appearance of facilities • Breakage • Criminal charges • Reduced social events • Reduced participation • Loss of community spirit and pride	• Tolerance of alcohol misuse • Incarceration • Poor societal norms • Reluctance to host social events • Reduced volunteer participation • Reduced tourism	• No serving to intoxication • Provision of low-alcohol and alcohol-free substitutes • Provision of food • Use of paper cups	• Increased involvement and participation by community members • Positive community image • Increased tourism • Increased attendance by low-risk participants • Pleasant environment free of broken materials

normally moderate consumer, a single excessive-drinking episode can have similar results should the drinking driver, whose job requires a vehicle, lose his/her licence owing to an impaired-driving conviction. The loss of the use of the family vehicle can also result in family members, especially children, dropping out of activities because they are dependent on an adult to drive them to their leisure activities. Children or their parents may drop out of groups owing to the transfer of funds from recreational pursuits to the payment of legal fees, fines, and increased insurance premiums.

Should a participant be served to a state of intoxication and be involved in an impaired-driving crash following a Special Occasion Permit event, the costs to the individuals involved in the crash, their families, the group running the drinking event, and the municipality can be enormous. In Ontario, people injured by those intoxicated can sue not only the impaired driver, but also those who served the patron to the state of intoxication or continued serving beyond intoxication. The courts have awarded damages in excess of $1 million (Solomon, Boake, and Gleason 1985). An impaired driver could lose all of his or her belongings and life savings; those managing the event and the club volunteers, as co-defendants, could also be affected. The municipality, as owners of the facility hosting the event and often as co-sponsors, could be held jointly liable and end up paying a large portion of the settlement, thus diverting tax dollars away from needed services. Solomon et al. (1996) have documented municipal liability both as providers of alcohol and as occupiers (for instance, ensuring that premises are safe).

Less dramatic events, such as violations of the Liquor Licence Act, could result in the loss of liquor-licence privileges. Therefore, the conduct of one group operating a poorly managed event could prevent other groups from operating an alcohol-related activity in that facility. This could result in lost income for charitable groups and in a decrease in municipal income. Should some of these cancelled events be festivals or community celebrations, the community could lose needed tourism revenues.

Other negative consequences experienced when a municipality permits the operation of poorly managed alcohol-related events include insurance disqualification or higher insurance premiums, and are displayed in table 4 (p. 238). Many of the previously noted MAP interventions are also identified. When the policy interventions are implemented, individuals, groups, and municipal corporate identities reduce their risk of suffering adverse consequences, and as a result they

TABLE 4
Some economic benefits of policy interventions

Short-term harm	Long-term harm	Policy intervention	Harm reduction benefits
Individual/family			
• Legal fines • Missed work days • Excessive spending to buy alcohol • Loss of driver's licence	• Jail term resulting in loss of income • Loss of insurance eligibility • Lawsuit • Poor work record	• Limited alcohol ticket sales per purchase • Refund for unused alcohol tickets • Lower charge for lower-alcohol-content drinks • Safe transportation options • Designated-driver program • Liability insurance purchased by event organizers	• Less money spent to purchase alcohol • Fewer arguments with patrons after the bar has closed • Decreased volume of alcohol per drink • Fewer vehicle accidents • Decreased liability risk for event organizers • Some financial protection in the event of a lawsuit
Community/societal			
• Increased maintenance costs • Increased cost of correctional system	• Loss of rental revenue • Lawsuit • High insurance premiums • Insurance disqualification • High health-care costs • Increased welfare costs • Increased unemployment • Increased levels of liability	• Decreased intoxication through server training • Decreased criminal activity through decreased intoxication	• Increased demand for and rental of facilities • Less stress on the justice and correctional systems • Decrease in liability risk incurred at a community level (municipality or First Nation)

can operate drinking events that contribute to the economic well-being of their community.

Policy Evaluation

Evaluations to date have consisted of a study of a community's receptivity to a municipal alcohol-policy campaign, an evaluation of the integrated server-training component, a survey of Ontario municipalities, and a collection of anecdotal accounts. A three-year outcome evaluation by the Addiction Research Foundation is currently in process (Gliksman et al. 1993).

Anecdotal information has provided feedback on MAP effectiveness. Facility managers and recreation directors have reported that some troublesome individuals, barred from social and recreational functions held in municipal parks and buildings, have modified their disruptive behaviour in order to be permitted to once again enjoy the privilege of attending events held in local facilities. Community members describe the pleasant change from the days when moderate drinkers were obliged to either tolerate the antics of the heavy-drinking crowd or avoid entirely those social occasions known to encourage excessive drinking. Cab drivers have commented on the increased use of their services following SOP events and on the decrease in the number of intoxicated passengers they see. In one mining community, doctors on call at the local hospital emergency service have reported a decrease in the number of injuries they have been required to treat as a result of weekend brawls. Police in an isolated rural area of northern Ontario have noticed a decrease in the number of arrests due to alcohol-related problems such as fights, vandalism, and impaired driving. One community was pleased to report that the picnic tables in its public parks were being used and enjoyed by families, friends, and other social groups rather than being demolished and used as firewood by intoxicated campers. Many communities have commented on the number of individuals who choose to leave their vehicles in the parking lot at the end of an event rather than drive home. In several communities, private clubs such as union halls and privately owned social clubs are using the MAP model to develop their own in-house alcohol policy. Private tavern owners have remarked on the decrease in the number of individuals arriving at their establishments already intoxicated after leaving an SOP event.

The first alcohol-management policy adopted by a municipality in Ontario was in the City of Thunder Bay in 1980. The policy, as a proposed intervention to reduce community alcohol problems being experienced in city-owned recreation facilities, experienced considerable controversy. To assess community receptivity to the policy, specifically the one-year promotional campaign introducing the policy to the community, a quasi-experimental evaluation was conducted. The researchers concluded that 'an advertising campaign that reports both the policy and the reasons for its incorporation can produce changes in attitudes and intentions of residents and increase the likelihood of voluntary compliance' (Gliksman et al. 1990: 414). This conclusion was supported by anecdotal reports by the city's community-services staff. For example, following the July 1 Canada Day Celebration in a park, few alcohol problems were experienced and city hall received over seventy favourable phone calls following the event, in contrast to the previous year's numerous complaints when no policy was in place. It was also reported that a community centre, known for hosting drunken events, was given permission to keep its liquor licence when the provincial review board learned that the centre's executive had agreed to conduct future alcohol-related activities within the guidelines of the new city policy.

As previously indicated, most Municipal Alcohol Policies require those operating with a Special Occasion Permit to have been trained in responsible serving practices. A review of the evaluation studies of server training programs by Eliany and Rush (1992) indicate that they are effective in reducing both intoxication and drinking and driving by patrons. The training program in use in Ontario received a quasi-experimental evaluation that, while it did not evaluate the impact of the training at SOP events, did test the intervention's impact in a sports bar, a neighbourhood tavern, a hotel lounge, and a skid-row hotel bar. The evaluators (Gliksman, McKenzie et al. 1993) reported that the training was effective in changing serving practices, with servers less likely to serve a patron to the point of intoxication.

Current prevention models, such as the Canadian federal government's Conceptual Framework for Preventive Action (Torjman 1986), Health and Welfare Canada's Prevention Framework for Native Communities (1993), and the Government of Ontario's Substance Abuse Strategy (1993), recommend integrating actions such as education programs, skills training, and policy development. Should combined, integrated, and sustained interventions yield more powerful results, then combining a policy intervention and server training program with a policy information campaign should produce a promising outcome for harm reduction.

In 1994, municipalities in Ontario were surveyed to determine the number of alcohol policies and their impact on reducing alcohol-related problems in municipal facilities. Of the 777 municipalities surveyed, 477 indicated that they had facilities that hosted drinking events. Of this latter group, 107 reported having a written policy in place, the majority having been developed in the last two years.

Forty-four of the communities felt that their policies had been in place long enough, exceeding six months, to observe changes. Of these 44 municipalities, 27 noted reductions in under-age drinking, 25 reported fewer fights and scuffles, and 24 experienced less vandalism. Sixteen encountered fewer police interventions and 14 received fewer public complaints. Reductions were also noted in the problem areas of injuries (8), legal action (8), unlicensed drinking (6), intoxication (5), LLBO penalties (4), and drinking and driving (1). Most of the municipalities reported reductions in at least two or three problem areas. (See Gliksman et al. 1995; Rylett et al. 1995; and Narbonne-Fortin et al. 1996 for additional results.)

In 1994, the Wellington Dufferin Health Unit and Homewood Community Alcohol and Drug Services surveyed fifteen municipalities that had received assistance from them in developing an alcohol risk-management policy. McCarty and Heath (1996) report that ten of the respondents indicated fewer confrontations, less rowdy behaviour, reduced citizen complaints, fewer minors being served, and a decrease in drinking in non-licensed areas.

To assess further the harm reduction potential of Municipal Alcohol Policies associated with Special Occasion Permit events, the Addiction Research Foundation (Gliksman, Douglas et al. 1993) is conducting a three-year quasi-experimental evaluation involving four communities with MAPs, compared to four communities with no policy initiatives. The paired communities involve matched large urban cities, rural cities and towns, and First Nations (Aboriginal) communities. In each community, public perception to policies will be compared through pre- and post-survey measures, as well as by assessing participant reaction to the drinking events and through the monitoring of problem incidents as reported by municipal staff.

Conclusion

While Municipal Alcohol Policies appear to be emerging as an important intervention for reducing potential harm caused by the inappropriate use and excess consumption of alcohol, it is worth underscoring the point

that the process of community participation in determining the risk
reduction strategies is as important in reducing harm as are the resulting
regulations. For policy to have a future in this public-health approach to
reducing harm, policy must be viewed as an incremental process, one
that progresses through a never-ending cycle of renewal. It is this process
of change that enables communities to review drinking norms, select
safer practices, and establish their choices in policy reflecting a new normative standard.

REFERENCES

Addiction Research Foundation. 1995. *Drugs in Ontario.* Toronto: Addiction
    Research Foundation.
Bruun, K., G. Edwards, M. Lumio, K. Mäkelä, L. Pan, R.E. Popham, R. Room,
    W. Schmidt, O.-J. Sog, P. Sulkunen, and E. Österberg. 1975. *Alcohol Control
    Policies in Public Health Perspectives.* Helsinki: Frossa, Finnish Foundation for
    Alcohol Studies.
Douglas, R.R. 1986. 'Alcohol Management Policies for Municipal Recreation
    Departments: Development and Implementation of the Thunder Bay Model.'
    In N. Giesbrecht and A. Cox, eds, *Prevention and the Environment,* 177–97.
    Toronto: Addiction Research Foundation.
Douglas, R.R., and N. Giesbrecht. 1993. 'Introducing Sully Ledermann to John
    Doe: Linking Theory to the Community Policy Agenda.' *Journal of Alcohol and
    Drug Education* 38(2): 1–13.
Douglas, R.R., K. Moffat, R. Caverson, E. Single, and M. Thomson. 1986. 'Drink-
    ing Practices and Some Implications to Managing Alcohol in Municipal Rec-
    reation Facilities and Parks.' *Recreation Canada* 44(2): 32–7.
Douglas, R.R., S. Pyette, and J. Anstice. 1990. 'Tehkummah's Alcohol Manage-
    ment Policy: A Model Policy That May Help Reduce Risks Associated with
    SOP Functions.' *Municipal World* 17(3): 14–18.
Eliany, M., and B. Rush. 1992. *How Effective Are Alcohol and Other Drug Prevention
    and Treatment Programs? A Review of Evaluation Studies.* Ottawa: Health Ser-
    vices and Promotion Branch, Health and Welfare Canada.
Else, P., R. Douglas, and B. Becks. 1992. 'Responding to the Challenge: Reducing
    Problems through Municipal Alcohol Policy Development.' *Public Health &
    Epidemiology Report Ontario* 20(3): 348–50.
Gliksman, L., R.R. Douglas, C. Narbonne-Fortin, and M. Rylett. 1993. 'Evalua-
    tion of the Municipal Alcohol Policy Program.' Research proposal. London,
    Ont.: Addiction Research Foundation, Social Evaluation and Research
    Department.

Gliksman, L., R.R. Douglas, M. Rylett, and C. Narbonne-Fortin. 1995. 'Reducing Problems through Municipal Alcohol Policies: The Canadian Experiment in Ontario.' *Drugs: Education, Prevention and Policy* 2(2): 105–18.

Gliksman, L., R.R. Douglas, M. Thomson, K. Moffatt, C. Smythe, and R. Caverson. 1990. 'Promoting Municipal Alcohol Policies: An Evaluation of a Campaign.' *Contemporary Drug Problems* 17(3): 391–420.

Gliksman, L., D. McKenzie, E. Single, R. Douglas, S. Brunet, and K. Moffatt. 1993. 'The Role of Alcohol Providers in Prevention: An Evaluation of a Server Intervention Programme.' *Addiction* 88: 1195–1203.

Government of Ontario. 1993. *Partners in Action: Ontario's Substance Abuse Strategy*. Toronto: Ministry of Health, Queen's Printer.

Health and Welfare Canada. 1993. *Prevention Framework for First Nations Communities*. Ottawa: Addictions & Community Funded Programs, Medical Services Branch, First Nations Printing Services.

Lauzon, R., D. Dawson, D. McLean, and R. Douglas. 1995. 'Small Community Offers Solutions to Alcohol Problems.' *OPP Review* (September): 8–10.

Liquor Licence Board of Ontario. 1995. *Licence Line*, 31 July: 4.

McCarty, T., and J.E. Heath. 1996. 'Minimizing Risk through Alcohol Policies: The Experience of Two Counties.' *Municipal World* 106(1): 6–7.

Murray, G., and R.R. Douglas. 1988. 'Social Marketing in the Alcohol Policy Arena.' *British Journal of Addiction* 83(5): May, 505–11.

Narbonne-Fortin, C. 1993. 'Chapleau: Working toward an Alcohol-Safer Community.' In G. Duplessis, M. McCrea, C. Viscoff, and S. Doupe, eds, *What Works!: Innovation in the Community Mental Health and Addiction Treatment Programs*, 321–9. Toronto: Canadian Scholars' Press Inc.

Narbonne-Fortin, C., M. Rylett, R.R. Douglas, and L. Gliksman. 1996. 'Municipal Alcohol Policies in Ontario: A Survey.' *Municipal World* 106(1): 4–5.

Newcombe, R. 1992. 'The Reduction of Drug-Related Harm: A Conceptual Framework for Theory, Practice and Research.' In P.A. O'Hare, R. Newcombe, A. Matthews, E.C. Buning, and E. Drucker, eds, *The Reduction of Drug-Related Harm*, 1–14. London: Routledge Publishing.

O'Hare, P.A., R. Newcombe, A. Matthews, E.C. Buning, and E. Drucker. 1992. *The Reduction of Drug-Related Harm*. London, New York: Routledge.

Pollard, A., T. Abraham, and R.R. Douglas. 1989. 'Avoiding Litigation: Elliot Lake's Alcohol Management Policy.' *Recreation Canada* 47(5): 12–18.

Rylett, M., R.R. Douglas, R. Bégin, H. Philbin Wilkinson, L. Gliksman, and C. Narbonne-Fortin. 1995. 'Municipal Alcohol Policies in Ontario: Facility Usage and Problem Reduction.' *Facility Forum* 5(6): 10, 16–18, 31.

Smart, R. 1988. 'Drinking under Special Occasion Permits: A Neglected Aspect of Alcohol Control Measures.' *Journal of Studies on Alcohol* 49(2): 196–9.

Solomon, R., B. Boake, and M. Gleason. 1985. 'One for The Road: A Tavern Owner's Liability as a Provider of Alcohol.' In E. Single and T. Storm, eds, *Public Drinking and Public Policy*, 258–76. Toronto: Addiction Research Foundation.

Solomon, R.M., S. Usprich, R.R. Douglas, L. Kiss, and L. Prout. 1996. 'Municipal Alcohol Policy: Liability, Prosecution and Risk Minimization.' Toronto: Addiction Research Foundation.

Symons, K., and R.R. Douglas. 1991. 'Community Policing in Action: Controlling Special Occasion Permit Drinking Events.' *OPP Review* 26(1): 6–8.

Thomson, M., and R. Douglas. 1983. 'A Peak into the Black Box: A Policy Development Model for the Resolution of Social and Health Issues in Municipal Recreation.' *Recreation Research Review* 10(1): 29–34.

Thomson, M., R.R. Douglas, G. Murray, and K. Moffatt. 1984. 'A Recreation Practitioner's Role in the Development of a Municipal Alcohol Policy.' *Municipal World* 94(9): 227–9, 250.

Thomson, M., K. Moffat, R.R. Douglas, G.G. Murray, and L. Gliksman. 1985. 'Implementing Policy to Manage Alcohol in Municipal Recreational Facilities: Influencing Participants to Play by the Rules.' *Recreation Canada* 43(3): 42–6.

Torjman, S. 1986. *Monograph 1: Essential Concepts and Strategies*. Toronto: Addiction Research Foundation and Health and Welfare Canada.

15 Harm Reduction and Alcohol Abuse: A Brief Intervention for College-Student Binge Drinking

G. ALAN MARLATT and JOHN S. BAER

How many college students drink, and what are the problems they experience with alcohol? A recent random survey conducted with 1595 students at the University of Washington (Lowell 1993) provides illustrative data from a large public West Coast university with a total population of over 35,000 students. More than half the students were light or non-drinkers, but undergraduates tended to be more extreme in their drinking patterns than graduate/professional students. Although there were more abstainers (28.6%) among undergraduates than graduate students (19%), among undergraduates there was a higher proportion (31%) of *binge drinkers* (defined as drinking five or more drinks on a single occasion) than among graduate students (17%). A significant minority of undergraduate students (11.4%) reported drinking more than eight drinks on a single occasion.

Binge-drinking rates among undergraduate students may be even higher on other campuses. In one survey of drinking practices among freshman-class students at fourteen colleges in Massachusetts, Wechsler and Issac (1992) found that over half the men (56%) and a third of women (35%) reported binge drinking. Over a third of the male and one-quarter of the female binge drinkers reported engaging in unplanned sexual activity, compared with only 10 per cent of non-binge drinkers. Binge drinkers were six times as likely to drive after consuming large quantities of alcohol and were twice as likely as non-binge drinkers to ride with an intoxicated driver (Wechsler and Issac 1992).

National surveys reveal that American college students have a slightly higher annual prevalence of any alcohol use (88%) compared to their age peers who do not attend college (85%); 43 per cent of college students report at least one episode of binge drinking in the last two weeks, compared to 34 per cent of their age peers (Johnston, O'Malley, and Bachman 1992). Other surveys indicate that heavy alcohol use is associated with a wide range of harmful consequences for college students, including school failure, relationship difficulties, vandalism, aggression, and date rape (Berkowitz and Perkins 1986; Engs and Hanson 1985). Alcohol-related accidents and injuries are the leading cause of death in this age group (National Institute on Alcohol Abuse and Alcoholism 1984).

Adolescent drinking patterns change over time (Grant, Harford, and Grigson 1988). Although drinking rates show a significant increase in the transition from high school to the college freshman year (Baer, Kivlahan, and Marlatt 1994), heavy drinking declines as students get older and assume increased adult responsibilities (Fillmore 1988; Zucker, in press; Jessor, Donovan, and Costa 1991). Although the majority of young adults show this 'maturing out' pattern over time, longitudinal studies have shown a continuity of drinking problems for a subset (approximately 30%) of heavy drinkers (Fillmore 1988; Zucker, in press). Among identified risk factors for continued alcohol problems in this age population, environmental factors such as residence (Larimer 1992) and 'party' settings (Geller and Kalsher 1990; Geller, Russ, and Altomari 1986), along with personal dispositional factors such as family history of alcoholism (Sher 1991) and history of conduct disorder (Jessor 1984) have all been identified in the literature. Our prevention efforts described below are designed with these two goals in mind: (1) to reduce the harm of alcohol abuse in adolescents who show a pattern of binge drinking and (2) to prevent the development of alcohol dependence among high-risk drinkers.

Background Research and Preliminary Studies

We developed our first alcohol harm reduction programs based on past research conducted in our laboratory on determinants of college-student drinking (Marlatt, Baer, and Larimer 1995). With our background and theoretical orientation in behavioural psychology and social cognitive theory, we were initially interested in psychosocial and environmental influences on drinking in this young population. Over the past two decades, our laboratory group has conducted a series of studies in which college students consumed alcohol under controlled experimental conditions (Caudill and Marlatt 1975; Collins and Marlatt 1981;

Collins, Parks, and Marlatt 1985; Higgins and Marlatt 1975; Marlatt 1978; Marlatt, Kosturn, and Lang 1975).

Based on these background research studies described above, we developed a cognitive-behavioural harm reduction program for college-student drinkers called the Alcohol Skills-Training Program (ASTP). We then conducted a controlled clinical trial to evaluate the impact of ASTP, presented in the form of an eight-week class (Kivlahan et al. 1990). The design of this study called for random assignment of student drinkers (N = 43) to one of three conditions: the ASTP experimental group, a comparison group called the Alcohol Information School, or to an assessment-only control group. Students were followed for a period of one year; a brief description of the study and the results follows.

Student volunteers were recruited to participate in the study by fly-ers, campus-newspaper advertisements, and class announcements ask-ing for participants who wanted to better understand or to change their drinking patterns. Subjects who qualified were paid for their time and effort for participation. To qualify, subjects needed to be heavy social drinkers who reported at least one negative consequence of drinking and who indicated no more than mild physical dependence on the Alco-hol Dependence Scale (Skinner and Horn 1984). The sample of students who completed the study was 58 per cent male and averaged twenty-three years of age. On average, baseline drinking averaged 15 drinks per week and subjects reported for the prior year an average of 7.5 occasions of driving after consuming four or more drinks.

Students assigned to ASTP completed an eight-week course (each weekly class was two hours long). Groups of eight students were led by male and female co-leaders. Each weekly session focused on a specific topic: (1) models of addiction and effects of drinking; (2) estimation of blood-alcohol levels and setting drinking limits; (3) relaxation training and lifestyle balance; (4) nutritional information and aerobic exercise; (5) coping with high-risk drinking situations; (6) assertiveness training and drink-refusal skills; (7) an expectancy challenge in which students consumed placebo beverages in a Behavioural Alcohol Research Labo-ratory (BARLAB, a simulated bar to study human drinking behaviour); and (8) relapse-prevention strategies for maintaining drinking behav-iour changes. In each class, a cognitive-behavioural psycho-educational model was adopted, with didactic presentations and small group dis-cussions.

In the Alcohol Information School control condition, students received an eight-week course required by the State of Washington for those convicted of under-age possession of alcohol or driving under the influence of alcohol. The program content was purely informational, and no new coping skills were taught. Lecture topics included the physical and behavioural effects of alcohol, dispelling myths about alcohol, alcoholism problems, and legal aspects of alcoholism. In the assessment-only control group, students participated in all assessment and follow-up measures, but received no prevention program until after the completion of the one-year follow-up period. The control-group data enabled an assessment of the effects of completing the assessment forms and self-monitoring drinking without any other intervention.

The impact of the prevention programs was assessed by student evaluations, self-monitored drinking rates, and estimates of weekly drinking rates. Self-monitored (daily drinking diaries) drinking rates were scored by computer to yield standard drinks per week and the peak (maximum) blood-alcohol level reached each week. At baseline, before program entry, students reported an average of fifteen drinks per week and a peak weekly blood-alcohol level of 0.13 per cent (0.10% or above defines legal intoxication in most states). At the one-year follow-up, ASTP subjects reported 6.6 drinks per week and a maximum blood-alcohol level of 0.07%, compared to 12.7 drinks per week and a maximum blood-alcohol level of 0.09% for students in the Alcohol Information School, and 16.8 drinks per week and 0.11% blood-alcohol maximum for assessment-only controls. Measures of self-perceived drinking patterns (in which subjects reported their drinking over a ninety-day period) showed students in the ASTP to have reduced their drinking significantly more than the other two groups when assessed at the one-year follow-up.

The results of this preliminary harm-reduction study were encouraging. Students involved in the research project reported that they significantly reduced their drinking and subjects in our ASTP condition showed the greatest changes at each follow-up period. Limitations included the small sample size, the use of only volunteer subjects, and the lack of collateral reports to validate self-report measures of drinking (the issue of the validity of self-report and the use of collaterals is discussed further below). In addition, subject recruitment was difficult; as expected, students failed to respond to an invitation to participate in an 'alcohol program.' Once engaged, however, the evaluation feedback indicated that the ASTP was perceived as just as helpful as typical alcohol-education programs.

The second trial of our alcohol harm reduction approach was

designed to evaluate the effectiveness of the ASTP program presented in different formats (Baer et al. 1992). Students ($N = 134$) were randomly assigned to one of three conditions: a classroom program (a replication of the ASTP program but reduced to six sessions from the original eight), a 'correspondence course' (the ASTP program content presented in a written six-lesson format), and a single session of 'professional advice' consisting of individual feedback and advice presented to the student. Although this third condition could be considered a minimal-contact control group, other studies indicated that just a single session of advice or motivational enhancement can have a significant impact on subsequent drinking behaviour, even for those with serious alcohol problems (Edwards et al. 1977; Miller and Rollnick 1991).

Student volunteers were again recruited from the campus population via flyers and newspaper ads, offering participation in a skills-training program to learn more about or change personal drinking patterns. As in the first study, subjects were offered monetary compensation for the time and effort involved in participating in a research program with multiple assessment periods. To qualify, students needed to report at least one significant alcohol problem and at least two days' drinking in an average week with blood-alcohol levels approaching 0.10 per cent or above.

The sample of 134 students who enrolled in the program was slightly younger (average age = 21) than those in the first study. Over half the sample consisted of females. Drinking patterns included an average of six alcohol problems; students reported drinking an average of twenty drinks per week spread over four drinking occasions (average drinks per occasion = five, the lower cut-off for binge-level drinking). Estimated peak blood-alcohol levels for weekly drinking averaged 0.14 per cent. Students assigned to the correspondence-course format were least likely to complete the assignment; less than half completed all six assignments. Drop-outs were less likely in the classroom-group condition, perhaps because of the peer support available in this format. The classroom condition was rated highest in the evaluation forms.

As in the first study, all students significantly reduced their alcohol consumption during the course of the intervention program. Average drinks per week declined overall from 12.5 to 8.5, and peak blood-alcohol levels dropped from 0.14 per cent to 0.10 per cent. Reported reductions in drinking levels were maintained significantly over the two-year follow-up period. At each assessment, subjects in the classroom condition drank the least, although differences between the conditions only approached statistical significance. It is noteworthy that the single session of professional advice showed results comparable to that of the more extensive prevention programs. On the basis of this finding, we decided to begin with a single session of advice as the first of a series of 'stepped-care' options. Our major study investigating the effectiveness of a stepped-care prevention model is described next.

Overview of the Lifestyles '94 Project

Rationale for Stepped Care and Study Design

The Lifestyles '94 project was designed to replicate and extend our earlier studies of brief, harm reduction programs with college-student heavy drinkers. The Lifestyles '94 study differed in several ways from our earlier studies. First, we did not wish to bias the sample by advertising for volunteers for a research program, but rather to apply this prevention to a cross-section of heavy drinkers in the college population. As a result, we screened all students in an entering college class and directly invited the heavier drinkers into a longitudinal study. Second, as we wished to test our interventions in a more preventive context, when students are younger and before problems develop, we focused on the first year in college (average age = 19) as the time for intervention (our previous samples were three to four years older on average). Third, we wished to test if our brief, one-hour feedback interview could be used as the first step in a graded program of interventions.

Our previous success with brief interventions suggested that motivational interventions such as feedback and advice may be sufficient to reduce harm associated with drinking among the college population. However, for those who did not respond, more intensive treatments were available. What is not clear is how to move students into more intensive and focused services. We felt that a brief, non-confrontational feedback session might be the best 'first step' in gaining rapport and access to students, hence facilitating the use of other, more intensive treatments as needed. Finally, the Lifestyles '94 study included specific research design improvements (from our earlier studies), including a much larger sample size, longer term (four-year) follow-up, the use of collateral reporters to confirm self-reports of alcohol consumption, and the assessment and analysis of individual-differences that may explain differential response to treatment. These individual-difference measures included gender, family history of alcoholism, history of conduct disordered behaviour, and type of student residence.

Subjects, Procedures, and Measures

Screening and Recruitment
In the spring of 1990, we mailed a questionnaire to all students who were accepted and had indicated an intention to enrol at the University of Washington the following autumn term (by sending in $50 deposit), who were matriculating from high school, and who were not over nineteen years of age. Each student was offered five dollars and entrance into a drawing for prizes for return of the questionnaires. Of 4000 questionnaires sent, 2179 completed forms were returned. Of these 2179, 2041 students provided usable questionnaires and indicated a willingness to be contacted for future research.

From the screening pool a 'high-risk' sample was selected. Students were considered high-risk if they reported drinking at least monthly and consuming five to six drinks on one drinking occasion in the past month, *or* reported the experience of three alcohol-related problems on three to five occasions in the past three years on the Rutgers Alcohol Problem Inventory (RAPI; White and Labouvie 1989). These criteria identified approximately 25 per cent of the screening sample ($n = 508$). An additional 'control sample' was randomly selected from the pool of 2041 responders to provide a normative comparison group ($n = 151$). As this sample was selected to represent normative practices, it was not restricted to those not previously screened as 'high risk.' As a result, thirty-three individuals were selected both as high-risk and as representing a normative comparison.

When they arrived on campus, students selected for the study were invited into a four-year longitudinal study of alcohol use and other lifestyle issues via letter. Phone calls were used to assure the receipt of the letter and to respond to questions. Students were asked to agree to be interviewed for approximately forty-five minutes and to fill out questionnaires for a $25.00 payment during the autumn academic term. Students in the 'high risk' group also agreed to be randomly assigned to receive or not receive individualized feedback the following academic quarter. All subjects agreed to additional questionnaire assessments annually for payment. Of the 508 'high risk' students invited, 366 were successfully recruited for the current study; 115 of 151 randomly selected subjects were similarly recruited (26 students were in both groups). Comparisons on screening measures between those subjects successfully recruited for the project and those not recruited revealed no significant differences in drinking rates (quantity and frequency), alcohol-related problems (RAPI scores), or gender.

Baseline and Follow-up Assessments
The initial or baseline assessment was used to guide individual feed-back sessions for those in the experimental group. The interview proto-col was based on three standardized interviews: the Brief Drinker Profile (Miller and Marlatt 1984), the Family Tree Questionnaire (Mann et al. 1985), and the Diagnostic Interview Schedule-Child, or DIS-C (Helzer and Robins 1988). From these protocols we assessed typical drinking quantity and frequency, alcohol-related life problems, history of conduct disorder, DSM-III-R alcohol-dependency criteria, and family history of drinking problems and other psychopathology. Interviewers were trained members of our research staff. In addition, students com-pleted questionnaires at baseline that included indices of the type of living situation, alcohol expectancies, perceived risks, psychiatric symp-tomotology (Brief Symptom Inventory, BSI; Derogatis and Spencer 1982), perceived norms for alcohol consumption, and sexual behaviour.

Students completed follow-up assessments through mailed question-naires in the Spring of the first year in college, and every autumn there-after throughout college. We have now analysed data from the junior year assessment, two years after baseline assessment. Note that the two-year assessment takes place in the junior year for those students who pursued their college education continuously (all subjects were fol-lowed regardless of enrolment or academic status). At each follow-up assessment students reported their typical drinking patterns, drinking problems, and alcohol dependency, in addition to measures of alcohol expectancies, life events, and psychiatric symptomatology. Details of these assessments are described below.

Measures

Drinking Rates
At all assessments, students used six-point scales to report their typical drinking quantity, frequency, and the single greatest amount of alcohol consumption (peak consumption) over the past month. A second mea-sure of drinking quantity and frequency was obtained at each follow-up assessment using the Daily Drinking Questionnaire (Collins et al. 1985).

Alcohol-Related Problems and Dependence
Alcohol-related problems were assessed with two different methodolo-gies at each assessment. As a measure of harmful consequences, stu-dents completed the Rutgers Alcohol Problem Inventory (White and

Labouvie 1989), rating the frequency of occurrence of twenty-five items reflecting alcohol's impact on social and health functioning over the past six months. Sample items include 'Not able to do homework or study for a test,' 'Caused shame or embarrassment,' and 'Was told by friend or neighbour to stop or cut down drinking.' The scale is reliable and accurately discriminates between clinical and normal samples (ibid.). Students also completed the Alcohol Dependence Scale (Skinner and Horn 1984), a widely used assessment of severity of dependence symptoms.

Other Risk Factors
Students were classified as family-history positive if they reported either natural parent or a sibling as being an alcoholic or problem drinker and reported at least two identifiable problem-drinking symptoms for that individual. History of conduct problems was assessed from fourteen items on the DIS-C that reflect common adolescent conduct problems, excluding alcohol or drug use (that is, truancy, fighting, stealing, school misconduct). These were coded as present or absent before age eighteen and summed to form a scale, with alpha = .65. College residence was coded as living off campus, in the dormitory system, or in a fraternity or sorority (Greek house).

Subjects
Description of this sample's drinking during high school and the transition into college have been described elsewhere (Baer, Kivlahan, and Marlatt 1995). Of the 366 high-risk students recruited, 11 were removed from randomization owing to extreme levels of drinking and drinking-related problems. These individuals were given our clinical intervention (described below) and referred for additional treatment. In addition, seven subjects returned questionnaires too late for the randomization. The final sample of 348 subjects were randomly assigned to receive or not receive intervention. At baseline, before randomization, 63 per cent of the sample of high-risk drinkers (188 females and 160 males) reported drinking at least 'one to two times a week'; 52.2 per cent reported drinking as many as 'three to four drinks' on a typical weekend evening of drinking; 61.4 per cent reported binge drinking at least 'five to six drinks' on a single drinking occasion during the previous month. Using the RAPI, the sample reported an average of 7.5 (sd = 5.86) alcohol-related harmful consequences as having occurred at least once over the six months before to the first-year autumn assessment; these students reported an average of 2.2 (sd = 2.83) problems occurring at least three to

five times over this same period. Students reported an average of 2.5 (sd = 1.94) conduct incidents during childhood, although the distribution was predictably skewed. Most high-risk subjects reported between zero and three previous conduct incidents (72.1%). Fifty-three subjects (12.9% of the sample) reported significant drinking problems in a first-degree relative (parent or sibling).

Procedures for Motivational Interviewing

The motivational intervention provided in the winter of the first year of college was based on prior research with brief interventions among the college students described above (see also Baer et al. 1992) and with motivational interviewing more generally (Miller and Rollnick 1991). Students assigned to receive an intervention were contacted first by phone and subsequently by mail to schedule a feedback interview (based on the data obtained the previous autumn term). Students were provided with alcohol-consumption monitoring cards and asked to track their drinking for two weeks before their scheduled interview.

In the feedback interview, a professional staff member met with the student alone, reviewed the self-monitoring, and gave concrete feedback about his or her drinking patterns, risks, and beliefs about alcohol effects. Drinking rates were compared to college averages, and risks for current and future problems (grades, blackouts, accidents) were identified. Beliefs about real and imagined alcohol effects were addressed through discussions of placebo effects and the non-specifics of the effects of alcohol on social behaviour. Biphasic effects of alcohol were described and the students were encouraged to question if 'more alcohol is better.' Suggestions for risk reduction were outlined.

The style of the interview was based on techniques of motivational interviewing. Confrontational communications, such as 'you have a problem and you are in denial' are thought to create a defensive response in the client and were specifically avoided. Instead, we simply placed the available evidence to the client and side-stepped arguments. We sought to allow the student to evaluate his or her situation and begin to contemplate the possibility of change. 'What do you make of this?' and 'Are you surprised?' were common questions raised to students in an effort to facilitate conversations about risk and the possibility of behaviour change. The technique is quite flexible. Issues of setting (life in a fraternity), peer use, prior conduct difficulties, and family history were addressed only if applicable.

From a motivational-interviewing perspective (Miller and Rollnick 1991), students are assumed to be in a natural state of ambivalence, and must come to their own conclusions regarding the need to change behaviour and reduce risks. Thus, the goals of subsequent behaviour changes were left to the student and not outlined or demanded by the interviewer. This style leaves responsibility with the client and hence treats all clients as thoughtful adults. Each student left the interview with a 'personalized feedback sheet' (that compared their responses with college norms and listed reported problems), and a 'tips' page that described biphasic responses to alcohol, noted placebo effects, and provided suggestions for reducing the risks of drinking. Students were encouraged to contact the Lifestyles '94 project if they had any further questions or were interested in any additional services throughout college.

Results to Date

Early results of this brief intervention with college freshman have been reported previously (Baer 1993). Summarizing, those receiving the feedback interview reported less drinking than those in the control group at the three-month follow-up. Longer-term outcomes will be described briefly here; a more thorough report of two- and three-year outcomes is currently being prepared. We have been generally successful in retaining the sample of students, with over 88 per cent providing data at the two-year follow-up assessment.

Multivariate analyses completed on one- and two-year post-baseline follow-up points revealed that, although all students on average reported reduced drinking over time, significantly greater reductions were continually reported by those given the brief advice intervention. Further, two different measures of alcohol-related problems (RAPI and ADS) revealed statistically significant differences between treatment and control groups, with results favouring the treatment group. Despite a general developmental trend of reporting fewer problems over time, examination of mean RAPI scores indicates that those given the brief intervention in the freshman year report on average 3.3 harmful consequences from alcohol use by the junior year, compared to 4.7 for the high-risk control group. Our random group, which serves as a normative comparison for high-risk students, reports on average 2.4 problems at the junior-year assessment. Thus, these differences, if reliable, reflect meaningful harm-reduction among those receiving the motivational intervention.

Analysis of individual differences that might relate to treatment response are complex: there are simply too many factors to analyse simultaneously and retain power to test all possible interactions. Therefore, a series of multivariate repeated-measures analyses of variance was completed to evaluate each individual difference factor (that is, family history of alcoholism, conduct problem history, type of university residence) as main effects and in interaction with gender and treatment in the prediction of drinking trends. Both alcohol-use rates and alcohol-related problems were evaluated as dependent measures. Analyses completed to date can be summarized by describing a few consistent trends in the data pertaining to the report of alcohol-related problems. None of the individual difference factors studied consistently interacted with treatment response: our treatment seems effective for all students regardless of risk status. However, several trends in our data suggested that not all students are equally at risk, and therefore treatment may be more important for certain individuals.

First, a family history of alcohol problems did not relate in any consistent fashion to changes to the self-report of drinking problems (no main effects or interactions). However, those with a history of conduct problems or delinquent behaviours reported more alcohol-related problems at all points in time (main effect). In addition, men living in fraternities reported more alcohol-related problems than women or those living elsewhere at all points in time (sex by residence interaction). Finally, compared to men, women reported greater decreases in problems over the two-year follow-up time period (sex by time interaction).

The treatment effects described above and the individual differences in developmental trends sum or compile to create a risky picture for certain individuals, in particular men with conduct histories living as members of fraternity houses. For women, our prevention program appeared to enhance a downward developmental trend for drinking problems, regardless of residence. For men a different and more troubling picture emerged. Men living in the Greek system reported more problems on average, and all men reported more consistent problems over time. Further, all of these trends were exacerbated by a history of conduct difficulties, and roughly two-thirds of those reporting conduct histories were men. As a result, individuals with multiple risk profiles (men living in fraternities who also have a history of conduct problems) showed the most severe pattern of harmful drinking over time and the least decline. These individuals, therefore, may benefit the most from our preventive programming. For example, in this study, men in the Greek system who did not receive treatment represented our only subgroup where alcohol-dependence scores actually increased during the first two years of college.

Our studies of college-student drinking described above naturally are limited by the self-report nature of the data pertaining to alcohol use and estimates of blood-alcohol levels. Although often criticized, self-reports of drinking behaviour often show considerable reliability and validity under conditions of confidentiality and safety (Babor, Stephens, and Marlatt 1987). We emphasize repeatedly to participants the confidential and non-evaluative nature of our data. Nevertheless, we cannot control completely for possible increases in the social desirability of reporting drinking reductions among those receiving treatment (and developing relationships with program staff) compared to those in the control condition. As a result of this concern we have spent considerable effort in our latest study collecting confirmatory data from collateral reporters. Collateral data serves two general purposes. First, the procedure communicates to the subject an emphasis on accuracy and a check on self-report. A long history of research on 'bogus pipeline' effects in social psychology suggests that this procedure should promote accurate reporting by subjects (Jones and Sigall 1971). Second, collateral reports constitute a separate data source. With collateral reports we can check if others perceive changes in our subjects' drinking.

In our current longitudinal study, collateral data have provided support for our self-report data. We asked collaterals to rate fairly specific aspects of subjects' drinking and the presence of low-level problems. Follow-up assessments resulted in reliable collateral assessments (both within collaterals and between subjects and collaterals); reliability for some responses are above r = .70. Further, these reports begin to confirm some behavioural differences based on self-report between treatment and control groups. In particular, collaterals perceive those in the treatment group as drinking less frequently and drinking to intoxication less often compared to those in the control condition. These trends appear most evident when collaterals report on female subjects, and less so with men. Treatment-group subjects are also more likely to be seen as having decreased their drinking than are control subjects. These data offer one important source of confirmatory evidence that our brief preventive intervention resulted in a decrease in drinking behaviour.

Harm Reduction and the Prevention of Alcohol Abuse

Our work on the prevention of alcohol problems with college students is best conceptualized as a harm reduction approach (Marlatt et al. 1993). We believe that harm reduction provides a conceptual umbrella that covers a variety of previously unrelated programs and techniques in the addictive-behaviours field, including needle-exchange programs for injection drug users, methadone maintenance for opiate users, nicotine replacement methods for smokers, weight management and eating-behaviour change programs for the obese, and safe-sex programs (e.g., condom distribution in high schools) to reduce the risk of HIV infection and AIDS (Marlatt and Tapert 1993). Our work in the prevention of alcohol abuse in college students fits well within this domain.

Habits can be placed along a continuum of harmful consequences. The goal of harm reduction is to move the individual with alcohol problems along this continuum: to begin to take 'steps in the right direction' to reduce harmful consequences. It is important that the harm reduction model accepts abstinence as the ideal or ultimate risk-reduction goal. But the harm reduction model promotes any movement in the right direction along this continuum as progress, even if total abstinence is not attained.

Clearly, the excessive use of alcohol is associated with increasingly harmful consequences as consumption increases. Harm reduction is based on the assumption that by reducing the level of drinking, the risk of harm will drop in a corresponding manner. By this logic, total abstinence from alcohol would seem to be associated with the lowest level of harmful consequences. In some areas, however, the benefits of moderate drinking may outweigh the harm reduction advantages offered by abstinence.

Moderate drinking can have both harmful and helpful consequences. Moderate to heavy drinking is reported to increase the risk associated with motor-vehicle crashes, birth defects, and harmful interactions with certain medications; yet it also associated with reduced risk of cardio-vascular disease (National Institute on Alcoholism and Alcohol Abuse 1992). Given the mixed risks associated with moderate drinking, arguments have been presented on both sides concerning whether abstinence or moderation should be recommended to the public concerning their use of alcohol (Peele 1993; Shaper 1993).

Harm reduction approaches are not limited to the type of individual clinical approaches or self-management training programs described in this paper. Changes in the physical and social environment can also be implemented, along with public-policy changes designed to minimize harm (e.g., legalization of needle-exchange programs). The best results occur when all three methods are combined. For example, to reduce the harm associated with automobile accidents it is possible to develop better driver-training programs (individual self-management or autoregulation), to construct safer automobiles and highways (changing the environment), as well as to introduce safety-enhancing public policies (e.g., a reduced speed limit or enhanced enforcement programs). To reduce the harm of drunk driving, it is again possible to combine these three elements: programs mandated for the drunk driver (that is, programs designed to modify drinking and avoid intoxicated driving), physical and social environmental changes (e.g., use of car ignition systems that are designed to foil the intoxicated driver; designated-driver selection), and policy changes (e.g., reducing the blood-alcohol minimum for legal intoxication while driving).

As documented in the present review, harm reduction can be applied to the secondary prevention of alcohol problems with moderation as the goal. In sharp contrast to the disease model and twelve-step programs that insist on abstinence as the 'first step' in dealing with any alcohol problem, harm reduction encourages a gradual 'step-down' approach to reduce the harmful consequences of alcohol or other drug use. By stepping down the harm incrementally, drinkers can be encouraged to pursue proximal sub-goals along the way to either moderation or abstinence.

NOTES

This research was supported in part by a Research Scientist Award and a MERIT award (grants #AA00113 and #AA05591) awarded to the senior author and by a research grant (grant #AA08632) awarded to the second author by the National Institute on Alcohol Abuse and Alcoholism.

REFERENCES

Babor, T.F., R.S. Stephens, and G.A. Marlatt. 1987. 'Verbal Report Methods in Clinical Research on Alcoholism: Response Bias and Its Minimization.' *Journal of Studies on Alcohol* 48: 410–24.
Baer, J.S. 1993. 'Etiology and Secondary Prevention of Alcohol Problems with Young Adults.' In J.S. Baer, G.A. Marlatt, and R.J. McMahon, eds, *Addictive Behaviors across the Lifespan*, 111–37. Newbury Park, CA: Sage Publications.
Baer, J.S., D.R. Kivlahan, and G.A. Marlatt. 1995. 'High-Risk Drinking across the

Transition from High School to College.' *Alcoholism: Clinical and Experimental Research* 19: 54–61.

Baer, J.S., G.A. Marlatt, D. Kivlahan, K. Fromme, M. Larimer, and E. Williams. 1992. 'An Experimental Test of Three Methods of Alcohol Risk Reduction with Young Adults.' *Journal of Consulting and Clinical Psychology* 60: 974–9.

Berkowitz, A.D., and H.W. Perkins. 1986. 'Problem Drinking among College Students: A Review of Recent Research.' *Journal of American College Health* 35: 1–28.

Caudill, B.D., and G.A. Marlatt. 1975. 'Modeling Influences in Social Drinking: An Experimental Analogue.' *Journal of Consulting and Clinical Psychology* 43: 405–15.

Collins, R.L., and G.A. Marlatt. 1981. 'Social Modeling as a Determinant of Drinking Behavior: Implications for Prevention and Treatment.' *Addictive Behaviors* 6: 233–40.

Collins, R.L., G.A. Parks, and G.A. Marlatt. 1985. 'Social Determinants of Alcohol Consumption: The Effects of Social Interaction and Model Status on the Self-Administration of Alcohol.' *Journal of Consulting and Clinical Psychology* 53: 189–200.

Derogatis, L.R., and P.M. Spencer. 1982. *The Brief Symptom Inventory (BSI): Administration, Scoring, Procedures Manual-I.* Baltimore: Johns Hopkins University of Medicine.

Edwards, G., J. Orford, S. Egert, S. Guthrie, A. Hawker, C. Hensman, M. Mitcheson, E. Oppenheimer, and C. Taylor. 1977. 'Alcoholism: A Controlled Trial of "treatment" and "advice".' *Journal of Studies on Alcohol* 38: 1004–31.

Engs, R.C., and D.J. Hanson. 1985. 'The Drinking-Patterns and Problems of College Students: 1983.' *Journal of Alcohol and Drug Education* 31: 65–82.

Fillmore, K.M. 1988. *Alcohol Use across the Life Course.* Toronto: Alcoholism and Drug Addiction Research Foundation.

Geller, E.S., and M.J. Kalsher. 1990. 'Environmental Determinants of Party Drinking: Bartenders vs. Self-service.' *Environment and Behavior* 22(1): 74–90.

Geller, E.S., N.W. Russ, and M.G. Altomari. 1986. 'Naturalistic Observations of Beer Drinking among College Students.' *Journal of Applied Behavior Analysis* 19(4): 391–6.

Grant, B.F., T.C. Harford, and M.B. Grigson. 1988. 'Stability of Alcohol Consumption among Youth: A National Longitudinal Study.' *Journal of Studies on Alcohol* 49: 253–60.

Helzer, J.E., and L.N. Robins. 1988. 'The Diagnostic Interview Schedule: Its Development, Evolution, and Use.' *Social Psychiatry and Psychiatric Epidemiology* 23(6): 6–16.

Higgins, R.L., and G.A. Marlatt. 1975. 'Fear of Interpersonal Evaluation as a

Determinant of Alcohol Consumption in Male Social Drinkers.' *Journal of Abnormal Psychology* 84: 644–51.

Jessor, R. 1984. 'Adolescent Development and Behavior Health.' In J.D. Materazzo, S.M. Weiss, J.A. Herd, N.E. Miller, and S.M. Weiss, eds, *Behavior Health: A Handbook of Health Enhancement and Disease Prevention*, 69–90. New York: Wiley.

Jessor, R., J.E. Donovan, and F.M. Costa. 1991. *Beyond Adolescence: Problem Behavior and Young Adult Development.* New York: Cambridge University Press

Johnston, L.D., P.M. O'Malley, and J.G. Bachman. 1992. *Smoking, Drinking, and Illicit Drug Use among American Secondary School Students, College Students, and Young Adults, 1975–1991.* Washington: National Institute on Drug Abuse, U.S. Department of Health and Human Services.

Jones, E.E., and H. Sigall. 1971. 'The Bogus Pipeline: A New Paradigm for Measuring Affect and Attitude.' *Psychological Bulletin* 76: 349–64.

Kivlahan, D.R., G.A. Marlatt, K. Fromme, D.B. Coppel, and E. Williams. 1990. 'Secondary Prevention with College Drinkers: Evaluation of an Alcohol Skills Training Program.' *Journal of Consulting and Clinical Psychology* 58: 805–10.

Larimer, M.E. 1992. 'Alcohol Abuse and the Greek System: An Exploration of Fraternity and Sorority Drinking.' Unpublished doctoral dissertation, University of Washington, Seattle.

Lowell, N. 1993. *University Life and Substance Abuse: 1993 Survey.* Seattle: University of Washington, Office of Educational Assessment, Report 93-4.

Mann, R.E., L.C. Sobell, M.B. Sobell, and D. Pavan. 1985. 'Reliability of a Family Tree Questionnaire for Assessing Family History of Alcohol Problems.' *Drug and Alcohol Dependence* 15: 61–7.

Marlatt, G.A. 1978. 'Behavioral Assessment of Social Drinking and Alcoholism.' In G.A. Marlatt and P.E. Nathan, eds, *Behavioral Approaches to Alcoholism*, 35–7. New Brunswick, NJ: Rutgers Center of Alcohol Studies.

Marlatt, G.A., J.S. Baer, and M.E. Larimer. 1995. 'Preventing Alcohol Abuse in College Students: A Harm-Reduction Approach.' In G.M. Boyd, J. Howard, and R.A. Zucker, eds, *Alcohol Problems among Adolescents: Current Directions in Prevention Research*, 147–72. Northvale, NJ: Lawrence Erlebaum and Assoc., Inc.

Marlatt, G.A., C.F. Kosturn, and A.R. Lang. 1975. 'Provocation to Anger and Opportunity for Retaliation as Determinants of Alcohol Consumption in Social Drinkers.' *Journal of Abnormal Psychology* 84: 652–9.

Marlatt, G.A., M.E. Larimer, J.S. Baer, and L.A. Quigley. 1993. 'Harm Reduction for Alcohol Problems: Moving beyond the Controlled Drinking Controversy.' *Behavior Therapy* 24: 461–504.

Marlatt, G.A., and S.F. Tapert. 1993. 'Harm Reduction: Reducing the Risks of Addictive Behaviors.' In J.S. Baer, G.A. Marlatt, and R.J. McMahon, eds, *Addictive Behaviors across the Lifespan: Prevention, Treatment, and Policy Issues*, 243–73. Newbury Park, CA: Sage.

Miller, W.R., and G.A. Marlatt. 1984. *The Brief Drinker Profile*. Odessa, FL: Psychological Assessment Resources.

Miller, W.R., and S. Rollnick. 1991. *Motivational Interviewing: Preparing People for Change*. New York: Guilford.

National Institute on Alcohol Abuse and Alcoholism. 1984. *Report of the 1983 Prevention Planning Panel*. Rockville, MD: NIAAA.

– 1992. *Alcohol Alert*. Rockville, MD: NIAAA.

Peele, S. 1993. 'The Conflict between Public Health Goals and the Temperance Mentality.' *American Journal of Public Health* 83: 805–10.

Shaper, A.G. 1993. 'Editorial: Alcohol, the Heart, and Health.' *American Journal of Public Health* 83: 799–800.

Sher, K.J. 1991. *Children of Alcoholics: A Critical Appraisal of Theory and Research*. Chicago: University of Chicago Press.

Skinner, H.A., and J.L. Horn. 1984. *Alcohol Dependence Scale* (ADS). Toronto: Addiction Research Foundation.

Wechsler, H., and N. Issac. 1992. '"Binge" Drinkers at Massachusetts Colleges.' *Journal of the American Medical Association* 267: 292–3.

White, H.R., and E.W. Labouvie. 1989. 'Towards the Assessment of Adolescent Problem Drinking.' *Journal of Studies on Alcohol* 50: 30–7.

Zucker, R.A. In press. 'Alcohol Involvement over the Life Span: A Developmental Perspective on Theory and Course.' In L.S. Gaines and P.H. Brooks, eds, *Alcohol Studies: A Lifespan Perspective*. New York: Springer.

PART IV:
LABORATORY, CLINICAL, AND FIELD STUDIES

16 Animal Self-Administration of Cocaine: Misinterpretation, Misrepresentation, and Invalid Extrapolation to Humans

JOHN P. MORGAN and LYNN ZIMMER

The increase in cocaine use in North America during the 1970s and early 1980s provoked a series of cautionary tales regarding its dangers, particularly its addictive powers. In the medical, clinical, and popular literatures, evidence of cocaine's addictiveness took two forms: (1) personal accounts of people who claimed to have lost control of the drug and (2) reports of laboratory experiments in which animals consumed enough cocaine to cause their own deaths. The second narrative was particularly important, given that cocaine was known to cause neither physical dependence nor withdrawal symptoms of the sort associated with opiates (Gawin and Kleber 1986). For cocaine to be accepted in the public mind as a highly addictive drug, it was necessary that alternative evidence, of a seemingly scientific nature, be offered.

Reports of studies showing that animals could be made to self-administer cocaine were in scientific journals for about ten years before anyone suggested that they offered insight into human cocaine use. Indeed, in most early reviews of the animal self-administration literature, researchers urged caution in extrapolating the findings to humans (Woods 1977; Byck and Van Dyke 1977; Fischman and Schuster 1982; Schuster and Johanson 1974). However, once cocaine's rising popularity became a focus of public concern and media attention, these words of caution were ignored, including by some of those who had originally voiced them.

Drug-abuse experts, particularly those involved in treating addiction, have been among the most ardent publicizers of the animal self-administration studies. In 1981, Sidney Cohen wrote in his *Drug Abuse and Alcoholism Newsletter*: 'Animals will work more avidly ... for cocaine than for any other drug. In an unlimited access situation, monkeys will self-administer cocaine by bar pressing for it until they die in status epilepticus ... They will work for cocaine in preference to food even though they are starving. They will continue to bar press even though a receptive female is in their cage. If humans had unlimited access to cocaine they probably would behave in a similar manner' (Cohen 1981). Cohen did not cite specific studies to substantiate these claims. Nor did drug-treatment providers Arnold Washton or Richard Schwartz:

Animal experiments dramatically portray the reinforcing and addictive powers of cocaine. When laboratory animals are given intravenous injections of cocaine, they will do almost anything to obtain additional injections of the drug. Animals will work harder and more persistently for cocaine than for any other drug, including heroin ... Hungry animals will preferentially bar press for cocaine rather than for food ... Male monkeys continue to work for cocaine even in the presence of a receptive female in their cage. In one experiment, monkeys continued to work feverishly at pressing a bar even though it took nearly 13,000 presses to obtain a single dose of the drug. Is cocaine addictive? The answer is an unequivocal YES. (Washton 1984)

Monkeys allowed an unlimited supply of intravenous cocaine died of convulsions within five days. They preferred cocaine to life – that's the bottom line. (Schwartz quoted in *Time Magazine*, 16 June 1986: 22)

Indeed, in textbooks for drug-treatment professionals, it is now common for cocaine to be identified as *the most addictive and most dangerous drug* that humans use:

Cocaine's most dramatic behavioural effect ... is its unparalleled rewarding potency. Animals become more readily addicted to cocaine than to any other drug and cocaine-addicted animals suffer more dysfunctional and lethal consequences than animals dependent upon other drugs. (Geary 1987: 19)

The strength of the addiction is illustrated by experiments performed on *Rhesus* monkeys ... All of the monkeys pressed the bar to receive the cocaine until inanition and death. The loss of control for self-administration of the cocaine was sufficiently potent to produce disregard for the instincts of self-preservation. The behaviour in the *Rhesus* monkeys is readily seen in humans who pursue it without regard for health and welfare, as manifested by their willingness to sacrifice large sums of money, liberty, and life. (Cocores et al. 1991: 346)

Journalists similarly began integrating the tale of animal self-administration into their coverage of the cocaine story. The following examples are illustrative:

Researchers who have studied cocaine's effect on the brain believe it interferes with normal biochemical agents that control the desire for food, sex, and sleep. Given a choice between food and cocaine in laboratory experiments, monkeys will become hooked on cocaine and take it until they starve to death. Humans become almost as manic. (*Time Magazine*, 15 September 1986: 63)

Cocaine is among the most 'reinforcing' of drugs. In an experiment ..., monkeys were allowed to self-administer intravenously a variety of chemical substances, including cocaine, caffeine, amphetamines, and nicotine. The monkeys went on binges with each of these substances, but only with cocaine did their use become so compulsive that they reached a lethal dose and died. (*Atlantic Monthly*, January 1986: 41)

Cocaine's power of reinforcement produces its most notorious effects: the desire to keep taking it as long as the drug is available. In one series of experiments ..., scientists let caged monkeys self-administer ... cocaine until they died ... The drug made them monomaniacal; in one ... experiment, a monkey was forced to press a bar 12,800 times before he received a dose of the drug. (*Rolling Stone*, 9 February 1989: 72)

Cocaine addicts tend to go on binges, and monkeys hooked up intravenously will inject themselves repeatedly, rejecting food, sex and sleep until they die. (*New York Times*, 14 June 1992: 7)

Even social scientists, who generally accept the limitations of pharmacologically-based explanations of drug use and abuse, have often found the image of animals self-administering cocaine so compelling that they present it without critical commentary. For example, in his widely used textbook, sociologist Erich Goode reports that '[i]n laboratory experiments, rats, mice, and monkeys will self-administer cocaine in preference to food and will even starve to death ... If experimental animals receive cocaine as a result of engaging in a certain activity, and the researchers then discontinue administering the drug, these animals will go on engaging in that activity – thousands of times in an hour – at a higher rate and for a longer period of time than will animals deprived of any other drug type' (Goode 1993: 240). In an anti-drug advertisement for the print media, the Partnership for a Drug Free America created a particularly provocative rendition of the story, claiming that monkeys had *smoked cocaine* when, in fact, almost all studies involve administering the drug through intravenous (IV) injection:[1] 'In animal studies, monkeys with unlimited access to cocaine self-administer until they die. One monkey pressed a bar 12,800 times to obtain a single dose of cocaine. Rhesus monkeys won't smoke tobacco or marijuana, but 100% will smoke cocaine, preferring it to sex and food – even when starving.'

The constant repetition of this narrative tale can best be understood in the context of America's most recent drug scare – that surrounding the use of cocaine, particularly in the form of 'crack,' by the urban poor (Reinarman and Levine 1989). In most of the popular literature on cocaine that appeared *before* the introduction of crack in the mid-1980s, the literature on animal self-administration was largely ignored. It was generally accepted that people could become addicted to cocaine, despite the absence of physical dependence (Grinspoon and Bakalar 1985), but the idea of cocaine being *more addictive* than other drugs – even more addictive than heroin – did not appear regularly until after the crack scare had begun. In the popular and medical literatures, the dangers of crack were exaggerated and distorted and, in the process, so were those of sniffed cocaine. Fairly typical is a passage from the journal *Science* that combines the animal self-administration narrative with a second one: that smoking cocaine (in the form of crack) adds substantially to the drug's addictive powers: 'A variety of species from mice to monkeys will learn to self-administer cocaine faster than any other drug and will do it until they die. In human terms it implies what has become self-evident in the inner cities – people get addicted to cocaine faster than they do to opiates and much faster to crack, which produces a vapor when burned that floods the brain indiscriminately in a matter of seconds' (15 December 1989: 1378).

Elsewhere, we analyse the claims regarding the hazards of smoking crack as opposed to sniffing cocaine powder (Morgan and Zimmer 1997). Herein, we review the animal self-administration studies on which the claims of cocaine's high addictive potential are based. At the outset we state our conclusion: the above quotes not only make inappropriate comparisons between animals and humans but grossly misrepresent the nature and findings of the animal self-administration studies.

Laboratory Conditions for Animal Self-Administration Research[2]

Animal self-administration studies follow the basic principles of operant conditioning. Typically, rats or monkeys are placed into a cubicle and trained to respond to a 'cue' – for example, a flashing light – after which their pressing of a lever delivers a predetermined dose of drug. For animals to self-administer drugs in this fashion, rather extreme conditions are necessary: they must be implanted with a catheter, to allow drug delivery; they must be tethered to the side of the cubicle, to protect the implanted catheter; and they must be kept isolated from other animals, who might destroy the equipment and/or distract them from their conditioned task. When monkeys are used, they are fitted with a stainless-steel harness and connected to the wall of the cage by a flexible hollow metal spring, through which a catheter delivers the drug from an external pump to a vein in the animal's neck (see figure 1). Essentially, all animal studies have been performed on animals isolated and tethered in this fashion. And because animals cannot easily be induced to swallow, sniff, or smoke drugs, most self-administration studies utilize automatic drug-delivery systems. Sometimes drugs are delivered directly into the stomach (Altshuler and Phillips 1978; Woolverton and Schuster 1983); sometimes they are injected into muscle (Katz 1980; Goldberg et al. 1976) or brain tissue (Goeders 1988); but most commonly, drugs are delivered to test animals by intravenous injection.

Early Studies Established Cocaine's High Reinforcement Value

Early self-administration studies, using primates and rats, established that cocaine was a powerful 'reinforcer.' That is, when each pressing of the bar delivered cocaine, animals could easily be trained to inject at regular intervals (Pickens and Thompson 1968; Deneau et al. 1969; Wilson et al. 1971). In fact, because it proved so easy to teach animals to inject cocaine, researchers who wanted to study the self-administration of other drugs – whether medications or illicit substances – often trained animals with cocaine before beginning the main experiment (Johanson 1984). In addition, cocaine has been used to test and modify the techniques associated with animal self-administration models (Grove and Schuster 1974).

To evaluate the relative reinforcement value of cocaine, researchers have conducted numerous studies, utilizing a variety of experimental designs and employing a variety of measures. Among the variables altered across experiments are dosage levels, response conditions, and frequency of drug availability. In some cases, researchers also present animals with negative reinforcers and, in others, with alternative posi-

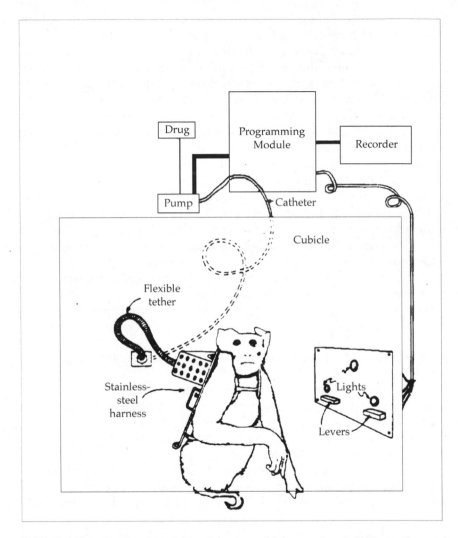

FIGURE 1 This picture, adapted from Schuster and Johanson (1974), illustrates the usual method for studying primate self-administration of drugs, using operant conditioning.

tive reinforcers (Johanson 1984 1988; Johanson and Fischman 1989). Together, this body of research, conducted with a range of animal species (although mostly rats and primates), has produced a complex set of findings that are sometimes contradictory.

Animal Self-Administration Studies under Conditions of Unlimited Access

A 1969 study offered rhesus monkeys an unlimited supply of cocaine, twenty-four hours a day, self-administered through an IV catheter (Deneau et al. 1969). Of the four monkeys originally used in the study, two initiated self-injection at a low dose, while the two others required higher doses before adopting the operant behaviour. A fifth monkey was added to the study at the higher dose, and all animals continued to be given unlimited access to cocaine. Overall intake varied considerably among the five, with some engaging in periods of voluntary abstinence lasting as long as five days. However, over the course of the study, all five monkeys exhibited dosage increase and, eventually, two of the monkeys convulsed and died – leading the researchers to abandon the project. Several years later, Johanson et al. (1976) provided rhesus monkeys with unlimited access to cocaine under similar conditions – and obtained similar results. All monkeys escalated their dose, and within five days, two of the monkeys were dead.

Animals self-administer cocaine at rates similar to those associated with many other drugs. Under unlimited-access conditions, monkeys quickly escalate their use of most psychomotor stimulant drugs, including some that are seldom misused by humans. For example, in the Johanson et al. (1976) study referred to above, animals that were given the anorectic medication diethylpropion not only *injected as frequently* as those given cocaine, but *died at a similar rate*. In another study, monkeys given unlimited access to methylphenidate – a drug commonly prescribed to children with Attention Deficit Disorder – were *more likely* than those given cocaine to self-administer to the point of fatality (Downs et al. 1979).

Under a variety of circumstances, animals will self-administer opiates even more commitedly than cocaine (Bozarth and Wise 1985; Johanson and Fischman 1989). However, the opiate self-administration story is much less dramatic because animals who continuously inject opiates seldom die. The reason for this is that although *a single large dose* of opiates may cause death – owing to respiratory depression – *continuous administration* of opiates produces *tolerance*, which protects animals (and humans) from the drug's potential lethality. Because stimulant drugs do not bestow a similar degree of protection against *stimulation* of the cardiovascular and neural systems, escalated use is associated with increased risk of physical harm, particularly in the form of seizures.

Thus, animals given unlimited access to cocaine are more likely to die than are those given unlimited access to opiates – not because cocaine is more *addictive*, but because at continuous high doses cocaine is more *toxic*.

After 1976, because of cocaine's known toxicity, animal experimenters seldom provided unlimited access – unless the study was of relatively short duration. One exception is a 1985 study by Bozarth and Wise, which gave isolated rats unlimited around-the-clock access to cocaine via an implanted IV catheter. Only a single bar-push was required to deliver cocaine, and injections were possible every ten seconds. Under these conditions – which were designed specifically to maximize self-administration – ten of the twelve rats acquired the operant behaviour and, predictably, nine of the ten died from cocaine toxicity. Despite the fact that this study contributed no new information, and merely reproduced results that had been reported nearly two decades earlier, it was accepted for publication in the *Journal of the American Medical Association*, where the authors warned physicians about its 'obvious implications for human drug abuse.'

Studies Employing Limited Access to Cocaine

Animal self-administration studies that offer cocaine under conditions of *restricted access* have consistently found more moderate patterns of consumption. As early as 1971, Wilson et al. showed that once monkeys were trained to self-administer cocaine on a limited fixed schedule (four hours per day), they ignored later opportunities to escalate use. Not only did they refuse to increase the number of injections during the four hours that cocaine was available, but when researchers increased the amount of cocaine per injection, the monkeys began injecting less frequently, thereby maintaining the daily dose that had been established previously.

Other studies, some employing more modest restrictions than those of Wilson et al., have similarly shown that once animals establish a stable daily intake of cocaine, they never exhibit the 'out of control' consumption pattern typical of animals trained under unlimited-access conditions (Johanson and Fischman 1989). Some researchers have found that increasing the dose of cocaine increases animal response rates, but this seems to occur when the dose increase is relatively small, and primarily in studies that provide a mandatory 'time-out period' following each self-administration episode (Balster and Schuster 1973). Most studies have found either a *flat* dose-response curve or an *upside-down U-shaped* curve, in which modest increases in dose result in higher rates of drug-administration, but more substantial increases suppress drug-taking behaviour (Dworkin and Smith 1988; Kelleher 1975; Goldberg and Kelleher 1976; Johanson 1982).

While the above studies seem to suggest that high doses of cocaine are *less reinforcing* than low doses, the diminishing animal response that accompanies higher doses may be a consequence of cocaine's *pharmacological impact on behaviour* (Johanson 1988; Dworkin and Smith 1988). Supporting this second conclusion are studies showing that, under some other experimental conditions, high doses of cocaine are *more reinforcing* than low doses. For example, when animals, at the beginning of limited-access studies, are allowed to choose between a high dose and a low doses of cocaine, they generally prefer the higher dose (Johanson and Schuster 1975; Iglauer and Woods 1974; Brady and Griffiths 1977; Johanson 1975). The broader point illustrated by this example is that animal responses can be a result of multiple drug effects, some of which may be induced by the conditions of the experiment, in interaction with the drug. Thus, with steadily escalating doses of cocaine, there may be a point at which the *animal's performance becomes impaired*, resulting in decreased responding – despite the potentially higher reinforcement-value of the larger dose. An understanding that drug effects sometimes *interact* to produce specific outcomes is necessary not only for making sense of the conflicting dose-response data described above, but for evaluating the additional research findings that will be discussed below.

Progressive-Ratio Studies

Some animal studies evaluate reinforcement by progressively increasing the number of responses required for an injection; the more committedly animals work for a drug, the more 'reinforcing' the drug is presumed to be. In 1973, Yanagita reported a progressive-ratio study using morphine and cocaine. After training monkeys in self-administration, he provided unlimited access and, every twenty-four hours, doubled the number of lever-pushes required for an injection. Of monkeys receiving morphine, some developed physical dependence and, not surprisingly, were more persistent bar-pushers than non-dependent monkeys; indeed, some of the former group pushed the lever 12,800 times to deliver a single dose of morphine. Of the four monkeys that received cocaine, two gave up early, but the other two matched the persistence of morphine-dependent monkeys, responding 12,800 times. However, this result was achieved only at the highest dose-schedule that Yanagita provided. At lower doses – similar to those used to establish animal self-administration of cocaine – Yanagita found lower 'breaking points.' Other progressive-ratio studies have similarly found lower 'breaking points' for cocaine, generally in the range of a few hundred responses (Bedford et al. 1978; Winger and Woods 1985; Griffiths et al. 1975; Griffiths et al. 1978; Risner and Silcox 1981; Risner and Goldberg 1983).

The fact that animals are willing to repeatedly push a lever to obtain cocaine is not necessarily evidence of the drug's reinforcement power. Confounding the results of all progressive-ratio studies is the fact that cocaine, whether self-administered or injected by human researchers, tends to produce heightened locomotor activity in experimental animals. And, at higher doses, cocaine often produces stereotypical repetitive behaviour – particularly in animals that have been 'preconditioned' in isolated research environments (Groppetti et al. 1973; Simon 1973; Post and Weiss 1988; Woolverton and Kleven 1988; Collins et al. 1979). In fact, no matter what task animals are trained to perform, they tend to perform it more commitedly when under the influence of cocaine (Spealman et al. 1977; Thompson 1977).

The willingness of animals to push a lever more than 12,000 times for a single dose of cocaine is almost certainly due, in part, to the pharmacological impact of the previously consumed doses of the drug.[3] Indeed, the fact that Yanagita found a substantially higher breaking-point for the highest dose of cocaine – despite the fact that, in other studies, higher doses of cocaine are not *more reinforcing* than lower doses – suggests that Yanagita was measuring cocaine's *psychostimulant properties* rather than its *reinforcing properties*. And because this problem affects all breaking-point studies, this measure of reinforcement – while useful for evaluating other forms of conditioned behaviours – is of little use when evaluating the reinforcing properties of cocaine.

Studies Employing Negative Reinforcers

The strength of cocaine as a reinforcer has also been studied under conditions of punishment – typically, by requiring animals to accept an electrical shock to obtain each dose of drug. In general, the more intense the shock, the more quickly animals decrease self-administration, regardless of the magnitude of pre-shock doses. And with sufficient shock intensity, all animals stop administering cocaine (Grove and

Schuster 1974; Bergman and Johanson 1981). However, over time, if shock intensity remains stable (and is in the low to moderate range) some animals will adjust to its presence and reinstate self-administration (Bergman and Johanson 1981).

Johanson's (1977) study of negative reinforcement required animals to choose between two dose-choices — the higher of which was accompanied by a mild electrical shock of constant intensity. When the shocked dose was twice as large as the non-shocked dose, most animals chose the lower dose, most of the time; however, as the shocked dose increased, more animals (and eventually all animals) chose the higher dose. This is not surprising, given that animals typically adjust to stable shock conditions and revert to previously established drug behaviour. If increases in shock intensity had accompanied the increases in dose, it is likely that some or all animals would have moved towards the lower dose. The fact is that although animals are willing to accept some amount of pain as a cost of receiving cocaine, they are unwilling to accept a lot of pain, regardless of the offered dose. In fact, animals exposed to very intense electrical shocks not only cease injecting cocaine, but never return to self-administration, even when non-punished sessions are once again offered (Bergman and Johanson 1981).

Studies Employing Alternative Positive Reinforcers

Some self-administration studies are designed to force animals to choose between cocaine and other positive reinforcers, including other drugs. Most common are studies pairing cocaine with another psycho-motor stimulant. Animals respond equally to some pairings (Woolverton and Johanson 1984), but when there is a strong preference for one drug over another, it is more often a preference for cocaine (Johanson and Schuster 1977, 1975; Johanson and Aigner 1981). Still, there is generally some dose at which other stimulants will be chosen over cocaine. And because the decision about what constitutes 'equivalent doses' of different drugs is to some extent arbitrary, there is a sense in which these studies are inherently incomparable.

Another set of studies requires animals to choose between cocaine and food. Aigner and Balster (1978) found that under unlimited-access conditions, monkeys chose cocaine most often. However, this does not necessarily indicate a *preference* for cocaine over food, and certainly does not indicate a preference for cocaine *over survival*. Because one of cocaine's pharmacological effects is appetite suppression (Angrist and

Sudilovsky 1976), once animals receive substantial doses of cocaine, their *attraction to food* is diminished. Indeed, in studies designed to evaluate operant conditioning with regard to food, animals pretreated with cocaine generally decrease food intake (Herling et al. 1979; Groppetti et al. 1973).

Other studies have similarly shown that when cocaine is available only at scheduled intervals, animals tend to eat normally; in fact, when the amount of food offered as an alternative to a stable dose of cocaine is increased, monkeys begin choosing cocaine over food less often (Nader and Woolverton 1991). There are also studies showing that animals *maintained on an adequate diet* before the experiment consume less cocaine than those 'primed' with food-deprivation (Carroll et al. 1979). Even animals initially deprived of food decrease their cocaine consumption when, during the experiment, they are offered sweetened water as an alternative reinforcer (Carroll et al. 1989). In short, only under extreme experimental conditions do cocaine-consuming animals fail to maintain an adequate daily food intake.

Despite the widely made claim that male animals choose cocaine over 'available receptive females,' we were unable to find a single study in which such a choice was offered. This is not surprising, given that self-administration studies require animals to be totally isolated and physically restrained. Indeed, as we discuss in more detail below, it is precisely because the experimental conditions under which animals self-administer cocaine are so different from the conditions under which humans take drugs that so little about human drug use can be learned from these studies.

Human Cocaine Use and the Limits of Animal Self-Administration Studies

In a recent anti-drug advertisement (quoted earlier), the Partnership for a Drug Free America followed its presentation of the cocaine-injecting monkey tale with the claim *'Like monkey, like man.'* Nothing could be further from the truth. To produce self-destructive cocaine use in monkeys, researchers must create an environment that bears little resemblance to the environment in which humans use drugs. Test animals are reared apart from other members of their species and are deprived of food before the experiment. During the experiment, they are tethered to an isolated cage and fitted with an injection apparatus that limits their movement. The drug must be continuously available to them, easy to obtain, and delivered immediately upon performance of a simple task. The dose must be neither too large nor too small; negative reinforcement must be absent; so must alternative positive reinforcers. Basically, all unlimited-access studies – regardless of the drug – are designed to 'push' animals towards maximum consumption.

To calculate the *relative reinforcement value* of different drugs, researchers compare patterns of self-administration under a variety of experimental conditions. However, this comparison does not provide a basis for identifying any drug as the *most reinforcing* since no drug uniformly scores high in all experimental settings. Nor does any drug always score highest on the various ways that self-administration intensity can measured – for example, number of doses consumed, frequency of consumption, degree of effort exerted per dose, amount of punishment accepted per dose, and so forth (Johanson 1988). Under some conditions, animals consume dangerously high levels of cocaine; but under others, rates of consumption for cocaine are similar to or lower than those for other drugs. Woolverton summarizes this well: 'Punishment, the availability of alternative reinforcers and response cost all determine whether or not cocaine has a reinforcing effect ... Although current rhetoric would often have one believe otherwise, these results emphasize that the self-administration of cocaine is governed by the same laws that govern behaviour maintained by other positive reinforcers' (1992: 158).

Even if it were possible to objectively rank drugs on the basis of their reinforcement power in laboratory animals, it would not provide meaningful insight into the use of these drugs by humans. There are drugs used recreationally by humans (for example, marijuana and LSD) that animals will not readily self-administer. And there are drugs readily self-administered by animals (for example, methylphenidate, procaine, and diethylpropion) that are rarely used recreationally by humans (Schuster and Johanson 1974; Brady and Lucas 1984; Kalant 1989). Indeed, there is no consistent relationship between a drug's reinforcement power in the laboratory and its popularity among human drug users.

The fact that almost all self-administration studies utilize intravenous injection further diminishes their applicability to humans. Injection is extremely uncommon among human drug users. According to a recent household survey, less than 8 per cent of the Americans who had used cocaine in the previous year had ever injected it; instead, the predominant mode of ingestion – employed by over 90 per cent of cocaine users – was to sniff or snort the drug (National Institute on Drug Abuse 1991a).

No studies have managed to induce animals to sniff or snort drugs, and the few studies using either oral ingestion or smoking have found *much lower* rates of consumption than those found in injection-studies (Siegel et al. 1976; Alexander et al. 1981). Thus, experiments that provide injectable cocaine to animals fail to predict patterns of use in animals offered cocaine through other means (Balster 1988). To an even greater extent, animal injection studies fail to predict cocaine-use patterns in humans.

Epidemiological data reveal that human cocaine consumption differs enormously from that of laboratory animals. Surveys conducted in the United States and Canada indicate that among people who have ever tried cocaine, only a small proportion use it more than occasionally and within this latter group, only a small proportion use it regularly for a prolonged period of time (Erickson and Alexander 1989; National Institute on Drug Abuse 1991a). Even people who become high-dose users tend to vary their intake over time, alternating periods of intense use with periods of moderate use and abstinence (Cohen 1995; Waldorf et al. 1991; Siegel 1985; Chitwood 1985; Erickson et al. 1987; Anthony and Trinkoff 1989; Gawin and Kleber 1985). At some point in their cocaine-use careers, many high-dose users report experiencing 'craving' and 'compulsion,' but even they do not behave like animals in unlimited-access laboratory studies – consuming cocaine continuously and single-mindedly, to the exclusion of all other activities, and inevitably causing their own deaths. Indeed, while negative health consequences never alter cocaine consumption in laboratory animals, the emergence of negative consequences is often an impetus for humans to reduce or stop use altogether (Waldorf et al. 1991; Cohen 1995).

The reason that cocaine-use patterns in laboratory animals bear so little resemblance to use patterns among humans is that animal studies are purposely designed to eliminate the 'set' and 'setting' factors that play a crucial role in human drug-taking (Zinberg 1984). Research by Alexander et al. (1981) shows that even animals reduce their drug intake when they are trained in groups, unrestrained, offered alternative activities and reinforcers, and allowed to interact with other members of their species. Numerous studies have also shown that researchers can induce animals to diminish drug consumption by requiring them to work harder for each dose or by attaching a punishment to each injection (Grove and Schuster 1974; Johanson 1977; Bergman and Johanson 1981; DeGrandpre et al. 1993). For humans, all drug use takes place in a social context that includes a vast array of positive and negative reinforcers – as well as a set of moral guidelines that influence drug-taking behaviour. Indeed, as Stanton Peele (1985) convincingly argues, 'addiction' itself is a human phenomenon, better understood as a response to life circumstances than to the biochemical properties of specific drugs. Thus, a problem with using animal self-administration studies to learn about *addiction* is not just that they fail to account for the numerous social and psychological factors that affect human drug use, but that they purport to measure in animals a phenomenon that is wholly human.

Animal self-administration studies are also used inappropriately, to warn about cocaine's potential *toxicity* in humans. Under conditions of unlimited access, animals can be induced to administer extremely high doses of cocaine, which then often produce physical harm and death. However, in limited-access experiments, cocaine toxicity does not emerge as a problem. Not only do participating animals survive such studies, but even after consuming cocaine *daily for months or years*, they show no signs of physical disease or impairment (Johanson 1984). In fact, using data from these limited-access studies, one could easily make the case that cocaine has been proved *remarkably safe* rather than *remarkably dangerous*. Of course, if humans were to consume large doses of cocaine, around-the-clock, via intravenous injection, they might very well – like animals in unlimited-access studies – harm themselves physically. But the fact is that human cocaine consumption is much closer to that of animals in *dose-restricted studies*. And there is evidence that cocaine use among humans rarely produces serious physical harm.

Data from the Drug Abuse Warning Network (DAWN) is often used to support the claim that dramatic increases in cocaine-related fatalities have accompanied the recent increases in cocaine use (U.S. Department of Health and Human Services 1992). However, independent reviews of coroners' reports have found that a majority of the deaths *officially labelled as cocaine-related* are not caused by cocaine directly; in fact, the most common causes of cocaine-related death were accident and trauma (Tardiff et al. 1989; Alexander 1990). DAWN reported 2500 deaths related to cocaine in 1992, but perhaps only a few hundred resulted from cocaine's pharmacological impact on the body. However, even if the 2500 figure were correct, the fatality rate for past-year cocaine users – who numbered nearly five million in 1992 – would be about .0005 per cent. This number, while perhaps still constituting a problem, is 1000 times lower than the 50 per cent fatality rate for monkeys in unlimited-access studies.

Science in Service to the War on Drugs

Although the consumption patterns of human cocaine users are much less dangerous than those of animals in laboratory settings, evidence from the animal studies is continually used to publicize cocaine's profound risk to humans. In a recent report, the National Institute on Drug Abuse stated that the animal model 'replicates the compulsive drug-seeking behaviour seen in people addicted to drugs' and was explicitly designed by NIDA-funded researchers in their 'search for an explanation of addiction' (National Institute on Drug Abuse 1991b: 16). However, the fact is that before cocaine's movement into the public spotlight in the mid-1980s, the animal studies – which had begun in the mid-1960s – had generally *not been used* as evidence of cocaine's highly addictive potential. For example, at a 1976 conference on cocaine sponsored by NIDA, none of the participants identified 'addiction' as one of the drug's important hazards (Peterson and Stillman 1977); and when data from the animal studies were mentioned, it was mainly to illustrate the health and behavioural consequences of high-dose use – not cocaine's addictiveness (Woods 1977). However, at a 1984 NIDA conference on cocaine (Kozel and Adams 1985a), several participants referred directly to the animal studies as evidence of cocaine's 'powerful reinforcing properties' and, therefore, its great addictive risk to humans (Clayton 1985; Cohen 1985; Kozel and Adams 1985b; Schnoll et al. 1985). Importantly, this focus on cocaine's addictiveness emerged despite the fact that, between 1976 and 1984, no important new findings had appeared in the animal self-administration literature.

Animal self-administration research continues to be conducted – today, mostly for the purpose of learning about cocaine's mechanisms of action within the brain's dopamine and serotonin systems. More so than in the past, animal researchers justify their work as offering 'valuable insight' into cocaine use by humans (Johanson 1984, 1988; Goeders 1988; Dworkin and Smith 1988). Probably most of them recognize the limits of such an application, but making it – if only in a cursory fashion – may be necessary for their obtaining government funding. Even if they report their findings accurately, with appropriate cautions about extrapolation to humans, the information they provide will almost certainly be used by others to generate terror tales for wider distribution.

It is among drug-treatment providers that evidence from the animal studies has gained the most currency. In fact, their descriptions of human cocaine users have come to closely resemble the narrative tales of experimental animals:

Given unlimited access to the drug, IV cocaine abusers will escalate the dose until they deteriorate physically and mentally. (Gold 1992: 208)

Richard and Eugene were preoccupied with cocaine. It had become their top priority – above physical well-being, above relationships, perhaps above basic survival instincts. (Weiss and Mirin 1987: 56)

Cocaine abusers will always crave more – and the more they receive, the more agitated and disordered they will become. (Rosental 1991: 233)

Affluence can still be a liability when it comes to cocaine. Like monkeys, some people will consume as much as they can get. The more they have, the more they use. Only exhaustion, debilitation, confinement, bankruptcy, or death can eventually stop them. (Washton 1989: 27)

These observations appear to have been *generated* by the animal studies rather than *predicted* by them. In other words, through their widespread dissemination, the animal studies have changed how cocaine use is viewed, interpreted, and described. The animal studies have even affected the way drug users themselves describe cocaine's powers:

So she said to me that I was going to have to make a choice – either cocaine or her ... It was clear to me there wasn't a choice. I love my wife, but I'm not going to choose *anything* over cocaine ... Nothing and nobody comes between me and my coke. (Quoted in Weiss and Mirin 1987: 55)

I was totally out of control. I didn't even realize it. That's what's crazy about cocaine. One night, my heart freaked out and I thought I was going to die. (Quoted in National Institute on Drug Abuse 1987: 4)

It was like – whoo! I can't really tell you how long I stayed high. It just made my body say "I want some more. I want some more. I want some more." ... [Now] I think I can say no. I hope I can. But never say what you'll do when it comes to cocaine. (Quoted in *Newsweek*, June 30 1986)

Conclusion

A small number of animal studies, employing highly contrived methods designed to maximize cocaine consumption, are now widely employed as rhetoric to label cocaine use as highly addictive and intolerably dangerous. Whatever the value of these studies to science and scientists, because they eliminate the sorts of factors that influence the drug-use decisions of humans, they contribute little or nothing to our understanding of cocaine in human cultures. In addition, their constant repetition – by persons involved in the drug research, drug treatment, drug policy, and drug journalism establishments – exaggerates the nature of the 'cocaine problem' and increases public support for harsh punitive responses. The problem is not in the science, but in the way drug-related science is funded, conducted, and reported under the current, highly politicized system of drug prohibition.

NOTES

1 In one of the Partnership's television ads, the route of administration is shown as oral consumption – also a misrepresentation. Indeed, virtually all aspects of animal self-administration research are misrepresented in this single anti-drug public-service announcement.
2 For a more detailed description of the techniques employed in animal self-administration studies, see Schuster and Johanson 1974 and Brady and Griffiths 1976.
3 Similarly, there are some drugs that when administered in operant-conditioning studies *reduce* the rate of animal responding, regardless of the task (Dworkin and Smith 1988).

REFERENCES

Aigner, T.G., and R.L. Balster. 1978. 'Choice Behavior in *Rhesus* Monkeys: Cocaine versus Food.' *Science* 201: 534–5.
Alexander, B.K. 1990. *Peaceful Measures: Canada's Way Out of the War on Drugs.* Toronto: University of Toronto Press.
Alexander, B.K., B.L. Beyerstein, and P.R. Hadaway. 1981. 'Effects of Early and Later Colony Housing on Oral Ingestion of Morphine in Rats.' *Pharmacology Biochemistry and Behavior* 15: 571–6.
Altshuler, H.L., and P.E. Phillips. 1978. 'Intragastric Self-Administration of Drugs by the Primate.' In B.T. Ho et al., eds, *Drug Discrimination and State-Dependent Learning,* 263–80. New York: Academic Press.
Angrist, B., and A. Sudilovsky. 1976. 'Central Nervous System Stimulants: Historical Aspects and Clinical Effects.' In I.L. Iversen et al., eds, *Handbook on Psychopharmacology,* 11: 99–163. New York: Plenum Press.
Anthony, J.C., and A.L. Trinkoff. 1989. 'United States Epidemiological Data on Drug Use and Abuse: How Are They Relevant to Testing Abuse Liability of Drugs?' In M.W. Fischman and N.K. Mello, eds, *Testing for Abuse*

Liability of Drugs in Humans, 241–66. Rockville, MD: National Institute on Drug Abuse.

Balster, R.L. 1988. 'Pharmacological Effects of Cocaine Relevant to Its Abuse.' In D. Clouet et al., eds, *Mechanisms of Cocaine Abuse and Toxicity*, 1–13. Rockville, MD: National Institute on Drug Abuse.

Balster, R.L., and C.R. Schuster. 1973. 'Fixed-Interval Schedule of Cocaine Reinforcement: Effects of Dose and Infusion Duration.' *Journal of Experimental Analysis of Behavior* 20: 119–29.

Bedford, J.A., L.P. Baily, and M.C. Wilson. 1978. 'Cocaine-Reinforced Progressive-Ratio Performance in the Rhesus Monkey.' *Pharmacology Biochemistry and Behavior* 9: 631–8.

Bergman, A., and C.E. Johanson. 1981. 'The Effects of Electric Shock on Responding Maintained by Cocaine in Rhesus Monkeys.' *Pharmacology Biochemistry and Behavior* 14: 423–26.

Bozarth, M.A., and R.A. Wise. 1985. 'Toxicity Associated with Long-Term Intravenous Heroin and Cocaine Self-Administration in the Rat.' *Journal of the American Medical Association* 254: 81–3.

Brady, J.V., and R.R. Griffiths. 1976. 'Behavioral Procedures for Evaluating the Relative Abuse Potential of CNS Drugs in Primates.' *Federation Proceedings* 35: 245–53.

– 1977. 'Drug-Maintained Performance and the Analysis of Stimulant Reinforcing Effects.' In E.H. Ellinwood and M.M. Kilbey, eds, *Cocaine and Other Stimulants*, 599–613. New York: Plenum Press.

Brady, J.V., and S.E. Lucas. 1984. *Testing Drugs for Physical Dependence Potential and Abuse Liability*. Rockville, MD: National Institute on Drug Abuse.

Byck, R., and C. Van Dyke. 1977. 'What Are the Effects of Cocaine in Man?' In R.C. Petersen and R.C. Stillman, eds, *Cocaine: 1977*, 97–118. Rockville, MD: National Institute on Drug Abuse.

Carroll, M.E., C.P. France, and R.A. Meisch. 1979. 'Food Deprivation Increases Oral and Intravenous Drug Intake in Rats.' *Science* 205: 319–21.

Carroll, M.E., S.T. Lac, and S.T. Nygard. 1989. 'A Concurrently Available Non-Drug Reinforcer Prevents the Acquisition or Decreases the Maintenance of Cocaine-Reinforced Behavior.' *Psychopharmacology* 97: 23–9.

Chitwood, D.T. 1985. 'Patterns and Consequences of Cocaine Use.' In N.J. Kozel and E.A. Adams, eds, *Cocaine Use in America: Epidemiologic and Clinical Perspectives*, 111–29. Rockville, MD: National Institute on Drug Abuse.

Clayton, R.R. 1985. 'Cocaine Use in the United States: A Blizzard or Just Being Snowed?' In N.J. Kozel and E.A. Adams, eds, *Cocaine Use in America: Epidemiologic and Clinical Perpectives*, 8–34. Rockville, MD: National Institute on Drug Abuse.

Cocores, J., A.C. Pottash, and M.S. Gold. 1991. 'Cocaine.' In N.C. Miller, ed.,

Comprehensive Handbook of Drug and Alcohol Addiction, 341–52. New York: Marcel Dekker.

Cohen, P.D.A., and A. Sas. 1995. *Cocaine Use in Amsterdam II: Initiation and Patterns of Use after 1986*. Netherlands: University of Amsterdam.

Cohen, S. 1981. 'Gift of the Sun God or the Third Scourge of Mankind?' *Drug Abuse and Alcoholism Newsletter* 10: 1–3.

– 1985. 'Reinforcement and Rapid Delivery Systems: Understanding Adverse Consequences of Cocaine.' In N.J. Kozel and E.A. Adams, eds, *Cocaine Use in America: Epidemiologic and Clinical Perspectives*, 151–7. Rockville, MD: National Institute on Drug Abuse.

Collins, J.P., H. Lesse, and L.A. Dagan. 1979. 'Behavioral Antecedents of Cocaine-Induced Stereotypy.' *Pharmacology Biochemistry and Behavior* 11: 683–7.

DeGrandpre, R.J., W.K. Bickel, J.R. Hughes, et al. 1993. 'Unit Price as a Useful Metric in Analyzing Effects of Reinforcer Magnitude.' *Journal of Experimental Analysis of Behavior* 60: 641–66.

Deneau, G., T. Yanagita, and M.H. Seevers. 1969. 'Self-Administration of Psychoactive Substances by the Monkey: A Measure of Psychological Dependence.' *Psychopharmacologia* 16: 30–48.

Downs, D.A., S.E. Harrigan, J.N. Wiley, et al. 1979. 'Continuous Stimulant Self-Administration in Rhesus Monkeys.' *Communications in Psychology, Psychiatry and Behavior* 4: 39–49.

Dworkin, S.I., and J.E. Smith. 1988. 'Neurobehavioral Pharmacology of Cocaine.' In D. Clouet, et al., eds, *Mechansims of Cocaine Abuse and Toxicity*, 185–98. Rockville, MD: National Institute on Drug Abuse.

Erickson, P.G., E.M. Adlaf, G.F. Murray, and R.G. Smart. 1987. *The Steel Drug: Cocaine in Perspective*. Lexington MA: Lexington Books.

Erickson, P.G., and B.K. Alexander. 1989. 'Cocaine and Addictive Liability.' *Social Pharmacology* 3: 249–70.

Fischman, M.W., and C.R. Schuster. 1982. 'Cocaine Self-Administration in Humans.' *Federation Proceedings* 41: 241–6.

Gawin, F.G., and H.D. Kleber. 1985. 'Cocaine Use in a Treatment Population: Patterns and Diagnostic Distinctions.' In N.J. Kozel and E.A. Adams, eds, *Cocaine Use in America: Epidemiologic and Clinical Perspectives*, 182–92. Rockville, MD: National Institute on Drug Abuse.

– 1986. 'Abstinence Symptomatology and Psychiatric Diagnosis in Cocaine Abusers.' *Archives of General Psychiatry* 43: 107–13.

Geary, N. 1987. 'Cocaine: Animal Research Studies.' In H.I. Spitz and J.S. Rosecan, eds, *Cocaine Abuse: New Directions in Treatment and Research*, 19–47. New York: Brunner/Mazel.

Goeders, N.E. 1988. 'Intracranial Cocaine Self-Administration.' In D. Clouet et al., eds, *Mechanisms of Cocaine Abuse and Toxicity*, 199–216. Rockville, MD: National Institute on Drug Abuse.

Gold, M.S. 1992. 'Cocaine (and Crack): Clinical Aspects.' In J.H. Lowinson et al., eds, *Substance Abuse: A Comprehensive Textbook*, 205–21. Baltimore: Williams and Wilkins.

Goldberg, S.R., and R.T. Kelleher. 1976. 'Behavior Controlled by Scheduled Injections of Cocaine in Squirrel and Rhesus Monkeys.' *Journal of Experimental Analysis of Behavior* 25: 93–104.

Goldberg, S.R., W.H. Morse, and D.M. Goldberg. 1976. 'Behavior Maintained under a Second-Order Schedule of Intramuscular Injection of Morphine or Cocaine in Rhesus Monkeys.' *Journal of Pharmacology and Experimental Therapeutics* 199: 278–86.

Goode, E. 1993. *Drugs in American Society*. New York: McGraw Hill.

Griffiths, R.R., J.V. Brady, and J.D. Snell. 1978. 'Progressive Ratio Performance Maintained by Drug Infusions: Comparisons of Cocaine, Diethlypropion, Chlorphentermine and Fenfluramine.' *Psychopharmacology* 56: 5–13.

Griffiths, R.R., J.D. Findley, J.V. Brady, et al. 1975. 'Comparison of Progressive-Ratio Performance Maintained by Cocaine, Methylphenidate, and Secobarbitol.' *Psychopharmacologia* 43: 81–3.

Grinspoon, L., and J.B. Bakalar. 1985. *Cocaine: A Drug and Its Social Evolution*. New York: Basic Books.

Groppetti, A., F. Zambotti, A. Biazzi, and R. Mantegazza. 1973. 'Amphetamine and Cocaine on Amine Turnover.' In E. Usdin and S.H. Snyder, eds, *Frontiers in Catecholamine Research*, 917–25. Oxford: Pergamon Press.

Grove, R.N., and C.R. Schuster. 1974. 'Suppression of Cocaine Self-Administration by Extinction and Punishment.' *Pharmacology Biochemistry and Behavior* 2: 199–208.

Herling, S., D.A. Downs, and J.H. Woods. 1979. 'Cocaine, d-Amphetamine, and Pentobarbital Effects on Responding Maintained by Food or Cocaine in Rhesus Monkeys.' *Psychopharmacology* 64: 261–9.

Iglauer, C., and J.H. Woods. 1974. 'Concurrent Performances: Reinforcement by Different Doses of Intravenous Cocaine in Rhesus Monkeys.' *Journal of Experimental Analysis of Behavior* 22: 179–96.

Johanson, C.E. 1975. 'Pharmacological and Environmental Variables Affecting Drug Preference in Rhesus Monkeys.' *Pharmacological Reviews* 27: 343–55.

– 1977. 'The Effects of Electric Shock on Responding Maintained by Cocaine Injections in a Choice Procedure in the Rhesus Monkey.' *Psychopharmacology* 53: 277–82.

– 1982. 'Behavior Maintained under Fixed Interval and Second-Order Schedules of Cocaine or Pentobarbitol in Rhesus Monkeys.' *Journal of Pharmacology and Experimental Therapeutics* 221: 384–93.

– 1984. 'Assessment of the Dependence Potential of Cocaine in Animals.' In J. Grabowski, ed., *Cocaine: Pharmacology, Effects, and Treatment of Abuse,* 54–71. Rockville, MD: National Institute on Drug Abuse.

– 1988. 'Behavioral Studies of the Reinforcing Properties of Cocaine.' In D. Clouet et al., eds, *Mechanisms of Cocaine Abuse and Toxicity,* 107–24. Rockville, MD: National Institute on Drug Abuse.

Johanson, C.E., and T. Aigner. 1981. 'Comparison of the Reinforcing Properties of Cocaine and Procaine in Rhesus Monkeys.' *Pharmacology Biochemistry and Behavior* 15: 49–53.

Johanson, C.E., R.L. Balster, and K. Bonese. 1976. 'Self-Administration of Psychomotor Stimulant Drugs: The Effects of Unlimited Access.' *Pharmacology Biochemistry and Behavior* 4: 45–51.

Johanson, C.E., and M.W. Fischman. 1989. 'The Pharmacology of Cocaine Related to Its Abuse.' *Pharmacological Reviews* 41: 3–52.

Johanson, C.E., and C.R. Schuster. 1975. 'A Choice Procedure for Drug Reinforcers: Cocaine and Methylphenidate in the Rhesus Monkey.' *Journal of Pharmacology and Experimental Therapeutics* 193: 676–88.

– 1977. 'A Comparison of Cocaine and Diethylpropion under Two Different Schedules of Drug Presentation.' In E. Ellingwood and M.M. Kilby, eds, *Cocaine and Other Stimulants,* 545–70. New York: Plenum Press.

Kalant, H. 1989. 'The Nature of Addiction: An Analysis of the Problem.' In A. Goldstein, ed., *Molecular and Cellular Aspects of the Drug Addictions,* 1–28. New York: Springer-Verlag.

Katz, J.L. 1980. 'Second-Order Schedules of Intramuscular Cocaine Injection in the Squirrel Monkey: Comparisons with Food Presentation and Effects of d-Amphetamine and Promazine.' *Journal of Pharmacology and Experimental Therapeutics* 212: 405–11.

Kelleher, R.T. 1975. 'Characteristics of Behavior Controlled by Scheduled Injections of Drugs.' *Pharmacological Reviews* 27: 307–23.

Kozel, N.J., and E.H. Adams, eds. 1985a. *Cocaine Use in America: Epidemiologic and Clinical Perspectives.* Rockville, MD: National Institute on Drug Abuse.

– 1985b. 'Cocaine Use in America: Summary of Discussion and Recommendations.' In N.J. Kozel and E.H. Adams, eds, *Cocaine Use in America: Epidemiologic and Clinical Perspectives,* 221–6. Rockville, MD: National Institute on Drug Abuse.

Morgan, J.P., and L. Zimmer. 1977. 'The Social Pharmacology of Smokable Cocaine: Not All It's Cracked Up to Be.' In C. Reinarman and H.G. Levine, *Crack in America,* 122–56. Berkeley: University of California Press.

Nader, M.A., and W.L. Woolverton. 1991. 'Effects of Increasing the Magnitude of an Alternative Reinforcer on Drug Choice in a Discrete-Trials Choice Procedure.' *Psychopharmacology* 105: 169–74.

National Institute on Drug Abuse. 1987. *Cocaine/Crack: The Big Lie*. Rockville, MD: National Institute on Drugs Abuse.

– 1991a. *National Household Survey on Drug Abuse: Main Findings 1990*. Rockville, MD: National Institute on Drug Abuse.

– 1991b. *NIDA Notes* 5(5).

– 1993. *National Household Survey on Drug Abuse: Population Estimates 1992*. Rockville, MD: National Institute on Drug Abuse.

Peele, S. 1985. *The Meaning of Addiction: Compulsive Experience and Its Interpretation*. Lexington, MA: Lexington Books.

Petersen, R.C., and R.C. Stillman, eds. 1977. *Cocaine 1977*. Rockville, MD: National Institute on Drug Abuse.

Pickens, R., and T. Thompson. 1968. 'Cocaine Reinforced Behavior in Rats: Effects of Reinforcement Magnitude and Fixed-Ratio Size.' *Journal of Pharmacology and Experimental Therapeutics* 161: 122–9.

Post, R.M., and S.R.B. Weiss. 1988. 'Psychomotor Stimulant vs. Local Anesthetic Effects of Cocaine: Role of Behavioral Sensitization and Kindling.' In D. Clouet et al., eds, *Mechanisms of Cocaine Abuse and Toxicity*, 217–38. Rockville, MD: National Institute on Drug Abuse.

Reinarman, C., and H.G. Levine. 1989. 'Crack in Context: Politics and Media in the Making of a Drug Scare.' *Contemporary Drug Problems* 16: 535–77.

Risner, M.E., and S.R. Goldberg. 1983. 'A Comparison of Nicotine and Cocaine Self-Administration in the Dog: Fixed-Ratio and Progressive-Ratio Schedules of Intravenous Drug Infusion.' *Journal of Pharmacology and Experimental Therapeutics* 224: 319–26.

Risner, M.E., and D.L. Silcox. 1981. 'Psychostimulant Self-Administration by Beagle Dogs in a Progressive-Ratio Paradigm.' *Psychopharmacology* 75: 25–30.

Rosenthal, M.S. 1991. 'The Logic of Legalization: A Matter of Perspective.' In M.B. Kraus and E.P. Lazear, eds, *Searching for Alternatives: Drug-Control Policy in the United States*, 226–38. Stanford, CA: Hoover Institution Press.

Schnoll, S.H., J. Karrigan, S.B. Kitchen, et al. 1985. 'Characteristics of Cocaine Abusers Presenting for Treatment.' In N.J. Kozel and E.H. Adams, eds, *Cocaine Use in America: Epidemiologic and Clinical Perspectives*, 171–81. Rockville, MD: National Institute on Drug Abuse.

Schuster, C.R., and C.E. Johanson. 1974. 'The Use of Animal Models for the Study of Drug Abuse.' In R.J. Gibbins et al., eds, *Research Advances in Alcohol and Drug Problems*, 1: 1–32. New York: John Wiley.

Siegel, R.K. 1985. 'New Patterns of Cocaine Use: Changing Doses and Routes.' In

N.J. Kozel and E.H. Adams, eds, *Cocaine Use in America: Epidemiologic and Clinical Perspectives*, 204–20. Rockville, MD: National Institute on Drug Abuse.

Siegel, R.K., C.A. Johnson, J.M. Brewster, and M.E. Jarvik. 1976. 'Cocaine Self-Administration in Monkeys by Chewing and Smoking.' *Pharmacology, Biochemistry and Behavior* 4: 461–7.

Simon, P. 1973. 'Psychopharmacological Profile of Cocaine.' In E. Usdin and S.H. Snyder, eds, *Frontiers in Catecholamine Research*, 1043–4. Oxford: Pergamon Press.

Spealman, R.D., S.R. Goldberg, R.T. Kelleher, et al. 1977. 'Some Effects of Cocaine and Two Cocaine Analogs on Schedule-Controlled Behavior of Squirrel Monkeys.' *Journal of Pharmacology and Experimental Therapeutics* 202: 500–9.

Tardiff, K., E.M. Gross, J. Wu, et al. 1989. 'Analysis of Cocaine-Positive Fatalities.' *Journal of Forensic Science* 34: 53–63.

Thompson, D.M. 1977. 'Effects of Cocaine and Fenfluramine on Progressive-Ratio Performance.' *Pharmacology Biochemistry and Behavior* 7: 555–8.

U.S. Department of Health and Human Services. 1992. *Statistical Series: Annual Medical Examiner Data 1992*. Rockville, MD: Public Health Service.

Waldorf, D., C. Reinarman, and S. Murphy. 1991. *Cocaine Changes: The Experience of Using and Quitting*. Philadelphia: Temple University Press.

Washton, A.M. 1984. 'Cocaine Epidemic in America: Prevalence, Problems and Policy.' Testimony before President's Commission on Organized Crime. Washington, 27 November.

– 1989. *Cocaine Addiction*. New York: W.W. Norton & Company.

Weiss, R.D., and S.M. Mirin. 1987. *Cocaine*. New York: Ballantine Books.

Wilson, M.C., M. Hitomi, and C.R. Schuster. 1971. 'Self-Administration of Psychomotor Stimulants as a Function of Unit Dose.' *Psychopharmacologia* 22: 271–81.

Winger, G.D., and J.H. Woods. 1985. 'Comparison of Fixed-Ratio and Progressive-Ratio Schedules of Maintainance of Stimulant Drug-Reinforced Responding.' *Drug and Alcohol Dependence* 15: 123–30.

Woods, J. 1977. 'Behavioral Effects of Cocaine in Animals.' In R.C. Petersen and R.C. Stillman, eds, *Cocaine: 1977*, 63–96. Rockville, MD: National Institute on Drug Abuse.

Woolverton, W.L. 1992. 'Determinants of Cocaine Self-Administration by Laboratory Animals.' In G.R. Bock and J. Whelan, eds, *Cocaine: Scientific and Social Dimensions*, 149–64. West Sussex: Wiley and Sons.

Woolverton, W.L., and M.S. Kleven. 1988. 'Multiple Dopamine Receptors and the Behavioral Effects of Cocaine.' In D. Clouet et al., eds, *Mechanisms of Cocaine Abuse and Toxicity*, 160–84. Rockville, MD: National Institute on Drug Abuse.

Woolverton, W.L., and C.E. Johanson. 1984. 'Preference in Rhesus Monkeys Given a Choice Between Cocaine and d,l-Cathinone.' *Journal of Experimental Analysis of Behavior* 41: 35–43.

Woolverton, W.L., and C.R. Schuster. 1983. 'Intragastric Self-Administration in Rhesus Monkeys under Limited Access Conditions: Methodological Studies.' *Journal of Pharmacological Methods* 10: 93–106.

Yanagita, T. 1973. 'An Experimental Framework for Evaluation of Dependence Liability in Various Types of Drugs in Monkeys.' *Bulletin on Narcotics* 25: 57–64.

Zinberg, N.E. 1984. *Drug, Set and Setting: The Basis for Controlled Intoxicant Use.* New Haven: Yale University Press.

17 Harm Reduction Interventions with Women Who Are Heavy Drinkers

GERARD J. CONNORS and
KIMBERLY S. WALITZER

Alcohol consumption and associated negative consequences among women are significant public-health concerns that may be alleviated in part through the use of harm reduction interventions. In this regard, one harm reduction intervention holding particular promise for heavily drinking women experiencing alcohol-related problems is drinking-moderation training.

This chapter accordingly will focus on several topics. The first section includes background information on alcohol consumption and related problems among women. There follows a discussion of drinking-moderation interventions as a harm reduction strategy. An example of such an intervention for heavily drinking women, the Women and Health Program, is described. The description of this program includes information on the demographic and drinking characteristics of the program participants, along with some preliminary outcome indications.

Drinking among Women

Survey data from a variety of countries have provided indications regarding the extent of alcohol consumption among women and the incidence of negative consequences. For example, Hilton (1987) reported that 25 per cent of all women surveyed in a United States national general population sample were 'frequent drinkers.' The combined category of frequent drinkers included three subgroups: frequent heavy drinkers (drink at least weekly and consume five or more drinks in a day at least weekly), frequent high-maximum drinkers (drink at least weekly and consume five or more drinks at a sitting at least yearly), and frequent low-maximum drinkers (drink at least weekly but never consume as many as five drinks at a sitting).

Problematic drinking (drinking representative of alcohol dependence) and tangible consequences of drinking (specific alcohol-related problems) are strongly evident among women drinkers in the United States (Hilton 1987). Fourteen per cent of non-abstaining women surveyed reported that in the past year they had experienced one or more alcohol-related problems (e.g., memory loss, tremors, morning drinking, binge drinking, or inability to reduce drinking). Seven per cent reported two or more alcohol-related problems in the past year and 4 per cent reported three or more problems. Sixteen per cent of non-abstaining women reported experiencing one or more tangible consequences from drinking in the past year (e.g., problems with spouse, work difficulties, legal problems, or health problems). Eleven per cent reported two or more tangible consequences in the past year, and 6 per cent reported four or more consequences. Comparable findings have been reported by Wilsnack, Wilsnack, and Klassen (1984) from their national survey of drinking among U.S. women.

Data on drinking among Nordic women have been reported by Järvinen and Olafsdottir (1989). They found that in three of the countries (Finland, Norway, Sweden), the percentage of alcohol-consuming women who drink beer once a week or more ranged from 14 to 17 per cent. The percentage for Iceland was only 3 per cent. The percentage of alcohol consumers who drink wine once or more a week ranged from 6% (Iceland) to 18% (Sweden). The percentages for spirits ranged from 6% (Iceland) to 13% (Norway). In looking at yearly consumption, 11 to 12% of the women drinkers in Finland, Norway, and Sweden consumed greater than 400 centilitres annually. The proportion for Iceland was 7%. Drinking to intoxication one to three times per month or more was reported by 30% of the women drinkers in Iceland, 13% in Finland, 11% in Norway, and 9% in Sweden. Finally, similar findings have been reported by Whitehead and Layne (1987) from a survey of young (ages 15 to 29) women in Canada. Heavy drinking, defined as four and a half or more drinks at a sitting, was reported by almost 15% of these women. The highest subgroup rate was 20% among women 18 to 21 years of age.

Studies such as the aforementioned have extended our knowledge and awareness about drinking and alcohol-related problems among women in several countries. It is noteworthy that many of these women likely would not meet commonly applied diagnostic criteria for severe alcohol dependence (at least based on the provided information on, for example, problem-drinking characteristics and tangible consequences) and that relatively few treatment services are geared towards the needs of problem-drinking women without histories of severe physical dependence on alcohol. Indeed, the vast majority of treatment services and resources worldwide are abstinence-oriented and directed at severely dependent alcohol abusers. Harm reduction interventions for alcohol abusers without histories of such physical dependence have been the exception to the rule, although interventions for these drinkers, including drinking-moderation training, hold significant promise for helping them reduce their alcohol consumption and concomitant risks.

Drinking-Moderation Interventions

Many of the secondary prevention/harm reduction efforts initiated with alcohol abusers in the past twenty years have sought to reduce drinking and alcohol-related negative consequences. Research has indicated that problem drinkers without histories of severe dependence on alcohol are particularly well suited for drinking-moderation interventions (Heather and Robertson 1981; Miller and Hester 1980; Rosenberg 1993). These drinkers typically have not experienced major losses because of their drinking and have not exhibited severe withdrawal symptoms (e.g., convulsions, seizures, or delirium tremens) upon cessation of past drinking. Successful responders tend to be in their mid-thirties and typically report fewer than ten years of problem drinking. The standard treatment has included a variety of behavioural self-control strategies (e.g., Miller and Munoz 1982; Sanchez-Craig 1984, 1993; Vogler and Bartz 1982), including self-monitoring, functional analysis of drinking behaviour, stimulus-control training, and strategies for modifying drinking behaviour (e.g., decreasing sip rate and amount, preplanning drinking, or setting drinking limits). These behavioural self-control packages consistently have yielded high improvement rates, frequently exceeding 60 per cent (with success generally defined as abstinence or at least a 30% reduction in drinking from baseline). Such outcomes have been reported by a variety of investigators (e.g., Alden 1988; Brown 1980; Connors, Tarbox, and Faillace 1992; Miller 1978; Miller and Taylor 1980; Sanchez-Craig, Annis, Bornet, and MacDonald 1984). Taken together, these data support the proposition that moderate drinking is a useful and effective treatment objective with this population.

Further evidence in support of moderate-drinking interventions has been provided by Sanchez-Craig and her colleagues (Sanchez-Craig

1980; Sanchez-Craig et al. 1984), who have documented problem drinkers' preference for a moderate drinking goal instead of abstinence. Problem drinkers assigned to an abstinence goal drank more during treatment compared to those assigned to a moderate-drinking goal. Furthermore, they developed moderate drinking on their own by the second-year follow-up (Sanchez-Craig et al. 1984), despite exposure to an abstinence-oriented treatment. When problem drinkers were given the choice of an abstinence or moderate-drinking goal, 80 per cent chose moderate drinking (Sanchez-Craig, Leigh, Spivak, and Lei 1989). Reduced drinking, relative to abstinence, appears to be a more palatable as well as effective objective for problem drinkers.

Two drinking-moderation studies have provided indications that women may be particularly positive responders to this form of harm reduction intervention. Miller and Joyce (1979), in reporting data on subjects from several previous treatment-outcome studies, found that women problem drinkers exhibited more success in achieving drinking moderation than did men problem drinkers. In another study, Sanchez-Craig et al. (1989) reported that women showed significantly greater reductions in heavy-drinking days at a twelve-month follow-up than did men, regardless of the treatment modality utilized. These reports provide an indication that moderate-drinking interventions may be the strategy of choice for reducing alcohol-related harm in this population of problem-drinking women.

The Women and Health Program

Based on this empirical and theoretical foundation, the Women and Health Program was developed to serve the needs of women problem drinkers experiencing mild to moderate alcohol problems. An overview of the program and participant characteristics is provided below.

Recruitment of Participants

Although participants were recruited through advertisements in a variety of mediums, the majority responded to newspaper advertisements. A typical notice was headed by the caption 'Women Drinkers,' followed by queries such as 'Are you worried about your drinking?' and 'Do you want to drink less?' The remainder of the advertisement provided a brief description of the Women and Health Program and a phone number that interested persons could call for further information and a brief telephone screening interview. The advertisement indicated that the program was only for women and that it was not geared towards the needs of alcoholic women. Other recruitment strategies included posters placed in various public locations, brochures, and radio and television advertisements. The program was provided free of charge.

Selection Criteria

Women were carefully screened in order to exclude those with histories of severe physical dependence on alcohol (for instance, marked tolerance, severe withdrawal, or morning drinking) and women for whom alcohol consumption was medically contra-indicated (through, for example, pregnancy or liver dysfunction). During the initial telephone contact, the following eligibility criteria were assessed: age twenty-one years or older, drinking at least fifteen drinks per week or drinking six drinks at least two days per week, and interested in reducing their alcohol consumption (as opposed to wanting to abstain). Exclusion criteria were previous hospitalization for alcohol or drug use, detoxification from alcohol or any other drug, current alcohol-related legal charges, current receipt of psychiatric treatment, hospitalization during the past five years for psychiatric problems, taking of psychiatric medications, medical problems contra-indicating moderate alcohol consumption, and pregnancy or current attempts to become pregnant. Several additional eligibility criteria were applied during a subsequent intake interview and medical evaluation: eligible women had to report no more than moderate levels of physical dependence (evaluated using a combination of interview and questionnaire measures) and normal liver-function tests.

Treatment Interventions

The treatment involved ten weekly two-hour small group sessions co-led by two female therapists. An overview of the drinking-reduction treatment components is provided in table 1. As can be seen, the program opens with considerable focus on self-monitoring and goal setting, themes that continue throughout the ten sessions. The majority of the following sessions focus on specific techniques for reducing drinking (e.g., reducing sip rate and amount and spacing drinks) and for developing alternatives to drinking (drink refusal, beverage substitution). The latter stages of the program key on maintaining treatment gains and

TABLE 1
General outline of treatment components used in Women and Health Program

---

Drinking-reduction focus
Session   1 Overview of program, self-monitoring, alcohol education, goal setting
      2 Goal setting, strategies (sip amount, sip rate, alternating beverages), functional analysis
      3 Strategies (counting drinks, spacing drinks, self-talk)
      4 Strategies (drink refusal, beverage substitution, self-rewards)
      5 Re-evaluation of goals, review of strategies
      6 Re-evaluation of goals, identification of high-risk situations, review of strategies
      7 Strategies (stimulus control)
      8 Strategies (preplanning drinking)
      9 Maintenance and relapse prevention, strategy review and consolidation
     10 Strategy review, maintenance, program feedback

---

avoiding relapses to previous patterns of drinking. Further information on the conduct of the group sessions has been provided elsewhere (Walitzer and Connors, 1997).

As part of the larger research design, a randomly chosen 50 per cent of the participants additionally were exposed to seven modules focusing on life-functioning skills. Each module keyed on a life skill (identifying and modifying negative automatic thoughts, problem solving, relaxation, communication, assertion, maintaining friendships, and building and using social support networks) and included discussion, modelling, role playing, and a 'homework' exercise. These modules were designed to develop and enhance participants' social, coping, and other life-management skills so as to maximally equip them not only to address those potential psychosocial/situational antecedents to problem-drinking situations but also to enhance their overall life-functioning capabilities. Following treatment, half of the participants were chosen randomly to participate in eight booster sessions during the six months following treatment.

Description of the Participants

Five hundred and thirty-two women called in response to the Women and Health Program advertisements. Of these, 300 were potentially eligible on the basis of the telephone screen and 192 attended an in-person comprehensive intake evaluation to determine final eligibility. From this group of 192, 144 were eligible on the basis of the in-person evalua-

TABLE 2
Demographic characteristics of Women and Health
Program participants

Age (years)	38.7 (10.0)
Education (years)	14.4 (2.2)
Marital status	
Single	24.3%
Married	43.1%
Separated	6.3%
Divorced	19.4%
Widowed	6.9%
Employment status	
Full-time	59.0%
Part-time	13.9%
Student	7.6%
Retired	1.4%
Unemployed	11.8%
Homemaker	6.3%
Racial/ethnic background	
White, not Hispanic	88.9%
White, Hispanic	0.7%
Black, not Hispanic	7.6%
Black, Hispanic	1.4%
Native American	1.4%

Note: Numbers in parentheses are standard deviations.

tion and a physical and laboratory work-up and initiated participation
in the treatment sessions. The data presented below are based on this
treatment sample of 144 women.

Demographic Data
The demographic characteristics for the treatment sample are provided
in table 2. As can be seen, the participants averaged almost thirty-nine
years of age. They were well educated, averaging fourteen years of
education. The modal categories for marital and employment statuses
were 'married' (43%) and 'full time' (59%). There was limited minority
response to the program recruitment efforts.

Drinking-History Data
Drinking-history characteristics are listed in table 3. The participants

TABLE 3

Drinking-history characteristics of Women and Health Program participants

Alcohol history	
Age drinking regularly (years)	20.4 (6.1)
Years of heavy drinking	5.4 (5.1)
Years of drinking problem	3.5 (4.2)
DWI conviction	5.6%
Drinking frequency (days/week)	4.6 (1.9)
Drinking quantity	
(mean drinks/day)	6.0 (3.5)
(mean drinks/week)	23.4 (9.1)
Alcohol Dependence Scale	12.6 (5.5)
Michigan Alcohol Screening Test	13.9 (5.9)
Monthly pretreatment drinking	
Abstinent (0 drinks) days	10.1 (7.6)
Light (1–3 drinks) days	6.1 (6.2)
Medium (4–6 drinks) days	8.0 (7.1)
Heavy (>6 drinks) days	5.6 (6.1)
DSM-III-R Alcohol Diagnosis (Lifetime)	
None	6.9%
Alcohol abuse only	0.7%
Dependence–mild	18.1%
Dependence–moderate	66.0%
Dependence–severe*	8.3%

Note: Numbers in parentheses are standard deviations.
*Women meeting DSM-III-R diagnostic criteria for alcohol dependence–severe had to score in the lower two quartiles of the Alcohol Dependence Scale in order to be eligible for treatment.

reported an average of 5.4 years of heavy drinking (self-defined) and 3.5 years of problematic drinking (also self-defined). They described drinking an average of 4.6 days per week and a mean of 23.4 drinks per week. A follow-back timeline procedure (Sobell and Sobell 1992) was used to collect information on daily drinking dispositions during the six-month period before treatment. Using this procedure, participants provided estimates of the amount of alcohol consumed on a daily basis during this period. These estimates were coded into four daily drinking-disposition categories: abstinent days; light-drinking days (defined as consumption of one to three standard drinks [SDs, defined as a beverage containing 0.5 ounce or 15 ml of ethanol]); moderate-drinking days (defined as consumption of four to six SDs); and heavy-drinking days (defined as consumption of >6 SDs). Using these definitions, it was determined that the participants were averaging approximately ten abstinent days, six light-drinking days, eight moderate-drinking days, and six heavy-drinking days per month during the six-month period prior to treatment. The majority of participants were diagnosed as having an alcohol dependency of moderate severity (Diagnostic and Statistical Manual of Mental Disorders [DSM-IIIR]; APA 1987), based on lifetime data gathered using the Diagnostic Interview Schedule-IIIR (Robins, Helzer, Cottler, and Goldring 1988).

Preliminary Outcome Indications

Attendance
The 144 women who initiated participation in the treatment sessions averaged attendance at 7.44 sessions (SD = 2.64, Range = 1–10). While the attendance rate averaged close to 75 per cent, it is instructive to divide the sample of 144 into treatment completers and treatment non-completers. For present purposes, treatment completion was arbitrarily defined as attending at least six treatment sessions (that is, over half of the sessions). Using this definition, 120 of the 144 subjects (83%) completed treatment and 24 (17%) did not. Treatment completers averaged 8.48 sessions (SD = 1.20, Range = 6–10) and treatment non-completers attended an average of 2.21 sessions (SD = 1.25, Range = 1–5). Nevertheless, the most notable point is that women who initiated session attendance tended to be engaged in the treatment process as evidenced by an average attendance rate of just under 75 per cent.

Drinking Outcomes
The follow-up phase of the Women and Health Program is now under way. Thus, only preliminary drinking outcome indications are available. Data on the six–month pretreatment, three-month treatment, and six-month post-treatment periods (collapsed across the treatment and booster-care manipulations) are provided in figure 1. Graphs are provided separately for the four drinking-disposition categories defined earlier: abstinent days, light-drinking days, moderate-drinking days, and heavy-drinking days. The most notable indications are changes in the occurrence of abstinent days and heavy-drinking days. Specifically, abstinent days are appearing to increase during the treatment phase, relative to pretreatment rates, and to be maintained during the six months immediately following treatment. Heavy-drinking days, a particular

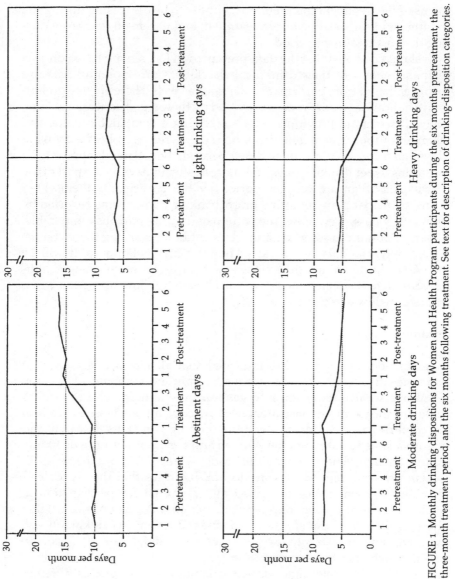

FIGURE 1 Monthly drinking dispositions for Women and Health Program participants during the six months pretreatment, the three-month treatment period, and the six months following treatment. See text for description of drinking-disposition categories.

focus of the treatment interventions, appear to be decreasing during the treatment phase, relative to pretreatment, and to remain decreased during the post-treatment period.

It should be noted that the data presented in figure 1 are based on participant reports of their drinking behaviour. Corresponding data are being gathered from participant collaterals as well. There are two preliminary indications from the data provided by these significant others. First, the collaterals are providing data suggesting a comparable pattern of changes in the participants' drinking (i.e., decreases in heavy-drinking days and increases in abstinent days). Second, the collaterals appear to be reporting fewer drinking days and more abstinent days on the part of the participants than are being reported by the participants themselves. Thus, participants are reporting more drinking than is being reported by the collaterals. Nevertheless, the pattern of findings remains comparable.

It is important to assert an important caution regarding these results. Specifically, the data presented in figure 1 are preliminary. It will be necessary to determine the extent to which the positive changes indicated to date are maintained over the extended follow-up period being studied in this investigation.

Summary

Epidemiological research has indicated that alcohol use is associated with negative consequences among significant numbers of women drinkers. A harm reduction intervention presenting much promise for reducing the negative consequences of drinking among women in a host of countries is drinking-moderation training. Previous research and data available to date from the Women and Health Program, a drinking-reduction intervention geared towards women without histories of severe physical dependence on alcohol, indicates that these problem-drinking women can be identified and recruited for participation in such secondary prevention/harm reduction interventions, and that these interventions can engender notable reductions in drinking. It will be important in later phases of the Women and Health Program to ascertain whether these outcomes are maintained over a longer follow-up period and to determine subject variables that may predict differential treatment attendance and outcome. Such determinations will be useful to clinicians and policy makers in a variety of countries in their efforts to assist individuals to reduce alcohol consumption and associated risks.

ACKNOWLEDGMENTS

Preparation of this report was supported in part by Grant AA08076 from the National Institute on Alcohol Abuse and Alcoholism. We gratefully acknowledge the efforts of the following research interviewers and therapists: Peg Duggan, Audrey Kubiak, Kathy Paradowski, Sheryl Allen, Tanya Bowen, Kathy Caproni, Claudia Casey, Paula Janicki, Gail Lehman, Danielle Maloy, Marilyn Meyers, Marianne Pansa, Kathy Ross, and Lisa Sanfilippo.

REFERENCES

Alden, L.E. 1988. 'Behavioral Self-Management Controlled-Drinking Strategies in a Context of Secondary Prevention.' *Journal of Consulting and Clinical Psychology* 56: 280–6.

American Psychiatric Association. 1987. *Diagnostic and Statistical Manual of Mental Disorders.* 3rd ed. rev., Washington: APA.

Brown, R.A. 1980. 'Conventional Education and Controlled Drinking Education Courses with Convicted Drunken Drivers.' *Behavior Therapy* 11: 632–42.

Connors, G.J., A.R. Tarbox, and L.A. Faillace. 1992. 'Achieving and Maintaining Gains among Problem Drinkers: Process and Outcome Results.' *Behavior Therapy* 23: 449–74.

Heather, N., and I. Robertson. 1981. *Controlled Drinking.* New York: Methuen.

Hilton, M.E. 1987. 'Drinking Patterns and Drinking Problems in 1984: Results from a General Population Survey.' *Alcoholism: Clinical and Experimental Research* 11: 167–75.

Institute on Medicine. 1990. *Broadening the Base of Treatment for Alcohol Problems.* Washington: National Academy Press.

Järvinen, M., and H. Olafsdottir. 1989. 'Drinking Patterns among Women in the Nordic Countries.' In E. Haavio-Mannila, ed., *Women, Alcohol, and Drugs in the Nordic Countries,* 47–75. Helsinki: Nordic Council for Alcohol and Drug Research.

Miller, W.R. 1978. 'Behavioral Treatment of Problem Drinkers: A Comparative Outcome Study of Three Controlled Drinking Therapies.' *Journal of Consulting and Clinical Psychology* 46: 74–86.

Miller, W.R., and R.K. Hester. 1980. 'Treating the Problem Drinker: Modern Approaches.' In W.R. Miller, ed., *The Addictive Behaviors: Treatment of Alcoholism, Drug Abuse, Smoking, and Obesity.* New York: Pergamon Press.

Miller, W.R., and M.A. Joyce. 1979. 'Prediction of Abstinence, Controlled Drinking, and Heavy Drinking Outcomes Following Behavioral Self-Control Training.' *Journal of Consulting and Clinical Psychology* 47: 773–5.

Miller, W.R., and R.F. Munoz. 1982. *How to Control Your Drinking*. 2nd ed. Albuquerque: University of New Mexico Press.

Miller, W.R., and C.A. Taylor. 1980. 'Relative Effectiveness of Bibliotherapy, Individual and Group Self-Control Training in the Treatment of Problem Drinkers.' *Addictive Behaviors* 5: 13–24.

Robins, L.N., J.E. Helzer, L. Cottler, and E. Goldring. 1988. 'Diagnostic Interview Schedule' (Version 3 revised). Unpublished manuscript.

Rosenberg, H. 1993. 'Prediction of Controlled Drinking by Alcoholics and Problem Drinkers.' *Psychological Bulletin* 113: 129–39.

Sanchez-Craig, M. 1980. 'Random Assignment to Abstinence or Controlled Drinking in a Cognitive-Behavioral Program: Short-Term Effects on Drinking Behavior.' *Addictive Behavior* 5: 35–9.

– 1984. *A Therapist's Manual for Secondary Prevention of Alcohol Problems: Procedures for Teaching Moderate Drinking and Abstinence*. Toronto: Addiction Research Foundation.

– 1993. *Saying When: How to Stop Drinking or Cut Down*. Toronto: Addiction Research Foundation.

Sanchez-Craig, M., H.M. Annis, A.R. Bornet, and K.R. MacDonald. 1984. 'Random Assignment to Abstinence and Controlled Drinking: Evaluation of a Cognitive Behavioral Program for Problem Drinkers.' *Journal of Consulting and Clinical Psychology* 52: 390–403.

Sanchez-Craig, M., G. Leigh, K. Spivak, and H. Lei. 1989. 'Superior Outcome of Females over Males after Brief Treatment for the Reduction of Heavy Drinking.' *British Journal of Addiction* 84: 395–404.

Sobell, L.C., and M.B. Sobell. 1992. 'Timeline Follow-Back: A Technique for Assessing Self-Reported Alcohol Consumption.' In R.Z. Litten and J.P. Allen, eds, *Measuring Alcohol Consumption: Psychosocial and Biochemical Methods*, 41–72. Totowa, NJ: Humana Press.

Vogler, R.E., and W.R. Bartz. 1982. *The Better Way to Drink*. New York: Simon & Schuster.

Walitzer, K.S., and G.J. Connors. 1997. 'Gender and Treatment of Alcohol-Related Problems.' In R.W. Wilsnack and S.C. Wilsnack, eds, *Gender and Alcohol*, 445–61. Piscataway, NJ: Rutgers Center of Alcohol Studies.

Whitehead, P.C., and N. Layne. 1987. 'Young Female Canadian Drinkers: Employment, Marital Status and Heavy Drinking.' *British Journal of Addiction* 82: 169–74.

Wilsnack, R.W., S.C. Wilsnack, and A.D. Klassen. 1984. 'Women's Drinking and Drinking Problems: Patterns from a 1981 National Survey.' *American Journal of Public Health* 74: 1231–38.

18 Two Steps Forward, One Step Back: Anti-User Bias in New York State's Approach to Needle Exchange

ROD SORGE and RUTH E. HARLOW

A Preliminary Note on the Nature of Harm Reduction

Harm reduction – when this term is used at all in the United States – has largely been and largely remains a synonym for needle exchange despite its much broader, more nuanced meanings. While needle exchanges have grown in number and visibility since the first such program was established in the United States in 1988, the concepts and definitions of harm reduction as an underlying philosophy have been much less extensively debated and formulated in the public realm. Some U.S. needle-exchange programs have developed sophisticated harm reduction analyses and approaches, but the public-health authorities and other government bodies that have given official support to needle exchange have been much more reluctant to discuss and adopt a harm reduction approach that extends beyond simply allowing the exchange of sterile injection equipment for used needles and syringes. Indeed, some of these government officials have placed restrictions on exchange programs that are substantially counterproductive to a harm reduction approach. This lack of common reference to an underlying harm reduction philosophy has resulted in U.S. needle-exchange programs that – although operating within the law or at least enjoying the official support of local or state government – are hindered by overburdensome regulatory schemes, conflicting laws, and the government's inability to effectively enforce its new legal protections for needle-exchange participants and workers. Under various government mandates, moreover, an anti-user bias has infected the provision of needle exchange, much to the chagrin of those directly involved with the exchange programs and other advocates of harm reduction.

To frame this paper's discussion of such difficulties in New York State, important elements of harm reduction bear emphasis at the outset. No precise and universal definition of harm reduction currently exists, in part because harm reduction itself demands different interpretations according to locale, population, and other parameters. International experience and research, however, have identified some characteristic and central aspects of this approach that have been supported and confirmed by the experience of needle-exchange programs in the United States (Des Jarlais 1995; Heather et al. 1993; O'Hare et al. 1992). For purposes of this analysis of HIV prevention efforts among injection drug users in New York, the most crucial elements of harm reduction include the following:

A genuine respect for the lives and abilities of users and a recognition of their critical role in harm reduction. Injection drug users must be actively involved in the design, implementation, and provision of needle-exchange services and policies. The all-important role of the injection drug user in facilitating HIV risk reduction and health promotion among other individual injectors and among social networks must be acknowledged and encouraged. Recognition of this central role requires the further acknowledgment that drug users have the *expertise* and can be *trusted* to carry out such tasks and are *as important as if not more important than* non-users who may be involved in harm reduction efforts. Finally, rather than requiring users to divorce themselves from the people, places, and communities that contribute to their life experiences and human identities, users' social contexts and physical environments should be used as vehicles for harm reduction.

*Policies and programs that enable **planned** risk reduction and **managed** safer drug use.* The extent to which drug users are able to practise harm reduction in their lives and more safely negotiate their worlds is influenced both by broad-based social and economic conditions (including official drug-control policy and the vicissitudes of the illicit drug market) and by the harm reduction materials, services, and interventions to which they have – or do not have – access. Programs that arbitrarily restrict the number of needles and syringes an individual may exchange or that unreasonably limit other supplies can stymie the careful planning many users engage in to avoid harm – a planning process that should be supported by harm reduction programs. Exchanges that require very frequent visits in order for users to obtain an adequate amount of equipment and supplies tend more towards the control of participants than towards HIV prevention or other harm reduction goals. Unlimited legal access to sterile injection equipment and other necessary supplies is a basic component of HIV prevention for drug injectors.

Accessible, relevant, and low-threshold interventions. It is clear that needle-exchange programs and other harm reduction interventions that are not geographically accessible, that place undue requirements and restrictions on participants, or that offer services deemed irrelevant by potential consumers are not well utilized by drug injectors (Vlahov et al. 1994; *Washington Post* 1994; Des Jarlais et al. 1994c). A particular brand or model of syringe purchased by a program because the price was attractive, for example, will not end up being a bargain at all if it is a product injectors will not use. Equipment and materials should be piloted among consumers before they are purchased in bulk for routine distribution. Interventions must be useful and easily integrated into users' lives.

The need for multiple and overlapping harm reduction options. Hinging sterile needle and syringe access on a single method, outlet, or program severely limits users' ability to plan and participate in harm reduction. A harm reduction philosophy instead contemplates as many options as possible, enabling the user to select one or several that suit his or her needs at a particular point in time.

As needle exchange in the United States (and elsewhere) is at last expanding and more public officials are recognizing the need for it, those in positions of power should critically examine existing programs and their surrounding legal schemes in order to shape future programs and policies for maximum effectiveness. Users, providers, and public-health officials must work together to define and shape a more holistic, broad-based *harm reduction* agenda. To that end, this article analyses recently legalized needle-exchange services in New York, highlighting some of the problems that arise when an intervention like needle exchange is implemented without a larger working concept of harm reduction behind it.

The Counterproductive Aspects of New York State's Approach

Needle exchange as an HIV-prevention measure has gained considerable ground in New York in terms of official support from local – and particularly the state – public-health departments and administrators. The most significant result of this support has been the preliminary legal reform, undertaken by the New York State Department of Health (NYSDOH), of creating a regulated exception to New York's criminal statute that outlaws the possession, distribution, or sale of injection equipment without a doctor's prescription. This regulatory change in 1992 enabled four needle-exchange programs that had been operating illegally in New York City to offer their participants and staff some degree of legal protection from the criminal statute and created a mechanism whereby other organizations could apply to the health department for similar status. By early 1997, twelve NYSDOH-approved and -regulated needle-exchange programs operated in New York State.

This attempt to broaden injection drug users' legal access to sterile injection equipment represents the most important and consequential action of its kind for the needle-borne HIV epidemic in New York to date. It not only altered the legal landscape (however imperfectly, as we will discuss), but also facilitated funding of the exchanges by the state and by private foundations. Evaluations of the now-legal New York City needle-exchange initiative demonstrate that these programs, as did their formerly illegal incarnations, are having a beneficial health impact on participants while engendering no new harms (Des Jarlais et al. 1994a). Specifically, the programs significantly reduce participants' risk of acquiring HIV and are associated with increases in valuable protective behaviours such as cleaning injection sites with alcohol pads before injection (Paone et al. 1993, 1994; Des Jarlais et al. 1994b; New York Times 1993).[1] Despite the extraordinarily encouraging experience of and data from these programs, however, convenient, legal access to sterile injection equipment remains out of reach for most injection drug users in New York State. In addition, most users still (correctly) regard needles and syringes as potentially risky contraband, even if they participate in a legal exchange program and understand the protection of the regulatory waiver.

This paper makes explicit and examines two related propositions: (1) that the regulatory exemption to the general criminal law keeps in place the prevailing cultural and prosecutorial views that have prevented users from accessing sterile needles and syringes for so long, and (2) that the specific regulatory scheme set up by the NYSDOH incorporates anti-user policies and attitudes that are fundamentally counterproductive to a harm reduction approach.

First, this movement towards legal reform has occurred against the backdrop of the criminal statute that is still in full force in New York State (N.Y. Penal Law §220.45),[2] creating a situation that limits the potential impact of the existing New York needle-exchange programs and that makes the widespread and speedy establishment of new ones unlikely. The uneasy coexistence of the criminal statute and the public-health exemption to that statute under which the legal programs operate interferes with maximally effective harm reduction, with one of the most serious problems being that enforcement of the exemption to protect program users is a difficult and ongoing struggle. The first part of this article highlights some of the problems that compromise exchange programs operating in this type of legal environment, and argues that total abolition of legal restrictions on injection equipment would better serve HIV-prevention efforts among injection drug users.

Second, in addition to the structural problems created by the two-tiered legal environment described above, the state has adopted policies to regulate needle-exchange programs that further circumscribe the maximum possible effectiveness of legal exchanges and broader harm reduction goals in New York. These policies, as discussed below, incorporate two counterproductive and troubling premises: that users cannot be trusted and that users cannot themselves effectively contribute to the diffusion of safer drug-injection practices or norms or assist in the distribution of HIV-prevention and harm reduction information and materials. Although needle exchange has greatly expanded in New York in terms of the number of sites and injectors contacted (in part because of the new regulations and attendant funding increases), NYSDOH prohibitions on 'secondary distribution' and on the handling of injection equipment by needle-exchange workers who are also drug injectors are two examples of policies that simultaneously reduce some of the potential impact of this expansion. This institutionalization of anti-user and anti-harm-reduction bias in state policies regulating needle-exchange programs reinforces the very negative stereotypes and assumptions about users that continue to hinder attempts at more widespread legal and public-health reform. This article argues that public-health officials, rather than socially reinforcing and codifying into law counterproductive biases against individuals who inject drugs, must fully involve those individuals in the creation and provision of harm reduction services and policies.

The Legal Framework

The Criminal Law

New York State first enacted its criminal needles offence and its prescription requirement in the second decade of this century, the period during which the 'non-medical' use of narcotics and other drugs – including for maintenance and detoxification therapy – was first widely criminalized and subjected to harsh penalties throughout the United States (Musto 1987; Courtwright 1992). It remains unclear exactly why, however, in the midst of adopting and institutionalizing a harsh, punitive approach to drugs and their users, New York and other state legislatures perceived the need to make hypodermic syringes and needles alone the basis for criminal prosecution. The needle offences may merely reflect the extremely zealous legislative response that drug use has periodically provoked during the twentieth century – if drugs should be outlawed, why not also outlaw the instruments of their use? An alternative explanation, with some support in the scant legislative histories of these provisions, is that law-enforcement officials and legislators viewed these offences as a means to a regulatory end: criminalizing injection equipment would make it that much easier to catch and punish users.[3] There is no record of the New York State legislature ever examining the precise goal(s) of criminalizing hypodermic equipment in careful detail. For present purposes, the relevant point is that this minor criminal offence – like similar ones long ago enacted by other states – is responsible for the firmly entrenched idea that needles and syringes are somehow themselves intrinsically 'criminal,' and therefore should remain illegal contraband, yet it rests on an uncertain premise for making injection equipment unlawful in the first place.

The Regulations Allowing Legal Needle Exchange

After years of pressure from activists who had been operating illegal programs in New York City and their supporters, the New York State Department of Health in May 1992 promulgated regulations designed to exempt state-approved needle-exchange programs and their participants from the needle-possession offence and prescription statute. The growing body of scientific evidence in support of needle exchange, a funding commitment from a major AIDS grant-maker for the New York City–based programs, and the reversal of opposition to needle exchange by several prominent New York City elected officials all contributed to the state's decision to finally make needle exchange an officially endorsed activity (*New York Times* 1991, 1992a, 1992b; *Daily News* 1992).

The NYSDOH used its powers under Public Health Law § 3381 to create the regulatory exception that, under certain circumstances, provides a shield from the criminal statute and prescription requirement for staff members, volunteers, and participants of state-approved needle-exchange programs. Non-profit organizations and government agencies within the state can apply for 'waivers' to the general laws. All individuals enrolled in state-approved programs are, at least on paper, protected from arrest and prosecution under the criminal statute as they exchange and possess injection equipment related to the programs. After several promulgations as emergency regulations, the final version became law in October 1993 (*Official Compilation of Codes*, hereinafter 'Regulations').[4]

As articulated in the regulations, the needle-exchange exemption protects only a limited number of behaviours: (1) the purchase and possession of injection equipment by staff members and volunteers of state-approved needle-exchange programs and the 'furnishing' (that is, giving) of this equipment to persons enrolled in state-approved programs; and (2) the possession by program participants of those needles and syringes obtained from a state-approved program (Regulations, at [a] and [e]). An individual must therefore be enrolled in a state-approved program, and be able to prove satisfactorily his or her enrolment if stopped by police, in order to lawfully possess equipment without a prescription. A technical reading of the regulations, moreover, indicates that this waiver from the criminal law applies *only* to those needles and syringes obtained from a state-approved program. All other aspects of the criminal law remain unaltered. And, significantly, a program participant may not give a needle or syringe to any other individual, regardless of whether the receiver is an injector or not, or a program participant or not, for the waiver to remain in effect for either the giver or the recipient (Regulations, at [e][3]). If a participant engages in such 'secondary distribution,' he or she falls back into the traditional status of an individual with works – an outlaw – by forfeiting the protection of the waiver. This last prohibition will be discussed at greater length below.

Problems Resulting from This Legal Structure

Incomplete Legal Protection

The net effects of the regulations coexisting with the criminal statute, as well as the narrow nature of some aspects of the regulations themselves, are several-fold. First, two 'classes' or groups of users are created – those enrolled in a state-approved needle-exchange program and therefore exempt from the criminal law under specified conditions, and those users who are not. This system creates the illusion of difference between those users who are within the law and those who remain – through no fault of their own – outside of it. The pretense of a 'better' injector is put forth, with which the programs are forced to collude in order to offer *any* user some amount of legal protection. The obvious need for the former group to be distinguished in some way from the latter under such a scheme has caused the state to mandate that programs issue identification cards for all participants. (The cards do not bear identifying information about the holder but do carry anonymous unique identifiers.) Users enrolled in approved programs must carry these cards with them whenever they are in possession of needles and syringes to have any realistic chance of coverage by the waiver.

This system burdens each needle-exchange program with the task of issuing identification cards to every new program participant and replacing lost or missing cards. Depending on the program's volume, at least one staff person's time must be spent exclusively on issuing and reissuing new or lost cards, leaving less time for more valuable interaction with exchangers. For these underfunded programs, one person can represent a quarter of its entire staff or outreach team. More important, however, one can easily imagine numerous scenarios, as well as document such scenarios in actual experience, where a user may not have her card with her (or may have her card destroyed by law enforcement officers) and therefore be subject to arrest – again, become an instant outlaw – simply on the basis of carrying a supply of needles and syringes. This 'slippery' protection under the law, tied to an identification card, underscores that the regulations decriminalize certain *persons* under certain *conditions*, not the injection equipment itself.

As should already be apparent, this tenuous form of legal protection requires the support and commitment of law-enforcement officers and institutions to make it a reality. With the long-standing general criminal law still in force and with most injectors in New York State still outside the exchange programs, there is not much incentive for law enforcement to learn about and follow the complicated new exemption. This is particularly true in locales where there are no programs at all. The idea of needles as contraband – as with anything having to do with drugs or drug use – remains firmly entrenched in the realm of law enforcement. This competing mindset has been sadly borne out by the experiences of the New York harm reduction programs and their users. The New York City Police Department (NYPD), for example, issued an 'Operations Order' informing all officers of the legal needle-exchange programs' authority to operate only several months *after* two of the programs had been state-approved, leaving users in 'legal' programs subject to arrest during this period (NYCPD 1992). While any user without a participant card is wide open to arrest regardless of their program status, even those with identification cards may be and have been detained while a police officer calls a program centre to ensure that a person is registered. As the programs are staffed only during daytime hours, users detained at night can remain in custody for considerable periods until a needle-exchange staff member is reached. And program participants routinely report that police officers disregard the identification cards altogether, sometimes ripping them in half while at the same time confiscating an individual's works or, for added humiliation, ordering the participants themselves to crush their works underfoot or throw them down a sewer (Bronx-Harlem Needle Exchange Program 1993; Lower East Side Needle Exchange Program 1994; *New York Newsday* 1994).

In addition to the NYPD, several other law-enforcement authorities operate in New York City, including those of the Metropolitan Transit Authority (MTA) and the New York City Housing Authority (NYCHA), which police the public subway and housing systems; the New York State Police; the New York City Sheriff; and the Parks Department Rangers, who patrol the city's public parks. Other individuals who may have authority of some kind over people carrying injection equipment – security guards at public shelters for the homeless, for instance – can also undermine the waiver system at their discretion, such as by preventing individuals with injection equipment from entering the shelter. All of these various law-enforcement authorities (and in cases like the shelter guards, the public social-service agency that employs them) must each be separately notified, educated, and convinced about the need to abide by the exchange-program regulations. Because the city and state have not succeeded in creating a law-enforcement culture that respects the need for harm reduction, the near-impossible onus of such educational efforts devolves to the already overburdened exchange programs themselves.

The extent to which the waiver is adhered to by law-enforcement organizations can also change with the local leadership of the moment and its approach to crime and drugs. Indeed, the law-enforcement officials with whom the NYSDOH and the New York City–based programs originally worked in 1992 to get an operations order issued were in 1994 replaced by a newly elected mayor who ran on a platform emphasizing 'get tough' measures on crime and drugs (*The Point* 1994; *New York Times* 1994a, 1994b). In May 1996, the police chief who had been appointed in 1994 resigned, taking with him most of his top officers, and was replaced by a new mayoral appointee. Again, needle-exchange programs must direct significant education efforts at top police officials. To work effectively, however, legal reform cannot be subject to the whim of politics, but must be accomplished on a broader, firmer scale.

Despite the fact that the programs may be technically legal and users of such programs technically exempted from the law, it is highly unlikely that such a complicated and ambiguous system will provide drug injectors – an extremely stigmatized and maligned group of individuals – with confidence-inspiring legal protection unless the ability to enforce needle possession laws is completely abolished. Normative change among law enforcement in this regard will come only when injection equipment has been completely decriminalized in every respect. The current system now in use is only incrementally better for some lucky users than no legal protection at all, with obvious, dangerous consequences for the HIV epidemic.

Limited Exchange Outlets

The second major effect resulting from this system of exemption and from the elaborate nature of the state's regulatory scheme is that only a very limited number of outlets at which injectors may legally obtain injection equipment have been authorized, and relatively few more will likely be established in the near future. Currently, there are only twelve such approved outlets in the expansive state of New York – a state with 260,000 injection drug users according to official estimates (New York State Office of Alcoholism and Substance Abuse Services 1992). Several of the smaller exchanges serve only a few hundred injectors each, and one serves less than one hundred people.

Because of the continuing validity of the general criminal prohibition on the sale of injection equipment without a doctor's prescription, important outlets for ready needle access – such as pharmacies, drug stores, *bodegas*, and convenience stores – are unavailable to injectors of illicit drugs. Only not-for-profit organizations and government agencies may even apply for a waiver to the criminal and prescription statutes. In addition to offering to make injection equipment available under safe conditions, any organization seeking such approval must also demonstrate many additional capabilities and institute many additional procedures to do so – including more than thirteen distinct reporting requirements and sixteen separate procedural requirements. Among them, for example, are 'referring program participants to services, including developing formal written agreements with service providers and documenting referral linkages'; maintaining a record of the number and types of services directly provided or provided by referral to participants; submitting 'a list of employees and trained volunteers who are authorized to obtain, possess and furnish hypodermic syringes and needles' to the NYSDOH; establishing procedures 'for obtaining and recording participant information,' including race, sex, and age; and providing a 'plan for evaluating program services and goals' (Regulations, at [g][14], [h][5], [j][6], [g][8], and [m][13]).

While the establishment and expansion of needle-exchange programs that offer comprehensive risk-reduction education, counselling, and other services either directly or by referral must continue, and proper procedures for waste disposal, avoidance of needle-stick injuries, and the like are necessary for any person or entity engaged in needle-exchange operations, many of the requirements in the waiver regulations are *simply not necessary* for safely and appropriately offering injectors legal access to sterile needles and syringes. In fact, they drastically limit the number of organizations that could serve as outlets. The financial and human resources required to start a needle-exchange organization, or for an existing organization to make needle exchange an additional service, are considerable as currently configured in the regulations. Although some public and private money for needle exchange has become available to the approved programs, it is grossly out of proportion to the need and thus the current programs suffer chronic funding shortages. It will remain impossible – financially, logistically, and as a matter of the realties of law enforcement – for all users, or even a significant percentage of all users, in New York to have access to sterile injection equipment so long as state-approved and -regulated needle exchanges remain the only lawful outlets for such equipment.

The Anti-User Bias in New York State's Implementation of This Scheme

Above and beyond the complicated map of legal access to sterile injection equipment described above, a second, more troubling aspect of the

New York scheme can be found in the assumptions about injectors undergirding some of the regulations developed by the NYSDOH and some of the supplementary policies to those regulations (New York State Department of Health, AIDS Institute 1993).[5] We will focus on two policies of the state – the explicit prohibition on 'secondary distribution' and the informal but very clear prohibition on active exchange workers handling injection equipment – to show how such requirements compromise the full potential of needle-exchange programs and institutionalize as official state policy assumptions about drug users that are antithetical to a harm reduction approach.

The Prohibition on 'Secondary Distribution'

The prohibition on 'secondary distribution' of injection equipment – that is, from a program participant to another injector whether or not he or she is also enrolled in a program – is one of the most explicitly anti-user provisions of the regulations (Regulations, at [e][3]).[6] Although it is impossible to effectively enforce such a provision, the NYSDOH has tried to minimize secondary distribution by mandating that programs place a limit on the number of needles and syringes that may be exchanged per participant per transaction, regardless of how many needles an individual may bring to return (New York State Department of Health, AIDS Institute 1994).

Secondary distribution occurs for a variety of reasons. As mentioned above, there are very few needle-exchange outlets. Owing to resource shortages, the programs that do exist typically operate less than five days a week for periods of only several hours at a time, and service small, fixed geographical areas of the city. (There are no programs at all in two of New York City's five boroughs.) Though it is not unusual for injectors to travel significant distances to use an exchange, most of the individuals who patronize a particular exchange program tend to live in areas near the exchange site. Thus, while the exchanges have been successful in attracting large numbers of injectors who use the programs on a regular basis, most injectors in New York State (programs are operating in Buffalo and Rochester as well) have no access to a needle-exchange program on the basis of their limited locations and hours of operation.

In addition to logistical issues, there are other factors – made more urgent by the legal picture – that make secondary distribution an attractive practice for users and that argue for its encouragement by harm reduction providers and policy makers as a sound public-health strategy. Many of the programs, for instance, operate exclusively in street-based settings with limited or no privacy. This strategy has been highly effective in reaching large numbers of users in certain street scenes, but it undoubtedly prevents others from taking advantage of such a service: those who may work or attend a drug-treatment program in the area and who could lose their job or be terminated from treatment; women who risk having their children taken away by the city if they are known to be drug users; individuals whose use of drugs violates their parole and subjects them to rearrest and imprisonment; or anyone else who would simply rather not have to subject themselves to stigma by exchanging their needles in a street-based setting.

The effects of a policy that prohibits secondary distribution are all counterproductive ones. By definition, this policy excludes shooting galleries as ongoing sites for needle-exchange provision, because even if a needle-exchange worker visits such locations, she cannot legally leave sterile supplies for future patrons. Secondary distribution could actually expand exponentially the number of injectors reached through a single needle-exchange outlet. Perhaps the most detrimental effect of the secondary-exchange prohibition is that it actively discourages 'peer education' activities among and between users, whether or not of a consciously educational or organized nature. The initiative and willingness of many users to exchange for others defies the notion that users interact with one another only in antagonistic ways, and indicates that protective behaviours may be being diffused and adopted on a subcultural level – an indication that needle exchange *is working*. In New York, however, the diffusion of safer injection and using norms – particularly to and among those who lack direct access to or choose not to use exchange programs – is undermined by the ban on secondary exchange. Indeed, this policy works directly against compelling findings that HIV risk reduction is in large part a social process and that involvement of peers in HIV prevention and harm reduction education is frequently more effective than that provided wholly by 'outsiders' – and in some cases is the *only* method to which certain groups or individuals respond (Grund et al. 1992a, 1992b; Springer 1992; McDermott and McBride 1993; Bottomley et al. 1995; Broadhead et al. 1995; Crofts and Herkt 1995). Enforcement of the prohibition through exchange caps on the number of needles per transaction is equally counterproductive. Individuals who before this regulation was instituted used an exchange site every several weeks or once a month are now forced to attend more often as a result of this policy, and those who regularly exchanged for themselves and one or more others may no longer be able to do so. Each of these scenarios potentially carries HIV infection risks, and users' attempts at *planned* hygiene and use are jeopardized by an approach that must seem arbitrary and is infantilizing to users.

At the core of the state's view of secondary distribution are the mistaken assumptions that users cannot responsibly or effectively pass on harm reduction information or materials to one another and that they can be only receivers of, not actors in, harm reduction. Requiring every single injector to come to a state-approved needle-exchange program (especially under current conditions) represents the social control of injectors rather than a reasonable means of maximizing injectors' access to sterile injection equipment. Further, an implicit power relationship based on the authority of needle-exchange personnel (assumed to be exclusively non-users) over participants is established by this rule, despite the fact that the programs themselves strive to eliminate such a dynamic by recognizing the competence and expertise of each user and by exchanging needles as individuals of equal worth (Lower East Side Needle Exchange Program Mission Statement; Elovich and Sorge 1991).

Such a policy implies a belief that human behaviour change is contingent exclusively upon an individual having (1) information, in this case about viral transmission, and (2) some form of access to materials – like condoms and sterile syringes – that can interrupt it. But this approach 'forgets' that it takes two individuals to share a syringe. It does not look beyond the individual injector to the context in which that person lives: social relationships and networks, living arrangements or lack thereof, the economics of drug sharing, power dynamics – including violence – within intimate relationships, social isolation, how one earns one's money for drugs and other necessities, and additional factors that can be as important as simple needle and syringe availability in determining whether or not safer injection and HIV risk-reduction practices are adopted and/or maintained. Needle exchange is most effective when it *supports* people's attempts to avoid harm through planning, initiative, and negotiation in their various worlds; whenever possible, the social and environmental context in which people live and the relationships that constitute their social world must be used to help this process along, not hinder it (Grove 1996).

The Prohibition on Active Workers Handling Injection Equipment

The most extreme anti-user policy put forth by the state health department in regulating needle-exchange programs is the prohibition on handling injection equipment (whether used or sterile) by active users who are also exchange staff or volunteers. While not encoded in the regulations, this prohibition is enforced 'informally' by the NYSDOH when programs applying for approval are required to state in their applications that staff or volunteers who are known drug users will not be allowed to handle injection equipment. Akin to the secondary-distribution prohibition, this rule enforces a destructive distinction between users and the staff of programs; an active user may never be a 'full' exchange worker. The implication of this policy – that users entrusted to contribute to harm reduction services as program volunteers or staff will inevitably end up stealing injection equipment or otherwise pose some danger or risk to the program and its other staff members – is based on the very assumptions about drug users that have hindered effective HIV-prevention and harm reduction services for so long. This time, however, it is official public-health policy under the guise of harm reduction.

It is important to point out that individual New York programs can and do 'neutralize' the anti-user bias incorporated in some of the NYSDOH regulations and policies, and make the best of the procedural requirements under which they are forced to work. The Lower East Side Harm Reduction Center (LESHRC), for example, awards free T-shirts with the program's logo to individuals whose anonymous unique identifier (code number) appears in *The Point*, a local users' newsletter, turning the state-imposed I.D. card system into a lottery that benefits program users. LESHRC and other programs also encourage and support user self-organizing initiatives to increase the power on the user side of the worker-user dynamic created by the NYSDOH requirements (Fishman 1996). And it is also important to mention that the legal shield that programs can offer users, as complicated as it is, has worked for some participants of approved programs. Because of the dedication and commitment of the programs, user-friendly, compassionate, and empowering harm reduction services are available in New York to those individuals able to access them. The energy and time it takes to provide such services is certainly increased, however, and the programs' overall ability to operate as effectively as possible decreased, when the regulatory policies under which they are required to operate are inconsistent with their goals and philosophy. Programs are forced to 'hustle' the system to provide services the way they see fit – the very same kind of hustle the programs themselves try to eliminate for users by meeting their needs openly and honestly. Moreover, such regulations may well have the effect of creating user-*un*friendly services if organizations not as familiar with a harm reduction approach, or fearful that their waiver application will not be approved or continued, closely follow the letter and spirit of the regulations in terms of program development and policy implementation.

Conclusion

There are several lessons to be drawn from the New York experience with legal needle exchange thus far. First, it is clear that laws or regulations enacted to widen drug injectors' legal access to injection equipment must be formulated in such a way that they are straightforward and enforceable. The option of legalized access to sterile equipment must also reach all users. The New York scheme excludes a huge number of individuals who could benefit from legal syringe access and offers only scant legal protection to those who have come within its reach. Worse, it creates a class system of 'bad' and 'better' injectors upon which the selective enforcement of the criminal needle-possession law is predicated. Policy makers and legislators in other jurisdictions – as well as those in New York – should study closely the New York situation so as to enact or amend laws that give *all* injectors the real ability to obtain and possess injection equipment without fear of arrest. Although not completely problem-free (Compton et al. 1992; Grund et al. 1995), the full decriminalization of needle and syringe possession, use, and sale would go farthest in accomplishing this end (Valleroy et al. 1995; Groseclose et al. 1995). Any action short of this will only prolong police harassment of users attempting to reduce drug-related harm and arbitrarily limit legal access to those users who happen to live near and feel comfortable using an exchange program.

Second, in terms of policy development and program regulation, it is clear that harm reduction is not best served by simplistic assumptions about drug users that are so often belied by experience and reality. The two state needle-exchange policies discussed earlier reinforce those very counterproductive assumptions. Such policies perpetuate the misguided notions – though virtual truisms in drug research and most social-service provision – that users are a 'hard-to-reach' population, significantly deviant from and less worthy than the 'general' population, to whom socially important information can be conveyed only by non-users. The essential contributions of the many users responsible for making the early underground New York needle-exchange programs successful, as well as their role in the now-legal programs, are erased. Without an understanding of this user involvement, it is easy to keep users on the receiving end of harm reduction initiatives and not in positions as actors, decision makers, and organizers – where they must be for the harm reduction approach to be maximally effective. Further, the anti-user notions embedded in certain NYSDOH policies will make it all the more difficult to bring about the basic, critical shift in thinking about drug-related harm that will one day hopefully convince sate legislators to abolish all legal barriers to sterile syringe access. In short, policy makers must analyse every aspect of the policies they create to 'help' drug users and realize the full effects of choosing the policy that subtly or overtly maligns drug users over one that recognizes users' competency, expertise, and personhood.

Most fundamentally, the mantra of 'user participation' in harm reduction program and policy development, so often intoned by public-health officials and service providers, must be made a reality. If self-identified drug injectors had been *literally* at the table when the New York State regulations had been drafted, department of health officials would have had a much harder time justifying the anti-user policies that resulted from their efforts.

NOTES

The authors wish to thank Allan Clear, Chuck Eaton, and Joyce Rivera for reading and commenting upon an earlier draft of this article.

1 These data from New York City–based programs are consistent with the findings of numerous other evaluations of needle-exchange programs (see, for example, Paone et al. 1995; Watters et al. 1994; Lurie et al. 1993; Des Jarlais and Friedman 1992; O'Keefe et al. 1991).
2 This criminal offence makes the unlawful possession, distribution, or sale of syringes or needles a class A misdemeanour. New York State also maintains a corresponding prescription requirement for the sale, furnishing, purchase, or possession of injection equipment (N.Y. Public Health Law § 3381), effectively banning over-the-counter sales of injection equipment without a doctor's prescription.
3 For example, a New Jersey law-enforcement official lauded that state's adoption of a hypodermic needle offence in 1956 by stating that it would be 'much easier to spot a narcotics violator with the restriction.' See 'Law to Curb Hypodermic Needle Sale,' *New Jersey Journal of Pharmacy*, March 1956: 6.
4 The total abolition of the criminal law can occur only through legislative action and is thus not within the power of the state health commissioner.

Legislative efforts in New York to fully decriminalize injection equipment on the grounds that it is an important HIV-prevention measure have unfortunately gained little momentum to date.

5 The regulations state that, in addition to their specific requirements, approved needle-exchange programs 'must adhere to policies and procedures developed by the department for the conduct of a hypodermic syringe and needle exchange' (at [g]).

6 'Secondary distribution' is a partial misnomer since individuals who exchange needles for injectors other than themselves often regularly re-collect and return to the program equipment they had previously distributed to friends and other contacts (Sorge 1992). 'Secondary exchange' might better describe much of the so-called secondary distribution that takes place.

REFERENCES

Bottomley, T., M. Smith, and C. Wibberley. 1995. 'Peer Education among Crack Users: Not So Cracked.' *Druglink*, May/June.
Broadhead, R.S., D.D. Heckathorn, J.-P.C. Grund, L.S. Stern, and D.L. Anthony. 1995. 'Drug Users versus Outreach Workers in Combatting AIDS: Preliminary Results of a Peer-Driven Intervention.' *Journal of Drug Issues* 25(2): 531–64.
Bronx-Harlem Needle Exchange Program 1993. 'Report to the New York State Department of Health AIDS Institute on Program Activities, July 24, 1992 – January 9, 1993.'
Compton, III, W.M., L.B. Cottler, S.H. Decker, D. Mager, and R. Stringfellow. 1992. 'Legal Needle Buying in St. Louis.' *American Journal of Public Health*, 82(4): 595–6.
Courtwright, D.T. 1992. 'A Century of American Narcotic Policy.' In *Treating Drug Problems, Volume 2*. Washington: National Academy Press.
Crofts, N., and D. Herkt. 1995. 'A History of Peer-Based Drug-User Groups in Australia.' *Journal of Drug Issues* 25(3): 599–616.
Daily News. 1992. 'They'll Give Out Needles in June.' 14 May: 5.
Des Jarlais, D.C. 1995. Editorial: 'Harm Reduction – A Framework for Incorporating Science into Drug Policy.' *American Journal of Public Health* 85(1): 10–11.
Des Jarlais, D.C., and S.R. Friedman. 1992. 'AIDS and Legal Access to Drug Injection Equipment.' *Annals of the American Academy of Political and Social Science* 521: 42–65.
Des Jarlais, D.C., S.R. Friedman, J.L. Sotheran, M. Marmor, S.R. Yancovitz, B. Frank, S. Beatrice, and D. Mildvan. 1994a. 'Continuity and Change within an

HIV Epidemic: Injecting Drug Users in New York City, 1984 through 1992.' *Journal of the American Medical Association* 271(2): 121–7.

Des Jarlais, D.C., D. Paone, M. Marmor, S. Titus, J.L. Sotheran, and S.R. Friedman. 1994b. 'New York City Syringe Exchange Program: Evaluation of a Public Health Intervention.' Paper presented at the 122nd Annual Meeting of the American Public Health Association, Washington.

Des Jarlais, D.C., D. Paone, S.R. Friedman, and N. Peyser. 1994c. 'Regulating Syringe Exchange Programs: A Cautionary Note.' *Journal of the American Medical Association* 272(6): 431–2.

Elovich, R., and R. Sorge. 1991. 'Toward a Community-Based Needle Exchange for New York City.' *AIDS & Public Policy Journal* 6(4): 165–72.

Fishman, E. 1996. 'Look for the Union Label.' *Harm Reduction Communication* 2: 17–19.

Groseclose, S.L., B. Weinstein, T.S. Jones, L.A. Valleroy, L.J. Fehrs, and W.J. Kassler. 1995. 'Impact of Increased Legal Access to Needles and Syringes on Practices of Injecting-Drug Users and Police Officers – Connecticut, 1992–1993.' *Journal of Acquired Immune Deficiency Syndromes and Human Retrovirology* 10(1): 82–9.

Grove, D. 1996. 'Real Harm Reduction: Underground Survival Strategies.' *Harm Reduction Communication* 2: 1, 6.

Grund, J-P.C., P. Blanken, N.F.P. Adriaans, C.D. Kaplan, C. Barendregt, and M. Meeuwsen. 1992a. 'Reaching the Unreached: An Outreach Model of "On the Spot" AIDS Prevention among Active, Out-of-Treatment Drug Addicts.' In P.A. O'Hare et al., eds, *The Reduction of Drug-Related Harm*. New York: Routledge.

Grund, J-P.C., P. Blanken, N.F.P. Adriaans, C.D. Kaplan, C. Barendregt, and M. Meeuwsen. 1992b. 'Reaching the Unreached: Targeting Hidden IDU Populations with Clean Needles via Known Users.' *Journal of Psychoactive Drugs* 24(1): 41–7.

Grund, J.-P.C., D.D. Heckathorn, R.S. Broadhead, and D.L. Anthony. 1995. 'In Eastern Connecticut, IDUs Purchase Syringes from Pharmacies but Don't Carry Syringes.' *Journal of Acquired Immune Deficiency Syndromes and Human Retrovirology* 10(1): 104–5.

Heather, N., A. Wodak, E. Nadelmann, and P. O'Hare, eds. 1993. *Psychoactive Drugs and Harm Reduction: From Faith to Science*. London: Whurr Publishers.

Lower East Side Needle Exchange Program, Mission Statement. No date.

– 1994. 'Summary of Law Enforcement Incidents, 1992–4.'

Lurie, P., A.L. Reingold, and B. Bowser, et al. 1993. *The Public Health Impact of Needle Exchange Programs in the United States and Abroad*, vol. 1. Atlanta: Centers for Disease Control and Prevention.

McDermott, P., and W. McBride. 1993. 'Crew 2000: Peer Coalition in Action.' *Druglink*, November/December.

Musto, D. 1987. *The American Disease – Origins of Narcotic Control*. New Haven: Yale University Press.

New York City Police Department. 1992. Operations Order no. 143. 11 November.

New York Newsday. 1994. 'Needle Battle: Experts Fear Arrests Hurting AIDS Fight.' 12 July: A23.

New York Penal Law, § 220.45.

New York State Department of Health, AIDS Institute. 1993. *Policies and Procedures – Hypodermic Syringe and Needle Exchange Programs*.

– 1994. *Annual Report of the New York State-Authorized Needle Exchange Programs, August 1992 – September 1993*.

New York State Office of Alcoholism and Substance Abuse Services. 1992. *Proposed 1993 Comprehensive Plan and Update for Alcohol and Substance Abuse Services in New York State*.

New York Times. 1991. 'Dinkins Panel Is Moving to Revive Needle Exchange to Combat AIDS.' 29 October: A1, B4.

– 1992a. 'Needle Swaps Gain Wider Acceptance.' 14 May: B1, B6.

– 1992b. 'Needle Swaps to Be Revived to Curb AIDS.' 14 May: A1, B10.

– 1993. 'New York Needle Exchanges Called Surprisingly Effective.' 18 February: A1, B4.

– 1994a. 'Giuliani and Bratton Start Effort to Shake up Top Police Ranks.' 26 January: A1, B3.

– 1994b. 'More Arrests, More Therapy in Drug Plan.' 27 January: B1, B3.

Official Compilation of Codes, Rules, and Regulations of the State of New York ('Regulations'), Title 10, § 80.135, 'Authorization to Conduct Hypodermic Syringe and Needle Exchange Programs.'

O'Hare, P.A., R. Newcombe, A. Matthews, E.C. Buning, and E. Drucker, eds. 1992. *The Reduction of Drug-Related Harm*. New York: Routledge.

O'Keefe, E., E. Kaplan, and K. Khoshnood. 1991. *Preliminary Report – City of New Haven Needle Exchange Program*, 31 July.

Paone, D., D.C. Des Jarlais, S. Caloir, and P. Friedmann. 1993. 'AIDS Risk Reduction Behaviors among Participants of Syringe Exchange Programs in New York City, USA.' Paper presented at the 9th International Conference on AIDS, Berlin.

Paone, D., D.C. Des Jarlais, S. Caloir, B. Jose, and S.R. Friedman. 1994. 'New York City Syringe Exchange: Expansion, Risk Reduction, and Seroincidence.' Paper presented at the 10th International Conference on AIDS, Yokohama.

Paone, D., D.C. Des Jarlais, R. Gangloff, J. Milliken, and S.R. Friedman. 1995.

'Syringe Exchange: HIV Prevention, Key Findings, and Future Directions.' *International Journal of the Addictions* 30(2): 1647–83.

The Point: Voice of New York's Lower East Side IDU Community. 1994. 'Rudy Crushes Poor, OK's Reign of Terror,' 1(3): 1.

Sorge, R. 1992. Testimony on Allowing Non-Prescription Possession and Sale of Hypodermic Syringes. New York State Assembly Committee on Health, Assembly Committee on Alcoholism and Drug Use, Assembly Committee on Codes, Senate Democratic Task Force on Access to Primary Health Care, New York, 20 February: 49–77.

Springer, E. 1992. 'Reaching the Unreachable: Street Work with Homeless Youth.' Paper presented at the 8th International Conference on AIDS, Amsterdam.

Valleroy, L.A., B. Weinstein, T.S. Jones, S.L. Groseclose, R.T. Rolfs, and W.J. Kassler. 1995. 'Impact of Increased Legal Access to Needles and Syringes on Community Pharmacies' Needle and Syringe Sales – Connecticut, 1992–1993.' *Journal of Acquired Immune Deficiency Syndromes and Human Retrovirology* 10(1): 73–81.

Vlahov, D., C. Ryan, L. Solomon, S. Cohn, M.R. Holt, and M.N. Akhter. 1994. 'A Pilot Syringe Exchange Program in Washington, DC.' *American Journal of Public Health* 84(2): 303–4.

Washington Post. 1994. 'Scarcely a Dent in the AIDS Menace – Needle Exchange Reaches Few Drug Addicts in D.C.' 18 April: A1.

Watters, J.K., M.J. Estilo, G.L. Clark, and J. Lorvick. 1994. 'Syringe and Needle Exchange as HIV/AIDS Prevention for Injection Drug Users.' *Journal of the American Medical Association* 271(2): 115–20.

19 Shopping, Baking, and Using: The Manufacture, Use, and Problems Associated with Heroin Made in the Home from Codeine-Based Pharmaceuticals

JULIA REYNOLDS, SIMON LENTON, MIKE CHARLTON, and JANE CAPORN

Prohibition can only be expected to be successful in reducing harm when there is little demand for the proscribed drug, controls are difficult to subvert, and similar drugs are unavailable or less harmful (Wodak 1993). This chapter provides an example of drug prohibition where these conditions have not been met. It describes the unintended negative consequences of heroin supply reduction and strategies employed in an attempt to reduce the harms associated with this situation. In parts of Australia and New Zealand the unmet demand for a preferred drug, white-powder heroin, has led heroin users to resort to manufacturing a much less desirable alternative that is associated with increased risk of harm to users and the wider community.

Australia is noteworthy in that in 1985 it adopted a nation-wide drug policy that aimed to 'minimise the harmful effects of drug use on Australian society' (Department of Health 1985). This national approach, which has now become the National Drug Strategy (National Drug Strategy Committee 1993) has incorporated both demand-reduction and supply-reduction initiatives to reduce drug-related harm. Since 1993 the government has specified that its policy aim is to reduce drug-related harm 'without necessarily eliminating use' (ibid.). One of the goals of the national strategy is the reduction of transmission of HIV/AIDS and other infections. To this end, needle exchange and provision schemes have been promoted and have contributed to successfully limiting the spread of HIV among injecting drug users (IDUs). For example, Western Australia (WA) appears to have one of the lowest rates of HIV infection among drug injectors in the Western world. Current data suggest that only about 1 per cent of IDUs in WA are HIV-infected (Loxley, Carruthers, and Bevan 1995). Despite this success, from the mid-1980s to the mid-1990s the use of 'homebake' became prevalent in WA. Homebake is morphine and heroin manufactured illicitly from codeine-based pharmaceuticals. Manufacture typically occurs in users' domestic kitchens. More recently there has been a decline in its manufacture and use that has coincided with an increase in the street availability of high-grade white-powder heroin in a market previously characterized by powder heroin of low purity and high cost owing to restricted supply.

This chapter is largely based on an investigation completed by the authors in Perth, the capital city of WA. The study was conducted in response to requests from drug users and treatment-agency staff for information about homebake to assist in reducing the harmful consequences of its use. In 1992, seizure data from WA police and health authorities confirmed anecdotal reports that many Perth heroin users were using homebake. However, a literature search yielded few articles on the drug and these did not provide information adequate for harm-reduction purposes (Bedford, Nolan, Onrust and Siegers 1987; Gordon 1985?; Manion 1986; Woollard 1986). Consequently, a survey was conducted to collect information about users' experiences with homebake. This appears to have been the first research to collect standardized information from users about the drug, its use, and associated hazards. Information was collected in questionnaire format from fifty homebake consumers, some of whom were also manufacturers of the drug. Although recruited from several sources, most respondents were clients of WA's only methadone program. There were approximately equal numbers of males and females and most were between the ages of twenty and thirty-nine years. Technical details of the study are provided in Lenton, Reynolds, and Charlton (1994).

History

Descriptions of significant use of homebake have been limited to opioid users in New Zealand and Western Australia. During the late 1970s, high-grade heroin from South East Asia became widely available in New Zealand for the first time. In 1980, a large international police operation led to the collapse of the 'Mr Asia' drug syndicate. This precipitated an abrupt, almost total, cessation of heroin importation into New Zealand. Almost overnight, heroin supply in that country was all but eliminated, yet there was no corresponding reduction in the number of users wanting the drug. Consequently there was a large unmet demand for heroin. At about the same time an article was published in a prestigious international chemistry journal that described the process by which morphine and heroin could be manufactured from codeine. A copy of the journal was held in the library of Auckland University, and is thought to be the original source of the homebake 'recipe.' Before this copy had been removed by the librarian, 'homebakers' were using it to manufacture 'bake.' The first homebake laboratory was seized in Auckland in January 1983. By 1986, ninety such laboratories had been seized across New Zealand (Bedford et al. 1987). The huge gap between supply and demand caused by the apprehension of the 'Mr Asia' syndicate was filled by the resourcefulness and ingenuity of the first homebakers.

It appears that the use of homebake by opioid users in Perth began about 1986 to 1987. From 1987, police reported that increasing numbers of 'bakers' were charged with offences related to manufacturing homebake. Edge (1992) found that in 1988–1989 there were five convictions for homebake manufacture in WA and this total had increased to nineteen convictions in 1990–1. A further indicator of increasing homebake use was found in the analysis of randomly selected urine samples from clients of WAs methadone program. When data for the years before 1990 were compared to those obtained for the year 1990–1, there was a substantial increase in the number of urine samples classified as being opiate-positive (Swensen et al. 1993). The presence of both morphine and codeine in half of these opiate-positive samples led the authors to conclude that much of the increase was due to the use of homebake. Indeed, when the survey of homebake users was conducted in late 1992, just over a third of persons presenting for methadone treatment in WA reported recent homebake use.

According to police intelligence data (ABCI 1994), clandestine homebake laboratories were found in only three Australian states during 1993. One laboratory was detected in South Australia, seven in Queensland and one in WA. In 1994, evidence of homebake manufacture was uncovered only in Queensland and WA (ABCI 1995). Furthermore, liaison with forensic experts in Australia and New Zealand, and an extensive literature search of international on-line databases failed to provide any evidence of homebake being used outside these two countries. The only related report (Jensen and Hansen 1993) was from Denmark, where some drug injectors had been separating codeine from pharmaceutical products containing aspirin and codeine, which is the first stage in the homebake process. However, it appears that these Danish users had been using the codeine itself orally, or by injection, rather than first converting it to morphine or heroin. Although the scientific literature suggests that it is only in WA and New Zealand that homebake has become a significant source of illicit opioids, the recent appearance of homebake postings on drug-related news groups on the Internet suggests that opioid users elsewhere in the world have been attempting to manufacture the drug.

Historically, the idiosyncratic geographical distribution of homebake is, in itself, of interest. There are several hypotheses to explain this. First, WA, like New Zealand, is somewhat geographically isolated. Although WA has been seen as a through port for heroin from South East Asia, heading for the larger, more lucrative, markets of Melbourne and Sydney on Australia's east coast, little of this heroin had typically reached Perth streets. As noted above, up until late 1994 street-grade heroin in Perth has been expensive and of low purity. Interestingly, there has never been evidence of significant homebake manufacture or use in Sydney and Melbourne, where users have had greater and uninterrupted access to opium-based heroin. Ross, Stowe, Loxley, and Wodak (1992) found that 14.4 per cent of injectors interviewed in Sydney reported ever having used homebake, compared to 75.3 per cent in Perth. Data obtained from the homebake survey are consistent with this restricted-supply hypothesis. While a small proportion of users stated that they used homebake because it was more potent than other available narcotics, most respondents indicated that they used homebake because it was cheaper or more available. One user summarized his views on homebake thus: 'It's pure brown poison, but it's "bloody cheap and nasty" and available more freely' (male, 30–39 years, using homebake for two years).

Another possible explanation is that the emergence of homebake in WA was the result of sizeable numbers of New Zealanders, including some members of New Zealand organized motorcycle gangs, migrating or travelling to that state. However, by whatever mechanism homebake manufacture and use was established in WA, it seems its existence could only be explained by a demand for heroin during a period of limited supply of traditional opium-based powder heroin. As the street availability of high-grade white-powder heroin has increased, indications are that the use of homebake heroin has decreased. According to the Drug Squad of the WA Police Department (personal communication), the availability and purity of white-powder heroin on the street began to rise around September 1994. From early 1995 to early 1996, the purity of heroin seized on the street in Perth increased from 12 to 20 per cent to around 60 per cent (Treweek 1996). In December 1992, 34 per cent of the last fifty people assessed for methadone treatment admitted to recent homebake use. In December 1993 the figure was 38%, in 1994 it was 14%, and in 1995 it was 12%.

Manufacture and Packaging

In order to appreciate the particular risks associated with homebake, it is important to have basic information concerning its manufacture and packaging. Homebake is usually made in domestic kitchens using rudimentary and easily portable laboratory equipment. The process takes about three hours to complete and requires a large quantity of codeine, several other chemicals and a 'recipe' that specifies manufacturing instructions. A number of illicit recipes are available, which sold for approximately A$500 during 1992 when data was collected for this study. When they first appeared in WA, recipes sold for five or six times that amount.

Typically, a small cooperative group of homebake users work together to buy large quantities of tablets that contain codeine. Commonly used drugs include Veganin, Panadeine, Codral Pain Relief, and Codiphen. In WA, these are available over the counter from pharmacies. There is also some indication of the use of Panadeine Forte by homebake manufacturers (Ilett 1992). This drug is available only on doctor's prescription and contains much more codeine than the other preparations. It is estimated that 250 Panadeine tablets would yield about 2 grams of codeine, which may yield 5 to 10 mls of homebake-heroin solution, containing somewhere between 10 and 40 mg of heroin per ml of liquid (Bedford et al. 1987).

There are three stages to homebake manufacture in the three-hour process. In the first step, codeine-containing tablets are crushed and codeine is extracted as a white to yellowish crystalline powder. Next, the codeine is converted to morphine, which tends to be a brown powder. This may be sold as 'powder' homebake. Finally, the morphine is converted to heroin as a dark brown paste that is diluted in water for injection. The final product usually also contains morphine, codeine, and, depending on the care taken, various quantities of the hazardous chemicals used in its manufacture. These chemicals are thought to be responsible for some of the idiosyncratic side-effects described below. The liquid residue from the manufacture is called the 'boil-up.' It contains higher concentrations of toxic chemicals, but may also be sold for injection. Powder homebake is often sold with a syringe of the corrosive

Acetic Anhydride (AA). Users will add AA to the homebake morphine powder in the spoon to convert it to heroin. They then attempt to burn off the excess AA before dissolving and injecting the mixture.

All respondents in the survey reported that they used intravenous injection to administer their homebake. The majority reported that they most often used the liquid form of the drug. Not surprisingly, none reported that they most frequently used 'boil-up.' The forms most often used were also those that were more available.

Hazards of Manufacture and Use

In addition to the risks usually associated with the intravenous injection of illicit narcotics, common practices employed in the manufacture and packaging of homebake increase the risks of harm occurring. There is a risk for contamination of the homebake as it is made in non-sterile settings, using makeshift equipment, by people who may be experiencing withdrawals or intoxication and under the constant stress of needing to conceal their operations. Not surprisingly, most of the survey respondents thought that homebake was not germ-free and were concerned about this. Other risks are associated with the dangerous properties of some of the chemicals used in homebake manufacture and with the increased potential for the transmission of blood-borne viral infections, particularly through the use of liquid homebake.

Chemical Hazards

Several particularly dangerous chemicals are used to make homebake (Woollard 1986). Many of these are believed to be present at various concentrations in the final product and may thus be injected intravenously by the user. In addition, many of the chemicals give off hazardous vapours and can pose an explosion risk during baking. Hazards associated with some of these chemicals are summarized in table 1.

Many subjects in the study were aware of some of the dangers associated with the use of these chemicals. For example, one subject expressed his concerns as follows: 'Disposal of reagents used in making homebake is a concern, dangerous chemicals are poured down the sink and put into the garden. Also in manufacture [the] use of Pyridine is a toxic process, gases and Hydrochloric acid etc. given off, often made indoors with small children about the house' (male, 30–39 years, using homebake for three years). Woollard (1986) has noted that the evaporation of

TABLE 1
Chemicals used in homebake manufacture and their hazards

Chloroform	Drowsiness and loss of consciousness
	Respiratory depression, heart problems, and seizures
	Liver and kidney damage
	Heating produces phosgene gas absorbed through skin and lungs, can cause severe pulmonary edema
Pyridine	Obnoxious odour
	As liquid is inflammable
	As gas is highly explosive
	Acute exposure can produce drowsiness and loss of consciousness
	Implicated in liver, kidney, and heart damage
Hydrochloric acid	Corrosive to eyes, skin, and lungs
Acetic Anhydride (AA)	Toxic upon inhalation, ingestion, and skin contact
	Corrosive to eyes and skin
	Explosion hazard

chloroform, particularly in a small enclosed room, like many kitchens, is extremely dangerous and spillage of chloroform onto a kitchen hot-plate can produce poisonous phosgene gas. Homebake users noted that many bakers wear masks and use extraction fans in an attempt to remove noxious fumes. Bakers run the risk that the pungent gases released to the environment by such fans can raise the interest of neighbours, who may alert the authorities.

Side-Effects
The homebake survey provided information about users' experiences with the drug and indicated that there were some unusual effects of homebake that were likely to be consequences of the chemicals used in the process of manufacture.

First, respondents to the survey were asked to indicate which of a list of side-effects they had experienced after using homebake. Relative frequencies of each side-effect for each form of the drug are summarized in table 2. Side-effects listed for liquid homebake such as itching, constipation, changed libido, and pain on injection are commonly found with any opioid use. However, some of the side-effects experienced are not typically associated with opiate use. Skin infections, rashes, and boils were reported following the use of powdered homebake. These were

TABLE 2
Percentage of respondents reporting side-effects of use for each type of homebake

	Respondents (%)		
Side-effects	Liquid	Powder	Boil-up
Headache	6.5	6.1	10.9
Constipation	8.4	10.4	8.7
Itching	9.1	8.7	6.5
Changed sex drive	8.1	8.7	6.5
Pain on injecting	7.5	6.1	6.5
Weight down	7.1	7.0	6.5
Skin infections sores and boils	3.6	7.0	4.3
Nausea and vomiting	6.5	5.2	6.5
Changes in vision	4.5	3.5	6.5
Appetite down	5.5	5.5	4.3

probably due to the injection of Acetic Anhydride (AA), that had not been burnt off efficiently after being added to the powdered morphine in the spoon. The headaches and changes in vision reported after boil-up use are possibly due to the high concentrations of toxic residues in this form of homebake. In addition, many of the users observed that, in their experience, the use of homebake led to a more rapid collapse of veins used for injection and that the veins that had collapsed in this manner took longer to heal than with other injected opiates.

Dependence and Withdrawal
The average length of time given by respondents to develop physical dependence on homebake was 10 days (range 4 to 27 days). This is probably not dissimilar from that for the street-grade heroin available in Perth during 1992. Respondents were asked to estimate the length of the period of abstinence necessary before a physically dependent person would experience withdrawals from homebake. The average length of time given by the respondents was 16 hours (range 2 to 36 hours). This is longer than withdrawal from heroin, which typically commences four to six hours after last use (Berkow 1982). This may be due to the inefficiencies in the manufacture of homebake that leave codeine in the final product. Withdrawals from codeine tend to appear about 8 hours after the last dose (Goodman and Gilman 1970). The majority of survey respondents found withdrawals from homebake worse than those from heroin but easier than withdrawals from methadone.

Respondents who stated they had at some time totally withdrawn from homebake without using alcohol or other drugs were asked which of a list of ten withdrawal symptoms they had experienced. Most endorsed items known to be common in opiate withdrawal, such as leg cramps, sleep problems, runny nose, nausea and vomiting, diarrhoea, and abdominal cramps. Two unusual symptoms reported were tremor and body odour, which were possibly due to impurities. Homebake users often give off a characteristic smell. This is probably due to the injection of Pyridine, which has a particularly nasty odour and vapours that can be secreted through the skin. One of the users in the study noted about withdrawal: 'When you "hang out" from homebake you ooze the smell, you taste it, you smell it' (female, 20–29 years, using four months).

Transmission of Blood-Borne Viral Infections

The second area of particular risk associated with liquid homebake involves the increased potential for transmission of blood-borne viral infections such as HIV and hepatitis B and C. The use of the liquid may be associated with risks for virus transmission that go beyond those documented for injectable drugs sold in powder form. These additional risks are associated with the possibility of direct transmission of viruses through the homebake liquid and the increased likelihood that injection equipment will be shared.

Potential for Infection through Liquid Homebake
It is at least theoretically possible that blood-borne viral infections can be transmitted in blood particles that find their way into the homebake solution itself. It is not thought possible for blood-borne viral infections to be directly transmitted through the dry-powder form of homebake.

There are anecdotal reports that indicate it is possible for infected blood and other contaminants to be inadvertently added to the homebake solution. For example, syringes are often used to measure out quantities of chemicals as they are added to the homebake during manufacturing. These syringes may have been used previously for intravenous injection. There have also been anecdotal reports of bakers injecting themselves with a syringe to sample the batch and then using the same syringe to measure doses of the homebake into multiple bottles for sale. In 1993 a user who became HIV-positive claimed that his only risk behaviour had been the use of liquid homebake and that he had contracted the virus directly from the liquid.

Just over half the survey sample thought it was possible for the home-bake to be contaminated by hepatitis viruses during the manufacturing process. Significantly fewer respondents thought that the homebake could be contaminated by the HIV virus during manufacture. However, most of the respondents who thought that either virus could contaminate the homebake also believed that injection of the contaminated homebake could lead to infection by the viruses. It seems likely that the respondents based their judgments of relative risk on the prevalence of the viruses in the local community. The rate of HIV infection amongst injecting drug users in WA is very low (approximately 1 per cent in the methadone-treatment population) in comparison to the very high rates of hepatitis C infection (approximately 90 per cent in the methadone-treatment population).

Virus Transmission via Needles and Syringes
Liquid homebake also presents the potential for virus transmission via the 1-ml 'insulin' syringes in which it is most often sold. The majority of respondents bought their liquid homebake already 'prepacked' in a syringe. In order for a syringe to be filled with homebake, it must be removed from its sterile wrapper. Unless users are present when the needle and syringe is removed from its wrapper and filled with home-bake, they cannot be sure that this injecting equipment has not been used before. Needles and syringes were seen as presenting a risk for transmission of both hepatitis and HIV by most of the respondents. One respondent explained: 'Homebake I feel is not a risk of infection while it is being made but maybe after it is completed and being transferred from bottle to fit, or fit to fit, that's where the risk is involved'* (female, 20–29 years, using homebake for eight months). There are also some indications that users may be more likely to share injecting equipment when using liquid homebake. For example, it was reported that young users with a low tolerance for opiates pooled funds and bought a syringe of homebake. They then shared this dose by using the same syringe to inject more than one person. These reports are of particular concern because there appeared to be significant use of homebake by the most vulnerable users. Evidence emerged of a new group of younger homebake users. Data collected in 1993 in a study of hepatitis C among 234 drug users aged from 15 to 20 years found that about one in three reported using homebake in the previous 12 months (Carruthers

---

* 'Fit' is users' term for a needle and syringe.

and Loxley 1994). Alarmingly, 60 per cent of the twenty young Aborigi-
nals in the sample stated they had used homebake in the previous
month. While there is no evidence that homebake use in these groups
has continued now that supply of white powder heroin has increased,
these data suggested that the use of the drug was not limited to those
with a long history of opioid use.

Harm Reduction Strategies

Strategies for reducing the impact of the additional harm associated
with homebake use may include interventions aimed at empowering
individual users to protect themselves and more systemic interventions
aimed at reducing the risks inherent in the use of homebake.

One intervention targeted at individual users was to provide them
with information about the hazards of homebake use and with strategies for reducing these hazards. Three-quarters of the survey respondents stated that they would like more information about homebake.
Their preference was for this information to be distributed in printed literature through the methadone clinic and needle-and-syringe distribution sites. Preliminary data from this study were included in an article
(Lenton, Reynolds, Charlton, and Caporn 1992) published in the Australian user magazine *Junkmail*. Copies of this magazine were distributed,
at no charge to the reader, through various sites in WA and other states
of Australia.

Thus, one of the main sources of information for harm reduction has
been that provided by users themselves. From the survey data, it is clear
that one of the main harm reduction strategies used by the respondents
was to manufacture their own homebake or to buy their drugs directly
from a baker whom they trusted. One respondent noted: 'I have only
ever had a habit on homebake, and since getting a habit have manufactured it myself. I am always meticulous about my equipment being
sterile and only ever use new syringes. It is always made under totally
germ free conditions' (female, 30–39 years, using homebake for sixteen
months).

However, becoming a baker may not be a very appropriate or palatable harm reduction strategy for many homebake users, particularly
given the risk of detection by law-enforcement officers and the severity
of sentences for manufacture of such a drug. Many respondents noted
that there were variations in the risks associated with individual manufacturers: 'Everyone bakes differently. Some do not take the time to

make sure everything is clean and sterile, also not making sure all chemical (as much as possible) has been taken out properly mainly because it takes longer to finish' (female, 20–29 years, using homebake for twelve months). As a consequence, familiarity with one's supplier and a knowledge of the process itself was seen by some users as one way of reducing the risks. An example of this strategy was given by one respondent who explained as follows: 'I know [that the] people I buy off are scrupulous in their methods to keep the equipment clean and to ensure only fresh, new syringes are used every time and I also ensure this is the case if I get any for anyone else, but I am aware that not everyone is as conscientious as this. People know about this [and] have remarked "One thing I know about you is that your gear is always clean." I pride myself on this. I've been tested HIV negative and intend to stay this way!' (female, 20–29 years, using homebake for thirteen months). Such an approach is also going to be inaccessible to many. Young and less-experienced users and people who use homebake infrequently are less likely to have extensive personal involvement in the manufacture of homebake. They may not be able to directly monitor the relative risks associated with any particular batch of homebake in the manner reported by many of the more experienced users surveyed.

It will be apparent that the risks of transmission of blood-borne viruses through the use of liquid homebake could be avoided by using the powder form of the drug. Several respondents suggested using powder homebake, rather than the liquid, where possible. For example, one respondent noted: 'As I make my own, I have no anxieties about impurities etc., but if I wasn't, I doubt very much if I'd buy it, particularly in liquid form – the powder would certainly be safer' (male, 30–39 years, using homebake for three years). Thus, powdered homebake was seen as somewhat less risky than liquid or boil-up. However, the survey respondents also indicated that powder was less freely available than liquid. Furthermore, there were anecdotal reports of some users accidentally injecting the syringes of AA that are sold with powder homebake to convert it from morphine to heroin.

In addition to the attempts made by individual users to reduce harm, systemic approaches need to be considered. Since March 1992, the Western Australian authorities have imposed limits on the supply of precursor chemicals and required that purchasers of large amounts of codeine-containing products provide proof of identification. However, the extent to which this has affected the availability of homebake is unclear. Police reports suggest there has been a marked decline in the number of homebake seizures in 1993, which they have attributed to the success of strategies to limit availability of precursor chemicals (ABCI 1994). It is not possible to definitively determine the relative impact on the levels of homebake use of increased purity and availability of opium-based heroin, compared to those steps taken to limit the availability of precursors and of codeine preparations. Actions to limit the supply of precursors and the codeine-based pharmaceuticals began in earnest in early 1992, yet even in December 1993 rates of recent homebake use among those seeking methadone treatment remained high. Falls in the prevalence of recent homebake use among those seeking methadone followed evidence of rises in the purity of white-powder heroin on the street towards the end of 1994. While both factors likely had some impact on homebake use, on balance such a decrease suggests that the increased purity and availability of opium-based heroin probably had more of an impact. In addition, we have noted that supply-reduction initiatives can result in increased harm where substitution of more harmful alternatives is possible. There was concern that restrictions on the chemicals used in homebake manufacture would lead to the use of other, even more toxic, chemicals. One respondent to the survey reinforced this concern: 'Now [that the] chemical AA has been banned – the bakers are using a more toxic chemical' (female, 20–29 years, using homebake for three years).

An alternative systemic intervention is to help manufacturers of homebake to make a product that is less harmful for users. In WA, non-government HIV outreach services for drug injectors have allowed their clients to obtain large quantities of new needles and syringes in an effort to encourage bakers not to recycle needles. Another possibility is to make information available that would allow bakers to further purify the homebake before it is distributed for injection. Further distillation and filtration of the liquid homebake may remove some of the remaining toxic contaminants. One baker commented: 'It's a shame that the homebake process isn't just a little more complete in the purification process as it's obvious that it is not as pure as white powder heroin.' (male, 30–39 years, using homebake for three years).

Conclusion

The development and use of homebake is an example of an unintended consequence of supply-reduction policies. It developed in a context of continuing demand for opioids, particular geographical and social factors, and policing of the importation and distribution of heroin. It is argued that these factors contributed to the establishment of a cottage industry where users could have more control over their supply, avoid risks of importation, and produce a drug that was attractive because of its price and availability, despite considerable hazards in its manufacture and use. The use of homebake persisted in Western Australia while high-quality opium-based heroin was in short supply. This occurred even though consumers experienced unpleasant side-effects and were concerned about heightened risk of virus transmission. It is suggested that high levels of homebake manufacture and use continued despite attempts to restrict access to the drugs and chemicals used in its manufacture. In this context, initiatives were employed that attempted to work with manufacturers and users to minimize harm. The recent decline in the use of homebake by opioid users in Perth appears to have been largely due to the increased availability of high-quality white-powder heroin, although strategies to limit supply of precursors and codeine based pharmaceuticals may also have been a factor. While homebake may historically have been largely limited to WA and New Zealand, its presence on the Internet suggests it may appear in pockets elsewhere in the world, particularly where the supply of opium-based heroin becomes restricted or is less attractive because of price or purity. The emergence of drugs such as homebake, and their associated problems, needs to be considered by those who argue for continuing prohibition and the war on drugs.

ACKNOWLEDGMENTS

We would like to thank the past and present clients and staff of the Western Australian Alcohol and Drug Authority's methadone program and Central Drug Unit, the Palmerston DRRA, and the Western Australian AIDS Council's Drug Outreach Program. The contributions of Susan Wilson, Mike Phillips, and Lim Tan are also appreciated.

REFERENCES

Australian Bureau of Criminal Intelligence (ABCI). 1994. *Australian Drug Intelligence Assessment 1993*. Canberra: ABCI.
– 1995. *Australian Drug Intelligence Assessment 1994*. Canberra: ABCI.
Bedford, K.R., S.L. Nolan, R. Onrust, and J.D. Siegers. 1987. 'The Illicit Preparation of Morphine and Heroin from Pharmaceutical Products Containing

Codeine: "Homebake" Laboratories in New Zealand.' *Forensic Science International* 34: 197–204.

Berkow, R., ed. 1982. *The Merck Manual of Diagnosis and Therapy*. Rahway, NJ: Merck and Co.

Carruthers, S., and W. Loxley. 1994. *Hepatitis C and Young Drug Users*. Perth: National Centre for Research into the Prevention of Drug Abuse, Curtin University of Technology.

Department of Health. 1985. *National Campaign against Drug Abuse: Campaign Document Issued Following the Special Premiers' Conference Canberra 2 April, 1985*. Canberra: Australian Government Printing Service.

Edge, J. 1992. *Homebake Fact Sheet*. Unpublished. Alcohol and Drug Information Service, Western Australian Alcohol and Drug Authority.

Goodman, L.S., and A. Gilman. 1970. *The Pharmacological Basis of Therapeutics*. 4th ed. New York: Macmillan.

Gordon, R. 1985? 'Homebake – the Drug.' *Metro*: 49–61.

Ilett, K.F. 1992. 'Is Panadeine Forte Being Over Prescribed?' *Medical Journal of Australia* 156: 583–4.

Jensen, S., and A.C. Hansen. 1993. 'Abuse of Codeine Separated from Over-the-Counter Drugs Containing Acetylsalicylic Acid and Codeine.' *International Journal of Legal Medicine* 105: 279–81.

Lenton, S., J. Reynolds, and M. Charlton. 1994. 'Shopping, Baking and Using: The Manufacture, Use and Problems Associated with the Use of Heroin Made in the Home from Codeine Based Pharmaceuticals.' Paper presented at 5th International Conference on the Reduction of Drug Related Harm, Toronto, 6–10 March.

Lenton, S., J. Reynolds, M. Charlton, and J. Caporn. 1992. 'Shopping and Baking: The Use of Homebake Heroin in Western Australia.' *Junkmail* 3(3–4): 22–6.

Loxley, W., S. Carruthers, and J. Bevan. 1995. *In the Same Vein: First Report of the Australian Study of HIV and Injecting Drug Use (ASHIDU)*. Perth: National Centre for Research into the Prevention of Drug Abuse, Curtin University of Technology.

Manion, R. 1986. 'A Life in the Day of a Homebake Shopper.' *New Outlook*, September–October: 55–7.

National Drug Strategy Committee. 1993. *National Drug Strategic Plan 1993–97*. Canberra: Australian Government Printing Service.

Ross, M.W., A. Stowe, W. Loxley, and A. Wodak. 1992. '"Homebake" Heroin Used by Injecting Drug Users.' *Medical Journal of Australia* 157: 283–4.

Swensen, G., K.F. Ilett, L.J. Dusci, P. Hackett, R.T.T. Ong, A.J. Quigley, S. Lenton, R. Saker, and J. Caporn. 1993. 'Patterns of Drug Use by Participants in the

Western Australian Methadone Program, 1984–1991.' *Medical Journal of Australia* 159: 373–6.

Treweek, A. 1996. 'Big Rises in Drug Deaths Alarm Police.' *Sunday Times*, 4 February: 7.

Wodak, A. 1993. 'Has Harm Reduction Been Effective in Australia?' Paper delivered at Winter School in the Sun, Brisbane.

Woollard, G.G. 1986. '"Homebake" Morphine: The Full Extent of the Problem.' *Journal of General Practice* 3: 1–5.

20 'Really Useful Knowledge': The Boundaries, Customs, and Folklore Governing Recreational Drug Use in a Sample of Young People

LAURA GAMBLE and MICHAEL GEORGE

Research into the recreational use of illegal drugs has never, arguably, achieved the prominence it deserves. 'Successful' recreational drug users may teach us more about treating problematic drug use than studying casualties whose drug use has become problematic or studying abstainers. Recent surveys of drug use amongst young people (Baldwin 1991) suggest that the prevalence of recreational or dance drug use as well as the use of cannabis and hallucinogenic drugs has increased substantially. Research that focuses on problematic or dependent drug use, therefore, fails to take account of the far larger cohort of drug users who maintain control over their intake. The beliefs and behaviours that underpin 'successful' recreational drug use combine to form the 'Really Useful Knowledge' that is the focus of this chapter.

This research is a slightly serendipitous adventure into the folklore, knowledge base, and tribal customs that govern this recreational drug use. The main corpus of research into controlled drug use dates back to the 1970s and early 1980s. It has been established that social sanctions, rituals, drug-taking environments, and cultural determinants all exert control on the quantity, frequency, type, and mode of drug use (Zinberg 1984; Zinberg et al. 1975). Presumably because it was the most topical drug of addiction, heroin is singled out in earlier studies (Powell 1973). In the 1990s, new recruits to opiate use appear to be dwindling and the use of psychostimulants and hallucinogenics appears to have eclipsed that part played by heroin. While tracking down long-term recreational opiate users is the ultimate challenge to outreach research (George 1993), there is an abundant sample of recreational stimulant and hallucinogenic users, many of whom are willing and able to discuss the unwritten rules that provide the informal checks and balances to their drug use. Previous studies have identified a range of factors that influence the use of substances by young people.

Wilks et al. (1989) review a significant corpus of research that demonstrates a powerful parental modelling effect for drinking behaviour. The authors comment: 'As modelling theorists would predict, the drinking behaviour of mothers and fathers was the best predictor of adolescent male drinking of beer, which is by far the most heavily consumed alcoholic beverage' (p. 627).

However, our study deals with a behaviour for which there is, by and large, no parental model: the use of illegal drugs. What then are the influences and sources of knowledge that shape illegal-drug-taking behaviour? The evidence would seem to implicate strongly the role played by peers. Swadie and Zeitlin (1980) identify peers as providing both a behavioural model and a source of information. 'It seems that differences between users and non-users exist in so far as the response to such information is concerned' (p. 154). Non-users favour 'professional' sources such as general practitioners, while users give more credence to information from other users or from ex-users. Neither group relied on parents as sources of information. The distinction that is probably being identified here is that between people who 'know what they are talking about' and those who do not. Predictably, in our study the only people who spoke positively of parental information or advice were those respondents whose parents used illegal drugs: 'My dad still smokes the ganja all the time. He still smokes it. But like my mum hasn't really tried anything. I have a smoke with my dad every now and again which is quite cool' (21-year-old female recreational user).

Grund (1993) studied the symbolic and ritualistic components of heroin and cocaine use in the Netherlands and noted that 'the ingestion of Heroin by both chasers and IDU's is subject to a fixed stylised and predictable behavioural sequence, which a user must master through practice, observation of, and instruction from more experienced users' (p. 295). These drug-use rituals are instrumental in the self-regulation of drug taking, and transitions between smoking or injecting or between heroin or cocaine in Grund's subject sample were often associated with 'attempts to regain control' (p. 296). Grund concludes: 'In contrast with stereotypical portrayals, it is concluded that the study participants put much effort in trying to control their drug use' (297).

The recent work of Grund draws heavily on the research on controlled intoxicant use carried out by Norman Zinberg (1984). Zinberg's seminal work influenced much of the subsequent research into the controlled use of drugs and deserves to be covered in some detail. He advocated the investigation of moderate drug consumption as a tool to discourage abuse and inform research into the treatment of addiction; he was not encouraging young people to use dangerous drugs on the basis that they were relatively harmless.

Zinberg pointed out that the historical legitimization of alcohol use, experimentation, and formal and informal teaching about alcohol's appropriate use have all combined to produce a situation in the twentieth century when most people use this drug harmlessly most of the time. This was not always so and, presumably, if alcohol were an illegal drug, would not be the case today. It takes several generations for the appropriate use of a substance to become woven into the customs, folklore, and accepted behaviour of a society. Zinberg's argument is therefore simple and persuasive. The illicit nature of many drug substances prevents the natural process of socialization and unconscious indoctrination of appropriate use through peer, parental, and community modelling. Teaching safe use is not intended to encourage use. Its main purpose is the prevention of abuse, just as the primary purpose of the few good sex-education courses in existence today is to teach the avoidance of unwanted pregnancy and venereal disease rather than the desirability of having or avoiding sexual activity.

The widespread belief that drug use, drug problems, and drug dependency are virtually synonymous further complicates the picture. While Zinberg argues that abuse flourishes in the educational vacuum that illegality promotes, Davies (1992) points out that the widely held belief that drug use tends inexorably towards loss of control can become a dangerously self-fulfilling prophecy. If people are taught that drug use leads to addiction, this belief and expectation will generate the very pathology it describes. Drug users will be more likely to see themselves, and be seen by professional agencies, as helpless, problematic addicts. Thus, a combined effect can be demonstrated that both denies the existence of controlled intoxicant use and promotes energetically the message that use results in uncontrolled use. These are presumably the beliefs and expectations that the novice drug user brings to his or her first tentative and ignorant experiments with illegal substances.

Despite these influences, there is increasing evidence for widespread recreational use of illegal drugs. Indeed, in some areas of the United Kingdom, controlled users are being recruited and trained to 'pass those skills onto others' (McDermott and McBride 1993). The introduction of this type of 'Peer Coalition' challenges drug workers to 'stop seeing themselves as the experts' (ibid.).

But what is the nature of the successful recreational users' expertise? In what ways is this relationship with drugs generated and how is it maintained? Who are these people who rarely present to drug agencies and who would be more likely to define their drug use as recreational rather than problematic?

To explore the possible answers to these questions, semi-structured tape-recorded interviews were held in pubs and clubs on the south coast of England with twenty-six young recreational drug users in the winter of 1993. The researchers commissioned to conduct the interviews were briefed by the authors to lead the discussion towards the following areas:

1/The parameters that govern the types of drug used, quantities of drugs used, and frequency of drug use.
2/The customs that had developed and were observed within the users' peer group relating to drugs and drug use.
3/The sources of the drug-related knowledge that informed and helped to govern the extent and type of drug use as well as the relative weighting or value bestowed on these various sources of knowledge by the user.

The typescripts of the semi-structured interviews were then analysed for content by the authors to 'map out' the self-imposed and external boundaries that governed individual drug use, the lessons the users had learned, the social and safety taboos, and the sources from which this folklore had been accumulated.

Because the two researchers commissioned to conduct the interviews were familiar with the entertainment scene around the town of Brighton on the south coast of England, they were able to conduct and facilitate informal discussion groups with the young recreational drug users. These groups were gathered by three main methods:

1/Young people who frequented particular music venues including pubs and clubs and who were approached at random.
2/Students outside one of the colleges of further education first con-
tacted on the street and then asked to an informal meeting at a public house. These individuals had also been asked to bring a friend if they so wished.

3/Acquaintances of the two researchers mainly interviewed in their
own homes or in the homes of the researchers. They, too, had been
asked to invite interested friends if they wished.

These contacts eventually formed the cohort of twenty-six respondents. All respondents were told the aim of the research and that it was
organized by the two agencies within which the authors worked. With
only one or two exceptions, everyone was eager to take part and most of
the respondents spent a lot of time discussing the issues, with only minimal prompting by the interviewers. This, perhaps, is one of the hallmarks of recreational drug users.

Because of the informality, anonymity, and non-directive nature of
our research, the profile of the subject sample is necessarily sketchy and
incomplete. This is both a strength and weakness of open-ended
research that encourages the respondents to explore their own agenda
rather than follow the agenda determined by the research worker.

Most subjects were in their early twenties. Four were younger than
twenty and one older than thirty. The youngest subject was sixteen
years old and the oldest thirty-four years old. Although two subjects
reported first using illegal drugs at the ages of eleven and twelve respectively, the majority reported their first illegal drug experiences between
the ages of fourteen and sixteen. Two subjects reported using their first
illegal drugs at the age of 20.

Nineteen talked about the first illegal drug they had tried. This had
been cannabis in fifteen cases, Ecstasy in two cases, amphetamine in one
case, and LSD in one case. All subjects were asked routinely which
drugs they had ever used. The following pattern emerged: cannabis
(88%), Ecstasy (81%), amphetamine (73%), and LSD (65%) were the most
likely recreational drugs in this sample. Approximately one-third of the
sample had used cocaine and one-quarter had used magic mushrooms.
Predictably, opiate use rated low; surprisingly, crack cocaine was only
reported by one individual.

Sixteen subjects mentioned drugs they would never use, although
once again this data set is incomplete. Fourteen subjects volunteered the
information that they would never use heroin, four indicated an unwillingness to use cocaine, four mentioned that they would never use
crack cocaine, and two mentioned that they would never use Ketamine
(special K).

Using the accepted methods of social ethnography in order to map
out the framework within which recreational drug use may thrive,

both authors listened to the recorded interviews and conducted independent content analysis of the typescripts. Key themes and issues gradually emerged. Subsequent comparison by the two authors revealed a reassuring measure of overlap. Core quotations dealing with each of the identified themes were selected to support the text and discussion.

The excerpts that accompany the following themes and sub-themes are reported verbatim from the original material and have not been altered in any way. While the grammar is sometimes inaccurate and the turn of phrase robust, it has been the authors' intention to render a faithful report of the selected material without imposing an academic bias that might radically alter its flavour and impact. The more obscure colloquial expressions are followed by bracketed explanations for those less familiar with 'street' idioms.

No attempt was made to investigate the validity or otherwise of any of the information given to the interviewers. It is therefore possible that the sample may have sought to 'fake good' for the benefit of the interviewers and appear to be more in control or having a better time than was actually the case. If this is true, it emphasizes once again that 'fun' and 'control' are highly valued attributes of recreational drug use that may be aspired to by some who have not attained them.

There is a further check imposed on the validity of the data. The categories, themes, and sub-themes were identified as significant by the authors because these issues emerged again and again. While only the most specific and cogent examples of the text are used, the themes to which they refer emerge again and again in the 'subject – subject' and 'subject – interviewer' discussions. Some themes, such as AIDS and hepatitis, are notable by their absence. It is unlikely, if these were central issues, that no reference would be made to them throughout the entire typescript.

The themes that emerged were classified into a hierarchy consisting of main categories, themes, and sub-themes. This 'road map' of motor ways, arterial routes, and country roads provides a working sketch of the internal and external boundaries that govern the establishment and maintenance of controlled recreational drug use.

The main categories that influence and control recreational use emerge as follows:

– Sources of drug-related knowledge
– Strategies for risk reduction

- Values and beliefs
- External controlling factors

Sources of Drug-Related Knowledge

The first of the main categories contains information about drugs, their effects, and the sources from which these data have been accumulated. The following themes and sub-themes emerge.

Experiential Learning

Experiential learning emerges as a major influence in relation to drug use. This theme deals with experiences that the subjects had themselves encountered in relation to drug use. These are therefore first-hand experiences and appear to draw their power and influence from this immediacy. Important learning experiences appear to include factors such as substance experimentation, dosage experimentation, and limiting experiences.

The subjects had experimented with a variety of substances. There is an underlying attitude that if an individual has not tried substance X, he or she has no right to be either promoting or deploring its use. Many had approached this experimentation with an open mind, eager for new experience and relatively unafraid of the consequences. The following quotation demonstrates how ignorance is seen as carrying greater risks than experimental use itself: 'When I first started taking drugs it was a sense of exploration and a sense of you've got to try everything once and that there was no way I could possibly comment on them or have an opinion on them if I hadn't experienced them and that was why I, you know, when I was first offered it, I'd have a go at almost anything. I think its been very useful and I've learnt a lot through doing that.'

Within the aetiology of recreational drug use it would appear that once a preferred substance has been chosen, or in the process of its choice, dosage experimentation does take place. It is not always assumed that 'more is better,' but sometimes this is a lesson that has to be learned. For most respondents this process of titration was a conscious and almost scientific process: 'I just upped what I was taking and experimented further and further until I reached a point when I thought, no, this doesn't feel so good, this is becoming unhealthy, the physical come-down off this isn't worth it. It was just a gradual process of trial and error.' They were aware when the optimum dose had been exceeded and would modify their intake appropriately. In some instances (for example, getting drunk and experiencing a hangover the following day), this experience was repeated on several occasions before the behaviour was modified.

Not all dosage experimentation was conducted purposefully. Some subjects had made mistakes and in several cases the unwanted experiences had been frightening: 'I just reached a point where I realised that it was affecting my personality and I was becoming very withdrawn and very insecure about things, but mainly very insecure about relationships that I had and there was a couple of times when I was taking acid [LSD] and there was one particular time that I remember where I just spent eight hours in a room full of people and I didn't say a word, I was just too scared and withdrawn to actually sort of actually participate in what was going on. Very, very frightening, I just couldn't say a word, not through anything physical, I was just very worried about what people would think if I said something. Whether I'd get shot down [criticized] That's really the time when I decided doing this was really going to fuck me up bad.' In some instances, these experiences occurred with familiar drugs that had been used on several previous occasions, and in some instances the drug (for example, ketamine) was being used for the first time. However, while these are predominantly negative events, these limiting experiences lead, in most instances, to increased insight, greater control, and the confidence that accompanies greater understanding of drug types and effects.

Observational Learning

This data set includes second-hand experiences that, while less powerful than those gained at first hand, have greater influence than academic information, unsubstantiated fact and rumour, and plain hearsay. Second-hand experiences include direct observation and the reported experiences of known others.

The example offered by those around the individual can be either positive (pro-drug) or negative (anti-drug). The ubiquitous principle emerges that the more significant the model, the more significant the modelling. The drug experiences of siblings, partners, and best friends are more persuasive than those of distant relatives and acquaintances: 'My sister's really fucked up about it. Like she's constantly on drugs the whole time. And she's like left home and stuff because she's really ratty [irritable] and stuff. And I don't want to get into heavier stuff like she did. Trips [LSD] like every day. Really bad. So I don't want to ... I keep it every weekend or something.'

Congruence also emerges as a powerful influence. If several acquaintances have a similar drug experience, it is more likely to be believed than in cases where the evidence is contradictory or equivocal: 'I'd also stop if any of my friends had a terrible experience on speed [Amphetamine], acid [LSD], Ecstasy. If I was there and had experienced it myself and seen it, I think I'd stop or cut down radically.'

In some cases, the subjects had not witnessed drug-related events (positive or negative), but had sought or obtained information from friends relating to experiences that had happened at another time or place: 'You pick up information here and there when you start getting into drugs and some of it's bullshit, some of it's truthful, and you have to hope that the people you have around you, who are supposed to be experienced, are actually experienced and not just feeding you crap, just talking bullshit. You've just got to learn by experience. If you have a dodgy E [adulterated Ecstasy], then you've gotta sort of learn the hard way really. And obviously not take too much of anything you're not sure about.' 'Whose information do you trust?' 'Um, friends probably. Best people to trust.'

Similar influences emerged. The more significant the informant, the more trusted the information and, therefore, one would assume, the greater the influence on the recipient.

Database Sources

These sources of knowledge are less influential than those deriving from experience or observation. However, this information, some of which is whimsical to the point of fantasy, forms a significant part of the portmanteau of dubious facts, influences, and attitudes that the recreational drug user carries around. It includes material taken selectively from a variety of sources that include folklore, academic research, parental advice, the education system, and the media.

The information that we label folklore is rarely attributed and often unattributable. Little of it is of any value and some is frankly misleading. Its attraction probably arises from its sensationalism. It concerns plots to create races of supermen, hospital staff driven to amphetamine use, and ketamine in bovine transportation: 'Smack Es [Ecstasy adulterated with heroin] generally give you wobbly legs and then on come down you feel really gouchy [sick] stomach-wise. You just feel really not too good. You're more prone to get paranoias on them as well 'cos they're mixed with other stuff. If it's good E you do not get paranoia.' 'Ketamine kills cows ...' cos they keep injecting them when they're moving them up and down the country. It's a very dangerous thing to get.' 'Yeah, it's not supposed to be orally taken. You're supposed to snort it.'

Regrettably, the drier and less imaginative information contained in the average drugs leaflet compares unfavourably with these examples! However, some respondents preferred to trust the written word. Unfortunately, the merit of the information appears to derive from its obscurity rather than its availability: 'I just ended up having to dig up some imported book from America. In order to find out about it I had to get a book imported from America from a dodgy London bookstall. You know, that was because I was specifically interested in it. Most people don't give a damn and don't know, which is why I think, you get so many people making so many mistakes.' The contention that high-profile drug information may be dismissed as propaganda deserves further investigation.

While parental attitudes and information are frequently cited by the subjects in the sample, rarely are they a valued source of information. Parents are either dismissed as being reactionary or praised for their laissez-faire attitude. Very few parents had been drug users themselves and therefore positive or negative modelling was unlikely. The hypocritical and contradictory distinction made by some parents between legal and illegal drugs emerges in the text: 'My dad's always buying me drinks. If he found out I'd ever had a joint [cannabis], he'd probably like hit the roof, you know. Which is like this really bad thing that old people have got. They just really don't understand about drugs at all.'

As with parental advice, our sample dismissed formal education as a source of valued drug-related knowledge. This data source was mentioned infrequently and only in a negative context. The information was described as tardy, inappropriate, and uninspired: 'Did you get any information at school about drugs?' 'Well, yeah. But it was just heroin, kind of jabbing needles into yourself. You know hard core drugs. That was the only kind of things they talked about. I mean, Acid wasn't mentioned or Ecstasy, anything like that.'

The arguments for improving the role and extent of drug education within the school curriculum have been rehearsed elsewhere. Our findings lend further support to the inadequacy of the current system in offering credible and relevant drug-related information.

Nor did the subjects in our survey rate the media highly as a source of drug-related knowledge. Only one program (a popular children's TV serial) is mentioned and immediately discredited. It is possible that the greater realism offered in contemporary programs about drugs will have a greater influence on the recreational users of the mid to late 1990s. It may be that the current trend towards including drug-related issues in popular adult serials will increase the credibility of the material for young people.

Strategies for Risk Reduction

The second main category that emerged from the raw data contains strategies for risk reduction built upon the information, experiences, and practices intended to minimize the dangers of drug taking. By definition, recreational drug use should maximize pleasure and minimize pain. Some of these strategies focus on identifying and reversing the trend towards escalation of use. Others deal with mental, physical, and environmental risk and contain advice about dealing with the bad drug-related experiences of oneself or others.

The issue of control runs like a thread that links the various aspects of risk reduction. These include quality-control measures to reduce the risks associated with the doubtful contents of the substance itself, identifying ways to control drug intake, and considering the physical and mental health risks that drug use entails in order to reduce them.

Quality Control

Illegal street drugs are not made to controlled pharmaceutical standards. Their very dangerousness arises out of uncertainties as to content and purity. In an uncertain world there are measures that the recreational user can easily employ to minimize the risks that accompany the use of substances of uncertain content. The first and simplest measure is to buy drugs only from known dealers: 'I'd never buy drugs from anyone I didn't know. Ever. If somebody walked up to me and goes, here do you want an E, do you want some speed? I'd just go, no. You don't know who they are and it's probably very very expensive. So I'd only ever buy it off people I knew and knew well.'

Anecdotally, individuals who have been 'ripped off' have bought from strangers. At best, harmless inactive substances are substituted, at worst dangerous poisons are consumed. Even buying from known dealers does not guarantee the purity of the merchandise. As one respondent declares: 'You're never going to stop people cutting drugs.' It is important for the recreational user to realize that this is the case and to be aware of some of the risks associated with the adulteration of illegal drug substances. In times of scarcity the practice of adulteration escalates while in times of plenty it diminishes: 'With Ecstasy or MDMA. It got to the point where people were knocking up [manufacturing] these, in little houses in back streets, they were knocking up thousands of these tablets and lacing [adulterating] them with anything they could get hold of. I've heard of Ecstasy being laced with strychnine.

This introduces another element to the Russian roulette of drug use. In the United Kingdom there have been fatal overdose epidemics (1993, 1994) in London and Brighton (Brind et al. 1993) associated with particularly pure batches of heroin. It is to be hoped that the wide media coverage these events have prompted has done something to alert the drug-using population to the increased risk specific to drug types and localities.

Intake Control

Addiction, tolerance, escalating intake, and overdose risks are identified as dangers to be avoided when possible. One of the probable hallmarks of successful recreational use is the recognition of 'drifting into dangerous waters' and the self-imposed corrective measures that this insight prompts. Various examples of this recognition and internal correction are contained in the interview data. Far from dismissing addiction as a myth or, like serious road-traffic accidents, something that only happens to other people, the cohort of recreational drug users interviewed recognize it as a reality to be avoided. This example is typical of the recreational drug users' awareness of this danger: 'I don't like to be on that drug that long. So if I'm like on speed for days on end I feel I might be getting a little bit addicted here – which is what you don't want. I'm quite good about just stopping and then carry on.'

Control, more than any other individual factor, appears to mark the boundary between recreational (non-problematic) use and dependent (problematic) use. To feel in control is the hallmark of success, to lose control the hallmark of failure. The successful drug user becomes adept at identifying control issues within his or her own drug use and that of others: 'They've always sort of said they were totally under control. But when you ask, how do you control it, does it affect your life, I think they ... particularly this one guy, my boyfriend's flatmate ... you put him on

the run [make him defensive]. Because, yes he doesn't end up collaps-
ing, nobody has ever picked him out of the gutter, the Salvation Army
are not yet involved, but he's missed work, he's lost money, he's been
crashed out in a sort of drugged-out haze and sort of ruined relationships. So it has affected his life. And to that point it has to be admitted
he hasn't controlled it that well.' It is tempting to speculate that our subjects may have found it easier to identify loss of control in their peers
than in themselves.

The danger sign most frequently mentioned by the subject sample is
that of tolerance or habituation leading to escalation, although these
technical terms are never used. The way in which tolerance is described
in the following excerpts illustrates the way in which it has been discovered experientially or anecdotally rather than assimilated as technical
jargon from a textbook. That which the professional drug worker refers
to as habituation, the user labels as 'not getting the reaction' or 'building
up a resistance' or 'taking longer to get that feeling.' Drug workers are
in danger of obscuring communication with drug users by replacing the
terminology of real experience with technical jargon.

Safe Use

Once the quality and quantity of drug intake have been established, the
recreational user can address the mental and physical risks associated
with illegal drug use.

There is no doubt that the possible mental-health risks of drug use,
especially involving psychostimulants or hallucinogenics, are recognized by the subject sample. LSD is the drug with the greatest reputation for compromising mental health, and a number of our respondents
spoke about 'acid casualties'; for example: 'I know a couple of acid casualties who are in institutions. I know about three of them, but I've only
known them more recently when they've been a bit fucked up anyway.
But then there was a friend of mine in Portsmouth who was ... he started
having these visualizations that he was murdering his girlfriend and his
parents had him sectionalized [confined to a mental institution] or
whatever.'

Although a somewhat devil-may-care attitude prevails as an under-
current in much of the typescript, the subject sample was neither
unaware nor unconcerned regarding physical-health issues. Some of the
reported measures are preventative (such as drinking water to avoid
dehydration), while others are reactive, such as abstinence prompted by

drug-related discomfort, whether physical or emotional. Adverse emotional drug reactions can range from the mildly unpleasant to the terrifying. From these experiences a tribal wisdom has accrued in dealing with unwanted effects: 'You get them into an environment where they feel safe, with people that they trust, friends or people who they know and you just keep saying to them and you keep telling them – it's not you, you're not going mad, there aren't people about to come to get you, you're on a trip, you're on acid, you're having a bad one. But you'll come down – you've taken it like four hours ago and you'll be coming down in a couple of, like three or four hours, and we'll be here for that time. We're fine, don't worry about it.'

Reassurance, companionship, and isolation from crowded or stimulating environments appear to be the chief components of this type of management. However, the process of drug experimentation and the establishment of recreational patterns of use are never without risk. Sometimes these effects can be dramatic and the user has to discriminate between milder reactions when the appropriate action is to lie down and 'chill out' and more dramatic and possibly life-threatening situations when the appropriate course is to seek hospitalization. On more than one occasion the interview data reveal a reluctance to seek medical advice because of the anticipated negative response of hospital staff: 'Like O.D.s [overdoses] and stuff up at the hospital, there're not really cared for, are they? So it's really hard to go and get help, 'cos they just think, automatically like, you're a waster, you're doing drugs. Or because, they're up where they are and unfortunately, we're where we are.'

This antipathy may have important implications. In a recent government anti-drug television commercial (United Kingdom, 1993), the friends who have brought an overdose victim to the hospital emergency room are chastised by emergency staff rather than praised for seeking treatment for their friend. This type of message may deter individuals from seeking hospital treatment in cases of emergency and could potentially lead to fatalities.

Values and Beliefs

The values and beliefs that surround the recreational use of drugs have evolved as a homeostatic mechanism that acts towards the preservation and integrity of both the individual and the group. These parameters seek to reduce behaviours that are unacceptable not so much by virtue of their dangerousness, but because of the threat which they impose on continuing group cohesion. Someone whose drug use is sliding out of control, for example, is not much fun to be with, while the negative image of excessive alcohol consumption presumably arises out of a desire to avoid the physical violence that often accompanies intoxication.

In this sense, the recreational drug-using peer group is no different from other social groups that seek to promote their own identity and values and thereby strengthen the group cohesion and reduce internal friction. The peer group does this by exerting positive peer pressure, by creating behavioural taboos, and by establishing appropriate links between chosen drugs and the environments in which they are used.

Positive Peer Pressure

The role of the peer group and peer environment in initiating first drug experience is well documented (Orford 1985). This form of peer pressure is usually seen as negative, and potential drug users are exhorted to 'just say no' and use the social skills of assertiveness and self-empowerment to overcome these influences. There is, however, a positive aspect to peer pressure that can tend towards control and moderation.

Individuals within the peer group feel they have a duty to others that appears to be reciprocal. Group members alert each other to their excessive or inappropriate drug use. In this way each becomes the guardian of the other. This monitoring role becomes more important in the light of our observation (see above) that it may often be easier to observe lapses of control in others than in ourselves. This extract from the original typescript illustrates the effectiveness of this peer-group monitoring function:

'How about your friends? Most of the people that you socialise with ... are they
  pretty sensible?'
'Yeah. All of them are. All my friends take them. There's not like anyone who
  doesn't. But, like no one goes over the top [uses too much] either.'
'Do you think you're in control of your drug use?'
'Um, I don't think I would be if I didn't have the friends that I do. Sort of saying,
  hold on, you want to take acid again, you only took it last week – come on,
  get a grip. In that way, because people around me are sensible as I hope I
  would be if they were doing too much, yeah, I think I am. But I can see myself

going completely overboard if there weren't the people to say, you know, come on don't do it too often, I think.'

Peer pressure can also positively influence drug choices. There is little doubt that some drug types have a particularly bad reputation, probably because of their perceived potential for addiction. Of the sixteen subjects from the original sample who made spontaneous reference to drugs they would never use, fourteen (87%) mentioned heroin. Four (25%) mentioned cocaine, and 4 (25%) mentioned crack cocaine. Notably, the words used to describe these drugs and their users evoke a sense of unattractiveness more that dangerousness. For some drug types, such as heroin or cocaine, this unattractiveness arises out of their 'sad' or 'dirty' image. Others, such as the hallucinogenic drugs, are seen as 'not sociable because they take you off on your own trip.'

While some of the survey sample spoke enthusiastically about alcohol consumption, either in isolation or in combination with other drugs, there was a significant anti-alcohol sentiment expressed by other peer-group members. Quite simply, alcohol and violence seem to be inextricably linked in the minds of these respondents, and violence appears not to be a highly valued behaviour in the recreational-drug-using peer group: 'I've met a lot of people during my life who were alcoholics. They're the worst sort, they're the worst. Like you can put up with E heads to an extent but piss heads [heavy drinkers] really do get on your nerves and you just don't want to associate yourself with them. They stink, they talk rubbish, they smash bars up, you know. Pick fights with you. It's got to be the worst one to be.'

It is possible that a similar peer group who had chosen alcohol as their drug of preference would hold a macho potential for violence or 'being able to look after yourself' in high esteem. Some of our interview subjects also took the opportunity to highlight the hypocritical inconsistency implied by society's widespread acceptance of a drug whose potential for devastating abuse has been adequately demonstrated in preference to their drugs of choice whose dangerousness might be more difficult to demonstrate.

Taboos

Associated with loss of control and antisocial activities that damage the integrity of the peer group are various taboos that, if ignored, threaten the credibility of individuals whose drug-related behaviour makes them look ridiculous in the eyes of their peers. People do not often want to make fools of themselves and, when they do, usually regret it afterwards. These incidents are observed and subsequently avoided by other members of the group. Looking ridiculous is another aspect of loss of control that lowers the status of individuals and that may demand care taking, which is provided resentfully: 'Friends of mine just go overboard and take lots of different drugs all at the same time. Pass out and collapse and all sorts of things. And they expect their friends to pick them up and look after them, which is not on really [not acceptable]. Ridiculous.'

There is also a welcome and reassuring taboo about drug administration by injection: 'I think the moment you decide to shoot drugs up then you're looking at a totally different situation. I think so anyway. I think then it takes on a completely different angle as far as drug taking goes. If you're prepared to go to those lengths to take the drug, prepared to abuse your body to that extent, then obviously you're in a very serious situation. I've never done that.'

It may be that the powerful anti-IV propaganda that has surrounded the HIV/AIDS publicity over the last decade has fuelled a healthy disregard for needles and syringes. It is also possible that injection itself is seen as a low-status activity since it is associated with low-status drugs (chiefly heroin and to a certain extent cocaine.) The combination of these factors has resulted in a welcome groundswell of anti-injection indoctrination.

A further taboo relates to age, and locates recreational drug use as a youthful activity. The comments on age and its relationship to drug use would appear to indicate that some recreational users would expect to become more and more selective as they become older, either abandoning the use of illegal drugs altogether or sticking to mellower drugs like Cannabis and abandoning the use of hallucinogenics and psychostimulants: 'I just see myself mellowing down. Less speed. Less trips, 'cos they make you go a bit off your rocker.' 'I think as I get older I'll just concentrate more on mellower stuff. Stuff like smoking hash [cannabis]. There're no horrible side-effects, no come down, no addictions.'

Contextual Choices

Much of the material we have presented suggests that the recreational use of drugs is more purposeful than haphazard. As well as making informed choices about types, quantities, and methods of administration, the peer group chooses environments and contexts to match the drugs they take. Some drugs are matched to pubs and clubs, others to isolated introspection, and others to pleasant countryside walks: 'You wouldn't just take it when you were sitting in your house. You only do it to socialize with other people. To be on the same level as the other people that are in that club. 'Cos you know near enough all those people are going to be taking that.'

Drug types become matched with contexts by experiential and observational learning, occasionally by advice from the dealer who sells them to the user, and sometimes by the desire to avoid becoming conspicuous: 'Living in a small town, the drug culture is very small so you know you're going to stick out like a sore thumb. You're very worried about the local constabulary. And eight of you going into a small pub, sitting in a snug bar if you're off your head [intoxicated] on acid is not done – not done.'

External Controlling Factors

The controlling factors that this paper has addressed thus far are generated largely by the individual or by the peer group to which he or she belongs. There are, however, external controlling factors that have little or nothing to do with the values, beliefs, and boundaries generated by the user group. Factors such as financial control, drug availability, legal aspects, and employment issues exist in the real world outside the peer group and have direct impact on the type and extent of drug use.

Financial Control

Unsurprisingly, recreational drug use is largely dependent on disposable income. Once again, important characteristics of recreational drug use emerge. There is little evidence that necessities are sacrificed in favour of drug purchase: 'I don't leave myself short with buying drugs if you know what I mean ... I always make sure I've got enough for everything else and if I can't afford them, I don't get them and that's that.'

Also, there is a useful comparison to be made between recreational and dependent drug use. While recreational drug use is controlled by disposable income, dependent drug use is more likely to be funded by acquisitional crime or other illegal means and therefore bears little relationship to legitimate income.

Availability

The close correlation between availability and extent of use is widely accepted. It is at the centre of the supply-side reduction policy and it is accepted as common sense that no one can use a drug that isn't there. The references to availability in our study would suggest that the quantity and quality of drugs available on the street is increasing: 'I've noticed that more and more people are taking cocaine. It's more available, it's there. And it was much harder to get three or four years ago. And having good cocaine, that was something that only happened at very special do's [parties].'

In the absence of successful supply-side interventions, the importance of demand-side management, a concept that includes successful recreational use, must be emphasized.

Legislation

Inspection of the data on which this study is based does not reveal much deterrent effect in anti-drug legislation. While the penalties associated with drug dealing may have deterred a number of people in our sample from this activity, little concern is expressed about the possible consequences of consumption or possession of illegal substances. A surprising level of familiarity with the drug categories and classes contained in the 1979 Misuse of Drugs Act was demonstrated by several subjects in the study, but this technical knowledge appeared to have little or no impact on their behaviour. The cautionary tales of police courts and prison sentences seem always to warn against dealing and never to warn against using.

Employment

The requirements and expectations that employment imposes on the individuals who had been working provided another external constraint: 'I was working for a bit and that stopped me, because I knew I'd feel like shit in the morning. It was quite a responsible job and so I didn't think I'd take too much then.' For these people the demands of the job had been a priority and had resulted in planned periods of abstinence so as not to impair their performance. The following extract reveals a level-headed pragmatism and sense of competing priorities that, arguably, is missing or severely compromised in dependent drug use: 'I've got to work. And so to work, that brings you down to a reality anyway. You just think, oh shit, I've got to work, which is like horrible really. That's what it is. It's priorities. Realizing you've got to survive.'

Once again, a boundary marker between recreational and dependent use emerges. When drug use and employment become incompatible, the recreational user modifies his or her drug use, while the dependent user modifies his or her employment.

Conclusion

This research has attempted to draw together the practices, beliefs, rituals, and sanctions that combine to produce the phenomenon of controlled recreational drug use. The research tool used was intentionally non-directive, allowing the priorities and concerns of the respondents to emerge rather than those of the research team. The subjects in this survey spoke a great deal about their drug use and very little about themselves. As a result, we have been able to make a detailed survey of the external and internal boundaries that maintain the controlled use of drugs, but we have been able to say very little about the people involved. Further research should attempt to address the variables that differentiated successful controlled users from dependent users who are, after all, unsuccessful controlled users. Few if any problematic drug users embarked on their drug career with the specific intention of losing control or becoming addicted.

We already have clear indications that, in terms of maintaining control, there is what we might call a 'hierarchy of dangerousness.' When we look at the specific drugs described by the controlled users, it is clear that some are protective of and some antagonistic to recreational use. The protective group of drugs are distinguished by the fact that their effects, their low prices, and their context of social use seem to enable the users to remain in control without becoming casualties. By contrast, the antagonistic group of drugs appears to create problems, high prices lead to financial difficulties, the context of their use points towards isolation and dislocation from the social group, and their effects can create mental and physical dependence.

This being so, it is perhaps not surprising that information campaigns that focus on drugs in an undifferentiated manner have not proved successful. Those that have highlighted a specific risk (for example, the spread of HIV from injecting drugs) are far more effective. It would seem that, in future, campaigns should acknowledge that not all drugs are the same and that not all drugs carry the same risks. Experience of locally based information initiatives, such as the series of FACTLINE campaigns in Brighton, England (Gamble and Boice 1991), illustrate the principle of emphasizing very specific risks to a targeted audience. This type of work can effectively build upon the control influences and boundaries already known to that audience and can reinforce existing knowledge and experience within the users' social group.

The area of peer training in drug education has received, deservedly, a high level of interest nationally. The peer-coalition work of McDermott and McBride (1993) has already been mentioned. It is a compelling argument that if, as our research shows, the greatest credence and influence derives from peer messages – especially those offered on the basis of experience – this resource should be mobilized and exploited in the campaign to reduce drug-related harm. The essential (and sometimes missing) ingredient is that the peer trainers should have a comparable knowledge and experiential base. Simply being of an equivalent age may be necessary, but is certainly not sufficient. Imaginative examples of this rule of thumb have been implemented. McDermott (1993) advocates the use of 'indigenous workers' in reaching out to high-risk drug users to progress HIV prevention. These people would be ex- or even current users recruited because of their ability to infiltrate and influence user networks in a way that the non-user professionals or volunteers could not.

Hanslope (1994) recruited sex workers in Liverpool to train them in the legal aspects of prostitution, safer sex and injecting practices, physical health, and 'tricks of the trade.' These women were then supported in passing on this knowledge to other sex workers with whom they came into contact. The evaluation of this project proved it to be 'an even greater success than was hoped.' The self-esteem of the recruited trainers was elevated and the harm reduction messages passed on effectively at street level.

There are further implications for information and education strategies, which are currently constrained by the unwillingness of most agencies in Britain to provide information about controlled use. The contrast between advice about alcohol use and advice about the use of illegal drugs is striking: in the case of alcohol, advice is widely available demonstrating the limits and boundaries of controlled use. Where illegal drugs are concerned, there is an apparent barrier to giving this kind of information at an appropriate age, either in the context of primary prevention or at the stage of early intervention – for example, with young experimental users. This barrier exists despite evidence that such intervention can reduce the dangers faced by young users.

The parallel situation can be seen in material for parents of teenagers: many of the messages in recent campaigns have presented *all* drugs as fear objects. A more helpful and realistic approach would educate about relative risks, and this would create more validity for the accompanying advice, which can be broadly summarized as 'don't panic.'

A greater focus on elements of control also has an impact on the ways in which health initiatives are delivered. In order to build on the protective control values within recreational drug use, the emphasis should be on new ways of providing outreach services to further develop the positive factors operating in the social context.

In terms of treatment strategies, a change in emphasis would be required in order to implement services driven by a similar philosophy. Rather than being either abstinence- or maintenance-oriented, the key concept would be re-establishment of control. This approach could be available, for example, as a short-term intervention to help people who become aware of a loss of control during a period of recreational drug use. The goal of such an intervention would be for the individual to regain control by building upon clearly identified protective factors – which we could perhaps term 'control counselling.'

There will, of course, still be a need for some services for users of antagonistic drugs (e.g., the opiates or crack cocaine), for whom traditional treatment models would still be the first choice. Apart from the direct benefits to service users derived from the differentiation of drug treatments proposed here, a second benefit would be to broaden the perception of treatment services held by the wider community, away from the narrow 'addiction' stereotype and towards a less marginalized view.

As acknowledged earlier in this paper, this research has the limitations imposed by the small subject sample and by the method of open-ended data gathering, which has resulted in some incomplete data-sets. Despite these limitations, the work has the strength of being driven by the perceptions of the subjects and they have generated some important ideas about successful recreational drug use. On this basis, we have attempted to make proposals that may inform future strategies in the areas of education, information campaigns, and service provision.

REFERENCES

Balding, J. 1991. *Young People in Schools.* Health Education Authority, National Drugs Campaign Survey (see also corresponding reports for 1990 and 1988).

Brind, C., A. Farrington, and A. Fraser. 1993. 'Solved by the Grapevine.' *Druglink*, July/August: 12.

Davies, J.B. 1992. *The Myth of Addiction: An Application of the Psychological Theory of Attribution to Illicit Drug Use*. Chur, Switzerland: Harwood Academic Publishers.

Gamble, L., and S. Boice. 1991. *I Don't Take Risks ... Do I? A Report on the FACT-LINE '90 Harm Reduction Campaign*. Unpublished, March.

George, M. 1993. 'The Role of Personal Rules and Accepted Beliefs in the Self-Regulation of Drug Taking.' *International Journal on Drug Policy* 4(1): 32–5.

Grund, J.P.C. 1993. *Drug Use as a Social Ritual: Functionality, Symbolism and Determinants of Self-Regulation*. IVO Reeks IVO Series 4. C.I.P. Rotterdam: Gegevens.

Hanslope, J. 1994. 'Healthy Women – Drugs/HIV Peer Education in Action Awareness. Brikenhead's Sex Workers.' *Druglink*, July/August.

McDermott, P. 1993. 'The Personal Touch.' *Druglink*, July/August: 13.

McDermott, P., and W. McBride. 1993. 'Crew 2000: Peer Coalition in Action.' *Druglink*, November/December.

Orford, J. 1985. *Excessive Appetites: A Psychological View of Addictions*. Chichester: John Wiley & Sons.

Powell, D.H. 1973. 'A Pilot Study of Occasional Heroin Users.' *Archives of General Psychiatry* 28: 586–94.

Swadie, H., and H. Xeitlin. 1980. 'Peer Influence and Adolescent Substance Abuse a Promising Side?' *British Journal of Addiction* 83: 153–7.

Wilks, J., V.J. Callan, and D.A. Austin. 1989. 'Parent, Peer and Personal Determinants of Adolescent Drinking.' *British Journal of Addiction* 84: 619–30.

Zinberg, N.E. 1984. *Drug, Set and Setting: The Basis for Controlled Intoxicant Use*. New Haven: Yale University Press.

Zinberg, N.E., R.C. Jacobson, W.M. Harding, and J. Amer. 1975. 'Social Sanctions and Rituals as a Basis for Drug Abuse Prevention.' *Drug and Alcohol Abuse* 2(2): 165–82.

PART V:
COMMUNITIES AND SPECIAL POPULATIONS

21 Alcohol and Other Drug Use in the Punjabi Community in Peel, Ontario: Experiences in Ethnocultural Harm Reduction

YUET W. CHEUNG, TIMOTHY R. WEBER, and PURVI BIRING

Over the past four or five years, the harm reduction approach has been broadened from one that deals more specifically with the prevention of HIV infection among intravenous drug addicts to one that is meant to be applicable to a wide range of illicit and licit drugs and different modes of substance use (Cheung 1994). While this search for a new 'paradigm' (Erickson 1992; Erickson and Ottaway 1994) has stimulated a great variety of new efforts in drug-abuse prevention, intervention, treatment, policy, and research (O'Hare et al. 1992; Heather et al. 1993), very few of such efforts have focused on harm reduction in ethnic communities. This chapter aims to fill this gap.

The resurgence of ethnicity has been a salient aspect of social change in the modern world (Glazer and Moynihan 1975; Driedger 1989; Alba 1990; Cheung 1993, 1990–1). In culturally pluralistic societies such as Canada, the United States, and Australia, ethnicity is very often a source of security and warm feelings for the individual, as well as an important basis of social organization and social action. It is no wonder, therefore, that ethnic groups not only survive, but also flourish, especially in big cities, which are major points of entry for continuous waves of immigrants (Glazer and Moynihan 1963; Reitz 1980; Breton et al. 1990). Some ethnic groups, especially visible minorities, are able to establish ethnic communities with high degrees of 'institutional completeness' (Breton 1964) – marked by the presence of a large network of interaction, channels of communication such as ethnic media, a variety of ethnic businesses and services, a number of social and cultural facilities, and political organizations. An institutionally complete ethnic community is able to attract a large number of people of the same ethnic origin and become a very concrete community, within the larger community or city, in which ethnic members interact and many of their activities take place.

As such, ethnic communities with high degrees of institutional completeness can offer excellent opportunities for the application of the harm reduction principle. Newcombe (1992) suggests that harm due to drug use may be divided into three levels: individual, community, and societal. Very often, harm reduction studies take 'community' and 'society' for granted and do not clearly define the empirical boundaries of these conceptual entities. This weakness could seriously hinder the assessment of harm at the community and societal levels, thereby limiting the reduction of harm to the individual level. As mentioned earlier, an ethnic community with a high degree of institutional completeness captures a great deal of its members' interaction and activities, and therefore provides a very concrete community for harm reduction efforts. Moreover, as the ethnic community and individual members of the community mutually influence each other, drug-related harm at the individual level would have implications for harm at the community level, and vice versa. In other words, the ethnic community becomes a very good focal point for examining harm at both community and individual levels.

The importance of the role of the ethnic community in health care, illness prevention, and addiction prevention, treatment, and rehabilitation has been widely recognized by researchers, professionals, and service providers[1] (e.g., Stimmel 1984; Westermeyer 1984; Lin 1986; Sabloff and Timney 1988; Cheung 1990–1; Trimble, Bolek, and Niemcryk 1992; Gordon 1994). The distinct cultural traits pertaining to health beliefs and health-seeking behaviour, the ethnic media, the concentrated residential and business locations, and so on, of an ethnic community are valuable resources that can be capitalized on for more effective prevention, treatment, and rehabilitation results. There is currently a strong quest for 'multicultural health care' – health care and addictions programs that are sensitive and responsive to different ethnic cultures. By the same token, for harm reduction efforts in culturally pluralistic settings to be effective, they also need to be ethnoculturally sensitive and responsive.

The Punjabi community in Peel, a regional municipality adjacent to and north-west of Metropolitan Toronto, is a good example of an institutionally complete ethnic community with a high degree of institutional completeness. This community, the population of which is estimated to be over 20,000 people (Statistics Canada 1992) has a highly concentrated residential and ethnic business locale within the cities of Brampton and Mississauga. It has an established network of television, radio, and print media that are widely used by ethnic members. The objective of this paper is to describe the efforts in reducing alcohol- and drug-related harm in this ethnic community, coordinated through the Punjabi Community Health Project, which will be described later. Specifically, the following questions are raised:

- What are the levels of alcohol and other drug use in the Peel Punjabi community?
- How 'serious' are the drinking and other drug problems in the community?
- How serious are the drinking and other drug-use problems as *perceived* by members of the community? Which groups in the community are at greater risk of alcohol/drug problems?
- What are the major reasons why some members of the community consume alcohol/drugs excessively?
- What are the appropriate strategies that can be developed for the reduction of alcohol or other drug problems in the community?

Despite the quest for culturally sensitive and responsive treatment and prevention programs in addictions and health care, there have been very few scientific studies of ethnic communities that provide data pertaining to the prevalence of alcohol and other drug use and the seriousness of alcohol/drug problems in these communities. The Peel Punjabi Community Health Project offers an example of what may perhaps be designated as 'ethnocultural harm reduction.'

Developed in the spring of 1991, the Punjabi Community Health Project in Peel was a collaborative initiative of the Addiction Research Foundation (ARF) in Toronto, the Peel Health Department (PHD), and a large number of social-service agencies and organizations serving the Punjabi community. The main goal of the project was to acquire the necessary information that could be used to develop strategies for the reduction and prevention of drinking problems in the Punjabi community and to improve the physical and mental health of community members.

Most of the results discussed in this chapter are based on the responses of 404 Sikh individuals, randomly selected from the city of Brampton voters' list. Information from focus-group discussions and interviews with key informants have also been used to supplement the quantitative data. Additional information on the methodology and other research findings for the Sikh component of this study can be found in two reports of the project (Weber, Biring, and Mutta 1994a, b).

TABLE 1
Demographics of respondents

Characteristics	N	%
Gender		
Men	228	56.6
Women	175	43.3
Total	403	100
Age		
14–29 years	109	27.5
30–39 years	142	35.8
40 years or more	146	36.7
Total	397	100
Marital status		
Married	350	86.8
Not married	53	13.2
Total	403	100
Education		
Primary/secondary	88	21.9
College/university	313	78.1
Total	401	100
Gross household income		
$40,000 or less	199	53.5
$41,000 or more	147	39.4
Don't know	26	7.0
Total	372	100

Note: This table and all those following are reproduced from Weber, Biring, and Mutta 1994a and 1994b.

Characteristics of the Sample

Table 1 gives the demographic characteristics of respondents of the sample, which consisted of 228 males (57%) and 175 females (43%). Twenty-eight per cent of the respondents were under the age of thirty, 36% were between the ages of thirty and thirty-nine, and 37% were forty or older. The majority (87%) of the respondents were married, and 9% had never been married. The sample had a relatively high level of education, as 78% of the respondents had either community-college, university undergraduate, or graduate education. It was not clear, however, whether the undergraduate and graduate levels of studies in Punjab and in Canada are equivalent to each other. Even with this possibly unclear definition, the fact that over half (54%) of the respondents had gross annual household income of not more than $40,000 was not consistent with three-quarters of the respondents having attained a college level of education or above.

The Punjabis have a relatively short history of immigration in Canada and the United States (Gibson 1988). The Peel Punjabi community is no exception. Ninety-two per cent of the respondents in the sample were not born in Canada. Table 2 (p. 370) gives further information about the respondents' lives in Canada. One-third of the respondents had been in Canada for ten years or less. Only 8.2% had lived in Canada for more than twenty years. The Peel Punjabi community is closely knit, as a highly concentrated residential location in the city of Brampton can be discerned. It is no wonder, therefore, that Punjabis have large percentages of friends who are of Punjabi background. For 31% of the respondents, one-quarter to half of their friends were of Punjabi origin, and for 54%, three-quarters to all of their friends were of Punjabi origin. Seventy per cent of the respondents spoke mainly Punjabi at home.

Ethnic media are very popular in this Community. Ninety-one per cent of the respondents either sometimes or often watched Punjabi television programs, 82% sometimes or often listened to Punjabi radio, and 65% sometimes or often read Punjabi newspapers, magazines, or books.

The lives of recent ethnic-minority immigrants are not easy. Over half (55%) of the Punjabi respondents reported that they sometimes or often experience racial discrimination. As many as 58% of the respondents considered life in Canada somewhat or very stressful. In spite of these stressors, the majority of the respondents (81%) were satisfied or very satisfied with their daily life.

In sum, the profile of the Punjabi community, as portrayed by the characteristics of the sample, is of a closely knit community of mostly recent visible-minority immigrants adapting to the Canadian environment and leading a stressful life owing to racial discrimination and downward occupational mobility in Canada. For the purpose of planning harm reduction work in such a community, we needed first to assess the extent of harm that was present in the community. To this end, we needed to find out the extent of alcohol and other drug use in the community and determine the seriousness of its alcohol/drug problem.

Levels of Alcohol and Other Drug Use in the Punjabi Community

Alcohol

The level of use of alcohol among the respondents can be seen in table 3.

TABLE 2
Culture and life in Canada

Characteristics	N	%
Years in Canada		
0–10	131	33.7
11–20	226	58.1
21 or more	32	8.2
Total	389	100
Language spoken at home		
Punjabi	280	69.5
Other, combination	123	30.5
Total	403	100
Stress of life in Canada		
Very/Somewhat	233	58.4
Not very/Not at all	166	41.6
Total	399	100
Frequency of discrimination		
Often/sometimes	217	54.5
Seldom/never	181	45.5
Total	398	100
Proportion of friends who are Punjabi		
None to < ¼	59	14.9
¼ to ½	123	31.0
¾ to all	213	53.7
No friends in Canada	2	0.5
Total	397	100
Satisfaction with daily life		
Very/satisfied	319	80.8
Neither	45	11.4
Very/dissatisfied	31	7.8
Total	395	100
Frequency of watching Punjabi television		
Often/sometimes	368	91.1
Seldom/never	36	8.9
Total	404	100

TABLE 2 (continued)

Characteristics	N	%
Frequency of listening to Punjabi radio		
Often/sometimes	330	81.9
Seldom/never	73	18.1
Total	403	100
Frequency of reading Punjabi newspapers		
Often/sometimes	264	65.3
Seldom/never	96 ·	23.8
Can't read Punjabi	44	10.9
Total	360	100

Almost half (49%) of the respondents reported that they had never used alcohol. Ten per cent had used it a year ago (past drinkers), and 41% had used it in the past year (current drinkers). Among male respondents, there were 66% current drinkers, but only 9% current drinkers were found in female respondents. These figures are substantially lower than those obtained in the National Alcohol and Drug Survey (NADS) conducted in 1989,[2] which show that 78% of the respondents were current drinkers, and that the percentages of current drinkers in males and in females were 84% and 72%, respectively (Health and Welfare Canada 1990).

Punjabi current drinkers drank as frequently as the national average shown in NADS. Sixteen per cent of Punjabi current drinkers used alcohol less than once a month, 41% drank one to three times per month, 18% used once a week, and one-quarter had consumed alcohol two or more times a week in the past year. Current drinkers in the NADS sample reported 26%, 25%, 19%, and 30% respectively for these frequency-of-drinking categories (Health and Welfare Canada 1992).

Other Drugs

As can be seen from table 4 (p. 373), the use of tobacco and several other substances was very low in the Punjabi sample. Thus, our attention will be focused on alcohol only.

In sum, alcohol was much more popular than other drugs in the Punjabi community. The level of use of other drugs, including tobacco, was very low. Alcohol use was predominantly a male activity. The level of use was comparable to the national average.

TABLE 3
Use of alcohol among respondents

Characteristics	N	%
Lifetime alcohol experience		
Never used	194	48.6
Used more than 1 year ago	40	10.0
Used in past year	165	41.4
Total	399	100
Ever had a drink?		
Men		
Never	43	18.9
More than 1 year ago	34	15.0
Less than 1 year ago	150	66.1
Total	227	100
Women		
Never	150	87.7
More than 1 year ago	6	3.5
Less than 1 year ago	15	8.8
Total	171	100*
Use of alcohol in past year		
Less than once a month	26	16.0
1–3 times per month	66	40.8
Once per week	29	17.9
2 or more times a week	41	25.3
Total	162	100**

*$p < .005$
**Responses for current drinkers only

The level of use of a drug is, of course, likely to be positively related to harm, but use alone is not enough to indicate the degree of harm. We need to examine the experience of harmful effects of alcohol in the Punjabi community.

Harmful Effects of Alcohol

First, we asked current drinkers in the sample to indicate whether they had experienced harmful effects of alcohol use on several aspects of life. From table 5, it can be seen that, in the past year, 13% of them had problems with physical health, 8% had problems with financial situation, 8% with home life/marriage, and 7% with friendships as a consequence of excessive alcohol use.

TABLE 4
Use of other drugs* among respondents

	N	Yes	%	No	%	Don't know drug	%
Tobacco	393	7	1.8	386	98.2	–***	–
Tranquillizers**	370	6	1.6	279	75.4	85	23.0
Cannabis	374	3	0.8	290	77.5	81	21.7
Stimulants**	369	2	0.5	270	73.2	97	26.3
Cocain/crack	372	1	0.3	290	78.0	81	21.8
Narcotics	372	1	0.3	295	79.3	76	20.4
Barbiturates**	369	0	0	266	72.1	103	27.9
Hallucinogens	372	0	0	286	76.9	86	23.1

*Refers to use only when residing in Canada
**Not medically prescribed
***Alternative not provided

TABLE 5
Personal consequences of excessive alcohol use (Current Drinkers Only)

Response categories	N	N responding 'Yes'	%
Experienced harmful effects in past year on:			
Physical health	148	19	12.8
Financial situation	149	12	8.1
Home/marriage	147	11	7.5
Friendships	149	11	7.4

	N	%
Frequency of impaired driving in past year		
Never	89	54.6
Once or twice	32	19.6
Three or more times	42	25.8
Total	163	100

The extent of the individual level of harm due to alcohol use seemed to be greater than that in the mainstream population. Findings from NADS reported that, within the past year, the percentage of current drinkers experiencing problems was 7% for physical health, 4% for financial situation, 3% for home life/marriage, and 5% for friendships.

Another indicator of the risk of harm due to alcohol consumption is

TABLE 6
Groups perceived to be experiencing problems, results
of, and extent of excessive alcohol use

Response categories	N	%
Groups perceived to be experiencing problems with alcohol		
Single men/blue collar	250	61.9
Married men/blue collar	231	57.2
Male teenagers	177	43.8
The elderly	89	22.0
Single men/white collar	82	20.3
Married men/white collar	56	13.9
Total	404	100*
Resulting problems		
Family disruption	234	57.9
Wife abuse	212	52.5
Drinking and driving	116	28.7
Health problems	109	27.0
Financial loss	108	26.7
Family break-up	94	23.3
Total	404	100*
Extent of problems		
No problems	4	1.0
Not widespread	30	7.4
Somewhat widespread	120	31.0
Very widespread	190	49.1
Don't know	43	11.1
Total	387	100

*Multiple responses permitted

drinking and driving. In the past year, 20 per cent of the Punjabi current
drinkers had practised impaired driving once or twice, and 26% had
driven while impaired three or more times. This figure is much higher
than the results obtained by NADS; 19% of current drinkers practised
impaired driving at least once in the past year.

Second, we asked all respondents to assess the seriousness of the
drinking problem in the Punjabi community, indicate which were the
groups at risk of excessive alcohol use, and relate problems resulting
from excessive alcohol use. Table 6 shows that alcohol use was perceived as quite a serious problem. Thirty-one per cent of the respondents felt that the drinking problem was somewhat widespread in the

community, and almost half (49%) of the respondents considered it very widespread in the community. Only 9% of the respondents did not regard drinking as a widespread problem.

Which were the groups more at risk of excessive alcohol use? Table 6 shows that the five groups that were perceived to have the most problem with alcohol, in order, were single men in blue-collar jobs, married men in blue-collar jobs, male teenagers, the elderly, and single men in white-collar jobs.

What were the problems that most often resulted from excessive drinking? From table 6 it can be seen that the five resulting problems, in order, were family disruption, wife abuse, drinking and driving, health problems, and financial loss.

Finally, the respondents were asked to assess the risk of taking one or two drinks nearly every day. Results (not shown here) indicate that as many as 19% of the respondents answered that they did not know about the risk of such frequency of alcohol use. Eleven per cent of the respondents did not think there would be any risk involved. For those who did attach some risk to such use, 20% thought the risk was slight, 16% thought it was medium, and only 34% thought the risk was great. These results reflect that perhaps there was a lack of adequate knowledge about alcohol and the risk of alcohol use among members of the Punjabi community.

In sum, although the level of alcohol use in the Punjabi community was similar to the average national level, Punjabi current drinkers were more likely than average Canadian current drinkers to experience more alcohol problems in various aspects of life. They were also more likely to drink and drive. Drinking was also perceived to be a widespread problem by a large percentage of members of the community, and single males in blue-collar jobs were the group perceived to be at the highest risk of alcohol-related harm. Also, there seemed to be a lack of adequate knowledge about the risk of alcohol use in the community.

Reasons for Excessive Alcohol Consumption

After assessing the extent of alcohol-related harm and identifying the high-risk groups in the Punjabi community, we needed to understand the major reasons behind excessive alcohol use before we could design appropriate strategies for the reduction of alcohol problems. Table 7 lists the major reasons for excessive drinking mentioned by respondents of the survey.

TABLE 7
Reasons for excessive alcohol use

Response categories	N	%
Reasons for excessive alcohol use		
Family problems	247	61.1
To reduce stress	168	41.6
To forget problems	148	36.6
Increased availability	133	32.9
Loneliness, isolation	105	26.0
Peer pressure	82	20.3
Total	404	100*

*Multiple responses permitted

The most frequently mentioned reason was 'family problems.' The questionnaire did not ask respondents to specify what types of family problems were being encountered, but interviews with key informants and discussions in focus-group meetings provided several explanations. Immigrant families like recent Punjabi families in Canada often encounter a host of problems resulting from the process of adapting to the Canadian environment. The relationship between husband and wife may change as the traditional woman's role of stay-at-home wife begins to be modified with more and more women taking up outside jobs; the traditional parent-child relationship may change as Canadian culture impacts on young people and their families; seniors may feel they are losing their traditional authority in the family and receiving less and less respect from young family members.

The second and third most frequently cited reasons were 'to reduce stress' and 'to forget problems,' respectively. Problems faced by immigrant families include men's desire to succeed financially in Canada being diminished when they experience downward mobility in the occupations they obtained in Canada; difficulty in adjusting to the Canadian culture; and racial discrimination. Alcohol use might have become a convenient way to cope with stress or to forget problems among many Punjabi men.

Another reason for excessive drinking was alcohol's 'increased availability' in Canada. It was reported that there was a larger number of beer and liquor stores in Ontario than in Punjab. An increase in the amount of disposable income available to individuals, when compared to Punjab, also increases the number of opportunities to purchase, or the availability of, alcohol.

Strategies for the Reduction of Alcohol-Related Harm

After we had determined the level of alcohol use, assessed the extent of alcohol-related harm, identified the high-risk groups, and understood the major reasons for excessive drinking, we were in a position to discuss the development of appropriate strategies for the reduction of alcohol-related harm in the Punjabi community. The findings presented above indicate that alcohol problems in the community were very likely induced by a combination of different kinds of factors:

- Culture-conflict factors: changes in the social relations and authority structure in the traditional Punjabi family in Canada, differences between the Punjabi and Canadian ways of life, racial discrimination, and so forth.
- Socio-economic factors: downward occupational mobility in Canada, discrimination in the job market and workplace, desire to financially establish oneself and one's family in Canada as soon as possible.
- Knowledge and information factors: The relatively high degree of drinking problems despite relatively moderate level of use and the relatively high frequency of driving under the influence of alcohol may reflect the situation that many Punjabis did not have adequate knowledge about alcohol and the risk of alcohol use.

In order to address some of the issues that the research had identified, it was important to consider all of these factors. Through further consultation with members of the community, steps have been taken to reduce alcohol-related harm in the Punjabi community.

Much of the dialogue has been directed through a community-based advisory committee or Community Action Group (CAG). This group includes representatives from the ARF, PHD, and other agencies serving the Punjabi community and has been in existence since early in the project. The original focus of this group was to provide advice to the research team on questionnaire design and research methodology and to assist in finding key informants. More recently, the group has assisted in the development of interventions based on needs identified in the survey and through their own experiences. The ultimate goal of this project is that the Punjabi community, through the CAG, will have complete ownership of this project, with the two mainstream organizations providing assistance only on an 'as needed' basis.

So far, the Punjabi community, the CAG, and the project have developed several interventions that are attempting to address the cultural conflict factors. One of the first responses to cultural conflict was a group developed by a group of university students. After participating in a focus-group session for this project, three enthusiastic individuals decided that it would be useful to have discussions amongst South Asian students on an ongoing basis. This group is currently entering its third year of operation and the focus of discussions has been on topics such as discrimination, dating and arranged marriages, and relationships with parents.

Other efforts are also under way to help the adult population better address some of the issues related to cultural conflict. Agencies serving Punjabis as well as other South Asians are assisting families in dealing with differences between Canada and India. These organizations are also helping to address some of the socio-economic factors individuals face by offering courses such as English as a second language, job-readiness training, and other counselling services. Periodically, the Punjabi media (television, radio, and print) are used to deliver messages to the community on issues such as relationships between parents and children and family violence.

Workshops and conferences aimed at service providers have been used to educate health-care and social-service professionals about some of the issues facing this community. Professionals who work within the Punjabi community have met to discuss how to best assist individuals living in Canada. As well, a workshop is being planned for mainstream professionals to assist the in better understanding the Punjabi culture.

Efforts to reduce alcohol-related harm have focused primarily on addressing the third set of factors: knowledge and information. It became apparent from the research that the community needed a better understanding of some of the consequences associated with excessive alcohol use and some of the options available for those encountering problems with alcohol. This information needed to be targeted not only at the broader community, but specifically at those working within the Punjabi community.

Brochures in English and Punjabi have been written to increase individuals' awareness of some of the issues related to drinking and driving. Similarly, a handbook and a video, also in English and Punjabi, have been developed to provide members of the community with some guidelines on sensible drinking habits, information on the effects of alcohol, and guidance on how to obtain treatment services.

A display has been developed by members of the CAG that has been used at cultural events, sports days, and religious ceremonies. In collaboration with members of the community, the group is developing a poster with a moderate-drinking message that will also be used at these types of events.

As mentioned above, Punjabi television, radio, and print media have been utilized to increase the community's awareness regarding a number of social issues. Several experts have talked generally about alcohol, family violence, and drinking and driving. These topics were chosen because they were identified as being important through the research component of the study. Similar information has also been disseminated through displays at a Punjabi sports day and at an agency's 'open house.'

These media have also been used to promote and generate interest in another source of information developed by the project team. Five pre-recorded tapes at the ARF are available in Hindi, Punjabi, and Urdu to telephone callers throughout the province of Ontario. Topics discussed on these culturally sensitive tapes include the effects of alcohol, prevention of alcohol problems, discussing substance abuse with teens, drinking and driving, and family violence and substance abuse. The names of three agencies serving the Punjabi community are provided at the end of the tape so that those seeking additional information can speak directly with a social-service worker. After one year of operation, the response to the tapes has been quite favourable; in the fall of 1994 it is anticipated that these tapes will also be available in Hindi and Urdu.

Punjabi students in local high schools also participated in a survey that attempted to determine the level of tobacco use amongst students. Data from this study have been presented to members of the community and efforts are now being taken to create an awareness-raising video and interactive display.

More focused information for men who are experiencing problems with alcohol has also been developed. A six-week-long 'support group' has been developed for these individuals in order to discuss the pharmacological and sociological effects of excessive alcohol use as well as coping strategies and treatment alternatives. The intent of this program is not necessarily to 'cure' those who are experiencing problems, but to assist South Asian men in making choices regarding their alternatives to decreasing their harmful use of alcohol.

Staff members of agencies who serve the Punjabi community have also benefited from the results of this project. Two training sessions on drug pharmacology, treatment alternatives, telephone counselling, and crisis intervention were developed specifically for these professionals.

Others have taken courses offered by the ARF in order to increase their knowledge on substance abuse and to 'network' with other addiction professionals. In 1997, professionals from a variety of health and social-service organizations will participate in a workshop in order to discuss some of the issues related the linkage between alcohol and family violence.

Finally, the research identified the family doctor as the person who would most likely be consulted if a person or someone they knew was experiencing problems with alcohol. Because of the importance of the family doctor, the ARF is attempting to collaborate with a group of family physicians who work within the Punjabi community in order to ensure that these individuals are able to serve their patients' needs. Seventy-four family doctors were surveyed in order to determine how they could better assist their patients. This consultation process led to the development of a one-day workshop on alcohol in April 1995. (Physicians who attended the session received a continuing-education credit from the provincial medical association.)

Concluding Remarks

This paper has described an exercise in the reduction of alcohol-related harm in a visible-minority ethnic community. From the experience of the Punjabi Community Health Project, we suggest that harm reduction for an ethnic community should include as its first step a scientific study that assesses the extent of alcohol/drug use, the seriousness of the alcohol/drug problem, the major reasons for alcohol/drug abuse, and the various forms of resources available in the ethnic community for facilitating harm reduction efforts. Such data are absolutely essential for the development of appropriate harm reduction strategies. One of the weaknesses of many harm reduction projects pertaining to ethnic populations has been the lack of a thorough examination of the nature and extent of the 'harm' in the relevant ethnic community that is supposed to be reduced. We hope that the experiences of the Punjabi Community Health Project will serve as an important reference for ethnocultural harm reduction efforts in the future.

NOTES

The authors wish to acknowledge the support to the Punjabi Community Health Project from the Addiction Research Foundation, the Peel Health Department, and the large number of social-service organizations, groups, and individuals in the Punjabi community in Peel and Toronto. Special thanks are due to Margy Chan, Norman Giesbrecht, Andrea Stevens-Lavigne, and Baldev Mutta.

1   A high degree of institutional completeness may also help facilitate a criminal subculture within an ethnic community, especially if members of the community are in poor socio-economic conditions and their opportunities to be upwardly mobile are blocked. See, for example, Ianni 1973 and Light 1977.
2   The sample of the survey consisted of 11,634 respondents who were fifteen years of age or older and were selected from ten provinces. For more details on the methodology and findings of the survey, see Health and Welfare Canada 1992.

REFERENCES

Alba, R.D. 1990. *Ethnic Identity: The Transformation of White America*. New Haven: Yale University Press.
Breton, R. 1964. 'Institutional Completeness of Ethnic Communities and Personal Relations of Immigrants.' *American Journal of Sociology* 70: 193–205.
Breton, R., W.W. Isajiw, W. Kalbach, and R.G. Reitz. 1990. *Ethnic Identity and Equality: Varieties of Experience in a Canadian City*. Toronto: University of Toronto Press.
Cheung, Y.W. 1990–1. 'Ethnicity and Alcohol/Drug Use Revisited: A Framework for Future Research.' *International Journal of the Addictions* 25(5A, 6A): 581–605.
–   1993. 'Approaches to Ethnicity: Clearing Roadblocks in the Study of Ethnicity and Substance Use.' *International Journal of the Addictions* 28(12): 1209–26.
–   1994. Review of *The Reduction of Drug Related harm*, ed. P.A. O'Hare et al., and of *Psychoactive Drugs and Harm Reduction: From Faith to Science*, ed. N. Heather et al. *Contemporary Drug Problems* 21(2): 341–9.
Driedger, L. 1989. *The Ethnic Factor*. Toronto: McGraw-Hill Ryerson.
Erickson, P.G. 1992. 'Prospects of Harm Reduction for Psychostimulants.' In N. Heather et al., eds, *Psychoactive Drugs and Harm Reduction: From Faith to Science*, 184–210. London: Whurr.
Erickson, P.G., and C.A. Ottaway. 1994. 'Policy – Alcohol and Other Drugs.' In P. Nathan et al., eds, *Annual Review of Addictions Research and Treatment*, 3: 331–41. London: Pergamon.
Gibson, M.A. 1988. *Accommodation without Assimilation: Sikh Immigrants in an American High School*. Ithaca: Cornell University Press.
Glazer, N., and D.P. Moynihan. 1963. *Beyond the Melting Pot*. Cambridge: MIT Press.
Glazer, N., and D.P. Moynihan, eds. 1975. *Ethnicity: Theory and Experience*. Cambridge: Harvard University Press.

Gordon, J.U., ed. 1994. *Managing Multiculturalism in Substance Abuse Services.* Thousand Oaks, CA: Sage.

Health and Welfare Canada. 1990. *National Alcohol and Other Drugs Survey: Highlights Report.* Ed. M. Eliany, N. Giesbrecht, M. Nelson, B. Wellman, and S. Wortley. Ottawa: Ministry of Supply and Services Canada.

– 1992. *Alcohol and Other Drug Use by Canadians: A National Alcohol and Other Drugs Survey (1989). Technical Report.* Ed. M. Eliany et al. Ottawa: Ministry of Supply and Services Canada.

Heather, N.A., E.A. Wodak, E.A. Nadelmann, and P. O'Hare, eds. 1993. *Psychoactive Drugs and Harm: From Faith to Science.* London: Whurr.

Ianni, A.J. 1973. *Ethnic Succession in Organized Crime.* Washington: U.S. Government Printing Office.

Light, I. 1977. 'The Ethnic Vice Industry, 1880–1944.' *American Sociological Review* 42: 464–79.

Lin, T.Y. 1986. 'Multiculturalism and Canadian Psychiatry: Opportunities and Challenges.' *Canadian Journal of Psychiatry* 31: 681–90.

Newcombe, R. 1992. 'The Reduction of Drug-Related Harm: A Conceptual Framework for Theory, Practice and Research.' In P.A. O'Hare et al., eds, *The Reduction of Drug-Related Harm*, 1–14. London: Routledge.

O'Hare, P.A., R. Newcombe, E.C. Matthews, E.C. Buning, and E. Drucker, eds. 1992. *The Reduction of Drug-Related Harm.* London: Routledge.

Reitz, J.G. 1980. *The Survival of Ethnic Groups.* Toronto: McGraw-Hill Ryerson.

Sabloff, A., and C.B. Timney. 1988. *Immigrant Clients in Alcohol and Other Drug Abuse Treatment Facilities: A Comparison of Two Surveys in the Metro Toronto Region 1983 and 1986.* Toronto: Addiction Research Foundation, Internal Document no. 95.

Statistics Canada. 1992. *Profile of Census Divisions and Subdivisions, Ontario – Part B.* Ottawa: Ministry of Industry, Science and Technology.

Stimmel, B. 1984. Special issue on 'Cultural and Sociological Aspects of Alcoholism and Substance Abuse.' *Advances in Alcohol and Substance Abuse* 4(1): 1–81.

Trimble, J.E., J.E. Bolek, and S.J. Niemcryk. 1992. *Ethnic and Multicultural Drug Abuse: Perspectives on Current Research.* Binghamton, NY: Haworth.

Weber, T.R., P. Biring, and B. Mutta. 1994a. *Punjabi Community Health Project: Summary Report (Sikh).* Addiction Research Foundation and Peel Health Department, December.

– 1994b. *Punjabi Community Health Project: Final Report (Sikh).* Addiction Research Foundation and Peel Health Department, December.

Westermeyer, J. 1984. 'The Role of Ethnicity in Substance Abuse.' *Advances in Alcohol and Substance Abuse* 4: 9–18.

22 Female Drug Injectors and Parenting

AVRIL TAYLOR

Drug-using mothers are generally regarded in negative terms (Perry 1987). Injecting drug use by mothers, in particular, is, at the very least, seen as putting children at risk (Mondanaro 1989) and can be regarded as a sign of outright unfitness in a mother (Densen-Gerber et al. 1972). Indeed, the unfitness to be a parent is one of the strongest stereotypical images of female drug injectors and can be the basis upon which policies relating to the care of their children are based.

But this image is to a large extent stereotypical rather than based on empirical evidence. Very little research has been undertaken to examine the behaviours and attitudes of injecting mothers towards their children.

So how does the female drug user relate to her children? How does she treat them? What effect has drug use on her ability to mother and, conversely, what effect has pregnancy and motherhood on her drug use? Do pregnancy and motherhood act as positive motivators for change? This chapter considers such issues. Based on fifteen months' participant observation with twenty-two drug-injecting females in Glasgow who were either pregnant, gave birth, or were in the process of bringing up one or more children during this period (Taylor 1993), this chapter examines the women's feelings when pregnant and their expectations before and after the birth of their children.

The results challenge the popular image of drug-injecting mothers, while at the same time explaining how these images arise and are maintained. Written from the women's own points of view, the findings also clearly demonstrate why drug-using mothers are reluctant to seek help for problems related to their drug use.

Pregnancy

It is often argued that within the female drug user there is a 'powerful drive' to become pregnant as a way of affirming her role as a woman and of achieving a close relationship in which she is needed (Densen-Gerber et al. 1972). While some of the women came to see an established pregnancy as perhaps helping them to change their lifestyle, none of them had deliberately set out to become pregnant for these reasons. Indeed, most women's pregnancies were unplanned and, as is the case with many non-drug-using women (Kitzinger 1978; Oakley 1979), pregnancy sometimes came as an unwelcome surprise. 'I was shattered, shattered' (Kate).

A common reason for not wanting a child was a feeling that they could not cope with the responsibility that motherhood would bring at that particular juncture in their lives, a feeling common to many other women. For this reason two women had had their pregnancies terminated. They did not, however, take these decisions lightly or for selfish reasons. Rather they felt that they could not give to the child the attention that it would need and it was out of consideration for the child and at considerable psychological cost to themselves that they had decided on this course of action. Vicky had recently had her termination and was still wrestling with ambivalent feelings: 'It's not what's best for me but what is best for the baby 'cause who knows what I'm going to be doing ... It doesn't matter what you do, I think you would feel guilty anyway. If you bring the baby into the world and you don't know what you are going to be doing and then if you give it away. I think it would have been a big mistake if I didn't terminate it. As I say, it doesn't matter what you do you are guilty anyway.'

But the knowledge that she is pregnant also brings the drug-injecting woman face to face with the possibility of one of the most serious repercussions of her injecting lifestyle. She may be HIV-positive and as a result her baby may be born infected. Fear that this may be the case led most women to be tested for HIV, with a view to terminating the pregnancy. Kate was waiting for her test result when she expressed how she felt: 'It might not be positive. But I don't think I could take that risk. If I have the virus, I'll get rid of it ... I don't think they really know the odds ... It means that you could be positive and the baby not but you wouldn't find out until it is eighteen months old. Imagine carrying a child and then having it for eighteen months and you don't know if it's contracted the virus or not. I'd rather go through the mental anguish of having an abortion rather than the mental anguish of having HIV in my baby. I mean the two of them – one is as bad as the other. But I could cope with an abortion, I couldn't worry constantly about a baby.'

Kate was negative and was among the majority of the women who, once over their initial rejection of the thought of motherhood, began to look forward to the event, not least because some saw it as an opportunity to begin a new life away from drugs. 'I didn't want it at first, but I love it to death already. I need something in my life. The responsibility will be good for me. It'll give me something to do, something to stay off for' (Liz).

There is a vast amount of literature on the possible deleterious effects on the foetus from continued drug use during pregnancy (Finnegan 1981). These include low birth weight, congenital defects, early gestation, and neonatal withdrawal symptoms. The exact mechanism of these complications is unclear, and it has been argued that other conditions such as inadequate prenatal medical care, poverty, and poor diet and tobacco smoking could all be contributory factors (Hepburn 1992). Nevertheless, continued drug use was regarded by the women themselves as the major threat to their unborn child. Accordingly, almost without exception they attempted to stop taking drugs during pregnancy. Women with established drug habits found abstaining from drugs a constant battle that, when lost, caused them bouts of guilt.

Helen had had a miscarriage the previous year. Just after the birth of a healthy child one year later, she spoke about her anxieties during her pregnancy: 'I never wanted a child until I lost that first one. When I got my pregnancy test and I was told it was definitely positive I was really, really happy. I said "That's it, I'm not taking another hit." I really thought I could do it. And I did cut it down and then I started smoking it instead of hitting it and for me that was really good. At first I thought I would have a miscarriage. When I was kind of over that stage and I went to the hospital and they said to me, "Do you want to hear the baby's heart?" I wanted to say "No" in case they couldn't find it and then when they did I was so happy. But I kept thinking the baby was going to be dead and right up until I saw her, even when she was born she was a funny blue colour and I got a fright, even up until that moment I thought I was going to lose her. I was scared to buy in for her in case she died. I only bought a couple of things just to show people I was buying things but I was so scared to buy things – not because it would be a waste of money if she had died – but because I would have to come home and see all her wee things.'

Helen's fear for her child's survival and her accompanying reluctance to provide for it gives an insight into why drug users are often accused of making little preparation for their forthcoming child (Finnegan 1981). It is not that they are feckless or hedonistic, but many of them have genuine fears that their pregnancies will not end in a live, healthy child, and they do not want to tempt fate by making plans and preparing for the child's needs.

The pregnant drug user, then, often has ambivalent feelings surrounding her impending motherhood. Some of these feelings are those experienced by non-drug-using mothers. Others are more specifically grounded in their drug lifestyle. The women are anxious to produce a healthy baby and remorseful if they feel they are putting this goal at risk by continued drug use. Some see their pregnancy and the forthcoming birth as a chance to move out of the drug culture, while still fearful that this will not prove possible. Above all they want to be 'good' mothers and are afraid that they will fall short of their ideal or, worse, that they will not be given the chance to prove their capabilities.

Motherhood

As with Dally's findings about 'ordinary' mothers (Dally 1982), for the drug injectors in this study 'good' mothering meant always being available for their children. 'I'm not saying I want her to have all these material things and that. I want her to have more than that. I want her to have me all the time, any time she wants me' (Frances).

Many, however, found that constantly caring for a small baby or toddler was stressful and tiring, as Lorraine tells us: 'See, when I had my kid I thought, "This is gorgeous, look what I've got, isn't he beautiful?" With lovely wee pram, lovely wee suit, beautiful wee baby. I didn't think you'd end up with shit and teething and vomiting and crying through the night' (Lorraine).

Like countless other women who are prescribed drugs to help them cope with the stresses of domestic life (Ettorre 1992), often the women's response was a return to or escalation in their drug use, which assumed a different function in their lives at this point: 'I felt as if I could cope with her a lot better because I didn't know how to cope with a baby and I had them to relax me a bit and I felt I could handle it a lot better. I used to take them for the sake of being full of it and having a good laugh but now when I've not got them I feel really lazy as if I can't do my housework or can't attend to the baby' (Jenny).

Apart from helping the women cope with the physical and mental stresses of child care, a return to drug use was also a way of helping them cope with the guilt brought about by the gap between their expectations of having a baby and the reality of the experience. The women had traditional attitudes towards motherhood and expected to find the role enjoyable and as fulfilling all their needs, and were distressed when this did not happen. This gap is also experienced by non-drug-using mothers and can be regarded as a consequence of the 'myth of motherhood' into which women are socialized (Badinter 1981). Those who are dissatisfied with this role are regarded as personally inadequate. As Oakley argues, only the most articulate and confident women are able successfully to challenge this interpretation (Oakley 1979). Others less fortunate, including the women in this study, labour under feelings of inadequacy and shame.

Returning to or continuing with drug use raises other problems somewhat akin to those of other mothers who return to work after the birth of a baby – the drug injector is torn between her desire to be a good mother and the demands of her injecting career.

Most of the women, including those living with a male drug-using partner, provided for their own drug habits and sometimes that of their partner (Taylor 1993). Where the demands of their career did not interfere with child care, it was regarded as worthy of praise, similar to the way in which working mothers are often admired for juggling the demands of their lives successfully. 'Fiona and Frances, fair enough they like their junk and they have their junk every day, but they have their children with them 24 hours a day. Nobody looked after their children, neither of their mothers, you never heard them mentioning, "My mother's got the baby." They have the children with them 24 hours a day, 7 days a week. When they went to nursery they were there to collect them on time. And their children aren't cheeky, they're great kids. Brilliant kids' (Judy).

All the mothers made attempts, most of them successfully, to balance the needs of baby and their career. Certainly in material terms the women's children were well cared for, all of them beautifully and often expensively dressed and provided with plenty of toys. But the women were also anxious that other aspects of their lives should not affect their children and, in particular, they made strenuous efforts to keep their drug life from impinging on their children: 'Like one day my pal came in to have a hit and she had the baby with her. I said to her to take her out. She says, "Why? She doesn't know what you are doing." And I said, 'I know, but that could stick in her mind – watching people having hits. I didn't want her in the room' (Sharon).

Keeping a drug habit going and looking after a child, particularly without support, do present difficulties that some women find too difficult to overcome. 'See, before Sally had her son taken off her? I mean the way she used to get money off that moneylender to buy drugs and not buy anything to eat for that child. It was a nightmare. He was eating dry cornflakes. A child getting up and eating bits of hard bread. She could live like that but a child can't' (Jackie). For three of the women, circumstances such as these resulted in what all drug-using women fear above anything else, their children being taken into care by the social-work department.

Social-Work Involvement

This fear of social workers did not arise because the women thought that they were incapable of providing proper care for their children. Most felt, and were correct in feeling, that their children were not neglected. What the women feared, and had to face the consequences of, was that service providers, such as social workers, held negative images of drug users and had the power to take away their children on this basis.

In particular, the women believed that social workers and other professionals with whom they came into contact through their role as mother saw drug use as an automatic indicator of unfitness in a mother. 'It's just not enough for us to look after our children. We've got to be drug free or we lose our kids' (Diane).

Moreover, the women believed that the images held of them by social workers were so strong that not only were they powerless to change them, but no matter what they did it would be interpreted as unacceptable behaviour. 'It doesn't matter what I do. If I'm not smiling, I'm not coping, and if I am smiling I'm not caring' (Michelle).

One consequence of this fear of having children removed from their care by social workers was that women who needed help were afraid to ask for it unless a crisis point was reached, such that they felt their drug use was putting their children at risk. 'Like me, I went to the health visitor. I know they are just as bad as the social workers. You think it will help you but ... but they don't. The majority of the time they don't. I just told her so she could pull a few strings to get my wee girl into nursery school so that I could get help with my drug problem. My mother couldn't look after her all day if I went into a rehab. But I was just stupid because she told my mother that when I came back if she sensed any drugs in me she'd phone the social services ... The way it came across to me was, if I need help, I risk losing my child' (Vicky).

Ironically, the effect on the women holding such beliefs, which were not unfounded, was that they developed attitudes and behaviours in response to their powerlessness that had the repercussion of confirming the negative views held not only by social workers but by people in general. Believing that social workers saw drug use per se as a reason to either remove children into care or at least apply for a care order, some women tried to avoid this result by lying about their current drug consumption.

After the birth of her child, Helen had been allowed to take her baby home. Her strenuous efforts to reduce her drug intake, together with the fact that she lived with her parents, had reassured her social worker that Helen's baby would be adequately looked after. She had been asked, however, if she would be prepared to accept a 'voluntary' arrangement of social-work involvement whereby a social worker would visit from time to time and Helen would provide urine samples as evidence of her drug-free state. She had agreed to this.

Helen had started using again on an intermittent basis, and one of her samples had shown positive. She was confronted by the social worker. Helen had been careful not to use drugs for several days before giving a sample and was convinced that her sample had either been mixed up with someone else's or someone had told the social worker that she was using again. Her social worker's accusation, she felt, was a test of her truthfulness and implicitly a test of her adequacy as a mother. 'I said to my social worker, "No, I'm not using it." And the reason I said it was because I don't need help the now. I just feel like a hit now and again and the baby is fine. The social worker herself said that. When she found out the sample was positive she said, "I'm not here to talk about the baby because she's fine even if you are using. But it's you I'm worried about because if you are using I would like to help you." But I don't trust social workers. A lot of people have told me that social workers act that nice and trusting towards you, but they're just trying to suss you out' (Helen).

Once a child is taken into care, access times are given to the mother, but these could be difficult to adhere to. 'Sometimes I get so upset when I leave him with his foster parents that I can't face the thought of going there' (Michelle). 'When she's been here to see me [in the rehabilation centre] and she goes away, she gets my mother uptight for about three days because she is upset. And that is very upsetting for me, so I sometimes tell my mother not to bring her' (Sheila).

Adherence to access times was, however, used by officials as an indication of the mother's interest in her child and, thereby, her fitness to have the child returned to her care. Without understanding of any difficulties experienced by the women, missed access times were often used as confirmation that the mother did not care and as a way of limiting future access times. This practice, confirming the women's powerlessness, could set up a vicious circle in which women would behave in ways that confirmed the image of them as out of control and therefore unfit to look after children. 'Monday, Wednesday and Friday from 12 o'clock until 3 o'clock, that was all I had her. One Wednesday my boyfriend had overdosed and he collapsed and it kept me twenty minutes late for the access because I took him to the hospital and the social worker said I loved my boyfriend more than my daughter. I put him first. There was another social worker there as well as mine and he said, "Oh well, you're too late for your access today." I could hear my wee girl shouting in the back. I said, "I'm not leaving here until I see my daughter." He said "We'll just send for the police." I said, "My wee girl's shouting on me. What's wrong I just can't go and see her. If I don't get my access today, just let me see her." By this time I was crying and all that. They said, "No, you're too upset now to see her." So I said, "Well fuck the lot of you, I'll go and find her then." So I started kicking in all the doors of the Social Work Department. I just couldn't take any more' (Diane).

Conclusion

Most drug-using mothers, like other mothers, attempt to do the best for their children. The majority of children encountered during fieldwork lived with their mothers and were loved, taken pride in, and well cared for. Pregnancy often provided, sometimes for the first time, the incentive to reduce drug taking. The women saw motherhood as an important function and adhered to the tradition that mothering should be their responsibility and totally fulfilling. However, the realization that it was not was the cause of much guilt and anxiety. On top of these reactions, the stress caused by the fear of losing their children and of having to prove their abilities as mothers in a way that other mothers do not, often resulted in a return to or escalation of drug use.

Despite this, these drug-using mothers were a far cry from the popular image of them as chaotic, out of control of their own lives, and therefore unfit to be in charge of anyone else's (Perry 1987). Indeed, in most respects drug-injecting mothers are no different from other mothers in general.

The role of mother does, however, bring female injectors face to face with some of the negative attitudes held by others about them. To protect themselves from the repercussions of these, the women adopted defensive stances and behaviours of their own. While these behaviours are understandable when seen from the point of view of the women themselves, often they resulted in confirming the unfavourable images of them held by social workers and society in general: that they are liars, deviant, and therefore unfit to be in control of their children's lives; and this view ultimately threatens their relationship with their children as well as the women's own well-being. Losing children can sometimes be the spur to coming off drugs. More often it can be the impetus to further drug taking and further integration into the drug-injecting culture. 'Look at Fiona. See since the children got taken away, she's just gone down and down and down. She's mad with it all the time and working up the town [prostituting] now to pay for her habit' (Judy). A year after this comment was made, Fiona was found dead from a drug overdose.

REFERENCES

Badinter, E. 1981. *The Myth of Motherhood*. London: Souvenir.
Dally, A. 1982. *Inventing Motherhood: The Consequences of an Ideal*. London: Burnett Books.
Densen-Gerber, J., M. Wiener, and R. Hochstedler. 1972. 'Sexual Behaviour, Abortion and Birth Control in Heroin Addicts: Legal and Psychiatric Considerations.' *Contemporary Drug Problems* 1: 783–93.
Ettorre, E. 1992. *Women and Substance Use*. Basingstoke and London: Macmillan Press.
Finnegan, L.P. 1981. 'Maternal and Neonatal Effects of Drug Dependence in Pregnancy.' In J.H. Lowinson and P. Ruiz, eds, *Substance Abuse: Clinical Problems and Perspectives*. Baltimore: Williams and Wilkins.
Hepburn, M. 1992. 'Pregnancy and HIV: Screening, Counselling and Services.' In J. Bury, V. Morrison, and S. McLachlan, eds, *Working with Women and AIDS: Medical, Social and Counselling Issues*. London: Routledge.
Kitzinger, S. 1978. *Women as Mothers*. Oxford: Martin Robertson.

Mondanaro, J. 1989. *Chemically Dependent Women: Assessment and Treatment.*
   Massachusetts/Toronto: Lexington Books.

Oakley, A. 1979. *Becoming a Mother.* Oxford: Martin Robertson.

Perry, L. 1987. 'Fit to Be Parents?' *Druglink,* January/February: 6.

Taylor, A. 1993. *Women Drug Users: An Ethnography of a Female Injecting Community.* Oxford: Clarendon Press.

23 The Harm Reduction Model: An Alternative Approach to AIDS Outreach and Prevention for Street Youth in New York City[1]

MICHAEL C. CLATTS, EDITH SPRINGER,
W. REES DAVIS, GLENN BACKES,
CHRISTOPHER LINWOOD,
MARIE BRESNAHAN, and STACEY RUBIN

Studies indicate that as many as two million adolescents in the United States are homeless, and that as many as 200,000 youth live as permanent residents of the streets (United States 1986). Although the size of the homeless and runaway youth population in New York City is not known with any degree of precision, available data suggest it may number as many as 20,000 (Gunn 1988; Schafer and Caton 1984). Many of these youth have lived for periods of time in shelters and welfare hotels, but many have spent at least some amount of time in which they were abjectly homeless, living on the streets, in abandoned buildings, subway tunnels, and bus depots. Degraded by the effects of street prostitution and the loss of their childhood, and overwhelmed by feelings of self-doubt and self-blame, many turn to the ephemeral comfort afforded by street drugs such as crack cocaine (Clatts 1990; Clatts et al. 1990). Quickly lost in a downward spiral of self-destruction, these youth become increasingly dependent upon the vicissitudes of the street economy – a system of exchange in which they are easily exploited and over which they have very limited power. Of particular concern in terms of risk for health are the high frequencies of both sexual and drug-related risk behaviours evidenced in this population that place them at high risk for HIV infection.

This chapter has two specific aims: first, to provide a brief overview of the demographic and behavioural characteristics of the street youth population in New York City; second, to describe the way in which the harm reduction model has been applied to the development of comprehensive AIDS outreach and prevention services targeted to street youth in New York City.

Demographic and Behavioural Profile of Street Youth in New York City

Until recently, demographic and behavioural information about the street youth population in New York City has been limited to information from a small number of studies conducted in institutional settings such as alternative high schools, prisons, shelters, hospitals, and drug-treatment facilities (Adams et al. 1985; Di Clemente et al. 1986; Hein 1988; Kegles et al. 1988; Rotherman-Borus and Bradley 1987; Yates et al. 1988). More recently, as part of a CDC-funded evaluation of the impact of street outreach on reducing high-risk behaviour among street youth, the Youth At Risk project acquired the first street-based, empirical study of the street youth population in New York City (Clatts and Davis 1993).[2] Between February and September of 1993, a total of 425 youth were recruited for baseline structured interviews using a time-by-location sampling plan that targeted several geographic locations in the central Manhattan area of New York City where street youth are known to congregate, including Times Square, Greenwich Village, the East Village, and the West Village piers.[2] Interviews followed a structured format that included questions about demographic characteristics, sexual activity, drug use, awareness of AIDS and sexually transmitted diseases, and contact with outreach and prevention services. Eligibility was restricted to youth between twelve and twenty-three years of age, who were homeless and/or dependent upon the street economy.

Nearly two-thirds of the youth contacted identified as ethnic minorities, primarily Black (24%) and Hispanic (39%) (see table 1, pp. 396–7). Most (72%) were between nineteen and twenty-three years of age. Nearly half identified as gay, lesbian, or bisexual (43%). Over half were homeless (55%), and well over half of these had been homeless for more than one year (61%). Over half (55%) were involved in sexual activity with more than one other person. Over a third (37%) were involved in prostitution. Youth reported the use of a wide variety of drugs, including crack (40%), heroin (37%), and LSD (38%). In the thirty days before the interview, over 11 per cent had injected heroin and roughly 9 per cent had injected cocaine. One-fifth (20%) had injected drugs at some point in the last five years. Despite high levels of drug use, less than a third (28%) had ever received drug treatment.

Many of these youth are at risk from both high-risk drug use and high-risk sexual activity. For example, youth who had ever injected drugs were less protected in all kinds of multiple-partner sex than those respondents who had never injected drugs (p < .05). Ever having injected drugs was also associated with several other variables, including prostitution (p < .01) and homelessness (p < .001).

In general, the AIDS education literature suggests that behaviour change is strongly associated with ongoing, consistent contact with prevention messages and resources. Yet, indicative of the inadequacy of prevention resources targeted at this population, less than half (49%) of the youth had ever talked with an outreach worker. Relatively few (10%) of those who had talked with an outreach worker said that they had done so almost every day in the last six months. Most troubling of all, however, is the fact that over half reported that it was 'somewhat likely' (40%) or 'very likely' (13%) that they would get AIDS. Less than a third (29%) said that it was not likely at all. Nearly 15 per cent (13.4) either did not know or could not estimate their risk.

History of AIDS Prevention Services for Street Youth in New York City

Clearly this is a population that is at very high risk for a wide variety of 'poor health outcomes,' including high rates of untreated tuberculosis, repeated exposure to sexually transmitted diseases, and high rates of unplanned pregnancies. The development of prevention services targeted specifically at these street youth began in the mid-1980s with a small number of community-based street outreach programs. Originally outreach programs were envisaged as means of preventing youth, particularly runaway youth, from becoming involved in the Times Square street economy by using street outreach as a means of bridging youth with the mainstream social-services system, including services that could return them home. Street outreach workers were deployed in geographic areas where these youth were known to congregate, providing food, crisis intervention, and referrals to mainstream services.

The youth population that outreach workers found on the streets, however, was quite different from that which had been anticipated. Most were from the New York City area, rather than being runaways from distant states. Many did not have families to which they could return. Others came from family environments that were themselves hazardous, and many reported that they could not return home (Clatts 1989). In general, the mainstream service-delivery system was ill equipped to meet the *demand* for services by this particular population. Drug treatment, for example, was very limited. Similarly, there were

TABLE 1

Demographic profile of the Youth At Risk (YAR) baseline treatment sample (N = 425)

Geographic region	N	%		Gender	N	%
Port Authority	177	(41.7)		Male	337	(79.3)
East Village	105	(24.7)		Female	87	(20.5)
West Village Piers	72	(16.9)		Unknown	1	(0.2)
Areas around Port Authority	48	(11.3)				
Central Village	23	(5.4)		Ethnic status		
				Black	102	(24.0)
Age				Latino	166	(39.1)
13–15 years old	9	(2.1)		White	113	(26.6)
16–18 years old	109	(25.7)		American Indian	4	(0.9)
19–23 years old	307	(72.2)		Asian	5	(1.2)
				Other/mixed	35	(8.2)
Residential status						
Homeless	235	(55.3)		Talked with outreach worker		
Some kind of housing	190	(44.7)		Yes	209	(49.3)
				No	215	(50.7)
How long homeless						
7 days or less	13	(5.6)		Frequency of OR contact in last 6 mos.		
8 to 30 days	15	(6.5)		Almost every day	23	(10.7)
30 to 60 days	10	(4.3)		60 days to 6 months	34	(14.7)
6 months to 1 year	17	(7.3)		Once/weel	42	(19.5)
More than 1 year	143	(61.6)		Once/mo.	42	(19.5)
				Less than once/mo.	85	(39.5)
				Never	23	(10.7)
					215	

TABLE 1 (concluded)

Sources of income		
Panhandling	148	(35.0)
Hustling/prostitution	157	(37.0)
Drug dealing	111	(26.2)
Pimping	9	(2.1)
Pornography	19	(4.5)
Rolling/mugging	41	(9.7)

Drugs used ever		
Crack	170	(40.0)
Heroin	161	(37.9)
Speed/amphetamine	114	(26.9)
LSD	162	(38.2)
Cocaine	247	(58.1)
Speedball	96	(22.6)

IV drugs used last 30 days		
Heroin	49	(11.7)
Cocaine	37	(8.9)
Stealing	90	(21.2)
Speedball	21	(5.0)
Speed/amphetamine	6	(1.4)
Injecting drugs in the last 5 yrs.	87	(20.5)
Ever an injecting drug user	117	(27.5)
Ever been in drug treatment	114	(28.1)

Sex with multiple partners		
Yes	234	(55.3)
No	189	(44.7)

Sexual identity		
Heterosexual	230	(54.4)
Bisexual	117	(27.7)
Gay/lesbian	66	(15.6)
Something else	10	(2.3)

How likely you will get AIDS		
Not at all likely	125	(29.5)
Somewhat likely	171	(40.3)
Very likely	56	(13.2)
Don't know	57	(13.4)
Has AIDS/HIV	15	(3.5)

virtually no services for gay and lesbian youth. Nor, for that matter, was the mainstream service-delivery system prepared to establish the *kind* of service-oriented relationships that are fundamental to effective work with these youth. Many youth came to the streets having already been exposed to profound emotional trauma, experiences that were exacerbated by the violence and exploitation that characterize the everyday life of street youth (Clatts 1990; Clatts and Atillasoy 1993). Mainstream adolescent services were often ill equipped to meet the complex social, economic, and emotional needs of these youth, a fact that has only served to further alienate this population.

In response to the unmet service needs of this population, many of the programs that had initially started by providing a limited set of street-based outreach services began to develop a wider range of services that included local drop-in centres where more intensive services tailored to the specific needs of this particular population of youth could be offered. Drop-in centre services included both daily living needs (food, clothing, showers, and so on) as well as a wide array of counselling, educational, and health services. Based upon their experience in having worked with this population in the context of street outreach, these services were designed in such a way as to afford youth with as much flexibility as possible, focusing particularly on needs identified by the youth and working at a pace that was in large part determined by the youth. Early in the AIDS epidemic all or most of these services included specific attention to AIDS education and prevention, a fact that is reflected in the relatively high levels of knowledge and information about AIDS that is evidenced in this population (Clatts 1989; Hersch 1989).

Applications of Harm Reduction to Outreach to Street Youth

As described in the preceding section, initially the services that were developed in these programs, including AIDS prevention services, had little or no basis in any of the mainstream intervention theories or models. Indeed, perhaps owing to the day-to-day frustration that outreach programs had in attempting to access services and resources for these youth, it is probably fair to say that there was some degree of antipathy towards both mainstream services-delivery strategies and many of the behavioural theories on which they are based. For example, outreach programs frequently found themselves at odds with other 'service-providers' interacting with the street-youth population, particularly those that took a punitive approach to drug abuse. Thus, for the most part, the approaches that have underpinned the development of these programs, including AIDS prevention activities within them, derived from the experiences and capacities of front-line project staff rather than in response to particular theories or models for behaviour change.

In more recent years, however, as increasing numbers of street youth have become ill with opportunistic infections associated with HIV, AIDS prevention has taken on an increased prominence in service delivery. The spread of AIDS among these youth served to heighten attention to the need for a systematic approach to service delivery, both in relation to HIV prevention as well as in terms of AIDS care. These developments prompted a new look at service-delivery models as well as at some of the intervention theories that have been applied to AIDS prevention among other groups at high risk for HIV infection (e.g., adult gay men and drug injectors). For example, a number of the projects experimented with the use of service-delivery models based upon Narcotics Anonymous. Following the NA model, project staff stressed abstinence as the only healthy and safe choice, an initiative that proved to be a wholesale failure among youth.

Generally speaking, outreach workers had been successful in learning how to engage street youth – in great part because of the principle of unconditional acceptance of each young person as an individual that each project embraced. Staff acknowledged that youth lived in dangerous conditions and that prostitution and criminal activity were part of surviving. Around issues of drug use, however, project services were sometimes denied to youth because of their continued drug use. The clear message was that drug use was wrong and that use endangered access to services, resources that are key to everyday survival on the streets. Implicitly, emphasis on an abstinence model also communicated that youth who failed to measure up to this standard were in some way wrong, deficient, and perhaps unworthy of services. Not incidentally, these are precisely the messages that street youth have come away with from the services system that has neglected them. Once internalized, these messages compound the acute sense of failure and powerlessness that is common among these youth (Clatts and Atillasoy 1993). In response, many drug-using youth became alienated from services, while others were inclined to misrepresent their drug use, negating any possibility of therapeutic discussion (including a critical opportunity for AIDS intervention).

It is important to understand that in many respects this population of youth has rejected mainstream services and mainstream approaches to service delivery, particularly services such as medical care and drug treatment that are typically delivered in a highly structured institutional environment and often in a highly coercive manner. Many of these youth are survivors of rape, incest, and sexual abuse, and other forms of physical and emotional abuse, largely at the hands of adults. After having been failed by their parents, many of them have suffered through an overcrowded foster-care system that is ill equipped to deal with their needs. Many of these youth survive through street prostitution – yet another experience of uncaring, exploitative adults. There should be little wonder that they are wary of authority figures and distrustful of the behavioural messages that these systems articulate (Clatts 1989; Hersch 1989).

Over and above the fact that this approach did not serve the youth, it should be emphasized that it also took an enormous toll on service providers. Many outreach workers felt they were in a near constant state of conflict with youth, and that they were expected to use the opportunity of outreach as an occasion in which to impose a set of behavioural goals that were not accomplishable given the limited choices that many street youth have.

In 1992, several of the outreach projects serving the street-youth population agreed to participate in a multi-city, CDC-funded, evaluation of the efficacy of street outreach services in relation to AIDS risk reduction. Participation in this study occasioned a re-examination of the service-delivery principles upon which services had been developed, and the harm reduction model was used as a theoretical foundation for this evaluation. One of the primary aims of the evaluation was to identify ways in which to enhance the organizational capacity of outreach programs in the hope that doing so would make for more effective and efficient delivery of street outreach services. To this end, a network of outreach programs – The Youth At Risk Cooperative-was developed, involving each of the five outreach programs that provide street-based services to the homeless-youth population in the central Manhattan area.[3] One of the primary functions of the YAR Cooperative was the development of an interagency training program for street outreach workers that serve homeless youth. Historically, outreach workers received little if any formal training, typically no more than an orientation to the agency itself rather than training in street outreach per se. Thus, outreach workers were often left to develop outreach skills principally by means of trial and error on the streets. Together with their own personal skills, this lead to some very innovative outreach approaches in the development of effective service relationships with a population that is both 'hard-to-reach' and 'hard-to-maintain.' However, the lack of any formal training made for inconsistency in the kinds of information and skills with which outreach workers were equipped, and hence in the kinds of messages that they provided. It also resulted in considerable staff burn-out and frequent staff turnover. Particularly in the context of a population in which the development of long-term service relationships is very important, this can limit the impact that outreach has in fostering sustained risk reduction.

The harm reduction model was used as the foundation for the training program for outreach workers and included skills-building exercises in using the harm reduction model specifically within the street milieu. Pre- and post-test evaluation of the training program indicates that nearly two-thirds of the outreach workers (60.6%) who participated showed improvement in post-test scores. Most (93.8%) of outreach workers found the training 'very relevant' to their work with street youth and most felt they would use what they learned 'extensively' in their work with street youth.[4] Perhaps more persuasive in terms of the potential of the harm reduction model as a service-delivery strategy for this population, however, are some of the case studies that were developed by staff who have integrated the model into their case-management activities.

'Frankie'

Frankie is a male Hispanic of approximately twenty-one years of age. He has participated in the Times Square street economy for several years, and was homeless at the time when he was first approached by outreach workers in the Times Square area.[5] One evening he approached outreach workers and apologized for the fact that he was 'high,' but requested the opportunity to talk to someone. The outreach worker took him aside, indicating that he would be happy to talk with him. Frankie further explained that if it were not for the fact that he had taken some dope, he would never have had the courage to come talk to the outreach worker. The outreach worker acknowledged that it is sometimes difficult to know who to trust on the streets and that some kinds of things were hard to talk about even with someone who could be trusted. The outreach worker also indicated that he felt it was good that Frankie had figured out a way to move beyond his fear, saying, 'Good, I'm glad you had a little dope then. What's up, what's bothering you?'

The client explained that he had tested HIV-positive six weeks before, and that he had been 'binging' on heroin and 'going crazy' (until the previous day, when he decided to do only six bags instead of twelve, and to try to talk to someone). At this point Frankie said, 'Sorry, I know I'm still messing-up and I want to quit using.'

Such situations always pose a quandary in working with street youth. Is the youth ready and able to abstain from drug use? Is he saying what he believes all social workers want to hear? Is he saying that he wants to abstain because he is afraid that if he doesn't promise abstinence that he will be denied services? In response, the outreach worker said, 'I'll help you with that if you want. If you want, we could work on finding you a place to stay, and on your medical stuff first. Whatever you want to do.' They went on to discuss whether there would be ways for Frankie to reduce his use of heroin to the extent necessary to attend important appointments related to obtaining housing. The outreach worker also explained ways in which Frankie could reduce his risk for complications associated with drug injection through proper needle-hygiene practices.

This first conversation lasted an hour, and was used by the counsellor to build trust and to share limited suggestions, such as 'How about doing a bag in the morning, then coming to see me? Or how about doing something else related to getting off the streets, and getting high only at night after these things have been taken care of?' The client agreed that he thought that these suggestions were possible. It was hoped that if the client successfully changes his or her behaviour to control the time and dose of the drug, the client will feel that he or she has some power over the drug, instead of the drug holding absolute power over him. Frankie began coming to the project the very next day, reflecting an engagement in the service-delivery system that would probably never have occurred if the service-delivery strategy employed by the outreach worker was not grounded in the recognition that prevention services must begin with the actual needs and capacities of the individual to whom they are directed.

'Lee' and 'Al'

Another example involves two youth – Lee, a black male eighteen years of age, and Al, a black male twenty-two years of age – who were encountered on the corner of Eighth Avenue and 44th Street in Manhattan. Noting the puddle of vomit by their feet, the outreach workers surmised that the two were stoned on heroin. One outreach worker

inquired, 'How's the dope?' Al replied, 'What? 'I ain't high.' The counsellor put his hand on Al's shoulder and asked, 'Who the hell stands
around a pile of puke, and looks so happy about it?' Al looked down at
the vomit, and then laughed. The outreach worker warned them not to
step in it, and for Lee to remember his appointment at the project the
next day.

'Angel'

Angel is a twenty-four-year-old black male transvestite. An outreach
worker observed that she used crack in a binge pattern of several days
and nights getting high and prostituting, followed by several days of
sleep and physical recovery. The outreach worker asked Angel what she
did when she wanted to end a binge. She replied, 'Two dime bags, and a
valium,' which she usually bought on her fourth day into a binge. The
marijuana, she said, stimulated her appetite enough to eat, and the combined effect of the depressant drugs and food allowed her to sleep for a
couple of days, after which she could usually abstain from the drug for
three days to a week.

'Binging' typifies the way in which many street youth use drugs, particularly stimulant drugs such as crack cocaine. This pattern of cocaine
and crack-cocaine use is one in which a youth abstains from drugs for as
long as is tolerable, and then is driven to consume large amounts of the
drug over a period of days, or even weeks, foregoing needed sleep,
food, and shelter. In both emotional and behavioural terms, periods of
binging are often the most risky periods in the daily life of street youth,
often marked by profound depression and feelings of self-destruction.
Binging is characterized by extremely high levels of drug consumption,
often using street prostitution as a means with which to obtain the
money. Outreach workers find that they can sometimes identify warning signs that prefigure binges. Dialogue between a youth and an outreach worker can sometimes assist in the formulation of plans to
interrupt this cycle, or at least to mitigate its harmful effects. As in the
previous case study, however, the opportunity for such a dialogue is
contingent upon the outreach worker being able to communicate acceptance, concern, and knowledge, and a willingness to provide an intervention environment in which a youth is assisted in directing his or her
own self-care plan. In talking with Angel, the outreach worker suggested that before she smoked any more crack she would invest in marijuana and valium, to be taken after the second full day of getting high.

Angel was successful with this plan, using this technique to shorten a binge and sometimes even to avoid one.

Discussion

It is beyond the scope of this paper to demonstrate in any formal sense that the harm reduction model has broad and sustained behavioural efficacy, or to compare its efficacy with competing behaviour-change models. Based upon the experience of service providers participating in the study, however, two salient features of the harm reduction model can be identified: first, as an approach to public-health policy, the harm reduction model is clearly predicated upon the recognition that some 'behavioural outcomes' have greater importance than others. Specifically, the harm reduction model prioritizes the prevention of HIV transmission. Second, as a strategy by which to achieve reduction in the transmission of HIV, the harm reduction model is the based on the recognition that particular behavioural goals must be tailored to the specific needs and real-life capacities of the individuals to whom they are directed.

In the context of outreach to a population such as street youth, for example, the principal public-health goal is one of providing risk-reduction *choices* to youth who occupy a particular niche in the street economy, rather than of seeking to impose a uniform code of behaviour or one that uses adherence to a particular code of behaviour as a condition for access to services. Here, the harm reduction model serves a service-delivery principle in which the task is that of providing risk-reduction education and tools that will enable an individual to make the most health-promoting choices possible in a particular place and time. As such, it contrasts rather sharply with approaches to service delivery that are predicated upon idioms of failure, blame, and deviance. It also contrasts with 'incentive' strategies for behavioural change that rely on the mediums of coercion, penalty, and criminalization. Thus, the harm reduction model contrasts with many of the more 'mainstream' behaviour change models whose behavioural goals are derived from outside the particular social and economic contexts in which they are to be applied.

In the context of the case studies discussed above, for example, it was more important that the outreach worker establish an effective relationship with Frankie than it was to tell Frankie that he should not use drugs. The health and well-being of the individual person, and a direct response to the needs that he or she defines as primary, are first-order goals of service delivery, not an abstract set of agency standards and procedures that match a given risk behaviour with a given behavioural expectation. In sharp contrast to rationalist models of service delivery, it is our experience that the harm reduction approach is much more likely to result in the development of the kind of relationship in which specific and realizable behavioural goals can be identified. Moreover, it is also the kind of service-delivery relationship upon which risk-reduction changes in behaviour can be supported, and thereby sustained. For example, it was more important to teach Angel how to minimize the potential harm of HIV infection from binging during prostitution than it was to direct her to stop using drugs and to stop prostituting – goals that at that point in time were not realizable given the social and economic options available.

Conclusion

Over the course of the last decade, several competing behavioural-change models have been developed in the attempt to forge a coherent public-health approach to changing behaviours that have been implicated in the spread of HIV infection. The scope of this chapter does not permit a detailed discussion of the complex theoretical issues that attend the development of these models, many of which implicitly (and often explicitly) underpin much of the publicly funded AIDS prevention effort, such as the Stages of Change Theory (cf. Fishbein et al. 1991), the Health Belief Model (Janz and Becker 1984), and the Theory of Reasoned Action (cf. Becker 1988). In general, these models focus on demonstrating a statistical association between individual psychological characteristics and individual behaviours, self-efficacy, and unprotected sex, for example. Indeed, it is precisely this kind of conceptual efficiency that is perhaps part of the great attraction of these models, for if historical and contextual factors are held constant these kinds of psychological properties are relatively easy to measure both over time and across risk groups.

It is noteworthy, however, that these models have limited the explanatory task to the 'search' for statistical associations among a narrow range of ill-defined and poorly operationalized psychological variables. Moreover, and particularly in the context of a population such as homeless youth, the relevance of these alleged psychological states to the structure of 'real life choices' is, at best, dubious.[6] For quite apart from the information an individual possesses about risk for HIV transmission, or the actions an individual may perceive as necessary in order to avoid it, or indeed what an individual might *wish* to do in order to avoid it – a number of complex structural constraints often serve as overwhelming barriers to an individual's capacity to engage in consistent risk reduction. The plain fact is that most of the people in the youth segment who will be at risk for AIDS in the coming decade will be at risk not because of inadequate knowledge, mistaken beliefs, or failures of intention, but rather because of the larger social and economic circumstances that govern their lives. Most will be subject to economic inequalities that have disparities of power and wealth at their core – inequalities exacerbated by factors of race, gender, and sexual identity (Clatts 1994b).

In contrast, service providers employing the harm reduction model have resonated with the 'non-judgmental' posture of the harm reduction model encompasses and with the attention to 'real life' behavioural choices that the model embraces when applied to a given clinical context. Thus, while the harm reduction model shares many of the same public-health goals (behavioural risk reduction) that are found in several of the more prominent behaviour-change models, it nevertheless reflects a substantially different orientation to the process by means of which behavioural risk reduction is sought to be accomplished. A central issue is one of power. We can all wish for a world in which young people were not living in the streets, a world in which sexual activity was always a nurturing and enriching experience rather than an opportunity for exploitation. Similarly, we can all wish for a world in which the best 'high' a youth could attain was achieved by their own creative expression, rather than through the ephemeral comfort found in a crack vial. Unfortunately, it is the latter that typifies the life of increasing numbers of homeless youth and, consequently, it is to these same circumstances that we must respond as thoughtful and creative service providers. In attempting to develop AIDS prevention services for these youth, it is critical that we remember to fit the service model to the youth, rather than the youth to the service model. The use of the harm reduction model has contributed to this process in several concrete ways that have been described here in the context of an outreach-worker training program. More generally, but no less substantively, the harm reduction model has also served to remind us that we cannot offer constructive assistance until we know that person to whom we are reaching out, and that we cannot know that person until we are prepared to listen.

NOTES

1 The research reported in this paper was supported by grant #U62/ CCU207192-03 from the Centers for Disease Control and was conducted under a collaborative agreement between Metropolitan Assistance (Victim Services/Travelers AID) Corporation, National Development and Research Institutes, Inc., The Hetrick-Martin Institute, and Community Health Project. The authors would like to specifically acknowledge the contributions made to the project by Richard Haymes, Frances Kunreuther, Helene Lauffer, John Santelli, M.D., and Mary Washburn. Correspondence should be sent to Michael C. Clatts, Ph.D., Youth at Risk Project/NDRI, 11 Beach Street, New York, NY 10013.

2 For a detailed methodological discussion of the sampling strategy, see Clatts, Davis, and Atillasoy (1995).

3 The idea for the development of the YAR Cooperative grew out a year-long community-assessment process in which ethnographic methods were used to examine the service-delivery infrastructure and to identify areas for potential enhancement. In the course of this assessment, it became clear that despite notable strengths in individual projects, there was little or no service-delivery infrastructure targeted to street youth, a fact that made for a service-delivery system that was minimally efficient and perhaps less than maximally effective. The purpose of developing the YAR Cooperative network was three-fold: (1) to coordinate street outreach services so as to ensure more consistent and efficient service delivery; (2) to develop an interagency training program for outreach staff, particularly in relation to AIDS risk reduction; and (3) to develop a computer system for client tracking, interagency case management, and systematic documentation of services at the community-wide level (Clatts et al. 1994). See also Reidel 1987.

4 The training curricula used in this program has been developed into a Resource Guide entitled *Innovative Approaches to AIDS Outreach & Prevention for Homeless and Runaway Youth: Applications of the Harm Reduction Model*. A copy may be obtained by contacting Michael Clatts, PhD, NDRI, 11 Beach Street, New York, NY 10013.

5 Names have been changed to protect the identities of the youths whose interaction with outreach workers are profiled here.

6 It is perhaps not accidental that these kinds of models have come to the fore at a time in which there has been a political premium placed on individual responsibility, indeed a political period in which disease discourse is infused with metaphors of guilt and blame (see Clatts and Mutchler 1989; Clatts 1994b).

REFERENCES

Adams, G.R., T. Gullotta, and M. Clancy. 1985. 'Homeless Adolescents: A
Descriptive Study of Similarities and Differences between Runaways and
Throwaways.' *Adolescence*, 20: 715–24.
Becker, M.H. 1988. 'AIDS and Behavior Change.' *Public Health Reviews* 16:
1–11.
Clatts, M.C. 1989. 'Substance Abuse and AIDS Prevention Strategies for Homeless Youth: An Ethnographic Perspective.' Paper presented at the Third International Gay and Lesbian Health Conference, San Francisco.
– 1990. 'Rage on Crack Street: An Ethnographic Journey.' *Family Therapy Net-
worker* 11: 37–41.
– 1994a. 'Getting "Real" about HIV and Homeless Youth.' *American Journal of
Public Health* 83(4): 1492–4.
– 1994b. 'All the Kings Horses and All the Kings Men: Some Personal Reflections on Ten Years of AIDS Ethnography.' *Human Organization* 53(1): 93–5.
Clatts, M.C., and A. Atillasoy. 1993. 'Where the Day Takes You: Homeless Youth
and the Structure of the Street Economy.' Paper presented at the Annual
Meetings of the Society for Applied Anthropology, San Antonio, 12 March.
Clatts, M.C., and W.R. Davis. 1993. 'A Demographic and Behavioral Profile of
Homeless Youth in New York City: Implications for AIDS Outreach and Pre-
vention.' Paper presented at the annual meeting of the American Public
Health Association, San Francisco.
Clatts, M.C., W.R. Davis, and A. Atillasoy. 1995. 'Hitting a Moving Target: The
Use of Ethnographic Methods in the Evaluation of AIDS Outreach Programs
for Homeless Youth in NYC.' In *Qualitative Methods in Drug Abuse and HIV
Research*, 117–35. New York: National Institute on Drug Abuse Research
Monograph 157.
Clatts, M.C., W.R. Davis, and J.L. Sotheran. 1994. 'At the Cross-Roads of HIV
Infection: A Demographic and Behavioral Profile of Street Youth in NYC.'
Paper presented at a symposium on Drugs, Sex, and AIDS: Prevention
Research 1995–2000. Flagstaff, Arizona.
Clatts, M.C., and K.M. Mutchler. 1989. 'AIDS and the Dangerous Other: Meta-
phors of Sex and Deviance in the Representation of a Disease.' *Medical Anthro-
pology* 10, no. 2(3): 105–14.
Clatts M.C., E. Springer, and M. Washburn. 1990. 'Outreach to Homeless Youth
in NYC: Implications for Planning and Practice in Social Services.' Paper pre-
sented at the Annual Meetings of the American Public Health Association,
New York.
DiClemente, R., J. Zorn, and L. Temoshok. 1986. 'Adolescents and AIDS: A Sur-

vey of Knowledge, Attitude, and Beliefs about AIDS in San Francisco.' *American Journal of Public Health* 76(12): 1443–5.

Gunn, B. 1988. 'Results of the Study of Street Youths and Runaways.' Office of the Mayor, New York.

Fishbein, M., S.E. Middlestadt, and P.J. Hitchcock. 1991. 'Using Information to Change Sexually Transmitted Disease-Related Behaviors: An Analysis Based on the Theory of Reasoned Action.' In J.N. Wasserheir, S.O. Aral, and K.K. Holmes, eds, *Research Issues in Human Behavior and Sexually Transmitted Diseases in the AIDS Era*, 243–57. Washington: American Society for Microbiology.

Hein, K. 1988. 'AIDS in Adolescence: A Rationale for Concern.' *New York State Journal of Medicine* 87: 290–5.

Hersch, P. 1988. 'Coming of Age on City Streets.' *Psychology Today* (June): 28–37.

– 1989. 'Exploratory Ethnographic Study of Runaway and Homeless Adolescents in New York and San Francisco.' Rockville, MD: National Institute of Drug Abuse.

Janz, N.K., and M.H. Becker. 1984. 'The Health Belief Model: A Decade Later.' *Health Education Quarterly* 11: 1–47.

Kegeles, D.B., N.E. Adler, and C.E. Irwin. 1988. 'Sexually Active Adolescents and Condoms: Changes over One Year in Knowledge, Attitudes and Use.' *American Journal of Public Health* 78: 460–1.

Reidel, M. 1987. 'Developing Multi-Level Service Delivery Networks for Runaway Youth.' National Runaway Network Annual Convention, Washington.

Rotherum-Borus, M.J., and J. Bradley. 1987. 'Prevention of HIV Infection among Adolescents.' In S. Bluumenthal, A. Eicheler, and G. Weisman, eds, *Women and AIDS: Promoting Healthy Behaviors*. Washington: American Psychiatric Press.

Shaffer, P.D., and C.L.M. Caton. 1984. 'Runaway and Homeless Youth in New York City.' A Report to the Ittleson Foundation, New York.

United States Department of Health and Human Services. 1986. *Fiscal Year 1985 Study of Runaways and Youth*. Washington.

Yates, G.R., J. Pennbridge MacKenzie, and E. Cohen. 1988. 'A Risk Profile Comparison of Runaway and Non-Runaway Youth.' *American Journal of Public Health* 78(37): 820–1.

24 Working with Prostitutes: Reducing Risks, Developing Services

SARAH CROSBY

Introduction

This chapter is based upon the experience and work of Manchester Action on Street Health (MASH), a voluntary organization providing an innovative, sexual-health service for street prostitutes in Manchester, north-west England.

The principle of harm reduction is central to the work of the MASH project. Harm reduction within the context of MASH focuses on the health risks associated with unsafe and/or injecting drug use. From this perspective, harm reduction can be conceptualized as a variety of interventions designed to reduce the potential harm to street prostitutes generated by their patterns of drug use and sexual activity. MASH recognizes that clients of its service are unlikely to change their lifestyles to the extent that they will stop injecting drugs or working as prostitutes in the short term. Consequently, MASH adopts a pragmatic approach by providing the means to practise safer sex and safer drug use through the provision of condoms and clean injecting equipment and, as a consequence, attempts to reduce the health-related harm to drug-using prostitutes, their immediate 'community,' and the wider society.

Concerns about the linkage between prostitution, drug use, and the spread of HIV have been recorded by several authors, both in terms of the connection between drug use and prostitution (Goldstein 1979; Day and Harris 1988; Kinnell 1989; Morgan-Thomas 1990) and the subsequent risks and levels of HIV infection (Goldberg et al. 1988; Barnard et al. 1990; McKeganey and Barnard 1992; Faugier et al. 1992). The evidence highlights the fact that sex workers face a potentially higher risk of HIV infection, and that this risk is substantially increased for drug-using sex workers.

Rather than concentrate on the relationship between prostitution, drug use, and the possible spread of HIV referred to above, this chapter will concentrate on the development of appropriate harm reduction strategies, targeted specifically at drug-using female and male prostitutes. The experience of MASH will be used to illustrate and discuss some of the issues and problems relating to the establishment of an easy-access, low-threshold service for prostitutes in an inner-city context.

Background: Prostitution and Drug Use in Manchester

The issue of prostitution and drug use is particularly applicable to Manchester, a large industrial city in north-west England, which has witnessed a dramatic decline in its traditional manufacturing base and increasing levels of unemployment and deprivation over the past two decades. During the 1980s the city, like others in Britain, experienced a high growth in the use of smokable heroin (Pearson 1987; Parker et al. 1988) and, partly as a consequence, the injecting of heroin and the use of a variety of other drugs remain widespread in parts of Manchester today.

Manchester also has an established 'sex industry,' which comprises both 'street' and 'indoor' prostitution. There are three main 'beats' ('red-light' districts) across the city, each with their own distinct characteristics:

City Centre. This area is unusual in that both women and men prostitutes work in the same vicinity. In recent years it has been the focal point for considerable investment, and there have been increasing pressures from local businesses to 'evict' prostitutes from this long-established 'beat.'

Whalley Range. This area, in the south of the city, has been a traditional red-light district for decades. However, unlike the city centre, it is largely residential, with many of the former grand Victorian houses now converted into flats. In recent years there has been vociferous opposition to street prostitution from local residents.

Cheetham Hill. North of the city, this is a multicultural working-class area and comprises a mixture of new council housing and older working-class terraces. It has a low-key street prostitution scene, and is the quietest of the three beats. There are also numerous other beats outside of the city, notably in smaller satellite towns in Greater Manchester.

Recent communication with the police suggests that within any given week approximately three hundred women work regularly in these red-light districts.[1] This is supported by official statistics which show that throughout Greater Manchester 278 women were charged with 'immoral offences' between January 1995 and December 1995.[2] It is likely that these figures represent a significant underestimate of the actual numbers.

Development of the MASH Service

There are clearly several health-related problems associated with the social context within which prostitution exists. This chapter will discuss the attempts of one particular voluntary agency to address these concerns, focusing on the development of the organization and its attempts to overcome institutional, cultural, and other obstacles, within the framework of an overall harm reduction strategy.

MASH developed out of the impetus of a number of outreach workers from across the city who were concerned about sensationalized media reports citing prostitutes as a 'reservoir of infection for HIV.'[3] Informal outreach work being undertaken with prostitute women, and the preliminary findings from a Department of Health funded study (Faugier et al. 1992), also suggested that this group was largely disconnected from any mainstream health-care provision.

Relevant workers were initially invited to a series of meetings in the autumn of 1990, and the principle of the MASH project was established. With a small grant, and the loan of a transit van from the Local Authority, MASH began operating its outreach service in February 1991. From its inception, MASH has operated as a non-statutory (voluntary) service, with charitable status, and has recently become a Company Limited by Guarantee. Its aims and objectives were to provide, in a harm reduction context, a sexual-health promotion/HIV-prevention service. MASH operates in the heart of the city centre's red-light area on three nights a week (Tuesday, Wednesday, and Thursday) from 8 pm to 1 am. Since July 1995, the service has operated from a custom-built trailer, providing the following:

- Harm reduction advice and information
- Condoms, lubricants, and spermicidal creams
- Pregnancy testing
- Genito-urinary medicine (GUM) service
- Needle exchange
- Input from a specialist Drug Liaison Midwife

- Input from specialist drug workers, including on-site assessments for drug treatment
- A link with primary health care and other appropriate agencies
- Staff who can undertake an advocacy role on behalf of clients
- Referrals to appropriate agencies and organizations
- Nursing input for minor-injuries treatment, first aid, and health advice

While MASH provides this range of services as part of its overall harm reduction strategy, one of the attractions to the client group is that it provides a place where prostitute women and men can have a break from work and a cup of tea. This approach made the service immediately accessible and, over time, allowed MASH to make the harm reduction interventions referred to above.

The service is staffed by a full-time outreach worker and a team of three trained volunteers, in addition to several staff members seconded from relevant agencies, including drug services. This ensures that a range of expertise is available on any given session. The MASH service has contact with between fifty and sixty clients per evening, and can offer immediate information, advice, and referrals, as well as ongoing support and advocacy. The needle-exchange scheme currently has over two hundred registered clients, and is one of the busiest exchanges in a network of twenty-two across the city.

Issues Relating to Service Development

Funding

Initially, the statutory funding bodies were cautious to support such an innovative service, and the MASH project was established on an extremely tight budget – a start-up grant of £1000 (approximately $2000 Canadian) in addition to the loan of a Local Authority vehicle. Staff worked on a voluntary basis, and supplies of needles and condoms were provided by the District Health Authority. The experience of MASH suggests that once such a small-scale initiative is actually 'up and running,' it is much easier to then convince the relevant fundholders that the project is a viable financial investment.

The MASH service was running for almost a year before funding for a full-time salaried member of staff was made available, but the project still managed to provide a professional, reliable service during this time.

While funding has subsequently been secured, and the service has continued to develop (MASH currently employs three full-time staff members), attracting adequate levels of funding is an immensely time-consuming process that inevitably diverts energy away from service delivery. Furthermore, when funding is received, it tends to be short-term and this inevitably makes longer-term planning difficult.

Attracting and Retaining a Client Base

If attracting and securing funding is the first major hurdle to overcome, then establishing and retaining a client base is equally important. It was vital that service delivery be compatible with the lifestyle of the potential client group (namely, chaotic poly-drug users who work late into the night). With this in mind, MASH situated itself in the heart of the red-light area and, from its inception, has operated as a low-threshold, easy-access facility. Female and male prostitutes and drug users are able to use all aspects of the service on a walk-in, no-appointment basis. MASH offers a full range of services and equipment that are made available at a 'one-stop' facility, without any of the perceived barriers sometimes inherent to statutory-drugs services. It operates at hours to suit its client group, as opposed to its staff. MASH is therefore in a unique position to make contact, and develop an ongoing rapport, with significant numbers of drug-using clients who are disconnected from other services. By delivering its service within a supportive and non-judgmental environment, MASH is in a unique position to engage clients in the adoption of harm reduction practices.

In the relatively short time that MASH has been in operation, it has become the major service provider for drug-using prostitutes in Manchester, and has contact with between 100 and 150 clients each week. Furthermore, MASH represents a particularly successful outreach model in terms of attracting a traditionally 'hard-to-reach' group of drug users, women. Statistics show that whereas the ratio of women to men using needle-exchange schemes in general across Manchester is 1:4, the MASH exchange has an equal ratio of female and male clients registered (University of Manchester Drug Misuse Research Unit 1994). In this respect, MASH is meeting recent government-endorsed recommendations that drug services should become more women-friendly, and include access to female doctors and counsellors, along with the provision of family-planning facilities (ACMD 1989). Effective outreach work, particularly with hard-to-reach populations, such as sex workers, has been highlighted as a key component of facilitating improvements in the health of drug users and in reducing the risk of HIV transmission. The Advisory Council on the Misuse of Drugs (ACMD) states: 'In terms of HIV prevention, the greatest benefits are to be obtained by maximising brief contacts with drug users who are out of touch with services. This implies a "front-line" role for outreach, with the emphasis on short-term contacts ... rather than on multiple contacts with established clients' (ACMD 1993). Given the potentially chaotic lifestyles of some drug-using prostitutes, it is important to establish a level of consistency in any service that attempts to attract and retain contact with this group. Prostitutes tend to be a very mobile population and information about the project is most commonly circulated by word of mouth. Therefore, the reliability of a service is crucial to its success. In recognition of this, and despite having a predominantly voluntary workforce, MASH has operated every night it has been scheduled to do so.

MASH provides a professional health-care service, but the service is purposely delivered within a non-medicalized context. This style of service generates a high level of credibility with prostitute women and men, as illustrated by the fact that MASH maintains long-term contact with a 'core' user group in addition to a steady flow of new clients.

It is also important to recognize that for the majority of prostitutes, male or female, drug users or non–drug users, prevention of HIV infection is not a particularly high priority in their daily lives. Issues around avoiding arrest, lack of money, social-security problems, housing, and, particularly, concerns about violence from 'punters' (male clients) are far more immediate and pressing matters (Synn Stern 1992; Green et al. 1993; Kinnell 1993; McKeganey and Barnard 1996). In this context, MASH does not consciously portray itself to its client group as an 'AIDS project.' Staff engage in a whole range of conversations, and only when a particular level of rapport has been developed, do discussions focus on more specific sexual health and drug issues. The trust established by this approach enables staff to make more focused interventions at a later stage without having alienated clients.

Working in Other Areas of the City

Central to the MASH philosophy is the need to deliver services directly to the client group. The project does not unrealistically expect women who work in other parts of Manchester to visit its city-centre facility. Consequently, in September 1992, MASH began operating a mobile 'satellite' service in the Whalley Range beat. Although this district is geographically close to the city centre (approximately two miles), very few of the women who work in this area had previously made contact with MASH. It was only when an easy-access service was effectively delivered 'to their door' that they began to utilize it.

As mentioned earlier, this district is a largely residential area with intense opposition to prostitution from many quarters of the local community. Operating a low-key approach to this element of MASH's work was essential, as was the support of the local police force. After initial wariness from the women, some of whom assumed we were 'vice' (plain-clothed vice-squad police officers), this service is now very well received. Many of the women come out from 'hiding spots' to use the service, and we have recently begun making 'door-to-door' deliveries for friends of those women who do not work on the particular night MASH operates. The service is continuing to make contact with increasing numbers of young women, many of whom are inexperienced as prostitutes, as well as being heavy and chaotic drug users.

Easy-Access Primary Health Care

As a street-based project, MASH seeks to make primary health care more accessible to a client group who have traditionally had little, or no, contact with mainstream health services. As MASH often provides the first point of contact into such services, the project is wary not to portray HIV and drug use as the only issues relevant to prostitute women and men. Drug-using prostitutes, in particular, often have multiple health-care problems including injecting-related infections, such as hepatitis B and C and septicaemia, as well as abscesses, thrombosed veins, skin infections, poor dental health, amenorrhoea, and general poor diet.

In this context, health advice is offered within the framework of a holistic service, which can make referrals or offer advice on a range of issues such as social, legal, financial, and general-health problems. With a full-time outreach worker available to undertake referral and follow-up work, MASH strives to direct clients into more formal mainstream services (e.g., community drug services, general practitioners, and Health Clinics) and, hopefully, counteract some of the negative experiences they may have had with these agencies in the past.

Studies clearly show that women sex workers, and particularly those women using drugs, experience high rates of infection from sexually transmitted diseases (STDs) (Darrow 1984; Plant 1990; McKeganey and

Barnard 1992) and face an increased risk of HIV infection. Yet, as previously highlighted, many of these women are disconnected from mainstream health-care services, particularly genito-urinary medical services (Kinnell 1989; Faugier et al. 1992; Green et al. 1993; Gossop et al. 1994). In a MASH survey (MASH 1994), 78 per cent of clients were not in contact with a GP, and only 14 per cent were in touch with a Community Drug Team. This data is further supported by evidence from a recent survey by the North West Regional Drug Misuse Research Unit which highlighted that approximately 60 per cent of clients of needle-exchange schemes in Manchester were currently out of touch with other drugs services (Donmall and Millar 1995).

In recognition of this lack of access to mainstream health services, in August 1993 MASH began offering its own night-time GUM facility specifically for women and men prostitutes. Funding was secured from the Regional Health Authority for a female GUM consultant and family-planning nurse to staff the service. The GUM service operates on a walk-in, no-appointment basis and offers screening and testing for STDs; counselling and testing for HIV; hepatitis B testing and vaccination; pregnancy testing; cervical smear tests; and contraception (including emergency contraception) and general advice on sexual health matters. The service can also make referrals for pregnancy terminations, and has been able to arrange hospital appointments at short notice. This targeted GUM facility is an innovative development that is available in few other areas in the United Kingdom.

A significant number of clients attending the GUM are diagnosed with, and receive treatment for, an STD, and requests for HIV testing and hepatitis B vaccinations are continuing to rise. The development of this GUM facility has enabled MASH to broaden the harm reduction aspects of its work, while simultaneously responding to the basic health-care needs of its client group. Nevertheless there are still aspects of the work that need to be developed. For example, the slower than anticipated take-up of the GUM service from male sex workers and the low re-attendance rate for test results in general both need to be addressed.

Working with Male Prostitutes

Working with male prostitutes has proved to be a more problematic area of work for MASH. In comparison with the recent growth of harm reduction initiatives in the UK that target women prostitutes, 'rent boys' have received far less attention. The lifestyle and working practices of male prostitutes, in the experience of MASH, tend to be quite distinct from those of women prostitutes. Their lifestyle is characterized by lower levels of injecting drug use and a greater degree of 'recreational' drug use. Prices charged by male 'rent boys' are lower, and there is less consistency in terms of charges for sexual services compared to women prostitutes. Sex does not always encompass a financial transaction, and can sometimes be provided in exchange for a bed for the night or a meal.

This lack of 'flat rates' for sexual services is also linked to the fact that many 'rent boys' have limited contact with other male prostitutes, and are less accustomed to negotiating rates for sex, which is usually paid after the service has been given (Morgan Thomas et al. 1989; Barnard et al. 1990; McKeganey and Barnard 1992). There also appears to be a lack of the sense of 'community' that characterizes female street-based prostitution. This factor also means that health-education, and specifically harm-reduction, messages are more difficult to disseminate.

Furthermore, research highlights lower levels of condom use, but higher levels of riskier sexual practices amongst male sex workers (Bloor et al. 1990; Barnard et al. 1990; Gibson 1992). Much of the available research underlines the fact that HIV transmission risks are higher among male prostitutes and clients.

While MASH recognizes these factors, attempts to devise and implement a service that will attract greater numbers of male prostitutes have proved problematic. The project is aware that for this group the availability of a needle-exchange scheme is not always relevant in terms of their drug-use patterns. It therefore attempts to encourage 'rent boys' to utilize the service through other means and concentrates on the sexual-health and safer-sex aspects of its service in attempting to make contact with this group. The project also maintains a wide selection of 'ultra-strong' condoms, which are more suitable for anal sex, and lubricants. Particular emphasis is also placed on encouraging male prostitutes to use the MASH GUM facility.

In the future, MASH hopes to recruit more male members of staff who have particular knowledge and expertise in this field of work. The project has also been working collaboratively with other local voluntary organizations whose client group may include male sex workers. Most important, MASH continues to develop a high level of trust with existing male clients, and attempts to utilize their informal networks to encourage more 'rent boys' to use the project.

Despite recreational and stimulant patterns of drug use being common among male sex workers, a focus on harm reduction is, neverthe-less, an appropriate and necessary strategy for working with this group. However, MASH recognizes that this area of work is immensely prob-lematic, particularly when male prostitution tends to be a far more covert activity than female soliciting, and the men and boys involved generally represent a much more stigmatized and ostracized group than female prostitutes.

Relationship with the Police

Crucial to the success of the MASH project is the good relationship it has developed with the police. Negotiations with the Greater Manches-ter Police (GMP) vice squad were initiated at an early stage in MASH's development.

In line with the general police policy towards needle exchanges in Manchester, MASH was assured that police officers would not enter MASH premises unless they had a warrant for an individual's arrest or were in pursuit of an individual who had committed a serious offence. This informal, but binding, agreement has been crucial to the success of the project and it is important to recognize that the police, more than any other organization, have the potential to stifle any outreach initia-tive simply through an unwarranted continual presence.

It has been extremely important to keep the police updated on any new developments relating to service delivery. For example, in initiat-ing the new service in Whalley Range, support from the relevant divi-sional inspector was obtained. As mentioned earlier, it was well known that there was vociferous opposition to prostitutes from local residents in this area, and MASH recognized that the support of the police could be vital if the project's work in this district were to become the focus of adverse publicity.

MASH has also undertaken several training/information events with the GMP. Initial discussions with GMP centred on the impact that MASH's work may have on the police's law enforcement role, but developed into a wider recognition of a lack of police information about harm reduction and HIV issues. At their request, MASH agreed to undertake a series of training events that would be attended by all vice-squad officers operating in the city centre.

The function of this initiative was fourfold: first, to educate officers about the issues relating to drug use, HIV, and the concept of harm-reduction; second, to inform local officers 'on the beat' about the work of MASH and, more specifically, to demystify some of the myths surrounding the project; third, to place MASH's work within the context of a broader harm reduction strategy relating to drug use; and, finally, to reiterate that this harm reduction aspect need not interfere with, or cause obstruction to, the police's law-enforcement role. Training sessions emphasized to officers that MASH would not act as a means to harbour any individual who had committed a serious offence or who had an outstanding warrant out for his or her arrest. In addition, all MASH workers carry identification cards with them when working, in order to avoid any unnecessary questioning from the police. These have proved to be particularly useful for male workers who could otherwise be arrested for 'kerb-crawling' (i.e., propositioning a prostitute for 'business'). The training sessions proved extremely useful from a 'public relations' perspective, and it was subsequently apparent that police attitudes towards the project and staff improved markedly. In addition, there were very few cases of officers approaching the night-time service out of curiosity. Furthermore, they even began informally referring women to the project whom they had cautioned or arrested.

MASH has also liaised with the police in attempting to encourage women who have been sexually and/or violently assaulted to report the incident. Any woman who has suffered such an assault can report the incident directly to a nominated female officer at GMP who has been specially trained to deal with the matter in a sympathetic manner. Alternatively, if the woman does not wish to report the attack in person, this arrangement allows for information to be directly supplied to the police in an anonymous, standardized format, with the woman's consent. Such information is currently recorded by the women who use MASH on a less formal basis in the form of a *Dodgy Punter's Notice Board*, which serves as a means of warning other women about particularly dangerous 'clients.'

While the experience of MASH has confirmed that it is possible and beneficial to work cooperatively with the local police, it is important to emphasize that such initiatives have developed within a context of an increasingly receptive attitude of many UK police forces towards harm reduction policies in recent years. Harm reduction is continuing to be viewed, particularly within the higher echelons of the Greater Manchester Police Force, as a credible approach in terms of reducing the levels of acquisitive crime committed by drug users to finance the purchase of street drugs (Greater Manchester Police Strategy [undated]: 20).

Relationship with the Media

Given the potential for hostility towards the MASH service, publicity about the project is restricted, as far as possible, to the client group, the statutory authorities, and other services. The nature of the work often leads to interest from the media, but while the chance to 'get the message across' and counteract some of the myths relating to prostitution is often appealing, the risk of sensationalist reporting represents a very genuine disincentive to do this, and consequently MASH purposely keeps a low media profile. However, while publicity about the work of the project is discouraged, MASH has actively developed effective links with other similar services operating both at a national and an international level. MASH played a key role in the establishment of a 'North-West of England Networking Group' that serves as a forum to discuss common practical issues, as well as providing an essential element of worker support.

Non-Commercial Condom Usage

There is increasing evidence that points to the reluctance of women prostitutes to use condoms in their 'private' sexual relationships, which clearly contrasts with the high condom usage reported for commercial sexual intercourse. The reasons for low non-commercial condom usage are well documented (Day and Ward 1990; Morgan Thomas 1990; Faugier et al. 1992; Barnard 1993; Gossop et al. 1994; McKeganey and Barnard 1996). While this reflects low levels of condom use in heterosexual relationships generally, the issue is an important one for MASH. The project is in contact with many of the male partners of prostitute women, mainly because the Manchester street-prostitution scene is largely devoid of 'pimps.' Many of the women work for themselves, but significant numbers also finance the drug habits of their male sexual partners. Many of these men are themselves registered clients of the MASH needle-exchange scheme, and spend considerable periods of time on the project while their partners are out working.

This level of familiarity and trust with the partners of prostitute women means that MASH staff are often able to engage both parties in discussions around safer sex in personal relationships generally, without them feeling threatened or 'lectured at.' However, the project is also realistic enough to understand the symbolic nature of sex between prostitute and partner without the use of a condom as distinct from 'business with a rubber,' and sensitive enough not to make assumptions about, or comment on, peoples' personal sex lives. In a similar vein, conversations can also be initiated around the issue of sharing injecting equipment and paraphernalia with others, including sexual partners. As McKeganey and Barnard (1992) have suggested, the 'passing-on' of injecting equipment can be an integral part of some drug-using subcultures.

Drug-Treatment Interventions

Approximately 75 per cent of the female prostitutes MASH has contact with are injecting drug users. This figure is considerably higher than that reported in other British cities (Day, Ward, and Harris 1988; Kinnell 1989; Morgan-Thomas et al. 1989), but this can partly be explained by the fact that MASH only has contact with 'street' prostitutes, who have a higher propensity to use drugs regularly than 'non-street' prostitutes. Heroin is the primary drug of choice, but a variety of others such as crack cocaine, amphetamine, Temazepam, and methadone are also used. The women's involvement in prostitution has to be seen in the context of the need to finance their drug use.

In relation to non-opiate drug users, MASH currently does not have access to any realistic treatment interventions, and the focus of work in relation to non-opiate use is one of harm reduction. A relatively high proportion of the needle-exchange clients are amphetamine users, and these amphetamine injectors are generally not in touch with any drug services other than the MASH needle-exchange scheme. Recently, the project has become more aware of an increase in the use of crack cocaine, which has become widely available in the city, and a substantial proportion of MASH clients are now using crack in addition to other street drugs. The use of crack cocaine on a national basis is a poorly researched phenomenon and, like other projects, MASH recognizes this usage is an area of increasing concern, particularly as sex workers will often work longer hours, see more 'punters' (paying clients), and, possibly, be more pressurized to accept offers of sex without a condom to finance their crack use.

The situation is more positive in relation to methadone prescribing in the city, and MASH has established good links with existing community drug services. However, many statutory services tend to have limited accessibility for our client group – they are only open during 'office' hours, and an appointment is usually required. MASH has therefore negotiated with the primary drug-treatment provider in the city to arrange for specialist staff members to be seconded to the MASH service. These staff provide regular input, offering specialist advice and information on issues such as safer injecting as well as undertaking on-site assessments for drug treatment (i.e., methadone prescriptions). Follow-up appointments at a local drug service are then made for those clients who wish to receive a regular prescription of oral methadone. While MASH is realistic enough to recognize that a methadone prescription in itself does not automatically stop opiate-using women from engaging in prostitution, it does lessen some of the pressure to 'do' a certain number of 'punters' and may reduce the likelihood of engaging in unsafe practices because of the intense pressure to obtain money for drugs (Matthews 1990; Bell, Hall, and Byth 1992).

Although the situation with regard to availability to a methadone prescription has greatly improved in Manchester, there is still a need for wider access to a range of prescribing services and, more specifically, for existing services to be flexible enough to accommodate the differing needs of drug-using prostitutes.

Conclusions

This chapter has illustrated how the general principle of a harm reduction strategy, which is fundamental to the work of the MASH project, is readily applicable to work with prostitutes. However, it is essential that attention is paid to the particular lifestyle differences and diverse needs of this community, and to the unique hostility that this type of street-based outreach work can provoke.

Resistance to this type of service provision can emanate from many sources: politicians, law-enforcement agencies, sceptical funding bodies, local residents, and even those practitioners opposed to the philosophy of harm reduction. Although it is necessary to recognize these hurdles, they should not be regarded as a barrier to getting a service off the ground. Once a service is established, resistance is likely to decline, or at least become more muted. It is particularly important to prepare the ground carefully for any proposed project. Clear aims and objectives, a shared understanding between management and 'grass-roots' workers, and an established history of interagency liaison are crucial factors during the preparatory stages.

However, the success of the service will depend much less on the attitudes of external agencies, and more on its ability to attract a significant client base among prostitutes and drug users. If it is ultimately to have any real impact in terms of harm reduction, an outreach-style service must be able to attract and retain its client group by designing a service that fulfils a wide range of criteria.

Because of the stigma attached to prostitution, there is an inherent mistrust of statutory services and, particularly for female clients with children, there is a very real fear of social-service agencies taking their children into care, despite government-endorsed recommendations that 'drug use per se is never ... seen as a reason for separating parent and child' (ACMD 1988). Therefore, if any work in this area is being planned, it is essential to define the basis on which the project will operate. Clearly a service that is viewed as separate from mainstream statutory agencies will inevitably be more approachable.

Once established, it is essential that the service be available in the vicinity where prostitutes work and operate opening hours that suit its clients' working patterns (i.e., late at night). It must ultimately strive to function as an easy-access, 'user friendly' service that is sensitive to the needs of an often marginalized and distrustful client group.

The service should, ideally, be staffed by a combination of specialist drugs/HIV staff in addition to generic workers who have other relevant skills and experience, such as ex-drug users and youth and community workers. Such a broad spectrum of staffing will be conducive to the provision of an approachable, non-threatening environment in which clients will feel at ease. Staff also need to be aware of, and sensitive to, the differences in working practices and lifestyles between female and male, and drug-using and non-drug-using, prostitutes, as well as the disparities between street sex workers operating in different 'beats' within the same city. In terms of service delivery, any agency should strive towards a more holistic approach incorporating, if possible, GUM, HIV counselling and testing, welfare rights, and midwifery input into the drugs and sexual-health aspects of the service.

Unfortunately, there are no ready-made formulae for success in terms of establishing a harm reduction strategy targeting women and men prostitutes. As Green states: 'The female streetworker prostitute is a complex phenomenon not amenable to simplistic evaluation or remedies' (Green et al. 1993: 331). However, there is evidence from within and beyond the UK that projects can work effectively in this potentially sensitive area and achieve demonstrable results, in both quantitative and qualitative terms (Kleinegris 1991; van Beek et al. 1993).

The essence of this chapter, however, is to emphasize that harm reduction as an isolated theoretical philosophy is limited. Only when significant numbers of drug users are attracted into appropriate services catering for their specific needs can harm reduction as a principle have any real impact on the overall quality of clients' lives. The experience of MASH has demonstrated that this particular approach can attract significant numbers of 'hard-to-reach' prostitutes and drug users, and facilitate an environment in which they feel comfortable enough to discuss issues around drug use and sex that can, in turn, bring about very real changes in relation to high-risk drug use and sexual behaviour. Over the last five years MASH has made a significant impact in terms of improving the health of this often marginalized and stigmatized group of drug users, and has clearly illustrated that a high-quality, professional service can be provided within an informal setting.

NOTES

1 Personal communication: Assistant Chief Constable, Greater Manchester Police Force.
2 'Persons Charged with Immoral Offences in Greater Manchester between January 1995 and December 1995.' Source: Police Principal Offence figures.
3 *Sunday Times* (London) 21 June 1987; *Daily Record* (Glasgow) 16 March 1988; *The Times* (London) 18 March 1988.

REFERENCES

Advisory Council on the Misuse of Drugs. 1988. *AIDS and Drug Misuse Part 1.* London: HMSO.
– 1989. *AIDS and Drug Misuse Part 2.* London: HMSO.
– 1993. *AIDS and Drug Misuse Update.* London: HMSO.
Barnard, M. 1993. 'Risky Business.' *International Journal of Drug Policy* 4:(3).
Barnard, M., N. McKeganey, and M. Bloor. 1990. 'A Risky Business.' *Community Care* 821: 26–7.
Bell, J., W. Hall, and K. Byth. 1992. 'Changes in Criminal Activity after Entering Methadone Maintenance.' *British Journal of Addiction* 87(2): 251–9.
Bloor, M.J., N.P. McKeganey, and M.A. Barnard. 1990. 'An Ethnographic Study of Male Prostitution and Risks of HIV Spread in Glasgow: A Report of a Pilot Study.' *AIDS Care* 2: 17–24.
Burke, T. 1991. 'Streetwise on Streetlife.' *Young People Now* 31: 23–5.

Cockrell, J., and D. Hoffman. 1989. 'Identifying the Needs of Boys at Risk in Prostitution.' *Children Worldwide* 14(3).

Darrow, W.W. 1984. 'Prostitution and Sexually Transmitted Diseases.' In K.K. Holmes, P.A. Mardh, P.E. Sparling, and P.J. Wesner, eds, *Sexually Transmitted Diseases*. New York: McGraw-Hill.

Day, S., and H. Ward. 1990. 'The Praed Street Project: A Cohort of Prostitute Women in London.' In M. Plant, ed., *AIDS, Drugs and Prostitution*. London: Tavistock/Routledge.

Day, S., H. Ward, and J.W.R. Harris. 1988. 'Prostitute Women and Public Health.' *British Medical Journal* 297: 1585.

Donmall, M., and T. Millar. 1995. 'Do Syringe Exchange Schemes Attract Different Clients from Services Providing Treatment?' University of Manchester Drug Misuse Research Unit, paper presented at the 6th International Conference on the Reduction of Drug Related Harm, Florence, Italy.

Faugier J., C. Hayes, and C.A. Butterworth. 1992. 'Drug Using Prostitutes, Their Health Care Needs, and Their Clients.' Manchester: University of Manchester, Department of Nursing.

Foster, C. 1991. 'Male Youth Prostitution: Perspectives, Policy and Practice.' *Social Work Monographs*, no. 100. Norwich, University of East Anglia.

Fuecht, T.E. 1993. 'Prostitutes on Crack Cocaine: Addiction, Utility, and Marketplace Economics.' *Deviant Behaviour. An Interdisciplinary Journal* 14: 91–108.

Gibson, B. 1992. 'Young Homeless Men Selling Sex in Central London: Identifying their HIV/AIDS Educational Needs.' Poster presentation at 8th International Conference on AIDS/STD World Congress, Amsterdam, July.

Goldberg, D.J., S.T. Green, J.C.P. Kingdom, et al. 1988. 'HIV Infection among Female Drug Abusing Prostitutes in Greater Glasgow.' *Communicable Diseases Bulletin* (Scotland) 88: 1–3.

Goldstein, P.J. 1979. *Prostitution and Drugs*. Lexington, MA: Lexington Books.

Gossop, M., B. Powis, P. Griffiths, and J. Strang. 1994. 'Sexual Behaviour and Its Relation to Drug Taking amongst Prostitutes in South London.' *Addiction* 89: 961–70.

Greater Manchester Police Strategy Plan (undated). *Drug Misuse Strategic Action Plan.*

Green, S.T., D.J. Goldberg, P.R. Christie, M. Frischer, A. Thomson, S.V. Carr, and A. Taylor. 1993. 'Female Streetworkers – Prostitutes in Glasgow: A Descriptive Study of Their Lifestyle.' *AIDS Care* 5: 321–35.

Kinnell, H. 1989. 'Prostitutes, Their Clients and Risks of HIV Infection in Birmingham.' Occasional paper. Department of Public Health and Medicine, University of Birmingham, Birmingham.

Kinnell, H. 1993. 'Prostitutes Exposure to Rape: Implications for HIV Prevention and for Legal Reform.' Paper presented to the 7th Social Aspects of AIDS Conference, June.

Kinnell, H., and S. Sandys. 1993. 'Services for Sex Workers.' In P. Scott, ed., *National AIDS Manual*, vol. I. London: N.A.M. Publications.

Kleinegris, M. 1991. 'Innovative AIDS Prevention among Drug Using Prostitutes.' Paper presented to the 2nd International Conference on the Reduction of Drug Related Harm, Barcelona, March.

McKeganey, N., and M. Barnard. 1992. *AIDS, Drugs and Sexual Risk – Lives in the Balance*. Milton Keynes: Open University Press.

– 1996. *Sex Work on the Streets: Prostitutes and Their Clients*. Buckingham: Open University Press.

McKeganey, N.P., M.A. Barnard, and M.J. Bloor. 1990. 'A Comparison of HIV Related Risk Behaviour and Risk Reduction between Female Street Working Prostitutes and Male Rent Boys in Glasgow.' *Sociology of Health and Illness* 12: 274–92.

MASH. 1994. 'Results from a Survey of 58 Service Users.' Internal report, Manchester Action on Street Health.

Matthews, L. 1990. 'Outreach Work with Female Prostitutes in Liverpool.' In M. Plant, ed., *AIDS, Drugs and Prostitution*. London: Tavistock/Routledge.

Morgan-Thomas, R. 1990. 'AIDS Risks, Alcohol, Drugs and the Sex Industry: A Scottish Study.' In M. Plant, ed., *AIDS, Drugs and Prostitution*. London: Tavistock/Routledge.

Morgan-Thomas, R., M.A. Plant, M.L. Plant, and D.I. Sales. 1989. 'Risk of AIDS among Workers in the "Sex Industry": Some Initial Results from a Scottish Study.' *British Medical Journal* 299: 148–9.

Parker, H., K. Bakx, and R. Newcombe. 1988. *Living with Heroin: The Impact of a Drugs 'Epidemic' on an English Community*. Milton Keynes: Open University Press.

Pearson, G. 1987. *The New Heroin Users*. Oxford: Blackwell.

Plant, M. 1990. 'Sex Work, Alcohol, Drugs and AIDS.' In M. Plant, ed., *AIDS, Drugs and Prostitution*. London: Tavistock/Routledge.

Synn Stern, L. 1992. 'Self-Injecting Education for Street Level Sex Workers.' In P.A. O'Hare, R. Newcombe, A. Matthews, E.C. Buning, and E. Drucker, eds, *The Reduction of Drug-Related Harm*. London: Tavistock/Routledge.

University of Manchester Drug Misuse Research Unit. 1994. 'Participation of Syringe Exchange Schemes in the Drug Misuse Database.' Drug Misuse Research Unit, University of Manchester, Manchester.

van Beek, I., R. Buckley, P. Hill, and J. Kaldor. 1993. *HIV Prevention in a Primary*

Care Setting. Paper presented to the 4th International Conference on the Reduction of Drug Related Harm, Rotterdam, March.

West, D.J, in assoc. with B. de Villiers. 1992. *Male Prostitution: Gay Sex Services in London*. London: Duckworth and Co.

25 A Harm Reduction Approach to Treating Older Adults: The Clients Speak

KATHRYN GRAHAM, PAMELA J. BRETT, and JANE BARON

Only a small proportion of persons who attend conventional addictions treatment programs are older adults (Ellis and Rush 1993; Moos et al. 1993). While this may partly be attributable to older people having a lower rate of alcohol problems compared to younger adults, it is also true that many people (both old and young) experience serious alcohol-related problems but are unwilling to participate in conventional addictions treatment programs. Although there has been increasing focus in the addictions field on early identification and on recruitment into treatment through workplace programs and the courts, there have been relatively few attempts to make treatment more acceptable to people by focusing on harm reduction rather than on the person's problem behaviour. This distinction is particularly relevant to older people who may be reluctant to enter treatment because (a) they do not wish to become abstinent in their remaining years or (b) they have tried treatment in the past and do not believe it will work for them. In addition, harm reduction is especially important for older people because their vulnerability to life-threatening health consequences of alcohol and drug use is greater than for younger people.

Just over a decade ago, a new approach was developed to intervene with older persons who were experiencing alcohol or drug problems, and two programs for older people based on this approach were developed at about the same time: the LESA program (Lifestyle Enrichment for Senior Adults; Bergin and Baron 1992) and the COPA program (Community Older Persons Alcohol Program; Graham et al. 1995). The programs were designed to reach a broad group of older people, including those who refused conventional addictions treatment. The approach was holistic and incorporated a non-confrontational model based on harm reduction and health enhancement.

Both LESA and COPA adopted an explicit harm reduction approach based on helping the person on his or her own terms and accepting improvement, rather than full remission, as a goal. The approach was based on the recognition that (a) many older substance abusers would die of the harmful effects of alcohol and other drugs before agreeing to abstain, and (b) many of these same persons, if counselled appropriately, could improve their lives substantially by reducing harmful use.

In particular, in order to reach older people, the new approach was pragmatic, focusing on making health changes rather than on breaking down 'denial.' The approach was based on the experience of health-care workers (Graham, Saunders, and Flower 1989) that older persons, who would not consider treatment for alcohol or drug problems or who had given up on conventional abstinence-oriented treatment, were often willing to become involved in programs where the focus was on reducing the harm caused by alcohol and drug use, rather than on their use per se.

These programs for older people were among the first to distance themselves from the traditional tenet that treatment would only be successful if the person admitted to and focused on the substance problem. The extent to which this was a radical approach is evident from the following quote from a recent article on controlled drinking: 'Many on the abstinence side of the issue are so strict about denial that they refuse treatment to any addict who refuses to abstain. They argue that a clinician who counsels an addict who is drinking is actually perpetuating denial by agreeing that the patient can get help without addressing the primary problem' (Morgan and Cohen 1993: 710).

Clearly, achieving specific goals with clients usually (although not always) involved reducing the use of or abstaining from alcohol and other problem drugs. However, the focus of the program on promoting healthy lifestyles and *reducing problems* rather than on substance use per se, was not simply a trick to entice clients into treatment. By focusing on the *harm associated with substance use* rather than solely on use, both the counsellor and the client could consider a broad range of solutions, of which abstinence was only one. For example, a person could be drinking because she is socially isolated; at the same time, her drunkenness may be causing others to avoid her. If suitable social options are made available to the person during the day, she might choose to delay drinking until evening, while still allowing herself the option of drinking the same overall amount per day (i.e., there is no explicit focus here on reducing use). However, the delay of drinking and the incentive to feel well for the next day's activities may result in a self-reinforcing reduction of alcohol use, with no feelings of loss or self-deprivation and with no specific focus on drinking or on being an 'alcoholic.' Similarly, a person who began drinking or using prescribed medications following the death of a spouse may find, in developing a rapport with the counsellor or group, that his desire to use substances is reduced because he has been able to deal with unresolved grief. Finally, the focus on problems rather than use reduces the stigma of slips and relapses.

In sum, the approach was developed to reflect a harm reduction/ health enhancement philosophy. However, although a holistic harm reduction approach guided the development of the program, there is an essential tension in a *treatment* program that is addiction-specific but not focused on substance-using behaviour. Namely, it is possible that the harm reduction aspects of the program are less apparent to the clients and that most clients ultimately perceive the program as a version of conventional addiction treatment. Certainly, there has been some research to suggest that patients have different perspectives on what is wanted, needed, and provided than do caretakers (Hornstra et al. 1972). Accordingly, it is an empirical question whether clients see the program as focusing primarily on reducing their problems (i.e., harm reduction) rather than on the substance use or abuse per se (i.e., the conventional approach). This study used qualitative analyses of interview data to assess the clients' understanding of this form of treatment, particularly their understanding of the program as one of harm reduction rather than conventional addictions treatment.

Method

This study was conducted at the LESA (Lifestyle Enrichment for Adults) program in Ottawa, Ontario.

Program Components

The LESA program contains three components: individual counselling, men's and women's group meetings, and social outings. Usually, in the beginning, the client is involved in individual counselling. When the person has been engaged in the process, he or she is invited to attend group meetings as well. The social outings occur about once a month and are open to everyone. All components are considered to be useful in helping the person make changes in his or her life. There is no set number of counselling sessions and clients may attend the group for as long as they choose. Usually, the frequency of individual counselling sessions decreases as the client improves until counselling is no longer needed. The group meetings and outings serve both as active treatment and as aftercare. In addition, individual counselling can be reactivated if clients in aftercare experience a period where they need additional support. Most clients receive at least some individual counselling, although a few have used the group meetings as their primary vehicle for change. Some clients prefer to receive only individual counselling and do not attend group meetings or outings. Others receive individual counselling and attend outings, but do not choose to attend group meetings.

Sample

The data were collected as part of a preliminary phase in developing a client-participatory evaluation study of the LESA program. Therefore clients were not chosen randomly for the case-study interviews. Specifically, the sample excluded clients who were at the early stages of involvement with the program, as this is a sensitive and critical time for engagement. Otherwise, clients were chosen to reflect a broad spectrum of backgrounds, substance-related problems, and phase of treatment (including clients who were no longer attending any parts of the program). Interviews were conducted with thirteen LESA clients (nine males and four females). The ages of the respondents ranged from 56 to 76. Table 1 (pp. 434ff.) provides a brief description of the cases who were interviewed for the study.

Format of the Interview and Analyses

The interviews were unstructured and conducted by researchers (Brett, Graham) who had no formal affiliation with the program. Clients were asked to be interviewed as part of work being done to evaluate and improve the program. The first question was generally something like 'Tell me about your experience at LESA.' The interviewer allowed the participant to respond to this question from whatever perspective he or she chose and encouraged elaboration and discussion of related topics. The interviewer tried to ensure that the following topics were discussed at some point during the interview: nature of involvement with the LESA program (i.e., individual counselling, group, social events), reasons for coming to the program initially, nature and extent of changes made while involved in the program, ways in which the LESA program helped the person make changes, and suggestions for improving the program.

Analysis of Clients' Perceptions of Harm Reduction

The interview did not include specific questions about 'harm reduction.' To address this issue, transcripts were examined to identify those aspects of the program that clients perceived to be directed towards minimizing problems related to alcohol and drug use and making their lives better generally, as opposed to those focused primarily on *use* of alcohol or drugs or on abstinence. Thus, for the present analysis, harm reduction was defined as the counsellor or program accepting the client's behaviour and attitude regarding substance use, and working within that frame to identify strategies for reducing the harmful effects of alcohol or drug use and improving the client's quality of life. The program is similar to conventional treatment programs in recommending abstinence as the most direct route to harm reduction. However, it is also similar to non-treatment harm reduction interventions in that the *primary* goal is reducing harm and improving quality of life (however that can be achieved) rather than the primary goal being abstinence or reduced use.

Results

Clients' views on aspects related to harm reduction will be described separately for each program component: individual counselling, group meetings, and social outings. Finally, a fourth 'component' of the program was identified by clients in the interviews. This component consisted of the availability of support from program staff generally (including the program secretary, often mentioned by name). Since this aspect of the program seemed to affect clients independently from the three identified components, this was deemed to be a fourth active component of the program.

Individual Counselling

Several aspects of individual counselling were identified as being consistent with a harm reduction approach: unconditional support, a broad focus on problem-solving, the non-confrontational attitude of the counsellor, and a general focus on overall lifestyle rather than on substance use.

TABLE 1
Characteristics of LESA clients who participated in the interviews

Age and sex	Substance(s) abused and substance-related problems	Duration and background regarding problem use	Participation in LESA program	Status at time of interview
73 M	Benzodiazepines, anti-depressants and analgesics. Overuse of prescribed medications.	Five years of using psychoactive medications, with the previous two years (since death of wife) involving misuse.	A counsellor had visited him regularly at his home and he had attended a few social outings.	Not using depressant or anti-depressant drugs.
65 M	Alcohol. He drank heavily every day.	He had a long history of very heavy drinking, including several attempts at treatment, but was socially stable (married, steady employment).	He had received individual conselling at LESA, counselling from a psychiatrist specializing in addictions, and attended group meetings and social events.	Abstinent (had two slips).
62 M	Alcohol. Heavy regular and binge drinking.	He had a long history of alcohol problems, including skid-row lifestyle at times.	He received some indivi-dual counselling at first, but most of his involvement was with the group and attending social outings.	Has the occasional drink.
58 M	Alcohol. Very heavy drinking with repeated admissions to detox before attending LESA.	He had a long history of heavy drinking and had attended numerous treatment programs, but none had been successful.	He had received individual counselling and had attended group meetings and social events.	Abstinent for several years.

Table 1 – continued

56 M	Alcohol. He had been drinking heavily and also experiencing panic attacks and depression.	He had a long history of problem drinking with a long period of abstinence during which he developed a problem with prescribed medications. He had received treatment previously.	He participated in individual counselling, group meetings, and outings.	Abstinent (with at least one relapse).
71 M	Alcohol. Moderately heavy drinking and possibly other psychiatric problems.	He provided little information on his drinking history.	Mostly he received individual counselling, but he reported attending two social outings. He had recently started attending a geriatric day program.	He reported that he had reduced his drinking from 4-5 nights a week to 3 nights a week.
65 M	Alcohol. [No information on pattern of use.]	He had experienced some alcohol problems over the years, but problems had worsened when his wife died.	He had been referred to LESA for aftercare following in-patient addictions treatment. He participated in individual counselling, group meetings and social outings.	Abstinent since in-patient treatment (a year prior).
76 M	Alcohol. He was a chronic heavy drinker.	He was a lifetime heavy drinker, but had a stable marriage and work history. Apparently no prior treatment.	He had received individual counselling and had attended some group meetings and a few outings.	Abstinent (significant health problems precluded current drinking).
56 M	Alcohol. At the time of referral he had been living on welfare and doing nothing but drinking. He also experienced depression and suicidal ideation.	He began heavy drinking when he split up with his wife.	He participated in individual counselling, group meetings, and social outings. He also saw a psychiatrist.	Intermittent bouts of drinking.

Table 1 – concluded

Age and sex	Substance(s) abused and substance-related problems	Duration and background regarding problem use	Participation in LESA program	Status at time of interview
67 F	Alcohol. She reported that she drank to lessen the pain of her psychiatric problems.	She had a long history of steady drinking. She had seen a psychiatrist in the past, but her first addictions treatment had been just before attending LESA.	Her involvement with the program consisted mainly of attending group meetings.	Abstinent
68 F	Alcohol.	She began to have serious alcohol problems following the death of her husband. She attended AA and a residential addiction treatment program, from which she was referred to LESA.	She participated in individual counselling and group meetings.	[Unknown from interview data.]
72 F	Alcohol. She drank heavily and was experiencing negative consequences from drinking.	She developed drinking problems after retiring. She had been referred for a psychogeriatric assessment following which she gave up drinking on her own but also became involved with LESA.	Mostly she attended group meetings, but a counsellor also visited her at home occasionally.	Abstinent.
57 F	Alcohol. Heavy drinking as well as health consequences related to drinking.	She had been a heavy drinker for many years, but her drinking had increased after retirement, resulting in hospitalization. She was referred to LESA from the hospital.	She participated in individual counselling, group meetings, and outings. She also attended a residential addictions program at the suggestion of the LESA counsellor.	Probably abstinent.

Note: These descriptions were derived from information provided during interviews with the clients and not from program records.

Unconditional Support
Harm reduction implies that help is not *conditional* on whether the person abstains from alcohol or drugs. When asked how exactly the counsellor had helped them, clients often described how nice the counsellor had been to them and how much this meant to them. Although clients did not usually identify unconditional support explicitly, not one of the clients described the counsellor's support as conditional on the client's avoiding alcohol or drugs (see quotes 1 and 2, table 2).

A Broad Focus on Problem-Solving
Clearly, one means to harm reduction is to provide clients with education not only regarding potential and observed harm from substance use and how to avoid this harm, but also introducing alternatives to substance use. Several clients described this educational element as one of the factors that helped them, such as education regarding non-drug alternatives to sleep problems (see quote 3, table 2). In addition, the broader focus beyond substance use was recognized and mentioned by several clients (see quotes 4, 5, and 6). Sometimes, the problem solving was quite practical, as in the instance of a client who was going through a particularly bad time in his life and had been focusing on jumping from his twelfth-floor balcony. The LESA counsellor helped him obtain an apartment on a lower floor!

Non-Confrontational Attitude of the Counsellor
Some of the clients described suggestions made by the counsellor about their alcohol or drug use, but none reported pressure from the counsellor. To the contrary, some explicitly described the lack of pressure and how well this approach suited them (see quotes 7, 8, 9, and 10). One interviewee, who had become abstinent at the time of referral to LESA and who had received individual counselling but had not attended group meetings, provided an interesting perspective on the non-confrontational aspect of the LESA program. Her comments also illustrate the logical conflict that can occur in a program that includes both addictions counselling and harm reduction:

(Looking at evaluating how well the program works for people, do you have any ideas how we might best ask people about that?) Well, no, not really. Although, it's funny you should mention that. I think it was before Christmas that at one of the outings, we were still around the table from eating and one of the, ahh ..., one of the counsellors, ... she was very jokey about it, 'How long has it been since anyone had a drink?' (Hmm, hmm.) So forth. Well, I think it took everybody by surprise. So somebody put her hand up and said 8 years. Well, that was terrific, so we all clapped I guess. But people seemed afraid. Now I don't think I put my hand up either, because I was going to say 2 years. And then I kind of chickened out for some reason or another. But you get the impression that nobody wanted to say because, and I'll tell you why nobody wanted to say was because apparently with the LESA they still can have a drink. (They still can?) Well, they seem to. You see that's what I told Christine, I can't understand. Why do they go if they still have drinks? (What did Christine say?) Well you kind of get the idea that – I don't know their policy is that if you want to have a drink you can have one, but they prefer that you didn't. They prefer that you don't, but they can't tell you that no, that no way can you drink. They won't dictate to you like.

Focus on Overall Lifestyle, Not Just Drinking or Drug Use

As described in the introduction, LESA is an acronym for 'Lifestyle Enrichment for Senior Adults.' And, while all the clients interviewed were aware that they had been referred to the program because of their alcohol or drug use, they all appeared to be clear regarding the broader focus of the program, as demonstrated by quote 11 in table 2.

Group Meetings

Over the years of the program and despite the changing membership, the men's group meetings have been particularly successful. Of the nine men interviewed, six had attended group meetings. All six were extremely positive about these meetings, with many indicating that these meetings were currently a critical part of their lives. Similarly, three of the four women interviewed had attended group meetings, and all three saw the group as a major factor in improving their lives.

Besides reporting generally that they enjoyed the group, all of those clients who attended group meetings identified similar aspects that they found helpful: contact with others who were the same age and had similar problems, the focus of the group on problem-solving in the here and now (rather than on past drinking problems), and the respect, support, and friendship that group members received from one another. These features were often contrasted to AA (the conventional treatment that most had either experienced or were familiar with). While comparisons of LESA with AA were not solicited by the interviewer, most interviewees had very definite ideas of how LESA meetings differed from those of AA.

TABLE 2
Harm reduction from the perspective of LESA clients

Program component	Quotes by the clients regarding that component
Individual counselling	
• Unconditional support	1 She's very available and she said to me a million times, 'Just give me a call. I'm here for you.'
	2 Well, she's such a, such a nice person and someone that you'd ... feel very comfortable with and you can talk to without being embarrassed about anything or feeling, well, do I have to say this or does it really matter. You just go ahead and say, and if she asks you a question you answer it honestly.
• A broad focus on problem solving	3 (In what ways did she help?) Well, by just talking to me really. It's, I, at that time when I got home I wasn't able to sleep and, not very good, and I wasn't eating, wasn't getting along very good for a while. She kept coming and just talking to me, and tell me about things I should do or try to do, and eventually it got back to normal again. I'm OK now. That was in January. I don't take any medications now.
-	4 But thanks to LESA I got, well, volunteer work at the hospital on Tuesday and Wednesday, and Thursday is LESA, and Friday and Monday is what I call my two days off. I keep that for shopping and all that. And plus LESA got me in contact with, well, different places where you can go to get like medical stuff.
	5 I started to feel I needed help somewhere else in the home. I never cooked a meal in my life. LESA saw to it that I had ... for instance, the Homecare, the VON, now I have the VON three times a week.
	6 Well, sometimes you want to know something about say the social services, or you want to know some clinics, or something, or some type of ... Like before that, I didn't know that there was foot doctor come here.
• Non-confrontational attitude of the counsellor	7 He would say, 'Try to cut down on your drinking.' Didn't tell you QUIT drinking cause I still haven't quit drinking, but I find it's easier to turn down a beer now than I did before.
	8 If anybody had pushed me I probably would have gone the other way. As a matter of fact, I probably would have said, 'Don't come and visit me again.' Because it makes you feel uncomfortable. You know that what you're doing is wrong. And you don't need someone

Table 2 – continued

Program component	Quotes by the clients regarding that component
	to tell you that. But somehow they manage to put that across without saying it. Umm, I'd like to know how they did that, too, now that I think about it (laughter).
	9 You know they are professional, those ladies, professionals. They don't come and say, 'Did you drink last night?' 'Can I look in your fridge to see if you have a case of beer?' I mean they don't go like that, because the door is there, this is my home not theirs.
	10 ... I had a relapse and it was a very bad experience. I could come here and just go on from where I finished before. Nobody made me feel guilty or anything like that.
• Focus on overall lifestyle	11 She visited, yeah. Yeah, well, when you first start they keep very close touch with you. So that, they come to see you almost once a week. Which is a great help. You know, because they come, they're very interested in how you're doing, and what's going on in your life besides drinking, or have you eaten right, and, you know, different things like that, are you, you know, or ... It's, it's, the idea I think that somebody, like, having somebody come over and visit you, they're interested in seeing how you are, and if you're sober, and, you know, that you're living, if you're living all right. It's not only the stop drinking, you got to live properly, too, you know.
Group meetings	
• Contact with others the same age	12 You look at the person and say. 'Now, that's a lady' and yet she has the same problem, exactly the same problem. Not exactly the same – everything is a little different, but as far as the drinking is concerned the pattern is the same.
	13 My contact with LESA was good because I met other people in the same boat that I was in – like recently retired and time on their hands.
	14 ... and plus I enjoy the meetings. You learn, you know, you do learn, I mean they, you know, they broach many subjects and, I just think you learn from other people as well. You know, they talk about a struggle that they had. Perhaps you didn't have that same one but you still find out that, you know, everybody went through a great deal to get to where they are right now.

Table 2 – continued

	15	And the thing is, even in the hospital, most of the other patients are at least 25, 30 or 40 years younger than you are, So, you seem to think, 'Oh well, I'm a completely isolated case.' You find out you're not. (When you're in these groups with LESA?) Yeah. 'Cause there are quite a few of older people – just single people or widows. Just happens, only they don't go to pubs or have parties or anything like that. (Like the younger people?) Yeah.
	16	The problem with AA is, there is too many drug addicts. We know it's all, you know, it's all the same, it's supposed to be the same thing. One you get the pill, one you get liquid. But to a person like myself that has nothing, has nothing to do with drugs, don't understand them, and people get up there and start telling you about smoking pot, taking needles and all that, you sort of lose interest, because you don't know anything about it.
	17	... and there are things there you learn from it, you know, I mean, things you didn't know. Some people have problems or something, and they bring that up, and somebody will have an answer for it, or where to go or what to do. I just see them there, listening they can – you know, I learned a lot about, you know, different things.
	18	And if you have a problem or have any questions you're quite free. You have your turn to speak. And you're heard and everybody listens and if anybody has an answer you find out. And if they don't, there is always somebody who has an idea of where you can go to get the answers.
• Focus of the group on current problems	19	With the LESA program, another thing I like about the LESA program, we don't harp on alcoholism. We talk about the weather, we talk about different things that's happening in the world, 'cause at our age, at 50 years or 55 or older ... We know we got the problem. You know what I mean? I mean we got enough brains upstairs to know that we got a problem. You know, the doctor will tell you that, or anybody even, you know. Why, why do we have to sit there for an hour and listen to somebody who lost his wife, lost a car, lost (...?), you know. (laughter) And they're 'has-beens' at 20 years old. Do you understand what I mean? Very ... to me it's very boring going to an AA meeting. I think it's a waste of time, you know.

Table 2 – continued

Program component	Quotes by the clients regarding that component
• Respect, support, and friendships of group members	20 ... because you know you're an alcoholic but you don't want to be reminded of it all the time. At least the group talks about everything. I talk about my daughter sometimes or just what you do through the week.
	21 And again, I must, I have LESA to thank for meeting people that have become good friends of mine – not in drinking, you know, but friends, you know.
	22 She's a real friend. If we hadn't met here, we wouldn't have met anywhere else. It's helped her and it's helped me.
Social Outings	
• A safe environment for socializing	23 ... I don't know too many people here in Ottawa, and when I was drinking I never went to too many places. I didn't want to waste my time going around – I stayed at home drinking. And, when I got into LESA program, at least I be in these outings, and they were good! ... Well, it helps, I mean, it's, it gives you, say you are, you go out and you play games and you want to, you don't have to, nobody's going to push you in. Or, if you want to say something, you can say something. Nobody's going to push you. But for an alcoholic, it takes them a long time before he say what he thinks.
• Enriching lives of people who have few options	24 ... you play lawn croquet or there's cards or bean bag. It seems to get everybody up and doing something. And then we have a bite to eat. The drive is always nice. We're always kidding someone on the bus about something. Only a few hours – but it's really relaxing. Just sit sit back, even fall asleep on the bus going out there you're so relaxed that it's ... (You don't go on any other trips like that with any other organization?) No ... Very helpful. Because if there wasn't any trips, I'd be stuck in Ottawa, nothing to do.
	25 ... and them trips are just terrific, get you out of town. Just marvellous. All of them trips, yeah. There's another thing that, you know, that makes them – some of them are boxed in a, you know, a bachelor apartment, or a one bedroom apartment. So they get out for a day and it's great.

Table 2 – concluded

| *General support from the program* | 26 | ... But I think maybe now that – I think she thinks I'm improved a whole lot since she first came, and she doesn't come as often now. That's the routine they have and, it's, and I find, you know, all the – there's Diane, and there's April, and there's Christine. A couple more. I forget their names now, but they're all nice and they're all willing to help, when we go on the trips, all of us, you know, to see that we're enjoying ourselves of – they're all well-liked, all the group likes them. |
| | 27 | They just seem to be there and they cared, give you a hug every once in a while ... Now, Christine is helping me and I don't know what I'd do without them really. As soon as I come in, I talk to Jane, I talk to Christine, I talk to April, or I go and see the doctor downstairs – It's just they're all there and you know they're there ... Well, I walked in off the street and whoever was here, I bent their ear. (laughter) Because sometimes I'm just feeling like drinking. And I walked into the hotel and I'd sit down. They'd say, 'Do you want a beer?' I'd say, 'No, I've forgotten something' ... and walk over here. |

Contact with Others the Same Age

There were several aspects of having contact with others of the same age that were identified as useful. First, for some people, finding others 'in the same boat' was reassuring (see quote 12). Having contact with people of about the same age and who had similar problems was also seen as important in that members of the group could understand one another (see quotes 13, 14, and 15). This was often compared to AA meetings, where some interviewees felt that the problems of younger people were so different that there was no common ground (see quote 16).

Focus of the Group on Current Problems

The aspect of the group that clients found most useful seemed to be the focus on current problems. The group was often cited as a source of information and problem solving (see quotes 17 and 18). Again, this 'here and now' focus of LESA meetings was contrasted to experience at AA (see quotes 19 and 20) and clearly demonstrates the harm reduction/health enhancement approach of the LESA group.

Respect, Support, and Friendships of Group Members

A number of people mentioned not only the conviviality of the group, but also that it provided a *trustworthy* social network. Perhaps because of the group's broad focus or because of the presence of a group facilitator, some members reported that they had found a safer environment for social relationships at LESA than they had experienced at self-help groups such as AA. One client was particularly clear in articulating the respect and trust of the group, especially in contrast with his experience at AA:

... I know that many times, because I have done it myself – just to get out of the cold I go to the meeting [AA] with a bottle on me. And sometimes a guy will say, 'Want a shot?' 'Sure,' you know. (At the AA meeting?) Yeah. And you always meet somebody there that ... and you know that he has money, well then you say, 'Ahh!' If we have a couple of drinks we can go at it again, you know. A lot of people go to the meeting for that, you know. (And why doesn't that happen with the LESA group?) Because ahh – I don't know, it's just different. If I take a drink, I wouldn't go. And that's the way many of us feel, that way. If you drink, why should you go there? ... A lot of these guys too, they go to these meetings [AA], they meet somebody and they borrow money off them, you know. I know, I never went to a meeting yet, that nobody asked me there if I had any change for the next bottle. But I've been going to these meetings [LESA] for two years now. Nobody asked me for a dime yet!

Several people reported that they had developed real friendships in the group (see quotes 21 and 22). Another interviewee had experienced success with AA, but when he relapsed following retirement he felt that his social relationships at AA had been dependent on his sobriety, and he contrasted his experience at AA with the less hierarchial acceptance of the LESA group:

Oh, they're friendly [AA contacts], but I don't go on out-of-town meetings with them and all that. They're clannish and they got this 20 years sobriety – will have 20 years and I would have got 20 years in June you see. Well they got this, they call it 'old timers' now. So I don't go with them anymore you see. I don't know what they think of me, 'cause I got a weak mind. I don't practise my steps and traditions. (laughter) I don't know. I could care less. The thing is I go to LESA and it's accepted here you know. So what, you're here today. There's no one-year medallion, there you did good, and all that. It's, I think LESA ... (They take you as you come?) As you come. Counsellors, counselling they will help you a lot to discover why you went back drinking. I mean we're all in the group together. Like in AA, 'Oh, he drank last year,' you know. 'He won't get his five years this year or 10 years,' you know. That kind of, what you describe, doesn't exist with LESA.

Social Outings

Early in the development of the LESA program, some clients described how, living in city apartments, they missed being in the country (where many had grown up). They often experienced a longing to get out of the city and go to the country to see the leaves change colour, and so on. In response to this expressed need, monthly outings were organized that include several trips per year to spend a day at a working farm, as well as other trips to see flowers, fall colours, ice sculptures, and so on. The outings involve lunch and an informal atmosphere – some organized activities are available (e.g., cards, croquet) for those who are interested. The formal program objective of the outings is 'to provide clients with the opportunity to consciously experience the health-enhancing effects derived from ordinary recreational activities' (Bergin and Baron 1992:

40). While a few clients interviewed did not seem to need the outings since they seemed to have successful social lives, most of those interviewed attended the outings and were very enthusiastic about them.

Those interviewed identified at least two therapeutic aspects of the outings: (1) the outings provide those who have been socially isolated or who have had long-term substance-abuse problems with a safe and accepting environment to practise their sober social skills; and (2) the outings enrich the lives of those who have few social/leisure options.

A Safe Environment for Socializing
Clients seemed to value highly the opportunity to socialize with others in the accepting environment of the outings (see quote 23).

Enriching Lives of People Who Have Few Options
Some of the clients, because of long-term health problems or lack of resources (sometimes related to long-term substance abuse), led very impoverished social lives. Several of clients mentioned the trips being one of the few real social events for themselves or for someone else (see quotes 24 and 25).

General Support from Program

Through the group, the social outings, dropping in to the program, and general interactions around appointments, most clients had contact with most or all of the LESA staff. Many commented on the helpfulness of the staff generally (see quotes 26 and 27). As stated by one client: 'I just started to feel at home here. I feel more at home here than at my own home. It's a nice feeling.'

Discussion

In this paper, 'harm reduction' as a treatment approach has been interpreted as a willingness to use a variety of strategies (not excluding abstinence) to reduce the harm caused by alcohol and/or drug use and to enhance the quality of life of the person who has problems related to alcohol and/or drugs. The two key features of the LESA program that define it as harm reduction and differentiate it from other addictions treatment program are (1) the client is not *required* to define substance-use goals or in any other way address *explicitly* their alcohol or drug use in order to receive services from the program; and (2) the goal of harm reduction/health enhancement is the primary goal of the program (with reduced use a potential means to this end).

It was apparent from the interviews that clients were quite clear regarding the harm reduction philosophy of the program. In part, their frequent references to AA reflected their recognition that the LESA program was different. Distinctions between LESA and AA that were recognized by clients included the non-confrontational approach of LESA, with much less focus on substance use; the orientation of the LESA program towards addressing current problems rather than discussing history of past use; and the lack of hierarchy based on years of sobriety. However, understanding the difference between LESA's harm reduction approach and more traditional approaches such as AA did not necessarily involve rejecting more traditional approaches. Some found it useful to attend both.

Also worth noting was the importance placed by clients on the social outings and the non-specific program support. The well-known high rate of relapse following addictions treatment attests to the problems some people experience in adapting to a sober life. One important area of this adaptation is learning to find pleasure in social events that do not involve drinking. It appears that these activities that are focused on pleasure not therapy may have had considerable therapeutic benefits for LESA clients. There appears to be no literature on the active therapeutic aspects of social outings, but from the interviews of the LESA clients, this issue merits further study.

The importance to the clients of the non-specific aspects of the program (e.g., chatting with the secretary) emerged because of the unstructured format of the interview and not as a targeted area of study. Program environment has received some attention in the evaluation of addictions treatment programs. Most noteworthy, Moos and his colleagues have examined the variability in the social climate of programs (Bromet, Moos, and Bliss 1976; Finney and Moos 1984; Moos and Finney 1988). In addition, client satisfaction measures often include items regarding the overall program and administrative aspects of the program, especially when these measures have been developed for a specific program (Graham et al. 1993). However, experimental evaluations of particular therapeutic techniques rarely take into consideration the overall context of the program environment. It may be that program atmosphere variables have little independent effect beyond the effects of the active treatment components. However, it may also be that program atmosphere has a synergistic effect with treatment or even an interactive effect (i.e., that certain treatments are only effective in specific contexts). The general program context may also be a factor in treatment retention. For example, involvement of clients in the broader program may prevent dropout associated with the unavailability of the primary counsellor (owing to illness or job changes). The program environment may be a particularly important issue when the focus is on harm reduction. In fact, a rigid and bureaucratic reception environment would be contradictory to a flexible and accepting harm reduction treatment program. This observation suggests that the overall program environment (including reception) may reflect the values and philosophy of the treatment modality. The extent that this may also influence treatment outcomes is worth considering.

The Value of Harm Reduction for Older Substance Abusers

The clients interviewed were clear and unanimous in valuing this orientation of the program. Many were in the process of restructuring their lives, either because of years of substance abuse or because they were dealing with issues of aging (e.g., retirement, losses, health issues, even taking advantage of seniors' discounts!). Accordingly, they valued the problem-solving aspects of the program, particularly the opportunities to problem-solve with their peers in same-sex groups. Many clients related how important it was to focus on current issues rather than dwell on drinking behaviours of the past as they perceived happened in AA (their perceptions of the focus of AA on past drinking have been supported by research on AA stories [Arminen 1991]). While this might be interpreted by some as 'denial,' there are several other potential explanations why this focus is particularly suited to older people. First, for some long-term alcohol abusers who have been marginalized and living on welfare, receiving the old-age pension brings greater relative wealth and greater status (i.e., being a 'pensioner' rather than a 'bum') (Graham et al. 1992). In addition, regardless of past history, clients alluded to using the program to address a variety of issues related to being older (e.g., accessing a foot doctor, finding out about activities for seniors). Moreover, problem-solving in the here and now also seemed to involve dealing with emotional issues, such as grief (including anniversaries of losses), family relationships, poor health, and dying. Finally, for some older people, the issue is not 'reforming' themselves or 'cure,' but rather making the best of their current situation. The harm reduction approach is particularly suited to this perspective.

The following conclusions can be drawn from this study of the older clients' perspectives on a harm reduction approach:

- Older persons appreciate and can make use of an approach that presents a range of options from which to choose.
- They appreciate not being 'pushed' and are able to describe how this lack of pressure worked for them.
- They see their lives in a broad context and value being able to address this context within the program.
- For some, a professionally run program provides a safer environment than they had experienced at self-help programs.

The Potential Generalizability of the Harm Reduction Approach

The harm reduction approach described here is based on helping people make the changes that they want to make in ways that they want to make them, rather than forcing people to accept the need for conventional treatment. Although developed for older people, this approach might also be useful for other age groups – not necessarily to replace traditional approaches, but rather to provide an alternative.

What about 'denial'? Previous research has demonstrated that this non-confrontational approach to older people who have alcohol or drug problems achieves considerable objective success (Graham et al. 1995). In particular, this prior research has demonstrated that acknowledging an alcohol or drug problem is not the *exclusive* road to recovery. The comments by clients described in this paper provide some insight as to how this approach is successful without the use of confrontation.

First, some clients argued that the less confrontational approach led to *greater* rather than lesser *honesty*. As one client stated, 'Why should you lie?' During the interviews, several people reported relapses and the lessons that they had learned from these relapses. Those who reported that they still drank did not provide any rationalization for this (as might be expected by someone in 'denial'). They simply stated that they drank and described various strategies they used to minimize their drinking and related problems. It should be noted that the program does *not* advocate moderate drinking; the program goal is better health, with abstinence the healthiest option. The clients appeared to understand this health goal and actively worked towards *minimizing* drinking as part of this goal. In this harm reduction/health enhancing framework, the clients, very appropriately, focused on their successes rather than on their failures. Ultimately, many clients did choose and maintain abstinence, but this was not the focus of their involvement in the program.

Second, the lack of confrontation allowed people to respond to the program in their own way and time. The value of the non-confrontational aspect of the program was particularly evident for one of the female clients. She had experienced years of drinking and psychiatric problems. When she finally entered a hospital-based addictions treatment program, she was particularly devastated by a film she saw there that emphasized the damage done to children growing up with an alcoholic parent. She reported that she was unable to respond to this intensive addictions program, even though she desperately wanted help. After initiating contact with LESA she started attending the women's group, but reported that she attended for a *year* before saying anything and only comprehending bits and pieces of what went on. Gradually, she became increasingly active in the group and at the time of the interview was actively engaged in reconstructing her life. She reported that the most important aspect of the group experience was the return of her sense of humour. Her experience in the LESA program corresponds quite well with the clinical model of recovery of chemically dependent women described by Hendrickson (1992) in which women are only able to take a proactive role in recovery after being in treatment for some time. The harm reduction approach provides an environment for each individual to engage in the process of change at his or her own pace.

These data illustrate the need and ability of persons who have alcohol and drug problems to benefit from non-addictions-focused interventions in resolving their addictions problems. Perhaps it is time for the addictions field (both treatment providers and researchers) to adopt a less dogmatic and more pragmatic approach to addressing alcohol and drug abuse, one that focuses on resolving problems. Harm reduction provides a useful framework for exploring different methods of achieving successful outcomes and recognizing that there are many ways of reducing the harm caused by excessive use of alcohol and other drugs. Although conventional approaches to treatment (including AA, as well as behavioural programs focused on drinking or drug use) have met with some success among those for whom this approach is suitable, there is no empirical support for the often stated belief that a person's drinking problem cannot be treated without a full acceptance of the problem *before* treatment. In fact, there is mounting evidence to the contrary. Similarly, there is no objective justification for addictions treatment research to focus solely on *drinking behaviour*, rather than on evaluating a range of treatment options to ameliorate problems.

REFERENCES

Arminen, I. 1991. 'Outline for Comparative Analyses of AA Life Stories: A Research Note.' *Contemporary Drug Problems*: 499–523.
Bergin, B., and J. Baron. 1992. *LESA: A Program of Lifestyle Enrichment for Senior Adults with Alcohol and Other Psychoactive Drug Problems*. Ottawa: Centretown Community Health Centre.
Bromet, E.J., R.H. Moos, and F. Bliss. 1976. 'The Social Climate of Alcoholism Treatment Programs.' *Archives of General Psychiatry* 33: 910–16.
Ellis, K., and B. Rush. 1993. *Alcohol and Other Drug Services in Ontario: Results of a Provincial Survey, 1992*. Toronto: Addiction Research Foundation.
Finney, J.W., and R.H. Moos. 1984. 'Environmental Assessment and Evaluation Research: Examples from Mental Health and Substance Abuse Programs.' *Evaluation and Program Planning* 7: 151–67.
Graham, K., B. Price, P. Brett, et al. 1993. *Directory of Client Outcome Measures for Addictions Treatment Programs*. Toronto: Addiction Research Foundation.
Graham, K., S.J. Saunders, and M. Flower. 1989. 'Approaches and Agenda of Researchers or Evaluators versus Those of Community Developers: Perspectives of the Program Developer, the Program Manager, and the Program Evaluator.' In N. Giesbrecht, P. Conley, R.W. Denniston, L. Gliksman, H. Holder, A. Pederson, R. Room, and M. Shain, eds, *Research, Action, and the Community: Experiences in the Prevention of Alcohol and Other Drug Problems*. Rockville, MD: Office for Substance Abuse Prevention.
Graham, K., S.J. Saunders, M.C. Flower, C. Birchmore Timney, M. White-Campbell, and A. Zeidman. 1995. *Addictions Treatment for Older Adults: Evaluation of an Innovative Client-Centred Approach*. New York: Haworth Press.
Graham, K., A. Zeidman, M.C. Flower, S.J. Saunders, and M. White-Campbell. 1992. 'A Typology of Elderly Persons Who Have Alcohol Problems.' *Alcoholism Treatment Quarterly* 9: 79–95.
Hendrickson, S.P. 1993. 'Women's Voices: A Guide for Listening to Chemically Dependent Women.' *Women and Therapy* 12: 73–85.
Hornstra, R.K., B. Lubin, R.V. Lewis, and B.S. Willis. 1972. 'Worlds Apart: Patients and Professionals.' *Archives of General Psychiatry* 27: 553–7.
Moos, R.H., and J.W. Finney. 1988. 'Alcoholism Program Evaluations: The Treatment Somain.' In D. J. Lettieri, ed., *Research Strategies in Alcoholism Treatment Assessment*. New York: Haworth Press.

Moos, R.H., J.R. Mertens, and P.L. Brennan. 1993. 'Patterns of Diagnosis and Treatment among Late-Middle-Aged and Older Substance Abuse Patients.' *Journal of Studies on Alcohol* 54: 479–87.

Morgan, P., and L. Cohen. 1993. 'Controlled-Drinking Advocates Challenge Use of Abstinence Model in Treatment of Addiction.' *Canadian Medical Association Journal* 149: 706–13.

26 Harm Reduction Efforts inside Canadian Prisons: The Example of Education

ANDRÉA RIESCH TOEPELL

In general, education is guided by several goals, including the intent to inform, raise awareness, or cause an effect (i.e., learn something new, revise previously learned information, change beliefs, attitudes, or behaviours, etc.). Education is inherently a beneficial facet of everyday life, and the dissemination of information through it is recognized as constructive.

Within the harm reduction model, education plays a critical role: it is the cornerstone of the model's many components. In risk prevention efforts (such as syringe-cleaning/exchange, safer sex, and substance-use alternatives), education is a vital component to successful risk reduction through behaviour change. In the promotion of policy reform, educating governments as well as the public is essential.

Despite its obvious benefits, the harm reduction perspective in education concerning safer behaviours can spark controversy. It can also intimidate, antagonize, and offend populations for whom the education is not intended. Others may ignore or simply reject such education for moral or other reasons. Implementing educational efforts in Canadian correctional settings has elicited all of the above reactions – but from people outside those for whom the programming was developed. Risk reduction education from a harm reduction perspective generated considerable consternation among correctional and public-health officials. At the same time, prisoner interest groups and community AIDS educators supported the undertaking.

This chapter provides an account of the processes involved in developing and implementing HIV/AIDS educational materials for the Canadian prison population. It describes the research and initiatives undertaken to ensure the production of accessible and prison culture–

sensitive resources, and the negotiative efforts necessary for these materials to be distributed in correctional facilities. It also discusses the politics that gave rise to controversy and censorship, and compares provincial prisons and federal penitentiaries with respect to the harm reduction efforts implemented in them.

As described by Cohen (1993), harm reduction is secondary rather than primary prevention. In contrast to primary prevention for risk behaviour, harm reduction education assumes that all persons sexually active and/or using syringes for drugs, steroids, or tattooing need information to make these behaviours safer. The intent of the educational initiatives described in this chapter is not to persuade inmates to become celibate, monogamous, or abstain from drug use – as this is a moral- and value-driven quest and not the goal of the author. Rather, the intent is to provide accessible information concerning risk behaviours in order to help prevent the spread of HIV and other communicable diseases in an effort to keep inmates healthy.

Background

When compared internationally, Canada is slow in addressing issues relevant to HIV in correctional institutions. Both the federal- and provincial-level prison systems struggle with internal resistance, political obstacles, and community pressures when attempting to respond to the distinctive circumstances and needs of inmates. It is well acknowledged and documented that risk behaviours in prison exist (Gaughwin 1991; Gaughwin et al. 1991; Horsburgh et al. 1990; Power et al. 1992; Shewan, Gemmel, and Davies 1994; Turnbull, Dolan, and Stimson 1991).

The prison environment and prisoners were first identified as 'high-risk' for the spread of HIV when Canadian government task forces examined the AIDS crisis in the general community (e.g., Royal Society of Canada 1988). Also, social scientists and epidemiologists who conducted the first seroprevalence studies in prisons (Hankins et al. 1989; Hankins et al. 1991) brought attention to the facts that infection rates were higher in prison than in the community, and that very little was being done about HIV and AIDS in prison settings. Numerous recommendations were put forward proposing harm reduction strategies to reduce the spread of HIV in prisons, and the need for education and availability of condoms and bleach was acknowledged. Soon thereafter various other federal groups made similar, if not identical, recommendations (Parliamentary Ad Hoc Committee on AIDS 1990; National

Advisory Committee on AIDS 1990; and the Federal/Provincial/Territorial Advisory Committee on AIDS 1991). As early as 1989, a non-governmental federal organization, the Canadian AIDS Society, published a report asking for a national AIDS strategy, in which recommendations specific to the prison population were also made. However, it would be several years before prevention strategies were considered by the correctional service systems in Canada.

Education is the least controversial aspect to an HIV preventive approach, in contrast to condom distribution or syringe exchange and bleach distribution. Yet the introduction of materials especially written and intended for inmates is often perceived as potentially threatening to the status quo found behind prison walls. Risk prevention education promotes concepts of self-worth and empowerment – and empowered people are perceived as more difficult to control behind bars.

In Canada, provincial institutions vary greatly from one another in their efforts to provide education and prevention tools. In October 1993, the introduction of condoms, dental dams, and lubricants in Ontario provincial prisons was implemented with tremendous resistance from correctional staff. Officers argued that condoms can be used to jam locks, employed as weapons against other inmates or in suicide (strangling), and can cause potential harm if used inappropriately (make water balloons with condoms, spread lubricant on the floor). In most Ontario provincial facilities condoms are made available through the health-care unit. Some provinces completely refuse to distribute condoms in their prisons. Federal penitentiaries across the country share a more consistent policy and have made condoms, dental dams, and lubricant available since January 1992. The distribution methodologies of these tools remain at the discretion of the individual federal institutions.

Researching Educational Needs

HIV/AIDS educational materials produced for the general public are neither appropriate for nor accessible to the prison population. Usually, these materials are written at higher literacy levels than that of the general prison population. The information may not reflect the realities of a typical inmate's life and can alienate the reader from the information being presented. For example, the majority of prisoners are greatly marginalized. For these individuals, HIV risk reduction is not a priority when they are coping with the effects of illiteracy, poverty, unemployment, homelessness, or substance dependency. Prevention education must be sensitive to these realities and make no assumptions concerning the resourcefulness and motivation of the reader.

Clearly, a need exists for tailored and culturally sensitive education for the prison population.

1. A Needs-Assessment Study

In 1991, the federal Ministry of Health funded Canada's first (and to date only) education needs assessment in the correctional setting. The intent of the study was to determine the gaps in knowledge and to collect information for the development of an HIV/AIDS education and prevention program, specifically tailored to the needs and preferences of the prison population. A year later, the study was completed (Toepell 1992a). A brief summary of the results collected from two Toronto, Ontario, correctional facilities is provided below.

Prisoners had a superficial understanding of HIV-infection prevention. Their primary source of information was the media (more specifically, a local news tabloid, the *Toronto Sun*). They did not understand the etiology of HIV; 93 per cent understood the benefits of protected sex, but only 15 per cent understood the link and distinction between HIV and AIDS (i.e., they did not grasp the concept of an exposure to the virus and possible infection due to exposure). Gaps in their knowledge, mostly owing to myths and misconceptions, were also revealed (e.g., 56 per cent believed that donating blood constitutes a risk for HIV infection, while 46 per cent believed the same for kissing). Others were convinced that sharing of toilets, cutlery, dishes, and food meant risk for spreading HIV, and that coughing and sneezing posed risks for contracting the virus as well. These fallacies can cause great distress to misinformed people who live in crowded environments with limited air ventilation, such as prisons.

It was also determined that, while living outside prison, inmates did not actively seek HIV/AIDS information made available to the general public – which is not to imply that these materials would necessarily be accessible or appropriately written for inmates. Prisoners strongly supported an HIV/AIDS education program in the prison setting, explaining that they would be most receptive to this education while incarcerated. Further, they supported and encouraged the distribution of 'exit kits' containing condoms and needle-cleaning agents upon release from institutions. Prisoners gave many suggestions and recommendations specific to education-program delivery and format; most favoured video presentation and the use of explicit or 'street' terms for describing safer behaviours.

2. A Knowledge, Attitude, and Behaviour Study

A knowledge-attitude-behaviour (KAB) study was conducted with the prison population in Toronto, Ontario (Toepell 1992b). From within the context of educational needs, the study examined attitudes towards HIV-infected inmates, correctional staff, and community groups, and towards HIV testing, and identified high-risk behaviours before incarceration (including sexual behaviour, injection drug use, and tattooing). Again, the goal of the study was to collect information that would assist in developing HIV/AIDS educational materials specifically tailored to the needs and preferences of the prison population, in this case focusing on attitude and behaviour change.

Prisoners expressed strong AIDS-phobic and homophobic attitudes. Further, they felt threatened by infected inmates living in their section, rationalizing that the infected individual could fight with or bite fellow prisoners and potentially spread the virus. Eighty-six per cent believed that separate facilities should be available to house infected prisoners exclusively. Over 75 per cent were of the opinion that prostitutes and gay men should be required to test for the HIV antibody, which sharply contrasted with their support (86 per cent) for anonymous and unforced testing in the community. Illustrated here is the misconception that mandatory testing and knowing a person's seropositive status will control the spread of HIV and thereby protect members of society from infection.

Prisoners demonstrated significant risk behaviours, despite their knowledge concerning risk prevention. They only used condoms with sexual partners they did not know well, and 52 per cent of condom users stopped practising safer sex with a new partner after an average of one month. Eighty per cent of prisoners who injected drugs shared their syringes. Prisoners who had tattoos done non-professionally shared the inks and equipment with friends during the tattooing procedure.

Findings or data concerning prisoners' educational needs specific to HIV/AIDS and risk behaviours are not available from other countries. However, several countries have initiated various educational programs within their prison settings, and these are briefly described later.

Responding to Educational Needs

Since the completion of the two research studies, a variety of educational materials have been produced for both federal penitentiaries and Ontario provincial institutions. These materials are described below, and all were developed and written by the author.

1. Education Concerning HIV/AIDS Knowledge

In response to the results from the above research, an HIV/AIDS education book was developed for adult male prisoners in Ontario provincial institutions (John Howard Society 1992a). The book is entitled *Get the Facts: Surviving in Prison and in the Community*. It was produced by the John Howard Society of Metropolitan Toronto, an agency serving male inmates, and was funded by the City of Toronto, Department of Public Health. The book, which has many unique features that address the educational needs and preferences of the inmate population surveyed, was prepared in consultation with ex-prisoners, prisoner interest groups, community AIDS educators, and representatives of the City of Toronto and the provincial Ministry of Correctional Services.

Get the Facts is written at a school grade 8 level, makes use of clear language techniques, and provides many illustrations. It is comprehensive in its approach and a wide range of topics are explained, including the transmission of, and protection from, the HIV virus both inside and outside of jail. It uses a non-condescending, non-judgmental tone, as well as explicit language and 'street' terms. When street terms are used the 'proper' or public-health term is followed in parentheses. A personal story written by an HIV-infected prisoner describes his experiences in prison after staff and fellow inmates were made aware of his HIV status. Testing and treatment options are explained, and a resource directory describes where to go in the community for additional information, free condoms, syringe exchange, bleach kits, treatment, legal assistance, and so forth.

The book was produced for adult male offenders in Ontario provincial prisons to receive while incarcerated and to take with them when released from prison. It became a controversial publication before its distribution at a local prison, and again after its distribution. These events will be described later.

The Correctional Service of Canada (the federal penal system) responded to the above research with the production of a five-pamphlet series, based closely in style and content on *Get the Facts*. The pamphlets are entitled *Men and HIV/AIDS*; *Women and HIV/AIDS*; *Needles and HIV/ AIDS*; *Testing for HIV/AIDS*; and *Living with HIV or AIDS*, and are bundled in packages of five (one of each pamphlet) (Correctional Service of Canada 1993). The bundles of pamphlets are intended for the 14,000 federal prisoners in Canada, and are available in both official languages.

The men's and women's pamphlets each provide general HIV education and prevention information. The pamphlet for women prisoners differs from the men's in that it addresses issues and concerns specific to women (e.g., negotiating safer sex with a resistant partner; childbearing and HIV). The pamphlet on needle use describes the importance of cleaning syringes when sharing them for injecting drugs or steroids, tattooing, and body piercing. Needle-exchange programs are described and their locations listed across the country. The pamphlet concerning testing provides details of the testing procedure and stresses the importance of pre- and post-test counselling. The concepts of anonymity and confidentiality are defined and discussion is given to the decisions of whether to test for the HIV antibody or to disclose a positive result.

The fifth pamphlet concerning living with HIV or AIDS is intended to give information to all inmates regardless of serostatus, although it is specifically written for infected inmates. This particular pamphlet is the forerunner to a much larger publication developed for inmates living with HIV or AIDS: a living guide/manual that is described later. The five-pamphlet series remains under review for distribution.

2. Education Concerning Attitudes

A pamphlet was produced addressing the documented homophobic and AIDS-phobic attitudes of prisoners (Toepell 1992b). It is entitled *Uncool Attitude ... Cool Attitude – What Do You Think about People with AIDS Inside and Outside of Prison?* (John Howard Society 1993a). This publication encourages healthier attitudes towards infected inmates and gay men, and explains why hostile attitudes are unnecessary and unacceptable.

Throughout the pamphlet, an inadmissible (*'un*cool') attitude is presented, an explanation is given as to why such a belief is unwarranted, and the original attitude is rewritten into an acceptable ('cool') attitude. Eight such examples are provided, written in an affirmative tone so as not to alienate the reader. It cannot be presumed that this pamphlet will singlehandedly affect malevolent opinions; however, it constructively raises awareness concerning specific inappropriate beliefs. As a publication, *Uncool Attitude ... Cool Attitude* is non-controversial and has successfully been introduced in local provincial prisons in Toronto, Ontario.

3. Education Concerning Risk Behaviours

As was indicated in the KAB study, prisoners practised significant risk behaviours (Toepell 1992b). Further, they expressed a powerless and defeated approach to HIV prevention. Some sentiments included 'It's [HIV] going to get me sooner or later – so why bother being safe?' and 'I'm not taking precautions, if it happens [becoming infected], it happens.'

In response to the above findings, a pamphlet entitled *Take Care – You're Worth It!* (John Howard Society 1993b) was developed to focus on risk-reduction behaviour change. The aim of the pamphlet is to nurture self-worth while emphasizing the importance of safer sex and needle use for tattooing, steroid use, and injecting intravenous drugs. The pamphlet encourages positive feelings towards one's health and identifies the person's own role in taking responsibility for his or her health. *Take Care – You're Worth It!* has become a very popular publication in the general community, as it addresses a significant factor in risk behaviour: lack of self-worth and self-esteem.

4. Education for Infected Prisoners

A living guide/manual entitled *Finding Out: What You Need to Know* was developed for federal male and female prisoners and is available in both official languages (Correctional Service of Canada 1994a). The manual is very comprehensive in its approach to educating the reader about living with HIV and AIDS both inside and outside prison.

Before developing the manual, it was assumed that infected inmates across the country had limited access to information concerning how best to live with HIV or AIDS. Any previous information available would have been brought into an institution through the initiative of a local community AIDS agency. As a result, the availability of information was sporadic and dependent upon individual institutions, and did not represent a consistent distribution of information across the country. Therefore, the *Finding Out* publication (funded and endorsed by the federal correctional system) is circulated throughout all federal penitentiaries. This book belongs to inmates, and they may keep it when released from the institution.

The living guide discusses expected topics such as HIV and the body, health and nutrition, the importance of safer behaviours, hygiene, medical information and treatment, financial and legal assistance, and disability and insurance. It also approaches many difficult subjects, including emotional reactions to testing positive (especially valuable for inmates who test positive while incarcerated), disclosure, discrimination and human rights, living with family/children, and arranging legal documents and funerals. The publication is written in a non-threatening and non-condescending voice, makes assurances throughout that the reader is not alone (while acknowledging how this is an understandable feeling during incarceration), and provides a list of telephone numbers that can be accessed for support and information.

Although the living guide is intended for the prison population, it is a valuable resource for any community member living with HIV outside of prison. This publication fills a gap found even in the literature for the general community living with HIV/AIDS.

5. Educational Programs in Other Countries

Internationally, efforts to provide prisoners with HIV/AIDS education are generally specific to individual institutions. That is, it is uncommon to find a standardized initiative implemented in each correctional facility in a country. The tendency is to create individual and innovative educational programs within a single institution.

In the United States, each state is responsible for educating the inmates housed in its county and state prisons. A national HIV/AIDS education strategy does not exist. The range of educational programming found in the United States is encouraging. For example, in many states inmates are trained to become HIV/AIDS educators and peer counsellors. A selection of peer education programs is found in New York: *P.A.C.E.* (Prisoners for AIDS in Counselling and Education) for men (Shippee 1993); *A.C.E.* (AIDS Counselling and Education) and *A.C.E. OUT* for women (Hernandez 1993); and *C.O.P.E.* (Committee on Prevention and Education for AIDS) for men (Aboussleman 1993). Many other such programs exist in various states, including *Project Alerta*, which attempts to empower women through HIV/AIDS education training at a local city/county jail in Albuquerque, New Mexico (Buffington 1993). In California, an educational video project exists designed to train young offenders as peer educators (Melrod, Burgess, and Charles 1993), while in Florida a *P.A.C.E.* program exists for young offending girls (Saiswick 1993).

As a national AIDS non-profit organization in England, AIDS Education and Research Trust (*AVERT*) develops and distributes educational packages to all correctional institutions across the country (Turnbull, Dolan, and Stimson 1991). As described in Fitzsimmons (1992), the Standing Conference on Drug Abuse (*SCODA*) developed a program in which volunteer correctional officers are trained as HIV educators to inform both colleagues and prisoners.

In Scotland a travelling theatre company has been introduced as a new method for educating inmates about HIV and AIDS, while additional efforts have been made to train 'prison buddies' (volunteers from outside the correctional setting) to offer individual support to HIV-infected inmates (Fitzsimmons 1992). Also, some prisons have developed drug-education programs for prisoners who disclose using injection drugs (McLaren 1994).

Several harm reduction strategies have been implemented in Australian prisons. Self-directed, student-centred learning has proven successful in institutions in South Australia (Behrens-Peters 1991), while a peer education program for inmates, in which correctional officers participate, is doing well in New South Wales (Mannion 1991).

Controversies Concerning Educational Materials

Get the Facts is Canada's first HIV educational resource developed specifically for the prison population. Ironically, the features making the publication unique and accessible to prisoners are also those that created extraordinary controversy – so much so that the funding agency for the book banned its distribution in Toronto just weeks after it was printed. A revised and rewritten version of *Get the Facts* was later negotiated, and another printing of the book was run (John Howard Society 1992b). In fact, both versions of the book met with controversy from separate sources, as described later.

At the time of printing the original version of the book, the political climate in Toronto changed significantly concerning the use of explicit street terminology in HIV/AIDS educational resources. In particular, the slang term for penetrative sex ('fuck') was identified as a term that could not be tolerated in printed resources funded by the Board of Health, City of Toronto. As can be understood, *Get the Facts* utilized this particular colloquial term in the sections concerning safer sex and safer-sex practices, as the term is commonly used and comprehended among the inmate population. Consequently, the language used throughout the book was censored when negotiating the revised version.

Further, senior officials of the Toronto Department of Public Health who had not seen the book in its draft forms disapproved of the harm reduction approach taken by the book. A position of harm elimination was preferred. At the time, provincial institutions in Ontario did not distribute condoms, dental dams, or lubricant. Implementing a harm reduction model was considered remote in the prison setting. Therefore, *Get the Facts* provided information specific to making sex safer in prison given the absence of condoms. A similar argument was used when the book was criticized for including information for making needle sharing safer without the provision of bleach (as bleach is still not available to inmates).

As a result of the above concerns, the original version of the book was never distributed, and a second version was rewritten. During the rewriting process, senior officials at the Ministry of Correctional Services took the opportunity to request that additional changes be made (despite their having approved the content of the book before its initial printing). This opportunity to further modify the book resulted in not only editing the text, but also censoring the content of illustrations. Three previously approved drawings were removed: one of inmates injecting together in prison; another of two inmates intimately holding each other; and a third demonstrating proper condom use – it was proposed that an excess number of drawn penises with condoms could offend the prison population. Modifications to the text included the removal of the following specific information: suggesting where to find bleach in prisons for properly cleaning syringes, and suggesting where to find materials in prisons for making sex safer (given the unavailability of condoms).

The revised version of *Get the Facts* was to be distributed at a local prison in Toronto as a pilot project. However, this venture was met with great resistance from correctional staff (in particular, from correctional officers). Officers literally revolted against the book and held a demonstration outside the institution protesting its distribution. They felt that the language used in the book was offensive (although the street terms had been already significantly modified), the tone and literacy level of the book were insulting to prisoners, and the illustrations were pornographic. The union representing staff issued formal complaints to the correctional service demanding that the book be removed from the prison, a request that eventually would be realized.

In an evaluation conducted six months after the distribution of *Get the Facts* began in the prison, it was evident that prisoners were in favour of the book and found it valuable (Toepell 1993). They expressed overwhelming support and appreciation for the book, found the language and use of street terms appropriate ('I've heard much worse in here [prison]'; ibid, p. 6), and admitted that they had learned more details about HIV and AIDS, in particular concerning transmission and how the virus is *not* spread. Prisoners also strongly recommended that *Get the Facts* be distributed across the province of Ontario and not exclusively in one prison.

The living guide, *Finding Out*, also spurred controversy in the federal prison system, in this case, among correctional officials. Although the language, which was 'toned down' from the outset of developing the manual, did not cause conflict, the information concerning syringe cleaning did. Officials would not approve the printing and eventual distribution of the living guide unless the cleaning instructions specific to sterilizing syringes were removed. It was feared that the government would be seen as condoning the use of syringes in prison, and contradict its own security policies specific to the possession of syringes (an institutional offence). After debating this issue for six months, the cleaning instructions were removed from the text, and the manual was promptly printed and distributed among federal penitentiaries across Canada without further incident. One year later, a second printing of the manual was necessary as the initial supply of 5000 copies was exhausted primarily owing to the manual's popularity outside prison in the general community and among AIDS service organizations.

Analysing the Controversies

Many fundamental issues are raised through the development and implementation of HIV/AIDS educational programming in correctional facilities. These include human rights, censorship, resistance from correctional staff, and the disregard for the prisoner's voice. Also, contradictions pertaining to correctional policies are highlighted.

1. Human Rights versus Corrections Policy

Although prisoners have a right to education and the means to protect themselves from HIV, the harm reduction strategies available in the general community outside of prison are not offered inside correctional institutions.

When attention is brought to the risk behaviours practised in the prison setting (i.e., tattooing, drug use, and sexual activity), it not only emphasizes the fact that the prison systems do not provide the necessary tools to make these behaviours safer, but also that these behaviours occur despite policies proclaiming their prohibition. Emphasizing the realities of risk behaviours creates distressing consequences for correctional officials, as the system experiences continued criticism for not implementing the harm reduction strategies found in the community and for establishing unrealistic policy. Arguably, this debate is one of human rights versus corrections policy. Health is neither a corrections issue nor a security issue; however, the reduction of risk behaviour for spreading HIV is perceived and treated as a correctional security issue.

Should the system implement recommended harm reduction strategies, it faces the likelihood of staff or the public viewing corrections as condoning sexual activity and drug use in the prison setting. A more responsible position to take (and one that honours the rights of prisoners) is one which demands that harm reduction strategies available outside prison be made available inside prison, and that policies be rewritten so as not to contradict harm reduction efforts. Whether behind bars or in the community, prisoners remain members of the general public. When living in our community, their health is a concern to society, therefore their health should remain a concern while they serve their sentences behind prison walls. The promotion of one's health should be seen as independent of one's criminal status.

2. Censorship

Censoring education that is intended to reduce the spread of HIV and is population-specific appears illogical. The aim of offering direct, tailored, and accessible education is to ensure that risk reduction messages are properly interpreted and understood. When language and pictorials are explicitly and clearly presented, information is more likely to be correctly comprehended. This strategy increases the chances of affecting risk-reducing behaviour change, which is the ultimate goal of harm reduction and HIV prevention.

The appeals to 'tone down' language and remove and modify both illustrations and syringe-cleaning instructions largely reflect the government's concern for its image – first, in funding the publications, and second, in distributing them. Also revealed is the discomfort over acknowledging the existence of risk behaviours in prisons and denial that these behaviours are widespread enough to warrant the implementation of harm reduction strategies. Furthermore, homophobic attitudes were exhibited by some officials and staff.

Despite documenting and substantiating the importance of using language that is most accessible to the prison population, the act of censorship ultimately prevailed. In order to ensure the printing and distribution of two valuable publications, the significant benefits to using specific language and illustrations were disregarded by government officials because of political pressures.

Finally, censorship concerning where to find bleach in prisons and the instructions on how to clean syringes before sharing is also an expression of nervousness. Corrections officials did not want to be seen as encouraging behaviours that are regarded as illegal in prison.

3. Resistance from Correctional Staff

Although many people are unaware of or deny the existence of risk behaviours as part of prison life, some members of the general public, including some correctional staff, feel strongly that prisoners are not worthy of the benefits of harm reduction efforts. Also, many people in the correctional services do not fully appreciate the pragmatics of a harm reduction approach or they simply misunderstand harm reduction. While everyone can agree with the obvious 'good sense' offered by a harm reduction perspective, resistance begins to mount as the practice of harm reduction efforts mirror programs available in the community. Attempts are made to maintain a clear distinction between 'life on the outside' and 'life behind bars,' without regard for the health of the prison population.

Further, many correctional officers have difficulty accepting any type of programming efforts for or consideration given to prisoners. There is resistance by some staff irrespective of what the initiative may be – simply because it is an effort intended to improve the situation for inmates, or give inmates choice, control, or opportunities to empower themselves. A common sentiment is that prison is a culture of its own in which inmates are undeserving.

The obvious discomfort that staff communicated concerning the illustrations accompanying safer sex instructions leads one to speculate on the reasons for their reactions. Perhaps this reflected embarrassment about sexuality in general and an overall lack of awareness concerning HIV and AIDS. The reaction of disgust and opinions that HIV/AIDS education is nothing short of pornographic material might also stem from the unfamiliarity with HIV prevention education and from an inability to see the illustrations in their intended educational context. Such perceptions reinforce homophobic and AIDS-phobic attitudes found among staff. Clearly, comprehensive HIV/AIDS education for correctional staff is indicated.

4. The Voice of Prisoners

The voice of prisoners is generally the last one heard and the one most likely to be ignored when negotiating harm reduction efforts in the correctional setting. Despite research documenting the preferences and needs of inmates, including focus-testing and evaluations of educational materials, their consultation is not deemed very valuable by most policy makers.

It is prisoners' interest groups, community AIDS educators and agencies, and social scientists that advocate on behalf of prisoners to have their HIV educational needs and choices met. Most federal institutions have a peer inmate committee (run by and for prisoners), which may or may not demand HIV/AIDS education programming, depending on the institution and the interests of the committee.

Current Directions in Correctional Settings

In the near future, it is anticipated that the Correctional Service of Canada will distribute a series of videos concerning HIV, hepatitis, and related communicable diseases in their federal penitentiaries. Discussions specific to initiating research studies in prisons (on high-risk behaviour, anonymous testing) are under way. The federal correctional system takes much of its direction from recommendations put forward by the Expert Committee on AIDS in Prisons (ECAP) in its report (Correctional Service of Canada 1994b). The committee reviewed issues raised by HIV and AIDS in prisons, and made multiple recommendations concerning harm reduction efforts in federal institutions.

Individual federal institutions have an inmate 'peer educator' who provides HIV/AIDS education to fellow prisoners. In the province of New Brunswick, a peer education program for inmates is currently implemented as a pilot project, complete with a comprehensive training and facilitator's manual. It is hoped that in the future a peer educator model will become standard in all institutions (both federal and provincial).

In the province of British Columbia, an educational program for both staff and prisoners is currently implemented in all the provincial prisons. Training sessions based on this educational program are currently offered to staff and inmates in selected federal prisons. Also, a bleach distribution program has successfully been under way for several years without incident in British Columbia, and the official distribution of bleach has been policy since July 1992. It is anticipated that a national bleach distribution program in federal penitentiaries will be implemented by the fall of 1996.

In other provincial prisons, many of the initiatives taken to educate prisoners about HIV and AIDS still come from the communities outside prisons. Many AIDS educators and agencies attempt to reach the prison population, but their success is dependent upon the receptiveness of individual institutions.

Although alien to a harm reduction perspective, the federal correctional system recently announced its intent to 'combat' and 'crack down' on drug use in penitentiaries. It proposes to increase effectiveness of drug detection, administer stronger punishments for smuggling and possession of drugs, and offer better access to substance-abuse programs. Increased detection methods include randomized urine testing of prisoners, use of trained detection dogs, and better training of staff in drug detection. The mandate of the 'crackdown' neither complements nor facilitates the efforts of a harm reduction model. In fact, it may create more harm by encouraging prisoners to consume injectable narcotics, which are detectable only for a few days in urine (heroine, cocaine, and amphetamines), as opposed to smokable drugs, which can be detected several weeks after consumption (cannabis, hashish) (White 1994). Further, the underground drug market in prison might see an increased demand in injection drugs, which could result in an increase in cost, drug-related violence, sharing of syringes, and, likely, overdoses. Now, more than ever before, is education specific to safer drug use and syringe cleaning needed in federal institutions.

Syringe exchange programs are essentially not being considered by Canadian prisons. On the provincial level, needle exchange or alternative options are not being discussed at all. In the federal prison system, the debate continues as the ECAP report addressed the controversial issue of needle exchange. It is yet to be seen how the federal system will respond to the ECAP's recommendations concerning needle exchange.

Internationally, syringe exchange programs do not exist in prisons – with the exception of one country. In Switzerland, a pilot project to provide sterile needles to inmates in a women's prison started in May 1994 (Jürgens 1994). This particular initiative is supported by the argument that inmates in the state's care should not suffer harm during their incarceration (including harms related to drug use) (ibid.). However, efforts to help free inmates from drug use are still offered.

Conclusions

As has been demonstrated, the unique features of educational materials that make them most accessible to the prison population are generally the same features that can ultimately prevent the materials from being distributed. Obviously, HIV/AIDS and drug use are very sensitive and politically laden topics in the prison setting. Controversial issues concerning harm reduction strategies can bring a halt to the implementation of such initiatives.

In the final analysis, the principles and ideology of a harm reduction approach are not currently realized in Canadian prison settings. Although senior officials, management of institutions, and frontline workers might agree to make some concessions, there is no appreciation for the pragmatic values of a harm reduction strategy. Only when harm reduction efforts are presented in the context of protecting the community at large (i.e., protecting inmates from contracting HIV because they might infect community members when they are released from prison) is there a shift in attitudes and some acceptance of harm reduction strategies.

Much of the resistance expressed by correctional staff is a result of the nature of the dynamic between staff and inmate. There is an important psychological facet to consider here, and it is a function of the psychology between the keeper and the kept. Correctional officers will typically feel that their safety is threatened as they are frontline workers, and that little to no consideration is given to protecting their security when harm reduction strategies are implemented in the interest of prisoners. Staff must be assured that an improvement to inmates' lives does not lead to a reciprocal worsening of their own.

While it is true that a continued drive for policy change is necessary (especially concerning educational initiatives and bleach distribution), one should not enter into the policy debate without taking into account the above described controversies. By acknowledging and addressing them and taking their political influences into account, we can best negotiate policy change to implement harm reduction strategies in Canadian prisons.

REFERENCES

Aboussleman, M. 1993. 'Committee on Prevention and Education for AIDS (C.O.P.E.).' Paper presented at the meeting of the National Conference on AIDS in Prisons, San Francisco, October.
Behrens-Peters, O. 1991. 'HIV Education Strategies within Correctional Services: The South Australian Experience.' In J. Norberry, M. Gaughwin, and S. Gerull, eds, *HIV/AIDS and Prisons, Proceedings of a Conference*, 199–209. Canberra: Australian Institute of Criminology.
Buffington, S. 1993. 'Where Has All the Power Gone?' Paper presented at the meeting of the National Conference on AIDS in Prisons, San Francisco, October.
Cohen, J. 1993. 'Achieving a Reduction in Drug-Related Harm through Education.' In N. Heather et al., eds, *Psychoactive Drugs and Harm Reduction: From Faith to Science*, 65–76. London: Whurr Publishers.
Correctional Service of Canada. 1993. *Men and HIV/AIDS; Women and HIV/AIDS; Needles and HIV/AIDS; Testing for HIV/AIDS; If You Have HIV or AIDS*. Ottawa: Author.
– 1994a. *Finding Out: What You Need to Know*. Ottawa: Author.
– 1994b. *HIV/AIDS in Prisons: Final Report of the Expert Committee on AIDS and Prisons*. Ottawa: Author.
– 1994c. *Correctional Service Announces Strategy to Combat Drugs in Federal Penitentiaries*. News release, communiqué. Ottawa: Author.
Federal/Provincial/Territorial Working Group 1988. 'Confidentiality in Relation to HIV Seropositivity.' Report accepted by the Conference of Deputy Ministers of Health and approved by the Interprovincial Meeting of Ministers of Health.
Fitzsimmons, L. 1992. *AIDS Education and Prevention Programs in Correctional Institutions Worldwide*. Ottawa: Health Canada.
Gaughwin, M. 1991. 'Behind Bars – Risk Behaviours for HIV Transmission in Prisons, A Review.' In J. Norberry et al., eds, *HIV/AIDS and Prisons, Proceedings of a conference held 19–21 November, 1990*, 89–107. Canberra: Australian Institute of Criminology.
Gaughwin, M., R. Douglas, C. Liew, L. Davies, A. Mylvaganam, H. Treffke,

J. Edwards, and E. Ali. 1991. 'HIV Prevalence and Risk Behaviours for HIV Transmission in South Australian Prisons.' *AIDS* 5(7): 845–51.

Hankins, C., S. Gendron, W. Handley, and M. O'Shaughnessy. 1991. 'HIV-1 Infection among Incarcerated Men – Québec.' *Canada Diseases Weekly* 17(43): 233–5.

Hankins, C., S. Gendron, C., Richard, and M. O'Shaughnessy. 1989. 'HIV-1 Infection in Medium Security Prison for Women – Québec.' *Canada Diseases Weekly* 15(33): 168–70.

Hernandez, M. 1993. *A.C.E.-OUT*, Women's Prison Association. Personal communications.

Horsburgh, C. Jr, J. Jarvis, T. McArthur, T. Ignacio, and P. Stock. 1990. 'Seroconversion to Human Immunodeficiency Virus in Prison Inmates.' *American Journal of Public Health* 80: 209–10.

John Howard Society of Metropolitan of Toronto. 1992a. *Get the Facts: Surviving in Prison and in the Community*. Toronto: Author.

– 1992b, revised. *Get the Facts: Surviving in Prison and in the Community*. Toronto: Author.

– 1993a. *Uncool Attitude ... Cool Attitude – What Do You Think about People with AIDS Inside and Outside Prison?* Toronto: Author.

– 1993b. *Take Care – You're Worth It!* Toronto: Author.

Jürgens, R. 1994. 'HIV Prevention Taken Seriously: Provision of Syringes in a Swiss Prison.' *Canadian HIV/AIDS Policy and Law Newsletter* 1(1): 1, 2–3.

Parliamentary Ad Hoc Committee on AIDS. 1990. *Confronting a Crisis: The Report of the Parliamentary Ad Hoc Committee on AIDS*. Ottawa: Author.

Power, K., I. Markova, A. Rowlands, K. McKee, P. Anslow, and C. Kilfedder. 1992. 'Intravenous Drug Use and HIV Transmission amongst Inmates in Scottish Prisons.' *British Journal of Addictions* 87(1): 35–45.

Prisoners with AIDS/HIV Support Action Network (PASAN). 1992. *HIV/AIDS in Prison Systems: A Comprehensive Strategy*. Toronto: Author.

McLaren, T. 1994. 'Drug Education and Harm Reduction in a Prison Setting.' Paper presented at the 5th International Conference on the Reduction of Drug Related Harm, Toronto.

Mannion, K. 1991. 'Educational Strategies and Policy Development.' In J. Norberry, M. Gaughwin, and S. Gerull, eds, *HIV/AIDS and Prisons, Proceedings of a Conference*, 193–6. Canberra: Australian Institute of Criminology.

Melrod, J., E. Burgess, and J. Charles. 1993. *Peer AIDS Education Video Project for Incarcerated and Probationary Adolescents*. Paper presented at the meeting of the National Conference on AIDS in Prisons, San Francisco, October.

National Advisory Committee on AIDS; Working Group on HIV Infection and Injection Drug Use. 1990. *Principles and Recommendations on HIV Infection and*

Injection Drug Use. Ottawa. Update (Nov. 1993) distributed at the 2nd National Workshop on HIV, Alcohol and Other Drug Use, Edmonton, Canada, February 1994.

Royal Society of Canada. 1988. *AIDS: A Perspective for Canadians: Summary Report and Recommendations*. Ottawa: Author.

Saiswaick, K. 1993. 'P.A.C.E. Center for Girls.' Paper presented at the meeting of the National Conference on AIDS in Prisons, San Francisco, October.

Shewan, D., M. Gemmell, and J. Davies. 1994. *Drug Use and Scottish Prisons – Summary Report*. Scottish Prison Service Occasional Paper, no. 5.

Shippee, B.S. 1993. 'Prisoners for AIDS in Counselling and Education (P.A.C.E.).' Paper presented at the meeting of the National Conference on AIDS in Prisons, San Francisco, October.

Toepell, A.R. 1992a. 'Prisoners and AIDS: AIDS Education Needs Assessment.' Toronto: John Howard Society of Metropolitan Toronto.

– 1992b. 'Prisoners and AIDS: Knowledge, Attitude and Behaviour.' Toronto: John Howard Society of Metropolitan Toronto.

– 1993. 'Evaluation of *Get the Facts* with Inmates at the Toronto Jail.' Report to the John Howard Society of Metropolitan Toronto.

Turnbull, P., K. Dolan, and G. Stimson. 1991. *Prisons, HIV and AIDS: Risks and Experiences in Custodial Care*. England: AVERT.

White, C.L. 1994. 'Harm Reduction/Health Promotion in Federal Prisons: Why "Blind-Eye" Policies Are Not Enough.' Paper presented at the meeting of the 2nd National Workshop on HIV, Alcohol and Other Drug Use, Edmonton, Canada, February.

Contributors

Bruce K. Alexander Professor, Department of Psychology, Simon Fraser University (Burnaby, British Columbia, Canada)

Glenn Backes Streetwork Project, Victim Services Agency (New York, New York, USA)

John S. Baer Research Associate Professor, Addictive Behaviours Research Center, Department of Psychology, University of Washington (Seattle, Washington, USA)

Jane Baron Coordinator, Lifestyle Enrichment for Senior Adults (LESA), Centretown Community Health Centre (Ottawa, Ontario, Canada)

Line Beauchesne Associate Professor, Department of Criminology, University of Ottawa, Ottawa, Ontario, Canada

Purvi Biring Former Research Assistant, Addiction Research Foundation (Toronto, Ontario, Canada)

Marie Bresnahan National Development Research Institutes (New York, New York, USA)

Pamela J. Brett Thames Valley Family Practice Research Unit, Family Medicine Department, University of Western Ontario (London, Ontario, Canada)

Jane Caporn Phlebotomist, Western Australian Alcohol and Drug Authority (Perth, Western Australia)

Mike Charlton Medical Officer, Western Australian Alcohol and Drug Authority (Perth, Western Australia)

Yuet W. Cheung Professor, Department of Sociology, Chinese University of Hong Kong (Shatin, New Territories, Hong Kong)

Michael C. Clatts National Development Research Institutes (New York, New York, USA)

Peter D.A. Cohen Associate Professor, Centre of Drug Research

(CEDRO), and Associate Professor, School of Environmental Science, University of Amsterdam (Amsterdam, The Netherlands)

Gerard J. Connors   Senior Research Scientist, Research Institute on Addictions (Buffalo, New York, USA)

Sarah Crosby   Service Manager, Manchester Action on Street Health (Manchester, United Kingdom)

W. Rees Davis   Research Associate, National Development Research Institutes (New York, New York, USA)

Ronald R. Douglas   Program Leader, Community-based Prevention Programs, Addiction Research Foundation (Toronto, Ontario, Canada)

Patricia G. Erickson   Senior Scientist, Addiction Research Foundation, and Professor, Department of Sociology, University of Toronto (Toronto, Ontario, Canada)

Benedikt Fischer   Scientist, Addiction Research Foundation, and doctoral candidate, Centre of Criminology, University of Toronto (Toronto, Ontario, Canada)

Laura Gamble   Acting Director, Drug Advice and Information Service (Brighton, United Kingdom)

Fernando Garcia Argañarás   Professor, Department of Political Science, Universidad Mayor de San Simon, and Director of Information and Research, Centro de Documentacion e Informacion-Bolivia (CEDIB) (Cochabamba, Bolivia)

Michael George   Director, Drug and Alcohol Services, Worthing Priority Care (Worthing, Sussex, United Kingdom)

Kathryn Graham   Senior Scientist, Addiction Research Foundation (London, Ontario, Canada)

Ruth E. Harlow   Managing Attorney, Lambda Legal Defense and Education Fund (New York, New York, USA)

Ralf Jürgens   Project Coordinator, Canadian HIV/AIDS Legal Network and Canadian AIDS Society (Montreal, Quebec, Canada)

René Lauzon   Program Consultant, Addiction Research Foundation (Timmins, Ontario, Canada)

Trudo Lemmens   Research Associate, Clinical Trials Research Group, Biomedical Ethics Unit, McGill University (Montreal, Quebec, Canada)

Simon Lenton   Research Fellow, National Centre for Research into the Prevention of Drug Abuse, Curtin University of Technology (Perth, Western Australia)

Christopher Linwood   New York Peer AIDS Education Coalition (New York, New York, USA)

G. Alan Marlatt   Professor, Department of Psychology, University of Washington (Seattle, Washington, USA)

John P. Morgan   Professor, Department of Pharmacology, City University of New York Medical School, Department of Pharmacology (New York, New York, USA)

Claire Narbonne-Fortin   Program Consultant, Addiction Research Foundation (Sudbury, Ontario, Canada)

Amanda Noble   Research Associate, University of California (Davis), and Research Scientist, California Public Health Foundation (Davis, California, USA)

Patrick O'Hare   International Harm Reduction Association (Rome, Italy)

Martin Plant   Director/Professor, Alcohol and Health Research Group, Department of Psychiatry, University of Edinburgh (Edinburgh, Scotland, United Kingdom)

Julia Reynolds   Senior Clinical Psychologist, Western Australian Alcohol and Drug Authority (Perth, Western Australia)

Diane M. Riley   Canadian Foundation for Drug Policy and International Harm Reduction Association (Toronto, Ontario, Canada)

Robin Room   Vice-President, Research, Addiction Research Foundation (Toronto, Ontario, Canada)

Marsha Rosenbaum   Director, Lindesmith Centre (San Francisco, California, USA)

Stacey Rubin   Streetwork Project, Victim Services Agency (New York, New York, USA)

Eric Single   Director of Policy and Research Unit, Canadian Centre on Substance Abuse, and Professor, Department of Preventive Medicine and Biostatistics, University of Toronto (Toronto, Ontario, Canada)

Rod Sorge   Director of Development, Harm Reduction Coalition (New York, New York, USA)·

Edith Springer   New York Peer AIDS Education Coalition (New York, New York, USA)

Tim Stockwell   Director/Professor, National Centre for Research into the Prevention of Drug Abuse, Curtin University of Technology (Perth, Western Australia, Australia)

Avril Taylor   Head of Behavioural Studies, Scottish Centre for Infection and Environmental Health, Ruchill Hospital (Glasgow, Scotland, United Kingdom)

Andréa Riesch Toepell   Assistant Professor, Health Studies Program, Brock University (St Catharines, Ontario, Canada)

Kimberly S. Walitzer   Research Institute on Addictions (Buffalo, New York, USA)

Timothy R. Weber   Research Associate, Addiction Research Foundation (Toronto, Ontario, Canada)

Govert F. van de Wijngaart   Psychologist, Head of Addiction Research Institute (CVO), Faculty of Social and Behavioural Sciences, Utrecht University (Utrecht, The Netherlands)

Lynn Zimmer   Associate Professor, Department of Sociology, Queens College, City University of New York (New York, New York, USA)